MARICOPA COUNTY COMMUNIT
WILLIAMS CAMPU
CHANDLER-GILBERT CC
7360 E. TAHOE AV
MESA, AZ 85212

Peacemaking

Peacemaking

From Practice to Theory

Volume 2

SUSAN ALLEN NAN, ZACHARIAH CHERIAN MAMPILLY, AND ANDREA BARTOLI, EDITORS

Foreword by Ekmeleddin Ihsanoglu

Praeger Security International

 PRAEGER

AN IMPRINT OF ABC-CLIO, LLC
Santa Barbara, California • Denver, Colorado • Oxford, England

Library of Congress Cataloging-in-Publication Data

Peacemaking : from practice to theory / Susan Allen Nan, Zachariah Cherian Mampilly, and Andrea Bartoli, editors.
    p. cm. — (Praeger security international)
  Includes bibliographical references and index.
    ISBN 978-0-313-37576-7 (set : alk. paper) — ISBN 978-0-313-37578-1 (v. 1) —
ISBN 978-0-313-37580-4 (v. 2) — ISBN 978-0-313-37577-4 (ebk.)   1. Peace-building.   I. Nan,
Susan Allen.   II. Mampilly, Zachariah Cherian, 1977–   III. Bartoli, A. (Andrea)
    JZ5538.P3744   2011
      303.6'6—dc22   2011016906

ISBN: 978-0-313-37576-7 (set)
      978-0-313-37578-1 (vol. 1)
      978-0-313-37580-4 (vol. 2)
EISBN: 978-0-313-37577-4

16 15 14 13 12   1 2 3 4 5

This book is also available on the World Wide Web as an eBook.
Visit www.abc-clio.com for details.

Praeger
An Imprint of ABC-CLIO, LLC

ABC-CLIO, LLC
130 Cremona Drive, P.O. Box 1911
Santa Barbara, California 93116-1911

This book is printed on acid-free paper ∞

Manufactured in the United States of America

Contents

VOLUME 1

Foreword by Ekmeleddin Ihsanoglu   ix

About the Contributors to Volume 1   xxiii

I. Peacemaking in Practice   1

Introduction   1
  Susan Allen Nan

1 Reaching Out to the Uninitiated: Engaging Youth to Combat
   Hindu Extremism in India   6
   Shabnam Hashmi

2 Switzerland's Peace Promotion in Nepal: Commitment,
   Discreteness, Flexibility   18
   Günther Baechler

3 Women, Resistance, and Peacemaking   36
   Vanessa Ortiz

4 10 Lessons from 10 Peace Processes   51
   Jan Egeland

5 Multi-Track Diplomacy—Its Origins and Some of Its
   Accomplishments   62
   John McDonald

6 A Reflective Practitioner's 40-Year Wilderness Journey
   Between Judaism and Conflict Resolution   76
   Marc Gopin

7 Noninstitutional Organizations and Conflict Resolution: Some
   Reflections on the Experiences of the Community of Sant'Egidio   92
   Mario Giro

8 NGOs and Mediation   107
   Andrea Bartoli

9 The Role of the ICC in Northern Uganda   122
   Adam Branch

10 Mediating Ceasefires and Cessation of Hostilities Agreements
    in the Framework of Peace Processes   135
    Nat Colletta

11 Peacemaking in a Relational Paradigm   148
    Harold Saunders

II. Toward an Inclusive Peacemaking   161

Introduction   161
   Zachariah Cherian Mampilly

12 Gandhi and Peacemaking   165
    Joseph Prabhu

13 Peacemaking, Conflict Analysis, and Resolution:
    The Legacy of Martin Luther King Jr.   179
    Johnny Mack and Maneshka Eliatamby

14 Buddhism and Peacemaking   192
    A. T. Ariyaratne

15 Confucianism and Peacemaking in Chinese History   211
    Victoria Tin-bor Hui

16 Islam and Peacemaking   228
    Sheherazade Jafari and Abdul Aziz Said

17 Jewish-Muslim Reconciliation: A Psychopolitical Strategy   244
    Joseph Montville

18 Reconciliation, Christianity, and Peacemaking   257
    Daniel Philpott

19 Peacemaking and African Traditions of Justice and Reconciliation   275
    Tim Murithi

20 Reclaiming Ubuntu through Multicultural Education: A Foundation
    for Peacemaking in the African Great Lakes Region   295
    Elavie Ndura, Apollinaire Bangayimbaga, and Vincent Bandeba

21 Inviting Persephone to Dance: Arts and Movement-Based
    Approaches to Peacemaking   308
    Michelle LeBaron and Carrie MacLeod

22 Narrative Approach to Peacemaking in Somalia 328
    Sara Cobb and Hussein Yusuf

23 Gender and Peacemaking: Women's Rights in Contemporary
    Peace Agreements 344
    Miriam J. Anderson

VOLUME 2

About the Contributors to Volume 2 ix

III. New Directions in Peacemaking 379

Introduction 379
    Andrea Bartoli

24 Building National "Infrastructures for Peace": UN Assistance
    for Internally Negotiated Solutions to Violent Conflict 384
    Chetan Kumar

25 Infrastructures for Peace 400
    Paul van Tongeren

26 The Responsibility to Protect and Peacemaking 420
    Abiodun Williams and Jonas Claes

27 Fact Based Approaches to Peacemaking: Global Peace Index 438
    Steve Killelea

28 Academic Diplomacy: The Role of Non–Decision Makers
    in Peacemaking 457
    Peter Wallensteen

29 Social Media: A New Track of Multi-Track Diplomacy 477
    Philip Gamaghelyan

30 Strategic Connectors: Community Strategies for Conflict
    Prevention in Times of War 492
    Marshall Wallace and Mary Anderson

31 Social Entrepreneurship: Paving the Way for Peace 502
    Ryszard Praszkier and Andrzej Nowak

32 Gang Intervention in the United States:
    Legal and Extra-Legal Attempts at Peacemaking 511
    SpearIt

33 Abraham's Path: The Path of a Thousand Negotiations 529
    Joshua Weiss

IV. Interpreting Peacemaking 545

Introduction 545
    Andrea Bartoli

34 Anthropological Examples of Peacemaking: Practice and Theory 550
    Douglas P. Fry

35 Ancient Peacemakers: Exemplars of Humanity   563
    Anthony Wanis-St. John

36 Spirituality, Emergent Creativity, and Reconciliation   585
    Vern Neufeld Redekop

37 A Social-Psychological Perspective on Peacemaking   601
    Morton Deutsch

38 Method in Peacemaking   610
    Jamie Price

39 The Hidden Dimensions of Peacemaking: A Systems Perspective   622
    Louise Diamond

40 A Dynamical Systems Perspective on Peacemaking: Moving
    from a System of War toward a System of Peace   637
    Peter Coleman, Lan Bui-Wrzosinska, Andrzej Nowak, and Robin Vallacher

41 Systemic Peacemaking in the Era of Globalization   651
    Monty G. Marshall

42 Theories of Change in Peacemaking   668
    Christopher Mitchell

43 The Contingency Model for Third-Party Interventions   683
    Ronald Fisher

44 Challenges in Peacemaking: External Interventions   701
    Louis Kriesberg

45 The South African Peace Process: An Urgency Theory Analysis   722
    Dean Pruitt

46 Peacemaking through Mediation: the Swiss FDFA in
    Israel-Palestine, Sudan, and Guatemala   741
    Simon J. A. Mason

47 Attending to Unfinished Business in Peacemaking: Preliminary
    Findings from the Reflecting on Peace Practice Project   761
    Peter Woodrow and Diana Chigas

48 The Dialogic Subject   780
    Ranabir Samaddar

Postscript   795
    Zachariah Cherian Mampilly

Bibliography   801

Index   851

About the Contributors
to Volume 2

Mary Anderson was cofounder of CDA, parent company to CDA Collaborative Learning Projects. She is author of *Do No Harm: How Aid Supports Peace— or War* and coauthor of *Confronting War: Critical Lessons for Peace Practitioners* and of *Getting It Right: Making Corporate-Community Relations Work.* Dr. Anderson, who received her doctorate in economics from the University of Colorado at Boulder, undertook her first overseas assignment in 1961 in the country then named Tanganyika. She remained actively involved in international work until 2009, when she retired.

Andrea Bartoli is director and S-CAR's Drucie French Cumbie Chair. He has been at the School for Conflict Analysis and Resolution (S-CAR) at George Mason University since 2007. He works primarily on peacemaking and genocide prevention. An anthropologist from Rome, Dr. Bartoli completed his Italian *dottorato di ricerca* (PhD equivalent) at the University of Milan and his *laurea* (BA-MA equivalent) at the University of Rome.

Lan Bui-Wrzosinska is assistant professor at the Warsaw School for Social Sciences and Humanities in Poland, where she is associate director of the International Center for the Study of Complexity and Conflict. Her research focuses on the dynamics of escalation in interpersonal and intergroup conflict, and especially on the changes of people's behavioral repertoire in conflict. She is involved in number of projects aimed at creating explanatory and predictive models and computer simulations of the dynamics of conflict in different cultural and social-psychological conditions.

Diana Chigas joined CDA in 2003 as codirector of the Reflecting on Peace Practice Project (RPP). She is also professor of the practice of negotiation and conflict resolution at the Fletcher School of Law and Diplomacy, where she teaches courses on negotiation and development and conflict resolution. Prior to joining CDA, Chigas worked as a facilitator, trainer, and consultant in negotiation, dialogue, and conflict resolution at Conflict Management Group, a nongovernmental organization founded by Harvard Law School Professor Roger Fisher (and now part of Mercy Corps). Her work included development of strategies, training and advice on preventive diplomacy in the OSCE, "track two" discussions in El Salvador, in South Africa, Ecuador, and Peru and in the Georgia/South Ossetia peace process, and facilitation of interethnic dialogue in Cyprus. Chigas became involved with RPP as a participant in the first phase, as CMG's programs in Cyprus and Georgia/South Ossetia were the subject of case studies.

Jonas Claes is program specialist at the U.S. Institute of Peace's Center for Conflict Management, where he conducts research on conflict prevention, the prevention of mass atrocities, and security issues in Central Asia. Claus is coauthor of a chapter on Leadership and R2P in the forthcoming *Routledge Handbook on "The Responsibility to Protect,"* edited by Andy Knight and Frazer Edgerton. He holds an MA in security studies from Georgetown University, an MA in international relations from the Katholieke Universiteit Leuven (Belgium), and a BA in political sciences from the Katholieke Universiteit Brussel. His personal research interests include the Responsibility to Protect and European conflict prevention capabilities. In 2008, Claes worked as a trainee at the Ludwig von Mises Institute-Europe in Brussels, where he represented the institute at policy debates at the European Parliament.

Peter Coleman holds a PhD in social/organizational psychology from Columbia University. He is associate professor of psychology and education at Columbia University, where he holds a joint-appointment at Teachers College and The Earth Institute and is Director of the International Center for Cooperation and Conflict Resolution (ICCCR) there. In 2003, he became the first recipient of the Early Career Award from the American Psychological Association, Division 48: Society for the Study of Peace, Conflict, and Violence. Dr. Coleman coedits *The Handbook of Conflict Resolution: Theory and Practice* (2000; 2nd edition 2006), and has authored over 60 journal articles and chapters. He is also a New York State certified mediator and experienced consultant.

Morton Deutsch is E. L. Thorndike professor emeritus of psychology and director emeritus of the International Center of Cooperation and Conflict Resolution at Teachers College, Columbia University. He has been much honored for his pioneering studies of cooperation-competition, conflict resolution social justice, interracial relations, and social conformity. He is considered to be one of the founders of the academic field of conflict resolution. His books include: *Interracial Housing*; *Research Methods in Social Relations*; *Theories in Social Psychology*; *Preventing World War III*; *The Resolution of Conflict: Constructive* *and Destructive Processes; Applying Social Psychology; Distributive Justice* and *The Handbook of Conflict Resolution: Theory and Practice.*

Louise Diamond is president of Global Systems Initiatives, bringing a whole systems perspective to critical global issues. She was the cofounder of the Institute for Multi-Track Diplomacy, where she worked as a peacebuilder in deep-rooted conflicts around the world. The author of four books on peace, Dr. Diamond received her PhD in peace studies from the Union Institute.

Jan Egeland is director of the Norwegian Institute of International Affairs and associate professor at the University of Stavanger. He was the undersecretary general of the UN for Humanitarian Affairs from 2003 to 2006 and UN Special Envoy to Colombia from 1999 to 2001. He has substantial experience in the field of conflict resolution as state secretary in the Norwegian Ministry of Foreign affairs (1990 to 1997) through the United Nations and NGOs, including Israel and PLO (Palestinian Liberation Organization), Guatemala, Sudan, Sri Lanka, Northern Uganda, and Colombia.

Ronald Fisher is a professor of international relations and director of the International Peace and Conflict Resolution program in the School of International Service at American University in Washington, DC. His primary interest focuses on interactive conflict resolution, which involves informal third-party interventions in protracted and violent ethnopolitical conflict, and his relevant publications include *Interactive Conflict Resolution* (1997) and *Paving the Way: Contributions of Interactive Conflict Resolution to Peacemaking* (2005), as well as numerous articles in interdisciplinary journals in the field of peace and conflict resolution. He holds a BA (Hon.) and MA in psychology from the University of Saskatchewan, Canada, and a PhD in social psychology from the University of Michigan.

Douglas P. Fry is professor and docent in the developmental psychology program at Åbo Akademi University in Finland and an adjunct research scientist in the Bureau of Applied Research in anthropology at the University of Arizona. Dr. Fry is author of *Beyond War* (2007), *The Human Potential for Peace* (2006) and coeditor of *Keeping the Peace: Conflict Resolution and Peaceful Societies Around the World* (2004) and *Cultural Variation in Conflict Resolution: Alternatives to Violence* (1997).

Philip Gamaghelyan is a PhD candidate at the School of Conflict Analysis and Resolution of George Mason University. He is also the cofounder and codirector of the Imagine Center for Conflict Transformation and the managing editor of the *Journal of Conflict Transformation: Caucasus Edition.* He initiated and facilitated numerous Azerbaijani-Armenian dialogue and training workshops and conferences with diverse audiences including students, politicians, and educators. Before establishing the Imagine Center and the *Caucasus Edition,* Philip served as a consultant, trainer, and facilitator for various Turkish-Armenian, Arab-Israeli, Indian-Pakistani, Afghani initiatives by Seeds of Peace, Harvard University, Brandeis University, and the Fletcher School of Law and Diplomacy. Philip lectured at Tufts University on the topics of collective memory and history in Turkish-Armenian reconciliation process. He has written methodological articles, book chapters, and manuals focusing on working with historical memory and with social media in conflicts.

Steve Killelea is an entrepreneur in high technology business development and leads philanthropic activities focused on sustainable development and peace. He is the founder of the Charitable Foundation, which specializes in working with the poorest communities in the world; the Global Peace Index, the first-ever tool for measuring the peacefulness of countries and identifying the correlations of peace; and the Institute for Economics and Peace, a research institute focusing on the linkages between business, peace and economics. He serves on advisory boards that include the International Crisis Group, the Alliance for Peacebuilding, and the OECD's Global Project on Measuring Progress of Societies, and he is an international trustee of the World Council of Religions for Peace.

Louis Kriesberg is professor emeritus of sociology, Maxwell professor emeritus of social conflict studies, and founding director of the Program on the Analysis and Resolution of Conflicts (1986–1994), all at Syracuse University. He received his PhD in sociology in 1953 from the University of Chicago. In addition to over 150 book chapters and articles, his recent books include: *Conflict Transformation and Peacebuilding* (coedited, 2009) and *Constructive Conflicts* (1998, 2003, and 2007). His current research and writing concern the field of constructive conflict, American foreign policy, and the Middle East.

Chetan Kumar is senior conflict prevention advisor, and team leader for conflict prevention and peace-building, with the Bureau for Crisis Prevention and Recovery of the UN Development Programme (UNDP). His current work focuses on building national and local capacities for the prevention or resolution of potentially violent tensions. Between 2003 and 2011, he has provided significant assistance for such initiatives—leading to the reduction of potentially violent tensions or the launch of sustained dialogue efforts—in approximately 18 countries, with results including the successful prevention of elections-related violence in eleven instances. He holds a PhD in political science from the University of Illinois at Urbana Champaign.

Zachariah Cherian Mampilly is an assistant professor of political science, international studies and Africana studies at Vassar College. His research focuses on the nature of contemporary conflict processes with an emphasis on Africa and South Asia. His first book, *Rebel Rulers: Insurgent Governance and Civilian Life During War*, was based on field work behind insurgent lines in

D.R. Congo, Sri Lanka, and Sudan. He received his PhD in political science from UCLA and his BA and MA from Tufts and Columbia, respectively.

Monty G. Marshall is a researcher and political consultant specializing in complex societal-systems analysis with emphasis on the issues of governance and development and the problem of political violence. He established and directs the Center for Systemic Peace. He has served as a senior consultant with the U.S. government's Political Instability Task Force since 1998. His systemic theory is detailed in *Third World War: System, Process, and Conflict Dynamics* (1999). He has held positions at the Universities of South Florida and Maryland and George Mason University and holds degrees from the Universities of Colorado, Maryland, and Iowa.

Simon J. A. Mason, Dr. sc. ETH Zurich, since 2005 senior researcher at the Center for Security Studies, ETH Zurich. His main research interests lie in the use of mediation in the peace process; the nexus between environment, natural resources and conflict; and the use of mediation in conflicts where religious and cultural issues play a key role. Besides training and process support, one of his main tasks within the Mediation Support Project is debriefing mediators of the Swiss FDFA and developing lessons learned.

Christopher Mitchell is professor emeritus at the School for Conflict Analysis and Resolution (S-CAR) where he was director between 1990 and 1994 and the second Drucie French Cumbie Professor, following Professor Mary Clark. Prior to that, he taught at University College, London and the University of Southampton and the City University, London. His work has included studies of mediation and problem solving workshops, as well as the initiation of peace processes.

Joseph Montville chairs the board of the Center for World Religions, Diplomacy, and Conflict Resolution at George Mason University. A retired career diplomat who served in the Middle East, North Africa, and the Department of State, he is also a founding member of the International Society of Political Psychology, which awarded him its Nevitt Sanford prize in 2008 for "distinguished professional contribution to political psychology." He is author/editor of *Conflict and Peacemaking in Multiethnic Societies, History as Prelude: Muslims and Jews in the Medieval Mediterranean,* and coeditor of *The Psychodynamics of International Relationships.* He has an AM from Harvard in Middle Eastern studies, and did doctoral studies (ABD) in comparative politics at Columbia.

Susan Allen Nan is assistant professor of conflict analysis and resolution at George Mason University. She is a scholar-practitioner of peacemaking, with current engagement in the South Caucasus region with Georgians and Ossetians. She has engaged practically in conflict contexts with the Alliance for

Conflict Transformation, the Carter Center, and was a founding member of the Alliance for Peacebuilding. Dr. Nan holds a PhD and MS in conflict analysis and resolution from George Mason University.

Andrzej Nowak is a professor of psychology at the University of Warsaw, Warsaw School of Social Sciences and Humanities, Florida Atlantic University, and a lecturer at Columbia University. His research interests include computer simulations of social processes, dynamic models of psychological and social processes, social influence, social change, social entrepreneurship, social networks, dynamics of conflict, self-structure, close relationships, and sports psychology. He is the author of several books and articles on the Dynamical Systems Theory and has contributed to the development of that field. Dr. Nowak has also inspired several generations of doctoral students to pursue their studies along those lines. He is the founder of the Center for Complex Systems Research in Warsaw.

Ryszard Praszkier, researcher at Center for Complex System, Institute for Social Studies, University of Warsaw. Main field of interest: studying the mechanisms of profound peaceful transitions, including social change processes facilitated by social entrepreneurs, with a special focus on the role and properties of social networks supporting durable social change. For over 15 years, Praszkier has been working for an international association, Ashoka, Innovators for the Public (www.ashoka.org), which has promoted social entrepreneurship since 1980 in over 70 countries, and is the author of several publications in that field.

Jamie Price is research professor of conflict analysis and resolution at George Mason University. He is also the executive director of the Sargent Shriver Peace Institute. He received his PhD from the Divinity School at the University of Chicago, and he works on the problem of peacemaking and religious conflict, with a primary interested in the problem of how to spiritualize politics without politicizing religion.

Dean Pruitt is distinguished scholar in residence at the School for Conflict Analysis and Resolution at George Mason University and SUNY distinguished professor emeritus at the University at Buffalo: State University of New York. He has received the Harold D. Lasswell award for distinguished scientific contribution to political psychology from the International Society of Political Psychology and the Lifetime Achievement Award from the International Association for Conflict Management. He is author or coauthor of more than 100 articles and chapters and the following books: *Social Conflict: Escalation, Stalemate, and Settlement*; *Negotiation Behavior*; *Mediation Research*; and *Negotiation in Social Conflict*.

Vern Neufeld Redekop is an associate professor in the conflict studies program at Saint Paul University. His involvement in training and program development has taken him to indigenous communities in Canada, as well as to Bosnia and Herzegovina, Sudan, Taiwan, and other countries. His theoretical and practical insights found expression in his book, *From Violence to Blessing: How an Understanding of Deep-Rooted Conflict Can Open Paths to Reconciliation*. Subsequent research has focused on protest crowds and police; the role of the church in the Rwandan genocide; reconciliation between Nuers and Dinkas in South Sudan; the concept of "teachings of blessing"; the nature of structural violence within economic systems; the potential for reconciliation through economic development; and spirituality, emergent creativity and reconciliation. His latest book (with Shirley Paré) is *Beyond Control: A Mutual Respect Approach to Protest Crowd—Police Relations*.

Ranabir Samaddar belongs to the school of critical thought in India. Earlier a professor of South Asian studies, he is now the director of the Calcutta Research Group. He was also the founder-director of the Peace Studies Programme at the South Asia Forum for Human Rights, Kathmandu. He has worked extensively on issues of justice and rights in the context of conflicts in South Asia. His particular researches have been on migration and refugee studies, the theory and practices of dialogue, nationalism and postcolonial statehood in South Asia, and technological restructuring and new labor regimes. He has worked on various commissions and study groups on issues such as partitions, critical dictionary on globalization, patterns of internal displacement in South Asia in the light of the UN Guiding Principles on Internal Displacement, institutional practices of refugee care and protection in India, rights of the minorities and forms of autonomy, and labor health and safety. He serves on the editorial boards of several journals and is the founding editor of *Refugee Watch*. Author of several acclaimed works, his chronicle of the history of the postcolonial subject is to be found in his newly published book, *The Emergence of the Political Subject* (Sage, 2009).

SpearIt is an assistant professor of law at St. Louis University School of Law. His expertise is in criminal law and corrections. In addition to teaching at San Quentin State Prison, he has researched gang culture at Homeboy Industries in Los Angeles. A philosophy major from the University of Houston, he earned a Master's from Harvard Divinity School, a PhD in religious studies from UC Santa Barbara, and a JD from UC Berkeley School of Law.

Robin Vallacher is professor of psychology at Florida Atlantic University and research associate in the Center for Complex Systems at University of Warsaw. His research focus is the adaptation of concepts and methods of complexity science to topics in social psychology, including self-concept, social judgment, conflict, and social change.

Paul van Tongeren established the European Centre for Conflict Prevention that, among others, published the *People Building Peace* volumes and the *Searching for Peace* series, describing the conflicts in different continents and who is working for peace. He was convener of the Global Partnership for the Prevention of Armed Conflict (GPPAC), established in 2003. In response to the call of UN Secretary-General Kofi Annan, GPPAC organized a conference at the United Nations Headquarters in New York in 2005 on the Role of Civil Society in Peace Building. Paul was secretary-general of GPPAC until 2010 and is now honorary chair.

Marshall Wallace is director of the Do No Harm Project and the Steps Towards Conflict Prevention Project at CDA Collaborative Learning Projects. He has been with CDA since 1997, during which time he has worked in over 30 countries with local people who are engaged in applying the lessons of Do No Harm. He has authored several articles and a widely used training manual on the subject of international assistance as it interacts with and either exacerbates local conflicts or, alternatively, as it can reinforce local connectors and thus support peace. Wallace has taught special courses at American University; Tufts University; Clark University; and the University of Massachusetts, Boston.

Peter Wallensteen holds the Dag Hammarskjöld Chair of Peace and Conflict Research, Uppsala University, Uppsala, Sweden (since 1985) and is the Richard G. Starmann Sr. Research Professor of Peace Studies, Joan B. Kroc Institute of International Peace Studies, University of Notre Dame, Indiana (since 2006). Wallensteen directs the Uppsala Conflict Data Program (UCDP), which publishes annual information on conflicts and peace efforts in the world (www.ucdp.uu.se). His *Understanding Conflict Resolution* (Sage, 2011, 3rd ed.) explains the basics of this approach and is used worldwide in teaching. Wallensteen also leads the Special Program on the Implementation of Targeted Sanctions, SPITS, (www.smartsanctions.se). A study of arms embargoes was presented to the United Nations in New York in November 2007 and International Sanctions. *Between Words and Wars in the Global System* (Frank Cass/ Routledge, 2005, edited with Carina Staibano) updates the field. Wallensteen has published works on third parties, conflict resolution, and mediation, most recently with Isak Svensson, *The Go-Between: Jan Eliasson and the Styles of Mediation* (US Institute of Peace Press, 2010).

Anthony Wanis-St. John is assistant professor in the International Peace and Conflict Resolution program at American University's School of International Service. He received his PhD and MALD from Tufts University's Fletcher School, and was a graduate research fellow at the program on negotiation at Harvard Law School. His research focuses on all aspects of international negotiation and peace processes, and he is the author of *Back Channel Negotiation: Secrecy in Middle East Peacemaking* (Syracuse University Press, 2011).

Joshua Weiss is a negotiation expert and the cofounder, with William Ury, of the Global Negotiation Initiative at Harvard University. He is also the managing director of the Abraham Path Initiative. He received his PhD from the

Institute for Conflict Analysis and Resolution (S-CAR) at George Mason University in 2002. Dr. Weiss has spoken and published on negotiation, mediation, and systemic approaches to dealing with conflict. In his current capacity, he conducts research; consults with many different types of organizations; delivers negotiation and mediation trainings and courses; and engages in negotiation and mediation at the organizational, corporate, government, and international levels. Weiss is the creator of the Negotiation Tip of the Week (NTOW) podcast. The NTOW has been in the top 100 iTunes Business Podcasts for the past three years and has been downloaded over 2 million times during that period. Weiss has conducted training and consulted with a number of organizations and companies, nonprofit entities, governments, and international organizations.

Abiodun Williams is vice president of the Center for Conflict Analysis and Prevention at the U.S. Institute of Peace. He worked at the United Nations for several years and served as director of strategic planning for Secretaries-General Kofi Annan and Ban Ki-moon. He has taught international relations at Georgetown, Tufts, and the University of Rochester. He holds an MA (Hons) in English Language and Literature from Edinburgh University, and an MALD and a PhD from the Fletcher School of Law and Diplomacy.

Peter Woodrow is codirector of the Reflecting on Peace Practice Project (RPP), based at the CDA Collaborative Learning Projects in Cambridge, Massachusetts. The RPP is an experience-based learning process that involves agencies whose programs attempt to prevent or mitigate violent conflict. Its goal is to improve the effectiveness of international efforts in peacebuilding. Woodrow is an experienced mediator, facilitator, trainer, and consultant. He is skilled in negotiation, collaborative problem solving, and dispute resolution systems design, and has mediated and facilitated issue resolution within organizations, as well as multiparty environmental and public policy disputes. He has also developed and implemented international programs in consensus building, problem solving, decision making and interethnic conflict resolution in Asia, Africa, and Eastern Europe. He has worked with the Peacebuilding Fund process in Liberia, the UN Bureau for Crisis Prevention and Recovery, and the UN Framework Team for Conflict Prevention. He is the coauthor, with Christopher Moore, of the *Handbook of Global and Multicultural Negotiation*. Woodrow holds a master's in public administration from the John F. Kennedy School of Government, Harvard University, and a BA in government from Oberlin College.

PART III: NEW DIRECTIONS IN PEACEMAKING

Introduction

Andrea Bartoli

Peace processes are on the rise. They happen more often, and they contribute more significantly to the international system as a whole. Peace processes are intentional, collective efforts to move human groups respectfully from active hostility to inquiry. We—as human family—are starting to recognize and comprehend them more precisely. We can document them, compare them, and study them in ways that are unprecedented. Because we live still in a nation-state centered system we tend to see these processes through that lens. We have complex databases tracking each state's peacefulness from year to year and tracking each conflict. Yet peace processes are more pervasive, vivacious, and creative than many have imagined. Peacemaking today happens in a world that is different from the world of 10, 20, or 30 years ago. We have e-mail, the Web, Twitter, and Facebook. The cold war gave rise to new international realities. The threats of global warming are becoming increasingly clear. The world is different. So although we salute the scholarship on peacemaking already available, we recognize the need to further our collective knowledge through new analysis and approaches that acknowledge today's peacemaking in today's world.

Peacemaking is difficult, fragile, and complex and emerges in multiple forms. In recent years, new protagonists have experimented with it, especially non-state actors. Recently, more conflicts have been addressed through negotiated settlement than previously known. The trend has been dramatic. "The Uppsala Conflict Data Program (UCDP)[1] reports that 119 armed conflicts were fought in the period 1989–2004. The warring parties signed peace agreements in one-third of all conflicts. A total of 139 agreements solving, regulating, or deciding on a process for how to regulate the incompatibility were found in the conflicts."[2] Yet this data is misleading. We are still constrained by a nation-state paradigm. What happens at the local level? What is the way to learn from those who are peacemaking at the level of villages, communities, and regions? And at the same time, what are the processes that we see emerging at the global level across nation-states?

We are at the beginning of a sustained practice-to-theory movement, a collective effort to learn from actual experiences, to update our understanding of peacemaking to reflect today's realities, to theorize properly, and to verify results. Many of the authors presenting in this section have their theoretical reflections emerging from actual experiences of the recent years' peacemaking. From the strategic connections identified by Marshall Wallace and Mary Anderson to the insights of Ryszard Praszkier and Andrzej Nowak on social entrepreneurs and their indirect approach to peacemaking, we see the promise of the practice-to-theory process. We know that experientially many make peace: what are the processes that allow that emergence? Complexity and adaptability are closely related to the emergence of peace in situation like gang violence, analyzed by SpearIt and infrastructures for peace presented by Chetan Kumar and Paul van Tongeren. Many human groups, sometimes nation-states and their organizations, sometimes non-state actors, are experimenting around peacemaking. They are trying new and old ways to handle conflict constructively, to respond to basic human needs appropriately and represent identities politically. Many of these entities are relatively new or refer to new constructs—like the Responsibility to Protect presented in the peacemaking context by Abiodun Williams and Jonas Claes. The pace of innovation is significant and takes new form when areas such as peace and economy are linked, as in the case of the Global Peace Index developed by Steve Killelea; or in the case of social media studied by Philip Gamaghelyan. When an established scholar such as Peter Wallensteen is writing about academic diplomacy, we see the emergence of a reflection about the very nature of the decision making that establishes the conditions for peace. In conflict situations, positions are hardened by numerous interactions. To let new possibilities emerge and be allowed is a difficult path, as testified by Joshua Weiss in his presentation of the Abraham Path, the effort to create a pathway through the countries of the Middle East following the traces of Abraham/Ibrahim.

What these contributions address is the relational and systemic dimensions of peacemaking today. Local groups and individuals as well as large political formations do peacemaking. At all levels successful peacemaking is innovating. It is innovating in relation to the conflict system by elaborating alternatives and implementing them. But is also innovating in the way peacemaking itself is conceptualized and actualized. Innovation seems to emerge especially along three axes: power, meaning, and relationships.

The literature on power is immense. For our reflections in this volume we are particularly indebted to the work of Peter Coleman who distinguished between constructive, destructive, and integrative forms of power. These different forms of power are significant in all conflicts and peacemaking efforts. Because all conflicts are relational, in that they occur between two or more parties, there is always a power structure that is created and operated. The structure can be balanced, participatory, and mutually empowering or, on the contrary, be asymmetric, exclusivist, and oppressive. Every conflict references power and the structures that power defines for the parties involved. Often, power is associated with respect, with the capacity to be properly recognized, listed to, appreciated, and valued. Change occurs and introduces disruptions in expected patterns that must be addressed. The conflict occurs when one or both parties do not wish to recognize the presence and power of the interlocutor, preferring to constrain the other's capacity for agency and freedom. Yet they are unable to win, to impose an outcome, a desired goal to the other that has become an adversary, an enemy. The relational system appears therefore to be inadequate because the power structure is unable to adjudicate and determine an outcome. Moreover, the system appears to be unstable because decisions need to be accepted by all to be sustainable over time. Who decides? Who is right? Once again, the conflict reveals something that the parties might not have been able (or willing) to recognize, address, and change: the inadequacy of power as it is experienced in that particular context. What the conflict reveals is not only the current structure of power but also the implicit call to change it. Adversaries can talk, but the communication can be inconclusive or even dangerous. Each party will police its own ranks to make sure that no one who is not authorized will approach the enemy. Those who connect with the enemy without proper instructions are traitors. In any violent confrontations, they are simply killed.

Peacemaking occurs when the parties become able to recognize each other's presence and power, acknowledging the need to understand each other and cocreate a power structure in which they both have a reasonable investment. Until that point, however, the conflict reveals the fragility of their interactions, of the frames that they are using and of the process that is at their disposal. The conflict reveals the inadequacy of the parties and of the system that is not allowing them to address the contention effectively. By expressing the conflict in adversarial terms, they position themselves one against the other. The power structure becomes open to escalation, responses that react to issues of power and its dimensions, especially respect and rank.

Power structures, defined as the operative links available to the parties to affect or resist change, can be oriented toward further destruction or toward constructive goals or be used in an integrative form. These choices are the key to the emergence of the learning about oneself, the other and the system in which the conflict is taking place. A solution of a conflict that does not address power either confirms the status quo or is unsustainable. One preliminary observation regarding power in a conflict resolution is that it pertains to who has the power to decide the process by which the outcome is determined. There are four modalities of decision making:

1. unilateral decisions
2. arbitration
3. mediation
4. negotiation

In unilateral decisions an actor has the power to decide for both parties. Many—especially in the United States—tend to associate this modality with adverse, exploitive outcomes in which the more powerful actor who is able to decide will necessarily take advantage and maximize gains against the other. However, this is experientially not true. Humans are perfectly capable of decisions that—while unilateral and taken only by one actor—have both parties' interests and needs addressed. Many power-imbalanced human relationships (e.g., parent–child; teacher–student) may lead to extremely creative and inclusive decisions that are not negotiated, mediated, or arbitrated. It is possible to do good unilaterally, to move human systems toward peacemaking unilaterally. It is not said that these moves would be effective, but individuals and groups can most certainly decide unilaterally to seek peace rather than more violent options. Both human and abstract entities constructed by humans (families, tribes, states, parties, and organizations) can make responsible decisions by themselves regarding a multitude of others. In certain cases, we routinely move in this direction. Think, for example, about how we make decisions regarding our health. We seek the expert knowledge of a physician. Although we might negotiate some of the doctor's decisions in general terms, when we are in the operating room, the surgeon is responsible for making sound decisions for all involved. It is important to remember that unilateral decisions can be caring ones. Unilateral decisions actually may describe very altruistic behavior. A caring mother does not need to negotiate with her child over why it is good to wash one's hands before meals. A unilateral decision made by a devout son to take in his elderly father and turn down a promising career move does not require an arbiter to be seen as good. What makes a unilateral decision proper in a situation of conflict is to consider all elements, aspects, and conditions that the inadequacy is revealing.

On the other hand, victimization results from unilateral decisions in which these considerations have not been made and one party is deprived of its ability to express its next move. Victims are acted upon by others. Perpetrators decide for themselves and the victim(s). The victims have no way to decide or to decide back. They are made victims; they do not decide to be victims. From cases of home violence to genocide, victims are deprived of their power and given one role, one status, one condition that they did not deserve and did not choose. If someone would seek a unified, comprehensive horizon for conflict resolution as a field of practice and inquiry, it should be "work for a world without victims." The power imbalance must be such that the victim cannot react and/or escape. Destructive conflict, degenerating into violence, always reveals constraints. The victim is deprived of the power to chose, to move, to inquire. The situation is determined by one party that is committed to violating the other and expecting not to be corrected. If any intermediary could act wisely and effectively, then there would be no need for violence. Parties could be helped by caring others to seek what is true and accept it together, joining forces to live fully. This is the extraordinary gift that has been brought to many involved in the restorative justice movement. Victims and perpetrators, families and friends of both, people affected by crimes, have been brought together by an open, honest, serious search of truth and reconciliation. The fruits of this work are beautiful and astonishing. Indeed, humans can find themselves again, together, in peace, after painful experiences of violence and hate.

Together these chapters confirm that peace is made continuously and in very daring circumstances, it is associated with innovation and creativity and can be analyzed further through a rigorous and systematic practice-to-theory process.

NOTES

1. http://www.pcr.uu.se/research/UCDP/ucdp_projects/peace_agreements. htm.

2. S. Högbladh, "Patterns of Peace Agreements—Presenting New Data on Peace Processes and Peace Agreements" (paper presented at the annual meeting of the International Studies Association, Town & Country Resort and Convention Center, San Diego, California Online, March 22, 2006, http://www.allacademic.com/meta/p99120_index.html).

Building National "Infrastructures for Peace": UN Assistance for Internally Negotiated Solutions to Violent Conflict

Chetan Kumar

THE LIMITS OF TRADITIONAL MEDIATION

Based on publicly available information on rising levels of interethnic tension, deep impasses on core issues, rapid onset of turbulence or transitions, or increased linkages between politics and criminality, 87 countries in all of the world's regions can currently be identified as facing the prospects of potential violence, prolonged deadlock, or a relapse into violent conflict over the next two- to three-year period. Of these, only 23 are currently receiving formal mediation assistance from the UN, including by the virtue of a peace operation.[1]

Some others have benefited from the peacemaking efforts of regional or nongovernmental organizations, but for the majority, there is no internal political consensus on receiving external assistance for mediation, especially where violent conflict has not erupted on a sufficiently significant scale. For many, external mediation would also constitute a fundamental interruption of sovereignty.

Beyond the lack of entry points for external mediation, the factors currently precipitating potentially violent tensions in many of the vulnerable countries may not be susceptible to external mediation alone. Yet, the need for peacemaking intended as intentional response to actual and perceived threats is great. Although mediation remains a critical tool, it may not be sufficient for the following type of situations:

1. Situations where the conflict is not limited to the primary protagonists alone, but extends through the different levels of society, from political and civic leaderships down through to communities; in these situations, which are especially correlated with interethnic tensions or exclusion based on identity,

an external mediator, even if backed by a very large team, may not be able to reach to and resolve every level and type of conflict.

2. Situations where ongoing or potential violence is not a variable of a centralized conflict, but decentralized violence over land, natural resources, allocation of mining and other land use rights, and chieftaincy which nevertheless affects national stability; West Africa in particular has been plagued by this type of conflict.[2]

3. Situations of deep, rapid, and continuous political or socioeconomic transformation, or even revolution, where the challenge is not the resolution of a specific conflict, but providing continuous accompaniment to all relevant actors engaged in a necessary transition so that the eventual outcome is based on inclusion and consensus and does not lead to more instability or repression; many countries in the Middle East are undergoing this transition.

4. Situations where potentially violent instability may result from the creeping influence of illicit trafficking, especially in weapons or narcotics, over the political system; the core conflict prevention challenge in these cases, mostly to be found in Central America and parts of Africa, is to build sufficient confidence between the state and communities so that they can work together to address chronic insecurity.[3]

In all these situations, attentive, intelligent, reasonable, and responsible actions are needed, reinserting peacemaking among the options available to all relevant actors. This is why external mediation may need to be complemented or substituted where entry points do not exist, with the development and application of national and local capacities for conflict prevention and for internal mediation. Such capacities can be described variously, but the best descriptions are offered by their users.

DEFINING NATIONAL INFRASTRUCTURES FOR PEACE[4]

Meeting in Naivasha, Kenya, in February 2010, representatives of governments, political parties, civil society, and UN Country Teams from 14 African countries agreed on a definition of infrastructures for peace, or the "dynamic network of interdependent structures, mechanisms, resources, values, and skills which, through dialogue and consultation, contribute to conflict prevention and peace-building in a society." Participants then committed to concrete plans to promote and develop this infrastructure in their countries. In doing so, they also agreed to draw on the experiences of countries such as Ghana and Kenya, which have recently developed and applied these infrastructures for resolving local conflicts or for ensuring a peaceful election (Ghana, 2008) or referendum (Kenya, 2010).

Such infrastructure, which can also be stated as constituting a society's collaborative capacity, can help a fragile, divided, or post-conflict society, or a society in rapid transition, to make and sustain peace by

1. managing recurrent conflicts over land, natural resources, apportioning of mineral wealth, and contested elections, especially where development itself has exacerbated these conflicts;

2. finding internal solutions, through a mediated consensus or a multi-stakeholder dialogue, to specific conflicts and tensions, especially in circumstances where concerns over sovereignty are paramount;

3. complementing external mediation targeted at the primary parties with internal negotiations that bring together actors at different levels of the society and polity, often inaccessible to itinerant external mediation, or a wider group of stakeholders, including civil society, thus broadening the base for peace; and

4. negotiating and implementing new governing arrangements in an inclusive and consensual manner, especially after periods of turbulent political or socio-economic transition.

The World Bank's World Development Report for 2011 focuses in particular on the challenges of addressing protracted and endemic armed violence and fragility through the reform of institutions, especially the security sector. In doing so, it highlights the extended period of time required for meaningful transformation, and the necessity in this context of internal collaboration, especially inclusive enough coalitions that can generate the collective political will for reform. The bargaining and internal mediation that is in turn required to sustain these coalitions highlights the necessity for infrastructures for peace, and the report mentions Ghana's National Peace Council (detailed later in this chapter) as one good example.

The United Nations system, and especially the UN Development Programme (UNDP) in close collaboration with the Department for Political affairs (DPA), is currently supporting efforts to establish such infrastructures or to conduct specific dialogue or conflict management activities leading to such infrastructures, in approximately 30 countries.[5]

Against baselines of previous rounds of violence, emerging patterns of tension similar to those that have led to violence in other countries, and prolonged periods of deadlock that have obstructed common efforts to achieve development objectives, successful conflict prevention in these instances is being measured through an increase in cooperative behavior leading to consensual solutions, peaceful political transitions, and reduction in levels of ongoing tension and violence. In the past five years, such results have been obtained with UN assistance in 15 countries, or one-third of the 45 countries where it is currently being provided.

An important emerging concept that relates to infrastructures for peace is that of insider mediation. In November 2010, a group of African nongovernmental organizations providing mediation assistance in different parts of the continent met in South Africa, with the support of the Peace Nexus Foundation, a Swiss organization, and UNDP to launch an "African Insider Mediators' Platform." As opposed to mediators who are invited from the outside to assist with the resolution of a conflict, insider mediators are seen as being endogenous to a situation, either by virtue of being resident in the country as part of permanent international presences, such as UN Country Teams, trusted bilateral partners, or regional organizations' offices, or by being viewed as neutral or autonomous citizens or domestic institutions with specific capacities and skills for mediation and negotiation.[6] Insider mediators are in a significantly better position to reach the different levels of conflict in a society and to also accompany protracted processes of change and institutional transformation.[7]

INFRASTRUCTURES FOR PEACE VERSUS TRADITIONAL APPROACHES TO CONFLICT PREVENTION

The emphasis on building and applying national and local capacities for conflict prevention, and the associated concepts of infrastructures for peace and insider mediation, marks an important departure from traditional approaches to conflict prevention:

- *First, the traditional dichotomy between structural and operational prevention, first proposed by the Carnegie Commission on Preventing Deadly Conflicts, is now transcended.* The UN's development presence is currently seen as an important vehicle for conflict prevention, not just by doing more or better-quality development, but also by equipping national and local actors with the skills and tools to manage specific conflicts and tensions in the short to intermediate term. Hence, development is the vehicle not just for structural but also operational prevention. Conversely, the political arm of the UN now increasingly supports the building of national capacities for conflict prevention (Ghana's National Peace Council received assistance from both UNDP and DPA) as complements or substitutes to more traditional diplomacy. Many of these activities can be described as preventive peacemaking, actions intentionally designed to reduce the occurrence and severity of violent, destructive conflicts.

- *Second, the traditional divide between development and diplomacy as distinct tools of promoting peace and security is also transcended.* On the one hand, development is now recognized as bringing new resources, actors, and interests into society and hence inevitably generating new conflicts which can lead to violence if not well managed and greater inclusion and progress if channeled into positive change. Again, the key difference lies in a society's collaborative capacity. Conversely, diplomats recognize that external interventions may at best freeze complex and multilayered conflicts if not accompanied internal or endogenous processes of change. Conflict sensitive development and effective diplomacy, therefore, require the same tools, which are national and local capacities for conflict prevention.

- *Third, the onus for action in this new approach shifts decisively to internal actors who are part of a situation, as opposed to external actors alone.* Bilateral and multilateral partners are no longer the ones preventing conflict, but are instead supporting a diverse group of domestic actors to do so. The upside of this approach is that it ensures both greater local ownership as well as the longevity of solutions thus developed. The downside is that where public or civic space is largely contested or polarized, widely trusted change agents or internal mediators either may not be available or may not have the political space in which to facilitate the right conversations or behavioral change.

- *Fourth, the profile of technical and professional staff employed by international organizations to support efforts to build national and local capacities for conflict prevention is also significantly different from the more conventional categories* and matches more closely the expertise found in professional civic or private organizations supporting conflict resolution and mitigation efforts. The UN, in particular, has taken the lead in moving beyond the traditional categories of diplomats, analysts, and program managers. UNDP and DPA jointly deploy peace and development advisers (PDAs)[8] through UNDP Country Offices to support national counterparts with their own conflict prevention and management efforts. These advisers combine strong skill for analysis, competencies for mediation and facilitation, and leadership of programmatic initiatives that help national and local actors acquire and apply skills and tools for conflict resolution. In other words, they are diplomats, analysts, and program managers rolled into one.[9]

- The presence of appropriately skilled staff is also crucial given that a focus on national and local capacities requires a nuanced, politically sensitive, and careful understanding and analysis of the actors who are best placed to support the transformation of conflicts into avenues for positive change or to promote the peaceful and consensual resolution of potentially violent tensions. UNDP, for instance, has developed and is currently upgrading a conflict-related development analysis (CDA) methodology[10] that brings together relevant national and international actors in-country, often facilitated by PDAs or similar specialists, to develop joint or shared analyses of the precipitants of possibly violent tensions or significant deadlocks that could stymie the achievement of key development goals, and to propose common solutions. The analyses then prepare the basis for appropriately equipped and autonomous forums or individuals to help move forward, in a negotiated and inclusive manner, the implementation of the commonly identified innovations and reforms.

- *Fifth, and finally, the new approach has helped move the discourse on conflict prevention more toward the global South.* Many developing countries, and especially rising powers such as Brazil, Turkey, and India, have traditionally been skeptical of the conflict prevention agenda as articulated by primarily northern institutes and think tanks, especially as the agenda has hitherto focused primarily on external interventions into internal conflicts. The emphasis on building national and local capacities for conflict prevention, and based primarily on southern experiences—such as Ghana's National Peace Council,[11] Kenya's increasingly functional system of "district peace committees,"[12] Nepal's Ministry for Peace and Reconstruction, and Timor Leste's Department for Peace-Building and Social Cohesion[13] in the Ministry of Social Solidarity—again places the responsibility and the onus for conflict prevention on the concerned governments and civil societies themselves. This has led to a significantly greater numbers of entry points for preventive action than is the case with the traditional, more interventionist approaches.

- For example, following the experience-sharing exercise in Naivasha referred to at the beginning of the chapter, Togo requested assistance for establishing a national peace architecture similar to Ghana's. The National Governing Council of the African Peer Review Mechanism Process of Uganda convened a high-level consultation in July 2010, based on feedback from the Ugandan delegation to the Naivasha meeting, on establishing a national peace architecture to address the country's burgeoning conflicts over land, natural resources, and traditional authority. The prime minister attended the consultation, and the process to establish a viable conflict management system is expected to gather momentum in 2011. Similarly, the Tanzanian delegation, which included the

Inspector-General of Police, applied ideas developed during the course of the Naivasha meeting to the peaceful and successful conduct of the Zanzibar referendum later in 2010.

The Naivasha meeting underscored the degree to which the sharing of experiences and learning among developing countries themselves remains underused as a tool for generating entry points for preventive action.

EXAMPLES OF RECENT UN ASSISTANCE

Much of the ongoing UN support for the development and application of conflict management capabilities is active in the approximately 45 countries in which it is being provided; that is, it involves ongoing and sensitive processes of internal dialogue and negotiation. Hence, an indicative sample and summaries of country-level results for 15, or one-third, of the countries are provided here:

1. *Guyana:* In 2006, after a period of rising political tension, Guyana conducted its first ever violence-free elections. An independent external evaluation conclusively attributed this result to a UNDP-supported national initiative known as the Social Cohesion Programme. A national dialogue, a network of local mediators to help ease tensions among communities, and agreements among political parties were some of the instruments used.[14]

2. *Bolivia:* In 2008, oil-and-mineral-rich Bolivia almost descended into social violence over a dispute over constitutional reform that followed a period of rising political tension. Working through instruments such as independent public surveys, credible information on the technical issues faced by the parties, and facilitation and observation through its country team when requested, the UN discreetly assisted internal negotiations in reaching consensus around a new constitution.[15]

3. *Ghana:* Ghana is West Africa's most stable democracy. Yet in December 2008, chieftaincy-related conflicts in parts of the country, and the discovery of oil led to new tensions as the country approached national elections, and the prospects for violence increased. When the elections were held, the narrowest margin of votes recorded in an African election—50,000 votes—separated the winner and the loser. With tensions rising, the National Peace Council, an autonomous national statutory body established with UNDP assistance, helped mediate a peaceful political transition. According to Emmanuel Bombande, a Ghanaian and the founder of the West Africa Network for Peace, "When it mattered most in an extremely difficult moment during Ghana's elections in 2008, the National Peace Council was there to save Ghana."

   Previously, the UN had discreetly assisted the mediation efforts of the Asantehene, the Ashanti king, and the Northern Region Peace Advisory Council (the precursor to the National Peace Council) in brokering peace in the long-standing violent conflict in the Dagomba kingdom on Northern Ghana, thus also ensuring violence-free elections in 2004.

4. *Ecuador-Colombia:* Over a five-year period from 2004 to 2009, a UN interagency initiative assisted national efforts to stabilize Ecuador's northern border region with Colombia. Already facing internal social conflict, Ecuador

was also confronted with spillovers from the activities of armed groups in Colombia, with communities along the border overwhelmed with refugees, gang violence, and illicit trafficking. By 2009, levels of crime and violence had been reduced in these areas, services improved, and dialogue established to resolve local conflicts. More importantly, despite upswings and downturns in Ecuador–Colombia relations, lasting bilateral collaboration had been established between both governments to address these issues.

5. *Kenya:* In 2010, Kenya, which is Africa's second-largest non-oil economy, held a constitutional referendum without single incident of violence. This followed the failed 2007 elections when 1,500 people were killed, and an additional 300,000 displaced. In advance of the referendum, UNDP provided quiet support for successful national efforts to reach a political agreement on the new draft constitution and helped government and civil society implement an early warning and response system—the Uwiano Platform[16]—that prevented over a hundred incidents of potential violence in the volatile Rift Valley region alone. Local peace committees were strengthened in all of the country's districts and played a critical peacemaking role during the referendum. Following the vote, UNDP is now assisting interparty dialogue on the implementation of the new constitution.

6. *Togo:* The 2005 national elections in Togo had seen about 250 deaths. However, in 2010, the establishment of a platform for political dialogue prior to national elections and the ability of civic actors to conduct a sustained peace campaign led to a reduction in tensions and peaceful elections, as well as a stable postelectoral period. Specifically, an agreement on critical postelection governance reforms was reached *prior* to the February poll; an agreement among political parties was reached in March 2010 to develop a national conflict management architecture (drawing on the experience of Ghana's National Peace Council was also reached); and a political party code of conduct and a public peace campaign were developed and implemented with UNDP assistance. The further development and consolidation of a national peace architecture will be a priority in 2011.

7. *Solomon Islands:* The 2005 national elections in Solomon Islands had seen the burning down of half of the capital city of Honiara, especially during the tense period of jockeying for the position of prime minister that followed the polls. In 2010, no violence occurred during or after the national elections. UNDP had supported a nationally led truth and reconciliation process that helped heal wounds from previous rounds of violence and therefore helped reduce tensions. During and after the elections, a small joint UNDP/DPA monitoring team assisted national negotiations with quite observation and facilitation.

8. *Timor Leste:* East Timor's fragile peace process almost collapsed between 2007 and 2009 as the return of refugees and internally displaced persons caused a significant increase in conflicts over land. With UN assistance, a network of community mediators was trained and deployed, and their conflict resolution efforts had enabled the return and resettlement of 13,000 families by 2010. In recognition of these efforts, the government is now working with UNDP to establish a new department of peacebuilding, in order for the country to have its own standing system for internal mediation.

9. *Kyrgyzstan:* In Kyrgyzstan, potentially violent tensions (after the April 2010 political regime change and subsequent violence) were de-escalated before and during the constitutional referendum and parliamentary polls later that

year, allowing these exercises to be conducted without violence. UNDP facilitated dialogue spaces between civil society, the Central Electoral Commission, and security agencies, hitherto suspicious of each other following events of April through June. It helped establish, and then supported the confidence-building efforts of, Oblast Advisory Committees (OACs) at the provincial, Local Authority Advisory Committees (LAACs), and district levels. For example, the OAC of Issyk-Gul facilitated dialogue between law enforcement agencies and youth and conducted awareness-raising campaigns on the risks of religious extremism.

10. *Sierra Leone:* Sierra Leone's 2007 elections marked the first transition of power since the end of the civil war. However, both prior to and during and after the elections, political tensions and the potential for violence were significantly high. UNDP equipped the Political Parties Registration Commission to play the role of an independent convener and mediator[17] and also supported the deployment of local level mediators, alongside a sustained advocacy campaign for peace, led and conducted by often disempowered youth. The elections and the subsequent transfer of power to the opposition were peaceful. More significantly, calls to violence by segments of the political leadership were not answered by the youth.

11. *Lesotho:* Lesotho's modern experience of democracy and constitutional monarchy has been characterized by prolonged deadlock, leading to violence that precipitated a SADC military intervention in 1998 and again raised potentially violent tensions in mid-2009. In the latter instance, a national church-led platform was formed to mediate among the major political actors and received very discreet UN support. While the mediation continues at the time of writing and has not yet resolved the primary political deadlock, it has lowered tensions that had brought the country to the brink again. The UN is now investing in a program to build the collaborative capacity of all key actors—government, political, and civic leaders and the private sector—so as to ensure that governance is not the platform for perennial deadlock, but delivers the services and participation that it is expected to provide.[18]

12. *Cyprus:* UN support for civil society–led track-two initiatives has strengthened communications across Turkish and Cypriot communities through media products jointly developed by the Cyprus Community Media Centre and through the Joint Contact Room (JCR) established to support the sharing of information between the police forces in the Turkish and Greek Cypriot communities, the first such instrument of its kind.[19] These and other targeted activities have led to a significant increase (as measured in terms of numbers of joint activities) in direct people-to-people contact across Greek and Turkish Cypriot boundaries in 2010 and in turn created greater political space for public leaders advocating for a resolution of the Cypriot conflict through UN-supported track-one diplomacy. As a result, the latter is expected to accelerate at the time of writing.

13. *Georgia:* The first ever systematic people-to-people contact and confidence-building, through civil society organizations working through the UNDP-assisted Confidence-Building and Early Response Mechanism (COBERM)[20] program, were initiated in 2010 across the administrative boundary line with Abkhazia by means of parallel technical assistance to organizations on both sides. These activities, which will be continued in the intermediate term, provide the basis for longer-term confidence-building and are significant in that,

for now, formal diplomatic options toward the resolution of Georgia's frozen conflicts have been exhausted.

14. *Nigeria:* Central Nigeria has provided the stage for significant intercommunity violence over the past 10 years. In what could be a model for other conflicts in that region, a long-standing violent conflict in the Agila local government area of Benue state in Central Nigeria was resolved in 2009 through local mediation efforts conducted by an Abuja-based women's organization, Women Environmental Development (WED), with support from local women's groups and from UNDP. The process employed modern mediation as well as traditional reconciliation methods, and the implementation of the agreement reached in 2009 combines efforts to improve both local livelihoods and the empowerment of women.

15. *Guinea-Conakry:* A national platform established in January 2010 with UNDP assistance to sustain multi-stakeholder dialogue and consensus during the political transition to civilian rule shepherded by Gen. Sekouba Konate. Together with regional diplomacy, its work led to a first round of peaceful presidential polls in June 2010 and the successful negotiation of the dates for the second round of presidential elections in October 2010. While interethnic and political violence occurred both before and after the second round of presidential polls in October–November 2010, its spread was contained through a combination of the work of the platform, together with regional and UN diplomatic efforts. UN efforts now continue to strengthen the country's own capacities for dialogue, conflict management, and interethnic reconciliation.

BEST PRACTICES AND POINTERS FOR FURTHER ACTION

Although a systematic analysis of UN's engagement in support of national conflict prevention efforts is still being undertaken, some preliminary best practices and pointers toward future conflict-prevention practice have emerged, as in-depth evaluations have been undertaken of efforts in particular cases, most recently Guyana, Ecuador, Kenya, and Ghana.

Complementarity between National and International Initiatives

When efforts to build and apply capacities have been undertaken together with regional or international diplomacy, they clearly demonstrate that the latter requires the former to achieve its full order of success. In Kenya, the "Concerned Citizens for Peace" initiative by a group of senior Kenyan leaders opened the domestic space for Kofi Annan's mediation following postelection violence in 2008. Subsequently, once the Kenyan leadership had declined further international mediation, internal efforts helped sustain negotiations over the draft constitution and other vital reforms. In Kyrgyzstan, local Oblast Advisory Committees were as critical as regional and UN diplomacy to maintaining peace on the ground during the referendum and parliamentary elections. However, as compared to resources currently invested in strengthening international ore regional diplomacy, relatively few efforts have been made to strengthen national mediation capacities.

The Importance of Accompaniment by Insiders

Behaviors and attitudes, vital to transforming conflicts into opportunities for progressive change, cannot be altered in consequential ways through one-shot itinerant diplomacy aimed at specific disputes or through time-bound projects aimed at limited results. Instead, the development and application of national and local capacities requires sustained accompaniment, wherein specialists assist their counterparts in overcoming initial suspicion and hostility by developing relations of trust, then impart skills for negotiation and mediation in a sensitive manner, and finally accompany them in applying these skills. In the process, they also assist them in thinking through and working together to install the institutional capacities necessary for longer-term conflict management (as indicated earlier, Ghana's National Peace Council emerged from efforts to resolve the violent conflict in the Dagomba kingdom).

Peace and development advisers, in that they play these roles and are resident in-country with UNDP, are seen as insider mediators by their counterparts, and not as external interveners. The same could also be true for other resident in-country staff of various bilateral and multilateral partners. Again, very few resources have been expended in ensuring that these staff have the requisite skills for analysis and facilitation, and the requisite political sensitivity, so that they can play the role of insider mediators when necessary.

In an increasingly turbulent world, cascading crises will often prompt rolling transitions like the ones that are currently being seen in the Middle East, and which will not take the form of specific conflicts amenable to traditional diplomacy, even where such diplomacy is invited (certainly Egypt, Tunisia, and Bahrain have not invited any). Hence, it will be increasingly critical that discreet resources are available in-country to accompany these transitions.

The Importance of Entry Points

Conflict prevention begins and ends with the way the case is made for it. Parties that are responsible for precipitating potentially violent tensions, either directly or inadvertently through their actions, are highly unlikely to accept the reality of emerging conflict and take remedial actions if confronted up-front with their own role in it, especially by external actors. They are more likely to get their backs up and close the doors to preventive action. Most initiatives to developing national capacities for conflict prevention start therefore with an elicitive approach, wherein pertinent actors are encouraged to analyze impediments to development (rather than the fact or potential for conflict) in a manner that does not immediately threaten anyone's positions or interests. Inevitably, as actors become more comfortable—as part of a structured, facilitated process—with confronting issues such as polarization, exclusion, or lack of ability to forge consensus, entry points emerge for preventive action, even as the attitudes of the participating actors begin to be transformed.

Governments and Other Actors Are Not Monolithic

Even under the most complex and rigid political environments, the exercise of power still leaves openings for some degree of constructive change. The trick is to identify those individuals and institutions that could be change agents and then find ways of assisting them without compromising them or using them to drive externally developed conceptions of the desired change. Efforts to develop and apply the skills and capacities for conflict management allow such actors to acquire credible roles as facilitators and interlocutors in neutral settings without being seen as serving external diplomatic agendas. For example, even in Zimbabwe's highly polarized setting, key individuals in government and academia opened doorways for UNDP and the UN Department for Economic and Social Affairs in 2002 for a nationwide effort to train members of parliament, civic organizations, the civil service, and the private sector in basic skills for conflict transformation and constructive negotiation. The program pointedly did not aim to resolve specific conflicts, but focused instead on building skills that all actors could find useful. Subsequently, individuals who were appropriately equipped through this program played key roles in the negotiation of the Global Political Agreement (GPA) when the conflict came to a head in 2008. Thereafter, the program has played a central role in keeping dialogue channels open and keeping the GPA from being abandoned. Although Zimbabwe's political crisis remains, the significant economic recovery attained as a result of the GPA has been sustained.

Similarly, in Fiji, once the military-backed government ended political dialogue in 2008, civic organizations, discreetly assisted by the UN, have supported key individuals in government, the private sectors, and civil society in establishing a viable dialogue platform to develop common perspectives on challenging issues pertaining to social, economic, and political reform. In an otherwise deadlocked environment, this remains the only channel for dialogue. Regional actors, who have boycotted the government until it holds elections, have also been supportive of this platform.

DIFFERENTIATING CORRELATES FROM CAUSES

Potentially violent tensions and conflict are often attributed to root causes such as the youth bulge, the resource curse, inequitable land distribution, ineffective policing, and so on. For instance, the wave of turbulence rocking the Middle East at the beginning of 2011 is already being attributed to the largely youthful populations of these countries. However, these same youthful populations have been the source of growth and innovation in India, Brazil, and Turkey, among other countries. Resources have caused violence through much of West Africa, but Ghana is developing a strategy for utilizing its new oil wealth through an inclusive process of dialogue, as did Sao Tome e Principe, with UNDP assistance, in 2004. Although many situations of conflict and fragility do correlate with issues such as unemployed youth and abundant mineral wealth, so do situations that are exactly the opposite. What makes for the difference? The UN's experience with providing assistance in this regard shows that the answer may lie in a country's collaborative capacity, its infrastructure for peace, or the internal ability to negotiate mutually acceptable outcomes across political and sectarian lines of division. The causes of conflict may not therefore be specific issues or challenges, but the manner in which they are addressed and the degree to which relevant decisions are made in an inclusive and consensual manner.

Elections Are Not about Elections

In recent years, elections have become a key focus for governments, civil society, and international partners. Free, fair, and peaceful elections are seen as vital to a country's stability, and the reverse is seen as an indicator of failing governance. Significant effort is therefore expended in ensuring that elections are sound from a technical perspective. However, elections concentrate many of the political rifts and tensions within a society. This is especially the case where leaders have not acquired the ability to be able to compete at the polls, but then simultaneously and subsequently collaborate in the national interest. Hence, ensuring stable political transitions through elections requires not only the right technical assistance, but also the building of infrastructures for peace well before, during, and after elections. Peaceful elections in Guyana in 2006, Ghana in 2004 and 2008, Sierra Leone in 2007, and Togo, Kyrgyzstan, and Solomon Islands in 2010 and the successful constitutional referendum in Kenya in 2010 all took place in the context of multiyear, UN-backed initiatives to develop and apply national capacities for conflict prevention and transformation. Three elements, all of which were developed over a two- to three-year period at a minimum, were common to all these cases:

- First, the presence of national platforms or mechanisms that enabled a minimum political consensus to be reached prior to elections, or which mediated high-level tensions during the elections themselves
- Second, the presence of significant conflict management and mediation capacities at the district and local levels, often in the form of local peace committees or similar mechanisms
- Third, the work of civil society, especially religious and traditional leaders, and mass membership civic associations, in carrying out systematic advocacy for peace, and engaging especially youth in these efforts

A strong pointer in this direction, and an example of the collective failure of the international community with regard to conflict prevention, is the situation that prevailed in Côte d'Ivoire at the beginning of 2011. Despite nearly six years of international peacekeeping and diplomacy, very little had been accomplished in terms of establishing viable internal mechanisms for binding better together the north and the south of the country at the political, cultural, and social levels. No major political party or a mass-based civic organization was in existence the work or agenda of which transcended the north-south divide. Prior to the 2010 elections where Gbagbo refused to concede defeat, no thought had been given to a broad-based consultation on an inclusive governing arrangement irrespective of the winner. When Ouattara defeated Gbagbo 52 percent to 48 percent, he did so essentially with northern votes, plus the small plurality provided by Bedie's support. Even Ouattara supporters in the capital were migrants from the north. At the time of writing, the country was polarized and on the brink of a return to violent north-south conflict. A concerted effort to establish a national infrastructure for peace in the previous decade might have averted this outcome. Alternatively, Gbagbo's refusal to step down could have been met with a massive national upsurge against his rule, rather than a further splintering and polarization of the country and the political spectrum.

Growing Interest and Ownership in the Developing World

Sierra Leone's Political Parties Registration Commission; Ghana's National Peace Council; Nepal's Ministry of Peace and Reconstruction, which has led the country's recovery efforts; Ukraine's Human Security Council for Crimea, which mediates majority–minority relations; Timor Leste's Department for Peace-Building; El Salvador's Economic and Social Council (a standing dialogue capacity that is also being developed by other countries in the region); and Kyrgyzstan's new Department on Ethnic, Religious Policy and Civil Society Interaction all point to a growing trend among developing countries to establish their own institutional capacities, albeit with varying effectiveness, for conflict management and peacebuilding. These capacities do not fit neatly into the traditional donor categories of crisis response or development. Alternately, they could neatly fit into either. What is critical is that they represent a growing ownership on the part of developing countries of the agenda for conflict prevention and peacebuilding. During a period of rapid onset of turbulence and transition, they also represent the core of the resilience needed by countries and societies. Hence, they deserve systematic support.

At the time of writing, Egypt, Tunisia, and Bahrain were in the midst of convulsive political transition as key actors sought to remake their systems of governance under runaway popular pressure. Although they had access to all the technical knowledge with regard to the pros and cons of different models for constitution-making and police reform, for instance, what they continued to lack were internal platforms and mediation capacities through which agreement could be built among contending actors on the best way forward.

CONCLUSION: CONFLICT PREVENTION WORKS AND NEEDS FURTHER ASSISTANCE

Traditionally, national and local actors did development—the vaccination of children and the building of roads—and international diplomats and nongovernmental organizations did conflict prevention or resolution, or the mediation of conflicts in primarily developing countries.

The examples in this chapter show that a new approach toward conflict prevention works and that it is indeed possible to equip national and local actors to resolve conflicts, prevent violence, and build consensus over contentious issues in an inclusive and credible manner. And this approach is cost-effective. Results in Guyana, Bolivia, Ghana, Kenya, and Timor Leste were achieved, for instance, for approximately only US$15 million. This is slightly less than the average cost of a DDR program in a post-conflict country.

In the case of the UN, a significant portion of this support was provided through UNDP's Bureau for Crisis Prevention and Recovery (BCPR) together with UNDP's regional bureaus; through the Joint UNDP-DPA Programme on Building National Capacities for Conflict Prevention (peace and development advisers are primarily deployed through this initiative), which is executed by BCPR; and through the Interagency Framework Team for Preventive Action, which is the UN's internal coordination mechanism on preventive action and is currently cochaired on a standing basis by UNDP and DPA and hosted permanently by UNDP. DPA's Policy and Mediation Division, together with the department's regional divisions, has also provided vital support to these initiatives.

However, compared to the amounts provided for the assessed budget for peacekeeping, and the US$350 million made available to the Peacebuilding Fund for post-conflict peacebuilding, the resources available for the work detailed in this chapter are a pittance, or about US$3 million a year. As a result, key initiatives are often not continued after the first year or two, despite concrete results, and the partner organizations (primarily UNDP and DPA) scrounge for funds to continue the deployment of peace and development advisers and similar specialists.

If the world's countries are indeed serious about building resilience to the turbulence that will increasingly be caused by cascading economic and climatological shocks and about responding more effectively and inclusively to rapidly mutating popular demands, then they will invest in building infrastructures for peace.

The views expressed in this chapter are strictly the author's, and do not in any way reflect any official positions of the United Nations or the United Nations Development Programme.

NOTES

1. This analysis, conducted by the author, draws on early warning information available through the UN Office for Coordination of Humanitarian Affairs; the Economist Intelligence Unit; Oxford Analytica; and fragility indices developed by several bilateral and multilateral organizations.

2. See, for example, the report on the Expert Meeting on Natural Resources and Conflict in Africa organized by the Office of the UN Special Advisor on Africa, Cairo, Egypt, 2006, http://www.un.org/africa/osaa/reports/Natural%20Resources%20and%20Conflict%20in%20Africa_%20Cairo%20Conference%20ReportwAnnexes%20Nov%2017.pdf.

3. The Government of Guyana–UN initiative on "Enhancing Public Trust, Security, and Inclusion" is a good example of an effort to address issues of decentralized violence and insecurity through the application of the "infrastructures for peace" methodology.

4. The term *infrastructure for peace* is attributed to Tobi Dress, an independent peacebuilding practitioner. The related term *building national capacities for conflict prevention* is similarly attributed to Andries Odendaal, a South African practitioner of peacebuilding. Over the past 10 years, the following individuals have played critical roles in assisting the UN in further developing these concepts and applying them on the ground: Chris Spies, Ozonnia Ojielo, Clever Nyathi, Dekha Ibrahim Abdi, and Tapio Kanninen, peacebuilding practitioners from South Africa, Nigeria, Zimbabwe, Kenya, and Finland, respectively; Howard Wolpe, former U.S. special envoy for the Great Lakes region; Kathleen Cravero and Jordan Ryan, the former and current directors of UNDP's Bureau for Crisis Prevention and Recovery (BCPR); Ragnar Angeby of the Folke Bernadotte Academy of Sweden; Youssef Mahmoud, Olara Otunnu, and Victor Angelo, all former special representatives of the UN Secretary-General; Gay Rosenblum-Kumar, the senior secretary to the UN Interagency Framework Team for Coordination on Preventive Action; Emmanuel Bombande and Paul von Tongeren of the Global Partnership on Prevention of Armed Conflict; the late Rick Hooper, Jack Christofides, Axel Wennmann, Alexandra Pichler, and Joao Honwana of the UN Secretariat; and Celine Moyroud (now with UNDP-Lebanon), Anita Ernstorfer, Jos de la Haye, Jelena Raketic, Devanand Ramiah, Emmanuelle Bernard, Anne Kahl, and Tajia Kontinen-Sharp of BCPR.

5. Formal collaboration between UNDP and DPA in this regard had commenced with the launch, by then–UNDP Administrator Mark Malloch Brown and head of DPA Kieran Prendergast, of the Joint UNDP-DPA Programme on Building National Capacities for Conflict Prevention in 2004. During the same year, both organizations took joint steps, in partnership with UNICEF and UN OCHA, to strengthen the Interagency Framework Team on Coordination for Preventive Action, which supports joint action by UN Country Teams in situations of early conflict prevention. In 2010, UNDP Administrator Helen Clark and head of DPA B. Lynn Pascoe sent a joint note to all UN Resident Coordinators and UNDP Country Directors and heads of political missions, highlighting steps to enhance collaboration on conflict prevention and to support field presences to undertake preventive action in complex political situations.

6. The Berghoff Foundation for Peace Support provides the following definition of *insider mediation*: "Situated within a conflict, these are trusted individuals (NGO leaders, traditional or religious authorities, former politicians, respected academics and social activists) who play the role of third parties. In particular, they serve as intermediaries, helping to exchange information and messages or testing the ground for (in)formal talks. Insider mediators are characterized by their in-depth knowledge of the conflict situation, cultural sensitivity and close relationships to the parties and, in some cases, their normative authority. Typically unofficial, the quality of their mediation is crucial: not only may it open doors for formal mediation, but it also can complement official negotiation processes" (http://www.berghof-foundation.de/en/glossary/insider-mediators).

7. See Dekha Ibrahim Abdi, "Insider Mediation in Kenya" (Swisspeace/CSS/Berghoff Foundation, 2008), http://www.berghof-peacesupport.org/publications/MED_Insider_Mediators_Kenya.pdf.

8. The term *PDA* is a generic term. Depending on the circumstances of each country, these specialists are variously referred to as *peace and governance advisers, collaborative capacity advisers, social cohesion advisers,* and so on.

9. Over the past six years, peace and development advisers as well as similar specialists have been deployed in at least 25 countries to support national and local initiatives for conflict prevention. Biannual global retreats of these advisers are convened by the UN Interagency Framework Team for Coordination on Preventive Action, which also

hosts a "community of practice" for them, thus allowing for knowledge and experiences to be shared and practice to be strengthened. Technical and operational support for the deployment of these advisers is provided primarily by UNDP's Bureau for Crisis Prevention and Recovery.

10. For the current version of the methodology, see http://www.undp.org/cpr/whats_new/cda_combined.pdf.

11. The concept behind the National Peace Council and the attendant National Architecture for Peace is detailed by the Government of Ghana at http://www.mint.gov.gh/dmdocuments/A_PEACE_ARCHITECTURE_FOR_GHANA_.pdf. The council was established as a government body by a cabinet decision in 2007 and by the Parliament as an autonomous national statutory commission in February 2011.

12. See AllAfrica.com, "Communities Forge Their Own Peace in the Rift Valley," October 26, 2010, http://allafrica.com/stories/201010280929.html.

13. See "The Ministry of Social Solidarity launches the Department of Peace-Building and Social Cohesion to celebrate World Human Rights Day," http://www.tl.undp.org/undp/The%20Ministry%20of%20Social%20Solidarity%20launches%20the%20Department%20of%20Peace-Building%20and%20Social%20Cohesion%20to%20celebrate%20World%20Human%20Rights%20Day.html.

14. For an independent evaluation of the program, see "Can Fostering a Culture of Dialogue Change the Course of a Nation?" (UNDP, 2006), http://www.undp.org.gy/pdf/final_SCP_evaluation.pdf.

15. See an account of the role of the UNDP program, PAPEP, in this regard on "PAPEP Project Was Presented at NORAD/UNDP Workshops on Governance and Political Economy Analysis," October 2010, http://www.gobernabilidaddemocratica-pnud.org/detalle_noticia.php?id_not=124. See, in particular, the comments from Jose Luis Exeni, the former head of Bolivia's National Electoral Court.

16. For an account of the work of the Uwiano Platform, see "Kenya: SOS by SMS," August 3, 2010, http://www.irinnews.org/Report.aspx?ReportID=90050.

17. According to an assessment of the elections conducted by UK's Department for International Development (DFID), "One of the innovations that the UN Development Programme has introduced into the electoral process is a Political Party Registration Commission (PPRC) . . . PPRC has played a useful role in promoting a Code of Conduct for Political Parties among activists and mediating the conflicts that have arisen—both during the elections and after them" (http://www.dfid.gov.uk/Documents/publications1/elections/elections-sl-2007-2008.pdf).

18. For more on support for the church-led mediation and wider UN efforts to enhance "collaborative capacity" in Lesotho, see http://www.undp.org.ls/democratic/Collaborative_Capacities.php.

19. More information on these initiatives can be found at the website of the UNDP Action on Cooperation and Trust Programme, Cyprus: http://www.undp-act.org/.

20. A more detailed description of COBERM can be found at http://www.undp.org.ge/files/78_914_211987_201012.pdf.

CHAPTER 25

Infrastructures for Peace

Paul van Tongeren

Infrastructures for peace is a relatively new phrase. It refers to a concept that has great potential and is sorely needed, but is barely known. Excellent policy documents from the governments of Ghana and Kenya on establishing an Infrastructure for Peace have escaped attention. Andries Odendaal, who himself played an active role in the peace structure of South Africa from 1991 to 1994, has published substantively on Local Peace Councils, but these papers did not circulate widely. I owe much to the inspiring examples in Ghana and Kenya and the groundbreaking research of Andries Odendaal.

Creating an infrastructure for peace means developing mechanisms for cooperation among all relevant stakeholders in peacebuilding by promoting cooperative problem solving to conflicts and institutionalizing the response mechanisms to conflicts in order to transform them. National, district, and local peace councils are cornerstones of such an infrastructure.

In the late 1990s, there were experiments in several countries with often informal local peace councils, although some had a formal national mandate. We will focus on those with a national mandate, as the impact of a formally recognized national peace infrastructure is higher.

The understanding that peacebuilding requires sustained and deeply transformative work has contributed to the development of the concept of peace architectures or infrastructures for peace. The well-known scholar and practitioner John Paul Lederach introduced this concept in his book *Building Peace: Sustainable Reconciliation in Divided Societies* in 1997: "I have a rather modest thesis. I believe that the nature and characteristics of contemporary conflict suggest the need for a set of concepts and approaches that go beyond traditional statist diplomacy. Building peace in today's conflicts calls for long-term commitment to establishing an infrastructure across the levels of society, an infrastructure that empowers the resources of reconciliation from within that society and maximizes the contribution from outside."[1]

His model included the need for structural transformation. Infrastructure, in his view, did not mean a rigid structure, but a process as a platform for change: a functional network that would span across the divisions and levels of society and that would ensure optimum collaboration between the main stakeholders. "As such, a platform is responsive to day-to-day issues that arise in the ebb and flow of conflict while it sustains a clear vision of the longer-term change needed in the destructive relational patterns. The creation of such a platform, I would submit, is one of the fundamental building blocks for supporting constructive social change over time."[2]

It took some time before the concept began to be introduced in official arenas: At the first Standing Conference on Stability, Security and Development in Durban in 2002, African leaders signed a resolution committing them to uphold their full responsibility to set up national institutions to manage conflict and work in partnership with their civil societies. In the 2006 Progress Report on the 2001 UN Report *Prevention of Armed Conflict*, Kofi Annan stipulated that "essentially, the aim should be the creation of a sustainable, national infrastructure for peace that allows societies and their governments to resolve conflicts internally and with their own skills, institutions and resources."[3]

In the April 2009 UN Secretary-General's report to the Security Council on enhancing mediation and its support activities, paragraph 52 pertains to strengthening national/local capacity for conflict prevention/resolution:

> Given the promise it holds for States to resolve inter-group tension without recourse to violence, the development of national and local mechanisms for addressing grievances and reducing tension through mediation, facilitation and dialogue has received surprisingly little attention. Recent efforts by the Inter-Agency Framework Team for Conflict Prevention and the joint program of the United Nations Development Program (UNDP) and the Department of Political Affairs on building national capacity for conflict prevention to place peace and development advisers in UNDP offices to build national and local capacity and mechanisms have begun to redress this. Although this work goes beyond mediation to include other peace processes, one promising approach is the development of a national architecture for dispute resolution through national, regional and district peace councils to provide mediation and prevent local conflicts from escalating and spreading. Given the African Union's call for all its members to establish, by 2004, national institutions or mechanisms for prevention, management and resolution of conflicts at community and national levels, much remains to be done.[4]

Two countries that are pioneering the implementation of infrastructures of peace are Ghana and Kenya. Both had general elections in recent years, and these structures (even partly implemented) helped in preventing and reducing post election violence.

The UNDP gave the approach more attention when it organized the Experience-Sharing Seminar on Building Infrastructures for Peace in Kenya in

February 2010 in partnership with NPI-Africa, WANEP, and GPPAC.[5] UN staff and national counterparts from governments and civil society from 12 countries in Africa were invited for this seminar, to share experiences of effective conflict prevention strategies, mechanisms, and projects; to develop an infrastructure for peace; and to inform and support the design of new initiatives in selected countries. The seminar was the first discussion among both Francophone and Anglophone countries in Africa on the issue of building national and local capacities for conflict prevention and management.

In a concept note, the UNDP described how conflict and development are linked and how the development process itself generates conflicts by changing the dynamics of economic, financial, and political power. The inevitable competition over the direction, resources, and distribution of development, if not well managed, can impede development and even reverse it if violence breaks out. Lasting peace and sustainable development often depend on an additional variable: the extent to which key sectors and groups are able to reach a stable consensus on national priorities and negotiate mutually agreed upon solutions to emerging disputes before violent tensions emerge.

To strengthen development, promote democratic processes, and prevent instability, it is imperative to ensure that better mechanisms for consensus building and dispute resolution are in place. This requires long-term, systematic efforts to raise awareness, impart skills, and strengthen institutions that will enable government and civil society representatives to respond to crises more effectively, bolster existing peace processes, and create procedures through which crises can be solved nonviolently, in other words, to develop a national infrastructure with these requisite capacities. We need a framework of relationships that allow us to manage crises and violent conflict and links different stakeholders and different levels, with national, district, and local peace councils, as further described in paragraph five.

There are different types of conflicts—on land, resources, religion, ethnicity/identity, chieftaincy, marginalization of communities, and many other issues. Often, countries lack both solid analysis of potential conflicts and the instruments and mechanisms to deal with them. We lack an overall systems approach to building peace: what are the capacities, tools, mechanisms, structures, and institutions we need to build sustainable peace?

Kai Brand-Jacobsen of the Peace Action Training and Research Institute of Romania (PATRIR) has made an interesting comparison between infrastructures for peace and those in the health care sector.[6] Similar comparisons could be made with many other fields, such as fire-prevention, education, and warfare. All involve awareness raising, training of professionals, capacity building, preventive policies, ministries, institutions, and the like. Peacebuilding needs a similar infrastructure.

THE DEVELOPMENT OF INFRASTRUCTURES
FOR PEACE IN AFRICA

Africa has gained some experience of this concept over the past two decades: a peace infrastructure was the product of the 1991 National Peace

Accord (NPA) in South Africa. Its main tasks were to create trust and reconciliation between leaders and to prevent violence and resolve disputes. Ghana and Kenya both experienced numerous conflicts over the last two decades and are pioneers in establishing an Infrastructure for Peace.

In all three countries, the leaders were convinced that a specific structure had to be established, because the existing ones would not be adequate to create trust and reconciliation, prevent violence, and resolve conflicts. In Ghana and Kenya, the violence escalated especially around elections, so the root causes needed to be addressed to avoid derailing future elections.

South Africa[7]

The transition from apartheid to the new democratic government in South Africa was served by a fairly well-developed peace architecture with local peace committees as the primary strategy to prevent violence. These structures operated between 1991 and 1994 and were discontinued following the successful national elections of April 1994.

The local peace committees (LPCs) were a product of the National Peace Accord (NPA), signed on September 14, 1991, by the 27 main protagonists in the conflict, the government, the main political parties, and the major liberation movements, due to escalating violence in the country. Between 1985 and 1990, more than 6,000 people were killed in incidents of political violence. When President de Klerk decriminalized the antiapartheid organizations and released imprisoned political leaders, the violence did not subside, contrary to expectations. Between September 1990 and August 1991, 2,649 people were killed. The sheer number of deaths was alarming, but even more so the perception that the violence was negatively impacting on the prospect of a negotiated settlement.

Part of the NPA described a peace architecture, comprising a National Peace Committee, consisting of all signatories, which was largely inefficient and met only twice; regional peace committees (RPCs) in 11 regions of the country; local peace committees (LPCs) in all affected areas; and a National Peace Secretariat to establish and coordinate the regional and local peace committees.

The RPCs consisted of regional representatives of all signatories with a presence in each region, as well as other relevant regional civil society formations including religious organizations, trade unions, business and industry, and traditional authorities. The police and defense forces were also represented, as were relevant government ministries. RPCs oversaw the establishment of LPCs, giving priority to those towns that experienced violence. LPCs focused on inclusivity, welcoming CSOs that wanted to be part of them. The main tasks of LPCs were to

- create trust and reconciliation between community leaders, including the police and army;
- prevent violence and intimidation; and
- resolve disputes that could lead to public violence.

The violence did escalate, but the general consensus is that the escalation would have been far worse if the LPCs had not existed.

LPCs facilitated dialogue at the local level where, for the first time, inclusive assemblies of stakeholders were able to address local issues jointly. However, LPCs were powerless in the face of spoilers or when political will was lacking. Much of the aggression was deliberately stoked by the so-called Third Force (sections of the security establishment), and the soft power of facilitation and mediation were unable to address the deliberate, planned violence.

Andries Odendaal identified some lessons that may have relevance for local peacebuilding processes elsewhere:

- The process of establishing a LPC was as important as the national mandate to establish them. In terms of legitimacy, they stood on two legs. One leg was the mandate by the NPA: without such a national agreement the establishment of LPCs in most places would have been met by resistance from all sides. The other leg was local buy-in into the concept: The NPA was an elite pact, and at the grassroots level, pockets of strong resistance existed. Presence of the police on the LPC, for instance, was very contentious: policemen were the face of the enemy in the townships. The establishment of an LPC had to be rooted in the conscious decision of local actors to engage with the peace process. Therefore, full-time field workers were employed and tasked with facilitating processes to establish LPCs, which happened only once all the significant actors had received a mandate from their members.

- The lesson is that it cannot be taken for granted that local communities will make peace just because national leadership has made that decision. The national agreement provides an opportunity, a framework and a legitimate mandate, but in the final analysis local actors must take responsibility for their own peace.

- LPCs and RPCs relied on a functioning peace architecture: They could not have operated in an administrative or logistical vacuum. The peace architecture that was set up provided support in terms of funding; a functioning network (LPCs were linked to Regional Peace Committees and the National Secretariat); the professional services of full-time staff; and the presence of UN and other international monitors;

- The NPA created space for substantial civil society involvement: Without the input by civil society the process would have had no chance of success. The NPA itself was the product of a joint initiative by the business sector and the churches. The negotiation of the text of the NPA was cochaired by Archbishop Desmond Tutu, on behalf of the churches, and John Hall, on behalf of the business community. The regional bodies and LPCs were chaired by civil society figures. They occupied the middle ground and kept all parties together, countering strong centrifugal forces, and carried out most of the facilitation, mediation, and violence prevention work. They can best be described by Lederach's term *insider-partials*. They were not impartial, but committed to the greater good of preventing violence and finding workable solutions. The lesson is that the business of peace cannot be left solely to the politicians. By creating a framework that allowed insider-partials the space to operate, the peace process gained much in depth and breadth.

- "[Establishing a peace architecture] was a move toward identifying key people in critical locations who, working through a network, would begin to build an infrastructure capable of sustaining the general progression toward peace. Central to the overall functioning of the peace process was the development of institutional capacities through the training of a broad array of individuals to respond to the volatile period of transition. What these approaches suggest is that the middle range holds the potential for helping to establish a relationship- and skill-based infrastructure for sustaining the peacebuilding process."[8]

Ghana[9]

Ghana has had a stable and democratic government since 1992, but is burdened with a troubled past of military coups and dictatorial rule. On the surface, Ghana is peaceful. "However, students of West African history would admit that a mere five years before the conflicts in Liberia, Sierra Leone and Côte D'Ivoire, no one in those countries could have predicted the occurrence of conflict. A perception of peace and stability is not a guarantee of long term peace."[10]

A study commissioned by the Ministry of Interior identified several conflict factors, including chieftaincy, civil and labor unrest, inter/intra–political party conflicts, land, religion, ethnic/identity conflicts, minerals, and economic resources among numerous others.

Twenty-three conflicts were recorded in the three northern regions of the country between 1980 and 2002. Many community-based and interethnic conflicts were intractable because the justice system was not functioning well and many court cases remained unresolved. When violence broke out, official commissions of inquiry were established, but their recommendations were not implemented. The official response to these conflicts was law and order based: The government deployed police and military units in conflict areas to keep the peace, with very limited official engagement on the structural issues underlying the conflicts.

One of these conflicts, the Konkomba-Nanumba war in 1994–1995, left 5,000 people dead. At this time, civil society organizations combined efforts to facilitate peacebuilding, and an Inter-NGO Consortium was formed. The consortium intervened by facilitating processes of dialogue and negotiation that had been successful in restoring peace in a number of these conflicts. Civil society's approach contrasted sharply to that of the government, by seeking to uncover the deeper sources of conflict and focus on dialogue, deeper mutual understanding, joint problem solving, and reconciliation.

In Ghana, two state systems exist in practice: a traditional state controlled by tribal chiefs, without formal political authority; and a modern state controlled at the local level by the district chief executive. In many communities, the real authority is the chief. In community conflicts, the district chief executive is expected to intervene and ensure the resolution of conflicts.

One eruption of violence led to the slaying of the king of Dagbon and many of his elders in 2002 in a conflict concerning succession to the chieftain's throne. The government of Ghana feared that these events might derail upcoming elections and declared a state of emergency in the region. The regional government established the Northern Region Peace Advocacy Council as a mediation and conflict resolution mechanism to deal with the issues of trust among the factions, as restoring confidence and relationships was crucial.

The council was composed of representatives chosen by the stakeholders themselves including chiefs, women, youth groups, and representatives of the security agencies. A series of capacity building and conflict transformation workshops were organized for stakeholder groups. The government had taken notice of the success of civil society's methodology and approached the UN for assistance. Following a UN mission, a peace and governance advisor was appointed.

With the success of the Northern Region Peace Advisory Council, the government decided to explore the possibility of extending the peace council concept to the rest of the country. A range of consultations was organized with many different stakeholders at local, regional, and national levels. The outcome of these consultations was the development of the national architecture for peace.

The National Architecture for Peace

The national architecture for peace works toward systematic change through changing the context in which conflicts occur and strengthening the institutions of the state to manage conflicts better. It consists of representatives of relevant stakeholders as well as individual Ghanaians who enjoy high levels of trust and respect in society. Councils exist at national, regional, and district levels with the mandate to facilitate dialogue, problem solving, and reconciliation processes at the level of their jurisdiction. They are served by a body of professional peace promotion officers connected to the 10 regional peace advisory councils. These are independent persons of integrity and credibility within the region, nominated by the regional governments in consultation with a broad range of stakeholders. They have been trained in conflict analysis, negotiation, mediation, and reconciliation as well as building trust and confidence among groups. They perform strategic roles advising regional governments on maintaining peace in the region, but they also coordinate civil society engagement in peacebuilding.

The NPC and RPCs were trained by the NGO WANEP, the West Africa Network for Peacebuilding. Furthermore, a Peace Building Support Unit was established within the Ministry of the Interior to oversee support and coordination from government agencies. The National Architecture for Peace in Ghana was issued by the Ministry of Interior in May 2006.

The process of establishing it is a work in progress: The National Peace Council (NPC) is in place and is an independent body, composed of 11 persons that carry leverage and high moral standing and respect with the citizens, including the Roman Catholic cardinal; the national chief imam; a bishop; a pastor; and a professor. The caliber of these individuals and the integrity they bring both individually and collectively to the NPC makes it a nonpartisan body providing a national platform for consensus building on potentially divisive issues as well as promoting national reconciliation. The NPC played a major role in ensuring peaceful elections in 2008 and a smooth transfer of power through discreet meetings with stakeholders that defused considerable tension. In March 2011, a National Peace Council Bill was unanimously adopted by Parliament, which will further strengthen Ghana's peace structure.

Regional peace advisory councils were established in most regions, but not all. In some regions, they were merged with regional security structures. The regional peace advisory council in the north also played a very constructive role in ensuring peace during the elections of 2008.

No district peace advisory councils have yet been established.

Conclusion on the Peace Architecture of Ghana

The National Architecture for Peace in Ghana is the first official national-level program on building peace in Africa, implementing the Resolution of African leaders in 2002 in Durban. Ghana's contribution to the peacebuilding field includes the acknowledgement of multiple roles that different actors and stakeholders are required to play in constructing peace in communities. Unless attention is paid to the structural issues in conflicts, peace may be temporary. Relationships need to be mended, yet those injured by the conflict need to be assisted to find closure: if they feel that justice has been done, their personal and group healing can move at a faster pace. With a historical legacy of oppression and dominance between groups, the process by which peace is constructed is as important as the issues that are discussed at the table: Acknowledgement of equality, participation, and respect contributes to empowerment and ownership of peacebuilding processes in communities.[11]

The success of the process of establishing the National Architecture for Peace in Ghana in Ghana had much to do with the quality support and capacity building provided by civil society and the UN system, and especially highly professional UN peace and development advisors. At the conceptual level, there is a clear distinction between the roles of the peace council and that of government structures. On the whole the architecture, as it exists on paper at the moment, is a textbook example of a well-designed infrastructure.[12]

Kenya[13]

Kenya is beset by a multitude of local conflicts that have the potential to escalate at any moment, as a result of resource crises, land tenure issues, and political machinations. It gives us a fascinating example of a bottom-up process to establish a peace architecture. The process started in 1993 with an initiative by a group of women of the Wajir district of Kenya, bordering Somalia and Ethiopia, in response to a highly destructive cycle of violent conflict in that region, and the failure of state institutions to regulate conflict, provide security, and promote development.

The initiative consisted of civil society actors working together to sensitize the population to the need for peace. They engaged the elders of the different clans and set up a mediation process between them. In this process, civil society actors worked with and involved representatives of formal authority, particularly the district commissioner and a member of Parliament. After some time, it became clear that some form of formalization was needed, so the peace initiatives were integrated into the one structure, the District Development Committee, in the district administration in Kenya that brought government, NGOs, and citizen groups together. In 1995 the Wajir Peace and Development Committee was formed, with the district commissioner as chairperson. Members included the heads of all government departments, representatives of the various peace groups, religious leaders, NGO representatives, chiefs, and security officers.

The success of the Wajir Peace and Development Committee in bringing peace to the district and in maintaining it soon led to the spread of the model to other districts in the northern part of the country.

The government was aware of the numerous types of conflicts in Kenya, including ethnic divisions, marginalization of communities, livestock rustling, land conflicts, and cross-border conflicts. In 2001, it established a National Steering Committee (NSC) on Peacebuilding and Conflict Management. The Office of the President, through the NSC, embarked on a process toward the development of a national policy on peacebuilding and conflict management in 2004. The National Policy, including the lessons learned from the postelection violence of 2008, was published at the end of September 2009 by the Office of the President. Both in the early years of the NSC and after the recent postelection violence, broad consultations took place, between the government and non-state actors—with all involved ministries, academia, development partners, regional organizations, CSOs, women, youth groups, communities, private sector, and local authorities—and in 12 regional Stakeholders' Validation workshops.

The vision of the policy is "a peaceful and stable Kenya." The mission is "to promote sustainable peace through a collaborative institutional framework between state and non-state actors." Further progress has been made recently by a constitutional referendum and the adoption of a new constitution in autumn 2010. All of this was accomplished without a single incident of violence.

The Peace Architecture

To achieve the vision and mission, the policy proposes a peace architecture with the following structure:

- *A National Peace Commission (NPC),* appointed by the president with approval by parliament, with 13 commissioners, one from each province and 5 others representing women, youth, civil society, persons with disabilities, and academia, all with a national reputation. The commission is to be supported by a secretariat, headed by a secretary. The work of the NPC shall be guided by bipartisanship and independence.

- *A National Peace Forum,* to be constituted as a platform for consultations, collaboration, cooperation, and coordination by all peace actors and stakeholders.

- *Provincial Peace Fora*, to be constituted as a platform for consultations and coordination at the provincial levels.
- *District Peace Committees (DPC)*, hybrid institutions that bring together synergies between traditional and formal mechanisms for conflict resolution.
- *NPC Secretariat*, to be the management arm of the commission.

Following the postelection violence in 2007 and early 2008, the National Accord and Reconciliation Act 2008 recommended the establishment of district peace committees in all of Kenya's districts, with priority given to the Rift Valley, the area where most of the violence had occurred.

The NPC and national policy and coordination strategies are incomplete. Those districts that already had peace committees reported much less violence than others during the conflict, a fact that considerably raised the importance of enhancing local capacities for peace. There is a fair amount of consensus among researchers and observers that the peace committees have, on the whole, been successful, especially in the pastoralist areas. They have demonstrated their ability to manage intercommunity conflict and to contain or prevent violence, were able to integrate a broad range of local stakeholders who were locally perceived as relevant for conflict resolution, and tackled cases of interethnic conflict.

Challenges and Dilemmas[14]

Similar to the Ghanaian situation, the peace committees in Kenya's pastoralist areas operated in the vacuum created by the weakness of government institutions, in particular the justice system, to provide security and justice to communities. This weakness was partly caused by the disjunction between two different paradigms of justice: that of the clans and that of the state. The mediation offered by peace committees involved more than problem solving; they also mediated at the level of fundamental values underpinning the justice system. At certain points they fundamentally contradicted the constitutional values of the state.

EXAMPLES OF INFRASTRUCTURES FOR PEACE IN OTHER CONTINENTS

Several countries have experience with infrastructures for peace in different modalities, different contexts, and sometimes different vocabulary, where the word *peace* is not mentioned. Sometimes these function only at the local or the national level, with varying connection to the formal governance structures of the country.

Nicaragua

In his book *Building Peace*,[15] Lederach describes peace commissions and elaborates on Nicaragua in the late 1980s and South Africa in the early 1990s. Throughout the 1980s, multiple internal wars raged in Central America. The

Central American peace accord that was signed in Guatemala by the five countries in the region provided mechanisms that dealt with the internal situations
of each country through a coordinated plan. The Nicaraguan government
moved quickly to set up a national peace commission, region-specific commissions, and a network of local commissions.

In fact, two independent systems of peace commissions were established. In
the south of Nicaragua, religious leaders joined forces at the peak of the war
to negotiate conflict-free zones, forming small commissions of local residents
to foster dialogue between the Sandinista government and contra rebels at the
community level. The original mission of the peace commissions was to document and investigate human rights violations. Over time, it came to include all
sorts of intracommunity disputes, land conflicts, and crime. By 1990, 60 commissions had arisen, performing communication and mediation functions to
promote dialogue between Sandinista and contra rebels.

The model for this conciliation effort was that of an insider-partial mediation effort, involving intermediaries from within the conflict who as individuals enjoyed the trust and confidence of one side, but who as a team provide
balance in their mediation work. Church leaders built durable local institutions for intracommunity conflict resolution.

The second type of peace commission, as a component of the regional
peace settlement, was the International Support and Verification Commission
(CIAV) of the OAS, which started work in 1990. It was originally charged with
overseeing the demobilization of over 22,000 contra combatants in the northern and western regions of the country. By 1995, the CIAV supported the creation of 96 peace commissions working on mediation, verification of human
rights protections, promotion of human rights, and facilitation of community
projects.

The peace commissions permitted an unprecedented space for dialogue in
which citizens could safely express their views.

The Philippines[16]

In 1986, the People Power Revolution in the Philippines led to the fall of the
Marcos Dictatorship. Subsequently, peace talks with all rebel forces were initiated, the peace process as a government policy was formalized, and the Office
of the Peace Commissioner under the Office of the President established.

The post of presidential adviser on the peace process (PAPP) with cabinet
rank, was created, charged with the management of the comprehensive peace
process, and assisted by a fulltime secretariat (OPAPP). Three underlying principles of the peace process were adopted (in 1993):

- A comprehensive peace process should be community-based, reflecting the
  sentiments, values and principles important to all Philippinos.

- A comprehensive peace process aims to forge a new social compact for a just,
  equitable, humane and pluralistic society.

- A comprehensive peace process seeks a principal and peaceful resolution of
  the internal armed conflicts, with neither blame nor surrender, but with dignity for all concerned.

In 2001 the government decided on a Policy Framework for Peace—affirming the guiding principles and the "Six Paths to Peace" of the previous administration—and formulated a National Peace Plan, with two components: (1) peacemaking and peacekeeping (seeking to end all insurgency-related armed conflicts through peace negotiations and to reduce the level of violence through local and civil society–led peace initiatives) and (2) peacebuilding and conflict prevention (seeking to address the major causes of insurgency, eliminate sources of grievance, rehabilitate and develop conflict-affected areas, and heal the wounds created by the long years of armed conflict).

The government established government peace negotiating panels for negotiations with the different rebel groups. OPAPP under the new administration did convene a consultation of civil society, in August 2010, who decided to loosely band together to share and develop strategies in engaging the peace process. The body is tentatively called Kilos Kapayapaan, or Action for Peace. It will serve as a de facto consultative cum advisory body to OPAPP but will remain independent of it.

Nepal[17]

In March 2007, the government of Nepal decided to create a Ministry of Peace and Reconstruction, becoming the second nation in the world with such a ministry after the Ministry of National Unity, Reconciliation and Peace in the Solomon Islands, and followed by Costa Rica in 2009 with a Ministry of Justice and Peace.

Root causes of the conflict in Nepal included feudalism, the exclusion of minorities, weak governance, and government neglect, with the result that most districts and villages had their tensions. The conflict in Nepal had rural roots and was partly a rural revolt against perceived discrimination and neglect. Peace at the local level had to be secured, or it would undermine the entire peace process.

The decision to establish local peace councils (LPCs) was taken as early as 2005, but the implementation was difficult and became contested. Some questioned the independence of the LPCs when they became closely linked with and reliant upon the later established Ministry of Peace and Reconstruction. There was reluctance to establish joint multiparty control over the peace architecture. Some 60 LPCs have been formed, but their effectiveness is an issue

ADDED VALUE OF THE CONCEPT

There are many different reasons to give far more focus and weight to infrastructures for peace and aim for a systemic approach to peacebuilding.

Development and Conflict

Development in itself generates new conflicts on top of existing root causes, by changing economic and power relations, and the current structures and mechanisms in many countries are not appropriate to deal with them. Community-based and interethnic conflicts are often intractable, partly because the justice

system is not functioning well, and the (local) government fails to provide security. Weak governments unable to deliver services again give rise to conflicts.

Sustainable Solutions Are Needed: A Systemic
Approach to Peacebuilding

When a conflict is escalating, it is not enough to look just at that specific conflict and address the symptoms only. The root causes should be addressed, and
sustainable structures and mechanisms established to transform the conflicts.
Otherwise, these conflicts will flare up during elections or other events.

Some countries have democratic processes and institutions that can help address conflicts. Many counties, however, lack the instruments and institutions
to address those conflicts systematically. In the cases of Ghana and Kenya—
countries perceived by many as peaceful—it is evident that many different
types of conflicts existed and that the governments came to the conclusion that
structural conflicts were continuing to destabilize the country, forming a threat
to development, security, and peace, especially during elections. These governments understood that we lack an overall systems approach to peacebuilding: what are the capacities, tools, mechanisms, structures, and institutions we
need to build sustainable peace in countries?

Electoral Violence

Elections are increasingly becoming contested, thus *triggering* underlying
tensions and root causes of conflict, as seen in the case of Kenya in 2008. Elections will be held in dozens of other countries in the coming years. There is
great concern in the international community that much more electoral violence may occur as a result.

Peace Councils Have Helped to Prevent
or Reduce Violent Conflict

It is often difficult to prove the prevention of violent conflict. We already
saw how in the early 1990s the South African LPCs contributed toward containing the spiral of violence, which observers agreed would have been far
worse if the LPCs had not existed. In Ghana and Kenya, the existence of these
structures helped in preventing and reducing violent conflict during recent
elections.

Expected Increase in Violent Conflicts

Another reason to speed up the establishment of infrastructures for peace is
that experts expect an increase in violent conflicts. The UN report on mediation states:

> Although there is solid evidence that efforts by the United Nations and our part-
> ners have made an impact in reducing the number of conflicts around the world,
> new dangers are on the horizon. Competition for scarce resources is a powerful

driver of conflict, especially when added to existing grievances between groups. As a result of the economic downturn, climate change and the growing depletion of resources, from arable land to water to oil, disputes within and between States may become more common in the future. Our Organization and our partners will need all of the knowledge, skill, wisdom and resources we can muster to meet this daunting challenge. . . . We, the United Nations, have a responsibility to "we the peoples" to professionalize our efforts to resolve conflicts constructively rather than destructively and to save succeeding generations from the scourge of war.[18]

With an expected increase in the diversity of citizens within each country, tensions will increase as well, and the promotion of social inclusion is very important.

We are not prepared for such an increase of violent conflicts.

Prevention Is Far Less Costly

If we wait until the conflict escalates, it is *more difficult to intervene* and *far more costly:* the toll in lives and in all other disastrous effects of violent conflicts, as well as the financial cost. Governments still spend 1,885 times as much on the military as they do on the prevention of conflict[19] and spend almost nothing on supporting civilians to stop violence. Peacekeeping troops in a country easily cost billions. Building the infrastructure for Peace in Ghana, on the other hand, cost only some 2.5 million dollars over the first three years.

A Positive, Proactive, Participatory, and Inclusive Approach

Responses to conflicts are often reactive, law-and-order based, top-down, and aimed more at managing the conflict than solving it. The infrastructures for peace approach, on the other hand, is proactive, participatory, inclusive, nonviolent, transformative, and principle based. It is positive in character and stimulates working with everything and everyone on behalf of the greater good.

One of the advantages of infrastructure for peace is that it makes the connection between the capacity and the conflict: people trained in conflict resolution and transformation are given a role in transforming the conflict.

The Approach Includes All Stakeholders at All Levels

A crucial component of such an infrastructure is to establish a platform for all peace actors and stakeholders for dialogue, consultation, cooperation, and coordination. Peace and peacebuilding are complex processes and urgently need such a platform. This approach acknowledges that sustainable peace needs a collaborative institutional framework between state and non-state actors.

MAIN COMPONENTS OF AN INFRASTRUCTURE FOR PEACE

The following main components were for the most part taken from the policy documents from the governments of Ghana and Kenya on their national peacebuilding architecture.[20]

- *National, district, and local peace councils.* The peace councils consist of highly respected persons of great integrity who are capable of bridging political divides and who possess competence, knowledge, and experience in matters relating to conflict transformation and peace, nominated by a broad range of different stakeholders. The councils' mandate will be to promote sustainable peace and human security. The work of the NPC shall be guided by bipartisanship and independence. The main objectives and strategies that LPCs have pursued in practice have been violence reduction, promoting dialogue, problem solving, community-building, and reconciliation.

- *National peace forum.* A platform for consultation, collaboration, cooperation, and coordination of peace actors and stakeholders.

- *A government unit or department on peacebuilding and a bill on infrastructures for peace.* One unit or department of the government will develop the overall government policy on peacebuilding together with the national peace council and the national peace forum and implement it.

- *A whole-of-government approach.* This unit or department will liaise and cooperate with other ministries or departments with related policies on peace, justice, defense, foreign affairs, social cohesion, conflict resolution in schools, environment, and social and economic development and health.

- *Building national capacities for peace.* The focus is to increase the capacity of peacebuilding institutions of government departments, peace councils, and others, including CSO groups. Broad-based skills training will be offered to functionaries, public servants, or members of civil society in peacebuilding and conflict management, including conflict analysis, conflict early warning and response, conflict resolution, and supporting dialogue processes.

- *Traditional perspectives on conflict resolution.* Traditional perspectives, understanding, and solutions to conflict will be offered and strengthened.

- *Promotion of a shared vision of society and a culture of peace.* Common values and a shared vision of society will be promoted and policies and structures established to implement them. Values of reconciliation, tolerance, trust and confidence building, mediation, and dialogue as responses to conflict will be highlighted. With an expected increase in the diversity of citizens within each country, the promotion of social inclusion and cohesion is more important than ever.[21]

- *Peace education.* Peace education and the celebration of the International Day of Peace, September 21, will be part of such an overall policy.

- *Establishing and implementing an infrastructure for peace.* In the initial phase of establishing an infrastructure, all stakeholders will be consulted: government and non-state actors and different sectors of society at the national, district, and local level. Analyzing the root causes of conflict in a country shall be a participatory and inclusive effort. When such a policy has been approved, it has to be operationalized, and regular assessments have to be executed.[22]

- *Budget.* Peacebuilding and conflict management intervention strategies require long-term funding by governments, donors, NGOs, and communities.

These components are not a straitjacket, but *possible* pillars for a national infrastructure for peace. It is essential that each process, structure, and mechanism is *authentic* and designed by the stakeholders themselves or in close collaboration with all stakeholders.

Listing the main components also aims to make more visible what a peace infrastructure can look like. It is an attempt at a systemic approach, a system with different components, but it should be context specific in each country.

CONCLUSIONS AND LESSONS LEARNED[23]

- The value of *bottom-up* and *consultative processes:* Meaningful experiences with a regional peace council in Wajir (Kenya) and in Northern Ghana worked well and helped de-escalate the violence toward more sustainable solutions and motivate national leaders to set up such structures at the national level as well. In both cases, informal LPCs inspired the formalization of LPCs, and a highly participatory and inclusive consultation process was chosen, which contributed to the legitimacy and success of the Peace Infrastructure.

- *Importance of a national mandate:* The existence of a national mandate for LPCs creates opportunities and can be supportive for the LPCs, but brings some challenges as well. Although the mandate confers legitimacy and access to state resources and national political leadership, it also opens up LPCs to political manipulation and makes them vulnerable to the fragility of a national peace process.

- *Composition:* The composition of LPCs is another important issue. They should be inclusive of the main protagonists, and they should include respected leaders from civil society who can lead the peace process. Any LPC has to include individuals that come from different sides of the conflict: both "doves," people who regard the achievement of peace as more important than pursuing sectarian interests, and "hawks," people that are distrustful of peace because they see their interests threatened by the necessary compromises of peace. With hawks absent, LPCs may lack credibility and local leverage. The ideal is to have a good mix of hawks and doves on the LPC. LPCs should include insider-partials, that is, persons typically drawn from civil society who are respected and trusted and have the personal integrity and gravitas to provide leadership to the peace process. Rather than politicians, these insider-partials should occupy the leadership positions on the LPC. What should be prevented at all cost is to allow one party to capture the leadership position of a LPC and dominate from there. The best is to appoint persons in this position on the basis of consensus. In South Africa, LPC chairpersons were elected on the basis of consensus. They were often from the religious or business sector. When LPCs failed to find a chairperson acceptable to all sides, two cochairpersons were elected. They proved to be very effective. Of all actors at the local level, the LPC chairpersons have made the most substantial contribution to local peacebuilding.[24]

- *Proven impact:* We saw that the South African LPCs contributed toward containing the spiral of violence. Observers agreed that the situation would be far worse if the LPCs had not existed. Ghana and Kenya both recently had elections, and the existence of these structures has helped in preventing and reducing violence. Based on studies of LPCs in 12 countries, Andries Odendaal concludes that LPCs can have the following impact:

  - LPCs can enable communication between former protagonists, thus dealing with potentially destructive rumors, fear, and mistrust.

- LPCs are effective in preventing or containing violence through a strategy of joint planning for, and monitoring of, potentially violent events.
- LPCs can facilitate or mediate in local peacemaking processes, leading to local peace agreements.
- LPCs can facilitate dialogue between various sections of the community, thereby strengthening social cohesion, which is a necessary precondition for governance.
- LPCs can facilitate reconciliation.
- LPCs can enable a flow of information between the local and national levels, so that peacebuilding challenges experienced at local level can receive proper attention at the national level.

CHALLENGES

What LPCs Cannot Do

- LPCs cannot *enforce peace,* especially not against spoiler groups that are bent on using violence.
- LPCs cannot deal with the *structural root causes* of conflict.

Relationship with the Government

A starting point for establishing an infrastructure in Ghana was the fact that the court system did not work and conflicts were not resolved; in Wajir (Kenya), the government failed to provide security. In the described cases of South Africa, Ghana, and Kenya, practical solutions had to be found for involving the government—for instance by making the district commissioner chair of the Peace and Development Committee in Wajir—while maintaining an independent position for the National Peace Council. When a government cannot respect this independence and tries to dominate the peace infrastructure—as happened in Nepal—it does not work. Colonial powers imposed a state model on their colonies that did not fit to their existing structures at that moment. We saw how the governments of Ghana and Kenya recognized the critical role of traditional conflict resolution mechanisms. The District Peace Committee in Kenya "is to be a hybrid institution that brings together synergies between traditional and formal mechanisms for conflict resolution."

- *Authoritarian governments.* Infrastructures for peace only work when governments are open for consultation and cooperation with civil society. What to do if they are not open for cooperation and when civil society is still weak?
- There seems to be a need for *hybrid political orders.*[25] Infrastructures for peace can be a bridge in this respect.
- *Electoral violence:* During elections, underlying tensions in society regularly come to the surface and lead to violent conflict. The dates of elections are often decided long in advance. Estimates about the potential for electoral violence can be made. This gives the opportunity to use the probability of electoral violence, to start preparing for peaceful elections long before they take place and aiming for establishing more sustainable peace structures in a country.
- *Lessons from other infrastructures:* Many sectors of society have some infrastructure with well-defined policies, training and education, strategies, ministries,

institutions such as hospitals and armies, and so on. What can we learn from other infrastructures in the fields of health, education, fire prevention, waging of war, and others?

- *Costs:* What is the cost-effectiveness of infrastructures for peace? What are the costs of establishing such an infrastructure, and what would be the costs if it failed or if it were not established at all?

EPILOGUE

Infrastructures for peace is a relatively unknown approach. Much more research has to be undertaken, but there are enough successful examples of local peace councils and of a provisional peace infrastructure in some countries that suggest that it works and helps in reducing and preventing violent conflict.

Taking into account that most countries have no adequate structure and mechanisms to deal with all their (structural) conflicts, a systemic approach is needed to establish such structures. Especially because an increase in violent conflicts is expected, we should prepare ourselves better.

Infrastructures at the Regional and Global Levels

One of the key principles of infrastructures for peace is the acknowledgement that the main stakeholders in peace should have a dialogue with each other and look for ways of consultation and cooperation. This counts not only on the *national* level, but on the *regional* and *global* levels as well. Regional organizations, the United Nations, governments, civil society organizations, and academia rarely meet to discuss how they could cooperate on specific issues of peace and conflict. There is a clear need for a *multi-stakeholder dialogue on peace-building* at the regional and global levels.

NOTES

1. John Paul Lederach, *Building Peace: Sustainable Reconciliation in Divided Societies* (1997), xvi and 49–51, on peace commissions; see also *The Little Book of Conflict Transformation* (2003), especially chapter 7, "Process-Structures as Platforms for Change," 40–48; and *The Moral Imagination: The Art and Soul of Building Peace* (2005), especially 47–49.

2. Lederach, *The Moral Imagination,* 47.

3. UN General Assembly, progress report on the prevention of armed conflict, 16, http://www.undp.org/cpr/documents/prevention/build_national/N0639322.pdf.

4. Security Council, Report of the Secretary-General on enhancing mediation and its support activities, April 8, 2009, http://www.un.org/Depts/dpa/docs/S-2009-189.pdf.

5. Background documents for the seminar can be found at http://www.gppac.net/page.php?id=1#par2544.

6. Kai Brand-Jacobsen, "Towards an Effective Architecture-Infrastructure for Peace: Learning from Medical Health," by Annex 2 of GPPAC (working paper on infrastructures for peace, July 2010), http://www.gppac.net/uploads/File/Programmes/EWER/I4P/Infrastructures%20for%20Peace%20July%202010.doc. Johan Galtung was the first to compare peace to health in "Theories of Peace, Theories of Health: Some Isomorphism" (1991) and "Health as a Bridge for Peace" (1997).

7. This short description is mainly based on the case report on South Africa, 1991–1994, in Andries Odendaal, *An Architecture for Building Peace at Local Level: A Comparative Study of the Use of Local Peace Forums.* The study is forthcoming from UNDP-BCPR; see also Susan Collin Marks, *Watching the Wind: Conflict Resolution during South Africa's Transition to Democracy* (USIP Press, 2000).

8. Lederach, *Building Peace,* on the cases of Nicaragua and South Africa, 51.

9. The section on Ghana is based on the following documents: *National Architecture for Peace in Ghana* (2006), issued by the Ministry of Interior; *National Peace Council Bill* (2011) and Andries Odendaal, *Local Peacebuilding in Ghana,* both at http://www.gppac.net/page.php?id=1#par2544; Dr. Ozonnia Ojielo, "Designing an Architecture for Peace: A Framework of Conflict Transformation in Ghana," *LEJIA* 7, no. 1 (2010); Emmanuel Bombande, "Ghana—Developing an Institutional Framework for Sustainable Peace—UN, Government and Civil Society Collaboration for Conflict Prevention," 46–54, in *GPPAC Issue Paper on Joint Action for Prevention: Civil Society and Government Cooperation on Conflict and Peacebuilding,* http://www.gppac.net/uploads/File/Programmes/Interaction%20and%20Advocacy/Issue%20Paper%204%20December%202007%20Gov—CSO%20cooperation.pdf.

10. Ozonnia Ojielo, *Designing an Architecture for Peace,* 9.

11. Conclusions from Ozonnia Ojielo, in *Designing an Architecture for Peace,* 9.

12. Additional conclusions from Andries Odendaal, in *Local Peacebuilding in Ghana.*

13. The section on Kenya is based on the following documents: Office of the President, Ministry of State for Provincial Administration and Internal Security, *National Policy on Peacebuilding and Conflict Management* (September 2009), and Andries Odendaal, *Local Peace and Development Committees in Kenya,* both at http://www.gppac.net/page.php?id=1#par2544; George Kut, "Towards the National Policy on Peacebuilding and Conflict Management," 38–45, in *GPPAC Issue Paper on Joint Action for Prevention: Civil Society and Government Cooperation on Conflict Prevention and Peacebuilding,* http://www.gppac.net/uploads/File/Programmes/Interaction%20and%20Advocacy/Issue%20Paper%204%20December%202007%20Gov-CSO%20cooperation.pdf. See also George Wachira, *Citizens in Action: Making Peace in the Post-Election Crisis in Kenya* (2008), 37, 61, http://bit.ly/KenyaCCP.

14. Andries Odendaal, *Local Peace and Development Committees in Kenya,* 14.

15. Ibid., 49; see also the case study of Andries Odendaal on Nicaragua in the discussion paper "An Architecture for Building Peace at Local Level: A Comparative Study of the Use of Local Peace Forums," forthcoming from UNDP-BCPR.

16. http://www.opapp.gov.py.

17. GPPAC issue paper 4: Manish Thapa, "Joint Action for Prevention: Civil Society and Government Cooperation on Conflict Prevention and Peacebuilding," *Nepal, Ministry of Peace and Reconstruction: A Foundation for Peace,* 55–61, http://www.gppac.net/uploads/File/Programmes/Interaction%20and%20Advocacy/Issue%20Paper%204%20December%202007%20Gov-CSO%20cooperation.pdf; Andries Odendaal and Retief Olivier, *Local Peace Committees: Some Reflections and Lessons Learned,* 7–10, http://www.gppac.net/uploads/File/Programmes/EWER/I4P/9.%20LOCAL%20PEACE%20COUNCILS.pdf.

18. United Nations Secretary-General. 2009b. *Report of the Secretary-General of the UN to the Security Council on Enhancing Mediation and Its Support Activities.* S/2009/189. April. New York: United Nations. http://daccess-ods.un.org/TMP/6862033.html.

19. OECD figures, from SMART POWER, International Taskforce for Preventive Diplomacy, February 2009.

20. *National Architecture for Peace in Ghana* (2006), issued by the Ministry of Interior; *National Policy on Peacebuilding and Conflict Management* (2009), by Office of the

President, Ministry of State for Provincial Administration and Internal Security, both documents at http://www.gppac.net/page.php?id=1#par2544.

21. The Club of Madrid Shared Societies project has developed a government audit of the Club of Madrid commitments for shared societies, www.thesharedsocietiesproject. clubmadrid.org/project-documents/commitments-and-approaches.

22. Ibid.

23. Most of the conclusions are taken from Andries Odendaal, "An Architecture for Building Peace at Local Level: A Comparative Study of the Use of Local Peace Forums," discussion paper, forthcoming from UNDP-BCPR.

24. Odendaal, Andries, and Retief Olivier. 2008. Local Peace Committees: Some Reflections and Lessons Learned. Report funded by USAID for the Nepal Transition to Peace (NTTP) Initiative, implemented by the Academy for Educational Development (AED) Kathmandu, Nepal, http://unpan1.un.org/intradoc/groups/public/docu ments/UN/UNPAN032148.pdf.

25. Volker Boege, Anne Brown, Kevin Clements, and Anna Nolan, 2009. "On Hybrid Political Orders and Emerging States: What is Failing—States in the Global South or Research and Politics in the West?" in *Building Peace in the Absence of States: Challenging the Discourse on State Failure*, ed. Martina Fischer and Beatrix Schmelzle, 15–35. Berghof Handbook Dialogue No. 8. Berlin: Berghof Research Center. Available at www.berghof-handbook.net/std_page.php?LANG=e&id=5.

CHAPTER 26

The Responsibility to Protect and Peacemaking

Abiodun Williams and Jonas Claes

Innovative ideas have played an important role in steering international responses to global threats and challenges. A notable example is peacekeeping, which was not envisaged by the framers of the United Nations charter, but is a critical instrument in the prevention, management, and resolution of international conflict. But no concept has moved faster in the area of global norms than what is commonly referred to as the Responsibility to Protect or R2P.[1] The concept emerged in 2001 and in a decade has become a prominent principle in international affairs with great potential to evolve into a norm that could reduce the frequency of future mass atrocities. During the 2005 UN World Summit, heads of state and government unanimously agreed to *act in accordance* with their responsibility to protect populations from genocide, war crimes, ethnic cleansing, and crimes against humanity, the four R2P crimes.[2] Their decision provided a solid basis for the development of R2P strategies at the global, regional, and local levels. But the normalization of R2P is a slow process, and many challenges remain before the principle can effectively prevent or halt mass atrocity crimes in a consistent manner.

"War makes rattling good history; but Peace is poor reading" observed the novelist and poet Thomas Hardy. Although our histories predominantly focus on wars, triumphs, and defeats, the enduring quest for peace is as old as humanity. Great philosophers since ancient times have pondered on the ideal of peace. The deep longing of peoples everywhere for peace is reflected in literature, music, art, and religion. The Nobel Peace Prize, established over a century ago, has not only become the most prestigious award on the planet, but an international institution in its own right. In the wake of the tragedy of the World War II, visionary and pragmatic leaders established the United

Nations "to save succeeding generations from the scourge of war."[3] The UN has survived 65 years of profound and turbulent global change, and it remains an essential instrument for dealing with dangerous crises and settling international disputes by peaceful means. But it is often forgotten that the United Nations was created because the *nations* were *united* in their commitment to peaceful conflict resolution.

The underlying assumption of this chapter is that the R2P and peacemaking agendas are fundamentally intertwined. The most effective way to prevent mass atrocities is to stop wars, and peacemaking—in its myriad forms—is a critical tool for the prevention of mass violence. In recent years, there has been a growing recognition that war and the suffering it engenders is a matter of responsibility for the international community as a whole. This is of particular importance since from Cambodia to Rwanda, from the former Yugoslavia to Sudan, the complex process of peacemaking is made even more difficult when it is overlaid with the legacy of genocide, ethnic cleansing, war crimes, and crimes against humanity.

The first section of this chapter places R2P in a broader historical context, including significant aspects of its evolution during the past decade. In the second section, we analyze R2P's current impact on peacemaking and identify some of the challenges hampering its implementation. The final section discusses R2P's potential contribution to peacemaking in the future.

PROTECTING POPULATIONS FROM MASS ATROCITIES

The end of the Cold War did not usher in an era of peace and tranquility as many had hoped. On the contrary, it removed superpower constraints on local conflicts and opened the door to civil wars on a terrible scale. Tragically, genocide, ethnic cleansing, the bombardment of cities, atrocities against civilians, and other war crimes became the hallmarks of the last decade of the 20th century. In 1991, former Yugoslavia disintegrated and descended into war and ethnoreligious violence; in Bosnia-Herzegovina alone, over 200,000 people were killed, 500,000 injured, and more than 2 million were displaced. The killing of thousands of unarmed men and boys in Srebrenica in 1995 was the largest and most brutal act of slaughter in Europe since the Holocaust. The Rwandan genocide of 1994 lasted about 100 days, and more than 800,000 Tutsi and 50,000 moderate Hutu were massacred, 500,000 were internally displaced, and more than 2 million fled to neighboring countries as refugees.[4] The conflict in Kosovo led to a 78-day NATO bombing campaign in the spring of 1999 to protect Kosovar Albanians against abuse by Belgrade, forcing Serb leader Slobodan Milosevic to capitulate. NATO's military intervention was controversial since it was undertaken without the authorization of the Security Council.

The Rwandan genocide, ethnic cleansing in Bosnia-Herzegovina, and the NATO operation in Kosovo dramatized the urgent need to develop a framework that, on the one hand, could help prevent or halt future atrocities in a legitimate and consistent manner, while, on the other hand, assuaging fears of sovereignty erosion through humanitarian intervention. In his speech on sovereignty and intervention to the General Assembly in September 1999, UN Secretary-General Kofi Annan articulated two notions of sovereignty—one for states, one for individuals.[5] As he put it, "State sovereignty, in its most basic sense, is being redefined by the forces of globalization and international cooperation. The state is now widely understood to be the servant of its people and not vice versa. At the same time, individual sovereignty—and by this I mean the human rights and fundamental freedoms of each and every individual as enshrined in our Charter—has been enhanced by a renewed consciousness of the right of every individual to control his or her destiny."[6]

In his Millennium Report in 2000, Annan posed this question: "If humanitarian intervention is, indeed, an unacceptable assault on sovereignty, how should we respond to a Rwanda, to a Srebrenica—to gross and systematic violations of human rights that offend every precept of our common humanity?"[7]

The International Commission on Intervention and State Sovereignty (ICISS) provided a comprehensive and well-crafted response to Annan's question in its seminal report *The Responsibility to Protect*. The Canadian government established the ICISS in 2000 to resolve this conundrum and with a mandate "to build a broader understanding of the problem of reconciling intervention for human protection purposes and sovereignty."[8] The ICISS report reframed the central issue of the debate on intervention and shifted the debate from a "right to intervene" toward a "responsibility to protect."[9] On the issue of sovereignty, the report stated that the notion of individual sovereignty should not be seen as a challenge to state sovereignty, but rather as "a way of saying that the more traditional notion of state sovereignty should be able comfortably to embrace the goal of greater self-empowerment and freedom for people, both individually and collectively."[10]

The publication of the ICISS report in 2001 was initially overshadowed by 9/11, and the main focus of the international debate in the aftermath of that tragedy was about intervention in self-defense against terrorism, as opposed to action to protect others from massacre and ethnic cleansing. However, the report lost none of its importance, and before long, R2P became the subject of much debate particularly at the UN General Assembly (UNGA) and within academic circles. R2P's focus on the protection of people from the most extreme humanitarian crimes and its victim-centered approach was particularly appropriate given the increased vulnerability of civilians in armed conflict. Most of R2P's components are not entirely new, but merely reaffirm existing international legal commitments.

Since 2001, R2P has undergone conceptual changes in which action thresholds were raised; criteria for the use of force were gradually removed; and the applicable crimes were narrowed down to four. Nonetheless, the core tenets of R2P have remained intact. State sovereignty implies responsibilities, and the primary responsibility for the protection of its people lies with the state itself.[11] Its application is not limited to traditional peacemakers. Instead, states carry primary responsibility to keep tensions from escalating within their borders. R2P is first and foremost a negative duty, an obligation for each state not to inflict harms that "shock the conscience of mankind," and a prima facie duty of the international community not to intervene in the internal affairs of sovereign states.[12] The international community—particularly neighboring countries, regional hegemons, and regional organizations—is responsible to assist other states in exercising this primary responsibility. When a state is unable to exercise its sovereignty responsibly and external assistance remains ineffective, the international community has a duty to prevent, halt, or reverse the effects of mass atrocities on vulnerable individuals.

The principle allows for a wide array of diplomatic, economic, legal, or military instruments under chapters 6 and 7 of the UN Charter, as well as chapter 8 operations undertaken by regional organizations. The focal point for responding to R2P situations remains the UN Security Council, while national governments are asked to act as good neighbors, generous donors, persuasive diplomats, and, if necessary, appliers of coercive pressure or military force.[13] The R2P toolbox consists of instruments that, depending on the local context, nonsequentially but often simultaneously contribute to the prevention of mass atrocities, the protection of civilians during ongoing conflict, and the stabilization of countries emerging from conflict. Structural tools to prevent, react, or rebuild include the promotion of membership in international organizations, support of equitable development, and security sector reform; examples of direct tools are preventive diplomacy, criminal prosecution, and humanitarian engagement.[14] Some of the instruments within mass atrocity toolboxes are not unique to R2P strategies, but overlap with the ongoing activities of development agencies, conflict resolution efforts, and human rights protection. Even when prevention fails, the international community's reaction is not necessarily military, but can also involve legal, political, economic, and diplomatic pressure.[15] Despite the emphasis on prevention and cooperative approaches, a flexible response through quick and decisive military action may be required when less coercive measures are unlikely to have a timely and decisive impact. However, the use of coercive military instruments under the R2P-label is only authorized as a last resort.

FROM THREE RESPONSIBILITIES TO THREE PILLARS

The ICISS report provided the conceptual foundations of R2P and the impetus for a decade-long debate about R2P's scope, its operational challenges, and its compatibility with existing norms. The commission introduced a framework with three responsibilities that follow the main stages of the conflict curve: the responsibility to prevent deadly conflict and other forms of man-made catastrophes; the responsibility to react to situations of compelling need of human protection; and the responsibility to rebuild durable peace.[16] States have the primary responsibility to protect their population, but if *unable or unwilling* to fulfill their duties, this responsibility would transfer to the international community.[17] The commission agreed that the UN Security Council should operate as the primary actor authorizing interventions, but this authority could transfer to the General Assembly or even ad hoc coalitions in case the council failed to act.

Even though R2P is often depicted as a Western concept, the first tangible progress was made on the African continent. The responsibility to protect was incorporated in both the African Union's 2002 Constitutive Act and the institutional structure of the Economic Community of West African States (ECOWAS). The concept was adopted in the 2004 Report of the Secretary-General's High-Level Panel on Threats, Challenges, and Change, "A More Secure World: Our Shared Responsibility," as well as Secretary-General Kofi Annan's agenda-setting report, "In Larger Freedom." The R2P agenda was also promoted through the advocacy of the Canadian Government, civil society organizations, and influential ICISS commissioners like Gareth Evans and Ramesh Thakur.

In 2005, R2P was adopted in paragraphs 138 and 139 of the World Summit Outcome Document after long and difficult political deliberations amongst UN member states. The consensus was hard won and largely unanticipated. In 2002, the Non-Aligned Movement (NAM) had blocked a Canadian draft of a technical GA Resolution committing the Assembly to deliberate on the ICISS report.[18] The humanitarian rhetoric applied by the Western coalition to legitimize the 2003 invasion of Iraq further jeopardized the survival of this nascent concept. The original language from the ICISS Report was softened to accommodate the concerns of R2P critics, particularly the United States, India, and other key players within the NAM.

Although the World Summit's decision was a significant achievement, the pragmatism which made the consensus possible was viewed with disappointment by parts of the humanitarian and NGO communities. The language on R2P in the Outcome Document was described as "R2P lite," and it was suggested that the principle had been watered down to such an extent that it would not afford protection to threatened populations.[19] Gareth Evans, one of R2P's founding fathers, described the Summit as "a huge wasted opportunity."[20] In order to achieve a political consensus a number of concessions were made, including the omission of decision-making criteria on the use of force, a code of conduct for P-5 members on the use of the veto, and the possibility of military intervention outside the scope of Security Council approval. The threshold transferring the Responsibility to Protect from the host state to the international community was raised during the very last minutes of the Summit negotiations, from the *inability or unwillingness* of states to protect their populations to a state's *manifest failure* to do so, a significantly higher threshold.[21] The Security Council was no longer the primary, but exclusive authority for mandating the use of force under the R2P label.[22] And whereas the ICISS version applied to large-scale loss of life, genocide, ethnic cleansing, crimes against humanity, situations of state collapse, and even overwhelming environmental catastrophes,[23] the Outcome Document limited R2P's application to four specific crimes: genocide, ethnic cleansing, crimes against humanity, and war crimes.[24] The Outcome Document also emphasized the role of prevention and the provision of assistance to societies under stress, reactive measures falling short of military action, and R2P's regional dimensions.[25]

Following the 2005 World Summit, R2P was further refined through Special Reports by UN Secretary-General Ban Ki-Moon, as well as debates and interactive dialogues in the General Assembly. The Security Council endorsed R2P in Resolution 1674 on the Protection of Civilians and Resolution 1706 on the situation in Darfur, and in 2009 the General Assembly passed its own Resolution on R2P.[26]

In his January 2009 report on implementing the responsibility to protect, which set out a comprehensive strategy to put R2P into practice, the Secretary-General incorporated the modified understanding of R2P into a new three-pillar approach:

1. The responsibility of each state to protect its population from genocide, war crimes, ethnic cleansing and crimes against humanity

2. The responsibility of the international community to assist states in exercising that responsibility through international assistance and capacity-building

3. The responsibility of the international community to take collective action in a timely and decisive manner through the Security Council and in accordance with the UN Charter, when a state is manifestly failing to protect its population from the four specified crimes and violations[27]

Secretary-General Ban appointed Francis Deng as his Special Adviser on the Prevention of Genocide and Edward Luck as his Special Adviser on matters related to R2P. At the time of writing, the financial and logistical details have just been arranged for the merger of their capacity within a new joint office for the prevention of genocide and the promotion of R2P. The principle was endorsed in both the 2010 U.S. National Security Strategy and the 2008 Report on the Implementation of the EU Security Strategy.

R2P'S CURRENT ROLE IN PEACEMAKING

R2P Invocations

Although conceptual ambiguities remain, a broad consensus has been forged on the core principles of the Responsibility to Protect. In the relatively short period of a decade, the Responsibility to Protect has received consensus-based approval among UN member states and is slowly becoming institutionalized at the global and regional levels. However, it is axiomatic that rhetorical commitments do not automatically result in operational effectiveness. Even though R2P has been invoked about 10 times in the past 5 years, selectiveness and inconsistency remain a political reality in the international community's response to mass atrocities.

At present, R2P functions primarily as a political tool bolstering the necessary will within the international community to halt and reverse ongoing atrocities. Since 2005, R2P has been invoked a number a times in response to crisis situations, with mixed success and a disturbing level of inconsistency. The invocations can be categorized in four groups based on their appropriateness and the effectiveness of the international response: (1) appropriate invocation and effective action; (2) appropriate invocation and ineffective action; (3) inappropriate invocation; and (4) non-invocation.

1. Appropriate Invocation and Effective Action: The Case of Kenya

Ideally, as long as R2P serves as an instrument to generate political will within the international community to assist or pressure governments to engage directly in a crisis situation, we should see formal invocations by world leaders, the Security Council, the General Assembly, senior UN officials, and regional organizations when R2P crimes are imminent or ongoing, resulting in a timely and decisive international response and policy changes by the local regime. The international diplomatic efforts in response to the violence following Kenya's disputed presidential election held on December 27, 2007, exemplify R2P's potential contribution to the prevention and mitigation of atrocities. Incumbent President Mwai Kibaki of the ruling Party of National Unity (PNU) was declared the winner over opposition candidate Raila Odinga of the Orange Democratic Movement (ODM).[28] The opposition charged that the election was fraudulent. A month after the election, the UN estimated that more than 1,000 people had lost their lives and 300,000 had fled their homes. As the violence increased early in 2008, former UN Secretary-General Kofi Annan noted the occurrence of "gross and systematic human rights abuses" in Western Kenya.[29] French Foreign Minister Bernard Kouchner asked the Security Council to take action "in the name of the responsibility to protect."[30] UN Secretary-General Ban, Special Adviser Deng, and the Security Council urged Kenya's leaders to exercise their responsibility to protect the civilian population and end the violence.

Kofi Annan led the mediation effort to resolve the Kenyan crisis as part of the African Union Panel of Eminent Personalities. Annan's team was supported by the United Nations, the European Union and the United States. After nearly 40 days, Annan negotiated a political settlement which included a power-sharing agreement.[31] In March 2010 the International Criminal Court investigated the occurrence of crimes against humanity that took place in Kenya, leading to the prosecution of six individuals including members of the Kenyan government.

The international community's response to the Kenyan crisis has been applauded as "a model of diplomatic action under the Responsibility to Protect."[32] This characterization is not accurate in the strict sense, as little action was taken in advance of the crisis, when corruption and impunity were widespread. Moreover, R2P was only invoked after the violence erupted, underlining the continuing reluctance of the international community to apply this concept, even to a crisis situation. Nonetheless, the invocation of R2P in the Kenya case certainly bolstered international efforts to resolve the crisis and increased pressure on Kenya's leadership to find an acceptable solution through dialogue and negotiation.[33]

2. Appropriate Invocation and Ineffective Action: The Case of Kyrgyzstan

In April 2010 riots broke out in Kyrgyzstan resulting in the deaths of about 100 people and the ousting of President Bakiyev, who fled into exile in Belarus. The Kyrgyz revolution in April was not the first time turmoil had taken place in Kyrgyzstan. There was interethnic violence between ethnic Kyrgyz and Uzbeks right after independence from the Soviet Union, and both before and after the 2005 Tulip Revolution, riots and crackdowns on political demonstrations were commonplace. On June 10, 2010 a new wave of violence erupted in the southern parts of Kyrgyzstan, resulting in killings, rape, and the widespread burning and looting of houses. The violence that month may have killed at least 371 people and left 400,000 homeless, mostly ethnic Uzbeks.[34] In response to the violence, the Interim Government, led by Roza Otunbayeva, declared a state of emergency and asked for international assistance to help stabilize the country.

The international response to the crisis and ethnic violence in Kyrgyzstan in the spring and summer of 2010 was demonstrably weak. Key governments, international, and regional organizations provided humanitarian relief and economic support, but were reluctant to take action to protect the civilian population and address security concerns. The Kyrgyz authorities' request for the deployment of a stabilization force remained unanswered. On June 15, Special Advisers Deng and Luck issued a joint statement urging the international community to "operationalize its responsibility to protect by providing coordinated and timely assistance to stop the violence and its incitement."[35] Six weeks later, the Organization for Security and Co-operation in Europe (OSCE) decided to deploy a small 52-member unarmed Police Advisory Group to the region.

As the Kyrgyzstan case amply demonstrated, neither early warning signs nor widespread ethnic violence automatically trigger a robust international response. The second round of violence in June highlighted the Kyrgyz interim government's inability to protect its ethnic minorities from the pogroms that were taking place in various parts of Southern Kyrgyzstan. The numerous pleas for military assistance by Kyrgyz interim President Roza Otunbayeva to regional organization and key regional powers fell on deaf ears. The international community's inability to develop an effective R2P strategy in response to the ethnic violence in Kyrgyzstan underlines the lack of both political will and institutional preparedness to act decisively to crisis situations.

3. Inappropriate Invocation: The Case of Cyclone Nargis in Burma

The cyclone that struck Burma on May 3, 2008, was not only a natural disaster, but provided a case study in the inappropriate invocation of R2P. Before 2008, R2P had been invoked appropriately by UN officials, human rights activists, and commentators in response to the rampant human rights abuses by the military junta, which according to Amnesty International constituted crimes against humanity.[36] For example, in the wake of the 2007 protests in Burma, the Fédération Internationales des Droits de l'Homme (FIDH) issued a press statement saying that "The Human Rights Council should call upon the UN Security Council, based on its "responsibility to protect," to take all concrete measures as necessary."[37] In October 2007, UNA-USA highlighted a call for action by former *New York Times* foreign correspondent Barbara Crossette:

"At the world summit in 2005 . . . scores of world leaders signed on to a concept (revolutionary for the UN) called the 'responsibility to protect.' In a groundbreaking and still controversial step, countries accepted that when a government will not stop abuses against its own people, the outside world has the right to act. If ever there was a perfect time to test this post-2005 principle it is now in Burma."[38]

In the aftermath of cyclone Nargis, the Burmese authorities prevented international humanitarian assistance and aid workers from entering the country, sparking an intense debate on whether the crisis caused by the cyclone could be considered an R2P situation. French Foreign Minister Bernard Kouchner's position on the matter was clear. Four days after the cyclone, he invoked R2P: "We are seeing at the United Nations whether we can implement the Responsibility to Protect, given that food, boats and relief teams are there, and obtain a United Nations' resolution which authorizes the delivery (of aid) and imposes this on the Burmese government."[39] Kouchner argued that the denial of humanitarian assistance contributed a crime against humanity.[40] His view was initially supported by some politicians and commentators, primarily in Europe and North America. However, it was immediately rejected by China and Russia, who argued that R2P did not apply to natural disasters. It also evoked concern from the UK, as well as from senior UN and ASEAN officials who maintained that R2P did not apply to natural disasters.

R2P was not the proper normative basis for international military action to force the delivery of aid against the will of the Burmese authorities. Linking R2P and the humanitarian crisis following Nargis is generally considered to be a misapplication of the principle.[41] But there is no consensus on the implications of the invocation of R2P during the cyclone Nargis crisis for the normalization of the principle. In the view of some scholars, the normalization process has been advanced by the misapplication: "Misguided justifications and attempted breaches of an emerging norm, when they are rejected, back-fire and actually have the opposite effect, thereby clarifying matters and fostering the norm."[42] Misapplications can thus arguably reinforce normative salience when strong voices persuasively contest the misrepresentation.[43] Others argue that the disagreement about R2P's application to the emergency in Burma complicated the general perception of R2P.[44]

4. Non-Invocation: The Case of the Democratic Republic of the Congo

One of the most striking cases where R2P has not been invoked is in relation to the ongoing conflict in the Democratic Republic of the Congo (DRC),[45] even though R2P crimes have clearly been committed against unarmed Congolese citizens. The conflict in the DRC remains one of the gravest humanitarian disasters of our time and is arguably the world's deadliest conflict since World War II.[46] According to a study by the International Rescue Committee, over 5.4 million people have died in Congo since the conflict began in 1998.[47] But despite the commission of war crimes and crimes against humanity, the case is not commonly approached through an R2P lens.

Some advocates of R2P justify this non-invocation on pragmatic grounds. In their view, the added value of R2P, at its current stage of development, lies not in dealing with cases of long-standing conflict, but in addressing those cases where new atrocities are imminent or very recent and the international community has not yet formulated a proper response. They also argue that the international community has a plethora of other peacemaking tools to deal with old conflicts that predate the R2P concept that are often much more institutionalized and better resourced than those within the R2P toolbox.

But this noninvocation is problematic for a number of reasons. As a principle aimed at protecting vulnerable populations from the most heinous crimes, R2P is certainly applicable to a country whose citizens are the victims of some of the worst atrocities we have seen in decades. A 2010 UNHCHR report noted that some of the systematic and widespread attacks "if proven before a competent court, could be characterized as crimes of genocide."[48] The controversial report also found the governments and militaries of a number of states culpable for carrying out mass atrocity crimes. The Human Rights Council passed two resolutions condemning the human rights abuses[49] and encouraging the government to "establish and implement the reforms needed to consolidate peace and national reconciliation."[50] In any case, the crimes that have terrorized the Congolese population for decades, including mass rape and the use of child soldiers, have certainly passed the R2P threshold. Morally, it seems appropriate to invoke R2P in relation to the DRC.

The inconsistent application of R2P also hampers the normalization of the principle. Double standards strengthen the suspicion of R2P critics that the underlying motives of R2P advocates are far from humanitarian. Admittedly, the international community is already actively engaged in addressing the humanitarian situation in the DRC. One could legitimately wonder what R2P can add to the ongoing international engagement in the DRC. But so far the UN Stabilization Mission in the Democratic Republic of the Congo (MONUC) has been unable to prevent the occurrence of mass rape or the widespread use of child soldiers. Approaching the case through an R2P lens could bolster additional resources and strengthen MONUC's capacity to prevent further atrocities and effectively implement its civilian protection mandate.

PERSISTING CHALLENGES

The R2P principle still confronts a number of conceptual, operational, and political challenges that hamper its implementation and potential role in peacemaking. Three particular challenges necessitate specific elaboration: the comprehensiveness of the responsibility to prevent; the warning-response gap; and the perceived incompatibility between civilian protection and national sovereignty.

The Comprehensiveness of the Responsibility to Prevent

International attention to conflict prevention has increased significantly during the past two decades. In his 1992 report *An Agenda for Peace*, UN Secretary-General Boutros Boutros-Ghali stressed the UN's role in preventive diplomacy. The Carnegie Commission on Preventing Deadly Conflict conducted a comprehensive three-year study of violent conflict from 1994 to 1997. Three fundamental observations formed the basis of the Commission's final report: deadly conflict is not inevitable; the need to prevent such conflict is urgent; and successful prevention is possible. Kofi Annan selected conflict prevention as one of his priorities during his tenure as Secretary-General.[51] It was the theme of his report on the *Prevention of Armed Conflict* and his 1999 Annual Report to the General Assembly. He encouraged member states to move the UN "from a culture of reaction to a culture of prevention." Conflict prevention is now officially supported by the UN, regional organizations, many governments, and nongovernmental organizations. But a gap remains between these rhetorical commitments and investments in institutional capacity to implement prevention strategies.

The comprehensiveness of the responsibility to prevent is one of the key remaining conceptual loopholes within the R2P framework. Scholars can be divided into two groups: *minimalists* and *maximalists.* The minimalists argue that R2P's prevention pillar refers to operational or direct prevention and should apply primarily to the use of direct and short-term prevention efforts in situations where mass atrocities are imminent.[52] The maximalists maintain that the responsibility to prevent includes structural or root cause prevention efforts and requires taking effective action as early as possible.[53] It also necessitates identifying situations at risk of deteriorating into mass atrocities.[54] The maximalist position is reflected in the ICISS report which suggests that combining crisis management and efforts to address deep-rooted structural problems allows for the greatest potential effectiveness.

The debate between minimalists and maximalists is exacerbated by the strong overlap between development work, conflict prevention, the protection of human rights, and the prevention of mass atrocities, both operationally and conceptually. For the minimalists, adopting a broad interpretation of the Responsibility to Prevent is considered a "short walk from maintaining that R2P includes a right to development."[55] In their view, the prevention and resolution of armed conflict poses one set of policy challenges, the prevention and curbing of atrocity crimes a distinct but related one.[56] Adopting an expansive conception of R2P could also undermine its political utility. The maximalists stress the similarity between the mass atrocity toolboxes and available tools to prevent conflict more broadly and argue that efforts to prevent violent conflict should be at the center of a structural R2P prevention strategy since atrocities mostly occur within the context of violent conflict.[57]

The Warning-Response Gap

A key operational challenge for the prevention of mass atrocities, as well as armed conflict more generally, is the disconnect between early warning and timely and decisive political action. According to Alex Bellamy, the question of how to translate warning signs into a commitment to act is the single most pressing dilemma in relation to the responsibility to prevent.[58] New communication technologies allow us to detect and flag signs of instability at an early stage. The number of actors providing early warning has also risen rapidly over the past decade. Early warning is now produced by NGOs, state actors, regional organizations, and risk assessment firms, for a wide array of phenomena, including armed conflict, atrocities, political instability, and natural disasters. But so far, the multitude of information produced has had a meager impact on international and local prevention strategies. This disconnect was not addressed in the ICISS Report, even though Alexander George and Jane Holl had already identified this challenge in a 1997 report on the warning-response gaps.[59]

Addressing this challenge will require adjustments on both the producer's and receiver's end. Conflict analysts and intelligence officials need to make sure their information is timely, precise, and accurate. Warnings also need to be actionable, including not only diagnosis but also prescription, linking warning with concrete response options.[60] Decision-makers should be more receptive to the analytical capacity of the intelligence community and warning producers and set up new procedures that will facilitate information sharing within their own governments and organizations, as well as externally with civil society, partner organizations, and allies. Both the UN and individual countries have taken steps to address this problem. The Office of the Special Adviser on the Prevention of Genocide (OSAPG) was mandated to collect information, act as an early warning mechanism to the Secretary-General, and make recommendations for the prevention of genocide.[61] But the OSAPG lacks the necessary resources to adequately fulfill its mandate. The creation of the new joint office is a promising new initiative to close the warning-response gap at the UN level. Once operational, this office will play a convening role, authorizing Special Advisers Deng and Luck to convene the relevant Under-Secretaries-General to develop policy options for civilian protection in case countries are "manifestly failing" to do so.[62] The August 2010 General Assembly Interactive Dialogue on Early Warning, Assessment and the Responsibility to Protect seemed to indicate that the UN was aware of this challenge and willing to meet it.

Civilian Protection and National Sovereignty

Concerns about R2P's compatibility with the non-intervention norm and the principle's potential to erode national sovereignty represent another formidable challenge to R2P's implementation with important political ramifications. A number of UN member states and scholars are convinced that R2P undermines national sovereignty as enshrined in UN Charter Article 2(7) and fear R2P could be abused to legitimize unilateral invasions. At the 2010 UN Security Council Debate on the Protection of Civilians, the representative from Venezuela urged others to "reject the concept of the responsibility to protect, for it disguises the violation of sovereignty in order to promote neo-colonial interests."[63] Concerns about the potential erosion of national sovereignty lies at the heart of the persistent political opposition to R2P within the General Assembly. Underneath the surface of expressed concerns about sovereignty erosion often lies a host of underlying motivations to oppose R2P, including a regime's own past or current human rights record, bad experiences with illegitimate or ill-functioning interventions, or strategic behavior within multidimensional negotiations.[64] Some of the concerns of R2P rejectionists are certainly legitimate, particularly with regard to the selectiveness of the international response to humanitarian disasters or previous illegitimate interventions by great powers or coalitions. But whether narrowly self-interested or legitimate, R2P rejectionism forms an important impediment to R2P's implementation. A number of states are reluctant to accept any internationally endorsed measures, even of the softest and most supportive kind, given their fear that internationalizing problems will result in further external interference and start down a slippery slope to intervention.[65] The failure to set up a centralized Early Warning Unit within the UN Department of Political Affairs with a capacity to collect information and inform the Secretary-General and Security Council, a long-standing proposal, is a direct result of these sensitivities. A reference to mass atrocities was also dropped in Special Advisor Deng's title after concerns were raised that an enlargement of his mandate could affect the sovereignty norm. Most recently, during the 2010 GA Dialogue on early warning, a number of participants were concerned that information gathering by the UN would compromise their own intelligence networks.

R2P advocates strongly oppose these "traditional nineteenth-century accounts of sovereignty with absolutist leanings."[66] They argue that there is no intrinsic competition between sovereignty and the collective protection of human rights as sovereignty has always entailed certain responsibilities.[67] R2P advocates are convinced national sovereignty and R2P are not in opposition, but mutually reinforcing. In this view national sovereignty does not merely derive from the quality of having supreme, independent authority over a geographic area,[68] but also from responsible behavior of the sovereign toward the population. In the words of the ICISS Report, "there is no transfer or dilution of state sovereignty. But there is a necessary re-characterization involved: *from sovereignty as control* to *sovereignty as responsibility* in both internal functions and external duties."[69] With R2P in place, governments would no longer be able to use sovereignty as a shield allowing them to commit or stand idly by in the face of mass atrocities committed within their borders.

R2P'S POTENTIAL ROLE IN PEACEMAKING

As the preceding account suggests, the influence of R2P on peacemaking has been rather mixed. However, the principle is still in its formative phase, and the process of its institutionalization at the international and regional levels is still evolving. In the short term, R2P could act as an effective catalyst for action. In the longer term, R2P has the potential to operate as a broader norm-based policy framework.

Short-Term Potential: An Effective Catalyst for Action

In the short term, R2P has the potential to operate as a political rallying cry effectively reducing the frequency, intensity, and impact of atrocities. Until R2P has developed sufficient normative strength and resulted in more consistent state practice, the principle can only function as a catalyst, elevating certain issues above normal politics.[70] Its short-term potential contribution to peacemaking lies in its relatively consistent use as a label applied to new and ongoing crises in order to generate political will and warn or deter potentially irresponsible leaders. Yet some level of inconsistency and double standards will undoubtedly persist. As Edward Luck has observed, "The intergovernmental bodies charged with making the toughest choices about how and when to respond . . . are intrinsically political bodies. . . . Politics and national preferences play a part."[71] International engagement to prevent or halt R2P crimes will remain conditional on a number of variables, including the complexity of the situation, the risks involved, the potential for success, the international financial and political climate, the geopolitical importance of the country, and host-state consent.

Once fully operational, the new joint office is expected to act as the vanguard office for R2P within the UN and mainstream R2P throughout the entire UN system. If this expectation is realized, the joint office could also provide options for the Secretary-General and the Security Council, including nonaction, in the face of imminent or ongoing atrocities, and render the existing tools within the UN system more effective in the prevention and mitigation of R2P crimes.

Given the limited capacity of the UN, an enhanced role for regional organizations in the implementation of R2P policies will be required to fulfill the promise of 2005. With the assistance of the UN, regional organizations can play a greater role in the principle's implementation. The interactive dialogue at the General Assembly on the role of regional organizations and R2P served as a recognition of the largely untapped potential of these institutions. Regional organizations have a number of advantages including a better understanding of local dynamics and sensitivities, and more cost-effective operations. But regional organizations also face major challenges, including a lack of resources, an overemphasis on secondary and tertiary prevention, and questions about their neutrality.

Long-Term Potential: A Norm-Based Policy Framework

In the long term, R2P could evolve into a norm-based policy framework. Even though many observers are frustrated about the slow pace of this norm-building process, in just five years R2P developed from a vague and controversial idea into a principle unanimously embraced by the world's leaders. Indeed, "a norm is emerging with considerable state practice behind it that articulates the collective international responsibility to protect human beings whose governments refuse to do so or are actually the cause of murder and ethnic cleansing."[72]

In the long term, R2P's concrete impact may not be restricted to crisis prevention and management. As its normative weight increases and its normalization advances, it could enhance local and international institutional capacities to assess and address the risk of atrocities at an earlier stage through primary prevention, ensure robust measures are taken to halt R2P crimes in a more consistent manner, and rebuild societies emerging from conflict. However, R2P will need to overcome the conditions that currently affect the likeliness of an international response, so engagement becomes contingent primarily on the severity of the situation.

CONCLUSION

The clear and unambiguous acceptance by all governments of the collective responsibility to protect populations from genocide, war crimes, ethnic cleansing, and crimes against humanity at the 2005 World Summit was an historic development in the age-long struggle to deter mass atrocities. For ethical and strategic reasons, the prevention of crimes of gravest concern to the international community must not be treated as something separate from peacemaking. Preventing mass atrocities is critical to achieving peace and stability because these crimes encourage other leaders to trample on human rights, impede peacemaking and peace implementation, and undermine the credibility of the international community.

Considerable strides have been taken since the World Summit to clarify, institutionalize, and operationalize the R2P principle against the background of the enduring challenge of bringing peace to the world's conflicts. However, much work still needs to be done on the conceptual, institutional, and political fronts. We still have a long way to go to ensure that R2P contributes to the prevention of mass atrocities consistently and effectively, but we have also come a long way from the unchallenged dominance of the state as the principal referent of security.[73]

The prevention of the most serious international crimes is a fundamental building block of sustainable peace. And the R2P principle may yet become an indispensable aid for peacemakers in the continuing quest for peace and stability within and among the nations of the world.

NOTES

1. Richard Jolly, Louis Emmerij, and Thomas G. Weiss, *UN Ideas That Changed the World* (Bloomington: Indiana University Press, 2009), 174.

2. "2005 World Summit Outcome," UNGA Res. 60/1, September 16, 2005.

3. United Nations, *Charter of the United Nations*, October 24, 1945, 1 UNTS XVI.

4. Scott R. Feil, *Preventing Genocide: How the Early Use of Force Might Have Succeeded in Rwanda* (New York: Carnegie Corporation, 1998); and Allison Des Forges, *Leave None to Tell the Story* (New York: Human Rights Watch, 1999).

5. Kofi A. Annan, "Two Concepts of Sovereignty," *The Economist*, September 18, 1999.

6. SGSM 7136, GA/9596 (September 20, 1999).

7. Kofi A. Annan, *We the Peoples: The Role of the United Nations in the 21st Century* (New York: United Nations, 2000), 48.

8. International Commission on Intervention and State Sovereignty (ICISS), *The Responsibility to Protect* (Ottawa: IDRC, 2001), 2.

9. The "right to intervene" approach was advocated by French Foreign Minister Bernard Kouchner in the 1980s and 1990s. This approach and the debate on humanitarian intervention focused on the modalities for military action in response to mass atrocities. See Bernard Kouchner and Mario Bettati, *Le Devoir D'ingerence: Peut-on les Laisser Mourir?* (Paris: Denoel, 1987).

10. ICISS, *The Responsibility to Protect*, 13.

11. Ibid., xi.

12. David Hollenbach, "Humanitarian Intervention," *Commonwealth*, November 3, 2010.

13. Gareth Evans, *The Responsibility to Protect: Ending Mass Atrocity Crimes Once and for All* (Washington, DC: Brookings Institution, 2008), 196.

14. Ibid., 252–253.

15. Ibid., 57.

16. ICISS, *The Responsibility to Protect*, 19, 29, 39.

17. Ibid., 17.

18. Alex J. Bellamy, *Responsibility to Protect: The Global Effort to End Mass Atrocities* (Cambridge, England: Polity Press, 2009), 70.

19. Michael Byers, "High Ground Lost on UN's Responsibility to Protect," *Winnipeg Free Press*, September 18, 2005, B3.

20. Gareth Evans, "The Reform of the United Nations" (address to Welt am Sontag/BDLI Forum on Reassurance at a Time of Insecurity, Berlin, Germany, October 24, 2005).

21. Bellamy, *Responsibility to Protect*, 90.

22. ICISS, *The Responsibility to Protect*, 48; and "2005 World Summit Outcome."

23. ICISS, *The Responsibility to Protect*, xiii, 33.

24. "2005 World Summit Outcome."

25. Evans, *The Responsibility to Protect*, 47–48.

26. A/RES/63/308, September 14, 2009.

27. Ban Ki-Moon, *Implementing the Responsibility to Protect*, A/63/677, January 12, 2009.

28. Dorina Bekoe, "Kenya: Setting the Stage for Durable Peace?" USIP Peace Brief (Washington, DC: USIP Press, 2008).

29. France 24, January 26, 2008. Available at http://responsibilitytoprotect.org/index.php/articles_editorial/1496?theme=alt1.

30. Bernard Koucher, "Violence in Kenya," *France Diplomatie*, January 31, 2008.

31. Evans, *The Responsibility to Protect*, 51.

32. Human Rights Watch, "Ballots to Bullets, Organized Political Violence and Kenya's Crisis of Governance," *Human Rights Watch* 20, no. 1 (2008): 67–68.

33. Cristina G. Badescu and Thomas G. Weiss, "Misrepresenting R2P and Advancing Norms: An Alternative Spiral?" *International Studies Perspectives* 11 (2010): 354–374.

34. "Where Is the Justice? Interethnic Violence in Southern Kyrgyzstan and Its Aftermath," Human Rights Watch Report, August 16, 2010. Available at http://www.hrw.org/en/reports/2010/08/16/where-justice.

35. "UN Special Advisers of the Secretary-General on the Prevention of Genocide and the Responsibility to Protect on the Situation in Kyrgyzstan," United Nations Press Release, June 15, 2010. Available at http://www.un.org/preventgenocide/adviser/pdf/Statement%20of%20Special%20Advisers%20Deng%20and%20Luck%20on%20the%20situation%20in%20Kyrgyzstan%2015%20June%202010.pdf.

36. Amnesty International, "Myanmar Ethnic Group Faces Crimes against Humanity," June 4, 2008.

37. International Coalition for the Responsibility to Protect, "The Crisis in Burma." Available at http://www.responsibilitytoprotect.org/index.php/crises/crisis-in-burma.

38. Ibid.

39. Claudia Parsons, "France Urges U.N. Council to Act on Myanmar Cyclone," *Reuters*, May 7, 2008, http://www.reuters.com/article/idUSL07810481.

40. Alex J. Bellamy, "The Responsibility to Protect—Five Years On," 152.

41. Russia also invoked the principle to legitimize its 2008 military operation in Georgia. This argumentation received hardly any support, as the intervention was not carried out consistently with the 2005 World Summit agreement.

42. Badescu and Weiss, "Misrepresenting R2P," 358–359.

43. Ibid., 361.

44. Lawrence Woocher and Paul Stares, "Enhancing International Cooperation for Preventing Genocide and Mass Atrocities: The Case for Transatlantic Cooperation" (paper presented at the International Symposium on Preventing Genocide and Mass Atrocities, Paris, November 15–16).

45. According to a number of scholars, including Alex Bellamy, R2P crimes were also committed after the U.S. invasion of Iraq, where over 100,000 civilians have been killed according to human rights group Iraq Body Count and a deterioration of the humanitarian situation is not inconceivable, as the United States continues to withdraw its troops.

46. International Coalition for the Responsibility to Protect, "Crisis in the Democratic Republic of Congo." Available at http://www.responsibilitytoprotect.org/index.php/crises/crisis-in-drc.

47. Benjamin Coghlam et al., "Mortality in the Democratic Republic of Congo, An Ongoing Crisis" (International Rescue Committee, 2009). Available at http://www.rescue.org/special-reports/congo-forgotten-crisis.

48. Office of the High Commissioner on Human Rights, "DRC Mapping Human Rights Violations 1993–2003." Available at http://www.ohchr.org/Documents/Countries/ZR/DRC_MAPPING_REPORT_FINAL_EN.pdf.

49. A/HRC/RES/S/8/1, November 28, 2008.

50. A/HRC/RES/13/22, April 15, 2010.

51. For a fuller discussion of Priority Setting for the Secretary-General, see Abiodun Williams, "Strategic Planning in the Executive Office of the UN Secretary-General," *Global Governance* 16, no. 4 (October–December 2010): 435–449.

52. Eli Stamnes, "Operationalizing the Preventive Aspect of R2P" (report by Norwegian Institute for International Affairs on the Responsibility to Protect, 2008), 6, http://www.globalr2p.org/pdf/R2P-1-Stamnes.pdf.

53. Evans, *The Responsibility to Protect*, 56.

54. Badescu and Weiss, "Misrepresenting R2P," 367.

55. Bellamy, *Responsibility to Protect: The Global Effort to End Mass Atrocities*, 101.

56. Edward C. Luck, "The Responsibility to Protect: Growing Pains or Early Promise?" *Ethics and International Affairs* 24, no. 4 (2010): 349–365.

57. Lawrence Woocher, "The Responsibility to Prevent: Toward a Strategy," in *The Responsibility to Protect*, ed. W. Andy Knight and Frazer Egerton (London: Routledge, 2011).

58. Bellamy, *Responsibility to Protect: The Global Effort to End Mass Atrocities*, 54.

59. Alexander L. George and Jane E. Holl, *The Warning-Response Problem and Missed Opportunities in Preventive Diplomacy: A Report to the Carnegie Commission on Preventing Deadly Conflict* (Washington, DC: Carnegie Corporation, 1997).

60. Christoph O. Meyer et al., "Recasting the Warning-Response Problem: Persuasion and Preventive Policy," *International Studies Review* 12 (2010): 556–578.

61. S/2004/567, July 13, 2004, 2.

62. A/64/864, July 14, 2010, 7–8.

63. Statement of the Bolivarian Republic of Venezuela: Ninth Open Debate on the Protection of Civilians in Armed Conflict, July 7, 2010, http://www.responsibilitytoprotect.org/Venezuala-%20Ninth%20Open%20Debate%20on%20the%20Protection%20of%20Civilains%20in%20Armed%20Conflict.pdf.

64. Claes, Jonas. 2012 (forthcoming). Protecting Civilians from Mass Atrocities: Meeting the Challenge of R2P Rejectionism. *Global Responsibility to Protect*.

65. ICISS, *The Responsibility to Protect*, 37.

66. Bellamy, *Responsibility to Protect: The Global Effort to End Mass Atrocities*, 60.

67. Ibid., 14, 33.

68. "Sovereignty," *Encyclopedia Britannica*, accessed November 24, 2010, http://www.britannica.com/EBchecked/topic/557065/sovereignty.

69. ICISS, *The Responsibility to Protect*, 37.

70. Bellamy, "The Responsibility to Protect—Five Years On," 159.

71. Edward C. Luck, "The Responsibility to Protect," 353.

72. Jolly, Emmerij, and Weiss, *UN Ideas That Changed the World*, 176.

73. Jolly, Emmerij, and Weiss, *UN Ideas That Changed the World*, 185.

CHAPTER 27

Fact Based Approaches to Peacemaking: Global Peace Index

Steve Killelea

The human experience can be defined as the search for happiness, and inner peace lies at the heart of being happy. But our outer world shapes our inner world, and without outer peace it is very difficult to shape inner peace. Today, the world is facing some of the greatest challenges that it has faced in its history, but challenges mean change and change means opportunity. With the right cultivation of our ideas the things that really matter will become our first priority—*such as peace.*

During the last 20 years, humanity has entered into a new epoch in its history. This has been brought about by a convergence of many factors.

Finite environmental barriers are now being reached, and on multiple fronts. World population is expected to reach 7 billion next year, and in many places it is already straining capacity. Technology is fueling change at an ever increasing pace that in many ways underpins the growth of globalization. The world is connected in ways that were unimaginable even 50 years ago. Wars are no longer economically viable, and change is occurring so fast that nations are struggling to keep up with both the legal and social ramifications of these changes. Even our language is changing daily, incorporating new words to describe our changing reality, and our notions and concepts of peace are changing with it.

WHAT DO WE KNOW ABOUT PEACE IN THE 21ST CENTURY?

Global challenges call for global solutions, and these solutions require co-operation on a scale unprecedented in human history. Peace is an essential prerequisite because without peace we will never be able to achieve the levels of cooperation, trust, inclusiveness, and social equity necessary to solve these challenges, let alone empower the international institutions necessary to address them.

Peace lies at the center of being able to manage these many and varied challenges, simply because peace creates the optimum environment in which the other activities that contribute to human growth can take place. In this sense, peace is a facilitator making it easier for workers to produce, businesses to sell, entrepreneurs and scientists to innovate, and governments to regulate.

But if peace is an essential prerequisite for solving our sustainability challenges and improving our economic and social well-being, then having a good understanding of peace is essential. This poses the question, "How well do we understand peace?" Fifty years ago, peace studies were virtually non-existent. Today there are thriving peace and conflict centers in numerous universities around the world. But most of these are centered on the study of conflict rather than on the understanding of peace.

A parallel can be drawn here with medical science. The study of pathology has led to numerous breakthroughs in our understanding of how to treat and cure disease. However, there is more than that to health. It was only when medical science turned its focus to the study of healthy human beings that we understood what we need to do to stay healthy: the right physical exercise, a good mental disposition, and a healthy diet. This could only be learned by studying what was working. In the same way the study of conflict is fundamentally different than the study of peace.

Over the last century, we have moved from having departments of war to departments of defense, and we are now seeing the emergence of organizations that are lobbing for the creation of departments of peace within governments. Although these changes are beneficial in improving our understanding of peace, peace is not yet seen as germane to the major academic disciplines, nor is there a methodological approach to the cross-disciplinary study of peace. There are no courses on the literature of peace in any of the literature departments of the major universities, yet there are profound works on peace. Similarly, there is no university chair of peace economics on any major economics faculties, yet most business people believe that their markets grow in peace and that their costs decrease with increasing peacefulness.

The simplest way of approaching the definition of peace is in terms of harmony achieved by the absence of war, conflict, or violent crime. Applied to states, this would suggest that the measurement of internal states of peace is as important as those external factors involving other states or neighbors. This is what Johan Galtung defined as negative peace—an absence of violence. The concept of negative peace is immediately intuitive and empirically measurable and can be used as a starting point to elaborate its counterpart concept, positive peace. Having established what constitutes an absence of violence, is it possible through statistical analysis to identify which structures, institutions, and social attitudes create and maintain peace?

The term *peace* means different things to different people. It spans from the mere absence of war or violent conflict to a state of personal well-being that could be characterized by the absence of any afflictive emotions.[1] However, the best definition of peace is entirely dependent on how it is to be used. Therefore, to measure peace, different definitions are applicable for an individual, community, or nation.

MEASURING PEACE

Measurement is the key to understanding any human endeavor and peace is no different. If we do not measure peace, then how can we know whether our actions are either helping or hindering us in the achievement of a more peaceful world?

In terms of measuring the peacefulness of nations, it is important to use a broad definition of peace that is generally acceptable, that is measurable, and that can also allow for a wide range of metrics to be incorporated within the definition. The Institute for Economics and Peace (IEP) has made substantial gains in the measurement of peace. It uses various states of peace to arrive at a composite index—the Global Peace Index—which measures both the internal and the external peacefulness of nations. For the purposes of this study, Zpeace is defined as the *absence of violence*, a definition with which most people can agree.

The compilation and analysis of the Global Peace Index is composed of a two-step process. The first step produces a scoring model that currently ranks 149 countries by their states of peace using specific indicators. Twenty-three indicators were selected, reflecting the best available data sets that reflect the incidence or absence of violence. Both quantitative and qualitative data have been used and are sourced from a wide range of trusted sources.

The GPI's second principal aim is to investigate the attributes of positive peace. It does this by identifying correlations between the results of the GPI ranking with other indexes, datasets, and attitudinal surveys as well as investigating the relative importance of a range of potential determinants or drivers that may influence the creation and nurturing of peaceful societies.

The GPI is developed under the guidance of an international advisory panel, with data collated and calculated by the Economist Intelligence Unit (EIU). The first Index was released in May 2007, and in only a few years the GPI has been able to "impact the peacemaking world in structural, attitudinal, and transactional ways."[2]

The GPI focuses on the positive, in an attempt to learn from the most peaceful countries. Prior to the GPI, hard data was primarily used to document what was lacking in a society, instead of determining what was working. The GPI may help lead to a paradigm shift as it has already helped change research agendas and spurred new work on understanding what creates a peaceful society.

The GPI and related research have encouraged a fresh look at peace and what leads to peace. As more data is collected, the initial analysis of trends in peacefulness can be strengthened to allow for cultural and regional differences.

Many NGOs and international organizations like the World Bank and the UNDP are using the GPI and the data it generates in their analysis and planning processes. Some universities have now started to include material from the IEP to better articulate how peaceful societies function, where different countries rank globally, the economic benefits of peace, and the relationship between business and peace.

The Index aims to change how businesses value peace by helping them see the link between the success of their business ventures and the peacefulness of the countries or the markets in which they operate and invest. Research conducted by Professor David Throsby at Macquarie University indicates that there is a positive relationship between peace and per capita income. This means that there is a strategic advantage for companies in learning how to factor changing peace into their business plans.

The index and peace metrics can also be incorporated in strategic corporate analysis. It is beneficial for companies to benchmark the levels of peacefulness in the markets in which they operate by cost components, margins, and price as violence creates friction and impediments that affect these items. For most products, certain baskets of costs must increase with lower levels of peacefulness, additionally, as there is a relation between peace and per capital income the size of markets should grow faster in more peaceful markets.

According to Ricigliano, the evolving methods of how to create peace is a pivot point in peace research. He states that "the GPI is contributing to changing the methods used by peace builders in doing their analysis by using their need for 'countables' to foster a macro-level view. By creating a quantifiable macro-level measure of peace it forces donors and other key peace building actors to see 'wholes' instead of just parts."[3]

A NEW APPROACH TO PEACEMAKING

The first study ever to rank the nations of the world by their peacefulness, the Global Peace Index has allowed a unique view of peace to be formed: fact based and constructive in its approach to working on the many and varied global challenges that humanity is facing.

The GPI provides a mechanism to statistically understand the factors that are associated with peace; this then forms the basis of creating a fact-based approach to understanding what creates a peaceful society. The data has enabled groundbreaking research in a number of areas, including the following:

- Understanding the structures and attitudes that lead to peace
- Analyzing time-series trends in peacefulness
- Valuing the monetary benefits brought about by peace
- Incorporating peace into corporate risk analysis.

In the following pages, we attempt at showcasing how the GPI and the underlying data can be used in these areas and present some results of the analysis.

What Creates Peace: Structures and Attitudes

Using the GPI, it is possible to analyze the relationships between peace and society so as to develop a fact-based approach to determining what types of societies will deliver the optimum environment for peace.

Based on statistical analysis and correlations between the GPI and a broad range of indicators,[4] the Institute for Economics and Peace has found that the most peaceful countries share a set of structures and attitudes. These structures and attitudes appear to be intricately linked to their peacefulness. When viewed together, they promote resilience in society, thereby allowing countries to overcome adversity and solve problems simply because peace is created by an environment that is optimal for many other endeavors. The analysis carried out to date has allowed the identification of the following factors:

- *Well-functioning government*—Strong relationships across a number of governance indicators show that well-functioning governments need to have many aspects working correctly if they wish to help create peace.

- *Sound business environment*—Business competitiveness and economic freedom are both associated with the most peaceful countries, as is the presence of regulatory systems which are conducive to business operation.

- *Equitable sharing of resources*—Low infant mortality and high life expectancy are characteristics shared by peaceful countries. The Gini coefficient (a measure of the equitable distribution of income) is moderately correlated with the GPI's internal peace measure, especially with crime statistics. Health metrics can also be used as a proxy for equitable sharing.

- *Acceptance of the rights of others*—A commitment to human rights is a key characteristic of peaceful countries, a claim supported by very strong correlations with three indexes measuring human rights. Also as important are the societal attitudes toward minorities, the disadvantaged, and foreigners.

- *Good relations with neighboring states*—Countries with positive external relations are more peaceful and tend also to be politically stable, have well-functioning governments, are regionally integrated, and have low levels of organized internal conflict.

- *Free flow of information*—Peaceful countries tend to disseminate information in a way that enables wide access to information. This leads to better decision making and rational responses in times of crisis. This can be epitomized through transparency and the freedom of the press.

- *High participation in education*—Higher average years of total schooling are closely related with the most peaceful countries. This also can be seen as a proxy for the equitable distribution of resources.

- *Low levels of corruption*—Strong correlations with corruption-related indexes suggest that the most peaceful countries are also often the least corrupt.

This fact-based body of analysis provides useful insights for a broad range of decision makers including policy analysts, business, academics, and other international institutions. It also serves to initiate wider debates and discussions.

Figure 27.1 provides a visual representation of the interactions between peace and each relevant element outlined previously. The three first-order structures of sound business environment, well-functioning government, and equitable distribution of resources have been identified as critical components within peaceful societies. The secondary elements—free flow of information, low levels of corruption, acceptance of the rights of others, high levels of education, and good relations with neighbors—are heavily interconnected to the first order structures.

These structures create an environment that is optimal for human potential to flourish.

Identifying and then potentially strengthening these so-called attributes of peace can lead to creating productive and resilient societies. A core finding of the research by the IEP is that *peace creates resilience*, allowing societies to absorb shocks more easily. Peace, when viewed through this lens, is a collection of activities that creates an optimal environment for human potential to flourish. The resilient nature of peaceful societies is one of the most profound observations of the GPI. In one sense, resilience is "merely the capacity of systems to absorb stress and maintain or ever repair themselves,"[5] yet it also accurately describes the inner toughness of countries that overcome

Figure 27.1
The Structural Attributes of Peaceful Countries

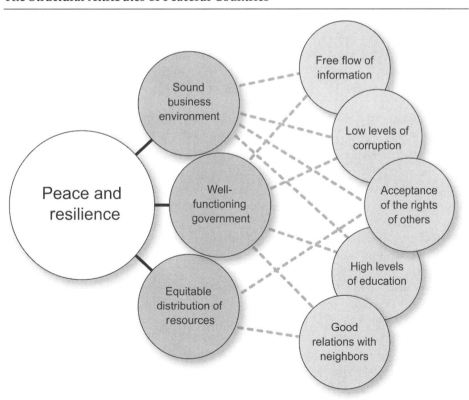

adversity and solve problems using peaceful methods. The characteristics that make countries resilient are also those that the most peaceful countries share in common.

To date, the overwhelming emphasis within studies relating to peace and conflict has been placed on understanding the causes of war. The GPI is a pioneering attempt to systematically explore the texture of peace and to advance our knowledge of the mechanisms that nurture and sustain peace.

Economic Value of Peace

The GPI and its underlying data are also instrumental in allowing a better understanding of the economic value of peace.

There have been numerous reports and studies on the cost of war. The IEP, with the GPI data, has enabled a better understanding of the monetary value of peace, or, in other words, the lost economic input due to violence.

The research found that peace does in fact have a monetary value independent of the human values associated with it. It can be expressed in terms of the additional value to global GDP that would ensue from creating a peaceful world.

If the cost of investing in proactive peace creation was minimal compared to the lost potential caused by violence, then would it not be apt for governments to free up the resources needed to build a more peaceful society? And would it not be fitting for business to engage with government and civil society to create peace in the markets in which they operate?

Shedding light on the economic impact of a more peaceful world can only help create a better business environment and create additional wealth whereby governments have an adequate tax base to provide a government that functions well, as well as helping to free up trapped productivity. These concepts can provide useful tools to peacemakers advocating for reductions in violence.

In 2009, the Economists for Peace and Security[6] used GPI data to calculate the monetary impact of violence to the world economy. The analysis concluded that a total cessation of violence would generate a peace dividend equivalent to approximately 13.1 percent of the 2007 gross world product. This was divided into two categories labeled dynamic peace and static peace. Dynamic peace referred to the total additional economic output likely to occur due to the liberation of human, social, and physical capital, which was suppressed by violence and was calculated at 8.7 percent of global GDP in 2007 or US$4.8 trillion. Static peace captured the economic activity that would be transferred from violence-related industries to peace-related industries; that is, expenditure on prison guards could be transferred to more teachers due to the need to imprison less people. This was calculated at 4.4 percent of global GDP or $US2.4 trillion. When added together, the static and dynamic peace dividends make up the total peace dividend of 13.1 percent or US$7.2 trillion.

The Institute for Economics and Peace commissioned an extension of this analysis for 2010 to identify trends in the peace dividend over time and to estimate the impact by industry sector for each of the countries included in the GPI. This additional analysis was carried out in collaboration with Dr. Jurgen Brauer,[7] professor of economics at Augusta State University in Augusta, Georgia.

Before presenting the outcomes of the research some simple observations based on the literature are worth considering.

- The figures used are conservative; estimates could place the peace dividend significantly higher.
- Additional world GDP growth in any one year could be at the minimum doubled if there was a cessation of global violence.[8]
- The global financial crisis saw the global economies contract 0.6 percent in 2008–2009. An economic downturn occurs about once every 10 years. However, world economic growth could have been 8.5 percent higher if the world were peaceful.
- Studies of violence in Latin American countries show that lost GDP growth through violence is not recoverable; that is, there is a compounding effect on the gap between the actual and the potential economy which increases with decreasing peacefulness and that when peace is improved the lost growth is not caught up.
- Countries with high per capita income, large GDPs, and lower levels of peacefulness have the largest possible gains in absolute terms. This is highly relevant for multinational corporations who have an interest in tapping into the peace dividend.

OVERALL COSTS OF VIOLENCE TO THE WORLD ECONOMY

The total economic impact from a cessation of violence is estimated to have been US$28 trillion for the last four years (2006–2009) or US$7.4 trillion (12.9 percent of gross world product) in the year 2009. This amount comprises the new economic activity that would have been be generated in peace (dynamic dividend) as well as the economic activity that would have shifted from violence-related activities to peace-related activities (static dividend, see Table 27.1).

One way to appreciate these numbers is by noting that the dynamic peace dividend is higher than the annual growth in total world economic output. Another way is to note that the world economic and financial crisis of 2008–2009 reduced gross world product by less than 1 percent. In contrast, the calculations of gross world product generated by peace suggest that violence has had a much higher impact on overall economic performance. The decline in per capita world economic output occurs on the order of once every 10 years, while the suppression of output due to violence is ongoing, in other words an annual affair.

This analysis seems to indicate that if policymakers had in the past spent as much time focusing on reductions in violence as they have spent on the global financial crisis the economic payoff could have been huge. Additionally, if we look at the mayhem caused by the global financial crisis, then

Table 27.1
Dynamic, Static, and Total Peace Dividend (in US$ billions), 2006–2009

Year	Actual GDP	Dynamic dividend	Static dividend	Total dividend
2006	$48,802	$4,026	$2,147	$6,173
2007	$54,975	$4,435	$2,418	$6,854
2008	$60,755	$5,112	$2,673	$7,785
2009	$57,522	$4,889	$2,531	$7,420
Total	**$222,054**	**$18,460**	**$9,770**	**$28,232**

improved peacefulness could easily have the opposite effect with substantial gains in profits, cooperation and well-being. This research can be a significant tool in the hands of peacemakers.

Additional economic wealth creates the opportunity to fund activities that may be difficult or unattainable to do in its absence. This is specifically relevant to many of the major challenges facing humanity today.

Although it is hard to imagine a world totally at peace, one in which there is no violence, it is, however, possible to imagine that a 25 percent increase in peacefulness is within humanity's grasp. If an improvement of 25 percent in global peacefulness could have been achieved during the past four years it would have unleashed an annual US$1.75 trillion in additional economic activity.

It is evident that only a partial reduction in violence would therefore yield a substantial increase in global GDP unleashing enough wealth to address many of the major challenges facing the world today. These funds could be used to fund a myriad of essential activities such as infrastructure investments, better social policies, renewable energy, debt repayment, enhanced global food security, or better water usage. As an example, the US$1.75 trillion would be more than sufficient to pay off Greece's debt, fund the achievement of the Millennium Development Goals (MDGs), and meet the EU's 20-20-20 climate and energy targets.

CUMULATIVE EFFECTS

Measuring the cumulative effects of peace on total economic output can highlight the development gap caused by violence. For the four years for which the calculations for the dynamic peace dividend have been calculated, the cumulative value of forgone output has reached US$18.4 trillion, which is equivalent to adding the combined economies of Russia, Brazil, India, and Indonesia[9] to the current world output.

The hypothetical example in Figure 27.2 shows how the GDP differential between a peaceful and non-peaceful country will increase forever, even for a relatively minor war of short duration.

The example shows two countries, marked with a triangle and a square, with five years of equal GDP growth (2 percent per person per year). In 1985,

Figure 27.2
Cumulative Peace Dividend

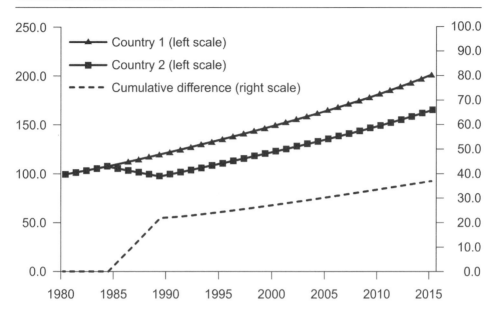

Country 2 (squares) experiences violence such that growth falls by 2 percent per year. Over the span of the 35 years depicted in the figure, Country 1's (triangles) GDP per person doubles from 100 to 200. By contrast, Country 2 lags behind by nearly 40 points (0.4 percent). The divergent paths of GDP are clear enough during the violence years, but because Country 2's base has been lowered during its war years, the GDP differential between the two countries will increase forever.

It can be shown that the gap between the triangle and square lines amounts, by 2015, to the equivalent of eight years of lost economic output. For Country 2 to catch up with Country 1 by the year 2015, Country 2's postviolence growth rate would have to equal 2.8 percent higher per year, that is, 40 percent faster than Country 1—a very difficult goal to achieve. Even then, the cumulative gap would have amounted to four times Country 2's initial GDP of 100, or the equivalent of four years of output loss.

Instead of speaking of Countries 1 and 2, consider the example of Costa Rica in Figure 27.3. Although that country did not suffer from war or civil war, its neighbors did—they fought a decade-long war in the 1980s. The spillover effects badly affected Costa Rica through the disruption of trade and tourism. By 2007, the country still had not recovered from the cost its neighbors had imposed, shown clearly by the light gray line in this chart.

Costa Rica faired well compared to its neighbor, Nicaragua, which did experience a war and has clearly paid a more severe price in terms of lost GDP output as can be seen in Figure 27.4. In this example the GDP[10] (light gray line) does not even begin to trend upward, let alone converge with the trend line based on the pre-conflict GDP growth average.

Figure 27.3
Real GDP per Capita, Costa Rica, 1950–2007

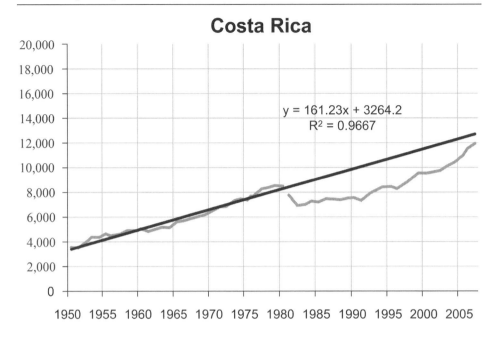

Figure 27.4
Real GDP per Capita, Nicaragua, 1950–2007

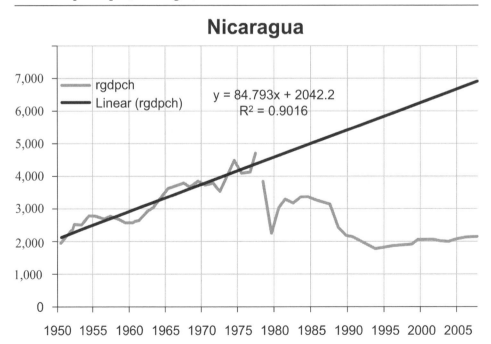

SECTORAL ANALYSIS

The research can also move more deeply into analyzing what would be the dividend from a reduction in violence to various economic sectors. This is done by calculating the overall peace dividend for a country and then allocating a value to each industrial sector depending on its share of GDP. The value of the peace dividend will vary from country to country depending on the size of each of these sectors. For example, India's economy is highly dependent on agriculture, which in 2008 made up 19 percent of the economy. Therefore, the peace dividend would amount to US$31 billion for the agriculture sector while the wholesale and retail sector's peace dividend would amount to US$26 billion. This compares with the United States, where the agriculture sector accounts for 1.1 percent of the economy and the wholesale and retail sector accounts for 15.2 percent. The peace dividend for these two sectors would be calculated at US$13.1 billion and US$185.01 billion, respectively.

Globally, it was found that two sectors in particular stand to benefit significantly from a decrease in violence. These are the global manufacturing sector, which in 2008 could have gained up to US$906 billion (17.7 percent of the dynamic peace dividend), and the global wholesale, retail trade, restaurants, and hotels sector, which could gain up to US$742 billion (14.5 percent of the dynamic peace dividend).

Table 27.2 summarizes estimates of the size of the peace dividend for each sector in billions of US$. There has been no attempt to estimate the static peace dividend for industry sectors as it is difficult to separate what portions of an industry sector is spent on violent or nonviolent activities. An example would be of a construction company: it could build either a jail or a power plant. This level of detail is not contained in national accounts. However, it would be safe to assume that the power plant would yield higher productivity than the jail. A shifting of economic activity that has been sunk into violence or protection against violence could be diverted to other activities that create future capacity or fund immediate needs.

The research carried out by the IEP based on four years of GPI data provides a quantifiable demonstration that improving peace can transform the global economy and unleash the wealth needed to tackle debt, fund economic expansion, and create a more sustainable environment.

Gross world product in 2009 reached just over US$57 trillion. On the baseline scenario, had the world been at peace, world economic output might have reached US$62.4 trillion, an increase of 8.5 percent and greatly exceeding the output losses due to the economic crisis of 2008–2009 of about negative 0.6 percent. A reduction in levels of violence of just 15 percent would in fact equal the output loss due to the world economic crisis of 2008–2009.

For the four years for which the calculations have been carried out, the cumulative value of forgone output has reached US$18.5 trillion. If we add the static peace dividend, then the total economic impact of a reduction in violence extends to US$28.2 trillion. The sums involved are large, and the case for peacemakers is easily made.

Table 27.2
Sectoral Allocation of Global Dynamic Peace Dividend (unweighted; US$ billion), 2006–2008

Sector[1]	2008	%	2007	%	2006	%
Agriculture, hunting, forestry, fishing	277.49	5.4	232.06	5.2	201.72	5.0
Utilities and mining	403.45	7.9	334.93	7.6	307.43	7.6
Manufacturing	905.97	17.7	777.84	17.5	703.80	17.5
Construction	291.41	5.7	250.76	5.7	226.52	5.6
Wholesale, retail trade, restaurants, and hotels	742.44	14.5	645.55	14.6	590.30	14.7
Transport, storage, and communication	368.75	7.2	319.91	7.2	288.73	7.2
Other activities	2,122.72	41.5	1,873.56	42.2	1,708.57	42.4
Total	**5,112.23**	**100.0**	**4,434.61**	**100.0**	**4,027.06**	**100.0**

[1] Sectors are based on the international standard industrial classification.

Strategic Business Analysis

The GPI can also be used by businesses to enhance their planning and strategic analysis activities.

Such new methods of analysis can help corporations increase their understanding of existing and future business environments. Existing planning techniques can be enhanced so that an additional dimension, peace, defined as the absence of violence, can be added.

Such a "peace analytics for business" can be an instrumental tool in peacemaking, as it brings peace to the attention of business and encourages investment in countries needing it the most. Areas that are reducing violence are good candidates for investment, thereby strengthening the peace process.

Research carried out by the Institute for Economics and Peace has uncovered a strong statistical relationship between increasing per capita income and increasing peacefulness, as well as increases in the size of various consumer markets.[11] Additionally, research carried out by Professor David Throsby from Macquarie University in Sydney, Australia, found that there are high correlations between the ease of doing business, competitive business environments, and peace. However, peace is rarely used in strategic planning or analysis due to the lack of defined analytical methods. To highlight this point, the United Nations Global Compact surveyed its members' companies in 2008, asking senior executives whether they thought that the size of their markets expanded with increasing peacefulness.[12] Eighty percent responded that it would. In addition, 79 percent thought that their costs also decreased with increasing peacefulness, yet only 13 percent knew of any tools or metrics that helped them understand the peacefulness of their markets.

The GPI, or any of its 23 indicators, can be individually applied to existing planning frameworks to better understand what effect changes in peacefulness may have on margin, cost structures, size of markets, product pricing, and competitive analysis. Differences in the overall score for a range of countries when benchmarked against a corporation's costs, margins, or market sizes can indicate what the likely effect of changes in peacefulness could have on these items.

As a quantitative measure of peacefulness, the GPI is comparable over time and therefore allows corporate decision makers to identify and understand peace trends in their markets of interest. Executives can monitor changes in certain GPI indicators to forecast the impact of changing peacefulness on their organization's operations, revenue, and profit. Comparing the cost structures, pricing, and margins indexed by peacefulness will allow companies to better understand the impact of peacefulness on these items.

Given that the vast majority of corporations prefer to invest their resources in less volatile markets, insight into which markets are trending toward peace can be a valuable source of competitive advantage.

Time-Series Analyses

Finally, a fact-based framework includes time-series analyses allowing an improved understanding of the trends in global, regional, and national levels of peacefulness. Such analyses will increase in value as more data is collected, but with four years of data now accumulated, some preliminary work has already been carried out.

Now in its fourth year, the body of research surrounding the GPI is growing, with more academics, researchers, and global think tanks using the data and results. The Institute for Economics and Peace has analyzed the four years of data to better understand the global, regional, and national trends in peacefulness.

The analysis shows that over the four-year period the world has become slightly less peaceful. However, the regions of Sub-Saharan Africa and the Middle East and North Africa have led the world by showing slight improvements in their peacefulness. Surprisingly, more countries decreased their military spending as a percentage of GDP than increased it, although total expenditure on the military did increase. The indicators that deteriorated the most in the four-year period were the number of conflicts fought, deaths from organized conflicts, and the number of homicides.

With the publication of the fourth GPI in 2010, it was possible to carry out a preliminary time-series analysis and identification of trends in peacefulness. To compare the time series accurately, only indicators and countries that have been constant throughout the four years were included in the analysis.

Table 27.3
Indicators Excluded from Time-Series Analysis

Indicator name	Reason for exclusion
UN troop deployments (percentage of total forces)	Replaced by UN peacekeeping funding in 2009
Non-UN deployments (percentage of total forces)	Discontinued in 2009
Funding for UN peacekeeping missions	Replaced UN troop deployments in 2009
Aggregate number of heavy weapons per 100,000 people	Methodology improvement in 2010
Number of displaced people as % of the population	Methodology improvement in 2010

Thus, the findings pertain to the original 120 countries and cover the 20 indicators for which the methodology has remained unchanged. Indicators excluded from this time-series analysis are listed in Table 27.3, with a brief explanation given for their exclusion.[13]

The methodology that was used in this analysis was to sum the scores by indicator, country, and region in 2007 and to then sum the scores again for 2010. The summed scores for 2007 were then subtracted from the summed scores for 2010, thereby arriving at the change figure for each indicator. This was then divided by the number of countries to give an average movement and converted to a percentage.

OVERALL FINDINGS

The research concluded that the world has become slightly less peaceful over the four years since the GPI's original publication in 2007. Table 27.4 demonstrates a slight improvement in peacefulness between 2007 and 2008, followed by a slight but steady deterioration in 2009 with an overall reduction in peacefulness of 2 percent occurring over the four-year period. It is interesting to note that the reduction in peacefulness coincided with the global financial crisis. For the period 2007 to 2010, the increase in overall GPI scores has been driven by a decrease in peacefulness for 75 of the 120 countries, or 62 percent of them; two countries recorded no change in their peacefulness, and another 43 or 36 percent of countries improved their peacefulness.

Low scores indicate more peacefulness while higher scores less peacefulness.

Although four years of data is still a short time series, it does give the ability to start to look at what global trends and events may be affecting the world and regional peacefulness.

The most significant event during the four years was the advent of the global financial crisis that occurred during 2008 and 2009. This event has been picked

Table 27.4
Average GPI Overall Scores* 2007–2010

Publication year	GPI average score	Number of countries whose score has improved	Number of countries whose score has worsened	Number of countries with no score change
2007	1.94	•	•	•
2008	1.92	68	39	13
2009	1.96	36	77	7
2010	1.98	41	75	4

* A higher score denotes higher levels of violence.

up in the 2009 and 2010 GPIs. This is because there is a one-year lag on data collection and reporting, as some of the data is sourced from other organizations.

The decline in peacefulness over the four-year period was primarily driven by increasing scores in the following GPI indicators: military sophistication, relations with neighboring countries, number of deaths from organized internal conflict, number of homicides, and number of external and internal conflicts fought.

Although many indicators did show declining peacefulness, there are some indicators that consistently improved over the four-year period. Military spending as a percentage of GDP and ease of access to weapons of minor destruction both improved. Some countries, Iceland for example, have demonstrated certain resilience with peacefulness returning quickly.

MOVEMENTS IN SPECIFIC INDICATORS

Another useful tool for policy makers would be to identify which particular aspects need special focus in order to increase peacefulness.

Of the 20 indicators included in the research, only 4 improved in peacefulness over the period 2007 to 2010 as can be seen in Table 27.5. Slight improvements were seen in the potential for terrorist acts and respect for human rights, whereas ease of access to weapons of minor destruction had a higher improvement. But the indicator with the most marked improvement was the percentage of GDP spent on the military. It is interesting to note that although on average more countries decreased their percentage of military spending as a portion of GDP, the overall global expenditure on the military increased.

The improvements in the ease of access to weapons of minor destruction indicator from 2007 to 2010 can be traced almost entirely to Sub-Saharan Africa. The eight largest score decreases (improvements) over the four years for this indicator were recorded by Angola, Cameroon, Equatorial Guinea, Gabon, Madagascar, Namibia, Senegal, and Zambia, all countries within this

Table 27.5
Indicator Movements*, 2007–2010

Indicator	Score change**	Change
Level of distrust in other citizens	0.72%	↓
Number of internal security officers and police per 100,000 people	0.58%	↓
Number of homicides per 100,000 people	5.13%	↓
Number of jailed population per 100,000 people	2.87%	↓
Ease of access to small arms and light weapons	−1.54%	↑
Level of organized conflict (internal)	1.75%	↓
Likelihood of violent demonstrations	1.57%	↓
Level of violent crime	0.33%	↓
Political instability	1.14%	↓
Respect for human rights	−0.16%	↑
Volume of imports of major conventional weapons per 100,000 people	1.04%	↓
Potential for terrorist acts	−0.20%	↑
Number of deaths from organized conflict (internal)	5.16%	↓
Military expenditure as a percentage of GDP	−6.44%	↑
Number of armed services personnel per 100,000 people	0.72%	↓
Volume of exports of major conventional weapons per 100,000 people	4.24%	↓
Military capability/sophistication	2.56%	↓
Relations with neighboring countries	2.76%	↓
Number of external and internal conflicts fought	15.57%	↓
Estimated number of deaths from organized conflict (external)	0.0%	•

* Based on 120 countries.
** Decreases in score denote improvements in peace.

region. This represents an improvement of 8.3 percent for the region on this indicator and highlights a regional trend toward peacefulness.

Relations with neighboring countries deteriorated globally over the four-year period, led by Central and Eastern Europe. In this region, only Macedonia improved its peacefulness in this score while Estonia, Hungary, Poland, Serbia, Turkey, Ukraine, and Uzbekistan all experienced worsening relations with their neighbors. Canada and the United States also deteriorated on this indicator, while most other regions moved only marginally.

The number of deaths from organized internal conflict has seen worsening scores overall but only from a very few countries. The Asia-Pacific region has experienced the biggest decline in peacefulness on this indicator, driven by Pakistan, Sri Lanka, and the Philippines. In other regions, Yemen and Kenya also significantly worsened their score over the four-year period.

Overall, the military sophistication increased leading to a deteriorating score between 2007 and 2010, driven primarily by Sub-Saharan Africa. Cameroon, Côte d'Ivoire, Equatorial Guinea, Gabon, Mozambique, Senegal, Sudan, and Tanzania were the worst performers. The Middle East and North Africa also deteriorated slightly, as did Central and Eastern Europe.

The respect for human rights indicator improved over the period, despite a significant decrease for Latin American countries.

A strong regional trend can be identified in relation to the indicator for the level of perceived criminality. This measure was static or positive for every region with the exception of Latin America, which registered a sharp deterioration for this indicator. Fifty percent of the countries in this region were rated less peaceful over the four-year period; one improved, while nine stayed the same.

CONCLUSION

This chapter on innovations in peace research demonstrates that an empirical, fact-based framework to evaluate the impact and value of peace is emerging. Such an approach can serve as a basis for building partnerships with policymakers and the business community in evaluating and realizing the benefits of increased peacefulness.

By measuring peace, creating baseline studies and monitoring change over time, new and innovative ways of applying this research will emerge. It is hoped that the improvement of peace will be seen to be as important to a nation's success as improvements in its economy.

NOTES

1. Trostle's (1992) Comprehensive definition of peace.
2. R. Ricigliano, *Making Peace Last* (Boulder, CO: Paradigm, 2011).
3. Ricigliano, *Making Peace Last*.
4. These include World Governance Indicators of the World Bank; Civil Liberties Index of Freedom House; Corruption Perceptions of Transparency International; Empowerment Rights Index of Cingranelli-Richards; Economic Freedom of the World Index of Fraser Institute; Global Competitiveness Report of the World Economic Forum; Freedom of the Press Index of Reporters without Borders; data from UN World Population Prospects; Ease of Doing Business Index of the World Bank and the Political Terror Scale.
5. A. Quinlan, "Building Resilience in Ontario: More Than Metaphor or Arcane Concept," *Resilience Science*, March 11, 2010, http://rs.resalliance.org/2010/03/11/building-resilience-in-ontario-%E2%80%93-more-than-metaphor-or-arcane-concept/.
6. J. Brauer and J. Tepper-Marlin, "Defining Peace Industries and Calculating the Potential Size of a Peace Gross World Product by Country and by Economic Sector" (2009), commissioned by Economists for Peace and Security USA for the Institute for Economics and Peace.

7. Dr. Jurgen Brauer is professor of economics at the James M. Hull College of Business, Augusta State University, Augusta, Georgia (http://www.aug.edu/~sbajmb) and visiting professor at Chulalongkorn University, Bangkok, Thailand.

8. In 2007, world economic growth was 5.2 percent, including 2.7 percent for advanced economies, 2.1 percent for the United States, and 7.9 percent for developing countries (IMF, *World Economic Outlook*, October 2009).

9. Russia $1.2T, India $1.2T, Brazil $1.6T, Indonesia $540B (IMF, *World Economic Outlook*).

10. Computed from Penn World Table, v6.3.

11. *Peace, Its Causes and Economic Value,* Institute for Economics and Peace, 2009.

12. UN Global Compact, *Response to Violent Conflict* survey, May 2008.

13. For this reason, the figures quoted in this section may not match those published in the IEP's 2010 Results and Methodology report or prior-year reports.

CHAPTER 28

Academic Diplomacy: The Role of Non–Decision Makers in Peacemaking

Peter Wallensteen

INTRODUCING ACADEMIC DIPLOMACY

This chapter aims at discussing the functions that third parties have in conflict resolution, although they are not the ultimate decision makers. There has been a growth in nongovernmental third-party activity, but its impact is often difficult to establish. It may, in fact, have impacts on lower levels of decision making rather than the ultimate decision makers. There has been some documentation on academics involved in peacemaking, or what here is termed academic diplomacy. Thus, this chapter provides a first glance at what may happen and suggests a way of evaluation. However, it should be recalled that the warring parties might employ academics as counselors for their particular side. Even if these academics are peace specialists who may bring peace perspectives to the parties, this activity is different from the independent third-party approach, which is the one in focus here. The idea of the third-party approach is to bolster those who are interested in peace on both sides of the divide and to give them tools in the internal battles on either side. Thus, by demonstrating reasonableness and possible routes forward, the chances of peace may be enhanced. Certainly, there are other forces operating at the same time: after all, this is a conflict, and academics may play roles that can deepen rather than bridge conflict.

This chapter develops a typology of third parties based on crucial elements in conflict resolution (the parties, the incompatibility, and the actions). This is illustrated with four cases that involved academics at the Uppsala University Department of Peace and Conflict Research. The question is raised whether these activities had a peacemaking impact on conflict dynamics in these four cases, and, if so, on what element(s) in the resolution process, and then for the short and long term? Peacemaking refers to the efforts to peacefully settle an ongoing armed conflict, including negotiation and mediation between the parties. Such efforts can be assessed in the immediate short term, that is, whether they actually served to end an armed conflict (or other types of armed behavior). The long-term perspective brings attention to its importance for the relationship between the warring parties, and potentially for peacebuilding after a conflict (Beardley 2008). In this way, long-term impact is different from whether there was a short-term impact or not. Obviously, immediate effects could be undone by the course of events after the third-party engagement. There could also be negligible short-term impact but a more significant impact for the relationships later or for other relationships involving the same actor or actors. Finally, some attention is given to the most difficult question: whether this impact can be attributed equally well to other factors than the third-party efforts.

MEDIATION: THE STATE OF THE ART

There has been considerable headway in the systematic study of international mediation. It has been made possible with the creation of large datasets, for instance the MILC dataset of the Uppsala Conflict Data Program (Melander, Möller and Öberg 2009) and other data collection efforts (Bercovitch and Gartner 2006; Greig and Regan 2008; Melin and Svensson 2009; DeRouen and Bercovitch (forthcoming). The mediators normally studied are states, international organizations (governmental or nongovernmental), as well as prominent personalities in particular situations and/or with a longer record of mediation. The studies are statistical and in that sense constitute significant brush-clearing operations and move the understanding of mediation forward.

There is also a more qualitative approach, which still is systematic. In a recent report, one and the same mediator was studied in six different situations that played out during a 30-year period (Svensson and Wallensteen 2010). It is a way to get closer to the craft of mediation, in terms of the fluctuations of particular mediation efforts and the many criteria that are required for an assessment of its contribution. In particular, this study wanted to demonstrate the styles of a mediator and their effect on process and outcome. Interestingly, at the same time several studies have been published on different national mediation approaches, for example, on U.S. negotiation behavior (Solomon and Quinney 2010). Mediation research may have arrived at a situation where different strands of thinking converge and where some important theoretical and empirical breakthroughs could be expected (Lindgren, Wallensteen, and Grusell 2010).

The studies have different foci. There is a vigorous debate on the motivation of the third-party and what impact that will have on the process and outcome. Bias has been a central concern to several studies (Kydd 2003; Svensson 2006, 2007, 2009). There has also been a concern about who is actually becoming mediator, at what moment in time such an actor appears on the scene, and the instruments available (Greig 2001; Greig 2005; Greig and Rost 2005; Smith and Smock 2008). For instance, is it important which actors offer mediation and if the warring parties will accept the bid. Offers tend overwhelmingly to be accepted (Greig 2005; Greig and Regan 2008), suggesting that there is considerable interaction between the warring parties and prospective mediators before decisions are made.

Organizing the discussion in what might be termed a process model, Svensson and Wallensteen distinguish between the third parties' activities when entering, pursuing, coordinating, and leaving mediation. These phases provide for very different types of third-party measures. Furthermore, the authors argue that it is important in what conflict phase mediation takes place (pre-violence, low/high intensity, after violence). The utility of these distinctions is demonstrated in the case of Ambassador Jan Eliasson (Svensson and Wallensteen 2010).

The third-party efforts that are typically included in these studies are those that can be documented the easiest, namely action on official, governmental levels, or what often has been termed as track I (Montville 1987). However, there has always been an undercurrent of other types of activities. Sometimes one may wonder if the official and publicly announced action is only the tip of an iceberg of activities. It is hard to know, as other interactions are likely to be secret, undocumented, or only known to some actors who also may not have the full picture. In due time, archives may open up and thus provide for more insight, but that should not prevent us from drawing tentative conclusions today, for the benefit of improving such measures in contemporary conditions. Interestingly, the data in the MILC dataset covering third-party action in internal conflicts, 1994–2003 does not demonstrate a particular increase in such activity, with the exception of the Israeli-Palestinian conflict, which actually takes a large portion of such official and publicly documented third-party measures (Melander, Öberg, and Möller 2009). The nonofficial third-party activity that is known to go on, is likely to be more difficult to systematically report on.

There may, however, be a possibility of gaining some insights from closer observation of one particular mediator, as is the case with Ambassador Eliasson that was just cited. There is also a category that is more likely than others to be willing to share some information on their activities, namely academics. It is often in an academic's own interest to document what goes on and make it available for deeper analysis. This furthermore may be done without jeopardizing confidence, political secrets, or creating dangers. Thus, this chapter takes up that particular category. There are academic institutions that have been involved in such work, in addition to their regular task, not only the department at Uppsala University or the International Peace Research Institute, Oslo (PRIO), but also the University of Notre Dame's Kroc Institute, George Mason University's Institute of Conflict Analysis and Resolution (ICAR), and activities based at Johns Hopkins University. It is of significance in itself to study such activities, of course, but it may also provide a framework for thinking of other third-party measures.

There is likely to have been a growth in such third-party activity since the end of the Cold War, although no numbers are easily available. It is reported that by 2007 there were more than 350 NGO affiliates engaged in peacebuilding work, compared to some 83 NGOs listed 10 years earlier, with slightly different definitions (Dayton 2009, 69). To this category belongs nongovernmental organizations specifically focusing on third-party work (Carter Center, International Alert, Conciliation Resources, International Crisis Group, U.S. Institute of Peace, Conflict Management Initiative, Center for Humanitarian Dialogue, Berghof Foundation for Peace Support, The Elders, etc.). There are also other bodies involved in conflict mediation but where the central mission is a different one. The circumstances lead actor into this, for instance, religious bodies (Quakers, Sant'Egidio, Sudan Council of Churches, Catholic Peacebuilding Network, World Council of Churches, etc.), humanitarian institutions (International Committee of the Red Cross, MSF, others), advocacy groups (Human Rights Watch), disarmament movements (Pugwash), and so on. In many of these cases, the actors may not even themselves think of this as third-party activity, but only as a natural way to sustain the work of the organizations. It is likely that many of these organizations do have records of their activities, but also that they prefer to keep their archives closed, as it may have impact on future work if history is revealed. Consequently, it is likely to be difficult to arrive at a full picture of all such activities, and even more difficult to assess their impact on conflict resolution.

Certainly, some of this work will be observed when it reaches into the domains of government action. This is also where it has to be observed if it is likely to have a direct impact on the actions a government takes in particular conflicts. Memoirs, diaries, and briefing papers would likely give us information. However, the experience is that this is far from complete. Comparing simple news reporting to the report by the third parties that were involved in the Burundi negotiations during the 1990s it was demonstrated that much information is left out in the participants' own accounts (Möller 2010).

EXAMPLES OF ACADEMIC DIPLOMACY

Seminars for Peacemaking

For researchers interested in conflict resolution and peace there is an expectation (raised by the academic themselves as well as from the community that supports such research) that the research results also should be applicable to reality. It would be satisfying to contribute in a tangible way to a nondestructive ending of a serious conflict. It would be ultimate confirmation that the theories are valid. There may also be other reasons for researchers to be involved in such work (moral commitment, personal interest, personal connection to particular conflicts, etc.). There could be inspiration from other fields, that is, economists advising governments on economic policies, natural scientists, engineers or legal experts working on major disarmament initiatives, medical experts involved in public health policy, and the like. It is not surprising to find academics involved in action. Some times their advocacy may result in more conflict if they are pursuing particular agendas. However, some have taken up the role of third parties, building on their position in academia.

A frequently used instrument to use academic insight to affect conflicts is the *problem-solving workshop*. This notion has had many names, but the substance is typically the same and is described in a handbook by experienced researchers (Mitchell and Banks 1996). In essence, it might not be more than an outgrowth of regular academic seminars and the academic culture of organized debates with opponents, respondents, commentators, and chairs that make it possible to clarify puzzles. Arriving at analytical clarity itself is often half of the solution. When entering into the realm of armed conflict, similar, probing approaches can help the parties understand their own conflict, both their own side and that of the opponent. Of course, stricter rules have had to be developed as to how to conduct such seminars and how to make them to productive in a short period of time. The meeting organized by John Burton is often credited of being the first of such meetings (Fisher 1997). However, the early Pugwash conferences did the same when delving into the nuclear disarmament issues and disaggregating the official positions of East and West (Rotblat 1972). With respect to armed conflict, such workshops have been documented for Cyprus, Lebanon, and Palestine. There have been attempts at systematizing the experiences. A prominent assessment was made by Fisher (1997, 187–212) building on some 25 published reports from 76 workshops of different types between 1969 and 1995. The workshops were run by a small number of researchers, Fisher notes (e.g., John Burton, Hal Saunders, and Herbert Kelman). They often encountered resistance from traditional diplomats or realists in academia and diplomacy (Fisher 1997, 198). A chief problem, according to Fisher, was to find ways in transferring positive experiences from the workshops to the policy makers.

Fisher divides the 76 cases into different schools for the conduct of these workshops. For instance, he thinks that a tradition from Burton is those workshops that aim at arriving at "a redefined relationship based on functional cooperation and political agreements" (Fisher 1997, 205). In a Kelman model, additional goals are included, notably the development of cadres of participants that later could play a role (a more educational ambition) and substantive inputs into the cultures on both sides. Kelman's activities focused on Israelis and Palestinians, and they also intended, over time, to promote a new relationship between these sides, which would be conducive for fruitful direct negotiations (Fisher 1997, 206). A third approach identified by Fisher is made up of the workshops led by Hal Saunders, the Dartmouth model. In this case, the ambition was to bring together persons with policymaking experience from the United States and the Soviet Union who attended the workshops with the approval of their respective leadership. They would thus have a more immediate impact on decision making.

Fisher's work summarized the situation at the early stage of the post-cold war period. As indicated the number of workshops organized by universities, nongovernmental organizations, religious movements and concerned citizens have multiplied. If Fisher could identify some 75 workshops during a 35-year period, it is likely that there would be an equal number every year today. The field of peace research has grown and so have the number of nongovernmental bodies. Arranging conflict-management seminars with academic input or

even leadership has become a customary activity. This is so even if Fisher did
not claim to make a comprehensive inventory. There might also have been
more going on during the time his assessment covers. For instance, the Pugwash workshops were not accounted for, nor were events that took place with
in human rights groups spanning the cold war divide in Europe.

Interesting observations stem from the Kelman seminars and their educational function. Education is what academics do, and thus, this is where one
would expect academics to be particularly useful. Kelman has outlined an
elaborate model for evaluating conflict-transcending seminars. Surprisingly,
making evaluations have seldom been part of the activities. That is a challenge
for newer efforts, and may also affect the way these events are organized. The
way the seminars have customarily been conducted may make it difficult to
study their impact, for instance, on the participants' attitudes toward each
other. If one were to administer a survey before and after, it might give the participants a feeling of being part of a scientific experiment rather than an event
that aims at change realities in life, according to Kelman (2008). Also, Kelman
outlines rules of conduct that are quite restrictive for the third party. This includes that that the seminar leadership should neither take part in substantive
discussions, nor give advice. The focus is on creating the conditions for ideas
to flow and providing the necessary trust for the participants (Kelman 2008).
The interaction is to take place between the participants themselves, who then
might undergo some form of attitudinal change. This, then, is what they might
bring with them when they return home after the experience. In this way, the
workshops contribute to a change of political culture in the society at large. In
a different design this might actually be probed further.

The academic style seminars may, however, serve many other functions. For
instance, if a there are a number of high-level participants from the opposing
sides then it is likely that interactions will also take place outside the formal
setting of the seminar. This opens for completely different types of contacts,
not controlled by the academics. In fact, the seminar may, from a political leadership's perspective, be only a convenient cover for establishing such connections. This gives the meeting a different function, where the academics are no
longer in control, as originally envisaged by Burton (which can be surmised
from his formulation *controlled communication*, [Burton 1969]). In fact, it is
even likely that powerful persons from one side are more interested in powerful participants from the other side, than in any of the others who happen to
be there. Politics is about power, and seminar deliberations can become a way
of measuring power. From a rational choice perspective, the seminar provides
an opportunity for information exchange directly between the parties. They
can communicate, receive information from the other sides, and thus learn to
assess the value of different types of information from the other side, notably
on the discrepancy between public pronouncements and private information.
It does not preclude them from bluffing, of course. That very discrepancy is
often where mediation finds a role, and that is also a role that the academic
third party would fulfill. Thus, the seminar can work as a mediation session,
whether intended or not by the organizers. This, then, leads us to a different
role for academics: the academic mediator.

The Academic Mediator

The accounts of academic third parties are scarce, even if some academics are known for engaging in such activity and may ultimately provide their own accounts. Professors John Paul Lederach and John Darby of the Kroc Institute, University of Notre Dame, are but two examples (see, for instance, Wehr and Lederach 1996). However, for confidentiality reasons, many refrain from talking about their experiences. There are, however, cases from recent history that shed light on such processes. An interesting account describes the work of Adam Curle, a professor of education at Harvard. Curle and a colleague were involved in secret diplomacy in the Nigeria-Biafra war in the period 1967–69 (Princen 1992, 186–214). Largely, they were acting as Quakers more than as academics. Still, this case warrants a closer look, as it bears similarities to the roles that academics can play.

Curle's engagement in the Nigeria-Biafra conflict was deliberately based on taking a low-key role, shunning media attention. It was in a way a demonstration of the "power of powerlessness" (Princen 1992, 210). For instance, the Quaker delegation was the only third party that was able to travel between the warring parties. The fact that neither of the warring sides made propagandistic points of this was seen as a signal that made the other side more convinced that this was a serious channel. The basic idea for the Quaker teams was to establish the conditions for a direct meeting between the two sides, but at times they also communicated entire proposals. No such encounter took place but no other third party managed even to get to the Biafra side, without this being used in the propaganda of that side. This was the fate of the missions of the Vatican and the World Council of Churches in 1967, for instance (190). The OAU Consultative Committee suffered the opposite fate of being embraced by Nigeria and largely taken its position in the conflict (189–90). Thus, potential third parties quickly lost the confidence of one or the other side. The Quaker team, however, maintained the relations throughout the war. In the short run, this did not matter. There was never a negotiation process and Biafra lost the war.

However, Adam Curle has often said that the efforts may have had a long-term effect on the way the Nigerian government handled its victory. The Quaker team could communicate to the Nigerian leadership that the Nigerian air raids and the economic sanctions did not have the effect Nigeria expected (Princen 1992, 193). It did not give the Biafrans confidence that they would be secure in a reunited Nigeria. Nigeria's actions, the team could tell the leadership, served to further alienate a population that was supposed to be turned into trusting citizens of the country. Curle argued that this information might have made Nigeria's President inclined to be more generous to the defeated enemy and the population than expected (Curle 1990, 55–56, 89).

This suggests that groups, such as neutral religious groups or academics, can play a more active role in affecting a conflict than only in the form of the problem-solving workshop. The mediator-academic is a different role, but one in which academic skills also can be useful. To this belongs an ability to listen and to distill points, as well as giving persuasive presentations, bringing attention to other relevant experiences, and draw conclusions from theoretical insights.

These are two roles, one that brings (representatives of) the parties together far away from the conflict zone; and other where the academic is traveling across the lines to talk to the parties. They are two endpoints on a continuum of possible actions. It suggests that there are many functions in peacemaking that have to be included. If the analysis starts with such functions, then other activities become more possible to grasp and evaluate. This means building a generic typology that may be of value not only to academic peacemaking activity but also for other efforts set up by those who do not have ultimate decision-making power. It is also a way to demonstrate where the strength is with mediators on higher levels, closer to the centers of decision making (such as official mediators from national and international bodies). This is why a typology may be of great help.

Developing a Typology

In conflict theory, a conflict includes three basic elements: the conflict parties and their mutual relationships historically, today, and with their resources; the disagreement or incompatibility, with all its connotations that color the attitudes between the parties; and the actions taken (i.e., the use of destructive methods between the opposing sides, combined with mobilizing actions within each side) (Wallensteen 2011b). Thus, the activities of the third party can be devoted to all the three aspects, but also focus on one. For instance, much confidence-building work deals with the action component: it aims at reducing the risk of misunderstandings, finding ways to inform the other side about intentions, and the like. Security-enhancing measures are there to guarantee the parties of their security, once a conflict has stopped. Activities searching for formulas deal with the disagreement itself. A central issue in conflicts with several parties—an increasingly common phenomenon (Harbom, Melander, and Wallensteen 2008)—is who should be involved in the negotiations and who will actually receive the mediator. All these matters ultimately involve decision by the parties themselves, of course, but the academic input (in the form of mediation, an academic seminar or other) can be instrumental in conveying ideas and information between the opposing sides.

Furthermore, the third party can be very active, bringing his/her own ideas to the parties, trying to directly contribute to a change of opinion. This is an assertive third party. It is often associated with the governmental level, but need not be the exclusive domain of powerful mediators. Then there are approaches of quiet diplomacy, where the facilitative roles of the mediator are emphasized, creating the conditions for exchanges of ideas. Ultimately, a settlement of a conflict will imply that actors, incompatibilities, and action have to change in important respects. Their postures will become less threatening, they will be more open to ideas, and they will scale down harmful action. This provides us with a typology of academic peacemaking diplomacy, which is presented in Table 28.1.

Table 28.1
Functions of Academic Diplomacy: Approaches and Conflict Components

Third Party Approach	The Parties	The Incompatibility	The Action
Assertive	I. Tackling the *problem of relevance:* Who should be at the table, and how relevant are they? *Example:* Invitations and commitments to participate; setting the agenda.	II. Finding the *formula for a settlement:* What are the possible solutions to the basic disagreement? *Example:* Autonomy and its contents.	III. *Building Confidence* by affecting the parties' actions against each other. *Example:* Cease-fire, confidence-building measures, repatriation.
Quiet	IV. Establishing direct *connection* between the parties. *Example:* Arrange and facilitate indirect and direct meetings	V. *Educate* the parties on processes, possible solutions and others' experiences *Example:* Training session, media attention.	VI. *Exchange of Information* to clarify positions. The difference between private and public information. Reduce hostile attitudes. *Example:* Academic seminars.

Table 28.1 outlines six different functions that the academic go-between could take up. The horizontal dimension captures the three basic components in a conflict, whereas the vertical axis has the two approaches identified previously. This provides six different functions of academic diplomacy.

Table 28.1 integrates the functions suggested by Fisher and Kelman, and they can also be found in accounts of third-party activities, such as the one Curle and his colleagues were undertaking in the Nigeria-Biafra conflict. It also locates some of the questions debated in the scholarly mediation literature, such as the commitment problem and the information questions, which are relevant for all the cells: will the parties abide by an agreement, and what hidden information could affect that assessment? This becomes particularly relevant in the case of an assertive third party. Will a mediator actually be able to deliver the other side to the bargain, and how consonant are such assurances with the information the party possesses?

This typology is now being applied empirically to four cases rooted in the Uppsala experiences of the 1990s. This means the cases are sufficiently historical to make possible a more detailed assessment. In the four cases, the question is whether the third-party activity added something to the situation and to what extent this can have had an impact on the courses of events.

All four cases belong to the period immediately after the end of the Cold War. It was a period of many peacemaking setbacks, particularly in the Balkans. It was also a period with a vigorous search for solutions.

Furthermore, all four cases belong to the same category of conflicts: they deal with state formation conflicts. This means that the central disagreement, the incompatibility, concerns the status of a particular territory. In all cases, forms of autonomy and independence are at the heart of the disagreement. This enhances the comparability of the cases and may make it easier to assess the functions academic diplomacy can play.

FOUR CASES OF ACADEMIC DIPLOMACY

BOUGAINVILLE 1990: ACADEMIC ASSERTIVENESS

(Source: Wallensteen 2009, 2011a)

The Bougainville dispute turned into an armed conflict in May 1989. The opposition movement formed itself as the Bougainville Revolutionary Army (BRA), and its demands no longer concerned only compensation for land destruction caused by a mining company but also independence for the island. This was something the national government of Papua New Guinea could not contemplate. Wallensteen entered as a third party in the conflict in January 1990, invited and being part of a group, the think tank from the local branch of the University of Papua New Guinea, and with support from local political leaders. In retrospect, one might say that the opportunity for negotiations was ripe at the time—January and February 1990. The government had attempted a military solution without success; the rebels had lost, they were pushed back, but not defeated. The offer of third-party action provided an opportunity to pursue a different course of action, for a time. However, the contacts made clear that the parties refused to talk to each other about a solution as long as there was fighting. Both sides expressed interest in the idea of an autonomy solution, but how far one could go was not possible to surmise under the tense conditions. Thus, the efforts turned into formulating a ceasefire arrangement and find a way to make sure such an agreement would lead to a sustained peace process. No side agreed to write this into the agreement, however. It had to rest on an explicit but unspecified understanding, further underscored by the fact that the ceasefire document was signed only by the military commanders. From a mediator perspective, it meant that instead of getting to cell II in the typology, third-party action concentrated on cell III, presumably as a first step.

The ceasefire was put in place on March 1, 1990, and was monitored by an international peace mission. It reported on a successful disarmament procedure and recommended that it was now time to take the next step of peacemaking. However, nothing happened after this. Thus, the months of March and April passed without government initiatives on this matter. In many ways, this was a lost opportunity. The BRA became increasingly anxious that the government was planning some surprise action and thus broke the ceasefire by breaking up the sealed arsenals to take out the weapons. The conflict since then saw a series of agreements, breakdowns, and restarts until 2001, when a peace agreement was signed granting regional autonomy to the island of Bougainville and specifying that a referendum on the status of the territory would take place 10 to 15 years after a functioning self-ruling administration was in place, which at this time means 2015 at earliest.

The autonomy idea was widely shared, and thus there was an understanding that a negotiated settlement had to deal with such an arrangement. It was not alien to the country, as the Constitution already had provisions for decentralization. However, negotiations lost credibility as armed action continued. Ending the violence became—unexpectedly—the primary assignment for the mediator. Certainly, he had to facilitate connections between the parties (the top leaders did not meet, however, and the connection was made through tape recordings carried across the dividing lines, a secret emissary and documents formulated by the third-party team). There was little opportunity to explain—even less to train—the parties in what the autonomy would mean. There was an exchange of information, in the sense that messages were delivered. But the quiet part of the diplomacy was of less significance. The third-party team acted more assertively, particular when pushing the ceasefire as such and ways to connect it to talks on the formula. The focus, in other words, was on cell III in this effort. The commitment of the parties to the agreement and to the process was continuously doubted by both sides. There was no way a guarantee could be found to safeguard a continuation—not even a signature on the paper. It is, furthermore, not in the power of an academic party to really deliver such a guarantee. Thus, to move the parties to cell I was not possible, on this score, the mediation stayed in cell VI. It was possible to set up a peace-monitoring mission, to ensure trust in the ending of military action (cell III), but nothing beyond that. It might require stronger outside forces to guarantee such a commitment. New Zealand was the broker that eventually found a settlement. It was not a regional bully, but an actor nevertheless committed to keep the parties within the agreed framework.

In sum, there was considerable short-term achievement. The ceasefire was visibly positive, the market opened, soldiers relaxed in the roadblocks and hoped to be able to go home. There was an opportunity to move forward. The parties could not grasp this chance, however, and in the intermediate term the venture failed. There were expectations, probably on both sides, that the war could be won, and thus risking renewed war seemed worth it. This is at least how BRA must have argued. However, negotiations were resumed at various intervals and eventually resulting in a peace agreement of reasonable quality (Regan 2010). The case recounted here became the first, but it may have set a pattern that any settlement required outside involvement, both in the negotiation process and in monitoring implementation. It also made the parties focus on autonomy solutions.

PALESTINE 1990: QUIET DIPLOMACY

(Source: Wallensteen 2010, 2011a)

In December 1988, PLO leader Yassir Arafat had agreed to denounce terrorism as a means for Palestinian liberation. This resulted in diplomatic relations between the United States and PLO. The Swedish government also wanted to create a link between Israel and PLO. In conversations with the Swedish Ministry for Foreign Affairs, the Department of Peace and Conflict Research at Uppsala

University was to hold an academic seminar on the situation in the Middle East in June 1990. It was to have participation from the PLO as well as Israel, as Israel encouraged its citizens to participate in international scientific conferences, particularly if they dealt with the Middle East. The seminar included three groups: Palestinians from the occupied territories as well as from the Diaspora, notably Tunisia (PLO); Israelis with political as well as academic backgrounds; and a group of neutrals, that is, Swedish and American academics, including Jewish personalities who had been important for the breakthrough in 1988. The seminar was conducted in June 1990 and achieved much of what is typical for such seminar: exchanges of ideas, personal connections, and in particular a feeling on the Palestinian sides that they were taken seriously. A comment after the seminar was that it helped also Israelis reducing their demonization of the opponent: They saw that there were reasonable people on the other side and thus constructive talks would be possible. The seminar achieved much of what is found in cell IV in the typology. It also suggested a number of ways forward. In fact, the whiteboard in the seminar room was full of such ideas, largely focusing on economic cooperation. By demonstrating the economic gains—also for Israel—of ending occupation and replacing it with economic integration, the participants hoped to find arguments for public acceptance of a two-state solution. To the Palestinians, the Intifada appeared to have created more equal relations and they hoped it would be possible to get mutual recognition. Confidence had been created and telephone numbers exchanged. This corresponds to the functions found in cell VI of the typology.

In sum, this seminar belongs to the realm of quiet diplomacy. The functions in cells IV and VI were those most relevant. In the short term, the result led to considerable continued interaction among the participants. Reports were going from the seminar, while it took place, to PLO headquarters, for instance. It cemented Swedish involvement in the Middle East.

However, the achievements suffered from what we can term an external shock (Lindgren et al. 2010). In August 1990, Iraq invaded Kuwait. PLO's inability to condemn this action, although most of the Arab governments turned against Iraq, brought to Israelis back a demonized picture of the Palestinians. In 1991, a new government took over in Sweden, with considerably less interest in the Middle East negotiations, and instead peace diplomacy passed on to Norway.

NAGORNO KARABAKH 1994: DIPLOMACY FOR A FORMULA

(Source: Svensson and Wallensteen 2010)

The conflict over Nagorno-Karabakh concerned the status of this territory in Azerbaijan. It was one of the many conflicts emerging during the period of the breakup of the Soviet Union (Melander 2001). Armenian forces gained the upper hand in 1992–93, taking de facto control over a large part of Azerbaijan's territory. To Azerbaijan, the conflict remains a matter of foreign occupation by Armenia. In 1994, Sweden was given the role as chair of the Minsk Conference, the committee within the OSCE that was assigned to mediate in the Nagorno-Karabakh conflict. Armenia and Azerbaijan were both members of this organization, which was to deal with security and cooperation in Europe. Ambassador Jan

Eliasson became the Swedish representative. He commented on this assignment "At first, I was skeptical—I do not believe that you can mediate in committees— but was later convinced, partly due to the possibility of also using the academic milieu in the mediation efforts" (Svensson and Wallensteen 2010, 29).

Azerbaijan lost badly in the battles during spring of 1994 and thus had to accept a ceasefire agreement in Nagorno-Karabakh. It had largely been brokered by Russian mediation, but engaged the Swedish mediation team as well. This was done without substantial political negotiations on the core issues of the status of Nagorno-Karabakh. It may well be that the ceasefire took away an incentives for the parties to resolve the core incompatibility of the conflict. In the period that followed, the Eliasson team tried to generate new moves. The hope was to get the parties to discuss this issue and develop a peace process, where also other issues would be tackled, for instance, international peacekeeping, refugees, and withdrawal from occupied territory.

Clearly, the most sensitive issue in the Nagorno-Karabakh conflict was the question of the definitive status of the region. The academic team that was formed in the department discussed various solutions to this end.[1] As part of these efforts, Assistant Professor Kjell-Åke Nordquist presented a matrix demonstrating various possible forms of autonomy. The vertical dimension included such issues as security (police, military dispositions), taxation powers, regional economic authority, political arrangements (local parliament, for instance), cultural provisions (protection of language, educational policy), and international aspects (guarantees, monitoring). Each of these issues could then contain different layers of power, which was demonstrated horizontally (low, intermediate, and high). The idea was to acquaint the parties with different forms of autonomy and initiate a discussion. Eliasson used this as a diplomatic non-paper: "I told each of the parties that I actually was carrying two hats. One was as the mediator, the other as a Visiting Professor at a well-known University. Let me now put on my academic hat and give to you a table of possible autonomy arrangements. Tell me what you prefer!" (Svensson and Wallensteen 2010, 44).

As an academic exercise this was a perfect assignment. It fits very well into cell V of the typology: it was a way to educate the parties about the notion of autonomy. Eliasson was operating in an official capacity, however, even if he handed this to the parties wearing his academic hat. It was not likely that they would only see it academically, in other words. To the parties, this was a matter of dealing with the incompatibility. That was something that belongs under cell II: finding a formula. However, it was done in an open and inviting way, and could then, presumably, be a start of a new process. None of the parties responded officially to this non-paper. Eliasson recounts that he met his former counterparts five years later, when he was no longer officially dealing with the case. The Armenian representative admitted that they had serious difficulties in formulating an answer. "You really gave us a lot of grief," Eliasson recalls him saying (Svensson and Wallensteen 2010, 44).

The academics in Uppsala continued to pursue this issue in a series of informal workshops during the following years, even including Armenians from Karabakh. However, there was little interest in formulating more closely what autonomy could possibly look like. It may not have been the preferred alternative of any of the parties. Azerbaijan wanted to restore the borders prior to the war; the Karabakh Armenians were striving for independence. The autonomy arrangement could be an outcome from a negotiation, not a starting point. It would, consequently, be something a negotiator could present at an appropriate moment in a direct negotiation. However, the parties were not inclined to go to a direct negotiation, particularly if they would not know what it was going to be about. Thus, preparations were needed, also on this possible compromise. In a sense, the non-paper was giving the parties a head start in thinking about solutions, but they were not willing to present their preferred options until there was a real peace process.

In sum, this case shows the impact of a semi-permanent ceasefire (cell III). The parties were not willing to start a new peace process, and thus peace initiatives found themselves in the more quiet dimensions of diplomacy. This meant to educate the parties on possible solutions (cell V) and provide them with informal direct connections (cell IV), thus, to some extent, contributing to cell VI information sharing functions. For humanitarian reasons, there was a necessary short-term measure of a ceasefire. It also prevented the defeat of either party. It established a status quo, which may have been comfortable to one side (Armenia) but managed also by the other (Azerbaijan, where the refuges population had no political influence and oil continued to generate revenue for the state, compensating for the costs of war). For the long term, the lack of a solution creates a permanent source for tension. There have been continuous flare-ups since the ceasefire, indicating the unsatisfactory situation. However, major powers, notably Russia, may also see the situation as sufficiently stable in an otherwise unsettled region, preferring not to expend energy on a long-term arrangement.

EAST TIMOR 1997–99: A FORMULA REQUIRES ELABORATION

(Source: Nordquist 2008)

East Timor was occupied by Indonesia in 1975, following a short armed conflict between groups in East Timor contending for power, as the colonial power Portugal withdrew. Indonesia quickly made East Timor into a separate province (its 27th) and tried to deal with this territory just like any other part of the country. However, resistance to the occupation continued through the 1970s and well into the 1980s. By early 1990s, tensions were again rising. A massacre in 1991 drew renewed international attention to the situation and the 1996 Nobel Peace Prize to two East Timorese nonviolent resistance leaders, José Ramos-Horta and Bishop Belo, resulted in pressure on the Indonesian government to find a constructive solution. The Asian economic crisis in 1997–98 further undermined the international and national position of the Indonesian military regime. It led to efforts by the United Nations to settle the matter. Seeing the possibility of change, a group of young Timorese—from different backgrounds in the previous civil conflict and with academic training—formed the intra-Timorese bipartisan advocacy group, based in East Timor, the East Timor Study Group. This group approached academics around the world, including Assistant Professor Kjell-Åke Nordquist at the department in Uppsala, who also involved Wallensteen. A chief idea from the outset was the exploration of alternative solutions to the question of the status of East Timor. The resistance movements, formed into an umbrella organization named CNRT (National Council for East Timorese Resistance), demanded independence; the Indonesian government could conceive of nothing that, in its view, threatened to break up Indonesia. Granting independence to one province might make others ask for the same. The autonomy solution appeared to Indonesia, as well as to pro-Indonesian groups in East Timor, to be a way out. It could be a formula that would be agreeable to the both sides in East Timor. Secret talks with representatives of Indonesia and CNRT suggested that there was some possibility of an autonomy solution, at least as an interim arrangement. For the Republic of Indonesia it might have been the final settlement; for the East Timorese resistance it would be a phase to allow for building state structures as a preparation for independence. Different time limits were discussed in the workshops that went on, for instance, in Sweden, in East Timor, and in Indonesia.

In a public statement in January 1999, the Indonesian president B. J. Habibie announced that East Timor was to have a referendum on its future status. The alternatives were to be autonomy and independence. His comment was made as a response to an unpublished letter from Australia's prime minister, John Howard, suggesting a longer period of self-determination for East Timor. Habibie had publicly discussed the East Timor issue since he took up the presidency in mid-1998, without giving a conclusive view (*The Australian,* August 29, 1999).

Nordquist notes that this surprising turnaround of decades of Indonesian policy "came just a few days after the first conference . . . in Jakarta ever, on the East Timor status issue. It was organized by Uppsala University, in cooperation with the Research Institute for Democracy and Development, Jakarta and with the East Timor Study Group represented as well." The conference dealt with the advantages and disadvantages of independence and autonomy (Nordquist 2008, 192). Its results were conveyed to the Indonesian and East Timor leadership, which was assisted by the fact that the East Timor leader Xanana Gusmão was in jail in Jakarta (Dewi Fortuna 1999). The direct connections between the seminar and the announcement can be debated and is not the most interesting aspect. Instead, by seriously working out advantages and disadvantages of different types of autonomy arrangements—whether interim or permanent—the political alternatives for East Timor became clear, comparable, and possible to debate, thus laying the basis for more informed political decisions.

The academic efforts during the 1996–1998 period focused on exploring the autonomy options, among others, as a theoretical exercise but with high-level participation. The conference in Jakarta in January 1999 aimed at making the notion better known also to the general public. However, Habibie's unexpected announcement made this impossible. As Nordquist observes, "a polarization took place" (2008, 192) that made this effort difficult. All attention was on the referendum. For East Timor's resistance movements this was an historical opportunity to liberate the territory from Indonesia. Certainly, this was a chance they were not going to miss. For those more sympathetic to Indonesia the referendum was instead a threat to the status quo, and to the benefits integration had given them. The disputes from the short conflict in 1975 resurfaced, although many had previously assured that such tensions were something of the past. In May 1999, an agreement was signed on the referendum, but it was not an agreement that formally involved the Timorese parties. It was signed under UN auspices by In-donesia and Portugal. There may have been some direct negotiations between Indonesian officials and the resistance leader Gusmão, however.

Following Habibie's announcement, Nordquist and members of the Study Group became engaged in finding ways to reduce tensions. Particularly the Cath-olic Church took an interest in preventive efforts, focusing on the internal splits in East Timor that the referendum activated. The August 30, 1999, referendum gave the independence option 78.5 percent of the votes. The losers went on a rampage in the country, 250,000 Timorese fled across the border, and an inter-national intervention became necessary.[2] Australia led the operation effectively, and, by the end of October, Indonesian military presence in the territory was ended. At that time, after Habibie's resignation, the new president, Abdurrahman Wahid (Gus Dur), agreed to rescind Indonesia's control over East Timor. As the president later told the present author, "I had met Gusmão, and he seemed to be a reasonable person, so why not accept East Timor's independence?" However, this left a major refugee problem, where many refugees in effect were controlled by pro-Indonesian leaders or warlords. In the following years, Nordquist was involved in negotiations that successfully brought refugees and leaders back to East Timor.

The focus here is on the autonomy solution, as an idea that was well suited for scholarly development. Academic diplomacy in this case benefited strongly from having a local base. Initiatives came from East Timorese, and they could also quickly make use of the information. Similarly, the renewed Indonesian interest in finding a solution after the fall of Suharto created links also to this side. The autonomy notions were known on the political level in both camps. However, when President Habibie suggested the two alternatives in the referen-dum, only independence had a ring to most Timorese. Schulze argues that the two concepts, independence and autonomy, did not exist in the local language, Tetum, and thus that the vote clearly became one for "troops out" (Schulze 2001, 81).

Summarizing this experience: In the short-term, this case of academic diplo-macy appears to have had an impact. The autonomy idea was embraced by the stronger party in the conflict. However, this was also the seed of its demise. The way Habibie presented the autonomy alternative made it into an Indonesian op-tion, not a Timorese one or one that had been jointly agreed upon. There was little chance that this option could win in a referendum. A quarter of a century of brutal Indonesian rule had not created a will for the majority in East Timor to stay with this state. The autonomy option served a political function for In-donesia, rather than becoming a real alternative. The referendum as such was a face-saving device where most analysts were convinced of the outcome. The academic explorations of the autonomy concept, thus, served as an issue for dis-cussion, but were probably not seriously considered by either party. Indonesia's attempts at selling the proposition were simply too feeble, and the East Timor re-sistance had consistently aimed for independence. Some realized that it would now come earlier and without preparation, which was a gamble. But to wait would be even riskier: the military leadership could well take over Indonesia again, and the result would be renewed repression in East Timor.

However, for the long term there might still be an impact, in Indonesia itself. Autonomy became a more well-known solution. It could be useful in another context. Thus, when the negotiations to end the war in Aceh were restarted in late 2004, the autonomy option was one of central interest. The mediated agreement in August 2005 made Aceh into a special autonomous region within Indonesia.

In terms of the typology, the approach of the East Timor Study Group and the academics focused on the incompatibility, finding a solution that would be agreeable to the two sides. Thus, the aim was to bring the discussions to cell II, but it necessitated its development, which is in cell V. There was a need to thrash out the idea and to educate the public about it. Political developments took over this function. The third-party approach had to be quiet, in the sense that there was little publicity around it for most of 1998, and indeed the conditions in Indonesia were still shaky. The military regime has just fallen (May 1998), and the future direction of the country was uncertain. With more time and more predictable circumstances, the solution may have had more of a chance, as also the developments in Aceh suggest. By 2005 Indonesia was a more stable country, with a more credible democratic order allowing for a more reasoned debate. However, third-party work in conflict seldom takes place under ideal conditions and political developments are always likely to generate surprises, or external shocks, to mediation processes (Lindgren et al. 2010).

THE PROMISE OF ACADEMIC DIPLOMACY

In this chapter, we have studied four cases of nongovernmental diplomacy in four highly charged armed conflicts. The forms have been different. Some have been direct mediation; others have been academic seminars; or channeling of ideas to official mediators and to the parties. In that way, they have involved decision-making levels without the third party being a decision maker.

Furthermore, all the cases have concerned conflicts with a strong territorial component. The status of a particular area has been the core issue. This has made autonomy a central, theoretically possible solution to the conflicts. In two cases, such solutions have actually materialized but not necessarily solved the conflict (Bougainville and Palestine), only to be regarded as temporary situations by leading actors. The academic diplomacy studied here does not claim credit for this. In two cases, such solutions were not entertained for the same reason: a better alternative seemed to exist to at least to one of the parties (for both Nagorno-Karabakh and East Timor: a complete break with the former controlling party).

The process, in all cases, unfolded differently than the academic participants had anticipated. In each of the four cases, the hope was to deal with the core issues of the conflict, the incompatibility, either by getting the parties to formulate ideas (that is, cell II in the typology) or to start an educational process to that effect (cell V). It was more difficult than anticipated, and often the mediating activities had to deal with issues relating to the parties actions rather than their disagreements.

In Bougainville, it turned out to be necessary to discuss a ceasefire (cell III) before approaching the originally intended focus on a possible solution (cell II), which thus only remained a sketch. In the case of the Middle East the focus was entirely on IV and VI, with little chance to move into an educated discussion on cell V, from which real proposals might have been generated, (e.g., a move to cell II). Possibly, the meeting was to early in a process for that to take place, in both these cases. The actions were pioneering and the parties had no previous experience of meeting for such serious discussions.

Also in the case of the more assertive efforts on Nagorno-Karabakh it turned out that the chances to discuss a compromise solution were not high. Thus, also this mediation effort came back to questions of the ceasefire, notably its monitoring by international peacekeeping (cell III). Finally, for East Timor the academic efforts were geared to developing formulas for solutions, but this was overtaken by events and the team had to deal with ways of defusing tension and dealing with the aftermath of the conflict (largely matters belonging to cell III).

Thus, we see that all efforts in fact came to deal with the action component of the conflicts, rather than the disagreement as such. This is remarkable, as the academic expertise was more on finding actual solutions. There is probably an important lesson here. The actions are what politics relate to, and to shift a conflict from destructive action and undoing the effects of previous destructive action, is probably an significant element of confidence building. As long as there is armed action, the parties are likely to have little confidence in the opposite side. Those engaged in negotiations will have difficulties in convincing their own side of the willingness of the other side to make a deal. New deeds will undermine what ever trust is created. At the same time, ceasefire by itself may also reduce incentives for compromise. This is a typical dilemma in negotiations to end war. Academic diplomacy confronted the same dilemma.

It was possible to an even lesser extent to raise issues with respect to the parties themselves. The negotiations took the parties for granted, although the most important elements in all the discussion actually were the intentions of the parties. Who were they willing to negotiate with, and what pledges were they willing to give to the opposing side? In the Bougainville case, there was minimal direct contact between the government and BRA. Similarly, the approach in the academic seminar was to assist in establishing a link between the Israeli government and PLO. A positive atmosphere was created and there was some momentum, for a short period, but nothing really happened within a reasonable period of time. In the case of Nagorno-Karabakh, the official mediator team had all the necessary contacts, but the parties were not willing to go beyond the ceasefire arrangement and clearly not officially engage in direct negotiations without certain preconditions being met. Finally, in the East Timor case, there appears to have been little direct contact between the Indonesian government at the time and the East Timor resistance leaders. For the parties to believe that a solution is going to last will require that there are clearcut commitments from the other side. Without direct relations, this is not likely to take place. It is, obviously, difficult for academic seminars to establish such links of any duration and quality.

All four processes were subject to an external shock, that is unexpected events that challenged basic premises of the negotiations. In the Bougainville case, the government faced internal military opposition (even a coup attempt) and then BRA broke the ceasefire agreement (thus undermining its credibility in future agreements). In the Middle East, Iraq's invasion of Kuwait completely derailed the track that had been established. In Nagorno-Karabakh, Russia clearly did not want negotiations to proceed beyond the ceasefire arrangement, which may not have been entirely surprising. In East Timor, the Indonesian government's unexpected endorsement of autonomy made it an impossible proposition. This suggests that academic and third-party diplomacy in general are highly vulnerable to events beyond its control. It is an expression of a lack of power, of course, but that very lack of power is also what makes such approaches interesting to the parties.

As this discussion makes clear, there are continuously other factors operating in the armed conflict situations. What achievements may be observed may in fact largely be the result of other parties exerting influence. As was demonstrated in the case of East Timor, Australia had direct relations to the Habibie government and may very well have convinced the president to make the announcement he made. Clearly, Australia had a great interest also in the Bougainville conflict and followed Wallensteen's action closely. It is not obvious what Australia did to promote or counteract, for instance, the autonomy proposal. In the same way, Russia was concerned about the developments in Nagorno-Karabakh and preferred to have Russian peacekeepers rather than international ones in the area. Indeed, Russia also pushed for the ceasefire agreement without paying attention to the larger settlement issues.

The United States showed little interest in any of these three conflicts, although it obviously was instrumental in getting Indonesia to accept the Australian peacekeeping operation in East Timor in September 1999. Its concern with East Timor related to its fear in 1975 that it would turn into another Cuba: the military government under Suharto was clearly the preference of the American government at that time. It is unlikely that East Timor was seen in the same light in 1999. However, the U.S. interest in the Middle East is a different matter. The Swedish idea in 1990 was to establish links between the three corners of the conflict: the United States, Israel, and PLO. The relations between the United States and PLO had been broken off two weeks before the academic seminar was held. This made the seminar particularly interesting also from the American side.

Furthermore, there is likely to have been many internal deliberation on each of the opposing side as to whether to participate in the activities, what goals one would have with participation, and how one was going to act. This is customary to consider during any time of diplomatic action, but it also applies to academic diplomacy. As is the case for traditional diplomacy, academics are likely to have little information on such internal deliberations. Signals and indications, rumors, and gossip becomes important also in this context, leaving the third party in a bind as to what is actually happening and what is then the best course of action.

Thus, what third-party diplomacy achieves or does not achieve may not only depend on the internal dynamics of the directly engaged parties. It will be decided on by the parties and the surrounding actors as well as unpredictable external shocks. What can be achieved, however, may be a shift in the agenda of the discussion, and that may help to ultimately bring forward viable solutions for a durable peace of higher quality than would otherwise have been the case.

ACKNOWLEDGMENTS

This chapter has benefited from valuable inputs from Isak Svensson, Kjell-Åke Nordquist, John Paul Lederach, John Darby, and Madhav Joshi. The responsibility for the text remains solely with the author. This chapter constitutes part of the Third Parties and Peacebuilding project managed jointly by the Uppsala Conflict Data Program, Department of Peace and Conflict Research, Uppsala University; and the Kroc Institute for International Peace Studies, University of Notre Dame, with funding from these institutions and the National Science Foundation, USA.

NOTES

1. The team was led by Peter Wallensteen and consisted also of Erik Melander, also from the Department of Peace and Conflict Research at Uppsala University, and Klas-Göran Karlsson from Lund University, an authority on the modern history of the Caucasus.

2. There seems to be dispute on the numbers: Schulze 2001:78 estimates the number of Timorese refugees to be 400,000.

CHAPTER 29

Social Media: A New Track of Multi-Track Diplomacy

Philip Gamaghelyan

The Internet and social media are revolutionizing all aspects of human communication. They are transforming the ways people and societies relate to one another, to themselves, and to other societies. Inevitably, technological advances have profound impacts on conflict dynamics and peacemaking. Even so, their effects have not been studied yet.

This chapter moves from acknowledging the impact of Web 2.0 revolution on social action in general to examining its impact on peacemaking practice. The chapter considers the Internet and social media as a new and emerging track in multi-track diplomacy that works in close interrelation with all others tracks to support or hinder peacemaking. The chapter presents the efforts of peacemakers in the Caucasus and elsewhere to incorporate this new track into conflict resolution work. It also examines cases in which these developments have contributed to conflict escalation. The chapter ends with a conclusion that notes the promises as well as the pitfalls that these trends present and suggests in-depth research to produce guidelines for the proactive use of the Internet and social media in peacemaking. Peacemaking here is defined as a targeted effort to contribute to cultural change that leads to positive transformation of relations among conflicting parties. The transformation of relations assumes rehumanization of the other, development of inclusive concepts of identity, mainstreamed critical thinking abilities, and constructive approaches to the phenomenon of conflict.

WEB 2.0 REVOLUTION

Clay Shirky's *Here Comes Everybody: The Power of Organizing without Organizations*[1] describes social media as having brought down the costs of coordination and organization. This makes it possible for otherwise unconnected individuals to initiate and coordinate large-scale social actions. Considering that such capacity of coordination and organization was previously inaccessible to individuals and limited for states or large organizations due to the high costs of communication and coordination, this development is unprecedented.

This seismic shift happened not because of the development and spread of the Internet or the consequent increased speed of communication per se. The Internet initially was just another means of communication that supported existing social norms and behavior. What made the difference, in the last few years, was the development of user-generated interactive social media platforms otherwise referred to as Web 2.0, as opposed to the author-generated and noninteractive Web 1.0 version of the Internet from 1993 to 2003. These platforms facilitate social action. Social networking websites such as Facebook have allowed physically unconnected individuals to easily find others with similar interests and rally around a common cause to coordinate collective actions with little or no cost. Quick information-sharing platforms such as Twitter have allowed real-time updates from conferences, protest actions, and court hearings, making it possible to organize a meeting or a demonstration at a greater speed than law enforcement agencies often can anticipate and prevent. The user-generated, interactive, and openly subjective wikis such as Wikipedia have become the preferred source of information for many people, often replacing objective books and encyclopedias written by professionals. Blogs, simple websites that anyone with Internet access can start, in some cases have readership comparable to top news outlets. Video-sharing websites such as YouTube broadcast material that otherwise would not make it to TV screens, including scenes of domestic violence, abuse in the army, and exposing and visualizing deep-rooted societal problems. Petitions to free jailed journalists that would gather few signatures in the past today can gather thousands of signatures online.

A recent example of social media-based action that challenges the way we are used to doing things were the protests across the Middle East in early 2011. They started in Tunisia and spread to Yemen, Jordan, Bahrain, Libya, Syria, and—most remarkably—Egypt, toppling the decades-long rule of seemingly invincible autocratic regime of Hosni Mubarak. What is particularly extraordinary about these social movements is that many of them had no center, institutionalized leadership, or formal organization.

Previously not connected groups of online activists were able to harness popular resentment against the injustice, repressions, poverty, and absence of freedom to build a critical mass of people ready to go out to the streets. These are remarkable cases of a new kind of revolution: revolution without leaders; political elites challenged not from within or not by competing elites, but by people that are now able to organize without organizations. The outcomes of these revolutions are unknown, because they have no precedents in history. However, they are likely to encourage many more social media–enabled popular revolutions.

Of course, it is not social media that creates social action. Activists all over the globe have long tried to challenge the status quo and fight for social change. What social media has done, as Shirky explains, is "remove obstacles to collective action,"[2] making possible even large-scale group action that was previously difficult to organize due to high costs of coordination and the need for institutional resources that activists typically did not possess.

What is particularly new about the potential of social media and what makes it so powerful is that it allows each person to determine what is important for her or himself and share that with a small group of friends and relatives who are likely to have similar interests. Therefore, instead of a more familiar world where few well-organized media outlets and professionals would decide what is important to broadcast, we now have millions of "sit at home broadcasters" deciding what matters to their immediate circle and making local news. Millions of Facebook and Twitter broadcasters of "small local news" then make a worldwide user-generated interconnected web of local news on a global scale.

The spread of social media has had implications for all types of collective action, from allowing for the facilitation of peacemaking to contributing to escalation of conflicts. Numerous groups have been created in social networking sites, connecting people from across conflict divides who were not able to connect previously. In many cases such contacts led to sustained dialogue and cross-border cooperation. Ongoing video-dialogues have been established, connecting people who are physically far apart from one another. Many peacemakers started adopting the emerging tools to improve the efficiency of their efforts. Workshops on social media and conflicts have become commonplace in the last two years, giving social media tools to peacemakers and conflict resolution tools to bloggers.

However, the reverse has also been true. The "power of organizing without organizations" has been beneficial not only for peace-oriented groups; this power is available to everybody, including nationalist and racist groups and various spoilers. As the examples in this chapter show, many peace activists have been harassed and attacked, often anonymously, through the same social networking sites; bloggers have been arrested for their virtual activism and put into very real jails. The conflicting sides have used social media to spread misinformation and messages of hate as well as engaging in information wars, taking advantage of the same benefit of reduced communication costs.

SOCIAL MEDIA AND SOCIAL CHANGE

We have become accustomed to thinking of the Internet and by extension of social media as communication tools. They are indeed, and as such, they mirror real life and are a continuation of already existent behavior and relationships, helping and enhancing both with greater speed and efficiency. As an example, for those already engaged in peacemaking, social media might be just a tool that helps preexisting behavior.

However, it would be misleading to think of social media *only* as a communication tool and as an auxiliary phenomenon. To build on the previous example, for many people who have never had the chance to see a person from the "other side" and are not professional peacemakers, social media *is* the change that makes cross-border communication even possible. Today, using Facebook and other online platforms, thousands of previously socially passive individuals become agents of change by engaging in cross-border and cross-communal dialogue, defying closed borders, societal taboos, and sometimes legal restrictions.

For already established media outlets, such as the *New York Times* or the *Guardian*, social media is just another tool to further promote their already existing work. However, for many pro-democracy bloggers, LGBT activists, or peacemakers around the world with no other avenues to express themselves, social media *is* the platform that makes it even possible to get their voices heard, to connect, and to mobilize others to action, even though they may be persecuted by political regimes and marginalized by self-censoring mainstream media. An emerging social media tool, Ushahidi,[3] has allowed individuals to record, track, and report cases of violence in postelection protests in Iran, becoming the main source of information in a controlled environment, exposing the conflict internationally and possibly containing further violence. Domestic violence and physical abuse in the army in Armenia has long been a well known phenomena for the local population, yet these issues were never addressed. In 2010, two relevant YouTube videos emerged: one was about a domestic violence case in which a young woman died as a result of a brutal beating by her husband and mother-in-law; the other showed the beating and humiliation of soldiers in the army. These videos led to nationwide protests prompting investigations. In October 2010, having seen the YouTube videos, representatives of the European Union visited the Parliament of the Republic of Armenia to discuss steps to be taken to prevent further cases of violence in the army.[4] A law against domestic violence is now under consideration in the Armenian parliament.

In 2009 two Azerbaijani youth activists—Adnan Hadjizadeh and Emin Milli—were arrested on false charges and sentenced to 2 and 2.5 years in prison, respectively. Luckily for them, Adnan happened to be a blogger. The arrest mobilized the small blogging community of Azerbaijan that felt threatened and decided to take the matter into their own hands. Immediately, news spread about their imprisonment using social media platforms and instantly became a cause for bloggers around the world. Twitter and Facebook were used to gather street protests in Azerbaijan during the court hearings, while updates from the courtroom were tweeted instantly and were followed by thousands around the world. The news then made it into the *New York Times* and onto CNN, as well as into other top media outlets, prompting U.S. Secretary of State Hillary Clinton to discuss the case of jailed bloggers with the president of Azerbaijan, Ilham Aliyev. A few months later, Reporters Without Borders reported that this time it was U.S. president Barack Obama who was "pressing Azerbaijan to free them."[5] The bloggers were set free after serving about half of their sentence.

SOCIAL MEDIA AND PEACEMAKING

Social media has gradually become one of the factors that affect the dynamics of conflicts and conflict resolution. Yet it is not yet adequately studied in the frameworks of conflict resolution. Social media does not even fit any of the tracks of multi-track diplomacy. The nine tracks identified until recently include the following:[6]

- Track 1—Government, or peacemaking through diplomacy
- Track 2—Nongovernment/professional, or peacemaking through conflict resolution
- Track 3—Business, or peacemaking through commerce
- Track 4—Private citizen, or peacemaking through personal involvement
- Track 5—Research, training, and education, or peacemaking through learning
- Track 6—Activism, or peacemaking through advocacy
- Track 7—Religion, or peacemaking through faith in action
- Track 8—Funding, or peacemaking through providing resources
- Track 9—Communications and the media, or peacemaking through information

Social media is interlinked with many of these tracks but effectively is a track on its own. While it is often assumed to be part of the "communication and media" track, it only partially fits the description. As communication and media, social media also contributes to author-generated information sharing. But unlike author-generated media, social media is also interactive, providing tools for networking, group forming, mobilization and management, dialogue facilitation, new forms of education, and relationship building. The subsequent examination in this chapter of recent peacemaking initiatives in the Caucasus and beyond illustrates the rationale for considering social media as a cross-cutting but independent track.

In 2007 Jale Sultanli (from Baku, Azerbaijan) and I (from Yerevan, Armenia) established a U.S.-based IMAGINE Center for Conflict Transformation, a small nongovernmental organization with a focus on peacemaking between Armenians and Azerbaijanis who share an unresolved conflict over Nagorno-Karabakh. Between 2007 and 2010, we organized a number of dialogue meetings, including problem-solving workshops and workshops on historical conciliation for young professionals, a number of conflict resolution and communication skills trainings, and a conference on Nagorno-Karabakh that was held in Boston in cooperation with the Fletcher School of Law and Diplomacy, along with a closed-door workshop with participation of experts and diplomats from both sides. Initially, all the initiatives were conducted behind closed doors, and social media and the Internet were not part of the toolbox. In 2009, IMAGINE held a project-planning meeting in Tbilisi with its program alumni in which the following problems for fostering cross-border dialogue and improvement of relations between Azerbaijani and Armenian societies were identified:

- Closed borders and absence of communication
- Difficulties for peacemakers to have ongoing communication with their colleagues across the border as phone lines between the sides have been cut, and the existing ones are closely monitored by National Security Services

- Absence of freedom of speech and tight government control over media
- Information wars and active cultivation of negative images of the other through education and media
- Stereotypes continuously reinforced and not challenged in the media as well as the Internet
- Widespread zero-sum vision of the conflict
- Absence of platforms for expressing or discussing alternative or pro-peace views and institutional obstacles for creating such platforms
- Peer pressure on peace activists and obstacles created on governmental and societal level, preventing the emergence of a community of peacemakers
- No space for self-critical voices

Considering the antagonistic attitudes of the governments toward cross-border initiatives and oversight of peacemaking activities and the tight government control over media and education, as well as the hostile attitudes in the society toward peacemaking, the aforementioned obstacles have prevented the creation of a peace community of any considerable size for more than two decades since the onset of the conflict.

During the 2009 meeting, the IMAGINE group had determined that social media tools can help to overcome almost all the previously mentioned obstacles. Using social networking sites could help overcome the isolation of societies from each other caused by closed borders and the inevitable high costs of meetings at a neutral territory; the social networking sites and online communication platforms such as Skype could allow regular, ongoing, and less controlled communication for the peacemakers; cross-border partnerships could be formed and sustained with daily and—if needed—hourly communication; online platforms could be created for critical voices and alternative ideas; social media tools can be used to create platforms for peacemakers to communicate, plan joint actions, and simply create an online community not to feel isolated; Twitter could help to communicate and share information on an ongoing basis; in the long term, online programs on peace education could be designed.

The statistics on Internet usage recently also provide encouragement. According to a 2010 report of Internet World Stats, 47 percent of the population of Armenia and 44 percent of the population of Azerbaijan were shown to be Internet users. Even if most of them were not yet actively using social networking sites and social media tools, the trend showed that significant and growing numbers of people could be reached through the Internet.

As a result of the project-planning meeting in 2009, the IMAGINE Center conducted a few social media tools trainings for young social scientists from Armenia and Azerbaijan. The focus was to incorporate social media into peacemaking work. The IMAGINE Center then moved on to creating an online platform: the *Caucasus Edition, Journal of Conflict Transformation,* at www.cau casusedition.net. In the same year, Arzu Geybullayeva, a regional analyst, blogger, and social media expert, joined the IMAGINE Center and further expanded the center's drive to improve the effectiveness of its peacemaking practices by connecting social media and conflict resolution.

The *Caucasus Edition* was created as a forum for Azerbaijani, Armenian, and international scholars, practitioners, policy analysts, novice researchers, and bloggers to provide critical analysis of the Nagorno-Karabakh conflict and explore alternatives for its resolution from diverse perspectives. Each issue features two analytical articles—one from Armenia and one from Azerbaijan (and occasionally from international experts), as well as a number of blog posts and personal reflections on the conflict. The website has an interactive feature and enables online sharing and commenting. From its launch on April 15, 2010, through the end of 2010, the *Caucasus Edition* had published 34 analytical articles by over 25 authors and over 50 blog posts by dozens of authors. The publication has attracted contributions of established researchers and experts but mainly has remained committed to its main goal of incorporating young and alternative voices within the peace process. Therefore, the majority of the authors have been graduate students, young professionals, or peacemakers whose voices in the peace process have not yet been heard.

Eight months after the creation of the *Caucasus Edition* website, by January 2011 the website had on average over 15,000 visitors each month or more than 500 visitors each day. The articles and the newsletters of the *Caucasus Edition* have been actively shared through various academic and other electronic lists, Twitter, Facebook, and other social networking sites.

The editorial board of the *Caucasus Edition* includes three Azerbaijanis, three Armenians, and an American, Susan Allen Nan, a professor at Institute of Conflict Analysis and Resolution of George Mason University. The Armenian and Azerbaijani members of the board have worked closely together daily, using social media tools such as Google Docs and Skype to edit the articles for balance of opinion and bias, providing feedback to the authors and maintaining a regular publication schedule.

Although it is still hard to assess the full impact of the *Caucasus Edition* as it is a young initiative and requires a systemic evaluation, some learning points can be discerned. The project started by navigating uncharted waters: the biggest concern when launching it was that as a jointly managed and openly peace-oriented Armenian-Azerbaijani venture it would be subjected to various pressures and attacks, including from the governments. Yet to our surprise we received only support. In fact, one of the very first articles of the *Caucasus Edition* was republished on the personal webpage of the president of Azerbaijan.[7] A number of leading researchers submitted articles soon after the publication was launched. This showed that the fears of persecution for cooperating with the other side that prevent many from engaging in peacemaking are somewhat exaggerated. That the *Caucasus Edition* survived the first few months encouraged many Armenians and Azerbiajanis who were hesitating in the past to consider engaging in cross-border cooperation, including through writing joint blog posts and articles.

Yet the statistics soon showed that the project, in its initial form, achieved only some of its objectives. The *Caucasus Edition* attracted a flow of Azerbaijani,

Armenian, and international bloggers and analysts concerned with Nagorno-Karabakh conflict and writing to contribute ideas to its analysis and resolution. A number of articles were jointly written by an Azerbaijani and an Armenian. So it became a platform where Armenians and Azerbaijanis who had never even met each other could analyze the conflict and engage in dialogue and joint thinking about the solution to the conflict. At the same time, the project failed to impact larger segments of the targeted societies, as only a small part of the readership initially came from Armenian or Azerbaijan and most of the readers were either from the United States, the UK, Russia, or Turkey. Internal evaluation showed that there were two main reasons for low interest toward the *Caucasus Edition* in Armenia and Azerbaijan. First, there was the language of the publication, which was English only: not many people in these countries spoke it. The second reason was the focus of the publication: while everyone found analysis of the conflict to be an important subject, not everyone was ready to read a strictly analytical publication regularly. These findings prompted the editorial team to consider adjustments.

In November 2010, the *Caucasus Edition* started a News Digest section presenting the summaries of English, Armenian, and Azerbaijani language articles related to Armenian-Azerbaijani relations and Nagorno-Karabakh conflict and peace process. Next, the Russian version of the *Caucasus Edition* was launched in April 2011, as many more people in Azerbaijan and Armenia read Russian than English.

The Neutral Zone—the blog platform of the *Caucasus Edition*—was launched at www.caucasuseditionblog.wordpress.com as a more open environment where the blog posts do not undergo the rigorous editorial process of the *Caucasus Edition*. It was created with the aim to tackle the problem of widely spread misinformation and negative attitudes between conflicting societies and to raise awareness and share information on pressing and critical issues for Armenian and Azerbaijani societies. With the help of social media tools, the Neutral Zone has given voice to an online community with alternative views who want to address deeply embedded stereotypes and contribute to a positive transformation of mutual perceptions. The sections of the Neutral Zone include parallel stories where the authors publish blog posts focusing on similarities as well as differences in both societies on topics such as culture, traditions, education, and health care; parallel posts on sensitive subjects and taboo topics in both societies, such as domestic violence, LGBT rights, minority rights, violence in the army, and the like; video surveys focusing on perceptions and stereotypes of the other in the streets of Azerbaijan and Armenia; an online interactive novel about the future of the region and solution of the conflict, for which readers suggest the story line.

IMAGINE is not the only group which has taken steps toward incorporating social media into peacemaking in the South Caucasus. In 2009 and 2010, a number of initiatives bridging social media and peacemaking appeared and their numbers have been growing as this chapter was written. A series of joint documentaries produced by Conciliation Resources called *Dialogue through Films*, on stories of peace and war, were produced in 2009.[8] Although social media can hardly be credited for the making of the documentaries, in the environment where such films cannot be screened on TV, YouTube, and other websites were the main platform for their dissemination. Other similar projects followed suit, such as two documentaries, *The Passenger* and *Image of Enemy*, sponsored by Eurasia Partnership Foundation as part of its Unbiased Media Coverage project.[9] In April 2010, Vermont-based Project Harmony International organized a conference, "Social Media for Social Change," in Tbilisi, Georgia, where social media experts from around the world and the peacemakers in the Caucasus shared experiences and ideas for contributing to social change using social media tools.[10]

In October 2010, the Eurasia Partnership Foundation organized an e-MediaBias workshop bringing together bloggers from Azerbaijan and Armenia to plan joint cross-border Internet initiatives on promoting mutual understanding and better e-media practices. *Global Voices,* a website that produces regular reports from what bloggers write around the world, has created a "Caucasus Conflict Voices" section producing reports from English language peace-oriented blogs in the Caucasus.[11] In December 2010, the Civil Society Institute (Armenia), Society of Humanitarian Research (Azerbaijan), and Conflict Transformation and Peace-Building Resource Centre in Stepanakert (Nagorno Karabakh) organized a series of video conferences between Armenia, Azerbaijan, and Nagorno-Karabakh called *Let's Peace Jam!*[12] A number of smaller-scale cooperative projects between Azerbaijani and Armenian individuals have also emerged.

Armenians and Azerbaijanis, of course, are not the only ones adopting social media for peacemaking. With the help of social media, peace activists contribute to attitude change, develop alternative ideas for peacemaking, and mobilize peace movements through online platforms that unite people who otherwise are not likely to meet or have a chance to engage in dialogue. Shalom-Salaam, one of the oldest Facebook peace platforms, unites over 3,000 members in its global group interested in discussing and contributing to the Israeli-Palestinian peace process.[13] Shalom-Salaam also has regional Facebook groups where members in a specific city or town coordinate online but also face-to-face events. Facebook itself created a *Peace on Facebook* page[14] where it tracks the number of connections created between people from various conflict regions. According to the page, Israelis and Palestinians, Albanians and Serbians, Indians and Pakistanis, and Turks and Greeks create tens of thousands of connections every day. A Washington, DC-based organization called Soliya, the pioneer in developing software for online dialogue, has been conducting dialogue between universities in the "West" and the "Arab and Muslim World"[15] for a number of years.

Through social media, groups already engaged in peacemaking maximize their impact. Combatants for Peace, an organization that unites Israelis and Palestinians who actively participated in the cycle of violence but later started a peace movement, have a Facebook page with over 2,000 fans and use it to organize and promote events, marches, and roundtables around the world. In 2009, a group of Turkish intellectuals appealed to Armenians through an online petition that became known as the "apology campaign" and that read, "My conscience does not accept the insensitivity showed to and the denial of the Great Catastrophe that the Ottoman Armenians were subjected to in 1915. I reject this injustice and for my share, I empathize with the feelings and pain of my Armenian brothers and sisters. I apologize to them."[16] The campaign gathered more than 30,000 signatories over the Internet.

Various online topical electronic mailing lists are less publicly visible but also a very potent tool that help peacemakers to network, build connections, share ideas, receive firsthand updates about the development in otherwise not easily accessible regions, and simply stay in touch with colleagues from across the conflict divide. The e-mail lists are particularly useful during crisis periods, serving often as a rare reliable connection between peacemakers from conflicting sides. As an example, during the war of August 2008, the number of interactions at the list of the Caucasus NGO forum that unites peacemakers from the Caucasus, including from Georgia and South Ossetia, grew to 147 a month compared to the average of 23 monthly connections during the rest of the same year.[17]

Social media tools are also widely used for organization and mobilization of pro-democracy, anticorruption, and human rights, social justice, and other movements that indirectly contribute to peacemaking.

SOCIAL MEDIA AND CONFLICT ESCALATION

Pro-peace, pro-rights, and prodemocracy movements are not the only ones who benefit from the technological revolution. To quote Shirky again, "falling transaction costs [that facilitate collective action] benefit all groups, not just groups we happen to approve of."[18]

Social media is actively used to identify and intimidate constructive or alternative voices. The Armenians or Azerbaijanis who befriend one another publicly on social networking sites such as Facebook or its Russian version, Odnoklassniki.ru, are often attacked, insulted, and called traitors online by their off-line friends and peers from their own society. Pro-democracy or pro-peace bloggers also get attacked both online and off-line. Any public expression of alternative views, criticism of one's own side, or simply public discussions of critical topics—all necessary components of successful peace process and sustainable coexistence with other groups—are actively discouraged. Anything but repeating the silently agreed-upon lines dictated by government propaganda becomes a taboo, and progress within each society is held hostage to a phenomenon of what an Armenian journalist termed "Shut Up! The Enemy Might Hear You!"[19]

Peacemakers or ordinary citizens are actively intimidated to prevent them from having contacts with the other side. People who have active Internet contacts with the "other side" are under constant surveillance and are subjected to questioning by the security services. Although most cases of such surveillance have understandably remained unpublicized, some cases become public. In 2009, a few dozen Azerbaijanis voted via their cell phones for an Armenian singer on a popular European song contest called Eurovision where both Azerbaijan and Armenia were represented. Soon after, the National Security Ministry of Azerbaijan summoned all 43 of them for questioning, revealing the degree of control and intimidation that exists over any kind of contact or positive interest in the other side. Such measures are not unique to Azerbaijan.

Therefore, the openness provided by social media tools is a double-edged sword. On the one hand, the costs of organization go down, and many more citizens engage in cross-border dialogue and cooperation than was possible before, while many others challenge the stereotypes and taboos and express alternative ideas. On the other hand, the open nature of social media exposes these people to the security apparatus and nationalists in their countries, thus subjecting them to government intimidation and peer pressure. These intimidation tactics then lead to self-censorship and restraint, thereby limiting the newly opened space for alternative opinion or open discussion.

Moreover, social media itself is actively used to promote hatred and xenophobia as well as to counter and intimidate peacemakers. In November 2010, a Yerevan-based NGO, Caucasus Center for Peace-Making Initiatives (CCPR), was planning to hold an Azerbaijani Film Festival in Armenia. After two decades of anti-Azerbaijani propaganda and the dehumanization of Azerbaijanis, the event was surely out of the ordinary, and some backlash could have been expected. Ironically, the Facebook page of the organizers of the Azerbaijani Film Festival itself became a platform to mobilize the Armenian society against the event.[20] The most problematic issue was not the opposition to the festival itself, but the way opposition to the event was voiced. While a few people raised their concerns in a respectful way, the loudest voices directed hundreds of insults and curses toward the organizers, potential attendees, and also Azerbaijani people and culture. Crossing every line, some went further and resorted to threats of physical violence. The trend was not limited to Facebook. It carried over to the blogosphere as well. Here are some quotes from a post of LiveJournal blogger "crazy-patriot":[21] "Grab him [the organizer of the festival] in the streets and break his neck; keep him in a basement for few days hungry, he might come to his senses . . . get him, put into a trunk of a truck, take him to Karabakh and put him into a jail there, let us see how many days he will survive . . . do this instead of 'promoting' his work on Facebook and other sources . . . are we really a nation that cannot 'take care' of such a jerk internally?"[22]

Crazy-patriot was not alone in his or her desire to "take care" of the organizers. The post was reposted on the Facebook page of the film festival on Tuesday, October 26, 2010, at 1:01 p.m. and "liked." Hundreds of other posts followed suit, threatening not only the organizers, but also the writer Lusine Vayachyan who created the event page on Facebook, as well as anyone who supported the idea. The future attendees of the festival were not only labeled "Azerbaijanis" (used as a derogatory term) and "traitors" but were also threatened with being "burned alive along with the organizers," "blacklisted," "taught a lesson," and the like. The Facebook page has also become a place for mass expression of open xenophobia and racism, often in a very proud manner. Someone even signed his post on October 28, 2010, "Respectfully, RACIST and NATIONALIST ARAIK," written in capital letters.

The film festival was ultimately canceled. According to the organizers of the festival, the reason for the cancelation was that the owners and managers of every possible venue where they tried to hold the event were threatened and had to withdraw support for the festival.

Many openly hate-promoting sites also make frequent use of social media, including two mirroring Facebook groups called "I hate Azerbaijan"[23] and "I hate Armenia."[24] Ramil Safarov, an Azerbaijani soldier who during NATO meeting in Budapest killed a sleeping Armenian colleague with an axe simply because he was Armenian, had a fan page that was promoting anti-Armenian messages and received thousands of likes, although it has been eventually removed after numerous protests from Armenians.

More developed and more damaging are the Internet information wars, often well-financed by the governments but also fed by the enthusiasm of armies of "patriots." The propaganda on these sites is subtler, and they are often presented as analytical, news, or historical publications and appear to present factual evidence. Often the factual evidence they appeal to is actually valid, however, the facts are selectively chosen to present one's own side in a positive light and the other in a negative one, thus drawing time and again on the "ideological square" of linguist T. A. Van Dijk, according to which the sides in conflict[25]

1. express/emphasize information that is positive about "us";
2. express/emphasize information that is negative about "the other";
3. suppress/underemphasize information that is negative about "us"; and
4. suppress/underemphasize information that is positive about "the other."

The most disturbing cases of the ideological square in action are the websites explicitly aimed at denying the atrocities committed by one's own side during the conflict. One such example is a website called Khojali: The Chronicle of Unseen Forgery and Falsification.[26] The Khojali massacre, the killing of hundreds of Azerbaijani civilians, was one of the worst atrocities of the 1991–1994 war over Nagorno-Karabakh. The website presents a few interviews intended to suggest that these were not Armenian forces but Azerbaijanis who massacred other Azerbaijanis in Khojali. The website then exposes some unreliable information on some Azerbaijani websites about Khojali to further question the Azerbaijani version of the events. Although all of that information might be worth considering in finding out the full truth about the Khojali massacre, the aim of the website is clearly not the search for truth. The website that fishes out everything that might be questioned in the Azerbaijani version of the event makes no mention of any of the evidence that points out the responsibility of their side, Armenians in this case, for committing the massacre. Yet such evidence is readily available, including reports by respected human rights organizations such as Human Rights Watch and Memorial; the interview of Thomas de Waal with the now president of Armenia Serge Sargsyan[27] where the latter is quoted as explaining why the Armenian forces had committed the massacre, thus indirectly taking responsibility for it; and the memoirs of the brother of a key Armenian military commander during the Karabakh War, Monte Melkonian, who writes that "Khojali had been a strategic goal, but it had also been an act of revenge."[28]

This website is unique in that it is available in Armenian, Azerbaijani, English, French, German, and Russian and thus becomes a potent weapon in the information wars. Most other sites are operating in one or two languages—typically in Azerbaijani and/or Russian or Armenian and/or Russian—yet the line of reasoning typically stays the same. Such websites promote evidence that casts "them" in a negative light and conceal the information that is negative about "us." By doing so, these websites contribute to the formation of a negative image of the other and a self-righteous image of self, reinforcing the negative stereotypes, promoting hostility and intolerance, and contributing to dehumanization of the other and leading the way toward a new cycle of violence.

CONCLUSIONS

Many of the initiatives described in this chapter affect the dynamics of conflicts and perceptions within societies contributing to peacemaking or to conflict escalation. They have implications for collective identities and relations between and within the conflicting sides, and they sometimes influence policy making. Yet almost none of the activities described in this chapter would have been possible just a few years ago. They became possible because the use of social media tools has become widespread.

The costs for creating and managing a joint Armenian-Azerbaijani analytical publication such as the *Caucasus Edition* would have been too high if it was not for the capacity of free blogging platforms such as WordPress, used to create and maintain the website. Should the platform have been created before the advent of Twitter and Facebook, it would have never reached thousands of readers all around the world in just a few months. In comparison, hard-copy free publications with a similar focus in Armenia and Azerbaijan get printed in no more than 200 copies as this is the maximum number of readers to whom publishers are able to distribute. Finally, the cooperative process of a group of Azerbaijani and Armenian editors—who have to work daily on recruiting authors, jointly editing articles and giving joint feedback, coordinating the publication schedule, and disseminating the journal—would not have been possible without Skype, Google Docs, WordPress, Facebook, and Twitter. Many marginalized young professionals with alternative views would hardly find a way to get their voices heard without social media tools and interactive online platforms such as Global Voices or the *Caucasus Edition*. Far fewer students in the West and the Arab and Muslim World would be able to engage in an ongoing dialogue.

Conversely, an Azerbaijani film festival would have taken place quietly in Yerevan, attracting a handful of people without causing a nationwide backlash or exposing widespread anti-Azerbaijani xenophobia in Armenian society.

The impact of social media will, of course, vary greatly from conflict to conflict. It would have a minimal impact, for example, in the war-torn Democratic Republic of Congo where the Internet penetration—according to Internet World Stats—is 0.5 percent, yet might have a much greater influence in Israel where the Internet penetration reaches 71 percent.

Far from suggesting that social media is *the* key to peacemaking or that it affects the conflict dynamics more strongly than politics, economics, traditional media, education, and the like, I want to acknowledge that social media today is a distinct factor that influences the formation and dynamics of personal and societal relations and has a major role in redefining and often defining behavior. Many of the old rules regarding cognitive patterns, group formation, and group action do not apply anymore. This change is not necessarily positive or negative. It is neutral. Yet its patterns and its effects on conflict dynamics are not studied and remain unknown.

Most of the attempts to bridge the worlds of conflict resolution and social media until today have been conducted by individual peacemakers or concerned bloggers. These are the groups who lead the way in attempts to conceptualize the impact of social media advances on conflicts by holding conferences and workshops on the topic. An example of such attempts was a workshop held by International Alert in Brussels in December 2010, where, among other things, a few bloggers and peacemakers, including me, agreed to cooperate on research aimed at understanding the impact of social media on the formation of the images of self and other in conflicts and developing recommendations for increasing the effectiveness of online initiatives working on the promotion of self-critical thinking, tolerance, and deconstruction of stereotypes.

Despite the good intentions, these are localized and short-term initiatives that lack adequate resources or methodology to conduct a long-term study identifying trends and dynamics. There is a need for rigorous studies of the impact of social media on conflict escalation and transformation and for the development of guidelines for more effective use of social media in peacemaking. Learning to effectively engage social media in peacemaking will require a partnership between pioneering practitioners and methodical social scientists. The ground has already shifted. Peacemaking today is treading new ground.

NOTES

1. C. Shirky, *Here Comes Everybody: The Power of Organizing without Organizations* (New York: Penguin Press, 2008).

2. Shirky, *Here Comes Everybody*, 153.

3. Ushahidi is a social media tool that was initially developed to map reports of violence in Kenya after the postelection fallout at the beginning of 2008. It allows any person or organization to set up a method to collect and visualize information using SMS (http://www.ushahidi.com/, accessed January 8, 2011).

4. The author of this chapter was visiting the EU office in Armenia when the representatives were preparing for the meeting in the Armenian parliament to discuss abuses in the army, and they shared that the source of the information was the YouTube videos.

5. Reporters without Borders, "Obama Presses Aliyev to Free Jailed Bloggers," September 27, 2010, http://en.rsf.org/azerbaidjan-supreme-court-refuses-to-hear-18-08-2010,37894.html (accessed January 8, 2011).

6. Institute for Multi-Track Diplomacy, "What Is Multi-Track Diplomacy," http://www.imtd.org/at-a-glance/mission/working-methods/what-is-multi-track-diplomacy/ (accessed January 8, 2011).

7. Gulshan Pasayeva, "Caucasus Edition: Reassessing the Nagorno-Karabakh Conflict in the Aftermath of the Russia-Georgia War," *Azerbaycan Prezidenti,* http://www.president.az/articles/247/print?locale=az (accessed February 8, 2011).

8. Concilliation Resources, "Dialogue through Film Project," http://www.c-r.org/our-work/caucasus/dialogue_through_film.php (accessed January 8, 2011).

9. Eurasia Partnership Foundation, "Unbiased Media Coverage of Armenia-Azerbaijan Relations Project," http://www.epfound.am/index.php?article_id=260&clang=0 (accessed January 8, 2011).

10. Social Media for Social Change, https://sites.google.com/a/ph-int.org/socialmedia2010/ (accessed January 8, 2011).

11. Global Voices, "Caucacus Conflict Voices," http://globalvoicesonline.org/specialcoverage/caucasus-conflict-voices/ (accessed December 8, 2010).

12. From the website of the British Embassy in Armenia, http://ukinarmenia.fco.gov.uk/en/about-us/working-with-armenia/embassy-projects/project-stories/peace-jam (accessed December 8, 2010).

13. The Facebook page of Shalom-Salaam Social Movement can be found at http://www.facebook.com/group.php?gid=2225147640 (accessed December 8, 2010).

14. *Peace on Facebook,* http://peace.facebook.com/ (accessed December 8, 2010).

15. Soliya, http://www.soliya.net/?q=why_we_do_it_overview (accessed December 8, 2010).

16. English-language text of Turkish apology from the official website of the campaign at www.ozurdiliyoruz.com (accessed December 8, 2010).

17. Caucacus Forum, http://groups.yahoo.com/group/Caucasus_Forum/.

18. Shirky, 208.

19. Anahit Shirinyan, http://caucasusedition.net/blog/shut-up-the-enemy-might-hear-you/ (accessed December 9, 2010).

20. The Facebook page of the Azerbaijani Film Festival can be found at http://www.facebook.com/event.php?eid=118393321556010&index=1 (accessed December 9, 2010).

21. http://crazy-patriot.livejournal.com/139595.html (accessed January 8, 2011).

22. Translated from the Armenian by Philip Gamaghelyan.

23. http://www.facebook.com/home.php?sk=group_170382072987153 (accessed December 8, 2010).

24. *I Hate Armenian and Block Page,* http://www.facebook.com/block.armenian.pages.groups (accessed June 16, 2011)

25. T. A. Van Dijk, "Politics, Ideology and Discourse," in *Encyclopedia of Language and Linguistics, Section Language and Politics,* ed. Ruth Wodak, http://www.discursos.org/unpublished%20articles/Politics,%20ideology%20and%20discourse%20(ELL).htm (accessed January 8, 2011).

26. *Xocali,* http://xocali.net/ (accessed December 8, 2010).

27. T. de Waal, *Black Garden: Armenia and Azerbaijan through Peace and War* (New York: New York University Press, 2003).

28. M. Melkonian, *My Brother's Road. An American's Fateful Journey to Armenia* (London: I. B. Tauris, 2008).

CHAPTER 30

Strategic Connectors: Community Strategies for Conflict Prevention in Times of War

Marshall Wallace and Mary Anderson

This chapter will discuss ways in which communities have built upon connectors in strategic ways in order to exempt themselves from conflict even in the midst of war. Based upon a project that has been looking at communities in conflict zones that consciously chose to stay out of the conflicts around them, the chapter will examine strategies around engagement with armed groups and the selection and maintenance of internal identity through connectors.

INTRODUCTION

As the Taliban moved across Afghanistan conquering each successive district, the people in Jaghori recognized that they too would soon be confronted by Taliban troops. A proud community with a strong history of fighting the Soviets, they considered, should they fight the Taliban, or was there another option? They had no intention of bowing down to Taliban rules. They were committed to their own way of worshipping, their own way of life, and their own culture, and they were determined to surrender these to no one. Of particular importance to them was their commitment to female education. A *shura* was called, and over two hundred leaders and representatives met for 10 days. With much consultation among communities, civic groups, and with religious leaders, the *shura* made the decision to approach the Taliban before they arrived and to negotiate a surrender in which they would assure the Taliban that they would not fight but in which they would exact a promise from the Taliban that they could continue to live according to their culture without interference. Over months of Taliban occupation, this community managed—through negotiation and trickery, through engagement and compromise—to maintain the values they shared internally while never succumbing to the Taliban agenda of dominance and rules.

Reflecting on the terrible ethnic battles of the 1990s, people in Sarajevo, Bosnia, say that their fellow countrymen in the city of Tuzla really did not "experience the war—they just did not take part." And the people of Tuzla agree. Even as ethnicity became the defining divider in the violence that consumed the regions of the Former Yugoslavia, Tuzla—as a city of over one hundred thousand people—managed to coalesce around their collective refusal to engage in the agenda of ethnic division. Although attacked by the Serbian army and subject to the propaganda of Bosniak national leaders, they asserted that their identity as Tuzlans was more important than their ethnic labels, and they maintained, as a city and a community, a commitment to interethnic cooperation and governance.

In a number of indigenous Colombian communities, sizable groups organized themselves into peace villages and refused all pressures to ally themselves with either the FARC or the government. Often threatened by violence from the troops of both sides, as well as the paramilitary forces that served the agenda of the government, they developed internal cohesion through systems of governance and communication by which they managed to maintain their separateness from this war that surrounded and, from time to time, invaded them.

In Chidenguele, Mozambique, as the protracted civil war destroyed physical and social infrastructure across the country, people of the Mungoi ancestry followed the decision of their deceased former leader that they should not engage in the violence nor be affected by it. The quite extensive area designated as under the wing of the Spirit of Mungoi maintained agricultural production, kept schools open and functioning, and maintained its road network in spite of the frequent incursions to their area by armed troops of both sides. Further, through the interventions of the Spirit, people in this group were exempted from fighting by the various armed groups and even were returned unharmed when kidnapped by a fighting force.

In Rwanda, as the genocide swept most people up into the fear and tension of violence, the Muslim community (which included Tutsis and Hutus) acted in concert to avoid participating in the killing and instead to rescue many others who were threatened by the *Interhamwe*. They chose to follow the leadership of the imams they admired rather than the political leaderships who urged them to identify as Hutus and Tutsis.

These examples—from Afghanistan, Bosnia, Colombia, Mozambique, and Rwanda—represent a large and as yet uncounted and unrecognized number of communities that, in the midst of their countries' wars, take conscious and collective steps to exempt themselves from participating. These communities, who manage to survive without taking part (or taking sides) as civil war rages around them and all the incentives suggest that they should join, demonstrate collective decisions and actions that challenge the broad international community concerned with conflict prevention. Although these groups do not prevent their countries' wars, they do manage to establish sometimes quite large and significant areas in which everyone, as a community, reject the agenda of the war. These communities do not claim to be pacifists or peace activists. Rather, they assert their separation from "this war" as a pragmatic choice based on calculations of gains and losses rather than as an expression of ideology.

In the following pages, we shall look at some of the experiences of these communities and analyze how they build on *strategic connectors* within their societies as they manage to stay apart from war.

WHERE THE EVIDENCE COMES FROM

Starting in 2002, CDA Collaborative Learning Projects began to collect the stories of such communities when two staff people were working with humanitarian agencies providing assistance in a number of war zones. Although international staff seldom mentioned these groups as significant, local people who themselves had participated, willingly or unwillingly in the war, often talked of a "group, over there, who did not take part in the war." Sometimes they expressed envy and always they expressed puzzlement. How was it that those people were able to avoid the war and not suffer its immediacy when they, the ones referring to the non-war community, did not want to participate but felt they had no choice?

Because such groups were mentioned in country after country, CDA decided to initiate a set of case studies to gather the experiences of these non-war communities and to compare them across contexts and time both to learn about them for their own value and to analyze their experience for its possible relevance to the conflict prevention efforts of the broader international community. If these groups, living in the midst of warfare and, themselves, embodying the divisions of the war, managed somehow not to take part—then it seemed they had in some sense been successful in conflict prevention.

The project was carried on over several years and included studies of 13 communities that, in their context, resisted the incentives that surrounded them to engage in war.[1] Through consultations in which people from the communities—as well as case writers and others—sifted through and compared these experiences, certain common themes were identified and lessons learned.

WHAT THE EVIDENCE SHOWED

The experiences of these non-war communities uniformly showed a cleverness and strategic sense that relied on identification of commonalities that united the community and that distinguished it from the dividers that drove the war. These *strategic connectors*—as we shall call them—will be illustrated through discussion of three areas where they were important in the sections that follow.

A Unifying Non-War Identity

The process of considering and then choosing the option of nonparticipation set these communities on a distinct path differing from those of their neighbors who engaged in their wars. In some way, each non-war group imagined the possibility that engagement was not inevitable or necessary. The process of doing this elicited, and depended on, the articulation of an alternative identity that both united the community around its non-war stance and distinguished it firmly from the identities that drove the conflict.

In Rwanda, the Muslim identity was a natural and immediate one. Isolated from political affairs for many years by successive Rwandan governments, Muslims quite naturally were connected through their faith and its rituals. However, a natural alternative identity is not always sufficient for nonengagement in conflict. It is well documented that many Christian groups, also sharing an identity of faith and ritual, nonetheless followed their Tutsi and Hutu identities as promoted by political leaders rather than their religious identity. Importantly, in this example, the Muslim leadership anticipated that the hate propaganda they constantly heard would, at some point, lead to massive intergroup violence. They therefore undertook a concerted and intense campaign in Friday prayers in the mosques, in Islamic schools, and even through public announcements aired on Rwandan radio, calling on all Muslims to be ready to act as Muslims, rather than as Hutu or Tutsi, if and when the violence began. They asserted the common, uniting identity that connected their community, and they heightened its importance relative to other identities people held. They chose to assert the primacy of the connecting identity that differentiated their community from the divisive identities that defined the war.

In Mozambique, the Spirit of Mungoi, channeled through a medium, insisted that all of his people learn their lineage back four generations on both their mother's and their father's sides, tracing it in relation to the Mungoi identity, in order to show their connection to this community. The Spirit of Mungoi granted his protection for all who could do this recitation of lineage, and perhaps more importantly, the recitation was also accepted as proof of protection by the commanders of armed groups, who had been convinced that Mungoi could exert supernatural powers that threatened the success of their military campaigns.

The unifying identity of the peace villages in Colombia was also natural in one sense in that they were made up of indigenous peoples who had lived on their lands for generations. However, not all indigenous groups identified as peace villages, and not all of them managed to maintain their unity when they were threatened by surrounding armed groups. The process of choosing to stay apart from the war called on their indigenous and landholding identity and reinforced it. Members of these villagers were constantly being threatened or courted by the opposing sides of the war, both of whom wanted to be able to claim the allegiance of the village. During some periods, many rural and disadvantaged groups would have had more identity with the rebel group than with the government. However, the peace villages knew that any show of favoritism toward one side would make them a target for attack by the other side. They also knew that such weakening of their independence was a threat to their landholding in that all sides regularly attempted to displace peasants so that they could take over their land. Thus, to reinforce their collective non-aligned identity, these peace villages eschewed any possible alliance with any side of the war, even requiring that not one of their small shopkeepers could sell a cold drink to a thirsty soldier, lest this be interpreted by the opposing army as showing favoritism.

In all of the non-war communities studied, similar stories were told of their selection and of the reinforcement of their unifying identity. In each case, an identity was chosen that was natural and familiar to the community (i.e., did not require that they adopt some new identity); that differentiated them from the dividers that drove the fighting; and that built on and strengthened values and principles that they held in common. These unifying identities were based on explicitly chosen and articulated strategic connectors.

Normalcy and Tradition

Even as they faced attacks, kidnapping, and sometimes, the death of some of their members, these non-war communities survived through conscious strategies for maintaining cohesion. The choice of a unifying identity was an important step in nonengagement but this choice needed regular and constant reinforcement. Again, these groups made use of strategic connectors in daily life and across time.

Normalcy

When fighting brought widespread destruction to national infrastructure and government services stopped functioning in many parts of the country, these communities developed systems and structures for maintaining some normal government services.

Not surprisingly, in the Jaghori District of Afghanistan, the most important and unifying service to be maintained was education, and under the threat of Taliban restrictions, especially female education even for older girls. Remarkably, this community also managed to start up an electrical cooperative, even as such services disintegrated across many parts of Afghanistan. In Mozambique, the function most important to the community's survival was agricultural production. In Tuzla, many people commented on how important it was, both for internal security and for its symbolism, that the city police force continued to be recruited from all ethnic groups in proportion to their representation in the population and that the police were never assigned paramilitary duties but performed strictly normal police functions.

In Colombia, peace villages focused on keeping open access to markets. Armed groups regularly tried to destroy the economic independence of these groups by erecting blockades or kidnapping traders as they moved from place to place. To address these threats and to ensure continuing economic viability, these peace communities developed strategies that relied on numbers. They organized themselves to travel to market in large numbers, relying on the public relations outcry that they could expect if entire communities were harmed by armed groups. This strategy often worked, and as it did so, this success clearly reinforced the spirits of the peace villages and encouraged continuing collective action.

One reason that providing some government services was important in the strategies of these non-war communities was that the normalcy that these services represented reassured community members of their collective strength and, through this, reinforced their connectedness. Interestingly, these communities also emphasized normalcy in another sphere that, at first, puzzled those of us engaged in reviewing the case studies. People in every community described events such as feasts, sports matches, fairs, and the like, that they planned and enjoyed throughout the war. To us, these activities seemed frivolous and superficial, but in conversations with people in each non-war community, they came up again and again. Finally, from the cumulative commentary on these ceremonies and festivals across countries and contexts, it became clear that events such as these also served to reinforce strategic connectors. They demonstrated that as others in communities around them were falling into distrust and fear, they remained connected both to each other—enjoying each others' company and sharing pleasures—and to their prewar normal life.

Maintenance of normalcy as a community, through government services or events enjoyed collectively, connected these communities to their histories of peace time, to their leadership and governance, and to each other. Again, these connectors had strategic import.

Tradition

Leadership in these communities was often shared, multilayered, and fluid. Leaders played many roles and led in unusually nonhierarchical ways by consultation more than by decree. Nonetheless, certain individuals did assume roles that the community recognized and welcomed as important to their collective identity. And contrary to a widely held assumption that conflict prevention requires new leaders with new skills, these non-war leaders were uniformly already in place prior to the crisis. That is, new leaders did not emerge to guide these communities to take the unusual step of exempting themselves from conflict. Traditional, preexisting leaders were the leaders that communities knew and trusted.

It should be said that not all preexisting leaders were equal, however. In many locations, through varying processes, these communities anointed some leaders to take them forward in their non-war strategies and rejected others whom they also knew. Those who were chosen by their communities (often informally, though sometimes through an election) seemed to have been chosen as a link to the known and trusted past but also because of the ways in which they led. To take the risks of nonparticipation in a war that raged around them, a community needed to trust that its leaders were reliable and knowledgeable and "durable," as a non-war community in Nigeria said.

One connector that these effective leaders used, therefore, was to call on tradition. Even as the community stuck out on an unfamiliar and risky path of nonengagement, these leaders regularly reminded people of experiences and values from their past that laid the groundwork for this decision. In a real sense, these claims were often disingenuous. Many of these communities had been active participants in previous wars, and most of them had explicitly considered the option of fighting even in this war before choosing the non-war path. Mungoi and other figures who became the reference point for their support of non-war had often been known historically as great warriors.

Nonetheless, the leadership of the effective non-war communities reviewed through this project strategically chose from their community's past those elements of traditional values and actions that buttressed the decision that the community now took. They cited tradition as it justified their nontraditional choices. In this, again, these communities made choices about their connectedness to their past that provided a sense of continuity and logic. And this shared sense of historical continuity, again, represented another form of strategic connector that helped these communities maintain cohesion in the face of threats.

Interaction with Armed Groups

Finally, each of the non-war communities studied also made strategic connections with the armed groups that surrounded and often threatened them.

As the case study project began, some people speculated that the communities we would study would be found to be militarily irrelevant. That is, their apparent success in avoiding involvement in war would be explained by the fact that they were either geographically remote or sufficiently small that they escaped attention from armed groups or that they were strategically unimportant in the agenda of the war. Further, people in a number of war zones have reported on the processes by which they unwillingly became embroiled in their country's civil war. Some have said that they hoped that by keeping quiet on the issues that drove the war, they could avoid being noticed and thus be able to sit it out. Others have said that, as war waged around them, they finally concluded that they must align themselves with one side in order to gain the protection afforded by its armies and/or in order to protect some value or ideal they believed in that was represented more by one army than the other.

The experiences of these non-war communities showed that they followed an entirely different and surprising strategy. In every case, as it made its choice not to fight, the community leadership went to talk with the various armed groups. They did not hide and hope to be ignored. They did not attempt to appear acquiescent in order to appease the fighters. With the exception of Muslims in Rwanda, they did they try to talk the armed groups out of fighting.

Instead, they went public with their non-war stance. They engaged the armed groups directly and openly. Every community took the initiative to negotiate with the armies early in their decision to not participate, and many did so regularly as the war continued. Occasionally these negotiations succeeded in establishing safety for the non-war community. Often they failed to achieve the specific agreement the community sought.

Even when they were unsuccessful about a specific point, however, these interactions seemed to force the armed groups to acknowledge the legitimacy of the non-war community. Through the very act of engaging armed commanders and getting these military people to engage with them, the communities signaled several important things. First, they indicated that they had no intention of fighting against the armed group and, by this, established a level of confidence. Second, they conveyed the message that they would not join this group and its agenda, but they did this in a way that asserted their human equality with the fighters in spite of their military inferiority in relation to them. Third, they clarified the values and issues that mattered most to them even though, in doing this, they exposed the areas where they were in disagreement with the agenda of the armed group and in which they were most vulnerable.

In one Colombian village, the community determined that they would completely exclude all arms within a certain perimeter. They sent this message to the armed groups in the area and erected a small, wire fence to delineate the boundary. Within a short time, armed men crossed this fence carrying guns in direct denial of the community's ruling. The community responded by moving the fence a bit farther into the village. Again, soldiers violated the space. To maintain its own right to set rules and demand that they be followed—but recognizing their inability to enforce their will on the armed group—the villagers then ruled that, although weapons were allowed within the perimeter, they could not be used.

As people in this village told this story, they did so to show how they were willing to compromise and adjust their strategies when the strategy did not work, but how they also managed to continue to engage the armed men in the negotiation regarding arms in the village in a way in which they finally prevailed. They did not claim that the armed group would never fire a weapon inside their village, even after this chess game of where weapons could be allowed, but they did feel as if they had managed to gain a recognition of their position from this armed group.

In Afghanistan, the Jaghori leadership proactively traveled to three areas where the Taliban leadership was headquartered (a national headquarters, a regional headquarters, and a religious headquarters) to negotiate their position before the Taliban troops arrived in Jaghori. The reason they gave for undertaking negotiations in these three locations was that they knew the Taliban leadership was not monolithic, and they wanted to see which of these headquarters would give them the best deal. In their negotiations, they told the Taliban that they would surrender their arms in return for assurances that they could maintain the values of their community. In particular, as we noted previously, they insisted that they be allowed to continue female education. The Taliban uniformly refused. The Jaghori indicated that they would continue to press for this compromise. The Taliban said they would allow primary education for both boys and girls but that young women would be forbidden to have secondary education. The Jaghori said they would continue to press for even higher female education. Over the years of Taliban occupation, the Jaghori did continue to educate their female children of all ages, finally gaining the complicity of the Taliban education officer who had been placed in Jaghori through offering to help him build his house and implicitly threatening that they could not ensure his physical safety if the people of the area really did not like him. This man became a tacit ally of the Jaghori in that he would warn them if a Taliban delegation were coming to visit the area so that the community could hide the fact that they still educated their girls of all ages.

Even in Rwanda, where direct negotiations with the *Interhamwe* were impossible, the Muslim community did not hide its position of noninvolvement. As noted, they publicly announced their refusal to engage in mosques, in schools, and even on national radio broadcasts.

As the preceding stories show, the engagement of non-war communities with their surrounding militaries involved direct negotiation and trickery, confrontation, and co-optation. In addition, many of the 13 communities included by this project maintained an open hospitality policy, welcoming all who wanted to come into their space so long as they did not bring their weapons or, as in the case of Colombia, use their weapons within the community.

In Mozambique, Mungoi's people consistently made clear that all people were welcome to come into their community for sustenance and rest. The Spirit also was reputed to be able to use his supernatural powers to trace lost and displaced people, and many people told stories about how he had reunited families within his territory. Former fighters in the Mozambican war tell how they would come to the Chidenguele District and leave their weapons at the border to go in to obtain food or to ask Mungoi for a favor of some kind. The Muslims in Rwanda also saved the lives of many of their neighbors by hiding them in their own homes, feeding them, and helping smuggle them to safety.

The non-war communities simultaneously guarded their identity that connected them internally as critical to the maintenance of cohesion under threat and, at the same time, established strategic connectors with others outside the community through engaging armed groups and welcoming anyone to enjoy their hospitality. Even as they set themselves apart from the agenda of the war, these communities used connectors beyond themselves to buttress strategically their positions of nonengagement.

CONCLUSION

The experiences of the non-war communities studied through this CDA project are complex and fluid—far more so than can be captured in this brief chapter. They differ across contexts and types of wars, and the strategies each pursued are embedded in each community's own history and circumstances. Even so, certain characteristics showed up across all contexts that suggest successful patterns for separating from war. The communities, themselves, do not claim to be models of conflict prevention. In interviews, the people of these communities often expressed surprise that their experiences would be of interest to anyone other than themselves. Most reflected on their choices and strategies modestly, often saying what they did was "only natural."

Still, as one looks at broad experiences in civil wars and listens to the stories of many people, the fact that these groups considered options and imagined that they could decide *not* to engage suggests this possibility to others.

Minimally, the experiences of these communities shows that normal communities have efficacy beyond that usually imagined in the context of politically charged environments. Choices can be made and strategies can be found that avoid the prevalent dividers of conflict and, instead, identify and build on—and even create—strategic connectors.

NOTE

1. The 13 case studies were conducted in communities in the following countries: Afghanistan, Bosnia-Herzegovina, Burkina Faso, Colombia, Fiji, India, Kosovo, Mozambique, Nigeria, Philippines, Rwanda, Sierra Leone, and Sri Lanka. The learning project was funded by German Church Development Service (EED), Ministry of Foreign Affairs of Denmark, Netherlands Ministry of Foreign Affairs (BUZA), Royal Norwegian Ministry of Foreign Affairs, and Swedish International Development Cooperation Agency (SIDA).

CHAPTER 31

Social Entrepreneurship: Paving the Way for Peace

Ryszard Praszkier and Andrzej Nowak

There are multiple paths to peace, some direct, in which issues of peace are addressed head-on; others indirect, which involve building preconditions for peace. One example of the direct approach is the ICT for Peacebuilding initiative (ICT4Peace),[1] an electronic fundraising and communications platform created by young people for the purpose of engendering support for various global peacebuilding initiatives. The indirect approach is observed in the far-reaching effect of international or intercultural exchange programs, which influence the mindsets not only of the participants but also, through a ripple effect, reach an extended audience; moreover, researchers found that the impact on secondary participants (chaperones, host families, and students and teachers in host schools) is greater than on direct participants (Olberding and Olberding 2010).

This chapter will address the indirect approach as demonstrated by the work of social entrepreneurs, who successfully address various pressing social problems by building social capital,[2] that is, by enhancing trust and preparedness for cooperation. Social capital, in the long run, contributes to peace: according to Bar-Tal (2000), the long-term peacemaking process requires the formation of relations based on mutual trust and acceptance, cooperation, and consideration of mutual needs.

Dr. Arnold Noyek,[3] a peace activist in the Middle East, provides an excellent illustration of how to pave the way for peace in the high-conflict-potential area. Under his tutelage, Arab and Israeli medical students and faculty work to promote health in the entire region. The strategy is to focus solely on medical issues, to the exclusion of all other concerns, including underlying political conflicts, unless those issues surface as a result of the group process. He reports[4] that at the outset of the joint Arab-Israeli seminars participants are usually extremely biased and negative, but when common goals are identified, a healing process ensues, and eventually leads to a shared-implementation phase. In the end, most participants are visibly moved when they express their regrets at initially expressing such aggressive, confrontational attitudes toward each other. This change influences others and spreads, palpably transforming mindsets over the conflict. Noyek also sponsors articles in professional medical journals, such as the *Lancet*, which focus on Arab–Israeli cooperation and peacebuilding through health initiatives (Noyek et al. 2005; Skinner et al. 2005).

We show that this sort of social-capital-building is also preventive with regard to potentially destructive latent conflicts. Our methodology uses a dynamical approach to analyzing social-change processes. It focuses on altering the equilibriums achieved by groups or societies (attractor theory) and the diffusion of change through employing growing novelty-clusters (bubbles theory). Our point of departure is an exploration of the phenomenon of social entrepreneurship and the social-change dynamics that it facilitates. Next we present the concept of sociopsychological preconditions for peace, and, finally, we provide case studies of social entrepreneurs paving the way for peace. We conclude with recommendations drawn from these cases.

SOCIAL ENTREPRENEURS

Social entrepreneurs address, mostly with extraordinary success, seemingly unsolvable social problems. In so doing, they not only manage to motivate the key players and influence people's mindsets but also generate a huge impact on the social landscape. They often trigger a bottom-up process, a sort of chain of change, involving and empowering groups or societies as a whole (Praszkier and Nowak 2012). There is an increasing interest in the field of social entrepreneurship (Brinckerhoff 2000; Gentile 2002; Leadbeater 1997; Martin and Osberg, 2007; Steyaert and Hjorth 2006). In the past decade, the field of social entrepreneurship has made a popular name for itself on the global scene as a new phenomenon that is reshaping the way we think about social-value creation (Mair, Robinson, and Hockerts 2006). The term *social entrepreneur* has sparked the interest of major foundations and private funders, spreading rapidly throughout the nonprofit sector (Kramer 2005).

Most authors (e.g., Dees 1998; Martin and Osberg 2007) see social entrepreneurs as playing the role of change agents in the social sector; they describe social entrepreneurship as:

- Adopting a mission to create and sustain social value; targeting underserved, neglected, or highly disadvantaged populations
- Recognizing and relentlessly pursuing new opportunities to serve that mission
- Engaging in a process of continuous innovation, adaptation, and learning
- Exhibiting a total commitment to their ideas of social change

- Acting boldly without being limited by resources currently at hand
- Exhibiting a heightened sense of accountability to the constituencies served and for the outcomes created
- Aiming at large-scale, transformational benefits that accrue either to a significant segment of society or to society at large.

Most definitions (e.g., Alvord, Brown, and Letts 2004; Bornstein 1998) of social entrepreneurs emphasize the innovative character of their initiative, indicating that social entrepreneurs:

- Open new possibilities by introducing innovative ideas
- Combine visions with down-to-earth realism
- Are creative and highly ethical problem-solvers

Ashoka: Innovators for the Public, operating since 1980, is known as the leading global association identifying, empowering, and linking social entrepreneurs in more than 70 countries. Ashoka's Founding CEO, William (Bill) Drayton, is credited with having coined the term *social entrepreneurship* (Hsu 2005; Sen 2007), which is considered the most comprehensive definition (e.g., Bornstein 2004). The selection criteria for Ashoka fellows are (Drayton 2002, 2005; Hammonds 2005):

- Having a new idea for solving a critical social problem
- Being creative
- Having an entrepreneurial personality
- Envisioning the broad social impact of the idea
- Possessing an unquestionable ethical fiber[5]

In sum, social entrepreneurs produce small changes in the short term that reverberate through existing systems, ultimately effecting significant change in the longer term (Ashoka 2000). This sort of change process merits taking a closer look, with a special focus on questioning what makes the change durable.

SOCIAL CHANGE FACILITATED BY SOCIAL ENTREPRENEURS

Social entrepreneurs, in a way, operate against the natural tendency of social systems to drift back toward a previously established stable state, regardless of actions taken to thwart this process. This stable state is called an attractor, which, metaphorically, attracts the system's behavior, so that even very different starting states tend to evolve toward the subset of states defining the attractor (Vallacher et al. 2010).

Social entrepreneurs often deal with protracted, insurmountable social conflicts or problems. The conflicts at some stage become a self-organizing structure (see Kauffman 1995, for discussion of self-organization), where different elements support each other. The adaptive structures generated around those situations over time, in a feedback loop, become self-perpetuating and counteract efforts toward change; they serve as equilibriums or attractors, preserving the status quo. Addressing such situations head-on with direct conflict-resolution or peace-building approaches usually fails, as the dynamics of the attractor, in the longer run, cause the situation to revert to the initial state. The effects of direct attempts to change the current state of a protracted conflict, even if successful, are likely to be short lived.

True change can be created by building new attractors toward which the system will naturally tend to drift, rather than by temporarily disrupting the state of a system within its old equilibrium (Nowak and Lewenstein 1994; Vallacher and Nowak 2007). In other words, creating positive attractors is often more successful than pushing for peace head-on. This means that the challenge would be to create a situation where peace becomes a collateral benefit, sneaking up on the parties involved before they realize it.

Computer simulations have documented that during social transitions, clusters (bubbles) of "new" appear and grow in the sea of "old" (Nowak and Vallacher 2000; Nowak, Vallacher, and Urbaniak 2005; Vallacher et al. 2010). The new attractors built by social entrepreneurs become the "bubbles of new in the sea of old," that is, bubbles of social capital, spreading and changing societal attitudes.

Social entrepreneurs find innovative ways to circumvent the intractable social problems or conflicts and to build areas of cooperation and trust "somewhere else" (Praszkier, Nowak, and Coleman 2010). For example, Noyek intentionally refrains from encouraging his mixed groups of Arab and Israeli medical students and faculty members to focus on issues of conflict and peace. Instead, he builds islands of cooperation "somewhere else," that is, around health. Students learn to cooperate, listen to each other, and share problems; finally, they start perceiving each other as individuals, not only as Arabs or Israelis. In a natural way, as this process evolves, the hurtful issues become a source of reconciliation, with students often finding themselves with tears in their eyes and asking themselves: What on earth have we been doing? Why did we hate each other? The real reconciliation appears indirectly, as a result of the new positive attractor employed outside the conflict area. In the following sections we will take a closer look at what it means to create a peace-supporting environment, enabling the appearance of new positive attractors.

SOCIOPSYCHOLOGICAL PRECONDITIONS FOR PEACE

Building a new attractor means creating a new, peace-supporting environment. Thus, the essential challenge is to transform the sociopsychological context so that it becomes a peace-enforcing environment (Lederach 2003; Miall 2004).

This approach would support the notion of "conflict transformation" rather than "conflict resolution" narrowly defined (Lederach 1996). The process must include the entire social and cultural context (Lederach 1996, 2003) and could be defined as perceiving and approaching the conflict dynamics as an opportunity for creating constructive change—in other words, envisioning conflict positively, as a natural phenomenon that creates potential for constructive growth (Lederach 2003). As such, the interaction becomes a process of engaging with and transforming relationships and interests (Miall 2004); conflict may thus be seen as an opportunity for change and become constructive. Similarly, from the dynamical point of view, true change could be created by building new attractors toward which the system will naturally tend to drift; this could be achieved by initiating small changes in the basic rules of interactions among people and groups, which can result in significant changes on the macro level over time (Praszkier et al., 2010).

Transforming conflict and creating an enabling environment for peace to materialize is especially essential vis-à-vis the social implications of a conflict that extends beyond the particular site of conflict per se (Miall 2004). Intractable conflicts in societies lead to developing a specific sociopsychological infrastructure, which includes collective memory, an ethos of conflict, and collective emotional orientations (Bar-Tal 2007). Societal beliefs (providing a collective narrative and a sense of what is unique to the society) are the basic components of collective memories and an ethos of conflict.

Research has confirmed that social entrepreneurs pursue their mission, whatever that may be, through building social capital, that is, trust and readiness for cooperation (Praszkier et al. 2009). This means that they succeed in creating a new, cooperative, trustful environment, often circumventing the areas of conflict (Praszkier et al. 2010). In the long run, this new environment also becomes transformative with regard to the properties of the conflict situations, making conflict irrelevant over time. The new, peace-enabling environment, through being advantageous, modifies the societal beliefs (narratives) into stories of success and future growth opportunities.

CONFLICT PREVENTION

Conflict prevention is an important dimension of this approach. While some conflicts are fully developed, visible, and obvious to all involved, in many situations, the conflict lurks, unseen, just below the surface. Protracted social problems often create high-risk areas for potential conflict, as there are usually multiple tensions involved. Social entrepreneurs, through building areas of trust and cooperation, are responsible for indirectly defusing those potential conflicts. In this way, social capital built by social entrepreneurs becomes a preventive force with regard to the conflict's potential outbreak. Following are some case studies illustrating this process:

Dr. Yehudah Paz, Israel

Social entrepreneur Dr. Yehudah Paz[6] is building islands of peace in the Middle East region—a place where distrust is the basic currency of cross-ethnic relationships. His core conviction is that mere conflict resolution is not enough, given that peace leaves a void, which is very often difficult to bear for people used to war, especially if they see no other prospects. Based on this philosophy, he is involving partners drawn from clashing groups in profitable joint ventures; through cooperating in these ventures, Israelis and Arabs experience the great benefits engendered by joining forces. Dr. Paz's ideas for joint ventures result in a peace imbued with new prospects based on trust and success. Not only are new enterprises blossoming, but a secondary effect is the empowerment of Arab women, who find themselves in the forefront of building a new economy for their families and their community. The joint Israeli–Arab approach is reflected in the structure of his organization, whose most active leader is an Arab woman, who not only seeds the new concepts, but also serves as a model for change. By building bubbles of trust and cooperation, Dr. Paz is also preventing the potential outbreak of dormant conflicts between the two communities.

Dr. Paz's efforts began in the Negev Desert, involving Bedouins, Arabs, and Israelis, and they are taking root in the entire Middle East, as well as in Sri Lanka, Kenya, China, and South Africa. He calls his approach an *integrated development*, combining trust, cooperation, and economic growth with education and orientation toward peace, yielding a widespread ripple effect, leading to his characterization of the phenomenon as *exponential spread*.

Krzysztof Czyżewski, Poland

In many places around the world, cross-ethnic, cross-religious, and cross-cultural conflicts are impeding economic development and fueling poverty, which in a feedback loop, accelerates conflicts. Krzysztof Czyżewski, a social entrepreneur from Poland,[7] has demonstrated that the attempt to overcome deeply ingrained cross-border and cross-religious prejudices can be far more effective when addressed through a variety of small, community-based initiatives rather than by tackling the issues head-on (e.g., through lecturing or patronizing members of the society). On the Polish–Lithuanian–Belarus border, a previously economically disadvantaged area, potential conflicts were brewing, each group blaming the other for ongoing setbacks. Czyżewski, operating in this area, focused on restoring the its historical roots; he encouraged children to publish a local chronicle, publicizing their efforts in collecting and exhibiting old postcards and photos and tracing the multi-ethnic history of the place. The historic Catholic, Jewish, Greek Orthodox, and Protestant roots in the region were thereby rescued from obscurity and disseminated throughout the community.

Other initiatives involve teaching traditional crafts and cross-cultural music lessons, where young people discuss the history and meaning of various traditions. Moreover, local youth, previously troublemakers and in conflict with the mainstream society, are now involved in reviving the indigenous Jewish folk music, and playing in a klezmer orchestra that performs locally and abroad. By transforming young people's perceptions and roles within communities scarred by historical divides, Czyżewki is creating a new vision for the future. His brand of entrepreneurship shows how many small initiatives can accumulate and foster a shift in the collective mindset of a community, which eventually engenders social and economic development.[8] This approach prevented the potential outbreak of underlying cross-ethnic conflicts.

ASAD DANISH, AFGHANISTAN

Asad Danish[9] is operating in Afghanistan and the Pashto tribal belt. He is bringing harmony and education through publishing and disseminating resources to illiterate people through radio transmissions. He is mostly recognized for his publishing house, Danish Publication Association, which prints learned books, and Pashto translations of books, encyclopedias, and magazines.

The foundation of Danish's idea for social innovation is the creation of educational hubs based in small-town libraries in Afghanistan (mostly located in schools for girls and boys); he created the concept of the *dynamic librarian*, enhancing the role of librarians and empowering them to spread reading circles to promote education in local communities. To provide educational resources on various levels, Danish's publishing association donates diverse books and magazines to those libraries. Moreover, he is establishing an FM radio frequency, which broadcasts local news and promotes Afghan culture and literature.

Through this approach, Danish is building bubbles of harmony and peace, especially around the dynamic libraries, where people are gathering, reading, exchanging thoughts, and learning about other cultures. The impact goes far beyond education, promoting peace, understanding of other cultures, and tolerance.

CONCLUSIONS

Protracted, insurmountable, and pressing social problems are usually areas at risk for conflict. Addressing those problems in a way that empowers groups and societies (through launching a bottom-up process of building social capital and, as a result, economic growth) becomes highly effective in decreasing the likelihood of outbreaks among groups in conflict. Social entrepreneurs address intractable social problems where various underlying potential conflicts are threatening to break through the surface. They are finding solutions that build trust and preparedness for cooperation. And through this approach, they are fostering economic growth based on a given community's own areas of potential. This tactic paves the way, often indirectly, for peace, enabling people to become optimistic and self-reliant, and to become aware of opportunities that cooperation can bring. And finally, the new socioeconomic infrastructure enables and augments peace.

This process requires the capacity for specific social empathy and the ability to build on people's potential (as opposed to imposing external solutions). It has been documented that social entrepreneurs avoid methods that do not build social capital, such as relying on external experts (Praszkier et al. 2009).[10] Social empathy also indicates a deep understanding of the existing and potential social process, as well as an ability to walk in the shoes of the target groups and societies (Zablocka-Bursa, forthcoming); for example, social entrepreneurs often spend a considerable amount of time with the groups or communities as insiders, so that they know through direct experience about their dreams, pains, desires, prejudices, history, needs, and areas of potential.

The social-capital-building approach to solving potentially high-conflict situations merits further exploration; moreover, it may be an important component of the curriculum for training future social activists involved in preventing manifestations of conflict. The training process could include a dynamical approach to analyzing social processes, as well as the use of computer modeling to enhance our understanding without experimenting on the real social fabric. An example of the latter may be computer modeling of the processes involved in potential segregation around ethnic issues ("Schelling's Segregation Model," Schelling, 1978).[11] The conclusion may extend even further to establishing special educational programs for conflict prevention.

Social empathy could be an important element of this sort of training curriculum, and it could be developed through field visits aimed at analyzing and identifying the latent tendencies and capacities of target groups and communities. A good example may be the way a social entrepreneur defused potential conflicts in an underserved, backward, and change-resistant community in Poland by uncovering, through field research, collective memories and historical documentation of a long-buried tradition of community bazaars, linking and bonding people, including the making and selling of handicrafts and offering public performances by community members. Resurrecting this sort of community-bazaar tradition, especially through involving the older citizens in brainstorming and the younger ones in implementation, launched a durable social process triggering various other initiatives and turning the previously lethargic community into an enterprising one.

As mentioned before, after conflicts break out and become intractable, the dynamics lead to developing a specific sociopsychological infrastructure, which influences the mindsets and, in a feedback loop, reinforces the conflict. The preventive approach pursued by social entrepreneurs triggers a bottom-up process leading to an alternative sociopsychological infrastructure, reinforcing peace and peace narratives and, as a result, diminishing the likelihood of an outbreak of accruing conflicts. It may be an important topic for future research to identify potential (dormant and lurking) conflicts in various communities and to capture the process of circumventing them through building alternative peace-enforcing attractors.

NOTES

1. See: https://ict4peace.wordpress.com/tag/peace-direct/.
2. Social capital understood according to Putnam (1993).
3. See: www.ashoka.org/fellow/anoyek.
4. Retrieved from an interview conducted by one of the authors of this chapter, Ryszard Praszkier, PhD, who worked for Ashoka for more than 15 years, providing second-opinion reviews of candidates for Ashoka fellowship.
5. See: Ashoka selection criteria explained: http://www.ashoka.org/support/criteria.

6. See: http://www.nisped.org.il/.

7. See: www.ashoka.org/fellows/krzysztof_czyzewski.

8. Krzysztof disseminated the Borderline Foundation's approach to many regions of conflict in central and eastern Europe, the Caucasus, and central Asia.

9. See: www.ashoka.org/fellow/5684.

10. Research conducted on the cohort of Polish social entrepreneurs, N°=52, in comparison with a group of leading social activists, N°=52.

11. See also a demo at: http://vimeo.com/1904652.

CHAPTER 32

Gang Intervention in the United States: Legal and Extra-Legal Attempts at Peacemaking

SpearIt

Before we can figure out what to do about gangs or what types of policies and interventions might be most effective, we need to devise analytic strategies that help us chart the real gang landscape and not just distorted images of it.
—Andrew V. Papachristos from "Interpreting Inkblots"

GANG INTERVENTION: FROM THEORY TO PRACTICE[1]

The concept of intervention refers to a third party that interferes or comes between the affairs of two other parties, whether by invitation or by force. In gang interventions, the idea is to "stop or prevent violence between gangs and the concurrent redirection of individual gang members and their families."[2] Typically, forceful intervention is designated as suppression, which takes place at the hands of law enforcement, courts, legislation, and corrections. Suppressive strategies, "loosely based on deterrence principles, have dominated gang interventions for a quarter century."[3] There are various types of gang intervention, including psychological, contextual, and criminal justice-based.[4] More broadly, social intervention involves utilizing socially oriented programming like the YMCAs and Boys' and Girls' Clubs as a means of gang intervention.[5] Community-based gang intervention "combines proactive and reactive approaches to improve the quality of life of communities," work primarily defined as violence-reducing and peace-promoting.[6] There is also general prevention, which may also be seen as a form of intervention. Many programs that attempt to reduce gang activity focus on a combination of prevention, community-based intervention, and suppression.

Trends in criminal justice demonstrate the law's attempts at intervention. In general, jurisdictions have relied on suppressive intervention such as gang injunctions, street sweeps, loitering laws, and curfew, among other forms of suppression. For example, California's influential STEP Act imposes significant sentence enhancements for those falling under the statutory definition of a gang,[7] while policing tactics concentrate on "hot spots"[8] and mandatory solitary confinement follows validation as a gang member. These laws and policies attempt to combat gang problems through legalistic mechanisms of control. The efficacy of these tactics is debatable, but their intended goal is to disrupt gangs, stem the violence, and deter individuals from associating with gangs—even if through sheer force or intimidation. In the case of the STEP Act, the prosecutorial bar is low, and a prosecutor does not even have to prove that one is a member of a street gang—active participation with one suffices for statutory purposes.[9]

Balancing suppression (cops/courts/corrections) and intervention (community) is not an easy task, and meta-analysis in gang research suggests that successful intervention strategy depends on a combination of both efforts. Although in theory, striking a proper balance between these forces is possible, in practice this has proven elusive. While there have been several major projects to integrate community and policing efforts, conclusions regarding their effectiveness do not exist as the programs were not properly evaluated.[10] Yet Papachristos has argued that doing something about gangs is more important than definitional disputes for "even the most well implemented gang strategies are rarely subject to rigorous evaluation."[11] As a guide to moving forward with what data are available, the Bureau of Justice Assistance has advocated three broad programmatic approaches that give a succinct outline of idealized gang intervention programming:

- Develop strategies to discourage gang membership.
- Provide avenues for youth to drop out of gangs.
- Empower communities to solve problems associated with gangs through collaboration with law enforcement, parents, schools, youth, businesses, religious and social service organizations, local government officials, and other community groups in a comprehensive, systematic approach.[12]

EFFORTS IN CRIMINAL JUSTICE

This alienation cannot be overcome by government anti-gang programs, a few jobs, better schools or "zero tolerance" police tactics. Some of these policies produce good effects, some bad, but most are irrelevant to solving the real problems of the underclass . . . And given the entrenched nature of inequality worldwide, I repeat, today's gangs are not going away soon no matter what we do.

—John M. Hagedorn from
A World of Gangs

The legal suppression of gangs is the preferred method of intervention among U.S. politicians. Technically, the aim of these efforts, however, is not necessarily to make peace between warring factions inasmuch as to make peace in the community—to stop the violence using other forms of the same. Whether by increasing law enforcement and patrols or developing gang squad units, the law can lay a heavy hand on gangs when it wishes.

The law also thrusts its force on gangs via legislation that targets gang membership for enhanced sentences. Anti-gang laws essentially make status as a gang member an aggravating factor for some crimes. Further, cities in California have championed the use of civil injunctions against gangs in public spaces, subjecting the mere presence of alleged gang members in public spaces to criminal liability for violation.[13] In courts, procedural barriers can hinge on gang membership. More specifically, prosecutorial allegations of gang membership can significantly increase bail amounts, leading to pretrial incarceration that inhibits an alleged gang member's ability to mount a proper defense.[14] In some jurisdictions, the prosecutor's allegation is granted tremendous deference, especially since the charges are based on "intelligence" collected by police officers, typically a system of data collection without rhyme or reason, which, among other problems, assumes that gang members never leave the gang.[15] Howell's study asked defense attorneys to attest to the accuracy of prosecutorial allegations of gang membership made against their clients. Of the 90 percent of defense attorneys who responded, less than 4 percent could attest to the accuracy of the allegation that "alleged gang members were active gang members."[16] Indeed, there was no evidentiary review of gang affiliation in 80 percent of cases where gang allegation was made in connection with high bail requests.[17]

Correctional facilities have added punitive burdens for validated gang members, who are likely to spend time in solitary confinement as result of validation. Such special lockdown conditions for gang members are widespread nationwide, yet there is no evaluation research of the effects of this technique.[18] However, the empirical literature on solitary confinement has painted an ominous picture when describing its negative effects on inmates. In many prisons, this confinement is typically 22 to 23 hours a day in an 8- by 10-foot cell, with breaks every other day for exercise and showers. One study on California prisons describes how these units produced a "deleterious effect on the mental health of all prisoners."[19] In solitary confinement, "prisoners with preexisting psychiatric disorders are at even greater risk of suffering psychological deterioration while in segregation."[20] This environment is known to induce intense rage and disorientation in prisoners.[21] Often death is the final act, as another California study shows how segregated inmates are prone to suicide; in 2003, 74 percent of all inmate suicides took place in solitary units.[22] These statistics might prompt one to ponder whether there is any connection between these negative outcomes and mandatory solitary confinement for validated gang members.

The banishment of validated gang members to supermax solitary units illustrates how law enforcement, legislation, and corrections have built a cottage industry around their concept of *gang*. Yet as scholars and researchers have opined, there is nothing close to a consensus of agreement in what determines a gang itself.[23] Even though criminal justice has dramatically upped the stakes for those alleged to be gang members, academics are still uncertain whether criminality is a predicate of what a gang entails.[24] These shortcomings have played out practically, and Howell has noted that "the basis for the allegation is not tested and defendants who face these allegations are often incarcerated when they would otherwise be released because the 'gang' label invokes fear of violence and organized crime."[25] More drastically, the tactics disproportionately burden minorities when conducted under implicit biases in law enforcement and the "refusal to recognize primarily Caucasian groups as gangs, even when they clearly meet the provisions [of law]."[26]

CULTURAL IMPACTS

> As I read on I felt the words seeping deeper into me, their power coursing through my body, giving me strength to push on. I was changing, I felt it. For once I didn't challenge it or see it as being a threat to the established mores of the 'hood, though, of course, it was. Muhammad's teaching corresponded with my condition of being repressed on the Rock. Never could I have been touched by such teachings in the street.
>
> —Monster Kody Scott from
> *The Autobiography of an L.A. Gang Member*

In addition to legal interventions there are community and culturally based efforts. Although it is difficult to measure their impacts, some have argued that culture is an "effective means of intervention for gang-involved and affiliated youth and their families," specifically invoking the arts as "the best path for change, peace, wholeness, and abundance."[27] Like arts-based gang intervention, the efforts of ex-gang members and religious organizations have been dedicated to the process of peacemaking, including groups like the Nation of Islam and the work of places like Homeboy Industries in Los Angeles, the brainchild of a Jesuit priest. As one study notes, "many people connect with one another by activities that enrich their spirits . . . All can be crucial in healing, creating community, giving back, and teaching."[28] In reentry this has proven so, and there is support for religious programming as a means of successful transition to community life and to "combat the negative effects of prison culture."[29]

MUSIC

Perhaps more than any other musical genre, hip-hop is an interventionist force that has tried to quell gang violence, quite literally, from coast to coast. However, scholarship has been tardy in recognizing the links between hip-hop and gang culture, or as Hagedorn writes, "gangsta rap and the worldwide embrace of hip-hop culture have been almost completely ignored by scholarship on gangs."[30] Yet the fact is that hip-hop culture itself was an interventionist strategy created to remedy gang violence in New York City.[31] Afrika Bambaataa, ex-leader of one of New York's largest street gangs, the Black Spades, was also the father of hip-hop, which he helped pioneer in the late 1970s. Bambaataa responded to drugs and violence in the South Bronx by organizing underground "block parties" in the name of peace and "no violence," which was especially enforced by Bambaataa. The paradigm of how hip-hop was to provide an alternative to gangs was exemplified by Bambaataa, who "redirected his life away from gangs and organized the components of this burgeoning cultural movement under the banner of the Zulu Nation, envisioning this new street movement as a 'revolutionary youth culture.'"[32] The Zulu Nation was hip-hop's first organization, and it borrowed from the Five Percent Nation of Islam's philosophy, which had influenced Bambaataa since his childhood.[33] The question of peace, then, was injected into the hip-hop culture with help from the likes of Bambaataa, who made the mantra "peace, unity, love, and having fun" staple fare for the hip-hop generation.[34]

In the hip-hop world order, as physical violence was the primary target of reform, enthusiasts displaced gang violence with the symbolic, spawning a cutting-edge competition in music, dance, and visual arts, based on the imagery of battle. Thus, instead of real wars, there were simulated battles—break battles on the dance floor, deejay and MC battles, and graffiti wars. The original crews that replaced the gangs were recruits from the gangs themselves, and so the culture had a direct impact on gang violence—many of the first hip-hoppers were gang members who had tired of the killings and sense of hopelessness. Although these new beats and raps started as a style of party music, engineered to pacify gang violence, the legacy of Bambaataa's music would be quickly taken over by a different type of message. This new incarnation, often labeled gangsta rap, took the music in a stark, violent direction, one that coincided with real-life gang war in the city streets.

During the most desperate of times, hip-hop would again intervene. In 1988, New York–based rapper KRS-ONE launched the "Stop the Violence" movement as an attempt to calm violence within both the black community and the rap community itself. The first widespread effort of this group was the release of "Self-Destruction," a song that featured collaborations among various rap artists. Among those advocating peace is Just Ice, who tells of his own escape from gang life and prison and admonishes,

> But believe me that is no fun—The time is now to unite everyone
> You don't have to be soft to be for peace . . . you don't have to be chained
>   by the beast

In 1990, the West Coast Allstars, a collaboration of mostly California-based rappers, released "We're All in the Same Gang," a song and message of anti-violence from some of the masters of gangsta rap themselves. This song featured the satirists Digital Underground, who launched a scathing critique on gang culture with a racial twist. In self-declared rage, they call out America, the "red, white, and blue," as responsible for the "blue and the red," the Cripps and Bloods' bloodshed; in other words, whites foment black-on-black violence and delight in the aftermath. Yet standing for "peace among brothers," they encourage,

> Do what you like—unless you like gangbangin
> Let's see how many brothers leave us hangin

According to these rappers, gang violence must cease because it is exactly what whites want for black people. From this perspective, the agency of gangs is undermined, since in whatever form it assumes, black-on-black violence is to the benefit and delight of whites. MC Hammer contributed especially pointed lyrics in a story that narrates the pain of gang life and violence under the sway of drugs, declaring,

> It's gotta stop, we don't need all the violence
> Peace in the hood and a moment of silence

As the lyrics attest, the power of music is an article of faith for antiviolence activism, and as Hagedorn notes, "it is in this power of identity, including the more life-affirming current within the hip-hop lifestyle, where we can nurture a cultural counterforce to youth's nihilism, misogyny, and self-destructiveness."[35] Of course more modern iterations of intervention through music have surfaced in hip-hop, including Lupe Fiasco's "The Die," the Roots' "Return to Innocence Lost," and the *No More Prisons* compilations.

RELIGION

The force of religion influences gang culture generally, and more specifically, through attempts to broker peace between warring gangs and help individuals out of the gang life. As Spergel notes, "rarely if at all, mentioned in social science studies is the influence of religious conversion in a youth's ability to leave the gang."[36] The following analysis builds from research into the works of Homeboy Industries in Los Angeles, California, and the Nation of Islam. These two operations exemplify how religious intervention can promote peacemaking efforts; both organizations show how the force of religion inspires both types of intervention—stopping literal bloodshed and getting and keeping people out of "the life." In the case of Islam specifically, perhaps no other tradition quite compares to its influence in three particular areas that relate to the present study: gangs, prison gangs, and hip-hop culture.

In prison, the links between gang culture and religion are profound, and Islam in particular can speak directly to a prisoner's current state of incarceration. Religious narrative based on Islam can make cosmic sense of a prisoner's current incarceration and infuse an inmate's life with meaning. For some converts, the resonance of Islam as a "warrior religion" has deep roots that trace back to the Crusades.[37] Many of those who are now law-abiding Muslims were once gangsters, or in Malcolm X's case, hustlers, an interface that Gardell describes as "gangland gangstas turning Gods."[38] Although for some gang members, the prison may already be pregnant with meaning, the racism, injustice, and brutality may communicate an even more coherent message of oppression under the sway of Islam. The existential power of these ancient narratives connects prisoners to the Messianic root of Islam—they are the modern-day version of the "household of the Prophet," who were incarcerated by non-Muslims over a thousand years before. For some converts, Islam is likened to the ultimate cosmic race, which may be attractive to gang members; under such a mentality, Islam may represent the largest gang of all.

A description of Islam's appeal to gang members is recorded in the autobiography of "Monster" Kody Scott during his incarceration at the California Youth Authority. Scott recalls how the only safe place for Crips to meet without detection was during Muslim services. Shortly after the first meeting, Kody encounters Imam Muhammad Abdullah, who ignites Kody's interest in Islam and forces him to reevaluate his definition of the "enemy." This encounter had a profound effect on Kody, who writes, "I put the word out that all Crips should come to Muslim services and hear Muhammad talk. Within three weeks attendance increased from nine to twenty-seven to forty and finally to eighty! The staff became alarmed, asking questions and even sitting in on some of our services, trying to grasp our sudden attraction to Islamic services. . . . After every service it was a common sight to see fifty to eighty New Afrikan youths mobbing back to their units shouting 'Jihad till death!' and 'Death to the oppressor!'"[39]

This prison's surveillance on Kody and his gang landed him a trip to the warden, who demanded an explanation of the unifying effect the Muslims were having on the gangs: "how do you explain twenty-three Eight Trays, fourteen Hoovers, eleven East coasts and a lesser assortment of bangers cropped up in a Moslem church for the past month, huh? Explain that!"[40]

Like Monster Kody's writings, other cultural productions offer poignant portrayals of Islamic outreach to gang culture. Films like *Boyz n the Hood* (1991) and *Menace II Society* (1993) and the HBO series *OZ* portray the links between Islam, gangs, and prisons. In *Boys n the Hood*, the opening scenes show what appears to be a Nation of Islam member, with suit and bow tie, selling bean pies on the corner. At the outset, then, the film's portrayal of gang life in Los Angeles reveals how Muslims are entrenched in the inner-city slum, preaching and trying to help the underclass. Later, the film's antagonist character, Doughboy, a banger, who himself is constantly in and out of prison, begins a discussion about God. When his brother appears, he tells Doughboy that he missed a talk given by their friend's father, Blaze, to which Doughboy replies, "Damn, Blaze is like Malcolm Farrakhan!" which ignites the whole set in reverential laughter and nods of approval. The reference here suggests that Blaze, who is perhaps the only positive male role model in the film, is a mixture of Malcolm X and Louis Farrakhan. In terms of cultural economics, this is a way of depicting Blaze as a man who commands the highest respect from these gangsters.

Islam's interventionist efforts are likewise expressed in *Menace II Society*, a film that depicts the violent and brutal dimensions of gang life. One of the core characters, Sharif, is a convert to the Nation of Islam, who nonetheless still hangs with his gangster homies, preaching when he can about Islam and the white man. In one scene, his gangster friends go to Sharif's father to try to get him to make Sharif stop talking religion and Islam. Yet the father tells them that the Nation of Islam has helped keep his boy alive, an answer they had not expected but one that affords them a new vision into what religion means to their friend. In this film, Islam penetrates the most hardened core of gang life, and although Sharif is ultimately shot dead by neighborhood enemies and left behind by his gangster friends, the scene conjures a heroic portrayal of Islam: Sharif's dead body lying in the street depicts how followers of Islam are willing to risk everything to reach out to the gangs in the hood, much like Imam Muhammad Abdullah in real life. The respect that the gangsters have for Muslims runs deep, and according to Dannin (2006), "so widespread is the fierce reputation of the incarcerated Muslim that the most ruthless urban drug dealers carefully avoid harming any Muslim man, woman, or child lest they face extreme prejudice during their inevitable prison terms."[41] Thus, the very presence of Muslims in a gang-infested community can have a peacemaking effect.

Islam is not the only religion that has worked with communities on these issues. Religion plays an important role inside prison, and it plays an equally important role outside it. Standing outside of 1916 East First Street in Boyle Heights, Los Angeles, is a dangerous act. Yet, for some, this place is the epitome of rehabilitation. This area is often designated by media and scholars alike as a "gang capital"—the heart of gang territory—that supplies future lifeblood to prison gangs. What is remarkable about this address, however, is not the future inmates, but the former ones. At Homeboy Industries (HBI), former inmates are learning how to live on the outside. The office is run like a business, and the people answering phones inside are confined to wheelchairs, their legs the victims of a more violent past.

Among the tattooed Chicano former gangsters works a Jesuit priest, who has dedicated his life to gang intervention and helping ex-prisoners rehabilitate. Father Greg Boyle is the founder of HBI, a mission that started with a small bakery shop. It was a business dedicated to offering jobs to the people who have the most trouble finding them: parolees, at-risk youth, and former gang members alike. Even those who had formerly tried to kill each other were welcome to work side by side with Father Boyle. The business has since expanded into screen printing and selling of merchandise and even has a new offshoot, Homegirls Café. With the proceeds, Father Boyle has extended his business ventures into charitable organizations and facilitated new services at little to no cost to his unusual clientele, including tattoo removal, counseling, and job training: everything one might need in trying to exit the gang. According to a HBI pamphlet, "*Jobs for a Future* creates opportunities so that at-risk youth can plan their futures and not their funerals. 'Nothing Stops a Bullet Like a Job' is our guiding principle. Gang violence is the urban poor's version of teenage suicide, and *Jobs for a Future* breaks the spiral of despair that holds so many youth in its grip . . . stands as a beacon of light for those who have lost their way in the darkness of senseless violence."[42]

HBI and Father Boyle's work have also been the subject of many media reports, and he has appeared repeatedly in academic studies, news reports, and books.[43] Although appreciated by many, the work of HBI is not welcomed by all. Previously, HBI ran a special division that cleaned neighborhood walls, removing gang graffiti and speaking out to the youth about the burdens of gang life. During the course of the program, however, two members of this team were gunned down during daylight hours as they attempted to carry out their duties of repainting defaced walls.[44] These events led to abandonment of the graffiti program, netting a victory for the gangsters. The deadly nature of what intervention can entail, especially for ex-gang members, shows a system so entrenched that it ensures the next generation gets caught up in the cycle. Compounding matters, HBI itself recently was forced to cut 75 percent of its work staff because of financial hardships, signaling perhaps another victory for the gangsters.[45]

GANGS AND EX-GANGSTERS

Using ex-gang members as a tool for intervention is not novel. Scholarly literature on gangs has outlined various successes, such as Brotherton's study of New York Puerto Rican gangs, which reported that the gangs "began to transform themselves into street organizations or cultural associations for self and community empowerment."[46] Yet there has been disastrous failure when intervention relies on the use of gang leaders to control and prevent violence.[47] Part of the problem therein is that *ex* is a far-from-clear concept, and many who are out of the life sometimes must return to it based on circumstances or emergencies. Such individuals might, by and large, be out of the gang but be forced into activity in the future; others, however, claim to be ex even though they continue working with the gang and committing illegal acts, including trafficking drugs. Thus, the porous nature of gang boundaries complicates strategies that can rely on the experiential power of gang culture itself. As history shows, ex-gang members, when they are really ex, have made sincere attempts at intervention. Although the success of these measures is debatable, former gang members have tried to stop violence by relaying their own experiences, like the Scared Straight tactics of old. Other times, the gang itself can be the main motivating factor for peace, and works like *Uprising: Crips and Bloods Tell the Story of America's Youth in the Crossfire* offer testimony of hardened core gang members and their admonition of the gang life as a means of teaching gang history so as not to repeat it.[48]

G-Dog and the Homeboys (2004), a book on Father Boyle and HBI, documents a telling example of how gangs can stop the violence, a twist in which intervention comes from gang leadership in California. In this episode, rival street gangs were about to wage an all-out war, pitting Chicano youths against themselves. At the moment when all hope had faded, with swords unshielded and gang members primed and readied, a truce was declared. But it was not the work of a do-gooder like Father Boyle that brought this conflict to an end before it had even begun. The message came from the beast itself: from the heart of Pelican Bay State Prison, word came from the *Carnales* in the Mexican Mafia, which established a strict set of war-rules that diffused the pending doom. The author recalls, "Whatever the motivation, the murky star of the *Carnales* has sent down a beam of light to intervene when all seemed lost."[49] This edict had nearly absolute power to back it up, too—hardly anyone, not even the most hardened street *veterano*, would profit by disobeying the orders of those higher-ups on lockdown. If anyone were bold enough to cross that line, he would eventually end up in prison, where the consequences of disobeying might be a terrible lesson learned.

In addition to the peacemaking efforts of gangs, there are intervention efforts of individuals. Many ex-gangsters find a calling in the quest for peace and helping young ones stay out of gangs. A most prominent example is Stanley "Tookie" Williams, cofounder of the Crips gang in the early 1970s in Los Angeles. Tookie's street reputation was immense, and in the course of his violent escapades, he was found guilty of four murders in 1979, crimes which earned him the death penalty. While awaiting execution in San Quentin's Death Row, however, Tookie underwent what seems to be a genuine transition to gang interventionist. After several years behind bars, he renounced his gang affiliation and became an advocate for peace. Part of his plan was to quell gang violence by targeting the youngest minds before the gangs got to them first, and so he penned several children's books. From his career as a banger, Tookie would transform into an anti-gang advocate who was intent on stopping violence and preventing others from joining gangs until the day he was executed by the state of California in 2005.

CONCLUSION AND PROSPECT FOR PEACE
THROUGH INTERVENTION

> The conclusion set forth is that the DOC gang policy is not merely unfair, or even cruel, it is counterproductive. Labeling and mistreatment actually encourages prisoner self-identification as gang members. Practices which reinforce gang member commitment to the group enhance gang cohesiveness and criminal capacity, undermining both prison security and public safety. Fair disciplinary policies that focus on prisoner conduct, staff training, and educational opportunities which offer an alternative identity to that of gang member, are more effective strategies for preventing prison disturbances and promoting safer communities.
>
> —Phillip Kassel from
> "The Gang Crackdown in Massachusetts Prisons."

Peacemaking through gang intervention is an uncertain strategy at best, both on the street and in prison. Perhaps the greatest difficulty is in predicting the efficacy of any given strategy in different contexts. Since gangs vary widely, as do circumstances such as social status, security, and economics, what may mitigate gang violence in some places may have different outcomes elsewhere. Since gangs themselves "are shaped by racial and ethnic oppression, as well as poverty and slums, and are reactions of despair to persisting inequality,"[50] addressing these underlying circumstances might be the proper target of intervention. There are also questions about scale and whether programs applied to small- to medium-sized prisons will work in places like Texas and California, two of the largest incarceration operations in the world and home to several super-gangs. Whether gang intervention can succeed behind bars is indeterminate, but on the outside, these states show, paradoxically enough, that interventions to ameliorate conditions of poverty and inequality may be disrupted by aggressive suppression and incarceration tactics that lead to further impoverishment and marginalization of at-risk communities.

In debates on intervention, it is often hard to determine whether a program is effective. As the gang literature describes, many formal interventionist programs are developed without evaluation plans, rendering the effect of any given program a largely unknown variable by dint of the program structure itself. For informal interventionist strategies, the problem is more acute, since there is even less possibility of systematic review of the program's success or failure. For example, "We're All in the Same Gang" was quite a commercial success and even garnered a Grammy nomination. But how might this translate on the street in terms of making peace? Is there any connection between this song and the lower rates of violence among gangs in the 1990s? Or what about the book *Uprising* or Tookie's books for children? How to assess their impact on diffusing gang warfare and gang recruitment efforts? Without doubt, these are impossible questions to answer. One would be remiss, however, in thinking that these interventionist efforts had little or no impact. Rather, it is safe to say that neither qualitatively nor quantitatively can these efforts be assessed, but at the same time, it is likely hard to find any gangster from the 1990s who is not familiar with at least some of the lyrics to these songs, or more recently who is not familiar with Tookie's efforts as portrayed through the TV movie *Redemption,* which tells the story of his turning away from gangs, a story that suggests lasting intervention must include an "identity alternative" to replace the self-identification linked to gangs and crime.[51]

CAUTION: A DOUBLE-EDGED SWORD

Examination of the legal and extra-legal attempts at gang intervention demonstrates that the very forces of intervention might also promote anti-intervention, a paradox in which gang experts, such as the police and criminal justice officials, "simultaneously cite suppression tactics as the most effective *and* the least effective strategies in addressing the gang problem."[52] One researcher reports, "Three related tendencies embedded in law enforcement and correctional approaches to gang intervention that contribute to counterproductive results. These are: (1) policies that proceed from an inaccurate view of what gangs are; (2) intervention strategies that enhance gang cohesiveness; and (3) misidentification of gang members. A fourth related factor, racial and cultural stereotyping, affects disciplinary and classification policies generally."[53]

Taken wholly, "relying on suppression alone will not produce long-term success. Intervention must include vigorous law enforcement to mitigate the negative consequences of gang activity, but they also have to focus on positive forces."[54] Thus, it has been recommended that policing practices adopt an approach that "combines suppression of youth gang criminal acts through aggressive enforcement of laws, with community mobilization involving a broad cross-section of the community in combating the problem."[55]

In addition, the harsh treatment and conditions of prison may be a factor that encourages gang membership, perhaps seen in those who turn to gangs for protection and connections once they are incarcerated.[56] "Having made a lifetime commitment to the prison gang," Petersilia writes, "the new members export these new connections, hostile attitudes and skills back to their home communities when they are released. California's 'catch and release' parole policies, which continually recycle inmates between prison and home, clearly facilitate this linkage."[57] This ironic situation is "cyclical and toxic," and Petersilia notes, "as prison gangs gain power, prisoners perceive the prison as being less safe and administrators in less control, causing more of them to join gangs for protection."[58] A side effect is that individuals who involve themselves with gangs for the immediate benefit of protection do not realize or even care that their affiliation might become a long-term commitment, maybe a lifetime commitment. Severe overcrowding, violence, and color codes can breed conditions where the only hope is to seek protection, or as one study found, "by imposing harsh, even tortuous conditions, the DOC only heightens the need for a 'sense of belonging,' which causes gang members to gravitate toward one another in the first place."[59]

In prison, Islam's positive influence on rehabilitation is legendary, yet at the fringe are elements that have helped spawned fears of "jailhouse jihad" or "terror recruitment." Although this issue is contentious, there is little doubt that the conditions under which prisoners live provide live ammunition for preachers. Such an environment has fostered "Prison Islam" or "Prislam," which is known for using select parts of the Quran to advance agendas which often include violence. According to one study, "as tensions have grown between the various factions, Prison Islam groups have increasingly become known for encompassing gang values and fierce intra-group loyalties,"[60] a phenomenon elsewhere described as "an amorphous presence in convict populations through which individuals may adopt Muslim names or idioms while dealing drugs, exploiting other prisoners sexually, and otherwise engaging in the typical activities of prison gangs."[61]

In the way that intervention efforts can go awry for criminal justice and religious intervention, the other cultural efforts can backfire as well. Hip-hop further exemplifies an art form born to reform gang violence, which would later be overtaken by rappers who would create gangsta rap. Today, the violent message comes with an ideological thrust, and the most recent forms of Islamic-based rap, sometimes called godcore or jihadi rap, are vehement calls to cease inter-gang war in the name of fighting a greater one.[62] Thus, despite whatever interventionist effect hip-hop music may have, these attempts must compete with violence in music that is the rule rather than exception.

THEORETICAL AND PRACTICAL
OBSTACLES FOR SUCCESS

Perhaps the first obstacle weighing against success in peacemaking is assumptions about gangs, U.S. gangs in particular. The gang form, in its various guises, is a permanent part of the American social fabric, developing spontaneously in marginalized groups from the colonial period through the Italian mafiosos in the modern era up to the present-day Mexican mafiosos, rendering the idea of eradicating gangs unrealistic.[63] A better understanding might premise itself on the idea that the gang problem cannot be eliminated unless the conditions that encourage gang membership are addressed. Acceptance of gangs as reflections of underclass struggles permits focus on the real problem—violence. Understanding that gangs will persist allows concentration on removing the violent elements from gang culture. In this regard, hip-hop culture is illustrative. As the culture was designed as an antidote to gang violence, it produced "crews," which in reality were like nonviolent gangs. They had practically all the elements, including criminality, of the gangs that preceded them, except that violence was somewhat forced from the repertoire. Instead, hip-hop created a means for displacing physical violence, even though practically everything else stayed.

The idea that gangs will one day be eradicated is a foremost obstacle to successful long-term intervention. The lure of street gangs directly links to strategies contemplating long-term intervention, especially since "no one has yet discovered any effective strategy for preventing the formation of youth gangs."[64] That gangs are here to stay should lead to a serious discussion about the relationship between street and prison gangs, a point supported by one study of gangs depicting that 8 out of 10 counties had active street gangs with strong ties to prison gangs.[65] Qualitative studies, documentaries, and other anecdotal evidence suggest that in places with heavy gang activity, those on the inside control not only the inside of a prison, but sometimes aspects of the outside as well, a situation described as "prison gang dependency."[66] A better understanding of the "deadly symbiosis" between prisons and ghettos is fundamental to intervention efforts, which render prison gangs as crucial members of the conversation.[67]

Plainly, gangs have been around in different forms due to circumstances of marginality.[68] From slave patrols to urban gangs to modern police gang units, the notion of a gang is seemingly endemic to U.S. history. Today, however, street gangs are a special target of social and political wrath. Today's heightened scrutiny of all things gang-related may be a Band-Aid where stitches are required. As long as perceptions of real danger in the ghettos persist, gang culture will persist as a way to secure oneself. As gangs are effective at providing economic opportunities, gang culture is seemingly inextricable from conditions in which security and economy are themselves unsecured and, indeed, sometimes impossible to secure. The will to gang formation may function like a contract made in the state of nature; the bindings of the agreement, as cumbersome as they may be, are nothing compared to life in the wild. Perhaps the only catch is that gang membership offers no relief from the wild, or if anything, increases susceptibility to violence.

As long as security is viewed as compromised, gangs will take up the slack, even if they are the cause of some of the fear in the first place. This point is bolstered by a study on St. Louis gangs that revealed that the most common reported reason for joining gangs was "a perceived threat and the hope for protection through gang membership."[69] This reality is more pronounced in prison, and research on the development of gangs in prison ranks "inmate requests for protective custody" as the number one indicator.[70] As opposed to seeking a safe haven from gangs, by doing the gang's bidding, the inmate has a world of benefits bestowed on him in a world where insecurity and indigence make the streets seem like paradise. Accordingly, as Spergel has noted, "gangs in prison cannot easily be ignored . . . Unlike their position in other criminal justice agency settings, gang members must be considered full-time participant members of the structure and organization of the prison or training school."[71] Thus, absent any about-face on sentencing practices, prison policies, and overcrowding, prisons will seemingly tend to foster conditions for gang recruitment.[72]

NOTES

1. For a historical overview of gang intervention, see Arnold P. Goldstein, "Gang Intervention: A Historical Review," in *The Gang Intervention Handbook*, ed. Arnold P. Goldstein and C. Ronald Huff (Champaign, IL: Research Press, 1993), 21. For a discussion on the current state of gang research, see Jack Katz and Curtis Jackson-Jacobs, "The Criminologists' Gang," in *The Blackwell Companion to Criminology*, ed. Colin Sumner, 91–124 (Malden, MA: Blackwell Publishing, 2004).

2. Los Angeles City Council's Ad Hoc Committee on Gang Violence and Youth Development, "The Community Engagement Advisory Committee's 'Community-Based Gang Intervention Model: Definition and Structure'" (2008), 4. Available at http://www.westernjustice.org/documents/GangInterventionModel.pdf.

3. James C. Howell, "Lessons Learned from Gang Program Evaluations," in *Youth Gangs and Community Intervention*, ed. Robert J. Chaskin (New York: Columbia University Press, 2010), 56; see also Anthony A. Braga and David M. Kennedy, "Reducing Gang Violence in Boston," in *Responding to Gangs: Evaluation and Research*, ed. Scott Decker and Winifred Reed (Washington, DC: Diane Publishing, 2002), 275 (citing the deterrent effects on violence from the presence of police officers, probation officers, and youth service caseworkers).

4. See, for example, Goldstein and Huff, *The Gang Intervention Handbook* (Champaign, IL: Research Press, 1993).

5. Irving A. Spergel, *The Youth Gang Problem: A Community Approach* (New York: Oxford University Press, 1995), 247. More drastic is intervention by limiting First Amendment rights; see generally Ann Kordas, "Losing My Religion: Controlling Gang Violence through Limitations on Freedom of Expression," *Boston University Law Review* 80 (2000): 1451–1492.

6. Los Angeles City Council's Ad Hoc Committee on Gang Violence and Youth Development, "The Community Engagement Advisory Committee's 'Community-Based Gang Intervention Model: Definition and Structure'" (2008), 4. Available at http://www.westernjustice.org/documents/GangInterventionModel.pdf.

7. California Penal Code §186.22 (2009); see Sara Lynn Van Hofwegen, "Unjust and Ineffective: A Critical Look at California's Step Act," *Southern California Interdisciplinary Law Journal* 18 (2009): 682. "As a result of the enhancement, criminal defendants may face sentences more than tripling the time in prison they would otherwise serve for the underlying offense."

8. J. Howell, "Lessons Learned," 57.

9. California Penal Code § 186.22(i) (2009).

10. Andrew V. Papachristos, "Interpreting Inkblots: Deciphering and Doing Something about Modern Street Gangs," *Criminology and Public Policy* 4 (2005): 643–652.

11. Ibid., 647.

12. Bureau of Justice Assistance, *Addressing Community Gang Problems: A Practical Guide* (Washington, DC: Bureau of Justice Assistance, 1998), xxii.

13. Cheryl L. Maxson et al., *Can Civil Gang Injunctions Change Communities? A Community Assessment of the Impact of Civil Gang Injunctions* (a report prepared at the request of the Department of Justice, 2005); Matthew M. Werdegar, "Enjoining the Constitution: The Use of Public Nuisance Abatement Injunctions against Urban Street Gangs," *Stanford Law Review* 51 (1999): 409.

14. Babe Howell, "Fear Itself: The Impact of Allegations of Gang Affiliation on Pre-Trial Detention," *St. Thomas Law Review* 23 (2010).

15. Terence P. Thornberry et al., *Gangs and Delinquency in Developmental Perspective* (Cambridge: Cambridge University Press, 2003); J. Howell, "Lessons Learned," 23–27 ("databases are bloated, the basis for inclusion obscured, and many males who have the misfortune of growing up in gang-dominated neighborhoods and sharing the ethnic or racial background of the gang run the risk of inclusion on these databases . . . most gang researchers recognize that individuals included on law enforcement gang databases have both active and inactive roles"). Yablonsky notes a class that moves out of the gang but "are too often identified by law-enforcement as gangsters who still belong to the gang. They are often erroneously arrested and prosecuted for crimes they did not commit." Jeffrey A. Butts and Caterina Gouvis Roman, "A Community Youth Development Approach to Gang Control Programs," in *Youth Gangs and Community Intervention*, ed. Robert J. Chaskin, 177 (New York: Columbia University Press, 2010). "Yet many [even most] gang youth are never more than peripheral members of their gangs, and most are involved for only short periods. In fact, the average period of gang involvement is around one year."

16. J. Howell, "Lessons Learned," 16.

17. Ibid.

18. Phillip Kassel, "The Gang Crackdown in the Prisons of Massachusetts: Arbitrary and Harsh Treatment Can Only Make Matters Worse," in *Gangs and Society*, ed. Louis Kontos, David Brotherton, and Luis Barrios, 232 (New York: Columbia University Press, 2003).

19. Terry Kupers, *Prison Madness: The Mental Health Crisis behind Bars and What We Must Do about It* (Hoboken, NJ: Jossey-Bass, 1999), xvi.

20. Jamie Fellner, *A Corrections Quandary: Mental Illness and Prison Rules, Harvard Law Review* 4 (2006): 391, 403.

21. Kupers, "Prison Madness," xviii.

22. Raymond F. Patterson and Kerry Hughes, "Review of Completed Suicides in the California Department of Corrections and Rehabilitation, 1999–2004," *Jail Suicide Mental Health Update* 17, no. 2 (2008): 7, available at http://www.ncianet.org/sui cideprevention/publications/update/Fall%202008.pdf.

23. See, for example, Spergel, *The Youth Gang Problem*, 24.

24. Malcolm Klein, *The American Street Gang* (New York: Oxford University Press, 1995), 25–27.

25. J. Howell, "Lessons Learned," 16.

26. Van Hofwegen, *Unjust and Ineffective*, 685.

27. Los Angeles City Council's Ad Hoc Committee on Gang Violence and Youth Development, "The Community Engagement Advisory Committee's 'Community-Based

Gang Intervention Model: Definition and Structure'" (2008), 9. Available at http://www.westernjustice.org/documents/GangInterventionModel.pdf.

28. Ibid.

29. Jeanette M. Hercik, "Prisoner Reentry, Religion and Research," *Department of Health and Human Services* 5, http://peerta.acf.hhs.gov/pdf/prisoner_reentry.pdf (accessed October 29, 2010).

30. Mike Davis, "Foreword" to John M. Hagedorn, *A World of Gangs* (Minneapolis: University of Minnesota Press, 2008), xxvii.

31. John M. Hagedorn, *A World of Gangs* (Minneapolis: University of Minnesota Press, 2008), 93–94.

32. Marcus Reeves, *Somebody Scream: Rap Music's Rise to Prominence in the Aftershock of Black Power* (New York: Faber and Faber, 2008), 17.

33. Jeffery O. G. Ogbar, *Hip Hop Revolution: The Culture and Politics of Rap* (Lawrence: University Press of Kansas, 2007); Samy H. Alim, *Roc the Mic Right: The Language of Hip Hop Culture* (New York: Routledge, 2006), 25.

34. Africa Bambaataa, *Renegades of Funk,* Tommy Boy Records, TB 839.

35. Davis, Foreword to *A World of Gangs*, xxv.

36. Spergel, *The Youth Gang Problem*, 107.

37. Reza Aslan, *No god but God: The Origins, Evolution, and Future of Islam* (New York: Random House, 2005), 79.

38. Mattias Gardell, *In the Name of Elijah Muhammad: Louis Farrakhan and the Nation of Islam* (Durham: Duke University Press, 1996), 285.

39. Sanyika Shakur, *Monster: The Autobiography of an L.A. Gang Member* (New York: Grove Press, 1993), 220.

40. Ibid., 221.

41. Robert Dannin, *Black Pilgrimage to Islam* (New York: Oxford University Press, 2002), 182.

42. Pamphlet given to author by Homeboy Industries Director Father Greg Boyle.

43. HBI has been profiled by Tom Brokaw and the *Los Angeles Times* and has been featured on *60 Minutes* and on A&E Television's *Gang Violence in America: 20th Century with Mike Wallace*. This organization has also been the subject of Celeste Fremon and Tom Brokaw, *G-Dog and the Homeboys: Father Greg Boyle and the Gangs of East Los Angeles* (New York: Hyperion, 1995), a journalist's perspective on the outreach work of Father Greg and his organization.

44. Hector Becerra, "Graffiti Project a Victim of Gang Killings," *Los Angeles Times*, August 7, 2004, http://articles.latimes.com/keyword/homeboy-industries (accessed October 29, 2010).

45. Jonathan Lloyd, "Layoffs Hit Homeboy Industries," NBC Los Angeles, May 14, 2010, http://www.nbclosangeles.com/news/local-beat/Layoffs-Hit-Homeboy-Industries-93778039.html (accessed October 29, 2010).

46. David C. Brotherton, *Old Heads Tell Their Stories: From Street Gangs to Street Organizations in New York City* (Chicago: Spencer Foundation, 1997), http://www.eric.ed.gov/PDFS/ED412305.pdf; Juan Francisco Esteva Martinez, "Urban Street Activists: Gang and Community Efforts to Bring Peace and Justice to Los Angeles Neighborhoods," in *Gangs and Society*, ed. Louis Kontos, David Brotherton, and Luis Barrios (New York: Columbia University Press, 2003), 107 (describing street activist typologies as "recovered gang member street activists," "OG street activists" and "gang member street activists").

47. Spergel, *The Youth Gang Problem*, 251; see George E. Tita and Andrew Papachristos, "The Evolution of Gang Policy: Balancing Intervention and Suppression," in *Youth*

Gangs and Community Intervention, ed. Robert J. Chaskin, 26–31 (New York: Columbia University Press, 2010).

48. See also Bill Piatt, *Black and Brown in America* (New York: New York University Press, 1997), 118–120.

49. Fremon and Brokaw, *G-Dog and the Homeboys,* 272.

50. Mike Davis, Foreword, xxiv.

51. Kassel, "Gang Crackdown," 241.

52. Tita and Papachristos, "Evolution of Gang Policy," 24, citing Irving A. Spergel and G. David Curry, "Strategies and Perceived Agency Effectiveness in Dealing with the Youth Gang Problem," in *Gangs in America,* ed. C. Ronald Huff, 288–309 (Thousand Oaks, CA: Sage Publications, 1990).

53. Kassel, "Gang Crackdown," 233.

54. Butts and Roman, "Community Youth Development Approach," 185.

55. Irving Spergel et al., *Gang Suppression and Intervention: Community Models* (Washington, DC: Office of Juvenile Justice and Delinquency Prevention, 1994), 5.

56. Ted Conover, *Newjack: Guarding Sing Sing* (New York: Vintage, 2001), 115.

57. Joan Petersilia, *Understanding California Corrections* (California Policy Research Center, 2006), 33. Available at http://ucicorrections.seweb.uci.edu/pdf/Understand ingCorrectionsPetersilia20061.pdf.

58. Ibid.

59. Kassel, "Gang Crackdown," 235.

60. Mark S. Hamm, *Terrorist Recruitment in American Correctional Institutions: An Exploratory Study of Non-Traditional Faith Groups Final Report* (commissioned report for the U.S. Department of Justice, December 2007).

61. Center for Islamic Pluralism, *Black America, Prisons and Radical Islam: A Report* (Washington, DC: Center for Islamic Pluralism, 2008).

62. SpearIt, "God Behind Bars: Race, Religion and Revenge," *Seton Hall Law Review* 37 (2007): 497.

63. See Matthew J. Cannata, "Achieving Peace in the Streets: How Legislative Efforts Fail in Combating Gang Violence in Comparison to Successful Local Community-Based Initiatives," *New England Journal on Criminal and Civil Confinement* 35 (2009): 246.

64. J. Howell, "Lessons Learned," 54.

65. Luke Dowdney, Neither War nor Peace: International Comparisons of Children and Youth in Organized Armed Violence (Rio de Janiero: 7Letras, 2006), 34.

66. See, for example, Avelardo Valdez, "Toward a Typology of Contemporary Mexican American Youth Gangs," in *Gangs and Society,* ed. Louis Kontos, David Brotherton, and Luis Barrios (New York: Columbia University Press, 2003), 22. Describes San Antonio's Nine-Ball Crew, which had "direct ties to a Chicano prison gang that controlled the heroin trade in this community."

67. See Loic Waqant, "Deadly Symbiosis: When Ghetto and Prison Meet and Mesh," *Punishment Society* 3 (2001): 95–134.

68. Diego Vigil, "The Established Gang," in *Gangs: The Origins and Impact of Contemporary Youth Gangs in the United States,* ed. Scott Cummings and Daniel J. Monti (Albany: State University of New York Press, 1993).

69. G. David Curry and Scott H. Decker, "Understanding and Responding to Gangs in an Emerging Gang Problem Context," *Valparaiso University Law Review* 31 (1997): 526.

70. Robert S. Fong and Salvador Buentello, "The Detection of Prison Gang Development: An Empirical Assessment," *Federal Probation* 55 (1991): 66.

71. Spergel, *The Youth Gang Problem*, 238.

72. See Louis Kontos, David Brotherton, and Luis Barrios, eds., *Gangs and Society* (New York: Columbia University Press, 2003), ix. Describes dangerous prison conditions: "Street-level dealer took the fall and subsequently came to rely on each other for protection in prison. It was out of this situation that the Latino 'supergangs' emerged."

CHAPTER 33

Abraham's Path: The Path of a Thousand Negotiations

Joshua Weiss

It was like a light coming on here. We got connected to the outside world and that makes us feel hope. Everyone in the village is always asking about when the next walkers are coming.

> —Hasan, a man involved in the Homestay program on the
> Palestinian segment of the Abraham Path[1]

WHAT IS ABRAHAM'S PATH?

Walking side by side. Sharing a meal and a story. Learning through this simple exchange of hospitality that, no matter what divides us, what unites us is far greater still. The ancient Path of Abraham/Ibrahim invites us to set out, in a spirit of friendship, on a journey through the heart of the Middle East to remember our common origins, respect our differences, and recognize our shared humanity.

Abraham's Path is a cultural route that retraces the remembered journey of Abraham and his family through the cradle of civilization 4,000 years ago. Abraham's Path connects many of the world's most fabled and cherished destinations, ultimately spanning 10 countries. The Path is at once a network of ancient walking paths, a place of courageous encounter across cultures, and an open-air university where people, young and old, can rediscover what connects us all.

Abraham's Path and Abraham Path Initiative

There is an important distinction to be made before explaining anything further—that of the difference between Abraham's Path and the Abraham Path

Initiative (API). Abraham's Path is the physical cultural route that is being developed in the Middle East, while the Abraham Path Initiative is a nonprofit entity based in the United States to support, promote, and inspire the creation of Abraham's Path. The two are clearly linked in many ways, but the most important point to be taken away from this distinction is that the Path is owned and nurtured by the people that live along it and not by the Initiative itself.

The Vision of Abraham's Path

Abraham's Path is not a typical peacebuilding project. Although the Initiative seeks to assist in the recreation of the ancient Path of Abraham throughout the Middle East, the vision is that the Path itself would become a vehicle for all kinds of interactivity and connection. The vision is that the route would be a vehicle, via cultural diplomacy, to bridge the widening chasm between the West and the Muslim population of the Middle East as well as a path that builds community in the Middle East through the very functional vehicle of responsible tourism.

While this vision is being achieved step-by-step, encounter by encounter, there is much more to the story. Since 2008, over 4,000 people have traveled the Path as of this writing, and in many different capacities—from classic tourism to voluntourism to youth exchanges. Moreover, part of the purpose of the Path is to project a different reality of the Middle East around the globe than people typically see through the media. The project seeks to take traveler's experiences to a much broader audience—thereby shedding doubt on their perceptions and stereotypes.

HOW DOES THE PATH CONTRIBUTE TO MORE PEACEFUL RELATIONS?

One might wonder how such a path might create more peaceful relations between peoples around the world and inside the region itself. Of course, the travel by people from around the world already alluded to—sometimes called peace through tourism—is one obvious focus. But more importantly, in the region itself, tourism is a key interest of all the countries in the Middle East. The Path seeks to harness the power of that functional industry to give people the opportunity to work together practically, improving their lives, and building relationships as they deem appropriate.

Shortly after the end of World War II, a Frenchman named Jean Monnet began an initiative called the European Steel and Coal Commission, which sought to use the steel and coal industry in a functional manner in order to bring the primary combatants of the war, France and Germany, into a working relationship around a common interest. That brilliant idea, in the ashes of Europe, would ultimately lead to the development of the European Union. Similarly, Abraham's Path seeks to pick up on the interests of all the countries in the region for tourism and to provide a platform for them to conduct their business very practically together. Given the nature of the tourism industry—including private enterprise, civil society, and local communities—a natural role emerges for these sectors and contributes to an infrastructure for peace while peoples' lives on the ground are being improved.

HISTORY AND EVOLUTION

The founding of Abraham's Path and the development of the Abraham Path Initiative began as follows:

One summer evening in August 2003, a group of old friends gathered for an informal dinner in Boulder, Colorado to discuss the Middle East. All the dinner guests were engaged in professional work promoting peace and intercultural understanding. Elias Amidon and his wife Rabia Roberts had just returned from the Middle East, where they had been organizing interfaith pilgrimages. William Ury, cofounder of the Harvard Negotiation Project and coauthor of the best selling negotiation handbook, Getting to Yes was also at the dinner. At the time, he had been working as a third party in a bitter dispute between President Hugo Chavez and his political opponents in Venezuela that threatened to turn into civil war, as well as an advisor to a peace process in Indonesia aimed at ending a 26-year-old civil war that had killed over 10,000 people.[2]

The dinner guests were alarmed by political developments in the Middle East. In March 2003, the United States had invaded Iraq and violence had escalated in the region. Reflecting on unresolved conflicts and escalating tensions between the West and the Muslim world, the friends met to consider what they might do as concerned citizens with professional expertise working in conflicts at the people-to-people level.[3]

During the evening over dinner with his Boulder friends, Ury observed that the current war was being staged in the ancient land of Mesopotamia, where Abraham, the common forefather of Judaism, Christianity, and Islam, heeded a call from God to go forth and found a new nation. Ury asked: Why not try to inspire the re-creation of the route that would retrace the journey of Abraham? What if a permanent pilgrimage route could be revived based on a commonality of cultures, rather than the conflict among them?[4]

Conceivably, Ury speculated, the Abraham Path could become part of the emerging sector of responsible tourism, which creates collaboration that gives back to local communities and benefits the local population from the business generated by tourists. The Path could also draw from the wider tradition of meditative excursions like the Camino de Santiago de Compostela, a collection of medieval pilgrimage routes across Europe, beginning for many at St. Jean Pied de Port in France and culminating in the city of Santiago de Compostela in Spain.[5]

After this initial conception, the author, Ury's colleague at Harvard, led a two-year research effort to study the idea and consult widely both inside and outside the region. Although many thought the concept was fascinating, there were plenty of doubts about the possibility of actually creating such a route, getting the different players to engage, and the issue of traveler safety. In November 2006, Ury and colleagues decided that what was needed was a trip down the Path to show its feasibility. So, 25 people from 10 countries embarked on a two-week Harvard Study Tour to hold a series of consultative meetings, test the idea further, and seek early partners. After that trip, the Path swung into full gear, with partners coming on board and segments of the Path developed over the following three years. To date, some 400 kilometers of Path have been developed in Turkey, Jordan, Palestine, and Israel and are in use to varying degrees.

MAPPING THE STAKEHOLDERS AND THEIR INTERESTS

The question was often asked of the organizers, "How do you go about such a challenge—trying to create such a long distance traveling route through a region with many different conflicts?" The first challenge of any negotiation, which the development of the Path represents in many ways, is to map the stakeholders and their interests. From a negotiation perspective, there were many challenges to manage—perhaps the most challenging of which were the vertical and horizontal levels of negotiation required to enable the Path come to life. By vertical and horizontal, I am referring to the negotiations at the official governmental level—necessary to work at other levels—and the negotiations with the private sector and down the ladder to the local communities who are the true owners and nurturers of the Path. For a graphical depiction of the interconnected nature of the negotiations required, see Figure 33.1.

Beginning at the bottom of the diagram, you can see the negotiations that the Initiative had to engage in at the international level. The international level was far from monolithic in terms of its interests in the Path. International Organizations, such as the United Nations Alliance of Civilizations, were most intrigued with the bridging power of the Path. Other institutions, such as the United Nations World Tourism Organization, were more aligned with the private tourism sector. The global citizenry's primary interest in the Path was in travel and learning about the culture and history in the Middle East in an authentic manner. Finally, interest in the Path in different countries around the world coalesced in the form of chapters who want to support the Path and its development through funding, travel, and promotion. The international level of involvement has provided the Path with significant credibility and support.

Moving up the ladder, the interests of the national governments in the Middle East region are, of course, varied and numerous. However, as explained previously, one underlying common interests of all the governments was for increased tourism—seeing this industry as a significant part of their future. This interest kept them involved in the Path to varying degrees. As anyone who has worked in the Middle East knows, nothing happens at the civil society or local level without the approval of the national governments. It is a hurdle that one must leap over, or progress becomes challenging as you move closer to the ground level. As you read on, you will come to understand the Initiative's successes and failures at this level.

Going up another rung to the civil society level, we encountered many different interests, from universities interested in research opportunities and student exchanges to oral history organizations interested in capturing the sto-

Figure 33.1
Vertical and Horizontal Negotiations to Develop Abraham's Path

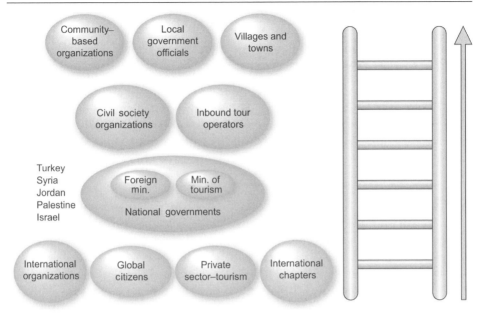

ries of Abraham/Ibrahim in the local communities, to archeological associations whose interest were in the preservation of historical/cultural sites and bringing people to appreciate such places. Another core entity interested in the Path were inbound tour operators who again desired to bring people to their country and show the social conditions as well as reap the economic benefits.

Finally, at the top of the ladder of stakeholders in the Path were the local communities, community-based organizations, and local governments. These entities were similar in some respect and different in others and, as such, need to be discussed one at a time. The local communities—from cities to towns and villages—have varied interests, which include economic benefits from the travelers (e.g., in the form of homestay programs, providing meals, selling handicrafts, offering classes), social interaction and encounter with people from around the world, local ownership and empowerment, and a recognition of their culture, heritage, and unique identity. In fact, it is this last issue of recognition of heritage and identity that many in the Middle East are sorely lacking.

Community-based organizations (CBOs) mirror many of the interests of the local communities themselves, but place more of an importance on the economic benefits and local ownership and empowerment. These CBOs reflect a collective desire to develop the Path in a manner that benefits the community writ large.

Local governments and municipalities are interested in the betterment of their people and their own political survival. The Path offers both of these—particularly through the improved lives of the people and through the publicity the Path brings. For these reasons and the involvement of many communities in national tourism strategies, there is a natural resonance in the Path.

In summary, some of these interests were very obvious, and like any negotiation, others took a good deal of time to try to understand in detail. Along the way there were numerous challenges to manage.

CHALLENGES TO THE DEVELOPMENT AND SUSTAINABILITY OF THE PATH

As with any project of this nature, there were a host of challenges that had to be confronted as the Path evolved. Some of these challenges were surmountable, whereas others we simply had to manage and recognize that they were creative tensions. These challenges are laid out in the following sections as well as the nature of each one and how they were or are being handled.

Meta Challenges

There were a number of meta-level challenges to the project from an early stage. The first meta-level challenge was the need to gain and develop credibility—at the international, national, and—equally important—city, town, and village levels. The second metal-level challenge faced in the project was the need to maintain a cultural diplomacy focus and not get pulled into the political realm. And the third and final meta-level challenge was rooting the Path on the ground with the local communities, showing progress, and taking steps toward long-term sustainability.

With regard to the first challenge of credibility, efforts were begun at the international level by trying to secure high-level partnerships so people inside and outside the region would take the Path seriously. Perhaps nothing went further to giving the Path credibility—at the international, national, and local levels—than the Path's affiliation with Harvard University. In addition, the partnerships built with the United Nations Alliance of Civilizations and the United Nations World Tourism Organization helped to confer legitimacy and put people's doubts and fears at ease. Sequentially, visits to the national governments were next on the list, with the goal of getting their blessing—not their significant involvement. Again, those who have worked in the Middle East learn very quickly that, at a minimum, you must get national governmental sign-off, or you will never have clearance to work at more local levels. In addition to this, endorsements of national associations and other national level entities were sought to further enhance support and trust. After doing all this it would still take quite a while to build and maintain trustworthiness at the local level—something that people are still trying to achieve in different places along the Path to this day.

The second challenge had to do with the focus of the Path being a cultural diplomacy project—not a political or religious effort. As one individual told the organizers early on, "I understand your desire to maintain distance from politics, but when it comes to the Middle East everything is political."[6] This advice was undeniably taken to heart, but steering clear of politics proved to be as difficult as this individual indicated. The reality was that if the Path succumbed to political pressure the project would get held back unnecessarily, and the challenge would become that much greater. Ultimately, it was clear that this was not a challenge that could be won, but rather one that was to be managed as best as possible.

The third meta-level challenge was to have the project take root on the ground, show continual progress, and move toward sustainability. So many projects come and go from the Middle East that it is critical to get a project rooted—particularly through local partnerships and empowering the local community to take the lead with the API supporting them, and not the other way around. But it is the exhibiting of continual progress—walking the talk that people on the ground watch so closely—and having a long-term sustainable plan that are the essential components of meeting this challenge. This meta challenge is a long-term one, and only time will tell if it will be overcome.

The final meta challenge emerged as a result of the use of the name and figure of Abraham. While the name Abraham and what he represents embodies a potential for unification around the world, the name and the figure also carries a tremendous amount of baggage in the Middle East region. The fear of land claims in the name of Abraham or Ibrahim by people on both sides of the conflict deepened people's questions and fears about the Path and its underlying intention. Was it a Zionist conspiracy? Was it an effort at normalization? Was it an Arab project that was seeking to reclaim ancient lands? All of these questions and more were asked and have been a persistent undertone to the Path's development. The way this has been managed is by staying true to the principles of the project and exhibiting the essence of the Path through actions on the ground (and not hollow words).

Midlevel Challenges

There were a host of other midlevel challenges—some of these issues created as many practical problems as the meta-level challenges mentioned previously. In particular, those that were ideological in nature have been particularly difficult to manage.

National and local connections posed an important challenge as the Path developed and took shape. While the importance of getting the national governments and entities on board BEFORE going to the local level was clear, this was easier said than done. But when national approval was accomplished to varying degrees, problems did not disappear. However, the most ardent supporters of the Path, particularly in Jordan and the Palestinian Territories, were those at the local level who wanted the project, were benefitting from it, and were given the opportunity to lead and own the Path from an early phase of the project. What was learned quickly by the organizers was the more local the decision making the more ownership was felt and the least amount of problems were to arise. If problems did surface, the local community would deal with them far more effectively than the API ever could—after all, they lived on the Path and knew the people and their mindset.

The other midlevel challenge has to do with the intricate relationships between dependency, interdependence, and independence. In order to get the project started, resources were needed, which helped to get partners and focus peoples attention on the Path. However, this also created a dependency issue that needed to be addressed if the Path would last over the long term. What was happening slowly, which has certainly been difficult at times, was a slow shift from dependency to interdependence—where the API and local partners recognized what each had to contribute to the effort in complimentary ways. This has continued to evolve into an increased desire from our partners on the ground for independence. Of course, ending up at a desire for independence on the part of the local partners is exactly what had been hoped for, but there were a number of problems along the way, including tension between international and local needs, decision-making issues, and effective cooperation to avoid problems of inefficiency.

As one might imagine, these challenges led to some fascinating stories that exemplify the process of creating the Path as well as some of the amazing outcomes that exhibit the power of the Path to transform lives and communities.

NEGOTIATION THEORY AND PRACTICE FROM AND ALONG THE PATH

Blueprint—What Blueprint?

From a negotiation theory and practice perspective there is a lot to learn and take away from the development of Abraham's Path. With a regional effort of this nature it was even hard to know where to begin. There is certainly no blueprint for how to make a Path come to life—even though there were very useful learnings that were culled from the development of other routes, such as the Camino de Santiago, the Lebanon Mountain Trail, the St. Paul Trail, and the Greenways of Europe. The issue of learning from these routes is not about comparing apples to apples, but rather apples to bananas, since none of these other routes traversed a region in conflict such as the Middle East.

Because there was no blueprint for breathing life into Abraham's Path, the organizers started with very small bite-size chunks—developing a short DVD to describe the Path, starting the diplomatic efforts at the international and national levels, reaching out to potential partners, and beginning to connect with the local communities to explain the project and seek their leadership and involvement. This reality would begin to blossom into many more moving parts as the Path began to take hold. However, underpinning the overall effort was an elicitive strategy—that is, taking a step based on consultation from certain parties, stopping and listening for feedback, and then taking another step. Many times the message came back that the action taken was not going to be successful, so a course correction was made until things began clicking on the ground.

A Key to the Development of the Path—Local Decision Making

One clear lesson was that the more local the decision, the more likely it was to succeed. As only one of many examples, take this situation involving attempts to get the Path started in Turkey.

In November 2006, Ury returned with the first study tour consisting a delegation of some 25 people from 10 different countries, to retrace the footsteps of Abraham from Urfa and Harran to Hebron, from Abraham's remembered birth cave to his death cave, from "womb to tomb" as Ury put it. In nearby Urfa, Ury and his colleagues met with the mayor of Harran and learned that a torrential flood had just occurred, leaving several hundred people without drinking water and significantly affecting his community. When the traveling group asked if and how they could help, the mayor indicated that drinking water would be most welcome. Ury decided on the spot to help, using private funds to purchase a truckload of bottled water: "how could we not, being there as we were at that moment? There was no quid pro quo expected or anything like that. It just seemed like the right thing to do since the very place we had come to honor was in dire need at that moment." Because of flooding in the region, the Deputy Prime Minister of Turkey came to Urfa to view the damage. Upon learning about the consultations and Harvard's involvement, he came to the meeting and endorsed it with a quote that opened the door to further conversation ("We're interested to learn more").

At the study tour meeting in Urfa, further issues—one in particular—emerged that would cause the project significant challenges. In preparation for the meeting, some of the Initiative's early partners in Istanbul suggested that the Armenian Patriarch, a Turkish citizen resident in Istanbul who enjoyed good relations with the Turkish state, should be invited. After all, the Abraham Path was about inclusion and healing of old wounds. Unfortunately, the presence of the Patriarch in Sanliurfa caused some significant concern among many citizens as to the true nature and intention of the project. Relations between Turks and Armenians in Sanliurfa were still sensitive and not nearly as well developed and positive as those in Istanbul. Rumors abounded: was the secret purpose of the API here to work on Turkish-Armenian relations? The study tour left an uneasy city with many unanswered questions and significant concerns.

Later, Ury, Yilmaz and I realized we needed to engage the community in Sanliurfa quickly. Yilmaz suggested that she go herself and meet with the mayor and governor. Yilmaz did and carried the message back to the API that if they wanted their project to work, they would have to do a better job of listening to the local leaders. Our response was "Okay, we understand, tell us what we need to do." The mayor and governor explained the importance of tourism to the area and suggested that framing in these terms be used going forward because the people in Sanliurfa would understand it. "Emphasize the tourism angle and show it to be true," they explained, "and you will gain the people's trust and confidence."

So in May 2007, Yilmaz, Daniel Adamson, Director of Path Development, and I went to Sanliurfa for a key meeting with representatives of the governor, mayor, and civil society representatives. At that meeting, the three of us expressed regret for the way things had transpired and that we were really there to listen to them and to have them take the lead with the Initiative supporting them. Yilmaz explained that this was a key moment for the project in Sanliurfa, but certainly not the end of the concerns.

In November 2007, the Abraham Path sponsored a tourism conference and trek in Sanliurfa and Harran, Turkey. I largely attribute the success of this event to Yilmaz's efforts on behalf of the Path:

> A lot of the credit for that goes to Arzu. She gained their trust and she's a city girl, you know, a Kurd again in a realm where there's tenuous relationships. She was magical in terms of getting the trust of the governor and the vice governor. Things had been fluid. One minute they were right behind us and the next minute, they couldn't support us. In 2007, in November, we had 170 people come to the tourism conference. One hundred people did the trek. We'd also planned a concert, but we cancelled because a few days before, some Turkish soldiers were killed and the local hosts thought that it would not be a time to celebrate and so we did not that out of respect. Part of the purpose was to try to change the image of the project there. We got tremendous publicity. The Ministry of Tourism paid for eight international journalists to come. There were seven national stories written, 25 local stories, TV spots, and thanks to our Brazilian colleagues we had a Brazilian TV company called Globo come and ultimately air a four-minute segment on *Fantastico* (the equivalent of *60 Minutes* in the United States) on Christmas Eve in Brazil which was watched by close to 40 million people. And so we got a tremendous amount of publicity. I was surprised that we succeeded at reformulating the project. We had made so many mistakes.

Prior to the Sanliurfa tourism conference, the Abraham Path Initiative had been the subject of threats from a small group of locals who opposed the initiative. Part of this opposition was due to the geopolitical situation at the time, which saw the United States and Turkey at odds over the handling of the Kurdish issue in northern Iraq. Furthermore, the U.S. House of Representatives had just passed a nonbinding resolution stating they believed that the situation in the early 20th century between the Armenians and Turks should indeed be labeled a genocide. Anti-American sentiment simmered among some in the local population. Threatening e-mails were sent to members of the Abraham Path Initiative staff. In the face of continuing conflict about the Initiative presence in the area, the author conferred with Ury about how they should proceed. Ury asked for my opinion. I reported that Yilmaz told him that the governor and mayor had acknowledged that there were threats but promised to do their best to provide security. The author recalled telling Ury, "We have to trust our partners. We've sought partnerships, saying we would take the lead from them." And Ury said, "Fair enough." I continued, "So we went ahead and while there were some small protests, everything went off without a hitch despite there being some tension in the air. It was good lesson that you have to put your money where you put your mouth."[7]

Sequencing the Negotiations to Develop the Path

As work on the Path began, emanating from the Global Negotiation Initiative at the Program on Negotiation at Harvard Law School, the question was often asked by interested observers—what does this Path have to do with ne-gotiation? The answer, of course, is that it has everything to do with negotia-tion. Abraham Path Initiative Board Member and Harvard Business School Professor James Sebenius often refers to the sequence of negotiations it took to develop the Path as a "negotiation campaign."[8] He compares this to a political campaign with the primary difference being that a political campaign has a fi-nite end, which makes it a lot easier to plan and fundraise for. But the most im-portant piece to this analogy is the issue of sequencing. Within any campaign there is an aspect of sequencing that is critically important because sequenc-ing is the type of issue that, if you get it right, nobody notices, but if you get it wrong, everyone blames it on how sequenced your approach.[9]

Previously, the sequence of how the API attempted to go about getting sup-port and dusting off the footprints was laid out. From the diagram depicted earlier it appears as if the process was a nice linear series of events, but in re-ality it was far more circular in nature. As was learned, certain actions were needed to gain permissions in order to do this work, but that was a *necessary but not sufficient condition* for success. There were so many other variables at play that it would have been foolish to think anything else. Furthermore, like most NGOs, much of what happens around the API is out of its control, and the people within the Initiative have to adapt to the changing environment they are working in. For example, when the war in Gaza erupted, the attention of the API shifted to Turkey and Jordan in the near term, thereby requiring that they wait until the situation in Israel and the Palestinian Territories settled to resume work there.

Time Was on the Side of the Path—Somewhat

Helping to support the creation of Abraham's Path is a long-term endeavor that could take a decade or more, given all the factors involved. In some re-spects that is a positive—that time is on the side of the Path, there is no hurry, and if challenges come up, they can be outlasted, or at least there is the ability to be patient until the situation changes. However, time has a funny way of also being an elusive concept. When you start working on the ground in con-flict zones, time is of the essence in the eyes of the people who live there. So many projects come and go in the Middle East, in particular, that resources, results, and progress are closely watched for their efficacy. The trick with re-gard to time is to see it as something to be worked with—recognizing that at certain moments things will become urgent, and at other moments, a longer-term perspective is needed and can be taken. The organizers have to remind themselves constantly that the development of the Path was a marathon, not a sprint. Even marathoners have to pick up and slow the pace at different times.

Creating a Broad Coalition Around a Key Issue

It should be very clear at this point that working at multiple levels was an essential ingredient to helping the Path come to life. Building a broad coalition—vertically and horizontally—was critical. And this was no more important than in the area of funding for the Path. In fact, one of the first things people wanted to know was "Who is funding the Path?" The danger of being brandished a project with a political or religious agenda was high given where the project emanated from (United States) and some of the early leaders (primarily of a certain religious background) of the effort. But since this was neither of those things, the organizers had to wage a conscious campaign that exhibited the broad cross-cutting and inclusive nature of the effort. As such, funding was secured from a wide variety of sources, creating a strong and diverse coalition, and making it very difficult for even the staunchest critics of the Path to attack this issue.

Two Powerful Interests on the Side of the Path

In spite of all the potential problems and opposition the Path faced, it still continues to this day. From a negotiation perspective, it is useful to ask, "Why is it persisting in the face of all these challenges?" The answer, while certainly complicated and not monolithic, comes down to two key interests found at multiple levels. The first is the story of Abraham/Ibrahim and the power it wields internationally and, more importantly, locally across the Middle East. The second is the desire and recognition by all the countries in the Middle East region that tourism is going to be a significant part of their future. Let's look at this powerful combination in more detail.

With regard to the power of the story of Abraham/Ibrahim, William Ury, the founder of the Abraham Path Initiative, calls this story the world's most widespread origin myth.[10] The fact is that at least 3.5 billion on the planet trace their history and lineage back to this story in some manner. For people around the world, there is a tremendous pull to connect with this story in different ways. This, of course, translates into the desire to travel the Path in the footsteps of Abraham. Those who cannot travel the Path for various reasons still have a desire to connect with the project by conducting walks in their own communities or by connecting with the virtual Path—the beginnings of which are in development.[11]

Interestingly, however, while the pull for people around the world is strong to connect with Abraham/Ibrahim, the bond to the story exhibited by the people of the Middle East region is much more intense. Abraham/Ibrahim is a living figure all throughout the region and is someone who is evoked constantly as a source of pride, guidance, and the basis for many of the vales the people live their life by. For example, Abraham/Ibrahim is associated with faith in the unknown, hospitality, and respect. The stories recounted in the Old Testament, and later in the Koran, bear testament to this fact. For example, in the book of Genesis, Abraham is asked to leave his home and go forth into the unknown. He knows not where he is going, why he is going, and for what purpose, and yet he goes with as much conviction as one can in those circumstances. Similarly, with regard to hospitality, it is said that Abraham's tent was open in all four directions as a sign of hospitality to guests and wayfarers. This tradition continues in the villages and towns of the Middle East today—as travelers show up and are treated better than most families treat their relatives. Finally, the notion of respect is also embedded in the story in a way that can only be described as genuine and based on esteem for the other, regardless of label. For example, an ancient Arab tradition dictates that when a guest shows up unexpectedly at one's home, it is the family's duty to provide shelter to that person or people for seven days before asking their name. This forces the family to get to know the stranger as a person first before bringing any preconceived notions to the situation.[12]

The second interest that was widespread and helps explain the different countries involvement in the Path is the touristic aspect of their future. As was previously mentioned, most if not all of the countries along the Path see tourism as an important part of their economic future as oil reserves and other traditional means of income dry up.[13] These countries are inherently political, but they are also pragmatic and entrepreneurial in spirit. Because the Abraham Path is a very functional effort with the promise of responsible tourism consistent with cultural norms and values, other business opportunities, and the strong potential to improve the lives of the people in the villages and towns, the people and national and local governments of the region found the entire concept intriguing and enticing. Most of the Ministries of Tourism have expressed strong interest in the Path, and some are working actively to make it come into being. Furthermore, the private section is increasingly getting involved and even beginning to offer trips down the Path on their own. Finally, a few local regions have already begun to form community-based organizations to take advantage of the opportunity and begin homestay programs, meal preparation, and offer handicraft classes. These two core interests—taken together—are at the heart of why the Path has evolved and why it has a strong chance to succeed in the future.

Getting Unusual Suspects Involved—Taking the Pressure Off

The last, and perhaps most important, lesson from the Abraham Path for the field of negotiation and peacemaking is the broad range of people involved in the effort. Given this is a Path of connection in a largely disconnected place, it also held open the opportunity to get unusual suspects involved—people who are typically not involved in various conflict resolution processes. The key to having these people involved was to take of the pressure of cross-border cooperation and leave that up to the partners and communities on the ground. What was asked of all the partners and teams on the ground was to work on their part of the Path and nothing more. This had the effect of easing people's fears, enabling them to build the Path in the way that *they* saw best and, in the process, honoring their own identities in a way that felt affirming and productive. Nowhere is this more the case than in the Palestinian Territories where the Palestinian partners have made the most progress in developing their part of the Path and in feeling empowered by the process. As one example, a few years back, as the Palestinian team analyzed their part of the Path, they felt a bit demoralized given all the restrictions of movement and other challenges they faced. They looked at other parts of the Path and saw beautiful landscapes and other aspects of the Path that they did not think they could compete with. But then one member of the team—after reflecting for a while—stated, "Wait a minute, we have something other parts of the Path do not . . . we have many of the sites directly related to Abraham! We have Nablus (ancient Shechem), Beitin (ancient Beth El), and Hebron (AKA Al Khalil)." From that moment on the Palestinians never turned back and saw this as a critical affirmation of their identity, which was a very important step toward any potential cooperation in the future. And that decision will be theirs and theirs alone. However, the chances of that happening are greatly increased when they are not forced to cooperate, but rather are able to see this happen naturally through functional avenues—such as travelers and other businesses that emerge along the way.

CONCLUSION

The Abraham Path did not start out as the Path of a thousand negotiations, but it has certainly evolved in that manner, and the success or failure of future negotiations will be a key reason the Path persists or fades into the landscape. From negotiations to gain credibility to negotiations to develop local support for the project, the Path continues to unfold step by step. Embedded in this ancient route, as the dust blows in the latest storm, are critical lessons for those involved in the development of the Path but also for the field writ large. And these lessons are there for people to read about or go experience for themselves—perhaps even culling further gems that will aid our work in the future.

NOTES

1. Kevin Rushby, "Walking in Palestine," *The Guardian*, September 4, 2010, 2–3.

2. J. Sebenius, K. Leary, and J. Weiss, *Negotiating the Path of Abraham* (Cambridge, MA: Harvard Business School Case Study, January 2010), 7–8.

3. Ibid.

4. Ibid.

5. Ibid.

6. Anonymous interview with Joshua Weiss, January 18, 2007.

7. Sebenius et al., 21–23.

8. J. Sebenius, "Beyond the Deal: Wage a 'Negotiation Campaign,'" *Negotiation Newsletter* 13, no. 11 (November 2010): 1–4.

9. For more on sequencing, see J. Weiss, *Which Way Forward? Mediator Sequencing Strategies in Intractable Communal Conflicts* (Saarbrücken, Germany: VDM Verlag Publishing, 2008).

10. An origin myth is a story or explanation that describes the beginning of some feature of the natural or social world. In this case, each culture has an origin myth about its development and beginnings that is relevant here.

11. See http://www.abrahamPath.org/virtual.php.

12 In fact, this tradition caused a bit of a challenge for the project because it was hard to explain the importance of charging guests to stay with them in order to generate economic resources for their families. People wanted to house these guests, not for money, but out of duty. Thankfully, some of the locals understood the concept of

tourism and were able to impart this concept to others who were skeptical. Similar traditions are found in the other religions associated with Abraham as well.

13. There are many articles and statistics on Middle East tourism and its importance. See, for example, http://www.eturbonews.com/10586/wto-middle-east-tourism-expected-rise and http://findarticles.com/p/articles/mi_m2742/is_341/ai_n250 81248/.

PART IV: INTERPRETING PEACEMAKING

Introduction

Andrea Bartoli

Peacemaking is a difficult choice, often not made and not supported. It is against the grain of the in-group and the wisdom of those who think that there is no other way than violence and war. Peacemaking is a hypothesis first. It is a potential that needs to be actualized. It is not certain, not definitive, not conclusive. It is a possibility offered in the midst of perceived impossibilities. This volume focuses on peacemaking as a shift, as a tangible result of human interaction, that moves individuals and groups from hostility to cooperation, from violence to coexistence, from war to peace. It assumes a dynamical system approach and understanding that consider war and peace as products, results of protracted human interaction. Thirty years ago, John Burton (1988) wrote,

> I wish to emphasize these precise uses of terms because clarifying their meanings goes to the heart of the problem we are discussing, that is, the separate but generic nature of disputes and of conflicts. If there were no difference between disputes and conflicts, if, that is, all human relationships could be regulated and controlled by an authoritative third party, then with sufficient courts and alternative means of settlement, and with sufficient means of enforcement, we could be assured of harmonious relationships domestically and internationally. History shows us that this is not the case: there are situations, both domestic and international, that are not subject to authoritative or coercive settlements.

The work of many, the deaths of too many more, the pain and sorrow of countless others, have brought the task of peacemaking to the forefront of our collective enterprise. The escalation that leads to violent destruction is often associated with a collapse in complexity, with the realization (or the illusion) that there is no other way, that violence is the only choice. There is an urgency to learn more about how to handle conflict constructively, how to face the challenges associated with conflict in ways that are not misguided, self-defeating, and hopeless. In the midst of conflict, we must be serious, we must dedicate ourselves to inquiry, and we must open up processes that might seem daring to some but will contribute to all. These pages guide us in considering peacemaking as an ever-occurring human experience. This section focuses on how we understand peacemaking, how we interpret it, how we make sense of it, and how we know it when we see it. By interpreting peacemaking, we find language with which to share our learning with others.

Peacemaking can be defined as an appropriate response of the actors involved in the conflict (either as party to it or as intermediary) that moves (or is intended to move) the human system away from violent confrontation toward cooperative inquiry. When these responses constructively address the needs of all involved and include procedures of adaptability within the emerging system, that will allow it to engage in self-correction and sustainability. Even in defining peacemaking, we are interpreting it. The definition focuses our attention to some aspects of peacemaking. Peacemaking is a long process that involves many decisions. It is through the analysis of patterns and long-term results that specific moments become turning points, opportunities for the whole system to be reoriented. The accumulation of free, verified, and adaptable responses can have positive cumulative effects on the parties, the conflict system, and all elements in the system. At least, many interpretations of peacemaking see it this way. It is imperative to foster a movement from practice to theory that is truly a collective and inclusive enterprise and allows multiple frames to illuminate peacemaking. By seeing peacemaking through different lenses, we learn different aspects of peacemaking. How we interpret peacemaking shapes how we practice peacemaking and how we teach peacemaking.

This last section of the volume, part 4, is dedicated to interpreting peacemaking and includes 15 chapters. The perspective is intentionally interdisciplinary and moves away from the narrow focus on official institutions and formal processes that dominates analyses of peacemaking but rather offers a more organic understanding of its true nature and potential. Just as humans could communicate before understanding linguistic theory, the study of peacemaking must begin with the recognition that humans have always been peacemakers. In this way, a more effective approach toward understanding peacemaking should take, as a starting point, the lived experiences of those engaged in seeking peaceful resolutions to violent disputes. Our intention is to refocus the study of peacemaking toward a systematic understanding of the various practices adopted by peacemakers around the globe. This is why this section is opened by an anthropological overview of peacemaking and reconciliation. Douglas P. Fry frames properly the exploration of peacemaking as an expression of human creativity and ingenuity. There are indeed human systems in which peace is sustaining and sustained. His examples question widespread assumptions about human aggressiveness and destructivity while inviting some further reflection on the very possibility of creating peacemaking human systems.

Peace does not happen by chance. It is the fruit of human choices. It is encouraged by cultures and expressed in social interactions. The break of peace is also not an expression of randomness alone but rather the systemic shift due to an accumulation of meaning. Peacemaking is highly dependent on the cultural variables that are available to individuals in a given context. A few chapters attempt to reflect on peacemaking from practice and have been placed in this section because they enrich the very understanding of peacemaking as process.

Anthony Wanis-St. John also addresses this relational capacity in his invitation to look at the animal kingdom for clues about peacemaking. He then uses passages from epic religious-mythological literature to support the contention that peacemaking has long been a universal part of human culture despite enormous cultural variation in practice today, despite, and perhaps because of, our long preoccupation with warfare. As we evolve, learn, and share in understanding, it becomes clear that indeed, as human we have the capacity to transcend constraints, to reframe them in through new meanings and new relational engagements. Vern Nuefield Redekop argues in his "Spirituality, Emergent Creativity, Peacemaking, and Reconciliation" that peacemaking is the deliberate effort to move human systems from destructive and violent patterns into constructive respectful ones. The role of spirituality and emergent creativity in these shifts is immense. When we examine each in the light of the other new understandings are highlighted. Spirituality is presented as the nexus of a source of inner strength, the establishment of rich transpersonal connection, transcendent understandings of the interconnections within the universe and awe at what has emerged, and an ethical vision of care. Emergent creativity is understood as a nonreducible and unpredictable transformation of a complex adaptive system such that the new product of the creative process is irreversibly established. At the core of the dynamism is human choice.

Morton Deutsch's approach on the "Social-Psychological Perspective on Peacemaking" presented in this section is in many ways the turning point, the moment of coalescence of contributions moving from practice to theory and vice versa. The margins for individual choosing within the parameters affect enormously the capacity to engage conflict constructively or destructively. The break of peace is not only an individual choice made by isolated individuals but rather a reasonable response to the current conditions. It must be noted that—in order to fully appreciate Deutsch's text—it might be helpful to recall the role of his research for some of the most relevant actors in the use of it in Poland. Two outstanding psychologists, Janusz Reykowski and Janusz Grzelak, applied some of his ideas during the negotiations between the Communist government and Solidarity that led to a peaceful transfer of governmental power from the Communist Party to Solidarity in 1989. Reykowski was a leading figure in the Communist Party, and Grzelak was a very important influence in the Solidarity movement. Each has indicated that Deutsch's work influenced him considerably in his approach to the negotiations, which facilitated a constructive resolution of the process. The observation is helpful to capture the dynamism of the theory-to-practice transfer. Once the ideas are shared, they belong to the reader, not only to the author, and peacemaking can be suggested by, supported by, and encouraged by relevant theories.

This exploration of the possible, of history in the making, beyond the constraints of what is perceived to be threatening, is core to the method in peacemaking formulated by Jamie Price that invites a reflection on, in Aristotelian terms, the *praxis* of peacemaking (what we do) from its *poiesis* (what we make[1]). It is a distinction that, for those familiar with Christian Scriptures, cannot go but in the direction of Jesus's expression "Blessed are the peacemakers," where the verb used is indeed *poiesis*. Peacemakers are indeed "peace-poets," people capable of finding in their own selves and in the environment the thoughts, words, and deeds that actualize something that would otherwise remain potential. As Price notes, peacemaking has to do with the range of actions and activities involved in defusing feelings of threat, deepening insight into the other, and otherwise healing, mending, and connecting relationships strained, broken, or disconnected by conflict. These choices create and orient systems as noticed—in different ways—by Louise Diamond, Monty G. Marshall, Peter Coleman, Lan Bui-Wrzosinska, Andrzej Nowak, and Robin Vallacher. Actual actors, as political subjects that are capable of peacemaking in highly contested conditions, shape the dynamism of these emergent systems.

Due to this interaction, change is omnipresent. Christopher Mitchell aptly delves into the theories of change that many prominent actors refer to when they reflect on their work. Similarly, Ronald Fisher offers a solid description of his contingency model for third-party intervention that explains many of the fundamental dynamics of human systems moving toward a peaceful resolution of conflicts. However, these interventions are not without challenges, and Louis Kriesberg focuses, in particular, on the tensions created by external ones. Differently, but always theorizing from actual cases, Dean Pruitt presents here for the first time his urgency theory, based on his in-depth analysis of the South Africa peace process; Simon Mason links peacemaking and mediation in actual cases; and Peter Woodrow and Diana Chigas elaborate on the rich finding of the Reflecting on Peace Practices project. Ranabir Samaddar concludes part 4 with an invitation to use peacemaking as a way to comprehend more thoroughly the political subject.

Some of the authors in part 4 belong to a generation that has contributed enormously to the conflict-resolution literature. We are very grateful to have them, together with other scholars who are now enriching a lively tradition. It seems appropriate to frame this current effort as a way to rediscover some aspects of the most relevant intellectual traditions that have contributed to the interpretation of peacemaking. From Kurt Lewin to Anatol Rappoport, from Elise Boulding to Sara Cobb, the field has expressed a richness that must be recognized and celebrated. In this trajectory, these contributions reaffirm three fundamentals: (1) interactivity, (2) relational responsibility, and (3) dynamism. Each conflict is relational, and each peacemaking conception and execution is relational. Interactivity is the locus of peacemaking. It is the fundamental dynamism that allows us not only to understand conflict and peacemaking accurately but also to respond to it constructively. The subject, in response to the environment, guides this interactivity.

However, the system in which the subject operates effectively constraints and orients her or his choices. This is why it is essential to introduce the notion of relational responsibility as the fundamental peacemaking orientation of those who act attentively, intelligently, reasonably, and responsibly in their relationships to others and the environment. Peacemaking occurs in all situations. It is an expression of and dependant upon human choices made by actual subjects in the most routine, or exceptional circumstances. This expression—while not Burtonian in its form—is embedded in John Burton's reasoning on "right relationships" and "provention." Finally, dynamism reminds us that everything changes over time, that conflicts in particular—while often products of recurrent patterns—do change over time. The constraints that human systems pose to movement and chance of time are at the core of the relational responsibility of the peacemakers who try to liberate human systems from these constraints.

While concluding the present work, part 4 invites all of us into the core of the practice-to-theory movement: the desire to acknowledge, understand, and strengthen peacemaking. We believe that this project, although rich and complex, is just a small and very initial contribution to this reflection. We expect new contributions to emerge, new interpretative frames to be tried, and new insights to be formed. Meanwhile, we are very grateful to the innumerable cohort of those who have been engaged in peacemaking and attempted to interpret it.

NOTE

1. Aristotle. 2009. *Nicomacheam Ethics*. Revised edition. Cambridge, MA: Oxford University Press.

CHAPTER 34

Anthropological Examples of Peacemaking: Practice and Theory

Douglas P. Fry

Anthropology provides diverse, sometimes fascinating insights into the ways that people sustain the peace and, in the event that the peace has been disrupted, how people restore it and reconcile their damaged relationships. Whereas looking at cultural diversity is a hallmark of anthropological comparisons, nonetheless, a cross-cultural view reveals certain recurring elements. In this chapter, a central goal is to look for themes in both peace sustainability and peacemaking across divergent cultures. The first part of the chapter focuses on how to prevent war, or to express this in the positive, on how to promote ongoing peaceful relations. The second part of the chapter examines ways of restoring the peace, once broken. Certain themes that emerge from a consideration of the cross-cultural data are used to organize the ethnographic material.

SUSTAINING THE PEACE AND PREVENTING WAR

Ethnographically, most societies engage in warfare, but some do not.[1] Non-warring societies can be found in various locations around the planet. Among the Hanunóo of Southeast Asia, "warfare, either actual or traditional, is absent."[2] The Saulteaux of North America "have never engaged in war with the whites or with other Indian tribes."[3] The Veddahs of Asia "live so peacefully together that one seldom hears of quarrels among them and never of war."[4] Pertaining to the Mardu of Australia, "there is no ethnographic evidence to suggest the existence of long-standing intergroup animosity akin to feud. There is no word for either feud or warfare in the language of the desert people."[5] And for the Machiguenga of South America, we have the report that "there is no warfare in their region."[6] Thus, war is not always and everywhere present.

Peace systems—groups of neighboring societies that do not make war on each other and sometimes not with outsiders as well—have been documented within Malaysia, Australia, India, Brazil, Canada, and elsewhere.[7] The Chewong, for instance, are one member of the non-warring peace system of Peninsular Malaysia that also includes such cultures as the Semai, Jahai, Btsisi, Batek, and other Semang groups.[8] In terms of values and behavior, these Malaysian societies emphasize conflict avoidance. And Howell notes that peaceful coexistence is their trademark: "None of these has any history of warfare, and overt acts of aggression are very rare."[9] The Malaysian peace system is not a new development, as evidenced by early accounts of these societies shunning violent resistance, even to slave raiders, and their "extraordinarily peaceful nature."[10]

An examination of non-warring societies and peace systems can provide insights into successful strategies for preventing intergroup violence. Peace-sustaining themes that we will consider in sequence include the creation and maintenance of (1) overarching social identities, (2) dense interconnections among subgroups, (3) interdependence, (4) values for peace, (5) ceremonies and symbolism that reinforce peace, (6) ritualization of competition, and (7) the development of overarching political institutions.

Social Identity: Expanding the Us

During times of conflict, certain psychological states can develop between groups. These psychological states include negative views and attitudes toward the other group, dehumanization, de-individuation, hostility, and competitiveness.[11] Separate identities tend to develop that distinguish the Us from the Them, a feature of de-individuation that redefines people not as individuals but as members of a social category. Group identification and the psychological states that tend to accompany it do not, in and of themselves, lead to war, but in times of conflict, Us-Them contrasting identities can augment hostility and facilitate intergroup violence.

At least some successful peace systems have psychosocial elements that counter tendencies toward us-them polarization by Expanding the Us to include the Them. For example, among the 10 tribes that make up four different language groups of the Upper Xingu River basin in Brazil, identities go beyond individual tribal membership.[12] The people of these 10 tribes have expanded the Us to include members of the other tribes as an additional social identity beyond the single tribe. Shared rituals and ceremonies reinforce the shared perception that each person is a member of a larger, peaceful social system that extends beyond the single tribe. As one Xinguano expresses, "We don't make war; we have festivals for the chiefs to which all of the villages come. We sing, dance, trade and wrestle."[13]

Darwin understood the Expanding the Us potential of human beings when he wrote in *The Descent of Man*, "As man advances in civilization, and small tribes are united into larger communities, the simplest reason would tell each individual that he ought to extend his social instincts and sympathies to all the other members of the same nation, though personally unknown to him. This point being once reached, there is only an artificial barrier to prevent his sympathies extending to the men of all nations and races."[14] Anthropological observations suggest that there are various ways for Expanding the Us, some of which we will now consider.

Nurture Interconnections

Social bonds among members of different groups, for instance, stemming from perceived similarity, mutual dependency, friendship, kinship, and so forth, discourage contentious practices and reduce the chance of dispute escalation.[15] Forming linkages that cross-cut different social groups is a very effective way to prevent violence among them. For example, due in part to "the multiple linkages (shared values, religion, worldview, Law, kinship, friendship and marriage alliances) joining every Mardu band to all others in their society, the arena of shared understandings is huge when groups need to resolve their differences."[16] The Mardu bands do not feud or make war. They allow open access to resources, and they solve disputes and conduct important ceremonies when they come together several times a year at big meetings.

Australian Aborigines in general are renowned within anthropology for their elaborate kinship systems. An illustration of how kinship ties help to sustain the peace comes from the Tiwi of northern Austria: "The bands were not firm political entities and therefore could not do battle, as bands, with each other. Everybody, on both sides, was interrelated in the same kinship system."[17] Among the Ju/'hoansi of Africa, who do not engage in warfare, each adult has trade partners in different groups, a fact that contributes another level of cross-cutting ties to the existing intergroup bonds of kinship.[18] The same principle is also illustrated from a very different cultural context as Glazer describes how special-purpose friendships that cross-cut antagonistic ethnic groups in New York can contribute to more amicable relations between the groups.[19] Intermarriage between groups can play a similar peace-sustaining role.[20] Within the Upper Xingu River basin peace system, for example, "intertribal marriage is a major source of peaceful contact with each of the Xingu villages."[21] Overall, we can propose that the existence of multiple types of cross-cutting ties among groups, ranging in character from ceremonial unions, kinship, and intermarriage to economic partnerships and friendships, dramatically reduces the possibility that conflicts will lead to intergroup violence.

Utilize Existing Interdependence and Create Even Greater Interdependence

Interdependence among groups is another factor that can contribute to peaceful intergroup relations. A classic script reads, when faced by a common enemy, drop your feuds, put aside your antagonisms, and cooperate to launch a united defense.[22] For example, once horse-raiding had become established among the Comanche, "fighting within the tribe was not to be countenanced when there were always outside enemies to be confronted."[23]

There are various types of interdependence, some imposed by circumstance and some purposefully created. At times, the harshness of the physical environment can be a unifying force, as occurs under ecological conditions when rainfall is sporadic and variable from year to year. The solution to harsh conditions in Africa's Kalahari Desert or Australia's Great Western Desert is for local groups to reciprocally allow each other access to water and food resources. Tonkinson points out that to allow disputes to harden into feuding or warfare under such conditions would be suicidal: "The situation is one of small and scattered highly mobile groups moving freely within large territories rather than highly localized, solitary corporate groups contesting resources and maintaining boundaries. . . . Everyone is mindful also of how much their survival rests on mutual hospitality and unfettered access to their neighbors' natural resources in both lean and bountiful times."[24]

Trade and exchange are antithetical to war. Exchange partners must be able to trust that items given away will be reciprocated in the future.[25] Trade helps to create the linkages among people that warfare casts asunder. Humans are adept at creating exchange relationships, which in turn contribute to economic interdependences and the maintenance of peaceful relations. Sahlins has called such pervasive exchanged balanced reciprocity.[26] Intertribal trade connects the villages of Brazil's Upper Xingu River peace system, for example.[27] The tribes of Australia's Western Desert have big meetings wherein they "exchange weapons, ochre, pearl shells, sacred boards and other objects and, importantly, resolve disputes, to maintain links of friendship and shared religion among the groups present."[28]

Promote Values for Peace

"In the Waurá view, self-control over violent aggressive impulses, compassion for children, and acceptance of the responsibility to share material wealth are all basic attributes of human beings."[29] Some value orientations are more conducive to peace than others.[30] Specifically, values provide the members of society with a motivational context that either accepts warfare as legitimate or not. Goldschmidt observes that "a veritable formula for war is for the society to place a high value on aggressiveness and ferocity."[31] On the other hand, values can promote peace. In the value system of the Upper Xingu tribes, peace is moral, and war is not: "The good citizen is therefore peaceful in response to both the moral imperative of peace and the aesthetics of behavior."[32] Thus, among these Xingu peoples, the warrior role is neither valued nor rewarded.[33]

The people of the Upper Xingu contrast themselves and their own peaceful value system to the values and behavior of neighboring warring peoples, a comparison that serves to remind them that warfare is morally repugnant and unacceptable in their own society. The Upper Xingu people see their own antiwar values as morally superior to those of the archetypal "wild Indian" who "splits peoples' heads with clubs. He kidnaps children and burns villages. He kills his own kin. War for him is a festival."[34] In that values become internalized within the minds of people and serve as guidelines for behavior, the promotion of antiwar values in society has a role to play in sustaining the peace.

Develop Unifying Ceremonies and Symbolism

Goldschmidt discusses social institutions of peace as "socially constructed patterns of behavior in which antagonism and competitiveness are expressed in ways that are neither lethal nor violent."[35] He suggests that the white deerskin dance of the Karok, Hupa, and Yurok of northern California; the potlatch among certain societies of the northwest coast of North America, such as the Kwakiutl; and the *kula* exchange system of Melanesia are institutions that reduce the chance of war by redirecting competitiveness to economic channels. The Kwakiutl called it "fighting with property," and Goldschmidt quotes ethnographer Codere on the historical shift in that society away from warfare: "'Fighting with property' instead of 'with weapons,' 'wars of property' instead of 'wars of blood,' are Kwakiutl phrases expressing what has proved to be a fundamental historical change in Kwakiutl life."[36]

The Upper Xingu peoples also engage in certain joint ceremonies that span tribal membership that serve to reinforce that they all belong to a common social system. They inaugurate chiefs at such overarching ceremonies as well as mourn the passing of former chiefs. Ceremonies such as these can contributed to feelings of unification and an expanded common identity.

Ritualize Competition

Social life involves certain tensions both within and among social groups. Various ethnographic descriptions from geographically disparate locations show that intergroup tensions can be channeled through nonviolent outlets. For example, after the Mendi of New Guinea were forced by the government to give up warfare, instead of meeting on the battlefield, competing clans expressed their rivalries in ritualistic form by hosting elaborate feasts. After years of planning and preparation, a clan would sponsor a huge gathering called a cassowary feast for a rival clan. Each member of the hosting clan displayed and then killed a cassowary bird to be ceremonially eaten. A few days later, the rival clan threw a reciprocal feast. In both cases, the rival clans gave away huge quantities of goods. "The cassowary contest now provides a replacement for inter-clan warfare. . . . As long as each clan has displayed the maximum generosity, both clans win. Honor and a new peace are achieved."[37]

The peoples of the Upper Xingu have a ritual, called *Yawari*, that includes mock aggression between related men from different tribes. In preparation for the ritual, arrowheads are covered with wax. Pairs of opponents take turns throwing and parrying the wax-tipped projectiles at each other as the others look on. The ritual entails the limited and controlled expression of hostility so that no one gets seriously hurt and ends with a reaffirmation of the bonds of kinship and friendship that link members of different tribes.[38]

Create Super-Ordinate Institutions and Practices

One structural or institutional way to bring peace to potentially or actually warring groups is to create or impose an overarching level of governance.[39] Externally imposed governance may bring peace but simultaneously comes with costs. On the other hand, when the constituent groups themselves decide to create a higher level of governance for their common good, a structural manifestation of Expanding the Us, the benefits may be substantial and the costs minimal. As an example, with the creation of the Iroquois League, six tribes from northeastern North America (the Oneida, Mohawk, Cayuga, Onondaga, Seneca, and Tuscarora) established a higher level of governance. The Iroquois League was ruled by a council of chiefs, and the creation of this confederacy brought peace among these societies. The Iroquois did not give up warfare against outsiders, but they did cease hostilities among themselves.[40]

RESTORING THE PEACE

Smith refers to humans as "the most dangerous animal." As the millions of war dead in the 20th century alone testify, humans are capable of remarkable carnage.[41] Nonetheless, humans also have a capacity to make peace and to live in social systems without war. The work of de Waal and his colleagues demonstrates that the ability to reconcile with opponents after engaging in aggression also exists in other species including many nonhuman primates.[42]

In humans, some of the same elements of individual peacemaking occur at the intergroup level. Specifically, individuals engaged in peacemaking may apologize, seek forgiveness, offer compensation, and accept punishment. Sometimes peacemaking rituals are employed during the peacemaking process, which bind the parties to peace accords and symbolize the reestablishment of amicable relations. Other people who are not directly involved in a dispute are instrumental and supportive of peacemaking, whether it occurs between individuals or between groups.

As we shift from a consideration of sustaining the peace to restoring the peace, this second section of the chapter examines several of the most prominent themes in the ethnographic data on peacemaking. The payment of restitution, the involvement of third parties in peacemaking, and reconciliation ceremonies and rituals will be considered in sequence.

Compensation

"A person could commit trespass or murder without being stigmatized as a criminal, but he could expect to be 'called to account' in quite a literal sense—being required to 'pay for his misdeeds,' not by undergoing punishment, but by paying indemnity in the form of shell money or other valuables."[43] This specific example speaks also for many similar cases in the worldwide ethnographic record: The payment of compensation is often a part of the peacemaking process between individuals, corporate groups (such as clans or lineages), and larger communities. For instance, among the Mea Enga of New Guinea, as in Melanesia more generally, negotiating the amount of restitution, to be paid in pigs as the currency of blood money for war dead, is a central feature of peacemaking.[44]

The key psychological feature of paying compensation for those lost in battle is to balance accounts, to even the score, which is a necessary condition that makes peace possible. In describing the peacemaking process among the Mae Enga as a complex series of often-heated negotiations over how much blood money is owed and will be paid in compensation for the war dead, Meggitt refers to the need to even the score and explains that "they should 'settle' the imbalance they have produced by making appropriate payments to the deceased's agnates."[45]

Third Parties

A variety of third-party roles exist from mediators to arbitrators, but a key factor in the effectiveness of third-party peacemakers is to be impartial in their efforts to help warring factions to put down their weapons. The pacification of blood feuds in Montenegro during the 1800s illustrates how arbitrators, called *Kmets*, restored the peace between clans.[46] The *Kmets* were men of high status with reputations for impartiality who assembled as the Court of Good Men. The central goal was to arrive at a compromise, so as to restore the peace and social harmony between clans and within the community overall.

In the 1600s, in South America, the members of a Yao village were instrumental in preventing bloodshed between the Caribs and the Aricoures. The Yao had amicable relations with both groups and hence did not want to see a bloodbath amongst their friends. After Yao intervention, in a dramatic display, the Caribs threw down their weapons and rushed to embrace the war party of Aricoures. To celebrate the end of longstanding enmity and to cement the peace accord, the Yao hosted both groups in their village for eight days.[47]

The importance of third-party impartiality is again reflected in an account of peacemaking between the Comanches and the Utes of the North American plains.[48] "A Ute woman who had been captured by the Comanches was with a band who were fighting the Utes. Her son was a Comanche brave and she feared for his life. Finally she rode out between the fighters and held up her hand calling for them to stop. She said she was on both sides; she a Ute, her son a Comanche, it was not good for them to fight." After some discussion and consideration the two sides made peace. Subsequently, a council of Ute chiefs paid the woman a special honor for her brave peacemaking deed. "They took her back to the main Ute camp where her father and mother were still living. They gave her a tipi with an antelope skin tied to the top of a pole for a special sign."[49]

Reconciliation Rituals

Peacemaking often incorporates reconciliation rituals.[50] A study of reconciliation across cultures reveals recurring themes.[51] Individuals and groups, when engaged in peacemaking, eat, drink, smoke, and celebrate together. Gifts are exchanged. In that engaging in trade is the antithesis of engaging in war, the reinstatement of exchange relations heralds the resumption of peaceful activities. Another element of peacemaking entails rituals that evoke the power of the supernatural to ordain by divine authority the peace accords and signal symbolically the shift in the nature of social relations from the bellicose to the peaceful. Third parties are often involved in peacemaking at various stages and in various capacities, as instigators of the peacemaking process, as mediators and arbitrators during the peacemaking accords, and as celebrants of the outcome. The cessation of hostilities and resumption of normal relations, whether between individuals or groups, are grounds for celebration that typically include oratory, drama, singing, dancing, and feasting.

Koch and his colleagues describe the ritualistic elements of reconciliation among the Jalé of New Guinea; the party that wishes to reconcile must find a curer to perform the required ritual that is rich in symbolic significance:

> The Jalé term for the condition described here as avoidance is *héléroxo*. The expression derives from *hélé*, denoting the ditch that separates two adjacent beds in a garden; the suffix—*roxo* corresponds to the English "-wise." In performing of the ritual, the curer, uttering esoteric formulae, smears a mixture of soil and blood drawn from the slaughtered pig on the hams of the antagonists. That act is called *kénangenep-tuk* ("soil them up"). Soil, or *kénan*, being the substance of that which *hélé*, divides, the metaphorical aspect of the rite becomes apparent, and the expression of "seal them up" aptly to connote the nature of the event.
>
> While at ordinary meals it is customary to tear off a portion of one's piece of food and hand it to a kinsman or neighbor present, on this occasion all participants, especially the reconciled parties, exaggerate these mutual exchanges. As the suspension of food-sharing has signaled the inception of the *héléroxo* relationship, so is its termination affirmed by the ostentatious resumption of commensal practice.[52]

Among the Omaha of North America, war was symbolically represented by the dark, stormy sky, whereas peace was symbolized by the cloudless sunny day.[53] The Omaha developed a peacemaking ceremony, rich in symbolic content, designed to establish between hostile groups a relationship analogous to that of the father and son. Since the warring groups lacked true blood relationships, the ritual aimed at establishing in symbolic form a close familial tie, with the meaning that fathers and sons do not harm one another in war. The peacemaking ceremony involved gift exchange, feasting, and smoking. "The leader of the party was . . . addressed as 'Father' and all his followers as 'Fathers.' The man who received the pipes was addressed as 'Son' and his party as 'Sons.'"[54] Singing was also part of the peacemaking ritual, and lyrics sung by the bearers of the pipes to the receivers helped to define the goals of the proceedings: "I have found the man worthy to receive the pipes and all the blessings which they bring—peace, the promise of abundant life, food, and happiness."[55]

FROM PRACTICE TO THEORY: THE ELEMENTS OF JUSTICE WITHIN PEACEMAKING

We have considered ways for sustaining the peace first and peacemaking second, but in times of hostility, the order must be reversed so that once the fighting stops, social institutions, practices, and values that support peace must be implemented to nourish the peace and reduce the chance of future wars. We started by examining ethnographic examples of peace maintenance that include both the creation and augmentation of overarching social identities (Expanding the Us), the weaving of interconnections among subgroups, the development of interdependence, the promotion of values for peace, the invention of ceremonies and symbolism which reflect new identities and bolster the psychosocial dimensions of peace, the ritualization of competition into nonlethal channels, and the implementation of governance that spans separate social entities. We next explored peacemaking processes recurrent in the cross-cultural literature including the payment of compensation, the participation of impartial third parties in peacemaking, and reconciliation rituals that mark the passage from a state of bellicosity into a state of peace. There are, of course, other ways to classify the ethnographic information on peace-sustaining and peacemaking than those used here, and other researchers might weigh the relative importance of these and other processes differently. I suggest that the features considered in this chapter include the most obvious processes identifiable in the cross-cultural data. What we have not considered, however, are topics such as peace through flight (avoidance), peace through subjugation, or peace through annihilation. Thus it is worth bearing in mind that wars sometimes end through very inequitable outcomes such as these that are a far cry from the peacemaking activities between more evenly balanced parties that we have been considering.

Many scholars have noted the interconnections of peace and justice. Lady Justice is portrayed in Western tradition as blindfolded and holding scales and a sword. Although a Western depiction, it may be that the symbols capture more universal aspects of justice and peacemaking. The blindfold represents impartiality on the part of the judge, a type of third party, and across cultural circumstances, the judicial process ideally must be impartial. Likewise, during peacemaking proceedings, third parties, whether they be mediators like the Yao between the Caribs and the Aricoures, arbitrators like the Montenegrin *Kmets*, or judges as in pacifying colonial powers, will not likely introduce a successful peace accord if they favor one side over the other.[56] A proposal will be perceived as unfair, and hostilities will likely continue under such scenarios.

The scales of Lady Justice represent fairness. The widespread use of compensation as part of the peacemaking process, as in the court of law, reflects the concept of fairness. Unless one side has such clear superiority of power that it can subjugate or annihilate the other, the deaths and damages must be balanced either through negotiations between the parties themselves or with the assistance of third parties. Otherwise, the brokerage of peace is unlikely. The Mea Enga haggle incessantly over payment of compensation for the war dead until both sides agree on restitutions that "settle the imbalance."[57] One variable behind the successful peacemaking between the Comanche and the Ute, when originally proposed by a daring woman, was that both sides had lost equivalent numbers of warriors, reflected in the Comanche leader reassuring his Ute counterpart at one delicate point in the peacemaking process, "things were even and there shouldn't be any trouble."[58]

The sword of Lady Justice signifies the power of the court to enforce its verdicts. This element of justice would seem to be the least applicable of the three principles to the peacemaking process. On occasion, third parties have the power to enforce a peace, as in the pacification of the Mendi by colonial administrators, but more typically neither party to the peacemaking process can unilaterally enforce the peace.

This is where the shift from the process of making peace to sustaining the peace becomes critical for a lasting accord. Peacemaking ceremonies and rituals of reconciliation can signify a new direction in relations between hostile parties, but such accords many times are fragile and must be strengthened through an active application of social institutions and practices for sustaining the peace.

ACKNOWLEDGMENT

Some of the data reported in this chapter were collected during research funded by the National Science Foundation (Grant number 03-13670), whose financial support is gratefully acknowledged. Any opinions, findings, and conclusions or recommendations expressed in this material are those of the author and do not necessarily reflect the views of the National Science Foundation.

NOTES

1. Douglas P. Fry, *The Human Potential for Peace: An Anthropological Challenge to Assumptions about War and Violence* (New York: Oxford University Press, 2006); Keith F. Otterbein, *The Evolution of War: A Cross-Cultural Study* (New Haven, CT: Human Relations Area Files Press, 1970); Quincy Wright, *A Study of War* (Chicago: University of Chicago Press, 1942).

2. Harold C. Conklin, "The Relation of Hanunóo Culture to the Plant World" (PhD diss., Yale University, 1954), 49.

3. A. Irving Hallowell, "Aggression in Saulteaux society," in *Culture and Experience*, ed. A. Irving Hallowell, 277–290 (Philadelphia: University of Pennsylvania Press, 1974).

4. Maurice R. Davie, *The Evolution of War: A Study of Its Role in Early Societies* (New Haven, CT: Yale University Press, 1929), 50 (quoting van Goen).

5. Robert Tonkinson, *The Mardudjara Aborigines: Living the Dream in Australia's Desert* (New York: Holt, Rinehart and Winston, 1978), 118.

6. Allen Johnson, "Machiguenga Gardens," in *Adaptive Responses of Native Amazonians*, ed. Raymond B. Hames and W. T. Vickers, 29–63 (New York: Academic Press, 1983).

7. Douglas P. Fry, Bruce Bonta, and Karolina Baszarkiewicz, "Learning from Extant Cultures of Peace," in *Handbook on Building Cultures of Peace*, ed. Joseph de Rivera (New York: Springer, 2008); Douglas P. Fry, "Anthropological Insights for Creating Nonwarring Social Systems," *Journal of Aggression, Conflict and Peace Research* 1 (2009); Marta Miklikowska and Douglas P. Fry, "Values for Peace: Ethnographic Lessons from the Semai of Malaysia and the Mardu of Australia," *Beliefs and Values: Understanding the Global Implications of Human Nature* 2 (2010).

8. Robert K. Dentan, *The Semai: Nonviolent People of Malaya* (New York: Holt, Rinehart and Winston, 1968); Robert K. Dentan, *Overwhelming Terror: Love, Fear, Peace, and Violence among Semai of Malaysia* (Lanham, MD: Rowman and Littlefield, 2008); Kirk M. Endicott and Karen L. Endicott, *The Headman Was a Woman: The Gender Egalitarian Batek of Malaysia* (Long Grove, IL: Waveland Press, 2008); Signe Howell, "From Child to Human: Chewong Concepts of Self," in *Acquiring Culture: Cross Cultural Studies in Child Development*, ed. G. Jahoda and I. M. Lewis (London: Croom Helm, 1988); Signe Howell, "To Be Angry Is Not to Be Human, But to Be Fearful Is: Chewong Concepts of Human Nature," in *Societies at Peace: Anthropological Perspectives*, ed. Signe Howell and Roy Willis (London: Routledge, 1989); C.M.I. Sluys, van der, "Gifts from the Immortal Ancestors," in *Hunters and Gatherers in the Modern World: Conflict, Resistance, and Self-Determination*, ed. P. Schweitzer, Megan Biesele, and Robert Hitchcock (New York: Berghahn, 2000).

9. Howell, "Child to Human," 150.

10. Kirk M. Endicott, "The Effects of Slave Raiding on the Aborigines of the Malay Peninsula," in *Slavery, Bondage and Dependency in Southeast Asia*, ed. A. Reid (New York: St. Martin's, 1983), 238 (quoting Skeat and Blagden).

11. Jeffrey Z. Rubin, Dean G. Pruitt, and Sung Hee Kim, *Social Conflict: Escalation, Stalemate, and Settlement* (New York: McGraw-Hill, 1994); Muzafer Sheriff et al., *Intergroup Conflict and Competition: The Robbers Cave Experiment* (Norman: University of Oklahoma Press, 1961).

12. Fry, *Human Potential*; Fry, "Anthropological Insights."

13. Thomas Gregor, "Uneasy Peace: Intertribal Relations in Brazil's Upper Xingu," in *The Anthropology of War*, ed. Jonathan Haas (Cambridge: Cambridge University Press, 1990), 113.

14. Charles Darwin, *The Descent of Man* (New York: Prometheus Books, 1998, originally published in 1871), 126–127.

15. Rubin, Pruitt, and Kim, *Social Conflict*, 127.

16. Robert Tonkinson, "Resolving Conflict within the Law: The Mardu Aborigines of Australia," in *Keeping the Peace: Conflict Resolution and Peaceful Societies around the World*, ed. Graham Kemp and Douglas P. Fry (New York: Routledge, 2004), 101.

17. C.W.M. Hart and Arnold Pilling, *The Tiwi of North Australia* (New York: Holt, Rinehart and Winston, 1960), 85; Fry, *Human Potential*, 153–155.

18. Fry, *Human Potential*, 210–211.

19. Ilsa Glazer, "Beyond the Competition of Tears: Black-Jewish Conflict Containment in a New York Neighborhood," in *Cultural Variation in Conflict Resolution: Alternatives to Violence*, ed. Douglas P. Fry and Kaj Björkqvist (Mahwah, NJ: Lawrence Erlbaum, 1997).

20. Klaus-Friedrich Koch et al., "Ritual Reconciliation and the Obviation of Grievances: A Comparative Study in the Ethnography of Law," *Ethnology* 16 (1977).

21. Gregor, "Uneasy Peace," 113.

22. Christopher Boehm, *Blood Revenge: The Enactment and Management of Conflict in Montenegro and Other Tribal Societies* (Philadelphia: University of Pennsylvania Press, 1987); Walter Goldschmidt, "Peacemaking and the Institutions of

Peace in Tribal Societies," in *The Anthropology of Peace and Nonviolence,* ed. Leslie E. Sponsel and Thomas Gregor (Boulder, CO: Lynne Rienner, 1994), 114; Mervyn Meggitt, *Blood Is Their Argument: Warfare among the Mae Enga Tribesmen of the New Guinea Highlands* (Mountain View, CA: Mayfield, 1977), 136–137; Rubin et al., *Social Conflict,* 129.

23. E. Adamson Hoebel, *The Law of Primitive Man: A Study in Comparative Legal Dynamics* (Cambridge: Harvard University Press, 1967), 139.

24. Robert Tonkinson, "Resolving Conflict within the Law: The Mardu Aborigines of Australia," in *Keeping the Peace: Conflict Resolution and Peaceful Societies around the World,* ed. Graham Kemp and Douglas P. Fry (New York: Routledge, 2004), 101; see also Eric Wolf, "Cycles of Violence: The Anthropology of War and Peace," in *Understanding Violence,* David P. Barash (Boston: Allyn and Bacon, 2001).

25. Thomas Gregor, "Symbols and Rituals of Peace in Brazil's Upper Xingu," in *The Anthropology of Peace and Nonviolence,* ed. Leslie E. Sponsel and Thomas Gregor (Boulder, CO: Lynne Rienner, 1994).

26. Marshall D. Sahlins, "On the Sociology of Primitive Exchange," *The Relevance of Models for Social Anthropology,* ed. M. Banton (New York: Tavistock, 1965).

27. Fry, *Human Potential,* 15–16; Fry, "Anthropological Insights," 6–8; Gregor, "Symbols and Rituals," 244.

28. Robert Tonkinson, *The Jigalong Mob: Aboriginal Victors of the Desert Crusade* (Menlo Park, CA: Cummings Publishing, 1974), 97.

29. Emilienne Ireland, "Cerebral Savage: The Whiteman as Symbol of Cleverness and Savagery in Waurá Myth," in *Rethinking History and Myth: Indigenous South American Perspectives on the Past,* ed. Jonathan Hill (Urbana: University of Illinois Press, 1988), 159.

30. Miklikowska and Fry, "Values for Peace."

31. Goldschmidt, "Peacemaking," 127.

32. Gregor, "Symbols and Rituals," 246.

33. Thomas Gregor and Clayton A. Robarchek, "Two Paths to Peace: Semai and Mehinaku Nonviolence," in *A Natural History of Peace,* ed. Thomas Gregor (Nashville, TN: Vanderbilt University Press, 1996), 162.

34. Gregor, "Uneasy Peace," 116.

35. Goldschmidt, "Peacemaking," 121.

36. Goldschmidt, "Peacemaking," 122.

37. Ira R. Abrams, "Kinship and Descent, Part 1," program 16 in the *Faces of Culture* series (Arlington, VA: Public Broadcasting Service, 1983).

38. Gregor, "Symbols and Rituals," 249–251.

39. Fry, *Human Potential,* 257–259.

40. Matthew Dennis, *Creating a Landscape of Peace* (Ithaca, NY: Cornell University Press, 1993).

41. David Livingstone Smith, *The Most Dangerous Animal: Human Nature and the Origins of War* (New York: Saint Martin's Griffin, 2007).

42. Frans de Waal, *Peacemaking among Primates* (Cambridge, MA: Harvard University Press, 1989); Frans de Waal, *The Age of Empathy: Nature's Lessons for a Kinder Society* (New York: Harmony Books, 2009).

43. William Bright, "Karok," in *Handbook of North American Indians, Volume 8, California,* volume ed. Robert F. Heizer, general ed. William C. Sturtevant (Washington, DC: Smithsonian Institution, 1978), 185.

44. Mervyn Meggitt, *Blood,* 113–143; Goldschmidt, "Peacemaking," 115.

45. Mervyn Meggitt, *Blood,* 123.

46. Boehm, *Blood Revenge,* 121–142.

47. Neil Whitehead, "The Snake Warriors—Sons of the Tiger's Teeth: A Descriptive Analysis of Carib Warfare ca. 1500–1820," in *The Anthropology of War*, ed. Jonathan. Haas (Cambridge: Cambridge University Press, 1990), 155.

48. E. Adamson Hoebel, "The Political Organization and Law-Ways of the Comanche Indians," *Memoirs of the American Anthropological Association* 54 (1940): 36.

49. Hoebel, "Political Organization," 36.

50. Goldschmidt, "Peacemaking," 115; Douglas P. Fry, "Conflict Management in Cross-Cultural Perspective," in *Natural Conflict Resolution*, ed. Filippo Aureli and Frans de Waal (Berkeley: University of California Press, 2000).

51. Fry, "Conflict Management," 345–347.

52. Koch et al., "Ritual Reconciliation," 272–273.

53. Alice Fletcher and Francis La Flesche, "The Omaha Tribe," *Annual Reports of the Bureau of American Ethnology* 27 (1911): 379.

54. Fletcher and La Flesche, "Omaha Tribe," 381.

55. Fletcher and La Flesche, "Omaha Tribe," 383.

56. Whitehead, "Snake Warriors," 155; Boehm, *Blood Revenge*, 121–142; Abrams, "Kinship."

57. Mervyn Meggitt, *Blood*, 123.

58. Hoebel, "Political Organization," 36.

CHAPTER 35

Ancient Peacemakers: Exemplars of Humanity

Anthony Wanis-St. John

History, mythology, religion, and literature of the ancient world provide glimpses into humanity's long familiarity with both conflict and cooperation. Prehistoric humanity did not leave archives, manuscripts, or recordings for subsequent study, but our genetic code offers insights into our slow but inexorable migration around the globe. In our long pilgrimage, we have learned to be warriors, but we have also learned to be peacemakers.

In this chapter, I analyze two sources of peacemaking behavior that attest to a long human engagement in peacemaking. First, I discuss the peacemaking behaviors of some of our nearest genetic relatives, members of the primate family. Our heritage as peacemakers and warriors is perhaps less a matter of human uniqueness and may be an essential part of life itself, combining biological disposition with cognition and social interaction. Living primates are directly connected to human evolutionary ancestry; thus, they offer us the possibility to make modest inferences about prehistoric humans. Second, I look at select passages from epic religious-mythological literature to support the contention that peacemaking has long been a universal part of human culture despite enormous cultural variation in practice today and despite (or perhaps because of) our long preoccupation with warfare.

Ancient traditions are full of parables, norms, and customs for resolving conflict, some attributed to divine figures, and some to human agency. That said, the record is by no means unblemished; both human and divine efforts to make peace are marked by success and failure. However, we should learn about the strategies and practices—even if not always successful—because they indicate the development of norms. Finally, I venture some tentative linkages between primate origins and cultural evidence of peacemaking.

In order to survive and thrive in a world full of danger, early humanity must have sought out solutions to destructive conflicts. The constant growth in the size of human communities and our incessant global migration over millennia created opportunities for conflict ranging from the slight and momentary irritations of everyday communal life to the existential and species-threatening patterns of destruction that we continue to develop into the present age. We have looked inward through introspection and reflection, trying to understand our fragile terrestrial existence, our need for community, and our sometimes destructive behaviors. But we must also have sought internal and external sources of peacemaking: We have created shared values and norms to ritualize the prevention and resolution of our conflicts. We have sought answers in the cosmic order attributed to divine figures that embody human and superhuman qualities. We must have constantly delved deep into our conscious and unconscious selves, collectively and individually, to reconcile with each other and create peace.

The human practices of peacemaking cannot be of recent origin. They must have emerged over hundreds of millennia, and perhaps are in part inherited from our evolutionary ancestors before the line of *Homo sapiens*. Along with the development of language and culture, we have developed strategies, techniques, and norms for peacemaking around the globe, some that bear the marks of deeply shared universal human heritage, while others are more contemporary, particular, unique, and localized.

HUMANS AS PRIMATES

The history of human evolution is in many ways a migration of human genes outward from the places of ancestral origin to the rest of the world, settling slowly, and moving on again.[1] Such a pattern requires strong adaptive strategies and skills. For either mobility or settlement, even small groups need coordination mechanisms, problem-solving skills, and the ability to communicate intelligibly. These are possibly the building blocks of conflict resolution practices. *Homo sapiens* and its ancestors moved about Africa and onto other continents in successive waves, encountering past population movements and possibly other subspecies that had gone before. Conflict likely emerged over how to compete for food or shelter, how to confront environmental challenges, how to share the responsibilities and spoils from hunting and gathering, mate selection, and group decision-making about anything related to group survival.

Movement, conflict, and conflict resolution were surely all interrelated. Movement, however, was also aided by the emergence of more sophisticated languages and tool making (including boat making), permitting our direct human ancestors to populate every part of the globe within perhaps 50,000 years from the first migration.[2]

Humans have been hunter-gatherers far longer than farmers or city dwellers. Hunter-gatherer groups brought together small numbers of families to improve the chances of survival. But larger groups probably meant even more conflict over food, mates, shelter, and perhaps control of the group. Douglas

Fry (see his chapter in this volume titled "Anthropological Examples of Peacemaking") has argued extensively that "the most basic, nomadic hunter-gatherer societies clearly are the best choice for gaining insights about the societies of our ancestors."[3] On the basis of anthropological evidence, he demonstrates that the image of humanity as instinctively inclined to warfare is the result of biases and assumptions that color how we have conducted research into aggression and violence. Fry describes the existing "non-warring societies" among contemporary foraging groups and links this to archeology to demolish the myth of "man the warrior."[4]

Many simple hunter-gatherer societies are more inclined to proactively manage conflict, encourage cooperation and reconciliation, and ritualize group conflict. Our ability to cooperate—even if that cooperation is limited to banding against a common foe—in all probability became a behavior that conferred evolutionary advantage on humans and our genetic ancestors. It is also likely that humanity and its ancestors demonstrated a strong desire to preserve stable social relationships for their own sake and not for any immediate benefit—the emergence of altruism beyond simple reciprocity has a long lineage. While there have been some indications of killings among our prehistoric ancestors, the absence of evidence for war may indicate a concern for peacemaking. William Ury notes that "the first 99% of human history reveals little conflict. Maybe they worked hard at reconciling and managing conflict."[5]

The transition from small hunter-gatherer societies to larger sedentary societies was unquestionably enabled by the parallel emergence of human agriculture approximately 10,000 years ago in the Americas, the Middle East, Southeast Asia, and Central Asia.[6] Agriculture began fueling a veritable explosion in population density that continues to this day. It is not difficult to imagine that competing uses of land became a node of conflict that we are still unfortunately familiar with, as foragers and pastoralists lost ground to farmers, and all lost ground to urban settlers. This shift to sedentary lifestyles is correlated with the emergence of ever more complex civilizations, with distinct cultures and languages and new forms of social organization and governance.

One of the earliest permanent human settlements, the ruins at Jericho's Ein al-Sultan, date to 9000 B.C.E. Archeologists note that, by 5000 B.C.E., Jericho was encircled by walls and defenses, and there is evidence of repeated destruction and rebuilding of those defenses.[7] The transition to living within walled settlements would seem to be a strong indicator of conflict and competition between those inside and those outside such walls.

The recorded history of our civilizations is in many ways the history of war, conquest, expansion, and resistance. Precisely because of this bellicosity, it is also the history of generating, making and preserving peace. Our written history began only about 5,000 years ago, and thus a mere 2 to 3 percent of our existence as a subspecies is recorded with language, symbols, and media that we have access to. There are no textbooks of peacemaking from the prehistoric world. Cave art, monoliths, and other markers of humanity before written language offer glimpses into our prehistoric past, but we are left to decipher and infer in order to try to know about the peacemaking practices of humanity before the written word could capture it.

In the absence of direct evidence of the peacemaking practices of prehistoric humanity and our genetic ancestors, we can infer that the conflict practices of our nearest genetic relatives offer some insight into the depth to which peacemaking is embedded in our existence. Therefore, I consider our primate relatives as evidence that peacemaking is a shared, evolutionary behavior.

Archaeological evidence suggests that the earliest anatomically modern humans or *Homo sapiens* appeared 195,000 years ago where Ethiopia is today located.[8] But ours is the most recent in a series of species within the genus that separated from our ancestor genus *Australopithecus* approximately 2 million years ago.[9] We know little about the conflict and peacemaking capabilities of our ancestral species such as *Homo floresiensis, Homo neanderthalensis, Homo habilis,* and others.

The point at which we would locate the most recent common ancestry for humans, chimpanzees, and bonobos (genetically our closest primates) dates to somewhere between 5 and 8 million years ago,[10] a mere .2 percent of the 3.5 billion–year history of life on earth. Humans, chimps, and bonobos *share* a further 20 million–year evolutionary heritage beyond that because the common primate stem that gave origin to all human and ape ancestors split off from other primate branches (the Old World primates, including baboons and macaques) about 30 million years ago.[11]

PRIMATE PEACE

Taxonomically, contemporary hypotheses based on DNA analyses affirm that among the hominoids, the Great Apes—chimpanzees, bonobos, gorillas, orangutans, *and humans*—are closely related to each other. Examination of the genomic record of both humans and chimpanzees leads to the conclusion that our genetic makeup and the patterns of evolution in our respective genes are extremely close.[12] Indeed, "some of the traits we have in common with other living hominoids exist today because we and they have inherited them from a common ancestor."[13]

In his research on primates, Frans de Waal has systematically gathered evidence of the peacemaking behaviors of animals, with special attention to primates, including human beings. His research questions the dichotomization of aggression and peacemaking, calling attention to their "intertwinement."[14] In the juxtaposition of conflict and peace, such researchers uncover a rich heritage of what humans might call conflict prevention, conflict management, and conflict resolution behaviors, all of which constitute different facets of the more global term *peacemaking.* Although nonhuman primates do not make war in the potentially genocidal way that we do, their peacemaking behaviors are worth understanding because they demonstrate remarkable parallels with our own practices.

De Waal argues that the commonalities and uniqueness among human and other primate peacemaking behaviors have "complex relatedness," including the possibility that in parallel we have learned to employ similar solutions to similar problems, and that biologically we share enough genetic material to explain our inclination to use such behaviors.[15] Based on his patient observation of nonhuman primates, he concludes that for humans "making peace is as natural as making war."[16] Human conflict and aggression operate "within a set of constraints as old as the evolution of cooperation in the animal kingdom."[17]

The work of primatologists and ethologists following this line of inquiry is not without controversy. Investigation into the possibly altruistic, reflective, or even moral behavior of nonhuman animals reopens philosophical and religious debates about human uniqueness (are we fundamentally different from nonhuman animals and to what degree?) and the nature of human nature (are we inherently beings given to selfishness, aggression, and lust who must be coerced into good behavior by human or divine authority?).

Formal debates about the place of humanity in the universe have concerned us since at least Aristotle. Jesuit priest and paleontologist Père Teilhard de Chardin saw little conflict between humanity's transcendent consciousness and the connection to prehistoric humanity and indeed to an ineluctable evolutionary process that began with the genesis of life.[18] Others, such as Jerome Kagan, propose that humans have both distinct abilities that separate us from primates and abilities that extend primate characteristics, although Kagan does not agree with the deterministic view that humans are inherently selfish. He would seem to support the idea that modern social conditions, and not human nature, have actualized negative behaviors that may have been better managed in early human societies that were small and mutually protective. Even in taking issue with de Waal, Kagan notes that "successful [human] adaptation required the suppression of excessive competition, selfishness and self-aggrandizement."[19]

There are good reasons for peacemakers and conflict resolvers to know something about primate peacemaking. One implication is that humans *may not* be unique in our peacemaking capacity. But this is good news: peacemaking is a deeply engrained part of biological and social existence. A second main implication is that the propensity for peacemaking may be more fundamental than the propensity for war. From this, it follows that our contemporary practices of massive, collective violence and war are not hardwired, but learned and by no means inevitable consequences of the way we have organized our world. Ferguson, in considering the extent and evolution of violence and warfare among ancient humans, concludes that "the multiple archaeological indicators of war are absent until the development of a more sedentary existence and/or increasing socio-political complexity, usually in combination with some sort of ecological crisis."[20]

Primate reconciliation, as used by the ethologists, refers to amiable affiliative behaviors among former opponents in a conflict. The usage is related but not identical to the reconciliation behaviors that humans have developed, although a complete dichotomy between human and nonhuman forgiveness is not justified.[21] Anthropoid primates are capable practitioners of peacemaking and, like us, will do so for a rich variety of reasons, including purely instrumental or opportunistic reasons (because it is expedient) but also for more altruistic reasons (restoring relationships for relationships' sake)[22] that bring no benefit, that bring considerable danger and cost to the doer, and that are not motivated by kinship.[23]

Such behaviors contribute to our collective survival as a species as well as to the success of individuals. The adaptive contribution of peacemaking goes against the grain of centuries of thinking that humans and other primates evolve and survive in part due to aggression, which has often been conceptualized as a biological imperative—weak practices, individuals, traits, and species giving way to more dominant ones. De Waal, acknowledging and embracing the inevitability of aggressive behaviors, nevertheless views aggression and conflict as intimately linked to countervailing and "powerful coping mechanisms" in our evolutionary heritage, including reconciliation and peacemaking.[24]

In order to be reconcilers and peacemakers, we primates need some basic capabilities, including, at minimum, the ability to distinguish individuals within a group, enough memory to recall a grievance or reciprocate a favor, the capacity to make emotional shifts "from anger to friendliness," along with the ability to be comforted by physical contact and other gestures, including primate "smiles."[25] Thus, we need to be able to differentiate those with whom we fight and with whom, therefore, we need to make peace. Memory must be developed enough to recall grievances, or there would be little need for explicit peacemaking as no one would remember being offended. Would-be peacemakers also need to remember to whom they should reciprocate a conciliatory gesture.

But we also need to have the cognitive ability to create and repeat successful practices of peacemaking and to adapt such practices when we find ourselves in new circumstances. Surely a prior condition of such peacemaking is that we value living in groups. Group living among animals is thought to result when the benefits of collective living are greater than the costs, but "some animals actively maximize the net benefits by reducing the costs in order to maintain group living."[26] Peacemaking behaviors, in this sense, reduce the costs of aggression to groups and their members by reducing the recurrence and victimization as well as the stress level of opponents and those around them.[27] These are patterns that humanity has certainly developed and refined in unique ways from culture to culture and from epoch to epoch. But they are not the exclusive domain of *Homo sapiens*.

PEACEMAKING AMONG CHIMPANZEES

Both in captivity and in the wild, chimpanzees (*Pan troglodytes*) are capable of extreme aggression, including the selective killing of members of outgroups and escalation of ingroup violence to the point of killing rival aspirants to a mate or to alpha rank. But even conflict and violence among these social animals provide opportunities to learn about their capability to de-escalate tensions among themselves and achieve reconciliations.[28]

Chimpanzees observed systematically while in captivity show an inclination to seek each other out after a fight by stretching a hand out to each other and eventually kissing. Chimpanzee bystanders will console participants in a fight by embracing the fighters (but not kissing them as this is a behavior reserved for the reconciling fighters). In fights between chimps of unequal status, an acceptance of an old or emerging asymmetric and hierarchical relationship by the less powerful chimp (submission) often brings forth reconciliatory gestures by the more powerful chimp. De Waal termed this adjustment of relationships "conditional reassurance" and noted that it works primarily because chimpanzees are highly concerned with the preservation of their social relationships. They may fear separation more than aggression and go to great lengths to remain with other companion chimps even if the latter have done them harm. The same extended hand gesture that chimps use to beg for food is also used to beckon a rival to reconcile. They make use of their relationships to proactively create and manage coalitions when in a conflict. Victims will appeal for and receive help altruistically when outnumbered by aggressors. Chimps will take strategic steps to isolate rivals from their supporters.[29]

While some of this sounds like conflict per se more than conflict resolution, their remarkable ability to create coalitions paves the way for peacemaking as well. If three chimps find themselves as rivals for dominance of a group, their "trilemma" resembles the negotiation dynamics that ensue from Raiffa's "hollow core" distributional bargaining problem.[30] Since no distribution of power is optimal, the animals create two-against-one coalitions that are in constant flux. Paradoxically, the excluded party exercises considerable leverage: he or she can and will pry away one of the members of the dominant dyad. The newly excluded chimp then resorts to the same strategy to create a new dominant dyad in which one member is the new alpha and the other a key supporter. Together, they form a blocking coalition, preventing the third from attaining dominance. Their constant bargaining eventually resolves itself into a new (albeit unstable) equilibrium. Triadic versus dyadic conflict and conflict resolution dynamics among humans are the subject of much inquiry, but are clearly not limited to humans alone.

Looking at chimpanzee gender differences, de Waal found that males were highly active in managing shifting coalitions in order to secure or improve their status in a group. Permanence among friends and enemies is scarce for males, and thus peacemaking and reconciliation behaviors are frequent, for "no male ever knows when he may need his strongest rival."[31] Females develop stronger and more permanent bonds with a smaller kinship group and work hard to reconcile conflicts *in this group.* Competing with other females over food for themselves, and less inclined to seek social dominance, they are more selective about whom they fight with and even more selective about whom they reconcile with.[32]

Chimpanzees are active mediators as well, regularly rebuilding bridges between parties who have fought and will not interact with each other. The third party invites the sullen fighters to groom *her* and then slips away, leaving them to groom each other. That they will avoid each other until a third party gives them a reason to come together peacefully indicates that the chimpanzees not only have a concern with saving face (they are reluctant to approach each other directly or make a first conciliatory move), but that they also value and rely upon the mediator's role in their groups.[33]

Chimpanzees apparently can play collective third-party roles as well: de Waal has described situations in which chimps that have fought will try to attract their adversary by "feigning interest in a small object to break the tension."[34] Other chimps will provide cover for the adversaries' rapprochement by coming over and pretending to be interested as well, before walking away and leaving the former adversaries to actively play with their new discovery, resume physical contact, and groom themselves into a reconciliation. The object per se is either trivial or nonexistent, but provides the pretext for a group to help fighters ease back into a restored relationship.

After intense violence, researchers have observed conflict prevention or mitigation behaviors: chimpanzees show an emotional and cognitive awareness of the gravity of what has passed and will take deliberate steps to prevent a recurrence of the conflict by "intensif[ying] their peace efforts."[35] Reconciliations can take place with greater frequency (there are many more attempts by fighters and mediators), as well as with greater efficiency (fewer peace overtures are rejected).

The collective impact of conflict may be linked to collective roles in supporting peace. A community of chimpanzees can be observed to wait in tense silence before rivals make up and then celebrate boisterously when they reconcile,[36] communally affirming the peacemakers. This supports the proposition that human peacemaking too needs a public dimension. Conflicts generate tensions within a group, and that tension is released when equilibriums are restored. Public participation in and celebration of peacemaking, for humans, extends this dynamic by contributing to the socializing of a new peace, minimizing discontent and spoiling, increasing accountability of the fighters while maximizing acceptance by the community.[37]

The fostering of a "shadow of the future" among rivals was described by Axelrod as a conceptual facilitator for the emergence of reciprocity, in place of outright dominance or submission.[38] Chimpanzees demonstrate the ability to encourage good will *later* by offering each other something of value *now*. For example, when hoping to have time to mate without being disturbed by rivals, chimpanzees can be observed to offer an extended grooming session to a sexual rival, who then demonstrates reciprocity by leaving his groomer to indulge in mating without the usual interference that otherwise characterizes these activities.[39]

PEACEMAKING AMONG RHESUS MONKEYS

Rhesus monkeys (*Macaca mulatta*) are Old World monkeys that, in the wild and in captivity, form matriarchal communities or troops that are arranged according to hierarchical status. They recognize each individual's family (matriline) and status within the group, frequently resorting to aggression to enforce or challenge hierarchy among them. Threats from dominant Rhesus females against lower ranking females are expressed with an open-mouth facial expression. Subordinate monkeys inevitably respond with what looks like a toothy, nervous smile or grin. The grin is always flashed by a subordinate to a superior and would appear to be a signal of nonthreatening intentions.[40] They also use a technique known as lipsmacking to signal friendly intentions, which involves lip and tongue movements with glances by one monkey to a partner. Rhesus monkeys in conflict will commit acts of aggression by displacing anger toward other members of the target's family. Although this has the potential to escalate violence, it may also play a deterrent role because it potentially raises the cost of conflict among them. Because eye contact and facial expression are important for engaging in conflict among the rhesus, they "avert their gaze during friendly approaches, including reconciliations."[41] Instead, rhesus monkeys seem to look for excuses to nonchalantly make physical contact after a serious fight, resorting to what observers call the *contact pass:* fighters on their way somewhere will pass close enough to each other to touch and then take advantage of the contact to resume grooming for peace—a kind of implicit reconciliation.[42] This seems also to be an uncertainty reducing move in which the potential for aggression is present, but since no aggression takes place, the fighters reconcile.

Contrasted with the chimpanzee, the remarkable hierarchy among rhesus monkeys correlates to a very different set of conflict behaviors, as well as conflict *resolution* behaviors. Hierarchy is a central component of the power distance concept among human cultures, described by Hofstede as the degree of acceptance of social inequality within a given cultural identity group.[43] Among humans, greater social asymmetries of power often lead to more indirect peacemaking practices. The greater the power distance, or the more accepted the hierarchy, the more likely that conflict parties need to save face and reconcile indirectly with the help of a third party.[44] Third parties facilitate implicit reconciliations that help the parties resume friendly relations, but without acknowledging shared contribution to the fight or assessing blame and responsibility.[45] The practices of the rhesus are reminiscent of human behaviors in cultural contexts that tolerate great power asymmetry.

Although hostility can sometimes spread beyond conflict parties among the rhesus, peacemaking, in the end, is made directly between the antagonists without mediators. Whereas conflict and aggression were traditionally thought to lead to dispersal among social animals, the rhesus monkeys systematically seek out their antagonists after a fight: "the former enemy is the preferred partner," for peacemaking.[46] Instead of avoidance, the rhesus, especially alpha males, demonstrate a proactive inclination to initiate friendly contact after a fight, particularly with second ranking members of the group, upon whom they rely to maintain a ruling coalition. Female rhesus monkeys focus their reconciliation efforts within their matrilineal groups, taking care to preserve the relationships among sisters, mother, and daughters. They are less frequently observed reconciling with monkeys from outside of their close circle and social class—they make peace more often with antagonists "whom they need for cooperation in a competitive world."[47] Their selective reconciliation strategy serves them better than strategies preferred by rhesus males who do not form the stable social groups that females do. Reconciliation and peacemaking are thus critical to individual survival as well. Predators and food scarcity pose less of a threat to a rhesus who maintains or improves his or her social position, sometimes by engaging in conflict, but also by strategies of reconciliation.[48]

The rhesus's preferential behavior for preserving relationships within the matriline and within the social class also correlates well to another human behavioral dynamic. Hofstede refers to the culturally informed disposition for either tolerating or feeling threatened by what is new and different as the degree of "uncertainty avoidance." He argues that human cultures confer different levels of tolerance for it among their members.[49] I have argued that uncertainty avoidance has important implications for the ways we negotiate and make peace and that practitioners and theorists have by and large ignored its role.[50] Specific uncertainties about peacemaking, such as the trustworthiness of adversaries and solidarity of constituents, impact our process choices, including decisions about whether or not to conduct peacemaking in secret or exposed to the wider community.[51]

The comparative implications of uncertainty in peacemaking include the relative willingness to escalate a simmering conflict and the relative unwillingness to initiate conciliatory moves. It may also involve preferences about reliance on elaborate rules, rituals, and practices to guide peacemaking rather than spontaneous, unstructured peacemaking.

PEACEMAKING AMONG STUMP-TAILED MONKEYS

The stump-tailed monkey, or stumptail (*Macaca arctoides*), like the rhesus, is more distant from human beings than great apes such as the chimpanzees and bonobos in taxonomic terms. It is remarkable in peacemaking for the overt sexuality of its reconciliation practices. After violence, stumptails of either gender embrace each other from behind, in what the ethologists call a "hold-bottom." During this encounter, at least some stumptails will physiologically achieve an orgasm (regardless of the gender of their former adversary). Although this does not take place in every fight, De Waal notes, "It is a revelation to know that nature has provided stumptails with a built-in incentive for making up with their enemies."

Stumptails, like rhesus monkeys, form matrilineal hierarchies, but are relatively more tolerant of confrontation between monkeys of different rank. They de-escalate potentially violent confrontations by engaging in a "mock bite," a method unique to them among primates. During a tense standoff involving threats, the dominant monkey may grab the wrist or foot of the offending monkey and bring it to her open mouth, but without causing any injury to the other. Subordinates will often proactively de-escalate a confrontation by *offering* a hand for the mock bite if the dominant monkey has not initiated this ritual conciliatory gesture.[52]

Compared to the rhesus, the stumptail is far less hierarchical, and there are implications for their conflict resolution strategies. Whereas the rhesus dominant tends to be the initiator of a conciliatory move (70 percent of the time) both dominant and subordinate stumptails have equal rates of initiating peacemaking moves. Stumptails in general are more proactive about peacemaking and will initiate reconciliation in about 56 percent of their conflicts, while the observed corresponding figure for rhesus monkeys is 20 percent. They also seek reconciliation quickly instead of letting conflicts simmer without resolution;

their time frame for initiating reconciliatory moves is less than two minutes after a confrontation. As noted, the gestures involved in peacemaking are located in the realm between sensuality and amiability: "most characteristic is the presentation of the rear end by one party, and a hold-bottom by the other."[53] Clearly, the stumptail way of peace is a gratifying affair compared to the strategic chimpanzee and the rigid rhesus.

PEACEMAKING AMONG THE BONOBOS

Bonobos (*Pan paniscus*) are as close to humans genetically as the chimpanzee and are highly social great apes whose proportions are thought to resemble *Australopithecus,* the ancestor of the *Homo* genus from which we descend. Female bonobos play a more central role in their communities than female chimpanzees do in theirs and maintain a more balanced relationship with the males. Bonobos demonstrate considerable self-recognition. They are capable of teasing each other (hauling up a chain after another bonobo uses it to descend into a moat) and possibly acting out of empathy (a third bonobo will drop the chain back down to the stranded bonobo), at least when in captivity. They can, with a simple look, coordinate team efforts to groom and thus pacify a surly dominant bonobo. They play games that require concentration and self-imposed rules, including their own version of blind man's bluff.[54]

Their uninhibited sexuality in conflict management also sets them apart from the chimpanzee.[55] Analyses of their social life in captivity (and to a lesser extent in the wild) shows that bonobos frequently reduce tensions among themselves with a wide variety of sexual play, across age groups, and in both homosexual and heterosexual orientations. Because bonobos are anatomically well suited for face-to-face sexual encounters, in contrast with chimpanzees, researchers documented hundreds of bonobo sexual encounters in which facial expressions and direct eye contact play an important role. They report that the "majority of mounts and matings occur in tense situations" in which reproductive concerns are not apparent. They seem particularly adept at managing the tension involved in claiming food and feeding by substituting erotic contacts for aggressive ones that pacify dominants. While bonobos employ grooming as an important social behavior, they diminish grooming before and after the outbreak of violence. However, their rate of embracing and sexual contact far exceeds their baseline behaviors during those same pre- and post-conflict periods. Hand and arm gestures, as well as genital presentations, are used by bonobos to invite their fight partners into a reconciliatory sexual moment.[56] Although such eroticism is (probably) absent from peace conferences to resolve an international or civil war, human beings in intimate relationships sometimes resort to amorous reconciliation after a fight.

Aggressors in a fight (often dominant bonobos) can be observed to initiate reconciliation "almost as if they regret having lost their temper," and victims of aggression often receive reassurance afterward. Despite his caveat that chimpanzees too were once idealized as gentle primates, De Waal's research suggests that bonobos in conflict appear to be efficient at de-escalation and that they act is if they had an "inner brake" of self-restraint that keeps their aggressive moments very brief compared to the more violent chimpanzee.[57]

Our primate relatives are clearly innovators and practitioners of diverse ways of making peace. Although their conflicts are less existentially threatening than ours, their genetic closeness to us and to *Homo sapiens'* predecessors offers support for the contention that humans have inherent and learned capacity for both conflict and peacemaking. It has sometimes been proposed that culture and learning are part of what distinguish us from other primates, and this has given rise to a belief that primate behavior is instinctive and human behavior learned. There may be no solid evidence that justifies such a dichotomy.[58] Human and nonhuman primates engage in both violence and peacemaking behaviors that may have biological bases but that are also learned, impacted by collective norms and individuality.[59]

Strikingly, nonhuman primates engage in altruistic behavior and actively manage tensions of their group coexistence. They deploy a sophisticated range of strategies that can only be either antecedents of human conflict resolution practices or corollary strategies that emerged in rough parallel with our own, or some combination of these two. Their proclivities as beings that foster social harmony even as they pursue self-interest, combined with practices such as alliance formation, mediation, ritualized fighting, reciprocity, and tension reduction through intimate contact, are all strategies with universal and ancient appeal to humans. We humans could benefit, not from needless idealizing or denigration of primates, but rather by seeing them as a kind of evolutionary companion in conflict reduction practices. While others will note their lack of other cultural and civilizational attributes, I would argue that the absence of genocidal conflict among them distinguishes them favorably, and their well-developed peace practices should inspire human reflection, and perhaps some measure of emulation, even as they shed light on the cultural origins of some of our cultural and universal preferences.

GODS, HEROES, HISTORIES, AND IMAGES

Mythology, religion, literature, and history all contain powerful images of violence, conflict, and aggression. Wars of extraordinary violence on earthly and celestial scales permeate mythologies from all over the world. Despite millennia of retelling and refinement, our stories rarely become more peaceful with time. The creation of the world and the birth of humanity are often correlated with violent events. Numerous traditions, including those of the ancient Sumerian, Hebrew, Mayan, and Andean people describe the destruction of humanity by discontented gods. These divine genocides often involve a great deluge, or flood story. (Re, the Egyptian deity, did it by unleashing another god, Hathor, on a killing spree against humanity.) Gods and semidivine figures battle with each other before humans emerge and contend with humans once they do. The Greek mythologies frequently detail divine intervention in the affairs of humans, including instigating cycles of war and peace.

Humans accepted or adopted new deities in order to further their own violent aims, as when the ancient Egyptians incorporated Ba'al into their pantheon in order to assist in their wars with the Hittites during the second millennium, B.C.E.[60] The Mexica (Aztecs) venerated the bloodthirsty Huitzilopochtli above other gods when they resorted to mass human sacrifice to expand their hegemony over neighboring tribes in the Valley of Mexico,[61] pushing aside the more compassionate divinity of Quetzalcóatl, for whom human sacrifice was hateful.[62] The values and teachings of ancient stories, religions, and myths are often structured around a conflict, and the virtues they promote are often attributed to victorious divine or human warrior figures.

Images of divine and human peacemakers are correspondingly rarer. It is difficult to find a divine figure who does not engage in violence on either a grand scale (warfare) or minor scale (blood sacrifices or self-sacrifice). Gods of peace in ancient cultures are hard to come by, whereas gods of war are ubiquitous. Nevertheless, divinely altruistic acts to create or rescue a nation, end a war, or prevent escalation can be gleaned in numerous traditions. Peace for later religious traditions is sometimes elevated to a transformative state of being, and not simply the absence of violence.

In this section, I offer some paradigms of peacemaking from several narratives of war: the *Epic of Gilgamesh*, the *Mahabharata*, and the *Iliad*. Somewhat ironically, images of how we make peace can be found in narratives of how we and our gods make war. On one level, this is predictable, for where else should we look? It is the warrior who makes peace; therefore, images of warrior and peacemaker are entwined. Examples of peacemaking are not always successful, but this does not invalidate their exemplary value. Even the failed attempts in myth and history offer important lessons for peacemakers.

An example in mythology comes from the succession conflict among the Egyptian gods Heru (Horus) and Set. The Egyptian goddess of war, Nit, is consulted as arbiter to resolve the issue. Under threat of bringing the sky down on Egypt, she decrees with some sense of divine equity that Heru should inherit the throne, and Set, despite having usurped the throne, should be compensated for his loss.[63] The gods, sitting in tribunal, remain divided on the question, and Set successfully undermines Nit's attempt to resolve the conflict peacefully, although it is Heru who ultimately inherits the throne.[64] The lesson is that even unsuccessful divine peacemaking may be preferable to successful conflict.

An historical example comes from Thucydides, who recounted the events of the Peloponnesian War by reconstructing dialogues among the protagonists. Greek religio-mythological elements are not privileged in Thucydides' accounts, as he strove for historical value, elevating the importance of human action rather than divine machinations. Several attempts to end the historic war resulted in only fragile truces and the resumption of fighting, provoked by the colonies and allies of Athens and Sparta rather than the gods on Olympus.

Late in the war, Athens sought to conquer a nominal Spartan ally, the island of Melos, in 416 B.C.E.[65] The Athenian invaders first come to Melos to demand surrender and are received by the Melian notables, who attempt to negotiate for their continued independence and survival. In the Melian Dialogue, Thucydides puts the reader virtually in the same room as the negotiators upon whose labors the fates of Melos (and ultimately Athens as well) depend.[66]

From the beginning of the dialogue, the tone of the Melians is portentous: "All we can reasonably expect from this negotiation is war." Yet later they invoke divine intervention: "We trust that the gods may grant us fortune as good as yours, since we are just men fighting against unjust." The Athenians (Thucydides himself perhaps) thought otherwise: "As far as the gods are concerned, we have no fear and no reason to fear that we shall be at a disadvantage."[67] The gods, however, are apparently not in a position to guarantee either peace for Melos or ultimate victory for Athens. Catastrophe comes in the end; the Melians, in seeking an honorable peace, cannot contend with the Athenians, who desire nothing less than total submission. In the lexicon of contemporary negotiation analysts, there was no zone of possible agreement between the reservation points of the two parties.[68] Within a few years of Melos' annihilation, Athens' imperial ambitions had taken it too far; Persia entered the war on the side of Sparta, and Athens' military power was destroyed. It may not have been Thucydides' intention, but the ultimate lesson of the Melian Dialogue is really about the futility of imperial war and the absurdity of predatory negotiation behavior.[69] It is, in a sense, a parable of the peace that we might have had.

The peacemaking mechanisms that we have evolved over the millennia are many and extraordinarily diverse. Nevertheless, certain strategies and methods present themselves in many places and times. In the remainder of this chapter, I try to illustrate five paradigms that are readily apparent in three ancient warrior narratives in which history, mythology, and religion converge. These sources, well known to specialists, are generally not considered in the study of peacemaking and come from traditions outside of the Abrahamic faiths. Some address the problem of initiating peace, while others are more useful to consolidate it and prevent recurrence of violence and conflict.

Adversaries interested in making peace can resort to multiple strategies or paradigms of peacemaking. They are described briefly here:

1. *Intimate contention.* Prove the mettle and valor of self and adversary through honorable confrontation, but only as a preliminary step toward friendship and reconciliation.

2. *Common enemy.* Create a coalition among former foes by identifying a new common adversary. Two variations on this are to

   a. create an alliance in order to *restrain another* who wishes to impose a new hegemonic order and
   b. create an expanding *coalition of the whole* so that all adversaries progressively become friends and allies.

3. *Mediators.* Restore and build peaceful relations among foes through the intercession of a third party acting as mediator.

4. *Magnanimity.* Show generosity in victory, protect the honor of adversaries, in expectation of forgiveness of the victor by the defeated, combined with submission of the defeated party.

5. *Ritualized combat.* Reduction of mass violence or warfare by limiting confrontation to a few designated fighters, for a limited period of time, space, and purpose.

Additional strategies and paradigms related to peacemaking that are found in many other ancient narratives but not considered here include the following:

- *Acts of restitution.* Offer restitution and recompense after having committed aggression.

- *Hostages.* Offer and receive reciprocal hostages as pledges of good conduct, non-hostility, and trustworthiness.

- *Intermarriage.* Strengthen good relations and lessen the likelihood of aggression among strangers by creating permanent relationships, including through intermarriage of ruling dynasties as well as common people.

- *Self-constraints.* Reassure and demonstrate good intentions by exhibiting self-constraint and limitations on action and reciprocal vulnerabilities.

- *New order.* Envision, demand, and create a more just new social and political order that transforms unstable, unjust relationships.

- *Interdependence.* Foster interdependence along numerous axes—social, political, economic, moral—on the presumption that those who need each other are less likely to engage in destructive spirals of violence.

THE EPIC OF GILGAMESH

In the first paradigm, adversaries identify each other as rivals and strive to overcome each other. In an otherwise honorable confrontation, however, they come to the realization that greater benefit would come from laying aside their enmity. The peace comes through a close, almost *intimate* conflict that leads to mutual respect and interdependence.

One of humanity's most ancient mythological narratives is *The Epic of Gilgamesh*, whose earliest versions date to approximately 2600 B.C.E. and were written in the Sumerian language, in cuneiform, on clay tablets. The main protagonist, King Gilgamesh, was an actual ruler of Uruk, a city-state in Sumer. The *Epic* portrays him as a semidivine figure given to excessive warmongering and sexual predation among his own subjects. His tyrannical rule cries out for some kind of counterbalancing force. The gods heed the lamentations of Gilgamesh's subjects and fashion a rival for him: the wild and savage Enkidu appears as the antithesis of the royal and civilized but undisciplined Gilgamesh, and they are destined to clash.[70] Their first confrontation, however, is also their last:

> For Gilgamesh, like a god, his equal has come
> Enkidu, at the gate of the bride house, planted his feet
> He prevents Gilgamesh from entering.
> They seized one another in the bride-house gate;
> They fight in the street, through the city quarter;
> [they break down part] of the wall.[71]

After the fight, Gilgamesh, who has barely won, praises Enkidu publicly in a show of magnanimity:

> Enkidu has no match . . .
> In the wilderness he was born; no one stands against him.

Enkidu stood there, listening to his words . . .
He sat down, weeping;
His eyes filled with tears . . . his strength left him.
They seized one another, embracing,
Took one another's hands like [brothers].[72]

Enmity turns to wonder, and violence yields to veneration as the victorious
Gilgamesh does not humiliate his foe but praises him instead, and this praise
is the catalyst for their reconciliation and forging of a new friendship. Together
as companions now they then turn their energies to heroic struggles against
new celestial enemies. The eventual death of Enkidu only deepens the significance of his arrival in the world, as Gilgamesh seeks out the greater meaning of
existence through the lamentation over the loss of his friend and companion.

The Gilgamesh narrative obviously involves at least three peacemaking paradigms I identified previously, even though the overarching theme is of conflict. The element of intimate contention gives way to reconciliation through
magnanimity and yields the benefits of peace for Gilgamesh's subjects. Gilgamesh's decision not to humiliate Enkidu and his concern for his foe's honor
and face permit the vanquished to be moved to tears and to seek friendship,
not vengeance: *generosity in victory* begets *forgiveness in defeat*. Consequently,
they create a new coalition and seek out new enemies. Their union of forces
and joint confrontation of other evils in the world and in the cosmos seal the
friendship and peace between them. Peace between the two protagonists is related to conflict with a third in a circular way: it acts as both cause and effect.
United, they can overcome other evils in the world, but also, the existence of
other evils in the world unites them.

THE MAHABHARATA

Another ancient war epic, *The Mahabharata*, contains a brief narrative of a
divine peace intervention. Written between 300 B.C.E. and 300 C.E., *The Mahabharata* recounts the mythical-historical Kurukshetra War of yet greater an-
tiquity. In the epic, the divine figure Lord Krishna attempts to forestall the
outbreak of war between two rival dynasties of the Kuru royal family, both
pretenders to the kingship of Hastinapur, in northern India. Since he is cousin
to both factions, Krishna wisely offers divine help to all, when each side tries
to get him to fight on its behalf: "soldiers, irresistible in battle, shall be sent to
one of you and I alone, resolved not to fight on the field, and laying down my
arms, will go to the other."[73]

After offering impartial assistance, Lord Krishna undertakes an ultimately
futile peace mission to achieve an honorable end to the conflict and prevent
the impending war. To King Dhritarashtra, Krishna-as-mediator delivers his
appeal in terms of making peace in order to create a *new coalition of the whole*
that no other adversary could overcome. If "thou hast both the Kurus and the
Pandavas at thy back, the sovereignty of the whole world and invincibility before all foes will be thine. All the rulers of the earth, O monarch, that are either
equal to thee or superior, will then seek alliance with thee."[74]

The *Mahabharata* illustrates at least two of the peacemaking strategies identified earlier—mediation and an appeal to unity in order to confront common foes. Krishna's peace bid, though not successful, remains an important ancient example of preventive mediation and diplomacy. Krishna is a proactive seeker of peaceful outcomes who nevertheless leaves the human parties to make their final choices with autonomy—in contrast with the coercive mediation strategies of other divinities and human mediators.

There are some who interpret the *Mahabharata* and one of its component narratives, the *Bhagavad-Gita* (the Celestial Song) as a spiritual allegory in which peace is the result of combating inner enemies. In the *Gita,* we delve deeply into the dialogue between Krishna and the Pandava prince who chose him instead of troops. Krishna urges Prince Arjuna into battle after the latter hesitates to go to war against his Kuru relatives. Krishna in this interpretation is not a warrior god; he sanctifies war only as a righteous inner struggle against the foes of worldly attachment and distraction, ego consciousness, and other spiritual vices.[75]

Only through robust confrontation with such inner foes can a new frontier of transformative peace be crossed. This concept of sacred struggle for self-realization, oneness with the divine, and inner purity has its corollary in other faith traditions, including the more recent Islamic *jihad al-akbar* (see the chapter "Islam and Peacemaking" by Said and Jafari in this volume). In either interpretation, the heroic, noble Krishna offers us an exemplar of peacemaking and peace-seeking.

THE *ILIAD*

Homer's *Iliad* recounts in mythological terms a fragment of the historic Trojan War.[76] The *Iliad* is a tragic and extraordinarily violent poetic heroic narrative. A diverse coalition of Akhaian (Greek) city-states lays siege to the Anatolian city of Troy to avenge the abduction of Helen, the Spartan Queen. Helen had been seduced by the Trojan prince Paris with the connivance of the goddess Aphrodite. The *Iliad* is also constructed around the consequences of another rivalry *within* the ranks of the Greeks. The commander of the Greek army, Agamemnon, seizes Briseis, a slave girl taken as war spoils by the semi-divine Achilles. In his rage, Achilles is tempted to kill Agamemnon, but the gods on Mt. Olympus intervene. Just as Achilles unsheathes his sword to slay Agamemnon, the goddess Athena appears to Achilles as divine mediator: "It was to check this killing rage that I came from heaven, if you will listen. Hera sent me, being fond of you both, concerned for both. Enough: break off combat, stay your hand upon the sword hilt. Let him have a lashing with words, instead: tell him how things will be . . . but hold your hand."[77]

Athena's divine mediation prevents a mutiny in the Akhaian ranks, but the rest of *The Iliad* is full of the tragic consequences for all as Achilles withdraws from combat and the tide of war turns in favor of besieged Troy. A delegation of Akhaian commanders tries to mediate again later in the story, even obtaining a pledge from Agamemnon to return Briseis and provide further recompense to the offended Achilles, but only the death of Achilles' friend, Patroklos, on the battlefield rouses him back to the war, where his own fate awaits him.

Still, these divine and human mediations are not for the purpose of ending the war, but rather to prevent the Akhaians from slaughtering each other. The fatigued and bloodied warriors take matters into their own hands after nine years of siege and warfare. Twice they attempt to achieve a longed-for peace by letting the outcome of the entire war turn on a single combat sanctified by ritual between the aggrieved Menelaus, Helen's husband, and Paris.

On the pacified battlefield, the Trojans and Akhaians pray together in a solemn ritual, sealing their truce with offerings of wine and sacrificial animals, pending the outcome of the ritualized combat. "Father Zeus, almighty over Ida, may he who brought this trouble on both sides perish! Let him waste away in the undergloom. As for ourselves, let us be loyal *friends in peace*."[78] But it is the gods themselves who subvert this attempt to end the war; Aphrodite whisks Paris the Trojan from the duel when things turn against him. Athena and Hera conspire to incite a Trojan bowman to shoot at Menelaus, breaking the sacred truce and plunging the two armies into full-fledged war again.[79] Mediation has its uses in *The Iliad*, but the warring sides themselves realize they are trapped in a tragic war and seek to escape it by ritualizing combat between the two individuals most intimately connected to the *casus belli*. Although one contender would have fallen, his death could have bought peace for the multitudes. Even if ultimately tragic, the *Iliad* gives evidence of divine and human mediation and of ritualized combat as a variant of intimate contention. Also, in at least two other passages in the narrative, Achilles, otherwise an unrepentant killer, is moved to act with magnanimity when approached by the parents of his victims, including a nocturnal visit by the Trojan King Priam, who begs to reclaim the body of his fallen son Hector. Achilles honors the request and even pledges 11 days of truce to let the Trojans bury their hero. In the midst of great violence, and divine traps to prolong it, latent peacemaking qualities can be discerned.[80]

Humanity has inherited a vast legacy of experience and knowledge through our genetic descent and our cultural patrimony. Part of this legacy—an important part—is the ability to simultaneously recognize our grievances while also forgiving the offender in order to restore or improve the social relationships in which conflict is embedded. The great apes and other primates demonstrate that our culturally informed conflict resolution norms are not totally unique to us, but that rather they are part of a wider set of adaptive skills related to the survival and flourishing of social individuals and groups. Our stories, mythologies, religious figures, and legends ennoble the pursuit of peace, even if they depict us as participants in a great cosmic drama in which conflict plays an inherent part. The peacemaking practices and tendencies of gods and heroes—even when they do not succeed—are sorely needed reminders and markers of our need to pursue peace with as much or greater zeal, skill, and strategy as how we pursue conflict.

The peacemaking practices of primates tell us that human peacemaking is enormously ancient and that our contemporary inclination to extraordinarily violent war is not predetermined. Their richly diverse methods of reaching and maintaining social equilibria have their echoes in our own familiar cultural patterns, including our needs—depending on cultural preference—to take refuge in mediators, hierarchy, physical consolation and intimacy, reciprocity, alliance formation, ritualized combat, and rituals of reconciliation. Empathy, altruism, and forgiveness are, apparently, capabilities shared by many primates. They help us to prioritize some level of collective well-being while also conferring important tangible benefits on the individual making her or his way in a conflicting and competitive world. These proclivities for peace are so important to us (and our ancestors) that our deities, heroes, and demigods are invested with them in mythical and religious traditions from diverse parts of the globe.

Our evolutionary, genetic ancestry as well as our cultural legacy, here considered together, suggest that even in the midst of contemporary conflict, an enormously ancient heritage of peacemaking resides within us.

NOTES

1. See, generally, L. Luca Cavalli-Sforza, Paolo Menozzi, and Alberto Piazza, *The History and Geography of Human Genes,* 3rd ed. (Princeton, NJ: Princeton University Press, 1994).

2. Cavalli-Sforza et al., 155.

3. Douglas P. Fry, *Beyond War: The Human Potential for Peace* (Oxford: Oxford University Press, 2007), 111.

4. Fry, *Beyond War,* 10–20.

5. William Ury notes that "the first 99% of human existence reveals little conflict. Maybe they worked hard at reconciling and managing conflict" (William Ury, "Violent Human Nature? Telling a New Story," presentation at Program on Negotiation, Harvard Law School, October 1, 1999. Lectures notes on file with the author).

6. Cavalli-Sforza et al., 106–107.

7. Michael Dumper and Bruce E. Stanley, eds., *Cities of the Middle East and North Africa: A Historical Encyclopedia* (Santa Barbara, CA: ABC-CLIO, 2007), 203.

8. National Science Foundation, "New Clues Add 40,000 Years to Age of Human Species," Press Release 05-024, February 16, 2005, http://www.nsf.gov/news/news_summ.jsp?cntn_id=102968.

9. Cavalli-Sforza et al., 61.

10. De Waal reports that the genetic closeness of humans to chimpanzees and bonobos has led to discussions about new taxonomies that either change our genus from *Homo* to *Pan* (thus humans would be *Pan sapiens* or "wise chimpanzee") or admit these two great apes into the *Homo* genus. De Waal, *Peacemaking among Primates* (Cambridge, MA: Harvard University Press, 1989), 172.

11. *Homo sapiens* is the only existing species in the *Homo* genus. The concept of human races, with diverse ancestral or evolutionary lines, based on the observable different human phenotypes, withers under the light of scientific scrutiny and is mostly used to create divisions that justify collective oppression and discrimination. It can be traced to several erroneous ideas, including the argument that different human groups evolved from different hominoid ancestors. Our shared biological heritage proclaims our shared humanity and discredits biases. Humans share genetic traits to such an extent that most genetic human diversity is found *within* human populations, and not

between or among them. About 84 percent of all human genetic diversity is "shared equally by all populations" (Alan R. Templeton, "Human Races: A Genetic and Evolutionary Perspective," *American Anthropologist* 100, no. 3 [1998]: 633; De Waal, *Peacemaking among Primates,* 172).

12. Tarjei Mikkelsen et al., "Initial Sequence of the Chimpanzee Genome and Comparison with the Human Genome," *Nature* 437 (September 2005): 69–87.

13. M. Ruvolo, "Genetic Diversity in Hominoid Primates," *Annual Review of Anthropology* 26 (1997): 515–540.

14. De Waal, *Peacemaking among Primates,* 236.

15. De Waal, *Peacemaking among Primates,* 230.

16. De Waal, *Peacemaking among Primates,* 7.

17. Frans B. M. de Waal, "Primates: A Natural Heritage of Conflict Resolution," *Science* 289 (July 28, 2000): 586–590.

18. Père Teilhard de Chardin, *The Phenomenon of Man,* trans. Bernard Wall (New York: William Collins Sons, 1959), 169.

19. Jerome Kagan, "The Uniquely Human in Human Nature," *Daedelus* 133, no. 4 (Fall 2004): 77–88.

20. Brian Ferguson, "The Causes and Origins of 'Primitive Warfare' on Evolved Motivations for War," *Anthropological Quarterly* 73, no. 3 (July 2000): 150–164.

21. "Reconciliation is best regarded as a heuristic concept capable of generating testable predictions regarding the problem of relationship maintenance" (de Waal, "Primates: A Natural Heritage").

22. Jessica C. Flack, Frans B. M. de Waal, and David C. Krakauer, "Social Structure, Robustness, and Policing Cost in a Cognitively Sophisticated Species," *The American Naturalist* 165, no. 5 (May 2005): E126–E139.

23. De Waal and Suchak distinguish individual motivations for conflict resolution behaviors and the evolutionary reasons for their persistence. "DNA data from the field demonstrates that most of the cooperative relationships among male chimpanzees are of a reciprocal nature and concern individuals without family ties" (Frans B. M. de Waal and Malini Suchak, "Prosocial Primates: Selfish and Unselfish Motivations," *Philosophical Transactions of the Royal Society B* 365 [August 2010]: 2711–2722).

24. De Waal, *Peacemaking among Primates,* 234.

25. De Waal, *Peacemaking among Primates,* 87, 243.

26. Nobuyuki Katsukake, "Complexity, Dynamics and Diversity of Sociality in Group Living Mammals," *Ecological Research* 24, no. 3 (2009): 521–531.

27. Filippo Aureli, Marina Cords, and Carel P. van Schaik, "Conflict Resolution Following Aggression in Gregarious Animals: A Predictive Framework," *Animal Behavior* 64, no. 3 (2002): 325–343.

28. De Waal, *Peacemaking among Primates,* 65–72.

29. De Waal, *Peacemaking among Primates,* 43–45, 46–51, 81.

30. Howard Raiffa, John Richardson, and David Metcalfe, *Negotiation Analysis* (Cambridge, MA: Harvard University Press, 2002), 436–449.

31. De Waal, *Peacemaking among Primates,* 53.

32. De Waal, *Peacemaking among Primates,* 53.

33. De Waal, *Peacemaking among Primates,* 21–22.

34. De Waal, *Peacemaking among Primates,* 238–239.

35. De Waal, *Peacemaking among Primates,* 77–79.

36. De Waal, *Peacemaking among Primates,* 5.

37. Catherine Barnes, "Civil Society and Peacebuilding: Mapping Functions in Working for Peace," *The International Spectator* 44, no. 1 (2009): 131–147; Robert Belloni, "Civil Society in War-to-Democracy Transitions," in *From War to Democracy:*

Dilemmas of Peacebuilding, ed. Anna Jarstad and Timothy Sisk (Oxford, England: Cambridge University Press, 2008); Jonathan Cohen, "Effective Participation of National Minorities as a Tool for Conflict Prevention, *International Journal of Minority and Group Rights* 16, no. 4 (2009): 539–547; Anthony Wanis-St. John and Darren Kew, "Civil Society and Peace Negotiations: Confronting Exclusion," *International Negotiation* 13, no. 1 (2008).

38. Robert M. Axelrod, *The Evolution of Cooperation* (New York: Basic Books, 1984); Robert M. Axelrod and Robert O. Keohane, "Achieving Cooperation Under Anarchy: Strategies and Institutions," *World Politics* 38, no. 1 (1985): 226–254.

39. De Waal, *Peacemaking among Primates,* 80.

40. De Waal, *Peacemaking among Primates,* 100–105.

41. De Waal, *Peacemaking among Primates,* 114.

42. De Waal, *Peacemaking among Primates,* 115.

43. Geert H. Hofstede, *Cultures and Organizations: Software of the Mind* (New York: McGraw-Hill, 2005).

44. Anthony Wanis-St. John, "Cultural Pathways in Negotiation and Conflict Management," in *The Handbook of Dispute Resolution,* ed. Michael Moffitt and Robert Bordone (San Francisco: Jossey Bass, 2005).

45. David Augsberger, *Conflict Mediation across Cultures* (Louisville, KY: Westminster John Knox, 1992), 187–228.

46. De Waal, *Peacemaking among Primates,* 119.

47. De Waal, *Peacemaking among Primates,* 121–126.

48. "Being at the top of the social ladder is not merely a pleasant comfortable position for a wild female monkey: it determines her life span and reproduction" (de Waal, *Peacemaking among Primates,* 128).

49. Hofstede, *Culture and Organizations,* 187–234.

50. Anthony Wanis-St. John, "Cultural Pathways in Negotiation and Conflict Management," in *Handbook of Dispute Resolution,* ed. M. Moffitt and R. Bordone (San Francisco: Jossey Bass, 2005).

51. Anthony Wanis-St. John, *Back Channel Negotiation* (Syracuse, NY: Syracuse University Press, 2011).

52. De Waal, *Peacemaking among Primates,* 157

53. De Waal, *Peacemaking among Primates,* 160.

54. De Waal, *Peacemaking among Primates,* 181, 193–195.

55. "Bonobos, in contrast [with chimpanzees], perform every conceivable variation, as if following the Kama Sutra" (de Waal, *Peacemaking among Primates,* 199).

56. De Waal, *Peacemaking among Primates,* 206–218.

57. De Waal, *Peacemaking among Primates,* 218–222.

58. Frans B. M. de Waal, "Evolutionary Ethics, Aggression and Violence: Lessons from Primate Research," *Journal of Law, Medicine and Ethics* 32 (2004): 18–23.

59. Gretchen Vogel, "The Evolution of the Golden Rule," *Science* 303, no. 5661 (February 20, 2004): 1128–1131; Frans B. M. de Waal, "Peace Lessons from an Unlikely Source," *PLoS Biology* 2, no. 4 (April 2004): 0434–0436.

60. C. Scott Littleton, ed., *Mythology: The Illustrated Anthology of World Myth and Storytelling* (London: Duncan Baird Publishers, 2002), 23.

61. Alfonso Caso, "El Pueblo del Sol," in *De Teotihuacán a Los Aztecas: Antología de Fuentes e Interpretaciones Históricas,* ed. Miguel León-Portilla (Mexico City, D.F.: Universidad Autónoma de México, 1983), 518–520.

62. Laurette Séjourné, "La Traición de Quetzalcóatl," *De Teotihuacán a Los Aztecas: Antología de Fuentes e Interpretaciones Históricas,* ed. Miguel León-Portilla (Mexico City, D.F.: Universidad Autónoma de México, 1983), 236–242.

63. *The Contendings of Horus and Seth,* transcription of the Papyrus Chester Beatty I, http://www.per-aset.org/ContendingsofHorusAndSet.htm. Also see Lucia Galin, *Egypt: Gods, Myths and Religion* (London: Anness Publishing, 2002), 64–67.

64. *The Contendings of Horus and Seth,* transcription of the Papyrus Chester Beatty I.

65. Thucydides, *History of the Peloponnesian War,* trans. Richard Crawley (Project Gutenberg eBook, 2009), http://www.gutenberg.org/files/7142/7142-h/7142-h.htm.

66. The Melian Dialogue appears in chapter XVII of *The History of the Peloponnesian War.* Thucydides does not give a literal account, but offers a reconstruction of the dialogue in the fateful negotiations between the Athenians and the Melians.

67. Thucydides, *History of the Peloponnesian War,* chapter XVII.

68. Raiffa, *Negotiation Analysis,* 110–112.

69. Heinz Waelchli and Dhavan Shah, "Crisis Negotiations Between Unequals: Lessons from a Classic Dialogue," *Negotiation Journal* 10, no. 2 (1994): 129–141.

70. Tablet I, *Epic of Gilgamesh,* in John Gardner and John Maier, *Gilgamesh: Translated from the Sin-leqi-unninni version* (New York: First Vintage Books, 1985), 68. This "late" Babylonian version was composed by the 13th century B.C.E.

71. Tablet II, column ii, *Epic of Gilgamesh.*

72. Tablet II, column iv, *Epic of Gilgamesh.*

73. *The Mahabharata,* Book 5, Section VII, trans. Kisari Mohan Ganguli, http://www.mahabharataonline.com/translation/mahabharata_05007.php.

74. *The Mahabharata,* Book 5, Sections LVIII–XCV, trans. Kisari Mohan Ganguli, http://www.mahabharataonline.com/translation.

75. See, for example, Paramahansa Yogananda, *God Talks with Arjuna: The Bhagavad Gita,* 2nd. ed., vols. 1 and 2 (Los Angeles, CA: Self-Realization Fellowship, 1995).

76. The survivors of the sack of Troy are said to go on to found Ancient Rome as well as the ancient Nordic and British cultures, according to sources in each of these cultures. See, generally, C. Scott Littleton, ed., *Mythology: The Illustrated Anthology of World Myth and Storytelling* (London: Duncan Baird Publishers, 2002).

77. Homer, *The Iliad,* trans. Robert Fitzgerald (Garden City, NY: Anchor Books/Doubleday, 1974), Book I, 18.

78. Homer, *The Iliad,* Book III, 78. Emphasis added.

79. Homer, *The Iliad,* Books III and IV, 81–91.

80. Homer, *The Iliad,* Book XXIV, 567–589.

CHAPTER 36

Spirituality, Emergent Creativity, and Reconciliation

Vern Neufeld Redekop

The study of spirituality, emergent creativity, peacemaking, and reconciliation together is a heuristically rich endeavor. In other words, it produces theoretical and practical results that can have a positive impact on humankind generally, guiding policies, strategies, and actions in the fields of conflict and peace. Furthermore, research on these four concepts can work reflexively to positively change researchers and the academic communities to which they belong. This chapter is a reflection on research in process; as such, it comes at a time when many insights about the relationship among these concepts are already emerging, and yet there is a realization that there is far more yet to come. These reflective results will be presented as follows: first, I will present a conceptual overview, describing how these concepts fit together. I will then examine each concept individually drawing out its fuller meaning. I will then return to the conceptual interconnections, showing how each shed light on the others while at the same time generating new insights. Finally, I will explore some of the practical implications and suggest new directions for further research.

> Before proceeding in a more formal way, allow me to present the *problematique* with a metaphorical presentation of an ancient text. It comes from Genesis 2:6–7, the second Creation story: A stream would rise from the earth and water the whole face of the *adamah*. (אדמה *adamah* is a word for ground, and the ground has a face; it is the female form of *adam* אדם the word for humankind and the designation of the first person created.) Then יהוה (this is the Name of God usually rendered "LORD") God, formed *adam* out of *adamah* (this cadavar was still lifeless). God breathed into its nostrils the breath of life, and the prototypic human, *ha-adam* (האדם) became a living being. (Genesis 2:7–8)[1]

Now, *ha-adam* (הָאָדָם) is the collective word for humankind; hence, in this case, it refers to the prototypic human that represents our collective humanity. The *adam* (ground formed in the shape of a human) was nothing until it was animated with spirit (note that the Hebrew *ruach* (רוּחַ) means breath, wind, and spirit). Using this metaphorically, we could say elements of peacemaking and reconciliation will not in and of themselves make reconciliation happen until "life is breathed into them." Suppose we designate spirituality as the "something"[2] that will animate the process of reconciliation. The question then becomes: What is the nature of this spirituality that prompts daring peacemaking? In other words: How is it possible for people who have hated one another to be turned around in their orientation such that they begin a transformative process such that they embrace each other at the end? It also raises the challenge of developing a discursive field around spirituality such that people of all persuasions can be meaningfully engaged on the subject (King 2008, 53–56).

RELATIONS AMONG KEY CONCEPTS

Peace is most needed wherever there is intense violent conflict between groups or individuals. Such conflict can be understood as the manifestation of mimetic structures of violence (Redekop 2002), where mimetic means imitative and reciprocal; structures are diachronic relational patterns; and violence is an orientation, attitude, and action intended to harm, diminish, eliminate, or disempower the other. War, genocide, and mass murder are extreme forms of mimetic structures of violence at the collective level; torture, rape, murder, and other forms of cruelty are evident at the individual level. Mimetic structures of violence can also be exemplified in subtle ways where people are undermined and destroyed through psychological abuse, betrayal, and character assassination through gossip.

Reconciliation can be understood as the transformation of mimetic structures of violence to mimetic structures of blessing in which actions are intended to and effective at mutual and reciprocal benefit and empowerment (Redekop 2002, 2007a, 2008). Benefit and empowerment can be understood as finding positive satisfiers for identity needs of meaning, action, connectedness, security, and recognition (Redekop 2002). Negative peace can be understood as diminished mimetic structures of violence and positive peace constitutes a context in which mimetic structures of blessing can be created and sustained.

Peacemaking is action that takes place in relation to mimetic structures of violence. It diminishes the violence and creates a space for the transformation of orientation, attitudes, and actions leading to peaceful coexistence (Chayes and Minow 2003), peacebuilding and eventually a culture of peace. This nonlinear process entails reconciliation, which results in new relationships, personal and collective healing, structural change (ranging from discursive structures to laws, customs and values), a capacity to transcend the previous situation (Redekop 2008), and a sense of justice.

Mimetic structures of violence, especially in their extreme form (e.g., war), are complex systems in which many factors play a role (Sandole 1999). These include mimetic desires and rivalries that can be manifest as greed on the material level and *hyperthumos,* meaning an exaggerated need for recognition (Fukuyama 1993). Violence is fueled by emotional, symbolic, and historical memories of past injustices (grievance). It is maintained through chosen traumas, narcissistic wounding, and a projection of all that is bad about oneself onto others (Volkan 1998). There may be hegemonic structures whereby the Other is experienced as having the power to set the agenda, make the rules, and exercise control that systematically disempowers the Self (Cummings 1993; Redekop 2002). Throughout runs a mimetic contagion that prompts a spiral of increasing violence (Girard 1987).

Given the complexity of mimetic structures of violence, peacemaking itself is a complex endeavor because it has to address the multitude of factors associated with conflict. Not only does it have to come to terms with the complexity of conflict, it also has to address the traumatic and systemic effects of conflict, the many actors involved in the conflict, those affected, and those wishing to intervene. There are also a number of processes involved—providing relief, diplomatic communicating, strategic positioning, negotiation, mediation, and the like. These factors, actors, and processes cannot be addressed in linear fashion because they are interconnected and constantly at play. Hence, complexity theory can be brought to bear on the situation. This introduces a dialectical paradox. On the one hand, peacemaking and reconciliation are goals with attendant processes which are well planned coordinated; on the other hand, complexity suggest that it is the unexpected event or action that precipitates cascading changes in the situation. Even the best plans are subject to the unexpected and outright chaos and runaway violence are always possible. Peacemaking can then be framed as staging the critical context for emergent creativity. To arrest the violence and create a space for something transcendent to happen in such a complex environment has all the characteristics of emergent creativity—it cannot be predicted, one change can have cascading effects, significant change can happen almost instantaneously, and consequences of any action can go far beyond what was intended (Kauffman 2008; Sword 2003). Emergent creativity entails both intentionality of action and a profound respect for the capacity of systems to self-organize. The latter can be seen as congruent with Eastern notions of nonaction. Hence, there are the constant paradoxes of acting and hopeful waiting, and speaking while being attentive to the unexpected and uncontrolled happening at the same time.

To engage in peacemaking in situations of chaotic violence might seem futile within the framework of utilitarian calculus of self-preservation, risk management, proven effectiveness, and realism. Peacemaking is an action within a complex relational system in which anything could happen. As such, it demands an inner strength and resilience, a capacity for paradox and complexity with an openness to that which is transcendent, an ability to connect with people at a profound level, and an ethical orientation and vision oriented toward the well-being of all of the parties implicated in the violence. In other words, peacemaking actions are motivated, initiated, and sustained by spirituality. We will now look more closely at the key concepts, beginning with spirituality.

SPIRITUALITY

The root metaphors for spirit are wind and breath, which you can't pin down exactly, making spirit hard to talk about. In the words of Jesus, "The wind blows where it will. You hear the sound it makes, but you don't know where it comes from or where it goes." (John 3:8, *The Inclusive Bible*) From this metaphor, there is openness to something that you cannot fully explain but is real and has an impact on our own lives. It also suggests that the spirit cannot be controlled or forced. Taking another approach, I did a thought experiment based on the medicine wheel of indigenous peoples of North America. One aspect pictures the human person as a circle divided into quadrants representing the emotional, physical, mental, and spiritual aspects that function in an integral way. My thought process was, "When we have a spiritual experience there is something emotional about it, right? Could we then collapse spirituality into emotion? Could we say we don't really need spirit, that it's only about emotion?" When we compare this experience with others that are only emotional, we sense that there is something else happening. Spirituality is more than emotion. The same could apply to the mental aspect: since our spiritual experience gives us an insight, there is something cognitive happening; hence, can we collapse spirituality into the mental-cognitive component? No. There is something value-added that goes beyond that. What about the physical? Mario Beauregard examines this connection between spirit and physicality and concludes that there is something value-added to our spirituality that cannot be reduced to physical explanations (Beauregard and O'Leary 2007). What is this value-added component that comes with spirituality?

Over the past few decades, spirituality has become the focus of academic study, with its own methodology and links to a variety of disciplines. One of these is transpersonal psychology, which examines our capacity to make profound links with others, to connect in a way that transcends language or physicality while implicating both along with thought, emotion, volition, and moral awareness. Another is growth in spiritual consciousness from an integral perspective and a third looks at spirituality as its own phenomenon. Jorge Ferrer, Ken Wilber, and Kees Waaijman respectively are advocates of these approaches. They offer some interesting observations and questions that can work heuristically in the development of an appropriate methodology.

Jorge Ferrer points out three methodological pitfalls in the area of transpersonal scholarship (Ferrer 2002): experientialism (emphasis on individual inner experiences), inner empiricism (a demand that inquiry needs to be empirically grounded), and perennialism (assuming that spiritual knowledge is universal) (Helminiak 1998). He argues for a participatory methodology that has the effect of freeing "individuals, communities, and cultures from gross and subtle forms of narcissism, geocentrism, and self centeredness"(Ferrer 2002) and positively "into intimate communion with the cosmos" (173). He also maintains that truth claims need to be subject to validation.

Using Wilber's integral methodology, we can attend to the interior and exterior dimensions of spirituality at the individual and collective levels (Wilber 2006). For Ken Wilber, Spirit occurs in the first, second, and third persons: an

Figure 36.1
Four Aspects of Spirituality

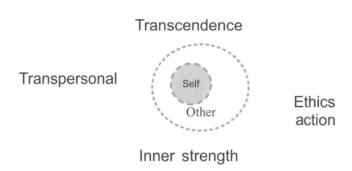

intrapersonal Spirit Witness of the first person; "the great You . . . the radiant living, all-giving God before whom I must surrender in love and devotion and sacrifice and release . . . I must love until it hurts" (159) of the second person; and the "Great It . . . this vast impersonal evolutionary System, the Great Inter-locking Order" (159) of the third person. Wilber's work also points to links between spiritual development and levels of consciousness (McGuigan 2006).

In his massive tome, *Spirituality: Forms, Foundations, Methods* (968 pages), Kees Waaijman distinguishes four methods of spirituality research: (1) Form-Descriptive, attending to spiritual biography; (2) Hermeneutical, attending to spiritual reading; (3) Systematic, attending to the reading community and thematic fields; and (4) Mystagogic, attending to spiritual accompaniment and spiritual transformation (2002).

Working synthetically within these parameters we can start to envision spirituality has having the following components: a source of inner strength, transpersonal connection, transcendence, and a capacity for ethical action. These can be pictured in Figure 36.1.

We note that spirituality can be found within a relational system that includes Self and Other. The boundary of the Self, like a cell, is open to information from outside the self (Moore 2008). The relational system itself is open, being influenced by other relational systems and fields. The four dimensions of spirituality impinge on Self and Other and the relationship between them.

- First, spirituality is a source of *inner strength*. Within most religious traditions are examples of people who were asked to do difficult things, who resisted but somehow found within their own spiritual experiences the strength to tackle overwhelming odds. Contemporary leaders who have made a significant difference in the interests of peace have drawn on spiritual resources: Gandhi, King, Tutu, Carter, and Romero. Quebecer Laurent Gagnon tells the story of being at a conference with Elijah Harper, who was the one person primarily responsible for the 1990 failure of the Meech Lake Accord, which was to bring Quebec fully into the Canadian family. He, with his people, had feelings of great animosity toward Harper. Despite his natural feelings, Gagnon found the inner strength to reach out to Harper, eventually becoming friends with him. Even those who have not worn religious affiliation on their sleeves have privately drawn on their own spirituality. One of the hardest tasks is to reach out to one's enemy as one dimension of a reconciliation process. I have witnessed the spiritual transformation of people who have had their families killed in genocidal action, allowing them to put their lives together and to empathetically reach out to those responsible for their suffering. One such person is Richard Batsinduka, who made a prison visit to the man who killed his brother during the Rwandan genocide.

• Second, our spirituality makes possible profound *transpersonal connections*. We talk about those with an *open spirit* or *generosity of spirit*. Those with whom we establish a close affinity are called *soul mates*. It is at the level of transpersonal connection that we experience caring love as givers and recipients. The unlikely but real transpersonal connections in times of violent conflict are evident at the individual and collective level. My friends Andre and Judith Schabraq were Holocaust survivors. They told stories of times when they crossed Nazi-controlled borders with false papers. On one occasion, the lone official gave evidence that he could see that their papers were false but with a knowing glance allowed them through the border. Collectively, the example is given of German and English soldiers in trenches opposite one another during World War II. On Christmas Eve soldiers on one side started singing Christmas carols. Soon they were joined by enemies on the other side. Eventually they got out of their trenches, mingled, and shared a meal together. After this event, the transpersonal connection precluded them shooting one another, and the units had to be changed.

• Third, *transcendence,* a word derived from Latin words meaning "to climb beyond," can be used in a number of ways in relation to spirituality. In a religious sense, it can refer to a connection to the Divine. We need not limit our understanding to this narrow use of the word. It can be thought of as reaching a more fully encompassing position such that clashes between Self and Other are reframed as each comprehends not only the position of the other but a transcendent perspective that includes them both. Another sense comes from Rwandan Oscar Gasana, who said it is like "getting out of the ditch onto the road again." Transcendence also refers to a vision of the interconnectedness of things. It is a well developed level of consciousness that results in a sense of awe at the diversity yet connections available within the biosphere and the noosphere. An example of this sense of awe comes from scientist-philosopher Michael Polanyi:

So far as we know, the tiny fragments of the universe embodied in man are the only centres of thought and responsibility in the visible world. If that be so, the appearance of the human mind has been so far the ultimate stage in the awakening of the world; and all that has gone before, the strivings of a myriad centres that have taken the risks of living and believing, seem to have all been pursuing, along rival lines, the aim now achieved by us up to this point . . . We may envisage then a cosmic field which called forth all these centres by offering them a short-lived, limited, hazardous opportunity for making some progress of their own towards an unthinkable consummation. (1964, 405)

The words following this interest panoramic vision of evolution acknowledge his own link with spirituality: "And this is also, I believe, how a Christian is placed when worshipping God" (Ibid.).

- Fourth, spirituality finds expression in a capacity for caring action. The fact that human beings have built ethical frameworks and moral principles that reinforce a capacity to do things intended to result in the well-being of others is another dimension of spirituality. When an ethics of care (Clement 1996; Held 2007) is present in a relationship, there is the potential for mimetic structures of blessing; that is, mutual reciprocal patterns of attitude and action that result in the well-being of Self and Other.

There is a diachronic side to spirituality. It is frequently presented as a journey (see Figure 36.2). In fact, the transpersonal dimension can be framed in terms of accompaniment.

Spiritual journeys involve the Self being accompanied by an Other as well as the Self accompanying the Other. There may also be times of profound alienation from others—a profound aloneness with a grasping for, an opening up of the self to, and a finding of a source to go on in the most trying of times. This is exemplified in Victor Frankl's *Man's Search for Meaning*, in which he describes how, even in the horrific circumstances of Auschwitz, he was able to control his own thoughts and discover meaning for himself in a time of suffering.

Figure 36.2
Spirituality as Journey through Time

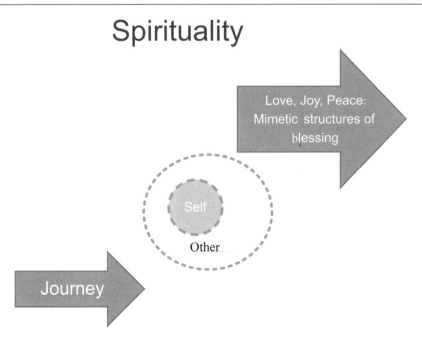

EMERGENT CREATIVITY

Stuart Kauffman's challenge is to find a framework for morality, value, agency, love, confidence, hope, good relationships apart from an established religious tradition. (Kauffman 2008) Similar to Polanyi, he views life through the prism of scientific methodologies; likewise he has sought to develop an epistemology broad enough to ground knowledge in realms of social science and ethics. Where Kauffman goes beyond what Polanyi could imagine is informed by chaos and systems theory. The "cosmic field that called forth . . ." that Polanyi refers to would be for Kauffman a universal principle of emergent creativity.

His first point is that the universe works in a nonreductionist way. Biology cannot be reduced to physics and systems cannot be reduced to their parts. Complex adaptive systems become a place within which there is one-way emergent creativity; that is, once something new emerges, it is not possible go back in time and undo this new development. Entropy functions in the same way: suppose you let a drop of ink fall into a Petri dish of water. It will diffuse, and all of the water will turn blue. However, this is not reversible, the ink will not naturally coalesce into one concentrated drop. Insights, to follow Bernard Lonergan (1957) and some others, are not reversible: once you have an insight, you can't go back and not have the insight. Creativity is not reversible; once you've created something, that new thing exists, and you can't go back to a state where it no longer exists.

Regarding work, he draws on Peter Atkins, a chemist, to say that work is really the constrained release of energy into a few degrees of freedom (Kauffman 2008, 90). So the physical definition of work is force applied through a distance but this is a little more abstract and general; there can be any of a number of kinds of energy. The energy is neither confined to a unitary direction and end, nor is it entirely diffuse. It is directed, but in an open-ended way. For Kauffman, a major aspect of the emergence of life was the development of a cellular membrane. The first cell had its boundary and could direct the energy so that the original DNA and self-replicating molecules would have a nice little space where they could do their developing. The porous boundary of the cell meant that energy expended by self-replicating molecules could be channeled into work, eventually giving cells a capacity for agency. The same principle of emergent creativity that made it possible for life to emerge, Kauffman sees operative within human systems such as legal and economic systems.

When we think about the initiative around creativity, it is work; it is energy directed into a few degrees of freedom. Those people who have made creative contributions have immersed themselves within a domain (Csik-szentmihaliy 1996), usually for about 10 years. This concentrated effort maps onto Polanyi's concept of indwelling—of building up a substantial tacit knowledge base around a *problematique,* such that it becomes a part of us (Polanyi 1964).

Emergent creativity in a really complex environment could be based on a variety of different platforms. An example of Kauffman's is an arithmetic operation that could be performed on a calculator, on a computer, or mentally, each of these can be thought of as a platform. One could use any of these platforms and get the same result, but the result could not predict which platform was used. So, in a complex environment where new things might emerge, it could take any of many platforms to bring a number of factors together that allows for the creative emergence of something new. Emergence happens in a really complex environment near the borderline of chaos and order. Something new is introduced that prompts systems to become self-organizing; they find a way of gravitating to something that introduces a new level of order. There is a tendency within the environment to move toward diversity, toward heterogeneity, to always be evolving new things. This happens in the biosphere and the noosphere through a constant sequence of dividing and reconnecting to something new. Creativity doesn't happen *ex nihilo*; it's always a recombining of what's there to produce something at a higher level of existence.

Criticality defines the circumstances in which emergent creativity is most likely to happen. It is a function of the diversity of resources and the number of ways they can be combined, including substitutes and complements. Figure 36.3 shows this relationship.

Above the criticality line in the graph is chaos—where anything could happen—and below the line is order. The further below the line the circumstance, the less likely anything creative will emerge; likewise, the higher above the line the less likely anything significant will be created. Criticality represents the edge of chaos in a complex system. Here are some simple examples, starting first with Lego blocks. There may not be very many kinds of Lego blocks, but there are so many thousands of ways that one could put them together that

Figure 36.3
Criticality

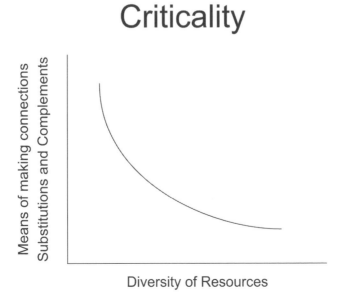

the creative potential of Legos is high. This example would be high up along the criticality line. Second, a designer with a display to decorate in a department store would have a vast array of resources with a limited space in which to put things together in a coherent way (a relatively small number of combinations); the potential for a new creative space to emerge would be high, a situation on the right end of the criticality line.

Substitutes and complements increase the potential for creativity. What this means is that the same item can be used for a number of different functions—some of which might be substitutes for other objects—and some might fill a unique but unintended role. A screwdriver is designed for turning screws, but it could be used to pry open lids, hold a door open, and so forth. The uses are endless. In the worlds of biology and economics, Kauffman argues, this happens all the time. Something new emerges, and it develops into the adjacent possibilities. The heart, for instance, emerged to pump blood but it produces sounds, establishes a rhythm, and develops neurological tissue, which contribute to the emotional and mental capacity of the body. New Internet-based technologies spawn new applications almost immediately, moving into adjacent possibilities.

When something significant emerges within a complex system, there is almost instantaneous change within the system as a whole. Every part of the system is reordered and there are new links among the parts, since all are interconnected.

After examining the concept of reconciliation, we will make links between emergent creativity and spirituality and how both can be seen as playing a key role in processes that address deep-rooted conflict.

RECONCILIATION

Reconciliation is a transformation of violent, deep-rooted conflict marked by resentments, hatred, and a passion for revenge into mutually respectful relationships in which Self and Other have a new identity defined not by violence but by creative blessing (Adams, 2000; Redekop 2002, 2007a, 2008). Reconciliation has political (Schaap 2005), social, and personal implications (Abu-Nimer 2001b; Bloomfield, et al. 2003; Helmick and Peterson 2001; Ismael and Haddad 2006; Nadler, et al. 2008). It involves symbolic gestures of conciliation, ritual and symbol (Schirch 2005), words of apology, acts of forgiveness, dialogue (Bohm 1997; Brown and Poremski 2005), and negotiation of new ways of being.

In the diagram of reconciliation (Figure 36.4), the heart of reconciliation is presented as a combination of discursive and symbolic transformative processes. Among the prerequisites for reconciliation are a vision, a mandate, and the resources to initiate processes with the goal of reconciliation. The meta-requisites include teachings of blessing—understood as principles, archetypal and inspiring stories, and insights derived from research on reconciliation (Redekop 2007b)—and GRIT, Gradual Reciprocate Initiatives in Tension-Reduction (Osgoode 1966).

Figure 36.4
Reconciliation

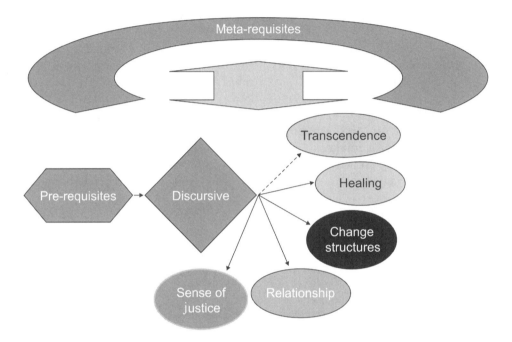

Reconciliation

The five result areas of reconciliation are interconnected. Personal healing—emotional, mental, and physical—enables the Self to reach out to the Other to establish new relationships (Herman 1997). New relationships can build sufficient trust for collaborative negotiations around structural change. Structures—understood as diachronic patterns of relating to one another expressed in norms, cultural expression, and laws—are indicative of and promote values of dignity, mutual respect, freedom, transparency, and capacity for agency. Mimetic (reciprocal, imitative) structures of blessing are marked by generosity of spirit. For perpetrators of violence this manifests as a concern to "make things right" (Radzic 2009) by empowering victims and their communities; for victims, this manifests as grace (the root metaphor is gift) to enable ever more profound forgiveness. The sense of justice derived from making things right and forgiveness contributes to healing and new relationships. At every step there is the possibility of transcendence—of seeing things from a new vantage point where the Self includes the perspective of the Other, of getting beyond the impasse that normally blocks progress in the other result areas, and of linking with some higher long-term process.

PEACEMAKING

There are two mutually enhancing approaches to an understanding of peacemaking that are applicable. The first comes from the literature around contemporary interventions in violent conflict; the second from biblical litera-ture. Regarding the first, peacemaking is placed at the point in waves or cycles of conflict where the fighting is the most intense (Lederach and Lederach 2010, 46–49). At this point peacemaking as an intervention is a decisive action to bring the fighting to a halt and the adversaries to the negotiating table. Within the context of violent conflict it may be a diplomatic intervention or a strate-gic offer of good offices of significant figures. It may be a threat of sanctions or the use of force from an international organization such as the United Nations, NATO, the Organization of African States, or another significant player.

In Jesus's famous Sermon on the Mount, one of the beatitudes begins "Blessed are the peacemakers . . ." (Matthew 5:9) The etymology of εἰρηνοποιοί, *peacemakers*, in this context is interesting and contains layers of meaning. This compound word includes *eirene*, the Greek word for peace, and *poioi*, the word for makers. *Eirene* carries with it two types of historical baggage. Jesus's Ara-maic version (the language he was speaking) would have been *shalom*, a word that conveys peace as wholeness along with overtones of peace with justice. The Greek word (the story was written in Greek) was rooted in Greek mythol-ogy with a rich overlay of related metaphors. The genealogy of the goddess/concept was as follows. *Uranus*, god of the heavens, was united with *Gaia*, god-dess of the earth. Their daughter was *Themis*, goddess of natural justice. *Themis* in turn had three daughters: *Eunomia*, goddess of good governance or good laws and teachings; *Dike*, goddess of procedural justice; and *Eirene*, goddess of peace. Hence we can see that however we understand it, peace is linked with justice—relational justice on the Hebrew side, and natural justice, fairness, bal-ance, and rightness—along with procedural justice on the Greek side. *Poiesis*, the word for "make," is the word used in Greek for the creative action of mak-ing something new and unique. It is from this word that we get the word *po-etry*, where the connotation is to compose something new (Ricoeur 2007).

Assembling the etymological and practical fragments, we can see the emer-gence of a concept of peacemaking that involves a call to turn things around. To turn from violence—a violent orientation, violent acts, and violent at-titudes—toward a new path that is directed toward a peace saturated with justice. The poetics—the creative work—of peace, calls on its ancestors, the wisdom of mother Themis, a spirit of justice, and its grandparents, Uranus—the heavens beyond one's ken—and Gaia, the earth, the mother, a grounded-ness in the concrete. The turnaround action of peacemaking is reminiscent of the Hebrew prophets calling on people to שוב *shuv*, to really turn around (New-man 2010). The prophets called on people to radically change their orientation when they perceived that the mimetic contagion of injustice, of lying, cheat-ing, treachery, murder, and the like, was destroying the human fabric. When the historical community was undoing itself, when the ethical vision of a fully human existence based on mimetic structures of blessing was unraveling, then *shuv*—reverse direction . . . or else—was the watchword.

INTERCONNECTIONS

I will now show how the interconnections among these concepts are heu-ristically productive. First, let us examine the linkages between reconciliation and spirituality. One of the prerequisites for reconciliation is a vision and man-date for reconciliation. Where do these come from and how are they derived? One can point to either a community or an authority that gives a mandate, but what about the first person who seeks such a mandate and develops such a vi-sion? Is it not because of a vision for something transcendent, something illu-sive, that a person wants to get a mandate to try what many might think of as being impossible? In other words, this impulse is based on hope, and what is hope but an openness, an anticipation, and a courage to be responsive to what might be an unlikely happening? If the future outcomes were certain and pre-dictable, the language of hope would not enter in. Does not hope then spring out of an intersection of transcendence and inner strength?

There is a strong connection between the impulse toward reconciliation and a longing for transpersonal connection. In the face of deep-rooted con-flict, every emotional impulse is geared to vengeance and continued violence. (Note that in international mediation there is the concept of a hurting stale-mate that can lead to negotiation. Such an impulse is geared toward settlement and does not entail forgiveness or a profound connection.) An ethical vision that values relationships and a vision for transpersonal connection prompt a desire to reconcile. It is this desire that may start with one of the parties or a third party that instigates the goal of reconciliation and sustains the process.

In a practical sense, the concept of a spiritual journey and concomitant ideas of spiritual accompaniment lead to the idea that within the reconciliation pro-cess, parties will need to grow spiritually and in many cases will need the sup-port of either spiritual mentors who can guide their grow or spiritual peers who can validate their experience and offer support through their transper-sonal connections. These peers and mentors are people who exemplify a good spirit—positive energy and openness to new possibilities. They can come from any religious or humanistic tradition.

What do we make of emergent creativity and its link to reconciliation? Deep-rooted conflict is a complex phenomenon that occurs within a relational system which is linked to a myriad of other relational systems. Likewise, reconcilia-tion is a very complex phenomenon; hence, the potential for the transforma-tion of mimetic structures of violence to those of blessing to meet the criteria of a complex adaptive system. Reconciliation can be understood as having the features of emergent creativity. It is non-reducible to the parts; the presence of all of the elements of reconciliation cannot guarantee it will happen. Rather they form a platform out of which reconciliation can emerge. What might be the trigger that starts the process of transformation is not predictable before-hand, but it is apparent after the fact. Reconciliation does not imply going back to a previous situation, but rather the creation of something new.

Each of the result areas for reconciliation represents an aspect of emergent creativity. New relationships in the wake of hatred and resentment show the creation of something new. Personal healing, especially from significant trauma, represents the construction of new neural pathways, representing physiologically, reconstruction, and emotional healing. It takes creativity to develop new structures—understood as laws, discursive patterns, and political arrangements—to allow for a nonoppressive life for all parties. The ability to find transcendence, to be able to remember rightly (Volf 2006) so that negative memories do not dominate the Self, to see things in a broader perspective, to see the Self from a transcendent position making it possible to be self critical—these demand emergent creativity and are irreversible. Finally, a sense of justice is itself something that emerges from the process.

Emergent creativity as a phenomenon of complex systems suggests that for reconciliation to occur it might be necessary to change some of the factors to approach criticality, perhaps by adding to the platform out of which it can emerge. This can take the form of adding new understanding in the form of teachings of blessing, introducing new parties to the process, finding resources, and providing contact with mimetic models, be they people or processes.

Reconciliation takes work, understood as the release of energy within a few degrees of possibility. It is not simply energy but energy directed toward a given goal. Another factor of emergent creativity is that reconciliation introduces adjacent possibilities. These possibilities could be internal to the relational system such as new potential for economic development or in other relational systems. For example, South African reconciliation, as fraught with problems as it continues to be, has nonetheless allowed South Africa to take the lead in many conflict resolution and reconciliation initiatives, and its Truth and Reconciliation Commission has been a model for other nations. Noteworthy was its use of Ubuntu—the concept that we find our fullness of being in the connection with and flourishing of the Other—as a conceptual basis for its work (Battle 1997).

What about going the other way: does reconciliation add something new to our understandings of spirituality and emergent creativity? At the outset, in relation to spirituality, it suggests that spirituality is not about convenient self-serving emotional highs. Rather spirituality is about doing the work needed to transform intractable situations and facing significant challenges. It also suggests that spirituality should produce results, results that have an impact on both Self and Other and on the relationship between them. These results should be open to scrutiny and should be subject to empirical validation. In relation to emergent creativity, reconciliation suggests that emergence, which is normally spontaneous, can take place within a process which has a sense of direction to it. There still can be a spontaneous action but it is within articulated parameters. Pursuing this could add theoretically to an understanding of the concept of emergence.

If peacemaking is understood as the beginning of a change from violence to peace, it comes at the nexus of two complex systems. We showed that violent conflict is a complex system and that reconciliation is a complex process. Hence, the point of change is a point of convergence of two or more complex entities that demand emergent creativity. It is a time when, out of the chaos of runaway violence, something new starts to happen. With the understanding that in complex systems something small produces huge results, we can start to see that there is at least the possibility of a turnaround in even the most dire situations (for examples, see Yoder 1983). The problem is, it is impossible to predict, a priori, what the precise action or event might be that starts a contagious rush toward peace. In both East Germany and Romania, the collapse of a violent order came about through crowds—crowds that the authorities wished to dismiss as mobs. However, when the people started chanting, "We are the people; we are the people," something turned around in the minds of the police and soldiers who had the power to crush the crowds (Redekop and Paré 2010). Eventually the crowd action brought the respective Communist regimes to their knees, creating the space for the emergence of a new order.

PRACTICAL IMPLICATIONS

If spirituality, emergent creativity, peacemaking, and reconciliation are complementary concepts that each add to their mutual understanding, the implications could be significant academically and for work in the field. First, the joint study of the concepts should have reflexive impact on researchers, enhancing spirituality, providing grounds for creativity and enabling them to work on reconciliation in the relational systems that they themselves find challenging. Second, those focusing on any of the individual concepts will be prompted to understand each more fully in the light of the others. Third, it suggests that spirituality should be seen as an important resource in reconciliation processes. This means that rituals, disciplines, and teachings that support spirituality should be drawn upon when initiating peacemaking and reconciliation processes. Fourth, the concept of emergent creativity should inspire hope in dire circumstances, prompting a strategic shift of circumstances that would increase the potential for something new to emerge. For example, the introduction of new parties to a process increases the ideas available, with the potential relational combinations thus enhancing criticality. In other instances, where too many interested parties might be together, separating people into subgroups could bring the situation closer to criticality and increase the chances for a breakthrough. It also suggests that nothing takes the place of hard work; that is, if people focus their energies, through research and process, on a given situation, the chances of reconciliation go up. Fifth, the methodological challenges indicate that empirical and theoretical work still needs to be done to validate the hypothesis of this chapter and to allow for new insights to emerge that might enhance our capacity as humans to live together in mutually helpful ways. Finally, instances of peacemaking (e.g., European Centre for Conflict Prevention 1999; Henderson 1996; Little 2007) need to be studied from the perspective of complexity theory, particularly to note the aligning of factors such that a certain action prompted the initial turning around of the hearts and minds of those involved.

CONCLUSION

By examining spirituality, emergent creativity, and reconciliation individually and then in relation to one another, significant insights were gained, thus demonstrating that the exercise was heuristically rich. These insights suggest new forms of action in relation to reconciliation processes and imply that the field of peacemaking would likewise be enhanced by attending to the potential contribution of spirituality and emergent creativity.

NOTES

1. Author rendition adapted from the New Revised Standard Version of the Bible.

2. Note that I am using an algebraic approach in which x is analogically *spirituality*.

CHAPTER 37

A Social-Psychological Perspective on Peacemaking

Morton Deutsch

My approach to peacemaking has largely been oriented toward developing theory and research that might be useful to peacemaking practitioners. Although my experience as a peacemaker has been mainly limited to working as a psychotherapist to individuals, couples, and small groups to deal with their conflicts in a more constructive and productive manner, this employment has had a considerable influence on my theoretical and research work. This chapter is divided into three main sections. The first presents a discussion of the processes involved in constructive and destructive conflict. The second is concerned with helping social actors (whether they be individuals, groups, or nations) to manage their conflicts more constructively. The third is focused on helping social actors reconcile after they have been through harmful, destructive conflict.

My discussion in the following sections of this chapter is meant to be quite general. I have sought to present my views about conflict so that they are applicable to conflict between groups of various sorts and sizes—between families, between groups within a community, between tribes, between ethnic groups, and between nations, as well as to interpersonal conflict. In doing so, I have ignored many of the differences that exist when the conflict is between different types of groups. My emphasis is on the similarities across different types of groups, rather than the differences, so that the reader may have a general framework for thinking about intergroup conflict. This framework needs to be supplemented and enriched by specific particularities when considering any actual conflict.

CONSTRUCTIVE AND DESTRUCTIVE PROCESSES INVOLVED IN CONFLICT

In my book *The Resolution of Conflict: Constructive and Destructive Processes* (Deutsch, 1973), I presented a detailed characterization of the nature of such processes. The main point that I made was that *a constructive process of resolving conflict is similar to a cooperative process of solving a mutual problem,* the conflict being the mutual problem. In contrast, a destructive process is like a competitive struggle to win the conflict. Below, I summarize the main features of these two types of processes.

Cooperative relations (whether within or between groups), as compared with competitive ones, show more of the following positive characteristics:

1. Effective communication is exhibited. Ideas are communicated and members of the different groups are attentive to one another, accepting of the ideas of the others and being influenced by them. They have fewer difficulties in communicating with or understanding others.

2. Friendliness, helpfulness, respect, and a minimum of obstructiveness are expressed in their discussions. Members of the cooperating groups also are more satisfied with the relationship between the groups and their solutions, as well as being favorably impressed by the contributions of the other group's members. In addition, members of the cooperating groups rate themselves high in the desire to win the respect of their colleagues. They also rate themselves high in a sense of obligation to the others.

3. The members of each group expect to be treated fairly by the other and feel obligated to treat the other fairly. In their relations to one another, justice is an important value.

4. Coordination of effort, division of labor, orientation to task achievement, orderliness in discussion, and high productivity are manifested in the cooperating groups (if the solution of the conflict requires effective communication, coordination of effort, division of labor, or sharing of resources).

5. Feeling of agreement with the ideas of others and a sense of basic similarity in beliefs and values, as well as confidence in one's own ideas and in the value that other members attach to those ideas, are obtained in the cooperating groups.

6. Recognizing and respecting the others by being responsive to the other's needs.

7. Willingness to enhance the other's power (for example, the knowledge, skills, resources, and so on) to accomplish the other's goals increases. As the other group's capabilities are strengthened, you are strengthened; they are of value to you as well as to the other. Similarly, the other is enhanced by your enhancement and benefits from your growing capabilities and power.

8. Attempts to influence the other rely on persuasion and positive inducements.

9. Defining conflicting interests as a mutual problem to be solved by collaborative effort facilitates recognizing the legitimacy of each other's interests and the necessity to search for a solution responsive to the needs of all. It tends to limit rather than expand the scope of conflicting interests.

In contrast, a competitive process has the opposite effects:

1. Communication is impaired as the conflicting parties seek to gain advantage by misleading the other through use of false promises, ingratiation tactics, and disinformation. It is reduced and seen as futile as they recognize that they cannot trust one another's communications to be honest or informative.

2. Obstructiveness and lack of helpfulness lead to mutual negative attitudes and suspicion of each other's intentions. One's perceptions of the other tend to focus on the other's negative qualities and ignore the positive.

3. Fairness to the other is not valued. Each group is willing to exploit or harm the other to advantage themselves.

4. The parties to the process are unable to divide their work, duplicating one another's efforts such that they become mirror images; if they do divide the work, they feel the need to check continuously on what the other is doing.

5. The repeated experience of disagreement and critical rejection of ideas reduces confidence in oneself as well as the other.

6. Attempts to influence the other often involve threats, coercion, or false promises.

7. The conflicting parties seek to enhance their own power and to reduce the power of the other. Any increase in the power of the other is seen as threatening to oneself and one's group.

8. The competitive process stimulates the view that the solution of a conflict can be imposed only by one side on the other, which in turn leads to using coercive tactics, such as psychological as well as physical threats and violence. It tends to expand the scope of the issues in conflict as each side seeks superiority in power and legitimacy. The conflict becomes a power struggle or a matter of moral principle and is no longer confined to a specific issue at a given time and place. Escalating the conflict increases its motivational significance to the participants and may make a limited defeat less acceptable and more humiliating than a mutual disaster.

9. As the conflict escalates, it perpetuates itself by such processes as autistic hostility, self-fulfilling prophecies, and unwilling commitments. *Autistic hostility* involves breaking off contact and communication with the other; the result is that the hostility is perpetuated because one has no opportunity to learn that it may be based on misunderstandings or misjudgments, nor to learn if the other has changed for the better.

Self-fulfilling prophecies are those wherein you engage in hostile behavior toward another because of a false assumption that the other has done or is preparing to do something harmful to you; your false assumption comes true when it leads you to engage in hostile behavior that then provokes the other to react in a manner hostile to you. The dynamics of an escalating, destructive conflict have the inherent quality of a *folie à deux*, in which the self-fulfilling prophecies of each side mutually reinforce one another. As a result, both sides are right to think that the other is provocative, untrustworthy, and malevolent. Each side, however, tends to be blind to how it, as well as the other, has contributed to this malignant process.

In the case of *unwitting commitments,* during the course of escalating conflict, the parties not only over-commit to rigid positions, but also may unwittingly commit to negative attitudes and perceptions, beliefs, stereotypes of the other, defenses against the other's expected attacks, and investments involved in carrying out their conflictual activities. Thus, during an escalated conflict, a person (a group, a nation) may commit to the view that the other is an evil enemy, the belief that the other is out to take advantage of oneself (one's group, nation), the conviction that one has to be constantly vigilant and ready to defend against the danger the other poses to one's vital interests and also invest in the means of defending oneself as well as attacking the other. After a protracted conflict, it is hard to give up a grudge, to disarm without feeling vulnerable, as well as to give up the emotional charge associated with being mobilized and vigilant in relation to the conflict.

FACILITATING THE DEVELOPMENT OF CONSTRUCTIVE CONFLICT MANAGEMENT

After much research by my students and myself into the development of constructive and destructive conflict (Deutsch 1973), I developed "Deutsch's Crude Law of Social Relations." *The characteristic processes and effects elicited by a given type of social relationship also tend to elicit that type of social relationship.* Thus, cooperation induces and is induced by perceived similarity in beliefs and attitudes, readiness to be helpful, openness in communication, trusting and friendly attitudes, sensitivity to common interests and de-emphasis of opposed interests, orientation toward enhancing each other's mutual power rather than power differences, and so on. Similarly, competition induces and is induced by use of tactics of coercion, threat, or deception; attempts to enhance the power differences between oneself and the other; poor communication; minimization of the awareness of similarities in values, and increased sensitivity to opposed interests; suspicious and hostile attitudes; the importance, rigidity and size of issues in conflict, and so on.

In other words, if one has systematic knowledge of the effects of cooperative and competitive processes, one has systematic knowledge of the conditions that typically give rise to such processes and by extension to the conditions that affect whether a conflict takes a constructive or destructive course. My early theory of cooperation and competition is a theory of the effects of cooperative and competitive processes. Hence, from the Crude Law of Social Relations, it follows that this theory brings insight into the conditions that give rise to cooperative and competitive processes. The Crude Law further suggests that *enhancement of any correlate of cooperation (e.g., trusting and friendly attitudes) would enhance its other correlates (e.g., an orientation to enhancing one another's power). Similarly, for competition, as any of its correlates are enhanced, this would lead to the enhancement of its other correlates.*

The Crude Law would suggest that constructive conflict management, successful negotiations, and peacemaking would be improved by any of the various characteristics of cooperative relations described in the preceding section. Thus, reframing a conflict so that it is viewed as a mutual problem to be solved by a cooperative process leads to successful peacemaking. Reframing has inherent within it the that whatever resolution is achieved it is acceptable and considered to be just to each party of the conflict when they recognize that their solution is such that they either sink or swim together, that each cannot achieve its goals unless they other also does.

Cooperative orientation in the conflicting parties facilitates reframing. As indicated by the Crude Law, a cooperative orientation is reflected in such behaviors as:

- Placing the disagreements in perspective by identifying common ground and common interests.

- When there is disagreement, address the issues and refrain from making personal attacks.

- When there is disagreement, seek to understand the other's views from his or her perspective; try to feel what it would be like if you were on the other's side.

- Building on the ideas of the other, fully acknowledging their value.

- Emphasizing the positive in the other and the possibilities of constructive resolution of the conflict. Limiting and controlling expression of your negative feelings so that they are primarily directed at the other's violation of cooperative norms (if that occurs), or at the other's defeatism.

- Taking responsibility for the harmful consequences—unwitting as well as intended—of what you do and say; seek to undo the harm as well as openly accept responsibility and make sincere apology for it.

- If the other harms you, be willing to forgive if the other accepts responsibility for doing so, sincerely apologizes, and is willing to try to undo it; seek reconciliation rather than nurturing an injury or grudge.

- Being responsive to the other's legitimate needs.

- Empowering the other to contribute effectively to the cooperative effort; solicit the other's views, listen responsively, share information, and otherwise help the other—when necessary—be an active, effective participant in the cooperative problem-solving process.

- Being appropriately honest. Being dishonest, attempting to mislead or deceive, is of course a violation of cooperative norms. However, one can be unnecessarily and inappropriately truthful. In most relationships, there is usually some ambivalence, a mixture of positive as well as negative thoughts and feelings about the other and about oneself. Unless the relationship has developed to a very high level of intimacy, communicating every suspicion, doubt, fear, and sense of weakness one has about oneself or the other is apt to be damaging to the relationship—particularly if the communication is blunt, unrationalized, and unmodulated. In effect, one should be open and honest in communication but appropriately so, realistically taking into account the consequences of what one says or does not say and the current state of the relationship.

- Throughout conflict, remain a moral person—therefore, a person who is caring and just—and consider the other as a member of one's moral community—therefore, as a person who is entitled to care and justice.

FORGIVENESS AND RECONCILIATION

After protracted, violent conflicts in which the conflicting parties have inflicted grievous harm (humiliation, destruction of property, torture, assault, rape, murder) on one another, the conflicting parties may still have to live and work together in the same communities. This is often the case in civil wars, ethnic and religious conflicts, gang wars, and even family disputes that have taken a destructive course. Consider the slaughter that has taken place between the Hutus and Tutsis in Rwanda and Burundi (Staub 2008); between blacks and whites in South Africa; between the Bloods and Crips of Los Angeles; the Protestants and Catholics in Northern Ireland; and among Serbs, Croats, and Muslims in Bosnia. Is it possible for forgiveness and reconciliation to occur? If so, what fosters these processes?

There are many meanings of forgiveness in the extensive and growing literature concerned with this topic. I shall use the term to mean giving up the rage, the desire for vengeance and a grudge toward those who have inflicted grievous harm on you, your loved ones, or the groups with whom you identify. It also implies willingness to accept the other into one's moral community so that he or she is entitled to care and justice. As Borris (2003) has pointed out, it does not mean you have to forget the evil that has been done, condone it, or abolish punishment for it. However, it implies that the punishment should conform to the canons of justice and be directed toward the goal of reforming the harm-doer so that he or she can become a moral participant in the community.

There has been rich discussion in the psychological and religious literature of the importance of forgiveness to psychological and spiritual healing as well as to reconciliation (see Minow 1998; Shriver 1995). Forgiveness is, of course, not to be expected in the immediate aftermath of torture, rape, or assault. It is unlikely, as well as psychologically harmful, until one is able to be in touch with the rage, fear, guilt, humiliation, hurt, and pain that has been stored inside. But nursing hate, as well as competition for victimhood between the conflicting parties, keeps the injury alive and active in the present instead of permitting it to take its proper place in the past. Doing so consumes psychological resources and energy that are more appropriately directed to the present and future. Although forgiveness of the other may not be necessary for self-healing, it seems to be very helpful, as well as an important ingredient in the process of reconciliation.

There are two distinct but interrelated approaches to developing forgiveness. One centers on the victims, and the other on the relationship between the victims and the harm-doers. The focus on the victim, in addition to providing some relief from PTSD, seeks to help the victim recognize the human qualities common to victim and victimizer. In effect, various methods and exercises are employed to enable the victim to recognize the bad as well as good aspects of herself and her group, that she has sinful as well as divine capabilities and tendencies. In other words, one helps the victim become aware of herself as a total person—with no need to deny her own fallibility and imperfections—whose lifelong experiences in her family, schools, communities, ethnic and religious groups, and workplaces have played a key role in determining her own personality and behavior. As the victim comes to accept her own moral fallibility, she is likely to accept the fallibility of the harm-doer as well, and to perceive both the good and the bad in the other.

Both victims and harm-doers are often quite moral toward those they include in their own moral community, but grossly immoral to those excluded. Thus, Adolf Eichmann, who efficiently organized the mass murder of Jews for the Nazis, was considered a good family man. The New England captains of the slave ships, who transported African slaves to the Americas under the most abominable conditions, were often deacons of their local churches. The white settlers of the United States, who took possession of land occupied by native Americans and killed those who resisted, were viewed as courageous and moral within their own communities.

Recognition of the good and bad potential in all humans, the self as well as the other, facilitates the victim's forgiveness of the harm-doer. But it may not be enough. Quite often, forgiveness also requires interaction between the victim and harm-doer to establish the conditions needed for forgiving. This interaction sometimes takes the form of negotiation between the victim and harm-doer. A third party representing the community (such as a mediator or judge) usually facilitates the negotiation and sets the terms if the harm-doer and victim cannot reach an agreement. It is interesting to note that in courts, such negotiations are sometimes required in criminal cases before the judge sentences the convicted criminal.

Reconciliation goes beyond forgiveness in that it not only accepts the other into one's moral community, but also establishes or reestablishes a positive, cooperative relationship among the individuals and groups estranged by the harms they have inflicted on one another. Borris (2003) has indicated: "Reconciliation is the end of a process that forgiveness begins."

Earlier, I discussed in detail some of the factors involved in initiating and maintaining cooperative relations; that discussion is relevant to the process of reconciliation. Here, I wish to consider briefly some of the special issues relating to establishing cooperative relations after a destructive conflict. Below, I outline a number of basic principles.

1. *Mutual security.* After a bitter conflict, each side tends to be concerned with its own security, without adequate recognition that neither side can attain security unless the other side also feels secure. Real security requires that both sides have as their goal mutual security. If weapons have been involved in the prior conflict, mutually verifiable disarmament and arms control are important components of mutual security. After violent conflict, fear that the other will violate an agreement to cease hostilities and will engage in violence again is slow to disappear. The intervention of powerful and respected third parties is often necessary to create confidence that the cessation of violence will be observed by both of the conflicting parties.

2. *Mutual respect.* Just as true security from physical danger requires mutual cooperation, so does security from psychological harm and humiliation (Lindner 2006). Each side must treat the other with the respect, courtesy, politeness, and consideration normatively expected in civil society. Insult,

humiliation, and inconsiderateness by one side usually leads to reciproca-
tion by the other and decreased physical and psychological security.

3. Mutual respect requires the belief that justice will be established in the relations between the conflicting parties. Doing so will involve the elimination
   of superiority, inferiority in rights and privileges, as well as exploitation in
   the relations between the conflicting groups.

4. *Humanization of the other.* During bitter conflict, each side tends to develop
   negative stereotypes of and dehumanize the other, which justifies images
   of the other as an evil enemy (Oppenheimer 2006). There is much need for
   both sides to experience one another in everyday contexts as parents, home-
   makers, schoolchildren, teachers, or merchants, which enables them to see one
   another as human beings who are more like themselves than not. Problem-
   solving workshops and dialogue groups along the lines described by
   Burton (1969, 1987) and Kelman (1972) are also valuable in overcoming dehumanization of one another.

5. *Economic security.* Basic supplies of food, shelter, and medical care are often
   seriously impaired during violent conflict. This lack of these basics must
   be addressed expeditiously if reconciliation is to be possible.

6. *Education and the media.* During a protracted, bitter conflict, the educational
   system as well as the media within each of the conflicting parties are often
   warped so that the in-group members are taught to view the out-group as
   an evil enemy and to consider its own heroes to be those who are most effective in destroying the enemy. A lasting reconciliation will require transformations in the educational system and the media within each group to
   achieve three objectives: (a) a nonpartisan view of the conflict and its history which is understood and essentially agreed upon by both parties (see
   Staub 2008); (b) providing knowledge and support for nonviolent constructive methods of conflict resolution; and (c) developing a positive image
   of the peacemakers and of peaceable persons.

7. *Fair rules for managing conflict.* Even if a tentative reconciliation has begun, new conflicts inevitably occur—over the distribution of scarce resources,
   procedures, and values, as well as perceived non-adherence to the terms of
   prior agreements. It is important to anticipate that such conflicts will occur
   and to develop beforehand the fair rules or laws, experts (such as mediators, arbitrators, conflict resolvers), institutions (such as courts) and other
   resources (such as neutral peacekeepers) for managing such conflicts constructively and justly.

8. *Curbing the extremists on both sides.* During a protracted and bitter conflict,
   each side tends to produce extremists committed to the processes of the
   destructive conflict as well as to its continuation. Attaining some of their initial goals may be less satisfying than continuing to inflict damage on the
   other. It is well to recognize that extremists stimulate extremism on both
   sides; it is an unwitting cooperation to keep the destructive conflict going
   by the extremists on each side. The parties need to cooperate in curbing
   extremism on their own side and restraining actions that stimulate and justify extremist elements on the other side. This is often difficult to do. Extremists will seek to provoke the other to engage in a destructive counteraction
   in the expectation that their counter-response will justify the negative view
   of the other as an evil enemy with whom one cannot have peaceful, coopera-

tive relations. In so doing, they will also try to discredit the moderates in their group as weak appeasers who are helping the enemy.

9. *Gradual development of mutual trust and cooperation.* It takes repeated experience of successful, varied, mutually beneficial cooperation to develop a solid basis for mutual trust between former enemies. In the early stages of reconciliation, when trust is required for cooperation, the former enemies may be willing to trust a third party (who agrees to serve as a monitor, inspector or guarantor of any cooperative arrangement), but not yet willing to trust one another if there is a risk of the other failing to reciprocate cooperation. Also in the early stages, it is especially important that cooperative endeavors be successful. This requires careful selection of the opportunities and tasks for cooperation so that they are clearly achievable as well as meaningful and significant. The development of superordinate goals (such as building a bridge, a school, or a hospital that would benefit both groups) is often an excellent way to develop cooperation.

I also suggest that it would be particularly useful to create cross-cutting groups whose members have common identities as well as the identities arising from their memberships in the reconciling conflicting groups. Here, for example, I am referring to such groups as health care workers, from both sides, working together to treat patients and to prevent diseases; as construction workers, from both sides, working together to repair roads and bridges, to build houses and the like; as educators working to develop joint curricula and other projects; and as lawmakers working together to develop fair laws and institutions. Many other types of cross-cutting, cooperative groups could be listed. In the initial stage of the development of such groups, it would undoubtedly be helpful if such groups had respected third-party facilitators who could help with the development of the cooperative process and with the substantive issues (e.g., health care) on which the group will be working. Levine and Campbell (1972) documented that destructive intergroup conflict is more conducive in pyramidal-segmentary social structures within a society than the cross-cutting structures proposed here.

CONCLUDING THOUGHT

Efforts to further reconciliation after bitter, violent conflict are important; but even more important is the prevention of such conflicts. As is true for many diseases, the prevention of the social disease of destructive conflict is easier and more effective than its treatment and remediation. Peck (1993), in a chapter on preventive diplomacy, has described how new regional conflict resolution centers (established under the auspices and direction of the UN) could provide preventive educational, mediation, and early warning signs that could deter the development of bitter, destructive conflict. And I (Deutsch 1994) have articulated a somewhat utopian proposal for actions that the United Nations, as well as the various institutions of national societies, could take in order to prevent destructive conflicts. These papers are suggestive efforts related to prevention that need considerably more work by many more scholars and practitioners in the field of conflict resolution.

CHAPTER 38

Method in Peacemaking

Jamie Price

This chapter concerns peacemaking. It also concerns method. Its purpose is to advance the possibility of developing method in peacemaking. But as a beginning, it is important to specify the meanings of these two terms and to pin down the performances they signify.

Peacemaking, of course, is the unifying theme of this volume. In my view, the editors have rendered a valuable service to the field by asking their authors to focus their reflections on the emergence of groups out of conflict, and in doing so to distinguish clearly between peacemaking and peacebuilding. As Susan Allen Nan explained the distinction to me, "Peacebuilding emphasizes structures and institutions. Peacemaking emphasizes the human dimension, creativity, openness, trust, and welcoming otherness."[1]

In Aristotelian terms, Nan is distinguishing the *praxis* of peacemaking (what we do) from its *poiesis* (what we build).[2] The utility of distinguishing these performances is that their functional relationship also becomes clear: for it is in the performance of making peace with others that we make possible the interpersonal and collaborative conditions necessary for creating and maintaining the institutions and structures required to sustain it. The praxis of making peace, then, is performatively and linguistically analogous to what we mean we say that we are "making up" with someone following an argument or a fight. As a technical term, *peacemaking* has to do with the range of actions and activities involved in defusing feelings of threat; deepening insight into the other; and otherwise healing, mending, and connecting relationships strained, broken, or disconnected by conflict. In a later section, we will attend more explicitly to the praxis of what we are doing when we are making peace. First, however, we must turn our attention to method, the other key term in this chapter.

As we do so, we might find ourselves spontaneously anticipating a discussion of tools and road maps, of qualitative and quantitative techniques. And although the equation of methods and tools certainly reflects a common understanding of the term, it is not the one I intend here. Instead, I invite you to differentiate methods and tools, and to reflect on method in a broader, more foundational sense: method not as technique, but as thinking cap; method as an investigative framework that enables scholars and practitioners to put their heads together to analyze and solve problems; method as a cognitive model that guides the way we use our minds to formulate questions, assess answers, transform the unknown into the known, options into decisions; method, in Bernard Lonergan's phrase, as a "framework for collaborative creativity,"[3] as "a normative set of related and recurrent operations yielding progressive and cumulative results."[4]

Admittedly, my account of this notion of method is highly generalized. Nevertheless, we can pin down its meaning by differentiating the inner experience of using our minds to analyze situations and solve problems from our reflexive awareness of the interpretive framework we employ to guide and direct those cognitional efforts.[5] Broadly speaking, this essay is an exercise in facilitating that differentiation.

So to bring this notion of method closer to earth—and to get a sense of its relevance to peacemaking—I invite you to consider the following two scenarios and to select the one you think is more likely to happen: the scenario you would put your money on if the scenarios were horses, and you were at the track.

- **Scenario One:** Biogenetic scientists and engineers will help to transform the growing crises in energy and climate change. They will successfully mount a collaborative effort to genetically engineer a photosynthetic organism that can directly convert sunlight into a safe, feasible, and effective source of hydrogen energy—making possible local development and distribution of clean, renewable energy for industrial and household use.

- **Scenario Two:** Peacemakers and peacebuilders will help to transform the global upsurge in religiously motivated conflict. They will successfully mount a collaborative effort that helps people of all religious persuasions to spiritually differentiate their religious commitments from the transcendent experiences of healing and compassion that called them forth—making possible the development of spiritually grounded policies, practices, and laws that directly serve human welfare and dignity without divisively politicizing religious belief and practice.

Which scenario do you find more likely? In my experience, nearly everybody would put their money on Scenario One, not Scenario Two. Why? Not because they overwhelmingly prefer the transformation of the global crises in energy and climate change to transforming the global upsurge in religiously motivated conflict. On the contrary, it comes down to a question of method. Based on their everyday experience of scientific discovery and development, most people have the sense that engineers and scientists are guided by methods that enable them to move creatively and collaboratively from questions to answers in solving complex scientific and technological problems. Thus, they believe that given the required time, effort, and resources, scientists and engineers might well discover how to genetically engineer a photosynthetic organism that produces hydrogen energy for industrial and household use.

In contrast, no equivalent methodological confidence exists when it comes to making peace. Based on their everyday experience of religion and conflict, most people believe it is far less likely that peacemakers and peacebuilders—regardless of the time, effort, and resources they put into it—will find it possible to transform and re-orient the spiritual and religious convictions, commitments, deliberations, and decisions that drive religiously motivated conflicts. Much as they might root for this horse, it is not where they would place their bets. Still, I suspect most would agree that the world would be significantly more peaceable if we were as methodologically advanced in peacemaking as we are in the natural sciences, if our efforts to make peace were guided by methods that enabled us—creatively, collaboratively, progressively, and cumulatively—to move from question to answer, from unknown to known, in our most intractable political, cultural, and religious conflicts.

So what then is method in peacemaking? What is the requisite framework for collaborative creativity? What is the normative set of related and recurrent operations yielding progressive and cumulative results in the healing, mending and connecting of relationships strained, broken or disconnected by conflict? Ay, there's the rub.

THE GALILEO ANALOGY

The field of conflict analysis and resolution is not yet the poster child for successful, methodological collaboration in this broader, foundational sense. Of course, there are many methods operative in this intrinsically interdisciplinary field, and there are pioneering efforts by individuals who attract disciples and adherents. But there does not yet exist a commonly affirmed interpretive framework to formally and informally link all these efforts in the field in a cumulative and progressive fashion. Indeed, I think it is difficult to imagine the possibility of collaborative creativity on such a scale, let alone the interpretive framework that might make it possible.

Thus, before directly addressing the problem of method in peacemaking, I will draw first on our comparatively greater familiarity with method in the natural sciences and attend specifically to the breakthrough performance that sparked the development of modern scientific method: Galileo's effort to understand the motion of falling objects.

Why Galileo? Because by deepening our understanding of what Galileo was doing when he revolutionized scientific inquiry in the early 17th century, we will discover an analogy for the kind of performance needed to revolution-ize peacemaking today. To be clear: the analogy lies in Galileo's performance, not his subject matter—though we can't reflect on the one without the other. Thus, drawing an analogy to Galileo is not about reducing peacemaking to physics, or equating the dynamics of conflict and meaning-making with the physical laws of nature. It is about trying to understand what Galileo was doing when he launched the development of a framework for collaborative creativity in his field—and what light that performance might shed on the development of method in ours.

Galileo Galilei (1564–1642) is probably known best for constructing the first functional telescope, using it to observe sunspots and Jupiter's moons, and being convicted of heresy at 69 years of age for arguing in print that the earth orbits the sun—a position the Holy Office of the Inquisition found troublesome because it aligned Galileo with Copernicus rather than with the Book of Joshua. However, Galileo's status as the father of modern science de-rives not from his study of the earth's movement around the sun, but from his study of the movement of physical objects on earth—studies he had conducted some 30 years before his trial, but found time to write up in his book, *Two New Sciences*, while under house arrest in the years following his conviction for heresy.[6]

The newness of these sciences is directly related to the newness of the in-terpretive framework that Galileo brought to bear on an ancient question, a question that had puzzled Aristotle some 2,000 years before, and that was still defining the frontier of physical science in his day: What causes objects to accelerate when they fall?

In Galileo's day, scientists operated within the reigning, Aristotelian ap-proach to scientific investigation. They studied the natural world, of course, and their own observations of moving objects reconfirmed what Aristotle had concluded long before: (1) that rest, not motion, is the natural state of physical objects; and (2) that if and when a physical object does move, its movement is caused by physical contact between the object and an external force—by a mover of one sort or another. Like Aristotle, they noticed that fall-ing objects pick up speed as they fall, and continue to accelerate the farther they fall, and they found themselves wondering: "Why?" Specifically, they wondered what the cause—what the mover—of this peculiar motion might be, since no physical cause was apparent.

Again, this essay is about method, not the motion of objects. And the key to understanding method lies in differentiating its role as an interpretive framework from the questions and techniques that framework inspires. Thus, the thing to notice here is that these scientists used their minds to won-der what caused the acceleration of moving objects, and that when they did so, they wondered about causes and movers because the interpretive frame-work they employed directed them to pay attention to such things.

What was that interpretive framework? In Galileo's day, scientists carried out their scientific investigations by using a form of speculative reasoning based on the ideals of logical argument set forth in Aristotle's *Posterior Ana-lytics*. They analyzed the natural world by seeking to reconcile the data they observed with the first principles of Aristotelian metaphysics, and as a result, they carried out their scientific investigations on the model of a logical proof. This is the way they used their minds. And they exercised critical control over the arguments they made and the conclusions they reached by appealing to the canons of good logic: clarity, coherence, and rigor.[7]

Over the centuries, therefore, Aristotelian philosopher-scientists extrapolated and deduced a number of logically valid solutions to the puzzle of falling objects. Aristotle himself speculated that the acceleration of falling objects is due to their growing exuberance as they approach their natural state of rest on the earth. Later philosophers argued that air causes objects to accelerate. They reasoned that the column of air above an object exerts a downward pressure that grows cumulatively stronger—propelling the object ever faster—as the volume of air beneath the object is progressively reduced throughout the fall. In Galileo's time, philosopher-scientists sought to integrate the internal and external aspects of these earlier positions by arguing that the acceleration of falling objects is caused by free-fall itself. They speculated that falling objects temporarily internalize the cause of their own motion by physically acquiring impetus or accidental gravity in the course of the fall. The farther an object falls (and the heavier it is), the more impetus it internalizes, and the faster it falls toward its natural state of rest on the earth.[8]

For his part, Galileo seems to have rejected the Aristotelian framework early on. A well-known story has it that as a 25-year-old instructor of mathematics at the University of Pisa, Galileo organized a public demonstration to formally disprove the Aristotelian teaching on falling objects. In front of the assembled crowd, Galileo climbed to the top of the tower, leaned out over the edge, and simultaneously dropped both a cannon ball and a musket ball. Contrary to the expectations of his Aristotelian contemporaries, the heavier cannon ball did not accelerate rapidly out ahead of the much lighter musket ball, but in fact, hit the ground first by only a narrow margin.

Despite the drama of the event, Galileo's demonstration seems to have impressed few people and changed no one's mind. Why? To question conclusions they had already reached, Galileo's contemporaries needed to use their minds in new ways. For this, they needed a new thinking cap, not a public refutation.

As it happened, Galileo spent the next two decades as a professor at the University of Padua clarifying and validating his own new thinking cap. During this time he mounted the famous experiment in which he and his assistants rolled a small bronze ball, many hundreds of times, down a groove cut in the center of an inclined plane.[9] In this experiment—now typically studied by high school students in introductory physics classes—Galileo revolutionized scientific thought by discovering that freely falling objects pick up speed in a regular, predictable pattern, and by demonstrating that this pattern can be understood and expressed mathematically.

We can discern three distinct yet related aspects of Galileo's performance. For one, he carried out an observable set of technical activities: he assembled the inclined plane apparatus, set the ball rolling, measured distances, marked times, and recorded results. For a second, he put his mind to use: he paid attention, raised questions, pursued answers, crosschecked findings, deliberated about next steps, evaluated his options, and decided what to do. For a third, he set aside the Aristotelian thinking cap used by his contemporaries and employed an interpretive framework based on mathematical reasoning. To be precise, Galileo used a mathematical model based on Euclidean geometry to guide and direct the way he used his mind and design the technical activities he carried out. Galileo was a mathematician who decided to use mathematics as an interpretive framework for studying the material world. In the process, he discovered that the material world is mathematically intelligible. Who knew? Before Galileo, no one did.

For most of us, Galileo's performance seems utterly predictable. We fully expect scientists to build their investigations around activities associated with measuring and quantifying. And culturally, our world is so completely steeped in the tools and concepts of standardized timing and measuring—schedules, deadlines, speedometers, and tape measures—that it is difficult to imagine a world without them. Yet before Galileo, people neither imagined nor valued the notion of standardized measures for time and distance. As Dava Sobel points out, "Galileo arrived at the fundamental relationship between distance and time without so much as a reliable unit of measure or an accurate clock. Italy possessed no national standards in the seventeenth century, leaving distances open to guesstimate gauging by flea's eyes, hairbreadths, lentil or millet seed diameters, hand spans, arm lengths, and the like."[10] So novel was Galileo's quantitative approach to scientific investigation that he found himself confronting a major practical and technological challenge: he had to devise his own tools and standards for timing and measurement.

Like any other interpretive framework, Galileo's mathematical approach shaped both *what* he thought, and *how* he used his mind. However, the way it enabled Galileo to use his mind—to focus his attention, to identify relevant questions, and to assess his answers—differed markedly from the cognitive performance fostered by the Aristotelian framework used by his contemporaries.

First, then, Galileo's new thinking cap focused his attention in a particular way. It gave him the working assumption that the most interesting and important aspects of the motion of falling objects would be those he could quantify and analyze mathematically. He therefore designed an experiment that enabled him to pay careful attention to such things: he imagined rolling a ball down an inclined plane, devised standards of measurement, and invented the timing mechanism.

Second, Galileo's interpretive framework guided the questions he asked and set up the insights he gained. Galileo observed the ball picking up speed as it rolled down the track, but he didn't grasp the mathematical intelligibility of that movement with his eyes alone. To grasp that intelligibility Galileo needed to perform an act of understanding; he needed to get an insight. But to get that insight, Galileo needed the right question: What is the relation of time and distance in the movement of the ball? And he could only ask that question because he had an interpretive framework that inspired him to ask it. Indeed, the utility of any interpretive framework lies in its capacity to put our minds in a position to grasp the insights we seek.

Third, since Galileo still needed to know whether or not his insights were correct, his interpretive framework guided his effort to critically assess his acts of understanding. However, unlike his Aristotelian counterparts, Galileo did not appeal to the standards of formal logic to verify his insights. Instead, the mathematical framework he was using steered his mind back to the aspects of the rolling ball he could measure and quantify, and he ran more comparative trials. It led him to settle any questions he had about his findings by appealing to a rigorous standard of empirical testing.

The point I would make here is that when it came to solving the age-old puzzle of falling objects, Galileo used an interpretive framework that turned out to be much better suited to the task than the one used by his Aristotelian counterparts. It liberated him to use his mind in new and perspicuous ways. It freed him to ask questions and to get insights that his Aristotelian counterparts could not get—not because they weren't bright enough, but because they didn't ask the same questions.

More significantly for the development of method in the natural sciences, Galileo's performance modeled a way for other scientists to liberate their minds too. For once Galileo published the results of his groundbreaking discovery, others began to ask the question with which we began: What was Galileo doing when he was investigating the movement of falling objects? Indeed, some of them also asked: How can I do that too? Thus, from its roots in Galileo's performance, what we now recognize as the normative operations of method in the natural sciences began to develop into a framework for collaborative creativity.

And it developed with remarkable speed.[11] For even in Galileo's own lifetime—and he lived only six more years after he published *Two New Sciences* in 1636—fellow scientists began to make his interpretive framework their own. Galileo's pupil, Evangelista Torricelli (1608–1647) used mathematical reasoning to empirically demonstrate the existence of atmospheric pressure, prompting in turn the discovery of the barometer and launching the scientific study of the atmosphere. René Descartes (1597–1650) formulated the modern principle of inertia by transposing the mathematical model Galileo used from Euclidean geometry to algebra.

In 1660, just 18 years after Galileo's death, the collaborative power of this newly emergent method inspired Christopher Wren, Robert Boyle, and 10 other natural philosophers in England to found a "college for the promoting of physico-mathematical experimental learning." The following year they secured the approval and support of King Charles II and dubbed their collaborative effort The Royal Society. In 1687—27 years after the founding of the Royal Society and merely 54 years after the Inquisition condemned Galileo for his views on the movement solar system—Isaac Newton (1642–1727), published his *Principia Mathematica*.

I trust there is no need to pile on evidence by rehearsing the entire history of the natural sciences or detailing the comparatively recent contributions of Einstein, Schrödinger, Heisenberg, and Dirac to the development of physics. For nearly 400 years since Galileo's breakthrough experiment, scientists have been using mathematical reasoning as an interpretive framework for investigating and solving scientific problems—a framework that has released a torrent of ongoing collaborative creativity that continues to drive major advances in mathematical modeling and to add to our knowledge of the material world. If that much is clear, let us now put this analogy to work: How can a grasp of Galileo's methodological breakthrough in the natural sciences help us toward an analogous breakthrough in method in peacemaking?

METHOD IN PEACEMAKING

We are now in a position to link our two key terms in the phrase, method in peacemaking. The term *peacemaking* directs our attention to the praxis of defusing feelings of threat, deepening insight into the other, and otherwise healing and connecting relationships wounded and broken by conflict. The term *method* directs our attention toward the answer to a more explanatory question: What is the interpretive framework that will enable us to generate progressive, cumulative, collaborative results in peacemaking? The Galileo analogy helps advance the answer to this question in at least three ways.

First, the image of Galileo rolling a small brass ball down an inclined plane, forced to invent measuring and timing devices of his own, makes it clear that the work involved in the early stages of a methodological breakthrough is detailed, painstaking, and multifaceted. Second, Galileo's breakthrough makes it clear that the key to successful methodological collaboration lies not in the repetition of particular techniques, but in the shared use of an interpretive framework that guides us to use of our minds to seek answers to the right questions. Third, a grasp of Galileo's interpretive framework makes it clear that a comparable breakthrough in peacemaking calls for the development an interpretive framework of a different order.

Why? The principle reason is that the data to be analyzed is fundamentally different. Galileo focused his mind on understanding the material world. Peacemakers focus their minds on understanding acts of meaning-making and the worlds of meaning they create. The praxis of peacemaking hinges on the creative and responsible use of our minds in mending relationships and discovering new possibilities for cooperation in situations broken and disaffected by conflict. Thus, if we are to get a handle on what we are doing when we are making peace, we need an interpretive framework that will help us to pay explicit attention to the way we use our minds when we make and mend worlds of meaning. I submit that the development of method in peacemaking calls for the identification and development of a critical, reflexive, philosophical framework that helps us to notice, identify, and verify the inner acts and patterns of consciousness associated with peacemaking in all its manifestations.

By no means is this a call for a return to the deductive argumentation modeled in Aristotle's *Posterior Analytics*. Nor is it an appeal to modern linguistic philosophy. But neither is it in the scope of this essay for me to clarify these differences or to critically assess the range of models and approaches that might be helpful in developing the critical, reflexive, philosophical framework I suggest we needed.[12] More helpful and to the point, I think, is an exposition of the methodological implications of a peacemaking effort guided by one such model, the philosophical thought of the Canadian philosopher, theologian, and methodologist, Bernard Lonergan.

Approximately 10 years ago, a group of scholars and practitioners located in Ottawa, Canada, began to use Lonergan's philosophical thought to help them understand the peacemaking processes involved in mediating interpersonal and small group conflicts. Cheryl Picard, an experienced mediator based at Carleton University, found that although she could regularly help parties locked in conflict to make peace with each other, she couldn't explain to her own satisfaction precisely what she was she was doing when she was making peace in her mediation practice. None of the existing theories of mediation adequately explained her performance either. So to explore this question she teamed up with Kenneth Melchin, a professor of ethics at St. Paul University, who suggested to her that the philosophy of Bernard Lonergan might be useful as an interpretive framework. Together, they designed a simple experiment. They videotaped one of Cheryl's mediation sessions and spent several months going over and over the tape, using Lonergan's philosophical thought as a framework to analyze the performance of peacemaking that took place during the course of the session.

Lonergan is not a typical philosopher in the sense that his philosophy is not based on a set of principles or axioms. The lynchpin of his thought is the twin recognition that human beings have minds and that we use them, and the focus of his philosophical analysis is what he calls the "data of consciousness"—the activities, patterns, and norms that mark the inner operation of our consciousness. In philosophical circles, Lonergan is perhaps best known for his analysis of insight, one of the basic operations of human consciousness.[13] In subsequent writings, Melchin and Picard dubbed his philosophical thought *insight theory.*[14]

Thus, when they donned insight theory as a thinking cap, it led them to pay careful attention to the data of consciousness evinced in the performances of the mediator and the parties on the videotape. It also put them in a position to ask what proved to be a very fruitful analytical question: What is the role of "getting insights" in creating conflict and making peace? Indeed, by paying attention to the act of getting an insight, Melchin and Picard discovered a fundamental intelligibility in the way we use our minds to lock ourselves into conflict with each other, an intelligibility that reveals its corollary in the performance of making peace.

Again, the scope of this essay does not permit me to do justice either to the intricacy of Melchin and Picard's analysis, or to the complexity of the dynamics of conflict itself. But for the purpose of indicating why I think a critical, reflexive philosophical framework is key to developing method in peacemaking, I offer the following sketch of a single component of their analysis.[15]

In analyzing the videotape, Lonergan's insight theory steered Melchin and Picard away from a focus on *what* the parties thought and *what* positions they staked out in opposition to each other. Instead, it directed them to wonder about the role that *getting* insights plays when parties lock themselves into conflict with each other. Of course, the basic moves in this dance are well known. One party will expresses an intention or make a decision that triggers feelings of threat in another, and the second party will respond with a decision or an action to counter the first. But the use of insight theory as an interpretive framework led Melchin and Picard to wonder in particular about the relationship between insights and feelings of threat, and they noticed that feelings of threat are in fact anchored by a particular kind of affectively charged insight. This is an insight that grasps a link between presenting circumstances and a dire future, an insight that typically provides an impetus for action.

Melchin and Picard refer to this confluence of insight and feeling as an experience of *threat-to-care,* and they note that it often consists in the strongly felt conviction that if the other party's decision or intention is allowed to stand, it will jeopardize something that the threatened party cares deeply about, and which must therefore be preserved and protected. Significantly, what Melchin and Picard also noticed is that a party's grasp or awareness of the insight that anchors their experience of threat-to-care is commonly murky or incomplete. They found that when parties lock themselves into conflict with each other, they are often not fully aware of the link they have grasped between present issues and future concerns. Their feelings of threat are activated, driving the conflict, but these feelings are often so quick and so immediate and so strong that they feel self-contained and self-justifying—thereby obscuring the parties' awareness of their own insight into the connection between present and future that triggered their feeling of threat in the first place.

Clearly, this discovery has direct implications for the praxis of peacemaking. It suggests is that a core element of peacemaking—of helping parties break out of a cycle of conflict—involves helping them to *get* insights. As Melchin and Picard make clear, this is not the same as *giving* them insights. This can't be done, anyway. It means helping parties to recover the insights that triggered their threat-to-care in the first place, and helping them to gain a self-reflective curiosity concerning their intelligibility or legitimacy of that link. Needless to say, this is easier said than done, and different levels of conflict present their own particular challenges to making peace. But it certainly helps to know what one is trying to do.

I have presented this sketch in broad strokes, of course. Melchin and Picard do not suggest that all parties in all conflicts are burdened by a lack of insight or affective self-awareness. Nor do they suggest that all insights generating feelings of threat-to-care are necessarily incomplete. But they do suggest that no conflict can be resolved—and no peacemaking carried out—unless parties deepen their insight into the feelings of threat-to-care that lock them into conflict with each other, and unless they grasp new, correcting insights that make it possible for them to delink the necessity of the threat that they feel. What is interesting about these suggestions, and interesting in particular for their relevance to method in peacemaking, is that all their suggestions are empirically based.

Thus, like all interpretive frameworks, insight theory provided Melchin and Picard with a standard for assessing their answers. But like Galileo's framework, insight theory led Melchin and Picard to settle any questions they had about their findings by appealing to a rigorous standard of empirical testing. The difference of course, is that whereas Galileo's mathematical framework led him to appeal to the data of his senses, insight theory led Melchin and Picard to appeal to the data of consciousness.

To illustrate: Do insights ground the experience of threat-to-care? Do these insights grasp of a link between present circumstances and dire futures? Is the cognitive dimension of this insight often obscured by the immediacy and power of the feeling it triggers? Each of these questions is a question for verification. Each can be settled by collaborative appeal to the data of consciousness: to the data provided by a critical appeal to the activities, patterns, and norms that mark the inner operation of our minds.

Melchin and Picard focused their investigation of the praxis of peacebuilding within the context of interpersonal and small group mediation. And the insight interpretive framework they used liberated them to use their minds in new and creative ways. I suggest that it can liberate the minds of other to do the same as they pursue the answers to their own questions. In the case of Galileo, the use and development of mathematical reasoning as a framework for collaborative creativity came quick quickly. Perhaps the use and development of insight theory—of a critical, philosophical framework that can assist us in carrying out self-aware, reflexive analyses of what we are doing when we are making peace—will come quite quickly too. If it does, we may have to revise our assessment of the two scenarios with which I began this paper. Certainly there is no shortage of further relevant questions.

NOTES

1. Susan Allen Nan, personal e-mail correspondence, January 30, 2011. Nan offers her distinction as an elaboration of the fundamental distinctions that Boutros Boutros-Ghali makes between preventive diplomacy, peacemaking, peacekeeping, and peacebuilding in *An Agenda for Peace*, http://www.un.org/Docs/SG/agpeace.html.

2. Aristotle, *Nicomachean Ethics*, 1140b, 1–5.

3. Bernard, J. F. and S. J. Lonergan, "A Post-Hegelian Philosophy of Religion," in *A Third Collection: Papers*, ed. Frederick E. Crowe (New York: Paulist Press, 1985), 205.

4. Bernard, J. F. and S. J. Lonergan, *Method in Theology* (New York: Herder and Herder, 1972), 4. See also Bernard and Lonergan, "Method: Trend and Variations," in *A Third Collection*,13–22; and Lonergan, "The Ongoing Genesis of Methods," in *Third Collection*, 146–165.

5. My use of the term *differentiation* is drawn from Robert Kegan's discussion of Piaget in *The Evolving Self: Problem and Process in Human Development* (Cambridge, MA: Harvard University Press, 1982), 28–31.

6. For my account of Galileo's life and work, I rely on Dava Sobel, *Galileo's Daughter: A Historical Memoir of Science, Faith, and Love* (New York: Walker and Company, 1999).

7. For a brief, detailed account of the scientific ideal set forth in Aristotle's *Posterior Analytic*, see Lonergan, "Aquinas Today: Tradition and Innovation," in *Third Collection*, 41–44.

8. Herbert Butterfield, *The Origins of Modern Science* (New York: Macmillan/Free Press, 1957), 16–17.

9. For Galileo's own account of this experiment, see Galileo Galilei, *Two New Sciences, Including Centers of Gravity and Force of Percussion*, trans. Stillman Drake, 2nd ed. (Toronto: Wall and Thompson, 1989), 178–179.

10. Sobel, *Galileo's Daughter*, 334.

11. The following account of this development is based on Butterfield, *The Origins of Modern Science*, 83–88.

12. For some important analytical work in this direction, see Michael McCarthy, *The Crisis in Philosophy* (New York: SUNY Press, 1989) and James Marsh, *Post-Cartesian Meditations: An Essay in Dialectical Phenomenology* (New York: Fordham University Press, 1988).

13. Bernard Lonergan, *Insight: An Essay in Human Understanding* (London: Longmans's Green & Co.), 1957.

14. For a detailed discussion of the relationship between Lonergan's philosophy and conflict resolution, see Kenneth R. Melchin and Cheryl A. Picard, *Transforming Conflict through Insight* (Toronto: University of Toronto Press, 2008), 49–101

15. See Melchin and Picard, *Transforming Conflict Through Insight*, Chapter 4.

CHAPTER 39

The Hidden Dimensions of Peacemaking: A Systems Perspective

Louise Diamond

Nearly 40 years ago, I was introduced to general systems theory. I immediately knew it as profound wisdom. How do living systems organize themselves, interact with their environment, manage differences, handle change, establish patterns, process information? What is the relation of the part to the whole? And what is the relation of the whole to the larger whole? How do the parts cohere around a common purpose or disintegrate into chaos? Exploring these and similar questions as they relate to human systems of all sizes has been a passion ever since. Exploring them especially in the context of peacemaking has been my focus since 1988.

In these four decades, the study of living systems has matured. Now we have complex adaptive systems, soft systems, dynamical systems, family systems, chaos theory, spiral dynamics, and many other lenses through which to understand the infinitely wondrous world of human dynamics. My own understanding of systems has matured as well. As the field of knowledge has become more intricate, I find that my direction has been to simplify, integrate, and apply.

For me, Einstein's famous words to the effect that you can't solve problems with the same mind that created them have become a guidepost.[1] It's all about how we think, for our actions unfold from our thoughts. Thinking systemically allows us to be effective and creative participants in our lives. My other favorite saying comes from my spiritual teacher, Venerable Dhyani Ywahoo. She says, "If it doesn't grow corn to feed the people, what good is it?"[2] Putting the two elements together—applying systemic thinking to actions that benefit the whole—is an approach I call applied systems thinking (AST).

In this chapter, I will explore four elements of AST as they relate to peacemaking: *interconnectedness, scale, field*, and *worldview*. I will apply them to three dimensions of peacemaking that I believe get little if any attention among peacemaking practitioners, researchers, or theorists: the *inner dimension*, the *energy dimension*, and the *evolutionary dimension*. In presenting this discussion, I draw on my two decades of peacemaking experience in places of deep-rooted conflict around the world, including in Cyprus, Israel-Palestine, Bosnia, India and Pakistan, Kenya, Liberia, and elsewhere. I also draw on 40 years of experience as an applied human behavioral consultant with human systems and organizations of all sizes. I begin first with a brief description of the four key AST principles.

INTERCONNECTEDNESS

That we live in an interconnected world has become a given. The Internet, the globalized economy, climate change—these and other modern phenomena remind us that, as U.S. President Obama said frequently during his presidential campaign, "We're all in this together." Whether we look at the microcosm of human beings at the level of atoms and cells, or at the macrocosm of global interactions, we see that everything depends on something or someone else. No one molecule, no one individual, no one nation exists alone. Every being, every part of every being, relies on others through an exchange of information, matter, and energy. As Mother Teresa is alleged to have said, "We belong to each other."[3]

SCALE

Think of those Russian dolls nesting within each other, from smallest to largest. Think of cells in the human body coming together to form tissues, organs, and eventually the circulatory, digestive, or endocrine system, and then the whole incredible human body. Not only is every part a whole in itself, but every part is also part of a larger whole, which in turn is part of an even larger whole. Although at each scale the parts may look and act differently, still they carry the same inherent pattern. In systems language, we say the part contains the whole. An acorn contains the pattern of the oak tree. Wherever on the scale of the system we focus, small to large, we can learn something that can be useful at other points on the scale. By changing one part, because of interconnectedness, we also effect change in the whole.

FIELD

What is the intangible medium within which all things are connected? What is the force that binds us together? Thought leaders, scientists, and mystics have been putting their minds to this question recently, and have begun to describe a *field of consciousness* or potential within which we all exist and from which all things arise. Although we are still exploring this phenomenon, what we do know is this: energy and matter are interpenetrating; our thoughts have consequences; and there is no such thing as an outside observer. Think of the Field as an ocean, an ocean of consciousness, where a single thought or feeling has its own frequency or note. Once sounded, that note resonates through the entire sea, sometimes meeting those of like or similar vibration to form large long rolling waves, or sometimes clashing with very different notes to create stormy, roiling seas.

WORLDVIEW

What we believe to be true, the assumptions we make, the mental models we hold—often unconsciously—determine our actions. Ultimately, it is what we believe about the nature of reality itself that forms the paradigm within which we act. Whether our reference point is the age of Aquarius, quantum physics, or the change from the industrial to the information age, we know that there is a big shift underway in our collective worldview. We are moving from the mechanistic to the holistic, from separation to integration, from reductionism to inclusivity. Because violent conflict is the ultimate expression of separation, and peacemaking the movement toward integration and inclusivity, this shift is extremely relevant to our work as peacemakers, as we shall see.

These four (out of many), key principles of AST, then, will be our lens throughout this chapter. One of the AST skills for peacemakers is what I call *telescoping*, being able to move in closer to ever-smaller parts and out again to ever-larger wholes, and seeing the relationships between them. So we will begin with telescoping in, way in, inside the heart and mind of the peacemaker him- or herself. Then we will telescope out to the process of peacemaking; not from a transactional or behavioral point of view as we usually view it, but from an energetic perspective, which is always present but often invisible to us. Finally we will telescope way out, to examine how peacemaking is part of that larger paradigm shift in the evolution of human consciousness—how it is both a leading and creative edge of that transformation and at the same time a result of even larger dynamics at play on the planet in these times.

I have called these the *hidden dimensions of peacemaking*. They are hidden only in the sense that we rarely turn our spotlight on them. Yet once we do, we can realize layers of meaning and potential that carry manifold possibilities for the peacemaker and for the success of his/her mission.

THE INNER DIMENSION OF PEACEMAKING

One of the common tools of peacemaking is the model of the iceberg. We show conflicting parties a drawing of an iceberg, with only a tip showing above the waterline and a much larger mass below it. Above the line is observable behavior—what we say and do. Below the line are all kinds of invisible dynamics that affect our behavior whether we're aware of them or not, which, if ignored, can figuratively sink the ship.

What we rarely consider, however, is that as peacemakers we have our own iceberg to contend with. Below the surface are the feelings, fears, experiences, assumptions, hopes, cultural and religious influences, values, individual and collective identity, history, intentions, political views, memories, and the like, that make us who we are. Some of these are unrelated to our role as peacemaker; some might be highly relevant and, if left unexamined, could become obstacles or influence our actions unconsciously.

For instance, if we have had experience with violence in our own lives—as a recipient, a perpetrator, or a witness—we are likely to come to a peacemaking scenario with whatever residue that experience has left in us. Are we afraid to be in the vicinity of physical violence? Are we ashamed of how we may have participated in violent acts—either physical or verbal—toward others? Have we experienced trauma related to conflict, directly or indirectly? Do we hate war? Have an aversion to conflict in general? Have we or any of our family members been in the military? Seen active duty in wartime? Been ethnically cleansed?

There is no linear set of correspondences here; we each bring our experience to bear on the peacemaking situation in our own unique way. It is important that we take the time to become aware of what we are carrying into the conflict situation, for, once we enter that system, its dynamics will magnify whatever lies within us.

In the mid-1980s, when I realized I was about to walk the peacemaking path, I took this inner inventory and discovered that indeed I had a strong aversion to violence from elements of my personal, philosophical, and political history (I am of the Vietnam War generation in the United States). Knowing I would be working in war zones with all kinds of armed actors, I undertook an intense program of desensitization.

At first, I couldn't bear to walk down the aisles of a video store and see titles and images of war movies. Nor would I consider sitting through such a movie, or reading a soldier's memoir. So I rented those films and bought those books, and slowly came to where I could sit through the bloody parts without covering my eyes, or read the violent parts instead of skipping ahead. Then an interesting thing happened. The more I read first-person accounts of battles, the more I became able not only to pay attention, but also to be deeply interested. Gradually, as I read and watched more, I began to discover within myself a certain excitement that I came to identify as the thrill of the kill. I understood bloodlust, the high of viciously hurting another.

At first I was horrified; how could a good Jewish girl like me feel vicarious bloodlust! Then I realized—these seeds are in all of us, as are the seeds of peace. I have never been in situations where I have had to commit violence against another, or fear for my life in every moment. I don't know what I would do, or how I would respond if exposed to those conditions day in and day out. I'm privileged not to have had to learn that about myself in a real situation, but others have not had that same privilege.

With that understanding, I was able to feel empathy for the warriors I knew I would be meeting as a peacemaker, rather than a certain overlay of disdain or aversion I might have felt had I not looked deeply inside at my own history, assumptions, and fears. With that empathy, I knew I could work in any war zone. That doesn't mean I suspend my moral judgment about behavior that harms others; it does mean I include myself in the system and acknowledge there are circumstances I have never had to face that might tip one over into otherwise incomprehensible behavior.[4]

Another inner dimension, having to do with intention, is also related to our history and opinions about violence and conflict. Why have we chosen peacemaking as our vocation? What motivates us to stay in this work? It's not a particularly lucrative profession, so money isn't likely to be the driver. Do we have a sincere commitment to assuage suffering in the world? A legalistic skill in mediating differences that we want to put to use? A passion to see justice done? A desire to see wounds mended or bridges built? What do we champion? To whom or what are we in service?

There are no right or wrong answers to these questions, and there will be as many responses as there are peacemakers. What's important is not only that we address these questions about ourselves, but that we create training and practitioner environments where we can share and discuss them.

In my own life, I had to confront this question after spending time in Israel and what was then called the Occupied Territories during the first *Intifada* in the late 1980s. I was so profoundly affected by the plight of the Palestinians under occupation that I felt a strong pull toward becoming a human rights activist. When I weighed that against the direction of peacemaking I found myself engaged in a deep assessment of my skills and values. What were my gifts, my passions? Where could I make the greatest contribution? From that point of view, and knowing there were other human rights activists doing an excellent job, I was able to make a clear and cogent choice for peacemaking as my path.

Another, potentially more difficult, hidden inner dimension has to do with how we are emotionally impacted by the conflict system. Because everything is interconnected, our emotions are involved as well as our minds, whether we wish it to be so or not. Conflict situations inevitably involve extreme emotions—fear, anguish, hatred, the desire for revenge, and more—and also behaviors that can set off strong reactions. As peacemakers, we like to think we are untouched, impartial observers, above the fray, but in fact two things are happening.

First, the emotional life of the conflict parties is always washing through the Field, thereby washing through and around us as well. Whether we're conscious of it or not, we are affected by this field of suffering. Second, if we attend to peacemaking with any kind of open-heartedness, we cannot help but be touched by the trauma in the system. Indeed, if we engage deeply and over a long time with a conflict system, if we are involved with a particularly brutal conflict scenario, or if we are in a position to hear many of the horrific stories of victims of war, rape, mutilation, ethnic cleansing, and such, we are at risk for contracting secondary posttraumatic stress syndrome (PTSD).

The final hidden aspect of the inner dimension has to do with taking on the dynamics of the system. This can be quite subtle, and has everything to do with the Field and interconnectedness. Conflict systems have usually developed their own set of dynamics, patterns, and games over the years. Many of these are unconscious and invisible, yet are playing out beneath the radar. For example, in the blame game, the parties give more attention to showing the other party in a bad light, even setting them up to fail as a peace partner, than to taking responsibility for their own contribution to sustaining the enmity. In the drama triangle, the two parties and the mediators may take turns playing the archetypal roles of villain, victim, and rescuer. A subset of this game that I call *eat the third party* happens when the third party speaks out on a sensitive topic and suddenly is attacked by the conflict parties, thus shifting from rescuer to villain and victim.

What often happens to us as peacemakers is that we unconsciously start playing out the dynamics and emotions of the system. If there is a lot of anger in the system, we may find ourselves expressing unusual degrees of anger at home or in the office. If there is a pervasive sense of hopelessness, we may get caught up in that downward spiral. If there is a conflict culture of scapegoating, we may discover that we, too, are consistently holding one party responsible instead of looking at the larger picture and seeing the mutual and multiple ways the conflict is perpetuated by several parties. If the parties excel in demonizing and dehumanizing the other, we may find ourselves making snide or demeaning remarks to colleagues about one or the other side.

Because we are all interconnected, and because of the phenomenon of the Field, once we engage with a system, we become part of it. We influence it and it influences us. Its dynamics play through us, and we resonate with its patterns depending on our own hooks and history. When we also apply the principle of scale, we understand that whatever is happening in our individual selves is likely a mirror for what is happening at the larger systemic scale, and vice versa. In fact, if we want to understand the conflict system better, we can look to our own emotional as well as physical, mental, and even spiritual experiences.

What are the implications for applying this knowledge of the inner dimension of peacemaking? First, there are implications for the training and maintenance of peacemakers. Where in our academic programs are these dynamics discussed? Do our practitioner organizations invite these conversations? Do our colleagues give us safe space for exploring our emotional reactions to the work? Are we considered weak if we absorb the trauma of the system and show signs of burn-out or secondary PTSD?

Competently managing the inner dimension of peacemaking requires specific personal and professional skills. We need to have a certain degree of emotional intelligence, to be able to first identify and then know how to manage our feelings. Next we need to sharpen our insight and analytical tools so we can identify system dynamics, and hone our intuition to notice when and how we are acting them out in our own lives or otherwise reacting to them. We need to have models of conflict resolution which assume that the material lying under the waterline, in both the conflict parties and in the peacemaker, is as important to address as the specific and presented content of the conflict. Finally, we need the tools of self-inventory to assure we are aware of how our own such material impacts our engagement with the conflict system.

THE ENERGY DIMENSION OF PEACEMAKING

Einstein told us that energy and matter are interchangeable, and physics tells us that what we think of as solid is really energy in motion—subatomic particles spinning within vast areas of space. My apologies to physicists as I try to simplify how I understand this as it relates to peacemaking.

If everything is energy in motion, then everything—tangible and intangible—has frequency, or vibration. We understand the notion of vibration experientially; think how we intuitively know when someone or some situation is emitting bad vibes or good vibes. Thus, our presence as peacemakers—our actions, our intentions, and even (perhaps especially) our thoughts and feelings—are all and always emitting vibrations into the Field, that sea of energy or awareness we described earlier. And what we send out has consequences, because through the Field others pick up on, harmonize with, clash with, or otherwise sense what we are sending.

We understand that energy follows thought, meaning that whatever we think about, we direct our vibration into that channel or direction, where it can be strengthened by resonating with similar vibrations in the Field and become substance or conditions. For instance, if one person thinks, "Those people are dangerous," he or she generates a vibration of fear. If thousands, or even millions, of people think the same thought, that vibration of fear becomes bigger and stronger until it's like a fog that permeates an entire environment or population; it becomes real, or true, or "the way things are."

Thus we are essentially cocreating our individual and collective reality all the time. This can be a scary realization once people understand it deeply, because the implication is that since we are always broadcasting into the universe with every word, every thought, and every act, we are essentially responsible for what we are generating and its impact on others. This is a deeper level of responsibility than most people are either aware of or willing to accept.

Let's look more closely at the notion of vibration. If we think about every thought or feeling as a vibration, we realize that peace, hatred, fear, pain, and other qualities associated with conflict each have their own frequency. This is easily tested. Imagine, for a moment, a feeling of deep peace. Now imagine something you are extremely afraid of. Can you feel the difference in your body? That difference can be felt around your body as well, in your energy field (yes, all living beings are energy in motion, which does not stop at the outside boundary of the physical skin; we all have an energy field around us.)

So the challenge—and opportunity—for the peacemaker is to be able to generate the frequency of peace at will. Many schools of meditation teach how to find and hold that deep inner well of peace that is often called center. Rarely, though, do our academic programs on peacemaking teach this. And yet, I would suggest it is an invaluable tool for peacemakers. Knowing what center and the peace vibration feel like for ourselves, and being able to go there at will, is critical for our own well-being amidst conflict situations. This is especially true when we are confronted with or surrounded by violent or dangerous energies. This is also what Gandhi meant when he spoke of "being the change we wish to see in the world,"[5] and what Thich Nhat Hanh refers to as "being peace."[6]

Even more important is the skill of being able to consciously radiate the peace frequency to change the Field. Most of us assume that our doing—our actions of mediation, intervention, negotiation, and so on—are what make the difference. In fact, it is our presence, our being, that can often tame very difficult situations. Many people around the world in the war zones I've worked in have told me that my skills were useful, but the quality of my presence made the most difference.

There were several times in my peacemaking career where, when the situation around me was especially dangerous or potentially violent and I went into a deep place of peace and emanated that frequency into the Field, the situation calmed noticeably, without my speaking a word. We cannot manipulate the energy field of others, just as we cannot ethically manipulate the behavior of others, but we can radiate the peace frequency and trust that it can touch that seed in others and through a resonance process, awaken it.

Another element of the energy dimension of peacemaking has to do with a new understanding of the nature of power. In most conflict situations power is about power *over*; that is, one party seeks to control the behavioral options and/or resources of another. But the true nature of power is quite different. Power is the potential for energy in action. So power *to* accomplish something, power *for* a particular goal, power *with* another to achieve something together—these are completely different ways of directing energy in peacemaking situations.

Much of peacemaking is about power *with*: that is, we bring conflicting parties together to change the relationship and explore new possibilities. When successful, peacemaking processes lead to the power *to* change the system, and the power of various sectors mobilized *for* peace. What we don't do is make this explicit. We don't name that we're using power—the potential for energy in action—in a new way. Yet by helping conflicting parties consciously redefine the nature of power, we empower them to cut the cords of power *over* and take creative action for something better and different.

Since power *over*, or dominance of one group over another, is often a core element of violent conflict, the only true scenario for peace is a shift to partnership, or power *with*. Helping parties realize how they are using their energy (thoughts, words, and actions) toward one another, and understanding the consequences, is a great contribution that peacemakers can bring to the system.

In the early 1990s, I had the chance to demonstrate this choice of partnership and collaboration over competition in peacemaking. A large grant to continue the work I had begun in Cyprus became available, but was slanted heavily toward another peacemaking organization whose work was at the transactional end of the peacemaking spectrum, while mine was at the transformational end. Rather than fight for the money, I extended an offer to the other organization to partner with them, and to use the opportunity to blend our different approaches, to learn from each other, and to essentially demonstrate this cooperative and cocreative model in the highly polarized Cyprus context. This partnership, between the Institute for Multi-Track Diplomacy and Conflict Management Group, was highly successful in delivering programs in Cyprus for several years, and led many of the local participants in those programs, having absorbed the message of power with each other and power to accomplish, to generate various groundbreaking bi-communal activities and events and to make significant changes in their societies.

The final aspect of the hidden energy dimension of peacemaking has to do with creativity. Resolving conflicts, transforming relationships, and securing peace require an ability to generate new ideas and breakthrough solutions. The much-quoted phrase, "If you always do what you always did, you always get what you always got,"[7] makes this clear. Most long-running and deep-rooted conflicts develop entrenched patterns and vicious cycles that become obstacles to peace—indeed, often become the very focus of negotiations.

Being able to see things differently and to generate new possibilities are necessary, then, for finding solutions, and requires the ability to access a realm of mind different from everyday, rational, linear thinking—the realm of creativity. If we think of the Field as a sea of infinite potential, creativity means being able to release our conditioned minds and be fully present to all that is possible. Peacemaking is more an art than a science, and art is the unique expression of infinite possibility.

This sea of infinite potential is accessible to us through intuition, dreams, meditation, and stillness, hardly attributes associated with the hard realities of war and peace. When we use the phrase *open to new ideas,* we are expressing a basic truth: possibilities exist in potential everywhere and always, and we can open our minds to them by relaxing the energetic structures of rationality and habitual thinking that limit our perspective.

What are the implications for applying this knowledge of the energy dimension of peacemaking? The most obvious is in the realm of training of practitioners. We need to design and incorporate methodologies for helping peacemakers sense and use their energy, and the energy of the system, productively. For this we need to call on a different set of disciplines than usually found in university or professional development programs: yoga, meditation, aikido or other martial arts, Reiki, and other energy-related fields. Even the U.S. military recognizes this, and has long brought some of the skills from these fields into the training of soldiers.

Next, we need our academic programs in peace and conflict studies to ground and validate this knowledge, giving what some would call flaky the credibility that comes with solid research and scientific exploration. They should include in their curricula courses that study some of the research results from neuroscience, mind/body disciplines, and martial arts, and show the relevance to peacemaking.

Finally, just as we need to change the culture among peacemakers to honor the inner and emotional elements, so we need to change the culture to honor the subtle, intangible energetic elements. Peacemaking is more than a rational process; it is multidimensional, holistic, and inclusive of all that we are as human beings and human systems. It is both transactional and transformational. Until this is recognized and given credence, we will be operating with only a portion of the resources available to us.

THE EVOLUTIONARY DIMENSION OF PEACEMAKING

We spoke earlier of a shift underway in the human family. When we step back and look at peacemaking in its largest dimension of scale, we begin to see it in reference to that shift. First, let us explore the shift more fully, and next consider where peacemaking fits within it.

Just as life-forms evolve over time, so does human consciousness, and along with it, human culture, science, education, economics, politics, religion, and all the ways we express our beliefs and values. Historically, as we have gained greater mastery of our physical environment, we have changed how we think about ourselves, others, and the natural world in which we live and on which we depend for life. In short, our worldview changes.

In the not-too-distant-past, Europeans believed the earth to be flat and the sun to revolve around the earth. We then translated that center-of-the-universe mindset in a belief in the divine right of kings, the natural order of feudalism, and the inherent right of the one true religion to slaughter or convert by force anyone believing otherwise. We have left those beliefs behind as we evolved through greater knowledge of how the universe actually works. We have had the age of reason and the age of enlightenment, the age of empire, the industrial age, and now the information age, periods of time in which new understandings emerge and change the very forms and foundations of how we live together.

We live in the midst of such a period today. Simply put, we are moving from the reductionist Newtonian view of the world to the holistic or quantum view. In the former, we believed that all matter was reducible to its smallest parts, and once we understood those parts, we would solve the mystery of how the parts fit together. The universe was conceived of as a big clock or mechanism, with each part doing its separate assigned task.

Twentieth-century physics opened a new perspective. What scientists discovered was that subatomic particles were not, in fact, discrete things, solid matter, but rather energy in motion that could appear as a particle or a wave, that was influenced by the observer, and that had properties suggesting consciousness. The universe is conceived of as an expanding and interwoven whole, with the parts dancing together in complex and ever-changing interaction.

If the keyword of the reductionist universe is *separation*, then the keyword of the quantum universe is *interconnectedness*. I think of it in terms of the classic description of human maturation through three levels:

- Dependence, when, as children, we need adults to care for our needs as we gradually learn basic life skills;
- Independence, or individuation, when, as teenagers, we push away from our parents and seek to discover our own unique identity and the freedom to choose our own way in the world;
- Interdependence, when, as adults, we bond with others to create our own new families, communities, and organizations.

In this mental model, the human family is in the midst of moving from stage two to stage three, and still very much in the transformation process. I say *transformation* rather than *transition* because this shift involves changes not only in our outer forms and structures but also in our most basic assumptions and ways of being. We are in a complex learning process as we access new information about our interconnectedness. With all our familiar beliefs and methods challenged, we are not yet sure what the new systems will look like. We have a natural resistance to change and fear of the unknown, even as we are excited about—and actively creative within—what is emerging all around us and on the horizon.

Let's put this in the context of peacemaking and global affairs. I like Joanna Macy's description best. She says, "The Great Turning is a name for the essential adventure of our time; the shift from the industrial growth society to a life-sustaining civilization."[8] The industrial growth society is the epitome of the dynamic of separation-in-action. We spent centuries organizing ourselves politically on the planet in terms of boundaries and power, ending up with a system of separate and sovereign nation states that make little concession to the multitude of different cultures and peoples living within them. On the contrary, many—if not most—nation states have assiduously repressed the unique language, culture, religion, and autonomy of the diverse peoples living within them—sometimes brutally.

In the economic sphere we assumed the natural world was an inanimate collection of things we could take and use at will to satisfy our needs and wants, and so we developed systems that essentially depend on the depletion of natural resources to fuel an ever-expanding need for more, and industries to manufacture the objects that define our lifestyle and satisfy the perceived march of material progress.

In both these systems, the underlying game is quantifiable—who has more, whether it be more money, more territory, more weapons, more access to resources, more power, more growth, more toys, more market share, and so forth. Because the view is about quantity, our economic and political systems rely on dominance to assure pre-eminence in the *more* department—of one country over another; of humanity over the environment; of men over women; of one religion over another; of one faction over another; of one company over others. And dominance, to be sustained, ultimately relies on violence, whether it be the violence of armed conflict or of environmental rape; the violence of racism, sexism, and colonialism; or the violence of tyranny, despotism, or indifference.

We have carried these two systems, and the assumptions behind them, to the point of collapse. Now we see that the challenges of climate change; criminal and terrorist networks; pandemics; peak oil, water, food, and resource scarcity; a vulnerable globalized economy, and many more, transcend national boundaries. We see that the groups of people we have held down will not be silent, but demand their rightful place in the collective. We see too that we have maxed out our ability to take from the natural world, and have brought ourselves to the brink of self-destruction through environmental degradation and change.

So the shift, in Macy's words, is to a life-sustaining civilization that acknowledges and indeed requires our basic interconnectedness—with others in the human family and with the living planet.[9] This requires an assumption of quality over quantity—the quality of life and of relationship rather than the quantity. Now we must learn collaboration, partnership, and connectivity rather than dominance. We must learn consensus, cocreativity, and cooperative problem-solving. We must learn to work for the good of the whole rather than the parts. In short, we must learn peace.

I suggest that peacemaking is both the vanguard of this shift and its natural consequence. Peacemaking is the leading edge because it is the action arm of the change from separation to interconnectedness. It works in situations where the separation has or could become violent and life-destroying to bring the parties into (or back into) some sense of harmony, shared purpose, and the realization of the need to work together for the common good. In this sense, it is acting as a bridge, not only between warring parties but between one worldview and another.

If we understand that our universe is a complex interdependent system, then wherever the connectivity has been forgotten or broken, our task is to connect that which is disconnected and heal the harm. That is exactly what peacemaking does. It's about weaving, relating, communicating, linking, and bringing together. It's about moving from dominance to partnership; about building viable and sustainable human systems. At its best, it's about creating new models for how disparate peoples can solve mutual problems and live together harmoniously.

It isn't just the actions of peacemaking that are leading the way to creating a new world. It is also the philosophy, or belief system, that says, "There is only one family of life on and with the planet. We are in this together; interdependent. Our interests are best met when we satisfy the legitimate interests of the other. We need each other. We are and always will be in relationship, and our task is to maximize the quality of that relationship. We are both the unity and the diversity; the yin and the yang of a single whole."

Peacemaking is also the result or consequence of the shift, in that it is, in a sense, mopping up the residue, the dregs, the sludge, and slag of the worst that separation mind has wrought on the planet. Whether working with human or environmental conflicts, peacemakers are dealing with the results of violence, dominance, trauma, and oppression. They are the cleanup crew.

There are three phases to any major change process: stopping the old behavior, making whole what has been broken, and crafting new ways. Peacemaking does all three. It helps parties in conflict cease firing at each other, literally and figuratively; it encourages healing and reconciliation; and it invites parties into a realm of creativity where new solutions and pathways can be found. Peacemaking is generative where there is human (and physical) destruction; it is life-giving in the midst of injury and death; it is the hope within the despair.

I think of my experiences in Bosnia right after the war that tore apart the interwoven communities of Croats, Serbs, and Bosniaks (Muslims). The Organization for Security and Cooperation in Europe (OSCE) was engaged there in rebuilding the country and organizing for elections, but soon realized those efforts would fail without communication, bridge building, and healing among the people. So, at their invitation, I and a team of colleagues ran a number of dialogues and workshops to provide that opportunity. Where people were too wounded to speak directly about their experiences, or to interact productively with each other, we used the metaphor of gardening. In that way, they were able to decide together what weeds needed to be pulled and thrown away from the desolate ground, how the soil could be prepared for new life, and what seeds they would plant and tend in order to feed the people in the next season.

Essentially, as in this case, peacemaking is the living embodiment of the archetypical phoenix bird, which burns itself to ashes and then rises up in a new and glorious form. As humanity takes itself ever-closer to self-destruction, peacemakers are busy both putting out the fires and assisting where new life is ready to emerge.

One of the larger dynamics of the shift underway has to do with a rebalancing of the masculine/feminine energies in the human family. As human consciousness evolves to a stage of greater inclusiveness, we realize that one of the defining elements of separation mind has been the repression of the feminine. This manifests as the oppression of women in all its myriad forms in cultures around the world and at every scale, from the intrapersonal to the interpersonal and societal.

But that manifestation is simply an out-picturing of a more subtle dimension. In our essence and totality, we hold both masculine and feminine energies. We are straightforward, linear, productive, and assertive, even as we are also receptive, relational, intuitive, and compassionate. We are both the line and the circle; the sword and the shield; the father and the mother.

Humanity has now lived through a long period of human consciousness in which this blend has been experienced as duality, a duality in which one must triumph over the other. And so, in religion, politics, economics, social relations, and other walks of life, we have subsumed the feminine and exalted the masculine. The damage from this over centuries, for individuals and for the collective, is incalculable.

As we come into a holistic age, there is a natural restoration of balance underway. The feminine is rising—not to replace the masculine in a power dynamic but to regain its rightful place in a harmonious dance that expresses all of who we are as human beings carrying the DNA of divinity, which is unity.

Peacemaking is an instrument of this dynamic as well. We invite people to sit in a circle; we bring the marginalized and oppressed into the conversation; we raise the issues of trust, forgiveness, reconciliation, and healing. We ensure that women as well as men are part of the process. We encourage inclusive and equal relationships. We promote dialogue over debate; co-creativity over the imposing of one will over another; collaboration over unilateral decision making. We work with metaphors, images, process, and intuition, as well as with rationality, metrics, content, and logic.

What are the implications for applying this knowledge of the evolutionary dimension of peacemaking? Again, we look at the training of peacemakers.

In university programs, we need a course on this global shift and its relation to peacemaking. Through the phenomenon of the Field, this shift in human consciousness is rapidly progressing. As peacemakers, we are central to this spread, and so should be aware of the large-scale context in which we are working. Otherwise, we are operating without all the vision and resources available to us, and remain disconnected from the very change process we are helping to engender.

We also need dialogues between peacemakers and evolutionary thought leaders, like Deepak Chopra, Hazel Henderson, Fritjof Capra, Joanna Macy, James O'Dea, Barbara Marx Hubbard, Duane Elgin, and others.[10] These two groups have much to share and much to learn from each other. Such conversations can help the peacemaking field ground itself in the bigger flow of energy on the planet in these times, and help the thought leaders see the application of their philosophy in some of the direst realities on the ground.

Finally, we need professional space in which to discuss these matters and share insights, to consider how evolutionary processes are unfolding around the globe, and to share reflections on implications of this for peacemaking. In a world where interconnectedness is emerging as the dominant worldview, peacemakers are the interconnectors. The more we know about both, the better we can function.

CONCLUSION

The inner, energy, and evolutionary dimensions of peacemaking are rarely discussed within our profession. They lie on the outer edge of our collective wisdom. Understanding how scale, interconnectedness, field, and worldview dynamics of applied systems thinking operate is key to supporting our awareness of these hidden elements of our craft.

Why should we care? What if these dimensions remain hidden? What is to be gained by lifting them into the light of knowing? The shift occurring on the planet now necessarily involves great chaos, as old systems built on outdated worldviews break down, and new systems built on the realities of interdependence rise up. Such breakdowns can easily lead to violence, as disparate groups grapple for power in the new order of things or as environmental challenges lead to greater scarcity of life-sustaining resources.

The peacemaking community has grown exponentially in the last 20 years, precisely because the need is so great. It, too, is evolving, and like other sectors, is gradually recognizing the full range of its resources. In that process, to only access the tangible and not the intangible would be to continue the separation dynamic of an older era. It's time to connect the disconnected, and reintegrate our inner, energetic, and evolutionary potential.

It's time, as well, to approach peacemaking with every possible tool, from the individual to the global scale, for peace is both the vision and the desperate longing of humanity in these times, and we are its instruments. We are called not just to make peace, but to be peace (the inner dimension), to resonate peace (the energy dimension), and to be the leading edge of peace (the evolutionary dimension) for a world in crisis. In this, we carry the legacy of the great peacemakers who have gone before us, and we are and will be the inspiration for the many who come after.

NOTES

1. Albert Einstein, in 1946, as quoted in Otto Nathan and Heinz Norden, *Einstein on Peace* (New York: Simon and Schuster, 1960).

2. Dhyani Ywahoo, from a lecture presented at the Sunray Meditation Society, Huntington, Vermont, 1983. Ven. Dhyani Ywahoo is a lineage carrier of the Tsalagi (Cherokee) ancient wisdom and Chief of the Green Mountain Band of the Aniyunwiwa. www.beautywayproductions.com.

3. Mother Teresa. BrainyQuote.com, Xplore Inc., 2010, http://www.brainyquote.com/quotes/quotes/m/mothertere107032.html (accessed October 19, 2010).

4. This same story is told in different words in a previously published book by Louise Diamond, *The Courage for Peace* (Berkeley, CA: Conari Press, 2000), 36–38.

5. Mohandas Karamchand Gandhi, (2002). As quoted in Michel W. Potts, "Arun Gandhi Shares the Mahatma's Message," *India-West* 27, no. 13 (February 1), A34.

6. Thich Nhat Hanh, *Being Peace* (Berkeley, CA: Parallax Press, 1987).

7. Author unknown.

8. Joanna Macy and her Work, http://www.joannamacy.net/resources/thegreatturning.html, accessed October 19, 2010.

9. See Joanna Macy and Molly Young Brown, *Coming Back to Life: Practices to Reconnect Our Lives, Our World* (Gabriola Island, British Columbia: New Society Publishers, 1998).

10. Deepak Chopra (www.deepakchopra.com) is a physician, speaker, and author of more than three dozen books, including *Peace Is the Way* (New York: Three Rivers Press, 2005). Hazel Henderson (www.hazelhenderson.com) is a futurist, evolutionary economist and author of more than a dozen books, including *Planetary Citizenship: Your Values, Beliefs, and Actions Can Shape a Sustainable World* (with Daisaku Ikeda), (New York: Middleway Press, 2004). Fritjof Capra (www.fritjofcapra.net) is a physicist and systems theorist and the author of five international bestsellers, including *The Tao of Physics* (Boston: Shambhala Publications, 2010). Joanna Macy (www.joannamacy.net) is an ecophilosopher and activist on issues of peace, justice, and ecology. Among her many books is *Mutual Causality in Buddhism and General Systems Theory: The Dharma of Natural Systems* (New York: State University of New York Press, 1991). James O'Dea (www.jamesodea.com) is the past president of the Institute of Noetic Scientists and previous director of Amnesty International in Washington DC. An author and public speaker, O'Dea teaches a seven-week course on *The Path of the Peacemaker*. Barbara Marx Hubbard (www.barbaramarxhubbard.com) is a futurist and evolutionary philosopher, a public speaker, and the author of five books, including *Conscious Evolution: Awakening the Power of Your Social Potential* (Novato, CA: New World Library, 1998). Duane Elgin (www.awakeningearth.org) is a speaker, a social visionary, and the author of several books, including *The Living Universe: Where are We? Who Are We? Where Are We Going?* (San Francisco: Berrett-Koehler Publishers, 2009).

CHAPTER 40

A Dynamical Systems Perspective on Peacemaking: Moving from a System of War toward a System of Peace

Peter Coleman, Lan Bui-Wrzosinska, Andrzej Nowak, and Robin Vallacher

Peacemakers today are confronted with progressively more complex cultural, economic, and social dynamics. The situations they face and the consequences of their actions often seem unpredictable. The demands of working with complex, dynamical social systems require that peacemakers understand situations of conflict and work with them in correspondingly complex and dynamic ways. Failing to do so typically results in a misreading of situations and in unsustainable, short-term solutions that can bring unintended negative consequences (see Dorner 1996; Peterson and Flanders 2002). Looking at most effective peacemaking efforts, such as the transition of South Africa to democracy, the peace process in Mozambique, or the signing of the Good Friday Agreement in Northern Ireland, we can observe intuitive actions rather than a rigorous application of theory-driven rules. In fact, most effective peacemakers would probably agree that their interventions were deeply rooted in the local context and, at the same time, influenced by their intuitions about global consequences of their actions. From a handbook perspective, what they accomplished in Mozambique, South Africa, or Ireland was simply impossible.

Although complex social systems have unpredictable dynamics, these successful peacemaking interventions and the behavior of similarly complex phenomena in other areas of science can enhance our understanding of how these systems work. We suggest that peacemaking—understood as a process—can be approached from the perspective of nonlinear dynamical systems, an approach that has revolutionized virtually all scientific domains over the last 30 years (Gleick 1987; Johnson 2001; Schuster 1984; Strogatz 2003).

Broadly defined, a dynamical system is a set of elements that interact over time in accordance with simple rules. Dynamical systems theory aims to describe system-level properties, identify system rules, and observe behaviors that emerge from their repeated iteration. In recent years, the dynamical systems perspective has been adapted to investigate personal, interpersonal, and societal processes under the guise of *dynamical social psychology* (see Nowak and Vallacher 1998; Vallacher and Nowak 2007). The most recent extension of this approach focuses on the defining features of conflict that are invariant across various levels of social reality, from intimate relations to international war (see Coleman, Nowak, Vallacher, et al. 2007; Nowak, Vallacher, Coleman, et al. 2009; Vallacher, Coleman, Nowak, et al. 2011).

Our aim is to introduce the dynamical perspective as a novel way of approaching conflict, particularly conflict that seems immune to intervention. In this chapter, we will explore the added value of this approach for understanding the qualitative transition of systems of perpetuated war toward systems of sustainable peace. First, we describe how systems of intractable conflicts are formed and sustained. Then, we discuss the case of Mozambique: a painful example of an intractable conflict that transformed into sustainable peace when it was seemingly impossible. We move to a detailed description of the dynamical features of conflict systems and the conditions under which such systems can make the transition to peace. In the last part of this chapter, we discuss the implications of this approach and suggest a set of guidelines for peacemaking strategies.

SYSTEMS OF INTRACTABLE CONFLICTS

Among the key challenges for the conflict resolution field are conflicts that are seemingly immune to peacemaking initiatives—for example, the conflicts in Sri Lanka, Israel, Lebanon, Afghanistan, and Sudan. We refer to them as *intractable* (Coleman 2003). Other researchers use different labels, such as *deeply rooted conflict* (Burton 1987), *protracted social conflict* (Azar 1990), *moral conflict* (Pearce and Littlejohn 1997), and *enduring rivalries* (Goertz and Diehl 1993). They all share three common characteristics: persistence, destructiveness, and resistance to resolution (Kriesberg 2005). These characteristics are present at all levels of social reality: they divide families, communities, and nations. Most do not begin as intractable, but they become so as escalation, negative sentiment, and hostile interactions change the quality of the conflict. Once a conflict becomes anchored in a pattern of destruction and hostility, a stable enmity system is established. From then on, the dynamical forces maintaining a state of conflict will counter any resolution attempts.

The forces at work in such systems can be made concrete by means of a hypothetical scenario in which conflict escalates to intractability. Let us investigate a conflict starting with an individual centering his or her thoughts on a particular incompatibility with another person. As separate, negative thoughts start to make sense together, a structure is gradually formed. This structure, which grows by assimilating an increasing number of different psychological processes, is integrated with negative emotions. Judgments affected by negative emotions become increasingly undifferentiated and unidimensional. They focus on the incompatibility with the other person. Communicating hostile intentions eventually initiates similar processes in the other person. If there are no suppressing mechanisms active at this stage, the two systems of conflict—existing at the personal level—reinforce each other and reduce the probability of positive interactions. The thoughts, feelings, and behaviors of both people are processed within the structure of conflict. Conflict now exists at the interpersonal level. Because both parties seek support from members of their respective groups, the conflict emerges at the social level, where it is sustained by links and positive feedback within the groups. Even if the person who initiated this process tries to disassemble conflict, it will be reinstated by the feedback from other group members. Growing conflict intensity and mutual negative feedback between the groups may lead to instances of hostility and violence. Such conflict is likely to start shaping the symbol system of the people involved: identities may be built around the incompatibility with the out-group. The terms used to refer to the out-group become dehumanizing and preclude positive interactions. Protracted conflict becomes embedded in the culture of the society, thus gaining a new means of maintenance and spread. Anyone adopting the culture is likely to adopt the conflict embedded within it. In this way, conflict is passed on through generations: in-group members who never had contact with the out-group are unlikely to form sustainable positive, or even neutral, relationships with its members.

The aforementioned scenario is a hypothetical model of how conflicts progress toward intractability. Even though this model may be different in real life, the forces at stake and the structure of the system will be the same: a multitude of positive feedback loops within and between the social levels will sustain and support the conflict, rendering fruitless any attempts to disassemble it (any disassembled part of the conflict will be reinstated in other parts of its structure). An intractable conflict can be seen as a "malignant" social relation (Coleman 2003) in which the multidimensionality of human relationships is reduced to the sole objective of sustaining enmity. When cancer penetrates an organism and enslaves essential body elements, they lose their original functions and begin working in service of the invader. The collapse of complexity is caused by intractable conflict in the same way. The psychological and social processes necessary for the maintenance of mental structures, religions, and societies become enslaved to the one-dimensional structure of conflict. Their original functions essentially vanish. In intractable conflict, love, friendship, or even professional contact between members of opposing parties will not be recognized as such, but rather will be interpreted as collaboration with the enemy, weakness, or treason.

In the light of this scenario, how can we advance our understanding of systems of intractable conflict that would allow for informed decision making? How can we foster the processes that could push such profoundly anchored systems of conflict toward peace? To demonstrate the practical utility of our perspective, we will discuss the 16-year civil war and the subsequent outbreak of peace in Mozambique in the early 1990s. Before discussing the case from a dynamical systems theory perspective, we will outline the historical context first.

THE EMERGENCE OF CONFLICT
AND PEACE IN MOZAMBIQUE

Mozambique was a Portuguese colony for more than 400 years. After World War II, when the process of decolonization made other European countries relinquish control of their colonies, Portugal resisted and engaged in a long and bloody war with independence forces in Mozambique, led by the Frente de Liberacao de Mozambique (FRELIMO). Although these forces were able to control some territory, they were unable to fully liberate the country until a leftist military coup in Lisbon in 1974 made the metropole grant independence to Mozambique. The enthusiasm for the newfound independence, which was formally declared on June 25, 1975, was evident. Authentic joy and pride were expressed across the country, from the capital in the south to the northern border with Tanzania.

Unfortunately, Mozambique's beginnings were far from auspicious. As Portugal used to have tight control over the country's administration, most qualified labor force left the country when it gained independence. Rhodesia and South Africa—at that time ruled by active white supremacists—immediately sought ways to destabilize the new government. Moreover, the initial enthusiasm of the population was misinterpreted by the FRELIMO leadership as "revolutionary fervor," setting the stage for harsh and demanding policies. Two of them were particularly relevant: (1) the mass relocation of the population and (2) the disempowerment of traditional authorities. The main aim of FRELIMO was to bring Mozambique together as a unified, socialist country, overcoming tribal and ethnic distinctions. However, the violent implementation of these policies and the lack of comprehension of the new identity imposed on the population led to the creation of the Resistancia National Mocambicana (RENAMO), a movement supported by Rhodesia and South Africa. The main aim of RENAMO was to make the functioning of the FRELIMO government impossible. It intentionally attacked civilians and forcefully recruited young boys to join its forces. The subsequent war ravaged the country for many years and involved many external actors. Exclusionary rhetoric and adversarial posturing were adopted, while moderate stands were marginalized or eliminated. Even at the end of this long and destructive cycle of violence, the interlocking dynamics made it very difficult to find the pathway to peace.

While FRELIMO and RENAMO were deeply entrenched in the conflict, an unexpected group of actors began to explore alternatives to the exclusionary policies of both sides of the conflict. It was a young, native, national bishop, Jaime Goncalves, representing a Catholic nongovernmental organization, the Community of Sant'Egidio. This community engaged in talks with the FRELIMO government to facilitate religious freedom as early as the second half of the 1970s. Their efforts led to the visit of Samora Machel, president of Mozambique, to the Vatican in 1986. After the unexpected death of President Samora, the new leader, Joachim Chissano, sought help from the religious leaders to establish contacts with RENAMO. Using their channels, members of the Community of Sant'Egidio were able to arrange a secret visit of Bishop

Goncalves to the RENAMO headquarters. Their first meeting in 1988 became a turning point of the conflict. At this meeting, Bishop Goncalves and Alfonso Dlakama, the leader of RENAMO, discovered that they were from the same ethnic tribe and spoke the same dialect. That meeting became the cornerstone of a peacemaking process leading to the signature of the General Peace Accords on October 4, 1992. It must be noted that Goncalves and the Community of Sant'Egidio never had the power to force the parties to reach an agreement. Although there were many earlier efforts to bring the two parties together, both by regional and international actors (Zimbabwe, Kenya, Malawi, private investors, etc.), they failed due to their inability to design a process that would be both engaging and respectful. Today, Mozambique is united, stable, prosperous, and at peace. In the following sections we investigate how it was possible to achieve this stability and peace.

UNDERSTANDING INTRACTABLE CONFLICT IN THE DYNAMICAL FRAMEWORK

One defining feature of intractable conflicts, like the civil war in Mozambique, is that they display strong resistance to intervention, even when rational considerations would seemingly defuse them (see Azar 1990; Bar-Tal 2007; Bercovitch 2005; Burton 1987; Coleman 2003; Goertz and Diehl 1993; Kriesberg 2005). Research has identified numerous psychological processes related to conflict intractability (see Bar-Tal 2007; Coleman 2003; Deutsch, Coleman, and Marcus 2006). Because intractable conflicts are entrenched in a wide variety of cognitive, affective, and social-structural mechanisms, they are effectively decoupled from the perceived incompatibilities that started them.

Attractor Dynamics

From the perspective of dynamical systems theory, conflict becomes intractable when various social and psychological processes interact over time to promote the emergence of stable and coherent patterns of thought and behavior organized around the perceived incompatibilities. These patterns function as *attractors* (Schuster 1984) for the system in that they constrain or attract the mental and behavioral dynamics of each party to the conflict. Metaphorically, the attractor serves as a valley in the psychological landscape into which psychological elements—thoughts, feelings, and actions—begin to slide. Escaping from such a valley, once trapped inside, requires tremendous will and energy and may appear virtually impossible. In other words, pushing a stone downhill is one thing, but pushing it back uphill is another.

This perspective provides a new way to conceptualize and address intractable conflict. Conflicts are commonly described in terms of their intensity (e.g., the amount of violence), but this feature does not capture the issue of intractability. Even low-intensity conflicts can become protracted and resistant to resolution. We suggest defining intractable conflicts as conflicts governed by strong attractors for negative dynamics and weak attractors for positive— or even neutral—dynamics. Hence, being aware of the attractor landscape of a given system—the ensemble of sustainable states for positive, neutral, and negative interactions—is critical for understanding the progression, transformation, and de-escalation of intractable conflicts. Conflict resolution attempts that do not work toward the achievement of a social capacity to maintain peace are likely to fail. They may lead to a temporary ceasefire but not to long-term coexistence. If there is no sustainable alternative to war, the first step of an intervention should be to establish one. Only after such a change has occurred can the system be effectively moved to a benign or positive state.

This scenario can also be seen in the case of Mozambique. The civil war there was characterized by the fact that the conflicted parties had little opportunity for movement (see Bartoli, Bui-Wrzosinska, and Nowak 2010); they were locked into enmity positions by power structures, meaning systems, and relational dynamics. Any alternative to the state of war was believed to be impossible; situations that could move the system in the direction of a peaceful resolution were intentionally avoided and strictly controlled. Even the idea of reconciliation was dangerous; any person broaching this topic could be executed as a traitor. The emergence of the system of peace was a consequence of movement. Actors from opposite sides of the conflict started to establish communication channels. Eventually, they became able to react to the arguments and could begin to gradually change their positions. The observed trajectory of the process moving from a tightly coupled, constrained system of enmity toward a more dynamic, and thus sustainable, peace can be understood as movement away from a very strong and limiting attractor for war to a much less constraining—but nonetheless stable—attractor for peace.

Attractors and the Collapse of Complexity

The relationship between conflicting parties may be characterized by incompatibility with respect to many issues. However, this state of affairs does not necessarily promote intractability. On the contrary, the complexity of such relationships may prevent the progression toward intractability and even enhance the likelihood of conflict resolution. Since either party may lose on one issue but prevail on others, conflict resolution is tantamount to problem solving, with both parties trying to find a solution that best satisfies their respective needs (Fisher, Ury, and Patton 1991).

It is the collapse of complexity that promotes conflict intractability. When distinct issues become interlinked and mutually dependent, the activation of a single issue effectively activates them all. The likelihood of finding a solution that will satisfy all the issues is drastically diminished. For example, a border incident between countries with a history of conflict is likely to reactivate all previous provocations, perceived injustices, and conflicts of interest. Consequently, the parties of the conflict may respond disproportionately to the magnitude of the instigating issue. Even if the instigating issue is somehow resolved, the activation of other issues will serve to maintain and even deepen the conflict. Mozambique is a good example of how single episodes were understood in the context of a general conflict reactivating the whole system. Even after signing the agreement, some violent incidents—most probably caused by communication errors—led to a resurgence of violence that threatened the peace process.

The loss of issue complexity is directly linked to the development of attractors. Interpersonal and intergroup relations are typically multidimensional, with various mechanisms operating at different points in time, in different contexts, with respect to different issues, and often in a compensatory manner. The alignment of separate issues into a single dimension, however, establishes positive feedback loops, such that the issues have a mutually reinforcing rather than a compensatory relationship. All events that are open to interpretation become construed in the same fashion and promote a consistent pattern of behavior toward other people and groups. The common state toward which diverse thoughts and behaviors converge represents a fixed-point attractor for the system. Even an unambiguous event that runs counter to the attractor can be assimilated to it. For instance, peaceful overtures by the out-group may be considered a trick if there is a strong antagonism toward the out-group.

Manifest and Latent Attractors for Conflict

A psychological system may have multiple attractors (e.g., love and hate in a close relationship), each providing a unique form of mental or behavioral coherence. When the system is at one of its attractors, others attractors may be invisible to the observers, even including the participants. Nevertheless, these latent attractors may be highly important in the long run, because they determine which states are possible for the system if and when conditions change. Critical changes in a system, then, might not be reflected in the system's observable state but rather in the creation or destruction of a latent attractor representing a potential state that is currently invisible to those concerned. The potential for latent attractors has important implications for intractable conflict (Nowak et al. 2007; Coleman et al. 2006, 2007). Although such factors as objectification, dehumanization, and stereotyping of the out-group can promote intractable intergroup conflict (Coleman 2003; Kriesberg 2005), their impact may not be immediately apparent. Instead, they may create a latent attractor to which the system can abruptly switch in response to a provocation that is relatively minor, even trivial. By the same token, efforts at conflict resolution that are fruitless in the short run may create a latent positive attractor for intergroup relations, thereby establishing a potential relationship to which the groups can suddenly switch if other conditions permit it. A latent positive attractor, then, can promote a rapid de-escalation of conflict, even between groups with a long history of seemingly intractable conflict. This possibility is consistent with research on the dynamics of social judgment (see Latané and Nowak 1994). When the judgment context has strong personal relevance, thoughts and feelings tend to sort themselves categorically, with each category representing a different value (very positive vs. very negative). If a person's judgment changes, it does so in an abrupt, nonlinear, qualitative manner rather than in a slow, linear, and incremental fashion.

Changing Attractor Landscapes

As attractors operate on a system, the manifest changes—visible as a more or less consistent oscillation of actions and events in social interaction—will tend to follow a nonlinear scenario (see Ruelle 1989; Thom 1975). These changes are linked to the shape of the attractor landscape: if an external event moves a system out of its attractor (e.g., by a momentary increase in hostility), the system will shortly return to its attractor (e.g., the parties will resolve the issue) and it will not respond proportionally to external influence. If a system is in the vicinity of an attractor, even minor forces will have important consequences and will lead to a qualitative shift. For example, once a strong attractor for conflict and hostility is in place, even a minor provocation can propel the social dynamics toward extreme violence. Conversely, if peace initiatives aimed at fostering a peaceful alternative to existing conflicts seem to have no effect, they have changed the attractor landscape by deepening the attractor of peace. Thus, even minor and local actions can initiate a series of events leading to peace.

However, in case of iterated provocation (e.g., sustained hostility by one party), the positive attractor may be weakened or replaced at some point with an attractor corresponding to negative interactions. There are two different routes by which this may happen. In a linear scenario, under conditions of high complexity, increased provocation on one side will result in a gradual change of the positive attractor to increasingly negative values (e.g., from friendly to neutral, unfriendly, and hostile). Although the value of the attractor changes, it represents the only attractor for the system. In a nonlinear scenario, under conditions of low complexity, the initial attractor for peaceful interactions does not change its value despite increasing provocation, but instead it becomes progressively weaker. Eventually, a second latent attractor at high values of negativity is created. With further provocation, the positive attractor progressively weakens and the negative attractor strengthens. At some point, the positive attractor loses its stability, and the relationship abruptly moves to the values defined by the negative attractor, which then governs the dynamics of the relationship. De-escalation scenarios mirror the escalation ones. In the linear case (high complexity), the attractor moves incrementally to positive values. In the nonlinear case (low complexity), reconciliatory actions weaken the negative attractor and reinstate the positive (latent) attractor. At some point, the system abruptly switches from negative values to positive values. In effect, the positive attractor becomes manifest, whereas the negative attractor becomes latent. This switch, however, is likely to occur at higher positive values of interaction than the values at which the system switched from positive to negative. The tendency for a system to remain at its current attractor, termed *hysteresis,* is a defining characteristic of nonlinearity. It should be noted, though, that even if the interaction between two parties changes to quite positive values, the presence of a latent negative attractor indicates the system's tendency to return to high negativity in response to even slight provocations.

IMPLICATIONS FOR PEACEMAKING: SOME GUIDELINES FOR NAVIGATING ATTRACTOR LANDSCAPES

In the next section we outline some general guidelines for working with long-term conflicts. These guidelines have emerged from our work or they are consistent with our framework and build on the work of other researchers of complexity and conflict from similar perspectives (see Conway, Suedfeld, and Tetlock 2001; Dorner 1996; Gersick 1991; Jones and Hughes 2003; Lederach 1997; Maruyama 1963, 1982; Morgan 1997; Pearce and Littlejohn 1997).

See the System

The main challenge for interveners in a conflict is to avoid oversimplifying the problems they face. They need to identify and work through the elements that drive or constrain change, bearing in mind the complexities of the situation. For example, the events in Mozambique were situated in a broader field of forces that played important roles in the destructive patterns that unfolded. Unlike in India, the decolonization process was not led by nonviolent visionaries such as Mohandas Gandhi. On the contrary, the long and bloody war of independence was led by a small group of committed militants who were constantly reminded of the power of arms by the violent Portuguese repression. The formation and growth of FRELIMO was also fueled by the Marxist-Leninist ideology. It was also affected by the framework of confrontation during the Cold War and by the white supremacist governments, such as Rhodesia and South Africa.

One of the first challenges for interveners working in systems showing a collapse of complexity (i.e., strong us-versus-them polarization) is to maintain or enhance their own sense of integrative complexity with regard to the case (Conway, Suedfeld, and Tetlock 2001). That is the capacity to view the system as a whole and to see its different aspects—and their interrelations—in order to use this knowledge to make informed decisions.

The dynamical systems perspective suggests that four key psychological and social mechanisms fostered intractability in Mozambique: (1) collapse of subjective and social complexity among many stakeholders, (2) loss of balanced feedback leading to escalation, (3) positive feedback between the levels, and (4) catastrophic changes in the quality of the conflict. For instance, the collective expression of enthusiasm over the independence victory was soon replaced by a very narrow ideological frame imposed by FRELIMO. Feedback was not welcomed unless it was supportive. Nonsupportive responses were labeled antirevolutionary and antipatriotic. Individuals and groups could either renounce their discontent and join the party line or harden the critique and be further marginalized.

The escalation of a new conflict directly resulted from this exclusionary approach, which sharply reduced the potential for self-correction within the system. Moreover, as the discontent increased, FRELIMO supporters felt more committed to the implementation of the policies of collectivization and nationalization. Agents at the local, regional, and national level became tightly coordinated to ensure that centralized directives would be implemented. This led to a catastrophic transformation when the violence—already present in the collective memory—was reoriented against FRELIMO, creating two active and self-reinforcing enmity systems.

This resulted in the emergence of a strong negative attractor that pulled the thoughts, feelings, and actions of the community into a self-perpetuating polarized dynamic. In this state, the resolution of specific issues—as initially attempted—did little to quell the tide of hostility and suspicion. More relevant was the role of catalysts like Jaime Goncalves, who was able to internalize various viewpoints and contradictions without being completely constrained by the enmity system. Supported by the Community of Sant'Egidio, Goncalves managed to stay connected with both enmity systems, which enabled him to challenge the tight structures of coherence built around the power, meaning, and relationships in both systems.

Take Time Seriously

The elements of complex conflict systems interact in a nonlinear fashion: a change in one element does not necessarily constitute a proportional change in the remaining ones. The recognition that conflict and peace arise and develop within complex, nonlinear systems suggests that we need to attend to temporal patterns and trends, not specific outcomes. This observation has two major implications for conflict transformation and peacebuilding.

First, it is important to recognize that a system's states and attractors change according to different time scales. Manifest conflicts can witness dramatic changes in their states: from relatively peaceful, through violent, to intensely destructive ones. This is observed when social processes move from one attractor pattern to another across what has been termed a *tipping point* (Gladwell 2000). However, such changes in the state of the conflict at any given moment should not be confused with changes in the underlying attractor landscape. Attractors tend to develop slowly and incrementally over time as a result of a host of relevant activities. In Mozambique, the first contact between the Community of Sant'Egidio and the FRELIMO government was established in the second half of the 1970s, almost 15 years before signing the peace agreement. This began the slow process of trust-building that established the conditions (an attractor) for facilitating talks. More than four years passed between the first meeting of Goncalves with Alfonso Dlakama, the leader of RENAMO, and signing the final General Peace Accords.

Second, the effects of different change initiatives also have different temporal patterns (Coleman 2006). *Episodic initiatives* are typically responses to crises associated with conflicts. Their aim is to quell outbreaks of violence or suffering and reinstate a sense of safety and stability. In Mozambique, the repressive and violent response to the expression of political dissatisfaction after gaining the independence escalated the conflict tremendously. A military response intended to quell discontent had the opposite effect. *Developmental initiatives* can have an eventual impact on conflict patterns, but such effects are typically gradual, particularly when introduced at lower levels of the system. *Radical initiatives* can trigger extreme shifts in attractor patterns (from destructive to constructive) through small but important changes (Gladwell 2000). For example, using the offices of a small and unknown nongovernmental organization to establish direct talks between FRELIMO and RENAMO was a small but radical step in addressing the dynamics of the enmity system in Mozambique. Nevertheless, it is not always easy to discriminate among the three qualifiers (episodic, developmental, and radical) prior to their effects. Intentionality is not always matched by results, and in a dynamical system the actual outcomes are often unexpected.

Take Peace Seriously

The idea of latent attractors demonstrates that conflict and peace coexist in every social system. Malignant thoughts, feelings, and actions characterizing a group's dynamics may represent only the most salient and visible attractor. In case of a long history of interaction with the out-group, there may be other potential patterns of mental, affective, and behavioral engagement with the out-group members, some of which may foster positive intergroup relations. Accordingly, identifying and reinforcing latent (positive) attractors, not just disassembling the manifest (negative) attractors, should be the aim of both conflict prevention and intervention.

In short, the identification and support of constructive actors and forces within the system is vital for increasing the probability for peace. There are many such tactics, including the following.

- *Support latent networks of effective action.* Virtually every conflict system, even the direst one, will contain people and groups who may be able to reach out across the divides and work to foster dialogue and peace. During the periods of escalation, these people and groups may be temporarily inactive—even going underground—but when conditions allow it, they are often willing to reemerge, becoming fundamental players in the transformation of the system.

- *Employ weak power.* Strong enmity systems are associated with stable states of hostility, strong attractors for destructiveness, and weak attractors for peace. Hence, they will typically reject most strong-arm attempts to promote peace. The events in Mozambique provide an example of the utility of weak power in such systems. During the conflict, the internal coherence of the two hostile systems was very high; ideologically, militarily, and politically, there was no communication between them. It was thanks to the nonthreatening communication processes that some key actors in the enmity system started to consider alternatives to the status quo at that time. These processes were made possible by the weaknesses of the propositions and of the proponents—that is, the Community of Sant'Egidio.

- *Employ negotiation chains.* An increasingly popular tactic employed in protracted conflicts is to use of negotiation chains (Pruitt 2007b). This practice involves a sequence of actors who may help start more formal talks. The talks transpire through a series of encounters between actors who are not constrained politically against speaking to each other and who have further contacts down the chain. This allows for communication between parties who (1) need to be able to maintain deniability in the talks and (2) who would otherwise not be able to communicate.

- *Identify discontinuities* (carefully increase complexity). Weak power third parties may be able to introduce a sense of doubt or dissonance in an otherwise coherent us-versus-them meaning system. The discontinuities may address the parties' sense of their enemies, the issues at stake, the history of events, their own in-group, and so forth. Although the introduction of dissonance may have no short-term effects, it can become important at a later point.

- *Work on positivity away from conflict attractors.* Recognizing that systems with strong negative attractors often frame peacemakers as part of the conflict system and position them in one camp or another, some interveners try to work constructively by circumventing the conflict. This tactic aims to reduce the misery associated with these situations but does so in a manner that is framed as outside the conflict.

- *Acknowledge superordinate identities and goals.* This classic approach to intergroup conflict involves the identification or development of joint goals and identities in order to establish a foundation of cooperation and eventually trust between parties (Sherif et al. 1961; Deutsch 1973). Even if peacekeeping missions, reconciliation processes, trust-building activities, and cooperative conflict resolution initiatives appear to be largely ineffective in situations locked in an ongoing protracted struggle, they may successfully establish a sufficiently wide and deep attractor basin for moral, humane forms of intergroup interactions that provide the foundation for a stable, peaceful future. Constructed gradually over time, a positive attractor may be imperceptible, but the process of its construction prepares the ground for a positive state otherwise impossible.

Reverse-Engineer Negative, Destructive Attractors

Establishing latent attractors for peace is only one part of the solution. The most obvious need is to quell violence and actively control destructive processes, which is often done by introducing peacekeeping troops. Even when systems de-escalate and appear to move toward peace, it is crucial to recognize that the potential for destructive interactions (destructive attractors) is still operative.

- *Decouple positive feedback loops.* The structure of conflict often binds together perceptions of all out-group members. Showing positive examples of specific out-group members can increase complexity, since a single judgment cannot accommodate all the out-group members. Another tack is to find an important in-group member (e.g., charismatic and of high status) who does not share the in-group's view of the conflict. If this person is sufficiently central, so that he or she cannot be marginalized within the group, the homogeneity of the in-group's perspective will be destabilized.

- *Introduce negative feedback loops.* One of the greatest concerns in Mozambique was the possibility of breaking the conditions negotiated during the first round of talks in Rome. It was agreed that military activity would be monitored by an independent commission. As in many other peacekeeping operations, the involvement of an independent agent drastically reduced the mistrust between the parties and the probability of conflict escalation. Peacekeeping is a critical basis for peacemaking activities not only because it sets the necessary safety boundaries for peacemaking but also because, by introducing negative feedback loops, it may alter some chronic dynamics and stop a vicious circle of hostile interactions. In Mozambique, an endogenous legend picturing "bad wind"—an evil force that sometimes takes people's souls and makes them commit atrocities—that turned out to be the key to peace and reconciliation. It introduced a negative feedback loop to the vicious circle of vengeance and guilt among Mozambicans.

- *Institutionalize more complex, alternative conflict narratives* (through media, textbooks, official accounts, etc.). Strong enmity systems typically have distinct and polarized narratives about the history of the conflict and its heroes and villains. Establishing mechanisms to monitor and revise such one-sided narratives plays a crucial role in preventing future generations from returning to the same destructive patterns. In Mozambique, the first step toward peace was made when the conflicted parties stopped using such derogatory terms as *macacos* (apes). Moreover, a new national identity—expressed in the peace treaty as "the Mozambican family"—eased the reconciliation of the two sides.

CONCLUSION

This chapter discusses some practical implications of the dynamical systems theory for peacemaking in protracted social conflicts. Moving beyond the language of interests and positions, a dynamical systems approach allows us to understand the contradictory and paradoxical moves that created the enmity system in Mozambique; maintained the conflict over time; blocked the system in recurrent, self-organized patterns; and made solutions highly improbable. It also allows us to better understand why an unknown external actor with little power (Sant'Egidio), working with a catalyst within the system (Bishop Jamie Goncalves), made the transformation possible.

There are several advantages of applying the dynamical systems perspective to the investigation of systems captured in patterns of destructive, intractable conflict. This perspective enables the application of insights from the study of other systems characterized by attractor dynamics, even though every conflict scenario is associated with a different set of factors. From the dynamical perspective, the development of a strong attractor responsible for intractability is due to the interplay of such factors across different levels of psychological and social reality (see Bar-Tal 2007; Coleman 2003). This interplay, in turn, reflects the manner in which the relevant factors are organized rather than their specific content. Despite the idiosyncrasy of the factors associated with a particular conflict scenario, the invariant features of conflict can be identified by focusing on the interconnection and feedback loops among whatever factors are operative in a given scenario. The conceptual tools of dynamical systems theory enable the study of the connection of factors operating at different levels of psychological and social reality (e.g., individual cognitions and properties of intergroup conflict). They can also identify and investigate the distinction between the manifest state of a conflict and the potential states of a system that represent latent attractors for the system's dynamics.

The dynamical systems approach enables us to see elements, trajectories, and relationships in a new and—we believe—powerful way. We are cautious about claiming too much at this stage and offer these guidelines in a spirit of modesty and humility. Although the transformation that made the emergence of peace in Mozambique possible is tangible and well documented, our understanding of the process is only rudimentary. Nonetheless, we hope that this contribution, in conjunction with the work of future dynamical systems conflict specialists, will increase the probabilities of peace.

CHAPTER 41

Systemic Peacemaking in the Era of Globalization

Monty G. Marshall

[O]ne day we must come to see that peace is not merely a distant goal that we seek, but that it is a means by which we arrive at that goal. We must pursue peaceful ends through peaceful means.

—Martin Luther King Jr.[1]

In the global context, the term *peace,* used on its own, may be viewed as indicating little more than the time period between episodes of open warfare, and, because episodes of open warfare have been a nearly constant feature in global politics throughout the recorded history of humankind, it can be understood as having little or no practical or applied meaning. The lack of an applied meaning would necessarily relegate the meaning of peace to an unattainable utopian ideal, a nonrelatable spiritual quest, or unknowable promise of an afterlife. The only practicable meaning for the term *peacemaking,* then, would be the act of warfare, which, through its emphasis on lethal violence, creates an applied pathway to the afterlife for large numbers of innocents for whom the promise of eternal peace is deemed most assured. The irony of war representing a pathway to peace is an extreme application of the peace paradox, in which the act of war defines the nature of peace. If peace is to have any real meaning, it must be a distinct condition independent of war. Peaceful relations can be neither created under nor enforced by the threat of war. The notion that peacemaking should, and can, have an applied meaning as a pathway to establishing an empirical peace on Earth must be, then, seen as the peace conundrum. The first step in practical peacemaking, which is the political process by which we attempt to solve the peace conundrum, begins with a question: How can we recast our notion of peace so that peace defines the problem of war?

The applied science of peacemaking necessarily seeks referents in historical and circumstantial empiricism.[2] In our written histories, war can be seen
to define both the state and civil society in a social Darwinian scheme of state
survival and supportive societal growth and expansion. Our notions of security have been largely defined by war; we even believe that we must fight for
freedom. Whether it is a Hobbesian, Machiavellian, or Marxist view of the relationship between the state and civil society or a Sun Tzuian or Clausewitzian
view of the relations between states, victory in war (or, better, victory through
the threat of war) empowers the state and conditions the subordination of civil
society. What we observe in such a historical review of the evolution of human
civilization are alternative examples of relative peace and separate peace,
where peace is conditioned and defined by its relationship to war.[3] The concept of relative peace is more accurately portrayed as the temporal, and temporary, condition of not war; it signifies the period of relative calm punctuated
by high levels of interpersonal violence and situated between episodes of collective violence or warfare. In this sense, peace is the preparatory process for
war situated within a culture of violence; peace exists primarily because war
cannot be sustained indefinitely. Warfare draws power from civil society and
applies that power to consume everything in its path, and so it stands as an
ultimately self-limiting social phenomenon. It ends when it has exhausted at
least one civil society. Populations are understood to be ripe for peace when
they can no longer effectively feed the appetite of war and can no longer reasonably envision a relational victory in war (a condition, perhaps, better considered war fatigue).[4]

The idea of a separate peace is predicated upon the spatial notion that a particular social group can somehow remove itself from the impetus, practices,
and consequences of war. Both these conditional forms of peace are achievable,
but neither are sustainable because both are entangled in the peace paradox
and are themselves essential elements of war: complementary components
that fuel war-making capacity and determine the self-limiting nature of warfare. Relative peace generates the potential for making war; separate peace
provides the incentive and motivation for war (i.e., the target or enemy). In
the act of being, the violence of war necessarily devours the power created by
a relative peace and transforms that power into violence to effect the destruction of a separate peace.[5] Even when the power of such a peace is completely
consumed by war, peace has consistently been observed to rise from its own
ashes as a Phoenix, recovering its veracity to empower the next cycle of war.
When we recognize that these forms of peace are both necessary and sufficient
conditions for war, we take the first step in recasting the relationship between
peace and war to one where peace defines war rather than war defining peace.
Peacemaking, then, should be understood as the self-perpetuating process of
making war by other means.

When war defines the peace, peacemakers are preoccupied with ending wars
or soothing the most brutal aspects of war and, in effect, acting simply to create the conditions for both a relative and a separate peace; they act, ultimately,
in service to war. The ending of a war does not create peace; it simply creates
a calm during which the creation of a meaningful peace can be reasonably

considered. This understanding helps to explain why, by interfering with the self-limiting nature of war, peacemakers may contribute to the creation of a self-limiting peace and, in so doing, further accentuate and entrench a political culture wherein peace is defined by war. War-ending is a necessary but not sufficient condition for a meaningful peace. Wars do not create peace, nor do the endings of wars; wars reinforce and accentuate the conditions that favored the onset of the previous war and create additional circumstances that favor the onset of a subsequent war. This is the nature of the war paradox that fortifies the war conundrum against halfhearted, disorganized, or ill-prepared attempts to resolve the problem of warfare. The peacemakers find themselves subservient to the war makers, and civil society is subordinated to the state. Under these circumstances and within this scheme, war makers are circumstantially empowered by the very conditions that present impediments to the peacemakers' attempts to resolve the war conundrum. From the feminist perspective, we can see that the peacemakers are relegated the role of cleaning up the war makers' mess, and this effort further distracts them from pursuing a more meaningful and productive role.

Thus, traditional forms of peacemaking have developed a preoccupation with the immediate challenges of ending wars prematurely and ameliorating the humanitarian crises and adverse conditions that wars create so that new wars can be waged. This is a most cynical perspective on peacemaking, but it is not without merit. It places war and peace in a comparative, developmental schema within which warfare can be seen as having differential effects. What seems to emerge most clearly from a comparative historical review of human civilization is that both violence and warfare are very strongly associated with lower levels of societal development and that the general pace of societal development has been spotty and slow, at least until the latter half of the 20th century. What most distinguishes the latter 20th century from all preceding periods is the general renunciation of war as a tool of statecraft.[6] This renunciation was led by the victors of war, where advanced societal development had empowered an independent civil society whose voice could compete with that of the war makers. The renunciation of war presents civil society's first systemic intervention in solving the war conundrum. Because war is a policy decision, the alteration of the war decision requires a superior act of political will.[7]

Whereas unsupportable rates of consumption limit the conduct of warfare, determined acts of civil disobedience have been found to limit the viability of warfare. The fact that, seen from the global perspective, societal development has been spotty and slow has provided the circumstances within which two world wars occurred in the earlier half of the 20th century that presented incontrovertible evidence that the true costs of war can no longer be discounted, nor can the severe externalities and consequences of war be ignored or denied, even by the victors of wars. The defining circumstances of the first two world wars, I believe, are three: spotty development created a spatial concentration of power in European states, slow development that contributed to strong competition among inefficient economies in Europe, and uneven development (i.e., an interaction effect of spotty and slow) that provided Europe a

relative advantage in exporting its war-making capacity in conquest of the nascent world system (thus reinforcing its preference of war making over peacemaking). As such, violent forms of social interaction should most properly be
considered as noncivil or uncivil impediments to societal development rather
than the proverbial stimuli for technological advancement, employment, and
economic growth as often claimed by the war makers. War, then, can be seen as
a problem of societal-system development.

It is tautological to observe that the victors in warfare are the parties to war
suffering the least (relative) destruction and enjoying the broadest access to
the resources necessary for postwar recovery. Should there be a war, there is
a distinct advantage in winning the war, and the more powerful states are
intrinsically rational enough to recognize and pursue their advantages.[8] The
vanquished are either incorporated to provide additional resources for the
victors, adding organizational complexity to the victor, or they are further
marginalized and denied access to vital resources (a process of ghettoization
of the disenfranchised). Societal complexity increases interest and identity diversity and, thus, drives organizational innovation to promote coherency and
cohesion in the victorious states. The vanquished tend to disintegrate into simple interest and identity constituencies; artificially imposed state structures
tend to be captured by key constituencies that reinforce social divisions and
promote simple interests, thus reinforcing uneven development in the nascent
world system.

Examination of the long-term, biased old historical record controlled by the
victors of war can be juxtaposed with an examination of the short-term, more
balanced, and detailed new historical record that has been collected largely
by elements of civil society and includes the experiences of the vanquished in
war.[9] The new historical record emerged as a consequence of the Second World
War and the critical examination of the war system that produced and prosecuted it.[10] The war makers were, at least temporarily, discredited by the scope
of destruction that the world's concentrated power was able to transform into
total warfare and project across much of the world, thus elevating the peacemakers' perspectives onto the policy agendas of the victors. Civil society leaders, following the example of those in the United States, also began to challenge
their traditional subordination to the state and demand greater influence in
the formulation of public policy in the world's still quite limited number of independent states.[11] In the nonindependent territories of the world, local civil
society leaders began to organize independence movements to pressure for
greater influence over local policy. The basic tenets of a systemic peace begin
to emerge at this time in conjunction with a shift in thinking away from globalism, the expansion of unilateral, and necessarily instrumental (coercive),
authority across the globe and toward globalization, the integration of social
units into a dynamic global system.

The two major, enduring accomplishments of systemic peacemaking in the
emerging era of globalization are the United Nations organization and the
largely negotiated end of the colonial world system. These accomplishments,
however, were largely overshadowed by the residual culture of globalism
driven by insecurities, empowered by the advent of nuclear weapons, and

manifested in a cold war competition between ideological camps threatening mutually assured destruction and empowering war makers in the newly independent states of the world by proxy. And, as a result, war quickly regained its predominance and, once again, defined peace in the emerging era of globalization. While *cold war* defined peace in the more developed regions of the world, *hot wars* defined peace in the less developed regions. This led to uneven development in systemic peacemaking as peacemakers attempted to constrain war makers in the more powerful states while struggling to formulate responses to the proliferation of wars in the less powerful states.[12] At the end of the cold war in the early 1990s, if we discount the more powerful democratic peace states of the global West, over one-third of the remaining (lesser developed) countries were embroiled in major episodes of warfare during the peak year (46 of 136 countries in 1992); nearly two-thirds had experienced some form of major warfare (usually civil warfare) at some time during the cold war period (92 of 139 countries; 41 countries experienced 10 or more years of warfare); and almost one-quarter of all country-years from 1946 to 1992 were marked by warfare (1,077 of 4,701 country-years).[13] Peacemakers, though active and enfranchised within the new historical record, were clearly overwhelmed by the imperatives of war-ending and the attendant humanitarian concerns of the cold war system. More generally, systemic development was severely constrained; third world dependency was simply an epiphenomenal outcome of the third world war.

What the new historical record does provide empirical researchers is a broader, less biased, more detailed, and more comprehensive tool for expanding knowledge and developing more meaningful understandings of the relationships between peace and war and the societal and systemic conditions that may increase the risks of warfare. Foremost among the risks for the onset of warfare is the general lack of societal development in a particular societal system; this risk is increased substantially when that lesser developed societal system is situated regionally among other lesser developed societal-systems (the bad neighborhood effect). Directly related to the risks of warfare in lesser developed societal systems is their proclivity to adopt autocratic forms of governance as the most readily attainable method by which to establish and enforce a social order. Autocratic governance regimes enforce a public order through the threat and selective use of violence against the leadership of oppositional constituent groups. This dependence on the instrumental enforcement of public order intimidates and subordinates civil society to the will and agenda of the autocratic regime and, in so doing, institutionalizes a polarization or factionalization of society into ruling and ruled groups that is further fortified by systematic discrimination against out-groups.[14] Periodic outbursts of political violence reinforce the conditions of lesser development by impeding progress or negating development initiatives, leading to what I have elsewhere called a "syndrome of 'societal underdevelopment' or *arrested development*."[15] Most importantly, research conducted using the new historical record has strongly confirmed systemic linkages among congruent qualities of governance, conflict, and societal (physical and human capital) development and among increasingly interconnected societal-system units comprising regional and global societal systems during the emerging era of globalization.[16] The war system is an integrated and mutually reinforcing set of systemic conditions in which the risks of war are reproduced by the dynamic logic of the system itself.

A new phenomenon emerged as a consequence of the cold war rivalry between the superpowers: the protracted social conflict that often persisted for decades due to the globalization of the localized war effort (i.e., the infusion of foreign governmental and nongovernmental material, military, and humanitarian support that interfered with and largely negated the self-limiting nature of warfare; with continual, external logistic support, localized wars can persist in perpetuity).[17] Protracted conflicts presented peacemakers with an almost insurmountable new complication of the peace conundrum: the intractable conflict in which coercion thoroughly subordinates cooperation as the society's organizational and aspirational principle and, thus, frames the prospect of war ending as an immediate and vital threat to the perceived well-being and security of the perversely affected society. Protracted war creates war-dependent populations whose sole source of livelihood is linked to external assistance and for whom continuation of war best ensures that their livelihoods will remain undisturbed. Warfare comes to be viewed as little more than an occupational hazard.

Despite these system distortions, the prospect of nuclear annihilation progressively disarmed the war makers in the more powerful states during the cold war period, and the rising influence of the peacemakers gained precedence in global policy. In the late 1980s, the dark shroud of the cold war system was discarded.[18] As the shroud was lifted, however, the peacemakers were faced with the sheer magnitude of the immediate and cumulative effects of warfare on the global system. Even though the peacemakers had succeeded in shifting the peace agenda to the forefront of public policy, the imperatives of war ending easily eclipsed all other considerations. The demise of the cold war system heralded the beginning of the era of globalization and the emergence of the global system; however, the severity of the cold war system's legacy has preempted and seriously constrained the systemic peacemaking agenda. Still, my own measurements of the amelioration of the cold war legacy show a reduction by nearly half of the number of states experiencing major armed conflicts between 1991 and 2009 (46 to 25; 46.7%) and a diminution of the summed magnitudes of all armed conflicts in the world by well more than half (179 to 77; 57.0%), bringing them to their lowest levels in 50 years (1970 and 1964, respectively). Of the 46 states experiencing warfare in 1991, 18 were experiencing protracted conflicts that had been going on for at least 10 years in 1991, and, of these, 13 were ended with only 4 recurring.

As mentioned earlier, the ending of existing wars is a necessary but not sufficient condition for promoting systemic peace. Because wars are costly in resources, lives, and welfare, there is little rationale for making or continuing warfare when less costly alternatives to war are available. The strong empirical relationship between low levels of systemic development and high levels of collective violence can account for a large part of the problem: the full costs of war are not known, and the alternatives to war as a method for conflict resolution and social organization are not available to the lesser developed societies. Under conditions of low integration, low interactive networking, and low knowledge and skills, the emotive content of uncertainty, insecurity, and ambition inordinately conditions rationality and motivates collective action in favor of unilateral strategies that are necessarily predisposed toward the use of coercive or instrumental tactics. The uses of force further accentuate emotive and dissociative responses in both actor and target, seriously distorting and diminishing the social rationality of the affected populations in favor of more individualized forms of rationality, further impeding sociation, negotiation, and the implementation of conflict resolution schemes short of victory or loss in war (or the perversion of warfare as organized crime and predation). These adverse effects are probably not remediable, particularly in the more directly and seriously affected portions of the war population. The amelioration of the adverse effects of violence then becomes a generational strategy of assisting the affected society to favor the sociational efforts of the nonaffected portion against the instrumental proclivities of the affected portion of the population; this requires external administrative assistance, implementation assurances, and accountability guarantees.

War-ending efforts are an immediate requirement for systemic peace, but these must be followed by commitments to longer-term war-amelioration assistance—that is, helping the war-ravaged society recover its lost power. Of critical importance are the regulation of the abnormally high and persistent emotive content of the war-affected population(s) and systematic treatment of the worsened civil society deficits that contributed to the societal system's prewar risks for instability and warfare. These key systemic deficits are low integration, low interactive networking, and low knowledge and skills. Strengthening the capacity of the state to impose social control and infusing the economy with transfer payments as short-term fixes for a weak state are likely to further polarize rather than integrate the state and civil society. The state can grow to depend upon or even prefer external assistance payments to the internal taxation of civil society, which imply service obligations by the state to civil society. Likewise, coercing a poorly developed or divided society to adopt democracy is more likely to heighten rather than lessen the emotive content of postwar societies, because democratic process tends to politicize and mobilize the entire population, especially in conjunction with elections. Still, warending and war-amelioration efforts are necessary but not sufficient conditions for systemic peacemaking.[19]

The key findings for systemic peace that come from empirical research of the new historical record derive from the ability to engage in process tracing so that we include in our analyses interactive sequences and structural factors that condition both actionable decisions and policy implementation. This frees behavioral analysis from inappropriate reliance on causal inferences so that responsibility can be assessed and accountability assigned. By moving away from causal determination to probability scenarios, we develop fuller understandings not only of the relationship among structural attributes and behavioral outcomes (events) but also of the societal-system dynamics that unfold or diverge into problematic behavioral outcomes. Political events result from critical decisions that take place in the context of issue and policy streams that are

themselves conditioned by circumstances and influenced by the varied interests of multiple players. Particular outcomes cannot be considered predetermined or inevitable but continually (re)directable, malleable, or transformable.
Political processes may have critical or definitive moments, but the decisions
made at those moments are single instances in an interactive stream of decision points, any of which can alter the trajectory or attributes of the process. As
such, critical points are as much defined by subsequent outcomes as they may
be perceived to define those outcomes and so are very often not easily identifiable as critical when they are made but only as they gain clarity in hindsight—
that is, as they are perceived to be related to outcomes of interest. Additional
process streams may intersect to alter trajectories; even seemingly unrelated
process streams can converge and alter outcomes. Yet social processes are not
necessarily random walks. Patterns of regularized and standardized behaviors
are associated with learned and conditioned strategic action. Institutionalized societal systems are complex, dynamic networks that are predominantly ordered by regularized (regulated and socialized) processes but that
are also subject to random and nonregularized processes. No matter how well
we understand patterned behaviors, new patterns may emerge to confound
analysis. Both prediction and control can only be partial in complex societal
systems; institutionalized administrative and management procedures are key
to isolating problematic sequences for special attention. Conflict processes are
a natural corollary to collective action that, when managed and governed properly, will minimize system disruption and generate sympathetic energy to perpetuate or pressure adaptations and trigger innovations in the societal system
in response to changing circumstances. Improperly managed, conflict processes
can disrupt or even derail societal systems.

Conflict is both a social phenomenon and stimulus to action that stands at
the nexus between war and peace; it is the social dynamic that drives technological innovation and, thus, ultimately defines societal development and
evolution.[20] Over time, social rationality has evolved an apparently innate capacity to constrain the warriors' appetite for consuming peace and redirect
the raw, emotive energy of combat toward more constructive modes of cooperation and competition. Although historically conditioned by the state and
war, societal development can be seen to evolve independently from either the
state or war. Peace as a societal concept finds its greatest strength in its nearly
universal, rational, and positive emotional appeal. It is a linking concept that
emerges from the nexus of reason and spirituality to encourage and accentuate political communication across experiential and social distinctions. Peace
is necessarily at war with war in the social context, a war that must be fought
in perpetuity by peaceful means—that is, a systemic peace.[21] Systemic peace is
not defined by the transformation of war to a corresponding (relative or separate) peace but, rather, through a myriad of everyday actions that together
improve societal performance and the effective and efficient management of
social conflict. War is a form of institutionalized violent behavior that is neither a natural nor inevitable feature of societal systems; it is a learned, strategic issue that can only be understood and managed within its appropriate
systemic context, that is, systemically.[22] The adverse effects of warfare diffuse

through social networks and spill across geographical space; they are a systemic problem requiring a societal solution.

As proposed here, the end of the cold war system coincided with the maturing of the era of globalization, giving way to the advent of the nascent global system and greatly improving the prospects for systemic peace. Early evidence drawn from the post–cold war record supports this prognosis. As mentioned above, the number of states experiencing major armed conflict and the total summed magnitude of the societal impact of warfare in the global system decreased to about half their numbers by 2009 since their peak at end of the cold war period. Measuring the quality of governance in these same states over the same period, we chart a global shift toward greater democracy in the global system whereby the number of democracies has doubled and the number of autocracies has been cut by two-thirds.[23] Using a comprehensive, aggregate measure of state fragility based on our empirical findings regarding the key impediments to societal-system resiliency (i.e., the developmental capacity to effectively manage societal conflict without resort to violence) and applied to the same set of countries as the measures of warfare and governance, we report a 20 percent reduction in aggregated state fragility in the global system. The net reduction in state fragility was found to be distributed fairly evenly across five of six regional subsets of countries despite substantive differences in the regional mean state fragility scores across the five regions (the sixth region, the North Atlantic region comprising the states of the West, measured little or no state fragility across the period). Non-Muslim Africa and the Muslim countries are the most fragile regions in the nascent global system, whereas Latin America and the former Socialist regions are the least fragile of the five non-Western regions and show the greatest net and proportional reduction in state fragility since 1995.[24]

Most importantly, however, global trends in measures of the quality of governance show a doubling of the global numbers of "anocracies" that coincides with the end of the cold war and the general shift from an autocratic-dominant cold war system to a democratic-dominant global system; the high numbers of anocratic states remain fairly constant across the post–cold war period (about 50 countries; nearly one-third of all countries).[25] The risk models developed by the U.S. government's Political Instability Task Force (PITF) identify anocracies, and particularly factional anocracies, as having the highest risks of onsets of armed conflict and regime instability.[26] Given the predictive accuracy of the PITF models, we should expect a concomitant doubling in the onset of political instability events in the post–cold war period. In fact, the frequency of onset of new political instability events remains constant across the cold war and post–cold war periods, while the annual number of ongoing episodes of political instability decrease substantively over the post–cold war period (as does the number and magnitude of armed conflicts, already mentioned).[27] In a separate study focusing on the particular outcomes of factionalism, we find that cases of factionalism are far more likely to transition toward democracy in the post–cold war period than trigger an autocratic coup or an onset of armed conflict, as was the predominant outcome during the cold war period.[28] The evidence cited here clearly supports the proposition that the post–cold war period and the nascent global system are characterized, in general, by substantive and comprehensive state-level improvements in the quality of governance, effectiveness of conflict management, and societal-system development. Systemic peace appears to be both a plausible and feasible attribute of globalization.

KEY ELEMENTS OF SOCIETAL-SYSTEMS ANALYSIS AND SYSTEMIC PEACEMAKING

Systemic peace refers to the means rather than any particular end of social endeavor and so should be understood as a variable function of systemic peacemaking, which itself must be viewed as a complex, conflict management approach to public administration that necessarily situates conflict processes in their relevant and comprehensive circumstantial context and within the dynamic societal system, accounting for and factoring in essential elements of both time (past, present, and future) and space (physical and relational). Indeed, it is the societal content of social conflict that makes its particular manifestations both comprehensible and manageable. The scope and effectiveness of systemic peacemaking is at once an evolutionary function of social learning and innovation and a developmental function of societal organization. The quality of systemic peace can only be assessed by measuring system performance from a holistic perspective; differential patterns and qualities of performance factors across the system provide crucial information for refining and sustaining systemic peace. An appropriate measure of systemic peace is to gauge the extent to which conflict processes are managed without resort to force and, particularly, without the use of violence and warfare.[29] Systemic peacemaking is a humanist approach to understanding peace and security wherein civil society defines the state and peace defines war.

As discussed above, systemic peacemaking is critically informed by societal-systems analysis. Traditional notions of peacemaking are largely the product of the old historical record written by the states that have emerged as the victors in war; that record is necessarily biased toward nationalist perspectives and unilateralist conceptions of peaceful relations. Traditional notions of peace and, therefore, peacemaking are defined by war and the war-making prerogatives of the sovereign state and within which civil society is subordinated to the state. Traditional peacemaking generally remains latent until spurred to action by the onset of war and is charged with ending the war or ameliorating the adverse effects of warfare. Perspectives on the potential for a perpetually vigilant systemic peace were generated by the socio-technological advent of world war, total war, and genocide in the first half of the 20th century and the culmination of war system logic in the threat of nuclear annihilation. With the technologies of warfare directly challenging human civilization and the sovereign state's limited capacity to restrain emotive affect and control perceptions regarding the rational utility of limited warfare, neither the war system nor the old world order can command the unconditional subordination of an ever-expanding and diverse global civil society.

Empirical evidence of the new activism and initiatives of civil society elements are found in the dynamics of globalization, primarily in the dramatic expansion and integration of private enterprise (multinational corporations, global markets, foreign direct investment), private media (journalistic and scholarly reporting, data collection, and, particularly, the Internet), and nongovernmental organizations and associations. Cold war characterized the transition from traditional perspectives on peace to elemental visions of a systemic peace. Key elements and principles of a systemic peace were encapsulated in the Charter of the United Nations; the organizational basis for a systemic peace was pushed forward by the dismantling of the Eurocentric colonial world system and finally realized by the reintegration of the Socialist bloc countries into an emerging global system.[30] The end of the transition to systemic peace is signified by the end of the cold war and the beginning of the era of globalization.

The concept of systemic peace differs from traditional conceptualizations of peace mainly in regard to the proposition that there is a knowable and manageable system that operates in regularized ways that, in totality, defines the existential quality of peace. This proposition is less controversial when applied to relatively small and well-structured organizations; it becomes increasingly controversial when applied to states, regions, and the world as a whole. Yet systems logic and systems analysis are increasingly recognized and embraced in the biosciences as essential aspects of learning, management, and treatment in organic systems. The term *system* did not enter the lexicon of Western political science until the mid-1960s and, then, only in reference to the inner workings of the Western state.[31] Neo-Marxist analysis brought about the concept of the modern world system by way of its critique of the continuing economic exploitation of the former colonial territories in the mid-1970s and neo-realists responded with reference to an anarchical world system in which a minimal pecking order of relative military capabilities conditioned relations among states.[32] At about the same time, neo-idealists began referring to increasing interdependence and interconnectedness among states in a world community or international society.[33] Scholars were beginning to acknowledge fundamental changes in the nature and quantity of interactions within world politics, but, to this day, many remain uncomfortable with or hostile to any claim that the density, regularity, and diversity of interactions, transactions, and communications constitutes the basis of an operational global system, despite the mushrooming of international intergovernmental and nongovernmental organizations and regulatory regimes. The end of the cold war appears to have stimulated consideration of the applicability of systems analysis in political science and public policy. However, statist approaches continue to be predominant in the early years of the 21st century and are unlikely to be supplanted by postmodern alternatives.[34]

A large part of the continuing reticence of scholars and analysts to consider systems approaches to political and policy studies is the difficulty of factoring dynamic complexities, multiple layers and loci of influences and effects, and alternative strategic avenues of interactive sequences with probabilistic consequences into critical analyses. This is certainly an issue of concern that would be prohibitive if it were not for the information and computation technological revolutions that have exponentially expanded analytic capabilities since the 1980s. However, the analytic difficulty of factoring complexity may be overstated, or overimagined, as the ordering principles and institutionalized structures of societal systems, by the rational nature of their operationalization, simplify and regularize dynamic factors imparting discipline on societal complexity and channeling otherwise chaotic action into coherent and cohesive systems. Systemization supports analytic parsimony by standardizing and regularizing complex dynamics and systemic effects. For example, the U.S. government's Political Instability Task Force has analyzed a single mode of inquiry for over 15 years beginning in 1994, both extensively (using every available information resource) and intensively (using every known analytic technique), and found that a model with only four general, observable conditions can explain the onset of political instability in any country in the world during the contemporary period, 1955 to 2003, with a remarkable degree of accuracy (distinguishing cases of impending instability from cases of stability at better than 80%); these four conditions are the general qualities of regime governance and immediate neighborhood level of development and state-led political discrimination.[35]

In developing the societal-systems analytic approach, I have posited that all social organizations (i.e., social identity groups) are based on the same fundamental organizational structure and are differentiated primarily on their association with a shared interest in a unique circumstantial/environmental context.[36] Social identity groups (i.e., societal systems) are understood to be organic systems—that is, self-actuating, self-organizing, self-regulating, and self-correcting. Societal systems are organized by some combination of instrumental (coercive) and sociational (cooperative) forms of within-group organization and conflict management; societal-system development, then, is seen as a function of the group-specific shift in reliance away from instrumental toward sociational forms. Reliance on sociational forms (systemic power) can be measured by the numbers of associational ties (i.e., societal complexity) and interactional densities (i.e., societal networking). Complex societal systems have incorporated and integrated tens of thousands of diverse social identity groups with particular shared interests over time; group membership is nonexclusive, meaning that any individual can be a member of more than one group.[37] In contrast, the system's reliance on instrumental forms can be measured by the numbers and magnitudes of potential and actual demonstrations of political violence and state repression. Within-group organizational strategies are independent from relations (potential organizational strategies) with other, nonintegrated groups; however, group associational disposition and potential are conditioned both by its within-group experiences and its prior interactions with out-groups (i.e., level of societal-system development and circumstantial history).[38]

Societal-systems analysis, then, is primarily concerned not with the specifics of what group members are doing or what they have produced at any point in time but rather with the group's capabilities and capacities for effective conflict management; this activity is associated mainly with the societal elite or protostate but is a function of the quality of development of the societal system as a whole (i.e., civil society). Obviously, this brief introduction is not intended to explain societal-systems analysis in detail but to convey the idea that complex systems can be understood and their performance can be monitored in standardized ways in which potential problems can be identified and treated in order to increase the probability of forestalling unwanted outcomes (here defined as conflict management in the interests of greater system integration and warfare prevention). Effective conflict management improves system efficiency mainly by limiting system atrophy and destruction and dampening the emotive content of conflict interaction associated with the resort to force.

The societal-systems approach to systemic peacemaking is primarily concerned, then, with systemic development—that is, the incremental process of transforming general system reliance from instrumental to sociational forms of conflict management—from enforcement to compliance norms. This approach is necessarily concerned with lessening differences in societal development across constituent units populating the global system to increase complementarity and thereby improve political integration. These systemic propositions do not imply advocacy of particularist values, such as egalitarianism or wealth redistribution; the principal implication is that societal systems have the right to free systemic association and the creative expression of societal values and goals. Systemic peacemaking does demand open information, an active and informed civil society, and broad and consistent engagement in conflict management initiatives directed at ameliorating the residual effects of the war system (i.e., ending current and preventing impending wars and assisting in the recovery of war-affected societal systems). The political economy of conflict management is determined by two principles, time-dependent economic functions of conflict processes: the exponential increase in the social costs of conflict management and the exponential decrease in the probability of successful conflict resolution over the course of a social conflict process.[39] The onset of violence marks the intersection of these two principle economic functions and signifies the point of diminishing returns on societal investments in that process. Efficient conflict management must act proactively to resolve conflict processes without resort to violence.[40] Systemic conflict management strategy avoids donor fatigue by avoiding the creation of aid dependencies through the proactive distribution of learning and application technologies and creative responsibilities to members of affective units to accomplish societal-system development according to local needs and aspirations.

The age of empires that dominated world politics for the past five millennia reached its natural, systemic crescendo with the "century of world wars" and must be abandoned to history. Systemic security during this formative period was determined largely by pervasive ignorance and uncertainty that came to define a national security approach to societal relations. Politics in the coming millennia will necessarily be determined by systemic complexity that will necessitate an age of empirics that will inform a human security platform for the management of global relations. Globalization, then, should be understood as a systemic process of self-actuation, self-organization, self-regulation, and self-correction for the emerging global societal-system. The challenges posed by complexity in a globalized societal-system encompassing more than six billion people can be overwhelming in and of themselves and have become even more so as they interact with the existential limits of the global ecosystem.

What has become clear is that the states comprising the global system can no longer afford to spend and invest their limited resources in the continuation of the man-made ecological disasters that are the essence of authoritarianism and war. If we accept that the phenomena of autocratic rule and warfare evolved as a circumstantial, societal response to promote and protect greater organization and development under the constraints of ignorance and uncertainty, then we must acknowledge that future organization and development must proceed under the more effective and efficient auspices of peaceful conflict management enabled by knowledge, communication, and system dynamics. Systemic peacemaking became possible with the general renunciation of war as *politics by other means* and the embrace of democratic governance.[41] Effective systemic peacemaking will require an irreversible shift in policy priorities away from the current emphasis on instrumentalities of force toward the promotion of efficient system management and effective humanitarian response to the real vulnerabilities of societal-systems to the complexities posed by natural, rather than man-made, boundaries and disasters.

NOTES

1. Excerpted from "A Christmas Sermon on Peace," delivered by Martin Luther King Jr. at the Ebenezer Baptist Church and broadcast by the Canadian Broadcasting Corporation on December 24, 1967.

2. Circumstantial empiricism emphasizes the importance of contextual factors in the examination and comprehension of social outcomes. See Muzafer Sherif, "A Theoretical Analysis of Individual-Group Relationship in a Social Situation," in *Concepts, Theory, and Explanation in the Behavioral Sciences*, ed. G. J. DiRenzo (New York: Random House, 1966) for an early treatment of the issue and Jared Diamond, *Guns, Germs, and Steel: The Fates of Human Societies* (New York: W. W. Norton, 1997) for a more recent elaboration.

3. Relative peace encompasses the notions of *cold war*, a term coined by George Orwell in 1945 to describe a collective, passive-aggressive response associated with (nuclear) deterrence (Orwell, "You and the Atomic Bomb," *Tribune*, October 19, 1945) and *cold peace*, coined by Brazilian diplomat Achille Bonitto Oliva in 1952 in reference to the tensions resulting from competing interests between the more developed societies of the global north and the less developed societies of the global south. Separate peace is closely related to Johan Galtung's notion of negative peace, where an absence of war is made effective by the separation or lack of relations between social groups (Galtung, "An Editorial," *Journal of Peace Research* 1, no. 1, 1964).

4. See, for example, I. William Zartman, *Ripe for Resolution: Conflict and Intervention in Africa* (New York: Oxford University Press, 1989). Victory in war is always relational (the victor emerges only in relation to the vanquished); while both victor and vanquished bear the extreme costs of warfare, the victor is relatively better off than the vanquished, and both are absolutely worse off than they had been prior to the war.

5. See, especially, Hannah Arendt's essay differentiating between power and violence in human social relations: "Violence can destroy power; it is utterly incapable of

creating it" (Arendt, "On Violence," *Crises of the Republic,* San Diego: Harcourt Brace Jovanovich, 1969, 155).

6. The first treaty among states to renunciate the right of states to make war was promulgated on August 27, 1928, as the General Treaty for the Renunciation of War (otherwise known as the Pact of Paris or the Kellogg-Briand Pact). Most importantly, this principle became a core precept of the Charter of the United Nations, signed on June 26, 1945.

7. Only in its most simple form can war be viewed as the result of a single declaratory decision. Wars are generally not declared but rather are the result of a series of political decisions in an interactive process. See John A. Vasquez, *The War Puzzle* (Cambridge, MA: Cambridge University Press, 1993).

8. See Bruce Bueno de Mesquita, *The War Trap* (New Haven, CT: Yale University Press, 1981) for a compelling treatment of the conditional rationality of war making by powerful states. See also Ted Robert Gurr, "War, Revolution, and the Growth of the Coercive State," *Comparative Political Studies* 21 (1988), 45–65, for a lucid argument for why victory in warfare entrenches a predisposition to war making in the leadership of states.

9. Franz Fanon, *The Wretched of the Earth* (New York: Grove Press, 1963) presents one of the more successful early attempts to bring the perspectives of the vanquished into the historical record. Karl Marx had earlier articulated a theory to explain the subordination of civil society to the war-making state.

10. See Richard A. Falk and Samuel S. Kim, *The War System: An Interdisciplinary Approach* (Boulder, CO: Westview Press, 1980). Critical reflection on the impetus to and conduct of war was given powerful public exposure with the Nuremberg trials of the major (German) war criminals held from November 20, 1945, through October 1, 1946, when Nazi Germany's surviving leaders were tried for crimes against peace, war crimes, and crimes against humanity.

11. Civil society in the United States, due to that country's geographical isolation from the European war system, was not traditionally subordinated to the state by a history of warfare with rivals. The principle of civilian control over the military is embodied in the U.S. Constitution, particularly Art. 1 sec. 8 and Art. 2 sec. 2.

12. Adverse public reaction to the world's first televised war taking place in Vietnam in the late 1960s combined with the nonviolent civil rights movement in the United States and anticolonialist sentiments to consolidate a systemic peacemaking agenda and elevate peacemakers into the public eye through mass media attention. Most civil wars in third world countries were largely dismissed as proxy wars between the world's superpowers. Public recognition of the breadth and severity of these wars came about only after the end of the Cold War; see Monty G. Marshall, *Third World War: System, Process, and Conflict Dynamics* (Lanham, MD: Rowman & Littlefield, 1999).

13. The democratic peace proposition is based upon the observation that "absence of war between democracies comes as close to anything we have to an empirical law in international relations." Jack Levy, "The Diversionary Theory of War: A Critique," in *Handbook of War Studies,* ed. M. Midlarsky (Boston: Unwin Hyman, 1989, 240). Democracies are not immune to civil warfare, however, and do make war with nondemocracies. Figures for warfare in states during the cold war period are derived from the Major Episodes of Political Violence, 1946–2009, dataset posted on the Center for Systemic Peace website (www.systemicpeace.org/inscr/inscr.htm, accessed on December 29, 2010).

14. See Jack Goldstone, Robert H. Bates, David L. Epstein, Ted Robert Gurr, Michael Lustik, Monty G. Marshall, Jay Ulfelder, and Mark Woodward, "A Global Model

for Forecasting Political Instability," *American Journal of Political Science* 50, no. 1 (2010): 190–208.

15. Marshall, *Third World War*, 146.

16. See Monty G. Marshall and Benjamin R. Cole, *Global Report 2009: Conflict, Governance, and State Fragility* (Arlington, VA: Center for Global Policy, George Mason University, and Center for Systemic Peace, 2009), www.systemicpeace.org/Global Report 2009.pdf.

17. See Edward E. Azar, Paul Jareidini, and Ronald McLaurin, "Protracted Social Conflict: Theory as Practice in the Middle East," *Journal of Palestinian Studies* 8 (1978): 41–60, and Edward E. Azar, *The Management of Protracted Social Conflict: Theory and Cases* (Aldershot, UK: Dartmouth Publishing Company, 1990).

18. The claim by the war makers in the West that the cold war ended in the military victory by the West is, at once, characteristic rhetoric and an absurd notion. The claim has, at least temporarily, rationalized popular support for maintaining the war system in the West. The global war on terrorism has, in many respects, supplanted the cold war rationale and places tangible limits on the influence of the peacemakers over public policy.

19. To be clear, I argue that the only legitimate use of force is to neutralize the perceived rational utility of force in political relations as explicitly prescribed in law. Marshall, *Third World War*, p. 14.

20. See, Lewis A. Coser, *The Functions of Social Conflict* (New York: Free Press, 1956).

21. Systemic peace, then, relates to Galtung's "positive peace" emphasizing interaction and integration of social groups but takes that notion a step further by proposing a proactive, holistic (multilevel) approach to peacemaking emphasizing complex societal-systems analysis and systemic conflict management functions. See also Immanuel Kant's 1795 essay "Perpetual Peace." Societal-systems analysis and an agenda for systemic peace are detailed in Marshall, *Third World War*, chapter 7.

22. As point of clarification, I argue that the impetus to violence is an inherent and thereby inevitable feature of the individuation process in the societal context, which characterizes systemic sociopaths and isolates and insulates them instrumentally from sociational pressures. The management of personal violence requires tactics that dissuade, dampen, deter, or contain violent impulse to minimize its influence on collective action. Collective violence, on the other hand, is a societal phenomenon that critically depends on social organization, which is fundamentally amenable to alternative management techniques and initiatives. Marshall, *Third World War*, chapter 3.

23. Marshall and Cole, *Global Report 2009*, 3–13. Measures of the quality of governance refer to the POLITY score produced by the Polity IV Project at the Center for Systemic Peace under the direction of the author of this study.

24. Monty G. Marshall and Benjamin R. Cole, "State Fragility Index and Matrix 2009" (www.systemicpeace.org/SFImatrix2009c.pdf, accessed December 30, 2010).

25. Anocracies are regimes with inconsistent or incoherent authority structures that combine autocratic and democratic modes of societal order or control. They may be considered alternatively as incomplete democracies, weak autocracies, or transitory regimes.

26. Goldstone et al., "A Global Model for Forecasting Political Instability."

27. Based on an analysis of the PITF State Failure Problem Set datasets posted on the Center for Systemic Peace website (www.systemicpeace.org/inscr, accessed December 30, 2010).

28. Monty G. Marshall and Benjamin R. Cole, "A Macro-Comparative Analysis of the Problem of Factionalism in Emerging Democracies," paper delivered at the annual meeting of the American Political Science Association, August 29, 2008, Boston.

29. This is also a standard measure of the quality of democratic governance.

30. Marshall, *Third World War,* chapter 1.

31. See David Easton, *A Framework for Political Analysis* (Englewood Cliffs, NJ: Prentice Hall, 1965).

32. Immanuel Wallerstein, *The Modern World-System I: Capitalist Agriculture and the Origins of the European World-Economy in the Sixteenth Century* (New York: Academic Press, 1974) and Kenneth N. Waltz, *Theory of International Relations* (New York: Random House, 1979). Waltz's theory was simply an updating of the basic classic precepts of the 17th-century Westphalian state system codifying the distribution of power in Europe following the Thirty Years War.

33. See, for example, Robert O. Keohane and Joseph S. Nye, *Power and Interdependence: World Politics in Transition* (Boston: Little, Brown, 1977) and Hedley Bull, *The Anarchical Society: A Study of Order in World Politics* (New York: Columbia University Press, 1977).

34. Societal-systems analysis proposes the state as the organizational and managerial component of any and every societal system. The integration of simple and lesser societal systems into complex and greater societal systems is accomplished through the articulation and recognition of what Muzafer Sherif has called "superordinate goals"; see *In Common Predicament: Social Psychology of Intergroup Conflict and Cooperation* (Boston: Houghton Mifflin, 1966). The coherence and cohesion of complex societal systems is predicated upon intersystem complementarity or symbiosis; this principle has been termed *subsidiarity,* wherein organizational management functions in complex systems should be guided by the most appropriate, competent authority in the system, usually the unit closest to the issue that enjoys comprehensive information and influence over policy outcomes. Subsidiarity is a natural, organizational corollary to accountability.

35. Goldstone et al, *A Global Model for Forecasting Political Instability.*

36. This organizational universality is an existential property in groups of statistically significant size: at least 100 members.

37. It is proposed that system resilience is a dynamic function of multiple-group identifications of system members and the general complementarity of group interests (i.e., associational ties and interaction densities of societal networks).

38. Marshall, *Third World War,* chapter 3.

39. See Figure 3.15 in Marshall, *Third World War,* 101, for a graphic depiction of the political economy of conflict management.

40. Legitimate enforcement of a formalized rule of law system should be considered the final arbiter of a conflict process; the use of force initiates violence into the process and must be considered a nonlegitimate resolution technique. The selective suspension of a societal-systemic interaction (optional play) is a superior strategy to the use of force in protracted conflict processes; see Marshall, *Third World War,* chapter 6.

41. See, Marshall and Cole, *Global Report 2009.* See also, Monty G. Marshall, "The Measurement of Democracy and the Means of History," *Social Science and Modern SOCIETY* 48, no. 1 (2011): 24–35; and Monty G. Marshall, "The New Democratic Order: Complex Societal-Systems and the 'Invisible Hand,'" *Harvard International Review* 33 no. 1 (2011): 95–106.

CHAPTER 42

Theories of Change in Peacemaking

Christopher Mitchell

On the one hand, the axiom can refer to the underlying contradictions that led to the dispute in the first place—the conflict that is initially caused by threatened values or by unfulfilled basic human needs. Sandole (1999) has referred to these as *start-up conditions* which, if left unaddressed, can get the rivalry, the hostility, the coercive behavior, and, ultimately, the violence going in the first place. On the other hand, *cause* can be used to describe factors that keep a conflict going over time and frequently lead to its intensification in terms of the damage done to the adversaries and their environment. Sandole talks about these as conditions for *continuation*, and they often present the most immediate difficulties in any peacemaking efforts.

Viewed in a slightly different manner, factors associated with cause in the first sense result in a conflict being *intractable*, because it is not over trivialities; those in the second sense lead to the conflict becoming *protracted* or to conflict perpetuation.

The dual nature of conflict causation demands from the field of conflict analysis and resolution somewhat different concepts, ideas, and theories to inform practical efforts to make peace and end a conflict. There are different answers to the questions "What changes are necessary in what, so that the patterns of coercion, hostility, and violence can be replaced by those of cooperation and trust?" and "What changes are needed to remove an inherent and fundamental incompatibility in goals, values, or needs?" As Burton (1988) has argued, the first query leads in the direction of settlement—to compromise, accommodation, and behavioral adaptation. The second and more difficult question leads to the holy grail of win-win solutions: final resolution and perhaps to the transformation of the relationship between erstwhile adversaries.

This chapter deals mainly with the concepts and theories that have arisen in the field to help bring about significant changes in the way adversaries and enemies behave toward one another, thus helping initial understanding of the causes of conflict perpetuation through coercion and violence—what causes conflicts to protract. I leave aside the whole issue of intractability and deep-rooted conflicts' resistance to final resolution, partly because this question requires much more concentrated and creative thought than has been devoted to questions of what makes conflicts continue beyond the point at which any rational observer would assume they should, logically, come to an end.

THEORIES ABOUT CHANGING MINDS: TIMING AND APPROPRIATE CONDITIONS

One of the first attempts to consider systematically the question of what changes are needed to move protracted conflicts in the direction of successful peacemaking and away from the simple repetition of coercive interaction was Zartman's work on the theory of ripeness. Central to Zartman's approach, which he summarized as an issue of "appropriate timing," was the idea that necessary change had to take place in the minds of enough key decision makers within the adversaries to enable a search for alternative strategies to begin. Basing his initial formulation on the empirical study of five successful peacemaking processes in Africa, Zartman (1989) characterized the essential change as being a movement from a mindset concerned with winning to one in which an alternative strategy of negotiation came to predominate. Initially, he argued that this change could come about through a recognition that both the parties to a conflict had arrived at a costly, hurting stalemate, in which no party had any prospect of winning and both were facing increasingly heavy losses from continuing the struggle. If this situation were to be accompanied by a looming catastrophe, which threatened to increase costs even more steeply to both, then this would also increase the likelihood that the necessary change in the minds of involved leaders would take place.

In this and subsequent works, Zartman (2000) and other writers elaborated the idea of ripeness and added to the list of factors that would increase the likelihood that a change of mind would take place. Some suggested that pressure from allies might have a similar effect (Stedman 1991); others that offers of disinterested help from third parties could open a window to the possibility of a peaceful, compromise settlement; still others that change could be brought about by the recognition of one set of leaders that what Kelman (1995) has described as "a viable negotiating partner" did, in fact, exist on the other side despite widespread belief to the contrary among rival domestic elites and rank and file followers. In Zartman's own words, quoted elsewhere in this volume, leaders came to see that "a negotiated solution is possible for the searching and that the other party shares that sense and the willingness to search too" (Zartman 2000, 228).

One researcher who has adopted a yet more flexible approach to the idea of alternative sets of factors that can bring about changes that could lead to negotiations—or, at least, a readiness to consider negotiating and an end to violent struggle—is psychologist Dean Pruitt. In a number of case studies (including one in this volume), Pruitt (2005, 2007a) has extended some of Zartman's ideas about what can bring about significant change. Originally entitling his approach "readiness theory," Pruitt argues that it is best to treat the causal factors in ripeness theory as variables rather than states and to accept that circumstances can arise in which one of the adversaries is experiencing a greater level of hurt than the other—an imbalance of distress that can change over time. In other words, while ripeness implies the need of equal hurt—and a looming catastrophe for both—far more often, one side will be more ready to consider an alternative than will the other. In a later extension of his theory, which he terms *urgency theory,* Pruitt (2011) combines variables that arise from the cost side of the conflict relationship with more optimistic ideas, including beliefs that some on the other side actually have the capacity to alleviate the hurt and minimize risks, the willingness to do this, and the capability of having any negotiated agreement accepted by their own rank-and-file followers.

It should be noted that in both versions of Pruitt's theories about change, the factors enabling a change of mind, and hence a change of strategy, are mainly psychological—a sense of pessimism about the current situation, a series of beliefs about the other side and its capacities and capabilities, an increasing consciousness of risk, plus a sense of optimism about the changed state of mind of rival decision makers. This approach does alter the focus of enquiry somewhat from what brings about change to who needs to change for peacemaking even to begin.

THEORIES OF CHANGING LEADERS

Among the most familiar approaches to the issue of why policies change is the time-honored tradition that involves the need to change those who are responsible for the conduct of a policy. Old leaders do not make peace, so the argument goes: new leaders must come to power and then they make peace. Many historical examples seem to bear out this conventional wisdom. The Bolsheviks come to power in Russia in 1917 and—admittedly reluctantly—sign the Treaty of Brest Litovsk. A year later, the imperial regime in Germany is overthrown, and a new civilian government concludes an armistice and then swallows the *diktat* of the Versailles Treaty. The Fascist regime in Italy is replaced in 1943; Il Duce is arrested and Italy changes sides to join the Allies.

Other cases, however, seem to support the reverse argument. Hitler and the Nazis stay in power until the bitter end, resulting in the wreck of Nazi Germany and eventual unconditional surrender. The case of Japan in 1945 gives pause to an uncritical acceptance of the old maxim. The same Japanese leadership did make a harsh peace with the Allies, even though there was much internal opposition from those who wanted to delay negotiations until the final battle on Japanese soil had been fought. More recently, existing governments in countries as different as El Salvador, the United Kingdom, Guatemala, and Indonesia have entered successfully into negotiations for peace with their own insurgents.

Such examples do make the point that it is not always necessary to change the leadership in order to change strategy in the direction of conflict resolution—existing leaders can change their minds, change direction, and seek a negotiated peace, but this is by no means easy. In one of the rare books written during the 20th century on the subject of changing a strategy of coercion to one of conversation, Fred Iklé (1971) remarked that the decision to seek peace as opposed to carrying on the struggle is one of the most difficult any set of leaders can confront. The results of facing such a dilemma—to continue or to quit—can result in major splits within any existing set of leaders as some change their minds while others adhere to the existing course of action. Such circumstances can result in the replacement (or physical elimination) of individual leaders or of an entire elite group, and its substitution by a pro-peace faction. They can result in an internal power struggle involving hawks and doves and a dynamic internal process that inevitably complicates strategy for the other side, uncertain about whom they should be dealing with, who can be trusted, and who can deliver on promises. Facing the prospect that one's country may be approaching the bitter end of a struggle can and often does bring about huge internal changes within an adversary. Even if one continues to take the approach to the issue of what needs to change that focuses on the perceptions, beliefs and aspirations at the level of individuals, the question remains: Who needs to change?

1. Key leaders
2. Elite groups of decision takers and opinion makers
3. Rank-and-file followers

Clearly, and despite the argument that successful peacemaking has to be a multilevel process involving leaders and those who are led, key decision makers must change in some manner if a peace process is to start and then continue toward an agreement. It is rare that individual leaders can, completely on their own, effect a total reversal of policy from high-level coercion to talks about talks and then to negotiations. Even the most charismatic leader needs advice and information. Perhaps one of the best examples of a leader almost single-handedly conceiving of a peace strategy and seeing it through in the teeth of strenuous, lethal, opposition would be President de Gaulle determining for himself and against his personal wishes that the armed struggle in Algeria could not be won through military means—no matter how (relatively) effective; then devising an alternative strategy leading to negotiation with the leaders of the National Liberation Front (Front de Libération Nationale, or FLN); and carrying such a peace policy through, despite the often violent opposition of domestic political rivals, of the community of over a million *colons* in Algeria, and of strong elements of the French military.

More usually, of course, the responsibility for seeking peace is a collective one, and a network of leaders can join together to change strategy and seek peace through negotiation rather than through victory. The ending of the nationalists' struggle in Northern Ireland in 1998 came about not through the efforts of a replacement set of Irish Republican Army (IRA) doves but from changes in the aspirations and expectations of some of those who, for years, had led the armed struggle against the continuation of British rule in the province—Gerry Adams, Martin McGinnis, and Mitchell McLoughlin. This group of previously committed hawks had to steer a new strategy through the bitter opposition of many other key leaders within the leadership of Provisional Sinn Fein and the IRA Army Council. Similar struggles between "hands-uppers" and "bitter-enders" (the labels put on Boer leaders advocating negotiations and those advocating fighting on against the British) can be witnessed within the FMNL (The Farabundo Martí National Liberation Front) over seeking a negotiated peace in El Salvador and between ETA-*politico* and ETA-*militar* (Euskadi Ta Askatasuna) in the Basque country over striking a negotiated deal with the Spanish government.

In recent years, this issue has been discussed as involving *spoilers*, a somewhat misleading title that has been applied to the members of an elite set of leaders who favor continuing the struggle to victory. The literature on spoilers is diverse and has yet to produce testable theories about the circumstances in which spoilers succeed in keeping the violence going by sabotaging plans for negotiations or undermining agreements concluded against their interests. At present, writers seem to be at the stage of classifying types of spoilers and speculating about their likely level of determination and their potential success levels in wrecking peace processes—or sell outs, as such processes undoubtedly appear to the spoilers themselves. In his initial formulation of the spoiler problem, Steven Stedman (1997) suggested analyzing the process according to whether new pro-peace factions found themselves facing "limited," "greedy," or "total" spoilers, while a later formulation drew an interesting distinction between "insider" and "outsider" spoilers (Zahar 2008). John Darby (2001) suggested that spoilers could be divided into "dealers," "mavericks," "opportunists," or "zealots." Both Stedman's and Darby's typologies were based on the possibilities for making a deal with various kinds of spoilers and on the tactics for outmaneuvering them by the doves. Darby's suggestion was that the lowest chances were those available to pro-peace factions facing spoilers of the zealots or total variety.

Much less attention has been paid to the question of why some elite factions do not change but remain faithful to their original goals and objectives while others changed and sought other means, even while maintaining their original, long-term goals. Who remain zealots and why? What might cause any elite faction to change and become dealers—or spoilers with limited rather than extreme goals? Do dealers ever go back to becoming zealots, and in what circumstances? All of these questions demand much more careful research.

The literature on spoilers seems mainly concerned with their behavior—steadfast, flexible, or unreliable—of elite leadership factions, but less systematic attention has been paid to the question of how the aspirations of rank-and-file followers—public opinion, domestic audiences, mass supporters, the street—can be changed in favor of negotiation in the short term, or of peace and compromise in the long term. This is by no means a trivial issue, especially when large numbers of people who have been bombarded with reasons for fighting and fighting on in the past are now required to accept a negotiation process that will undoubtedly produce an outcome short of well-deserved victory. Mass rejection has undermined numerous negotiation possibilities as well as initialed agreements, from the mass protests by Protestant Unionists against the 1974 Sunningdale Agreement to the rejection by both Israeli and Palestinian "streets" of the elite-level agreements arising from the Oslo process in the mid-1990s.

It is often as difficult to change the minds of enough supporters to enable a peace process to start up or to continue as it is to sell a less-than-victorious agreement to a public that has been told for some time that victory is just around the corner or that there is light at the end of the tunnel. On the other hand, it has often been the case in the past that once a community or a whole society has reached the point of extreme war weariness, they will give support to anyone who promises to lead them out of the cycle of violence and counter-violence, no matter what the hawkish section of the elite continue to promise will be the result of one last heave. In the late 1950s and early 1960s, the weariness of the French people with the continuing colonial struggle in Algeria and their abandonment of the perception that Algeria was really part of France enabled General de Gaulle to face down the most ferocious opposition from the settler population of Algeria and to start serious negotiations with the FLN. Anecdotal evidence indicates that such large changes in public mood often enable pro-peace elite factions to capitalize on the changes and start a search for a way out of such quagmires. On the other hand, there are many examples of established elites resisting growing antiwar sentiments and simply carrying on with the struggle despite its unpopularity. To some extent, unwillingness may be connected to the fact that a particular elite group of leaders may feel themselves trapped in a set of behavioral patterns that allows them no chance of an exit without unacceptable costs to their group.

THEORIES ABOUT CHANGING PROCESSES

The third manner in which change can contribute to the start of a peacemaking process, apart from changing minds and changing leaders, involves changes in behavior by one or both of the adversaries. As I have argued elsewhere (Mitchell 2006), one way of conceptualizing this necessary type of change is to frame it as a reversal of a number of common patterns of behavior that contribute to an increase in the scope and intensity of the conflict—in other words, that develop a conflict-intensifying dynamic.

Many years ago, Morton Deutsch (1973c) characterized such a relationship as adversaries being involved in a "malign conflict spiral." More commonly, the relationship is characterized as the end result of a process of escalation, which needs to be reversed if the parties involved are to move toward a negotiated peace. However, using the broad term *escalation* (and thus calling for *de-escalation* as necessary preliminary for successful peacemaking) conceals to some extent the complexity of such a reversal. At the very least, such major reversal involves the need to bring about change in a number of complex interlinked processes that contribute to the intensification—or at least the continuation—of any intractable conflict. Elsewhere (Mitchell forthcoming),

I have tried to delineate six of these conflict-intensifying dynamics that usually need to be reversed if a peace process is to have any chance of success. Clearly, one of the most important of these dynamics takes the form of the interchange of damaging, coercive, and usually violent actions aimed at the adversary with the idea of increasing the level of loss to the point where the other's leadership will give up. In this more limited sense of escalation—increased coercion and violence—it seems reasonable to argue that a change in the direction of de-escalation—decreases in cost-imposing activity—is a key behavioral change that needs to precede talks about talks—or even a recognition by some that Kelman's (1995) "viable and reasonable negotiating partner" exists on the other side.

A second equally important dynamic that needs to be altered involves the many changes that have occurred within combatant parties once a conflict has intensified and reached a protracted and intractable stage. Pruitt and Kim (2004) talk about this as *mobilization*—a complex process that involves, among other characteristics, the diversion of resources (time, effort, material) to the actual prosecution of the conflict through coercion; the focusing of information and attention on the conflict as the main, or even the sole, concern of the community; major efforts to establish and maintain unity of purpose and an absence of internal dissent within the embattled population; and a shift in the balance of influence within leadership circles to those directly concerned with the coercive prosecution of the conflict. *Demobilization* in this broad sense thus encompasses efforts to change all of these common intraparty factors as part of a peace process—which seems a pretty tall order, to say the least.

The same can be said about the need to reverse other dynamics that contribute to conflict perpetuation; *polarization* of relations between adversaries, whereby rivalry over one set of issues becomes a matter of constant opposition across a wider and wider range of issues, leading to local, regional, or even global confrontations or cold wars that can perpetuate over decades: *enlargement*, whereby other parties are drawn into a protracted conflict as patrons or allies, often complicating the original disagreements and introducing other issues into the mix, making the search for a peaceful solution more difficult and less likely; and *dissociation*, whereby the contact and communication processes between adversaries becomes attenuated and coarsened, often narrowing to accusation and counteraccusation or propaganda efforts intended to undermine the others' will to fight.

Equally complex in its nature and challenging in its requirements for reversal is the dynamic of *entrapment*—the process by which structural, political, economic, and psychological factors combine to make any kind of major change of course in the direction of a negotiated peace increasingly difficult. Through a variety of circumstances—investment of economic and human resources plus political reputation in the struggle, cultural norms and psychological commitments to success or to not backing down, the manner in which previous sacrifices (sunk costs) seem to increase the value of the goals being fought over, and the apparent absence of any graceful or low-cost exit from the conflict—elites become increasingly entrapped and see no alternative to continuing the struggle to the end, no matter how bitter this may turn out to be.

In summary, there is a need to reverse a number of common dynamics that exacerbate a conflict and to substitute processes that lead to those which assist in emplacing a benign spiral leading to talks and solutions:

Conflict Exacerbating	Conflict Mitigating
Escalation	De-escalation
Mobilization	Demobilization
Polarization	Amalgamation
Enlargement	Disengagement
Dissociation	Recommunication
Entrapment	Decommitment

Of all the dynamics that contribute to the continuation of a conflict that need to be reversed, demolishing a sense of entrapment through a process of de-commitment is the most crucial type of change needed, at least in the initial stage of any peace process. The question is how to achieve this in any practical sense, especially once elites have committed their country or community, their reputation, and themselves to a struggle involving much loss and sacrifice—the factors which, in themselves, become strong reasons for continuing.

THE ART AND PRACTICE OF DECOMMITMENT

Despite its central place in any strategy of starting peacemaking, the process of decommitment is lamentably lacking in conceptual clarity and theoretical understanding. It is generally accepted that, for parties in an intractable conflict, a strategy of making firm and credible commitments is a way of: (1) conveying to the other side that one is totally determined to use all means available to gain one's goals and continue on to victory; (2) to convey to one's followers that their effort and sacrifice is necessary to achieve success in the conflict; and (3) to convince any doubters that the leaders will never betray them or their aspirations in some compromise deal with adversaries characterized as untrustworthy and undeserving. As rallying cries, statements such as "There is no alternative," "No surrender," and "The choice is a suitcase or a coffin" (alternatives alleged by hardliners to confront French *colons* in Algeria) serve to mobilize support and resources and to silence doubt and potential opposition.

There is, of course, a major downside to the constant repetition of such statements that commit a party in an intractable conflict to continuing the struggle. By making it more difficult for leaders to change direction should circumstances require, high levels of commitment may help to make the conflict even more intractable. Elites become further entrapped by their own convictions and enmeshed by their own rhetoric. To be sure, there are various types of commitment and various levels of entrapment that make the obstacles to changing course somewhat less difficult to overcome. One of the reasons for any change in the direction of abandoning coercion by new leaders being easier is that the latter usually start with a clean slate. Newcomers can argue that they are not responsible for the commitments made by their often-discredited predecessors.

Commitments fall into a number of types, each presenting different kinds of obstacles to escape, should the desire to escape arise. Commitments can be addressed to different audiences. In some cases, commitments are mainly addressed internally to rank and supporters—to the mass followers whose own commitment to the struggle must be encouraged, partly through the belief that their leaders are equally committed. Others can be addressed to the adversaries to convince them of the leaders' determination to see the struggle through to a successful conclusion. Still others can be aimed at allies and patrons, who might need proof of the protagonists' steadfastness in the pursuit of shared aims.

Apart from the question of the main target of the commitment, some commitments can be very precise in the limitations they impose, while others are very broad and sweeping but also somewhat imprecise. Some can deal with things that will not be done, others with things that will continue to be done—or will be achieved at some future date. Some can be conditional ("We will continue the struggle until . . .") and others unconditional ("We will never, under any circumstances . . ."). Some can be made verbally either off the cuff on one occasion (George H. W. Bush's "No new taxes. Read my lips") or repetitively and by many leaders (the IRA's "Not a bullet not an ounce" of explosive to be surrendered), thus reinforcing their impact but also the difficulty of decommitment.

Probably the commitments that pose the most difficulty for leaders to abandon or modify are those that have been enshrined in documents—declarations, policy statements, sets of principles, charters, or constitutions. These can become formidable weapons, which factions seeking to continue can use to belabor and discredit those seeking change. The difficulties experienced by the pro-negotiation factions within the Palestine Liberation Organization (PLO) leadership in abandoning the commitment to the destruction of the state of Israel enshrined in the PLO constitution—and now in the founding documents of Hamas, including its charter—illustrate the limits imposed by such documentation. Another recent entrapping example involves the Lithuanian parliament's hasty formal declaration of independence from the Soviet Union in March 1990, which—firmly adhered to thereafter by the Lithuanians—precluded compromise and sparked off a major crisis in the Baltics and in other fringe areas of the Soviet empire. Sam Goldwyn may have been right in his pronouncement that "verbal agreements aren't worth the paper they are written on," (see Easton 1976, 150–155; Lipson 1991) but once commitments are formally enshrined in legal documents, they take on a (long) life of their own, most effectively binding the hands of future generations.

Imprecise and conditional commitments can allow leaders more opportunity for changing course than precisely delineated statements made without the possibility of arguing that they contain a loophole of modifying conditions. Absolute prohibitions limit absolutely. However, even apparently unbreakable and precisely delineated conditions might allow leaders to argue that particular commitments are not quite absolute. Different levels of commitment can be illustrated by a common dilemma that affects parties in an intrastate conflict when the incumbents state categorically—and often—that they will never open negotiations with "terrorists" until the latter have abandoned violence or laid down their arms or undertaken a genuine ceasefire. The second level of commitment—the laying down of arms—is unlikely to happen, as the arms usually appear to the insurgents to be the only means by which they have convinced the leaders of the other side that there are serious issues that must be addressed, plus the fact that retaining them is the "protection of last resort." Abandoning violence seems to offer opportunities for entrapped incumbents to argue that, at some point, their adversaries have made their own commitments to abandon violence if, in turn, certain other conditions come about. The third level of commitment, a ceasefire, certainly allows some debate about the nature of a "genuine" ceasefire, and while a temporary, bilateral ceasefire is always revocable, at the least it can be argued that it is genuine as long as it holds.

STRATEGIES AND TACTICS OF DECOMMITMENT

Unfortunately, much of the existing literature on how to avoid becoming entrapped in failing policies takes the form of anticipatory decisions made at the initiation of the commitment (see, e.g, Simonson and Staw 1992). Initially setting clear and agreed-upon limits on investments of time, effort, and resources is one common strategy, while distributing responsibility for the policy in question is another. A third involves the prior establishment of minimum target levels that, if not achieved, can act as opt-out points. However, while fine in theory, such strategies seem most applicable to commercial and industrial enterprises where decision makers face choices about terminating unambiguously loss-making projects. Prior, built-in checkpoints that enable a less-fraught withdrawal from a losing strategy seem to be a rarity in highly ambiguous enterprises, particularly protracted, socio-political conflicts. In such cases, the questions become: Are there any general patterns in the way in which leaders manage to change violent policies in the direction of peacemaking *well after* the initiation of the conflict? How can serious obstacles to change be overcome?

To a large degree, the kind of decommitment strategies necessary depend first on the nature of the commitment now seen by some to pose an obstacle. Second, change strategies can involve a minor adjustment or—with greater difficulty—a complete reversal of direction. One way of approaching this problem of strategies to avoid commitments that create obstacles to change is to consider the actual nature of the commitments—what they focus on. There seem to be at least three important foci for prohibition:

1. Commitments regarding values
2. Commitments regarding goals and outcomes
3. Commitments regarding strategies or tactics

At first, it seems to be the case that decommitting from the pursuit of specific goals—usually seen as the abandonment of an important prize, worthy of continuing sacrifice—is the most difficult type of commitment to give up or even modify. Objectives such as "a united Ireland," "independence for the Basque country," or "majority rule for Ruritania" seem to be unambiguous as well as unmodifiable.

However, there are a good number of historical examples of an embattled party abandoning specifically enunciated goals by arguing that the continued pursuit of those goals has turned out to undermine important national values, which can be supported by pursuing alternatives. This is often a difficult line of argument to present convincingly, unless it is avowed by a new leadership with little responsibility for previous policy, but it can be done. In the early years of the French Fifth Republic, President de Gaulle made much of the argument that a nonmilitary solution to the Algerian conflict short of independence—a negotiated association—was much more in keeping with the traditions of France as a great and civilized nation than a military victory over the ALN (Armée de Libération Nationale)—an argument that was generally accepted by the majority of people living in France, even if not by the *colon* community in Algeria itself.

Another strategy that enables pro-change leaders or factions to change radically current policies involves arguing that goals have not changed but that circumstances have changed so that the sure achievement of those goals can be attained by different tactics. Sometimes, such a change can be based on adopting a different time scale for success. A good example of this strategy of abandoning violent means arose for the nationalist movement in Northern Ireland during the 1990s, once the British government had irrevocably announced that it would not stand in the way of whatever choice the majority of people in the province might make regarding their future. This declaration enabled the IRA to abandon its commitment to armed struggle, to adopt a Totally Unarmed Strategy and to enter into negotiations—all of which could justifiably be based on the argument that, in the long run, demographics would produce a majority for union with the Irish Republic. This, it was argued, rather than the continuation of guerrilla violence, would lead to the defeat of the British and the Ulster Unionists and, ultimately, the achievement of the desired goal of Irish unity.

Both of these examples underline that at least one basic strategy for altering or abandoning commitments involves shifting the argument between levels. Decommitment can be achieved by reframing the debate about continuing or quitting as a choice that does not involve abandoning goals but by changing over to tactics that will achieve those goals. Alternatively, the argument can be made that change does not involve abandoning basic values, but it substitutes alternative goals that will fulfill values in other ways.

Other historical examples in which firm commitments to carry on the fight to the bitter end have been abandoned to suggest other principles upon which a strategy of decommitment can be based. Many fall into three basic categories, and pro-change factions often take up one of these lines of argument. They can:

Argue that Circumstances Have Changed Radically, Necessitating a Major Reconsideration of Current Policies

Arguments by pro-change factions that take up this basic idea are usually possible when a conflict has protracted and commitments made several years previously can be undermined as being out of date, given that circumstances have changed radically in the meantime. One common reason for contemplating a new policy is that the leadership has changed on the other side, so that an olive branch might have a better chance of success than in the past (Mitchell 2001). Alternatively, the adversary might have indicated a change of aspirations and expectation by a change in its own policy, as when the British government in the early 1990s announced through the secretary of state for Northern Ireland that it no longer had any "selfish interest" in the future of Northern Ireland and that the people there should determine their own future.

Apart from internal changes in the adversary, there is always the possibility that what might be termed *major tectonic changes* can take place in the international system whereby changes in one's policy can be justifiably considered and undertaken. The collapse of the Soviet Union had this effect on a wide variety of local and regional conflicts and freed up many sets of leaders from previous positions, policies, and commitments in places as far apart as Latin America, Africa, the Middle East, and Caucasia. In South Africa, the end of the Soviet Union meant that it became harder to view the African National Congress as an agent of international communism and easier to contemplate negotiations. It became somewhat easier for the conflict between Israelis and Palestinians to be viewed as a regional conflict rather than as an extension of the global cold war. Similar global upheavals are admittedly rare (the change in the 1970s from widely available cheap oil to the situation where demand outstripped supply might be another recent example), but when they do occur, many leadership factions are given the opportunity to make substantial changes.

Argue that New Information—that Could not Possibly Have Been Known Previously—Has Come to Light and Necessitates Policy Revision

This is a familiar decommitting tactic for incoming leaderships that have gained office by promising action that they now find difficult to execute. On many occasions, new leaders have abandoned previous firm commitments on the grounds that they did not know how serious things were until they actually entered office. This was a major justification offered by some among the Obama administration on taking over a shattered U.S. economy in January 2009 from the second Bush administration.

Apart from similar examples of breaking commitments to bring about change, new information can also be used to justify the abandonment of current and long-supported policies, even by incumbents responsible for those policies. Such justifications for abandoning previously firm commitments can be made more acceptable and credible by a variety of framing tactics. One of these suggests that focusing attention on the alternatives that are being sacrificed by continuing the current course of action helps to justify change. Emphasis on the details of opportunity costs has been effective in reducing tendencies to maintain or escalate commitments in experimental situations

(Northcraft and Neale 1986) and also in many real world situations. "Let us all be clear about what is being sacrificed through the present policies!" One of the major factors influencing President de Gaulle's government to change policy away from retention of Algeria was the fact that continuing the policy of trying to maintain *Algerie Francaise* meant that France could not afford the resources and effort needed to modernize the French armed forces for the nuclear age (see Horne 2006).

New information can be discovered or emphasized by a pro-change faction, or it can arrive suddenly and be utilized to argue that a policy change is now necessary. At the start of the 20th century, the realization that the kaiser was not going to come to the aid of the Boer forces fighting the British in South Africa was a major help to those Boer leaders such as Smuts and Botha arguing for a negotiated settlement with the British. Alternatively, new information can arrive gradually until it builds up an overwhelming case for a change, realization often being triggered by an ostensibly trivial event that proves to be the final straw. A Karl Deutsch and Richard Merritt (1965) pointed out, a steady drip of negative information about a policy can frequently be ignored or argued away until some event—a changed vote in an international organization, the abrupt lessening of support from an important patron, or the fall of a symbolic site to the adversary—triggers the need for a policy review.

Argue that the Original Commitment Has Been Misunderstood, Misinterpreted, or Misapplied and that It Was Never Intended to Be as Constricting on Alternatives

This is probably the most frequently employed decommitment strategy, but it is also the most difficult to bring off convincingly, given that there will always be pro-continuation factions willing to point out the true limitations set up by the original commitment and to cry treachery. The strategy is particularly hard to use convincingly when the commitment is clear and unambiguous, but easier when it is capable of a number of interpretations. The ruling pigs in *Animal Farm* might have been able to get away with reinterpreting the commandment that "No animal shall drink alcohol" by adding the phrase "to excess," but such blatant reinterpretations seldom work fully in real life. One common tactic that sometimes enables a change of policy to be accepted smoothly by rank-and-file supporters might be termed *exceptionalism*. whereby it is argued that the original commitment to continuing a policy of fighting on was never intended to cover *this* particular situation. Various reasons can be adduced for supporting such a change of policy, among them the argument that the situation is entirely new and unique, calling for a new—and also possibly unique—response. It was used by Japanese leaders in August 1945 once the Allies were found to possess a "new and terrible weapon" capable of devastating whole cities. It was used by the leaders of the Boer commandos facing a situation whereby their British adversaries were removing the entire civilian population from the farms on the veldt and putting them all in the first concentration camps.

In actual situations in which leaders are struggling to free themselves from the entrapment caused by prior commitments, a combination of all types of decommitting tactics and arguments is usually employed. The overriding objective is for leaders to release themselves from a narrow corner into which they have been painted—or painted themselves—by previous statements and promises. Only when decision makers have been shown—or constructed for themselves—some kind of credible escape hatch from the trap they or their predecessors have built up will change seriously be contemplated.

CONCLUSION; CHANGE, COMMITMENT TO GOALS, AND DURABLE PEACE

This chapter has examined three kinds of change that help to start some form of peace process. It discusses changes of mind, changes of leadership, and changes in behavior, as well as some of the factors that make possible alterations of policy in the direction of talks about a negotiated peace.

However, it is always necessary to end on a word of caution and with a warning that one should not always regard change as unambiguously for the good. It always depends on the values of those involved and whether factions involved in any proposed change value peace above all else. Spoilers and bitter-enders are viewed differently—they are those who remain true to a party's original goals and are not willing to abandon them for some compromise with the enemy.

Revisiting the ideas of decommitment for one last time, is it necessarily the case that commitments to a cause and resultant entrapment in coercion is always a bad thing bringing about bad results—and for whom? As noted previously, in March 1990, the newly elected Lithuanian parliament made a firm and—as it turned out—virtually unbreakable commitment to Lithuanian sovereignty and independence from Mikhail Gorbachev's Soviet Union. Absolute Lithuanian independence thus became an unmodifiable goal for Lithuanians. The situation deadlocked as the Kremlin refused to begin discussions with Lithuanian leaders until the March 11 declaration was retracted, while the Lithuanians were equally committed to not retracting.

A variety of tactics were subsequently employed by both sides to reframe their commitments to make some room for compromise. In May 1990, the Lithuanian legislature voted to suspend all legislation passed since the declaration (much of it damaging to Soviet interests) if Moscow would agree to open negotiation on independence. The Soviet leaders initially insisted that the declaration itself had to be repealed and Lithuania accept the new Soviet law on secession, which involved referenda and a five-year cooling-off period.

Efforts to provide formulae that would enable talks at least to begin—ideas offered by outsiders, including U.S. Secretary of State James Baker—eventually succeeded, and conversations took place between Gorbachev and the leaders of all three Baltic countries. However, talks broke down on the Lithuanian commitment to the principle that they should already be treated as an independent actor, while the Russians insisted that their adversaries needed to acknowledge that they were still a part of the Soviet Union. Damaging economic sanctions had already been imposed by the Soviet Union, and in January 1991 there was an attempted *coup de main* by the military in which Soviet forces attempted to take over Vilnius and key communications points throughout the country. In these January events, 14 Lithuanians protecting these targets nonviolently were killed, and more than 700 were wounded.

At this point, it seemed that neither the leaders in Vilnius or Moscow were able to change and that both were trapped in unsustainable positions by previous unmodifiable commitments. However, from the Lithuanian viewpoint, their commitment to full independence, unmodified and unchanged, succeeded triumphantly. By September 1991, it had been recognized by a growing number of countries, most importantly by the Soviet Union but also by the United States. In the same month, independent Lithuania became a full member of the United Nations. By 2004, Lithuania had joined the European Union, and in the same year, the country became a member of the North Atlantic Treaty Organization. Change, flexibility, and the abandonment of commitments were, for Lithuanians, neither acceptable nor successful, any more than they were in 1961 for the FLN in Algeria once the French began to offer major concessions or for the British in June 1940, following the collapse of French resistance to the Nazis.

Sometimes steadfastness and commitment work—at least for one side and in the long term. Sometimes there really is light at the end of the tunnel.

CHAPTER 43

The Contingency Model for Third-Party Interventions

Ronald Fisher

The development of the field of peace and conflict resolution has shown considerable interest in the process of negotiation by which contesting parties interact to seek arrangements that will manage the issues arising from interdependencies between or among them. Accordingly, the field has also become concerned with methods of third-party intervention, especially mediation, through which a relatively impartial and trusted intermediary assists the negotiation process in seeking a settlement of the dispute. While negotiation and mediation are appropriate and effective in managing substantive conflicts over tangible issues, such as territory, resources, or trade relations, they have proven less effective in addressing destructive and intractable conflicts between distinct groups, which are rooted in or escalated by intangible issues related to security, identity, recognition, or cultural values that are not amenable to negotiation. Thus, alternative forms of third-party intervention have emerged that are directed toward managing the subjective elements of identity group conflict and toward improving the relationship between the parties, placing them in a better position to negotiate on the tangible issues. The development of these relationship-orientated methods has evolved over the past 50 years, as has the articulation of ways that they can serve a complementary function to the more established methods of negotiation and mediation. Unfortunately, some scholars in the field have attempted to incorporate these newer, innovative and distinct methods into wider definitions of mediation, thus ignoring their unique qualities and contributions to peacemaking. Some have even evaluated them in terms of their capacity to deliver a settlement on substantive issues, when this has never been articulated as an immediate objective.

Thus, it is essential to assert the fundamental distinctions among various third-party methods rather than attempting to lump all forms of pacific and impartial interventions into the same category. When unique elements have been articulated, the immediate and obvious question then becomes which method might be the most effective under what conditions or at what point in time in the life cycle of a destructive conflict. A second question relates to the sequencing and coordination of methods, given that one method may be the most useful lead intervention to be followed by other methods to address additional elements of the conflict. These are the questions that drive the search for a contingency approach to third-party intervention, in which the choice and sequencing of methods is made contingent upon selected aspects of the conflict.

These questions will first be approached by briefly describing the development of newer, process-orientated third-party methods that address the perceptual, cognitive, and relationship aspects of escalated, destructive conflict between identity groups. These methods include the prototypical problem-solving workshop and other approaches to dialogue, conflict analysis, and problem solving, grouped under the rubric of interactive conflict resolution (ICR), which is roughly equivalent to track-two diplomacy. Next, these methods, as captured by the term *third-party consultation*, will be placed in a taxonomy of third-party methods ranging from conciliation to peacekeeping, and varying largely in terms of the degree and forms of power that are used to influence the parties toward settlement and resolution. The primary clue as to which method might be most useful at what point will be addressed by presenting a stage model of escalation, which will then be placed in relation to the taxonomy of methods to produce a contingency model of third-party intervention. Finally, some case analysis evidence for the contingency model will be provided, prior to drawing conclusions that will stress the need for further theorizing and research to develop and assess the model, and for coordination among third-party methods in practice so as to maximize complementarity and effectiveness.

THE DEVELOPMENT AND EXPRESSION OF
INTERACTIVE CONFLICT RESOLUTION

The genesis of this bundle of third-party methods is generally attributed to the work of John Burton and his colleagues, who brought together influential yet unofficial representatives of parties engaged in destructive international and intergroup conflict to partake in a mutual analysis of their dispute, guided by a panel of scholar-practitioners in a small group setting characterized as a combination of an academic seminar and a problem-solving team. Burton's approach was predicated on an alternate paradigm of international relations, which stressed the pluralistic, systemic nature of global relations along with the importance of the subjective elements of conflict, all in contrast to the prevailing realistic model rooted in conceptions of power and cost-benefit analysis. Burton's early success in contributing to the resolution of the destructive conflict between Malaysia and Indonesia in the mid-1960s caught the attention of the conflict resolution field and stimulated a variety of kindred experiments, mainly by other academics, to address intractable ethnopolitical conflicts in a similarly innovative manner.

A survey of approximately 25 years of these unofficial third-party interventions led to an initial definition of interactive conflict resolution as "involving small group, problem-solving discussions between unofficial representatives of identity groups or states engaged in destructive conflict that are facilitated by an impartial panel of social-scientist practitioners."[1] In addition to the work of Burton, this review highlighted the contributions of Herbert Kelman and his colleagues in developing a model of interactive problem-solving and applying the method to the Israeli-Palestinian conflict and similar intractable disputes. In particular, Kelman has articulated the theory of practice for the problem-solving workshop (PSW) and has indicated how the method is rooted in assumptions and a rationale derived from the field of social psychology.[2] For my own part, I articulated a model of third-party consultation and have applied it to identity group conflict in organizational and community settings well as at the international level.[3] While this model captures the essential elements of the method, it provides particular emphasis on the identity, role, and functions of the third-party facilitators who organize and moderate PSWs. As the conflict resolution field has grown, the academic pioneers of ICR have been joined by a variety of other actors, particularly retired diplomats and members of nongovernmental organizations, who have extended and proliferated the method of the PSW or have developed their own models of unofficial diplomacy through induction from various practices.[4]

This growing variety of applications has been demonstrated to generally have positive and contributive effects on peacemaking practice; at the same time, the majority of the evidence has been based on anecdotal or case study descriptions, thus demonstrating potential more than definite effects. This proliferation of methods also required a broader definition of ICR as "facilitated face-to-face activities in communication, training, education, or consultation that promote collaborative conflict analysis and problem solving among parties engaged in protracted conflict in a manner that addresses basic human needs and promotes the building of peace, justice, and equality."[5] Throughout the development of ICR, scholar-practitioners have not been attempting to take over the role of diplomats in crafting, negotiating, or mediating peace agreements, but they have been looking to play a complementary role to official actors by addressing the subjective factors (misperceptions, negative attitudes, hostile emotions, relationship issues) that often get in the way of rational and cooperative interaction leading to conflict settlement and resolution. Thus, the intent of ICR practitioners has been to broaden the definition and practice of peacemaking beyond the traditional methods, specified, for example, in the charter of the United Nations, as negotiation, good offices, conciliation, mediation, arbitration, and adjudication.

A TAXONOMY OF THIRD-PARTY INTERVENTION

The first step in constructing a contingency model of third-party intervention is to define a typology or taxonomy of such interventions. However, developing a concise list of pacific, impartial third-party interventions in situations of conflict is not an easy task, especially if one attempts to define different types of intervention in a mutually exclusive manner. As Loraleigh Keashly and I point out in our initial attempt at this task, the number of different third-party roles in the literature is large and is being added to by the development of hybrid roles, such as mediator-arbitrator.[6] Furthermore, the strategies or functions indicated under individual labels can vary, such as in different forms of arbitration or mediation. In addition, different labels can be used for the same method, such as conciliation and mediation, both essentially meaning to assist parties in their negotiating efforts. Nonetheless, we took up the challenge and developed a taxonomy of six identifiably different types of intervention, which in its current expression is as follows:[7]

1. *Conciliation,* in which a trusted third party provides an informal communicative link between the antagonists for the purposes of identifying the issues, lowering tension, and encouraging direct interaction, usually in the form of negotiation.

2. *Consultation,* in which the third party works to facilitate creative problem solving through communication and analysis, making use of human relations skills and social-scientific understanding of conflict etiology and dynamics.

3. *Pure mediation,* in which the third party works to facilitate a negotiated settlement on substantive issues through the use of reasoning, persuasion, effective control of information, and the suggestion of alternatives.

4. *Power mediation,* which encompasses pure mediation and moves beyond it to include the use of leverage or coercion on the part of the mediator in the form of promised rewards or threatened punishments and may involve the third party as monitor and guarantor of the agreement.

5. *Arbitration,* wherein the third party renders a binding judgment arrived at through consideration of the individual merits of the opposing positions and then imposes a settlement that is deemed to be fair and just.

6. *Peacekeeping,* in which the third party provides military personnel to monitor a ceasefire or an agreement between antagonists and may engage in humanitarian activities designed to restore normalcy in concert with civilian personnel, who may also assist in the management of political decision-making processes such as elections.

In contrast to traditional conceptualizations of third-party intervention, this taxonomy is notable for two additions and one now largely accepted distinction. First, the addition of consultation (i.e., third-party consultation) acknowledges the development of ICR in line with the initial definition of that label offered previously. Second, the inclusion of peacekeeping as a conflict resolution method acknowledges that classic peacekeeping is a pacific method in contrast to traditional military intervention and is a move that has been appreciated by scholars in the peacekeeping field. In addition, the distinction initially made by others between pure mediation and power mediation, although these methods involve some overlapping functions, has been regarded as capturing an important difference in practice that carries implications in terms of third-party ethics and relationship to the parties. By and large, the taxonomy distinguishes the methods in terms of their overall purpose, gives attention to both objective and subjective elements of conflict, and orders the methods in terms of increasing control of the third party over the settlement of the conflict and the behavior of the parties. The articulation of the taxonomy thus allows us to go to the next step in the development of the contingency model.

THE STAGES OF ESCALATION

Conceptually, one could speculate that a number of characteristics of conflict could serve as potential cues for the application of different third-party actions. For example, the basic source of incompatibility in the conflict might call for different interventions, such as miscommunication being a call for conciliation, or resource conflicts such as over territory being an occasion for arbitration, or power conflicts being a target of power mediation. Nonetheless, the primary aspect of conflict that has most entered into contingency thinking is the level or stage of escalation—that is, the degree of emotional and behavioral intensity and the magnitude of the stakes at issue. However, it should be noted that level of escalation is inherently related to the objective and subjective mix of human social conflict. It is generally accepted that most conflicts originate in objective sources—that is, competition over resources or other interests, which may, of course, be driven in part by differing values or the need for power. As conflicts escalate, it is also accepted that subjective factors, such as miscommunication, self-serving biases, cognitive distortions, enemy images, and entrapment, become more prominent. Thus, different methods of intervention are likely required to address, at least initially, the mix of subjective and objective factors at a given level of escalation. Ultimately, it is likely that a number of third-party interventions are required to address highly escalated and protracted conflict between different identity groups.

The initiation of contingency thinking based on level of escalation appears to have occurred in the subfield of organizational conflict management, where a number of scholars considered the links between escalation and type and timing of third-party intervention. For example, Blair Sheppard developed a complex procedural framework for different types of interventions, which specified the form of control exercised by the third party (process, content, outcome) at different stages of escalation and resolution.[8] A simpler framework offered by Hugo Prein relates the choice between mediation and consultation to the characteristics and context of the conflict. Through the analysis of multiple cases of organizational conflict, he finds (in line with the aforementioned rationale) that mediation is more successful when substantive issues predominate, whereas consultation is more effective when miscommunication and mistrust are high.[9] The most explicit attempt to develop a contingency approach is found in the work of Friedrich Glasl, who developed a nine-stage model of conflict escalation based on changes in the parties' behavior, patterns of interaction, perceptions, and attitudes.[10] Six different third-party interventions are then connected to the nine stages, where they are seen as having the most potential effectiveness. This articulation thus proposes that all the common forms of intervention have utility if applied at the appropriate level of escalation and also suggests that a third party may begin with one form of intervention and then shift to another to complete the process. The next step in forming a contingency model is to conceptualize the possibility that different methods might initiate the intervention process and then be sequenced and coordinated to provide a comprehensive third-party initiative to de-escalate and resolve the conflict.

In terms of stages of escalation, the work of Glasl and Prein at the organizational level was combined by Loraleigh Keashly and I with that of Wright[11] at the international level to produce a model of escalation encapsulating four stages of increasing intensity (see Table 43.1).[12] The four stages (discussion, polarization, segregation, and destruction) are distinguished by important changes in (1) the communication and interaction between the parties, (2) their perceptions and images of each other and the nature of their relationship, (3) the overt issues at the fore of the conflict, and (4) the perceived possible outcomes along with the parties' preferred strategies for addressing the conflict. In reverse, the escalation model can be seen as one of de-escalation, although other elements relevant to de-escalation would need to be added for a full description of the process of descending intensity.

Fisher and Keashly succinctly describe the process of conflict escalation as follows:

> Briefly, as conflict escalates, communication moves from direct discussion and debate between the parties to reliance on the interpretation of actions rather than words, to the use of threats, and finally to direct attacks. Thus, communication is carried out through increasingly aggressive forms of interaction between the

Table 43.1
Stages of Conflict Escalation

Dimensions of the Conflict			
Communication/ Interaction	Perceptions/ Relationship	Issues	Outcome/ Management
STAGE			
I Discussion/ debate	Accurate/trust, respect, commitment	Interests	Joint gain/mututal decision
II Less direct/ deeds not words	Stereotypes/other still important	Relationship	Compromise/ negotiation
III Little direct/ threats	Good vs. evil/distrust, lack of respect	Basic needs	Win-lose/ defensive competition
IV Nonexistent/ direct attacks	Other nonhuman/ hopeless	Survival	Lose-lose/ destruction

Source: Adapted from Fisher (1990) and reprinted with kind permission of Springer Science and Business Media.

parties. Accompanying this breakdown in open and direct communication is the replacement of accurate perceptions with negative and simplified stereotypes to the point where the other party is regarded as evil and nonhuman. The relationship moves from one of trust, respect, and commitment to one of mistrust, disrespect, and, finally, hopelessness in terms of possible improvements. In terms of issues fueling the conflict, the emphasis shifts from substantive interests and positions to concerns regarding the relationship, to basic needs or values, and ultimately to the very survival of the parties. In line with these changes, the possible outcomes begin with joint gain, or win-win, options, move to compromises, then to win-lose results, and finally to lose-lose results, in which the objective is to minimize one's own losses while inflicting maximum costs on the other party. In attempting to achieve these outcomes, the parties' preferred methods of conflict management move from joint decision making through negotiation to defensive competition, and ultimately to outright attempts at destruction. Although the stage model presents a simplified picture of conflict escalation, it does provide an accurate and detailed enough picture so that different third party interventions can be linked to different stages, which is the essence of the contingency approach.[13]

The final step in constructing a contingency model is to link the taxonomy of third-party interventions with the stages of the model of escalation by specifying the lead intervention most appropriate at each stage followed by the subsequent interventions deemed to be necessary to de-escalate the conflict to the less intense stage(s).

THE CONTINGENCY MODEL

Given the characteristics of the different stages in the model of escalation, it is apparent that different challenges exist at each of the four stages in terms of what symptoms and issues predominate in driving and protracting the conflict. Thus, it is proposed that different interventions are more effective as the lead intervention at each stage. This is in contrast to the traditional practice of third-party intervention in international conflict, where the application of mediation is often attempted repetitively, regardless of the state of the conflict, supported by the notion that sooner or later the timing will be right. At times, of course, peacekeeping is also applied in situations where violence is rampant and a ceasefire can be attained, and mediation is again used in the hope of reaching a settlement. Unfortunately, both of these traditional methods more or less ignore the relationship issues and the frustration of basic human needs that drive existential conflicts between identity groups.

The contingency model developed by Loraleigh Keashly and I is presented in Figure 43.1, which shows how the four stages of escalation are addressed with a lead intervention drawn from the taxonomy, followed by additional interventions to de-escalate and resolve the conflict. The detailed rationale for each sequence of intervention is provided by Fisher and Keashly[14] and will be briefly summarized here.

At the first stage of escalation, conciliation is the prescribed lead intervention, because the primary challenge is to improve communication between the

Figure 43.1
A Contingency Model of Third-Party Intervention

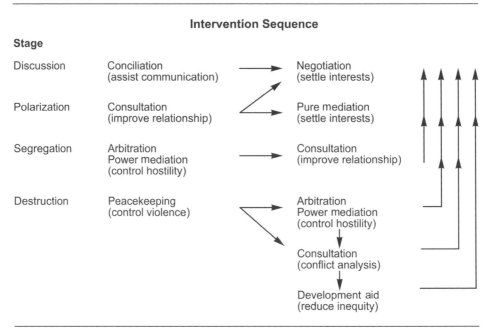

Source: Adapted with revisions from Fisher (1990) and reprinted with kind permission of Springer Science and Business Media.

parties so that they can clarify, elaborate, and justify their interests. Often in addressing important and difficult issues, parties will escalate their rhetoric and move into debate mode and other forms of adversarial behavior, which means that they are not listening to each other and are not seeing common interests or the potential for integrative outcomes. A skilled third party can facilitate clear and open communication that assists the parties in initiating or moving back to negotiation to settle their interests in a mutually satisfactory manner.

At the second stage of polarization, consultation is the prescribed lead intervention to address emerging relationship issues in which trust and respect are threatened and in which simplified stereotypes and other cognitive distortions arise. Once these problems are addressed and a cooperative relationship is reestablished, the parties are in a better position to address the substantive issues in dispute in a clearer and more rational manner. Thus, they may be able to move back into negotiations, but, given the importance and complexity of the interests, which in part induced escalation, it is more likely that a complementary third-party intervention of pure mediation is called for. The prior intervention of consultation should improve the chances for success in mediation, because relationship issues and other subjective elements will be less likely to contaminate and derail the negotiation process.

In the third stage of escalation, the conflict has reached a point where it is threatening one or both parties' basic human needs for security, identity, freedom, justice, or other deeply held principles and values. Of course, such needs often underlie the many interests and relationship qualities that are salient in stages one and two, but at those levels of escalation, basic needs are not threatened and can be satisfied through mutually acceptable arrangements between the parties. The difficulty with stage three is that the parties engage in unilateral and adversarial tactics to coerce the other into acceding to their demands, which often hardens resistance and escalates countermeasures. Given that the parties are exercising greater power in executing the conflict, the lead intervention by the third party needs to involve greater control over both the process and substance of the conflict. Thus, arbitration or power mediation are the interventions of choice to control the rising hostility, provide a cooling-off period, and possibly bring about some immediate settlement on surface issues. The follow-up intervention is then seen as consultation to address the relationship issues that fueled escalation, and to begin the de-escalation process in which pure mediation and negotiation also play important roles.

At stage four, the unilateral and coercive strategies of the parties have escalated to the use of violence to prosecute the conflict, thus inducing and reinforcing subjective elements in their most extreme form, wherein the other party is regarded as nonhuman and all manner of tactics are justified. To control the use of violence and the mutual intent of the parties to annihilate each other, a powerful third-party intervention is required in the form of peacekeeping. This can be peacekeeping as originally conceived, wherein the parties agree to a ceasefire and the imposition of the third-party force, or it can be the latest version of more robust peacekeeping in which force is used to subdue the parties' violent behavior as required. The central point is to stop the violence, not only to protect human lives but also to stop egregious human rights abuses that become additional issues in the conflict. At this point, all of the activities common to post-conflict peacebuilding become required elements of de-escalation and resolution. However, in terms of third-party interventions, actions involving arbitration or power mediation by a governing authority may be required to prevent hostility from breaking out again in violence. At the same time, interventions involving consultation toward a full and mutual analysis of the conflict, along with addressing relationship issues, would be prescribed to help de-escalate the conflict. At the same time, development aid in a variety of forms would be necessary to rebuild political, economic, and social institutions and practices in ways that meet the basic human needs of the parties in a mutually satisfactory manner.

The contingency model thus provides a road map and a rationale for applying and sequencing third-party interventions to deal with escalating, destructive conflict, primarily at the intergroup level between identity groups whose satisfaction of basic human needs is under threat or attack. The taxonomy of interventions and the stage model of escalation were induced primarily from efforts at the organizational (largely intergroup) level and the international level (inherently intergroup). Thus, the application of the contingency model is most appropriate to conflicts between distinct identity groups in the organizational, communal, and international domains. Real-world applications of contingency thinking appear to be rare, and the practice of conflict resolution is thus challenged to think and act in more comprehensive and coordinated ways if overall effectiveness is to be increased. Conflict resolution efforts also need to be integrated into the wider practice of peacemaking and peacebuilding if they are to make a significant contribution to achieving the outcomes inherent in the contingency model. These intentions are supported by other contributions to the contingency approach and more recently by evidence that contingent and coordinated interventions are more effective in meeting the challenges of destructive intergroup conflict. Contingency approaches, including the present model, have been criticized on a number of grounds.

VARIATIONS AND CRITICISMS OF THE CONTINGENCY APPROACH

The decade of the 1990s in the field of conflict resolution witnessed a number of attempts to develop contingency thinking in the area of third-party intervention, some of which intended to improve upon or provide a broader alternative to the contingency model. Throughout this period and beyond, Louis Kriesberg has been an active supporter of contingency thinking and has advocated for multiple and coordinated interventions that are linked to the expression of the conflict at different points in time.[15] Rather than using a model of escalation, he developed a four-step model of de-escalation: (1) de-escalation initiatives including prenegotiation, (2) explicit negotiations, (3) explicit agreements, and (4) implementing agreements. Kriesberg then relates the four steps to a variety of intermediary activities carried out by different third parties—for example, providing good offices, reframing the conflict, adding resources to a settlement. Some of these activities are more prominent at particular stages, even though he maintains that each type of activity can occur at every stage but in different forms. Activities by unofficial parties that are directed toward reframing the conflict, such as through PSWs, tend to be more aligned with the initial stages of de-escalation, while official activities to support negotiations and agreements tend to be more prominent in the later steps of de-escalation. While Kriesberg asserts that a variety of simultaneous (rather than sequenced) activities are useful, his idea that unofficial parties and interventions may be more helpful in the prenegotiation stage does support some of the rationale for the contingency model.

In a broad, multimodal approach to intractable conflict, Dean Pruitt and Paul Olzack proposed an intervention model designed to deal with the dynamics of conflict as represented by five basic modes of human experience: motivation, affect, cognition, behavior, and social environment.[16] Depending on the state of the conflict, these five modes become the targets for interventions that are selected and sequenced to de-escalate the conflict. In a highly escalated conflict, there will be hostile elements in all modes of experience;

in a mildly escalated one, only one or two modes will be problematic. Pruitt and Olzack identify seven modules of conflict intervention (e.g., negotiation and mediation, inducing ripeness, developing trust, conflict resolution training, PSWs), and describe how problematic conditions in the modes can be addressed in sequence by the interventions. For the sake of brevity, it will simply be noted that their model prescribes a deep analysis of the conflict using methods such as PSWs to move toward lasting resolutions in intractable conflicts. To address the question of sequencing the conflict modules, Pruitt and Olzack draw a parallel to the contingency model, asserting that conflict analysis and the development of motivation to escape the conflict must precede the negotiation of concrete interests.

David Bloomfield has accepted the basic rationale of the contingency approach and has built upon the contingency model in developing a broader model of complementarity in third-party intervention with specific reference to the conflict in Northern Ireland.[17] He sees the contingency model as acknowledging the important distinction between conflict settlement and conflict resolution and as affirming the necessary complementarity between these two broad approaches rather than casting them in opposition and competition. Nonetheless, he criticizes the model for its linear nature, whereas the conflict reality on the ground is one of chaos and recycling, with different constituencies within the parties expressing different levels of escalation at the same point in time. Therefore, he prescribes multiple interventions occurring simultaneously (in addition to sequential ones) to deal with different constituencies (e.g., political elites, peace activists) at different junctures. He does note that the contingency model is open to simultaneous interventions, and he acknowledges the importance of working on subjective elements of the conflict alongside the substantive issues. Mainly, he argues for complementarity among interventions directed toward different societal levels to address the complexity of intractable intergroup conflict. In defense of the contingency model, it must be noted that the model was not designed to address multiple constituencies within societies but to focus primarily on the political level of influentials and decision makers and to prescribe complementarity between unofficial (largely prenegotiation) processes and official attempts at settlement through mediation and negotiation. Thus, Bloomfield's treatment, while extending the scope of contingency thinking, does not invalidate the essential nature of the contingency model.

The rationale of the contingency model is well supported by Chester Crocker, Fen Hampson and Pamela Aall in their realistic and practical exposition of multiparty mediation, in which a variety of third-party actors make contributions to peace processes in different ways and at different points in time.[18] As with the contingency model, these authors use the level of violence (i.e., escalation) of the conflict as the critical cue for the choice of the most effective third-party interventions. Different forms of intervention (i.e., track one and track two—read mediation and consultation) are then linked to the current level of violence (low, medium, high) in the conflict. However, unlike the contingency model, interventions are paired or coupled at each level of escalation with an indication of which form of intervention comes first. At all levels, track-two diplomacy by unofficial actors is the lead intervention designed to gain entry and is followed by different forms of mediation to deal with the substantive issues in the conflict. Their model is thus more sophisticated in specifying the identity of the most appropriate actors for both track one (nongovernmental organizations, scholar practitioners, small powers) and track two (great powers, coalitions of states, international and regional organizations) at each level of escalation. In addition, their model prescribes whether the interventions should be simultaneous (at level one) or sequential (at levels two and three). Along the line of Bloomfield's work, this analysis also envisages multiparty mediation directed toward both elites and various constituencies in civil society. Their work thus extends the reach and the specificity of contingency thinking in useful directions, even though it does not incorporate as wide a range of third-party interventions as the contingency model.

Christopher Mitchell also makes use of the contingency model in developing his process model of mediation in international conflict resolution.[19] Rather than matching interventions to characteristics of the conflict, such as level of escalation, Mitchell casts mediation as a complex process over time to which many different actors can make contributions, either simultaneously or consecutively. In addition, Mitchell does not cluster various third-party functions into broad traditional roles, such as mediation or conciliation, but divides these into more fine-grained roles, such as convener, facilitator, fact finder, enskiller, and guarantor. He provides the specific tasks and functions that define each of these roles and asserts that a variety of external actors need to play these roles at different points in the mediation process. His analysis thus draws attention to the succession of barriers that must be overcome in a mediation process and makes it clear that no one third-party intervener is capable of de-escalating and resolving an intractable conflict. Thus, Mitchell's analysis shares some assumptions with the contingency model and also provides a much finer-grained exposition of the numerous tasks required in a successful peacemaking endeavor.

EVIDENCE SUPPORTING THE CONTINGENCY MODEL

The contingency model has an appealing logic in its rationale, linked to the dual importance of subjective and objective elements in escalated conflict and to the assumption that predominant subjective aspects need to be addressed to some degree before both elites and societies on both sides of the conflict can move toward and support peace processes. However, much of the evidence supporting the various hypotheses that are embedded in the model (the most effective lead intervention, the sequencing of interventions) is largely anecdotal or case-study based, and does not provide the strength of assurance that social science would consider adequate to advise policy or practice. Only recently has serious and detailed comparative case analysis been carried out to assess the validity of the model,[20] and yet we find an increasing acceptance of the logic and assertions of approach in the conflict resolution field. This part of the chapter will briefly review some of the evidence and identify some of the supportive commentary that has been brought forward on contingency thinking.

In one of the first expositions of the contingency model, Loraleigh Keashly and I applied it retrospectively to the intractable conflict on the island of Cyprus between Greek and Turkish Cypriots, including various interventions by third parties to help resolve the dispute.[21] The major events in the conflict were charted over five decades and divided into the four stages of escalation. Then, third-party interventions following the definitions in the taxonomy were aligned with the stages, and their effectiveness in contributing to de-escalation and/or settlement was assessed. In a somewhat biased analysis (we wanted to show the potential utility of consultation), we concluded that the application of power mediation by the involved states (mainly the United Kingdom) was ineffective at stages one and two, whereas conciliation or consultation followed by pure mediation might have led to a settlement that was accepted by the parties on the island. Furthermore, we noted that two applications of consultation in the form of PSWs (one by John Burton and his colleagues) were successful in encouraging a return to stalled mediation, as specified in the model. However, the analysis was most useful in identifying the possible misapplication of power mediation along with the potential utility of consultation, had such interventions been more readily available.

Although not directly assessing the contingency model, my review of 75 cases of various types of consultation interventions (mostly PSWs) demonstrated a clear theme of unofficial contributions to peace processes.[22] The reported outcomes of multiple cases of intervention in a variety of intractable conflicts over four decades by various interveners (mostly academic scholar-practitioners) indicated that positive influences on peace processes (positive attitudes, improved public discourse) occurred in about 40 percent of the cases, while direct contributions to peace processes (plans, initiatives) happened in 17 percent of the cases and to negotiations (analyses, frameworks) in 26 percent of the cases. These results are based on analyzing the self-reports of the interveners, which can be positively biased. In addition, only one hypothesis of the contingency model is being addressed: the utility of consultation as a prenegotiation or paranegotiation intervention to help prepare the way for more effective mediation.

A systematic analysis of a smaller set of more carefully selected cases is provided in my 2005 book: *Paving the Way: Contributions of Interactive Conflict Resolution to Peacemaking.*[23] Using the structured and rigorous method of comparative case analysis, nine instances of apparently successful consultation interventions were analyzed in terms of the characteristics of the conflicts, the nature of the interventions, and the occurrence of transfer effects to official peacemaking. All the cases involved escalated and intractable ethnopolitical conflicts between identity groups or states and were drawn from four decades of unofficial interventions covering most regions of the world. The analysis of transfer effects is relevant to the contingency model and demonstrated that most interventions were designed to help prepare the ground for mediated negotiations and then to support these processes once they were underway. All the interventions claimed positive cognitive changes among participants (e.g., new realizations, changed attitudes) and most produced novel ideas or options for addressing the conflict (e.g., principles for a solution, proposals for cooperation). In addition, most evidenced a revolving door between the unofficial meetings and track-one interactions in that a number of participants later moved into official roles in negotiations or policy making. Thus, these results again support the utility of consultation as a preparatory intervention at escalation levels three or four to assist mediation efforts, although they are again vulnerable to a positive bias as the cases were written up by the practitioners themselves or sympathetic researchers.

An explicit test of the contingency model occurs in a more focused comparative case analysis of 5 of the 2,005 cases in which consultation appears to have made important contributions, mainly by serving a prenegotiation function.[24] The five cases include conflicts in different regions of the world at different points in time over the last 45 years. The five interventions typically employed problem-solving workshops, and generally followed the contingency model in that they occurred at a high level of escalation (typically between stages three and four) after the imposition of peacekeeping or a period of stalemate and failed or nonexistent mediation. The analysis of transfer effects from the unofficial interventions to official interactions indicated that each of the consultation interventions made useful contributions to the de-escalation and/or resolution of the conflict. However, only two cases showed clear and complete support for the sequencing of interventions in the model, thus demonstrating the complexity of dealing with turbulent international conflicts. For example, in one case, the consultation intervention began in the midst of a civil war with peacekeeping only coming in as a later intervention to control the violence. In another case, consultation began in a situation of armed stalemate where power mediation had failed to move the parties toward resolution. Nonetheless, in all cases, consultation appears to have assisted in a return to mediated negotiations or the initiation of such negotiations. It was also clear in the analysis that there is generally very limited coordination among third-party interveners, a point borne out by a related analysis of coordination efforts, which demonstrated that unofficial interveners often approach and inform official third parties of their intentions and plans but that there is very little reciprocity on the part of official actors.[25] Clearly, if the contingency approach is to be implemented effectively, there is much need for various forms of coordination between the various third parties involved in resolution efforts on the same conflict.

Contingency thinking appears to be coming into vogue in the field of conflict resolution, even though there is a need for models of greater conceptual sophistication and for stronger evidence to support the approach. In one popular and comprehensive text, the authors acknowledge "attempts to suggest that different types of third-party interventions are effective at different stages of the conflict process, that they can be seen as complementary, and that the type of appropriate intervention is contingent upon the nature and stage of the conflict. . . . The argument is that softer forms of intervention are more appropriate when miscommunication and mistrust is high (when the subjective elements are strong), whereas harder forms of intervention are more successful when substantive interests are at the forefront."[26] In a similar vein, Louis Kriesberg in his very inclusive treatment of conflict analysis and resolution, notes the increasing attention of analysts to the type of intermediary interventions that are appropriate to different stages of a conflict and points out that "various intermediary activities also differ in their likely effectiveness for different kinds of conflicts and at different phases of a conflict. Thus, consulting and conveying information between the adversaries is likely to be more effective than strong, deal-making activities at the prenegotiation stage of a conflict."[27] Further, in his concise survey of developments in the conflict resolution field, Kriesberg, in noting matters on which there is consensus, states that: "There is general agreement, at least in principle, that specific CR strategies and tactics fit particular kinds of conflicts and conflict stages. . . . Attention has been devoted to the various methods that are appropriate for intermediaries trying to hasten de-escalation at different stages of a conflict, referred to as the 'contingency approach.'"[28] It thus appears that contingency thinking is permeating the field in terms of both theory and practice and that to pursue its continued development, application, and evaluation is a worthwhile goal.

CONCLUSION

The development of contingency thinking in the conflict resolution field now goes back about three decades, if we begin with the seminal thinking in the subfield of organizational conflict management. In the international domain, the idea that problem-solving workshops could play an important prenegotiation role goes back even further, but that notion does not constitute a fully developed contingency model incorporating all the common forms of intervention. That development awaited the formulation that was first articulated in the late 1980s and that gained increased visibility in 1991 with the publication of the article in the *Journal of Peace Research* by Loraleigh Keashly and me.[29] The stimulus for contingency thinking came largely from the development of process- and relationship-orientated methods of third-party intervention, the creators of which were looking to see how these different methods could be integrated into the wider domain of conflict management along with the more traditional methods. These methods, captured under the rubric of ICR or track-two two diplomacy, are increasingly regarded as having applicability and utility by established theorists and practitioners, and this gives prominence to the question of how different methods can work effectively together. The contingency model and other similar formulations attempt to provide an initial answer, at least conceptually. As critics have indicated, the model can be seen as simplistic and formulaic, and yet it may capture the essence of the contingency process. Thus, as subsequent formulations have indicated, there is a need for elaboration of options and sequences and flexibility in their application. For example, as the initial work on the model admitted, there may be occasions when the simultaneous application of different interventions may be more effective than their sequencing. At the same time, it is not helpful to succumb to the chaos of highly escalated real-world conflict and attempt to address every eventuality and nuance that such complexity brings forward. Better yet to bring focus and along with it some insight and control to the process of how third parties can more effectively manage chaotic situations. In this regard, the contingency model is a useful initial step that needs conceptual elaboration, practical implementation, and rigorous evaluation.

In terms of conceptual work, the model does not specify but rather assumes the identity, skills, and resources of various third-party actors who can implement the different interventions in the taxonomy. It would be useful to specify this aspect to better understand which actors are capable of which interventions and what institutions need to be established or changed to provide the full gamut of interventions at the global level. In terms of the practice of peacemaking, there is a wide gap between the potential of unofficial, process-orientated interventions and what is actually occurring. The needs for training, funding, institutionalization, and professionalization identified almost 20 years ago for the effective practice of ICR still go largely unaddressed.[30] Also, in terms of practice, the awareness and the need for the critical element of coordination among third parties to implement the model require a great deal of attention. In terms of research, the past reliance on anecdotal and case study evidence has been augmented somewhat by recent comparative case analyses, but the results are encouraging rather than conclusive. Younger scholar-practitioners should understand that acceptance in principle of contingency thinking does not constitute an adequately solid base for drawing conceptual conclusions or for supporting the necessary practice. There is much work to be done before the contingency approach can take its potentially very useful place in the wider domain of peacemaking.

NOTES

1. Ronald J. Fisher, "Developing the Field of Interactive Conflict Resolution: Issues in Training, Funding and Institutionalization," *Political Psychology* 14 (1993): 123.

2. Herbert C. Kelman, "Interactive Problem Solving: A Social-Psychological Approach to Conflict Resolution," in *Dialogue toward Inter-Faith Understanding,* ed. William Klassen (Jerusalem: Ecumenical Institute for Theological Research, 1986).

3. Ronald J. Fisher, "Third Party Consultation: A Method for the Study and Resolution of Conflict," *Journal of Conflict Resolution* 16, no. 1 (1972). Ronald J. Fisher, "Third Party Consultation as a Method of Conflict Resolution: A Review of Studies," *Journal of Conflict Resolution* 27 (1983). Ronald J. Fisher, *Interactive Conflict Resolution* (Syracuse, NY: Syracuse University Press, 1997).

4. Joseph V. Montville, "The Arrow and the Olive Branch: The Case for Track Two Diplomacy," in *Conflict Resolution: Track Two Diplomacy*, eds. John W. McDonald and Diane B. Bendahmane (Washington, DC: Foreign Service Institute, Department of State, 1987). Harold Saunders, *A Public Peace Process: Sustained Dialogue to Transform Racial and Ethnic Conflicts* (New York: St. Martin's Press, 1999). Vamik D. Volkan, Joseph V. Montville, and Demetrios A. Julius, eds. *The Psychodynamics of International Relationships*, Vol. 2. *Unofficial Diplomacy at Work* (Lexington, MA: Lexington Books, 1991).

5. Fisher, *Interactive Conflict Resolution*, 8.

6. Ronald J. Fisher and Loraleigh Keashly, "Third Party Consultation as a Method of Intergroup and International Conflict Resolution," in *The Social Psychology of Intergroup and International Conflict Resolution*, ed. Ronald J. Fisher (New York: Springer-Verlag, 1990).

7. Ronald J. Fisher, "Methods of Third-Party Intervention," in *Transforming Ethnopolitical Conflict: The Berghof Handbook*, Vol. 2, eds. Martina Fischer, Hans J. Giessmann, and Beatrix Schmelzle (Berlin: Barbara Budrich, 2010).

8. Blair H. Sheppard, "Third Party Conflict Interventions: A Procedural Framework," *Research in Organizational Behavior* 6 (1984).

9. Hugo Prein, "A Contingency Approach for Conflict Intervention," *Group and Organization Studies* 9 (1984).

10. Friedrich Glasl, "The Process of Escalation and Roles of Third Parties," in *Conflict Management and Industrial Relations*, eds. Gerald B. J. Bomers and Richard B. Peterson (Boston: Kluwer-Nijhoff, 1982).

11. Quincy Wright, "Escalation of International Conflicts," *Journal of Conflict Resolution* 9 (1965).

12. Fisher and Keashly, "Third Party Consultation as a Method of Intergroup and International Conflict Resolution."

13. Ibid, 236.

14. Ibid. Ronald J. Fisher and Loraleigh Keashly, "The Potential Complementarity of Mediation and Consultation within a Contingency Model of Third Party Intervention," *Journal of Peace Research* 28 (1991).

15. Louis Kriesberg, "Formal and Quasi-Mediators in International Disputes: An Exploratory Analysis," *Journal of Peace Research* 28, no. 1 (1991).

16. Dean G. Pruitt and Paul V. Olzack, "Beyond Hope: Approaches to Resolving Seemingly Intractable Conflict," in *Conflict, Cooperation, and Justice: Essays Inspired by the Work of Morton Deutsch*, ed. Barbara B. Bunker and Jeffrey Z. Rubin (San Francisco: Jossey-Bass, 1995).

17. David Bloomfield, "Towards Complementarity in Conflict Management: Resolution and Settlement in Northern Ireland," *Journal of Peace Research* 32, no. 2 (1995). David Bloomfield, *Peacemaking Strategies in Northern Ireland: Building Complementarity in Conflict Management Theory* (London: Macmillan, 1997).

18. Chester A. Crocker, Fen Osler Hampson, and Pamela Aall, eds., *Herding Cats: Multiparty Mediation in a Complex World* (Washington, DC: United States Institute of Peace Press, 1999).

19. Christopher Mitchell, "The Process and Stages of Mediation," in *Making War and Waging Peace: Foreign Intervention in Africa*, ed. David Smock (Washington, DC: United States Institute of Peace, 1993).

20. Ronald J. Fisher, "Assessing the Contingency Model of Third Party Intervention in Successful Cases of Prenegotiation," *Journal of Peace Research* 44, no. 3 (2007).

21. Loraleigh Keashly and Ronald J. Fisher, "Toward a Contingency Approach to Third Party Intervention in Regional Conflict: A Cyprus Illustration," *International Journal* 45 (1990).

22. Fisher, *Interactive Conflict Resolution.*

23. Ronald J. Fisher, ed. *Paving the Way: Contributions of Interactive Conflict Resolution to Peacemaking* (Lanham, MD: Lexington Books, 2005).

24. Fisher, "Assessing the Contingency Model of Third Party Intervention in Successful Cases of Prenegotiation."

25. Ronald J. Fisher, "Coordination between Track Two and Track One Diplomacy in Successful Cases of Prenegotiation," *International Negotiation* (2006).

26. Oliver Ramsbotham, Tom Woodhouse, and Hugh Miall, *Contemporary Conflict Resolution*, 2nd ed. (Cambridge, UK: Polity Press, 2005), 51.

27. Louis Kriesberg, *Constructive Conflicts: From Escalation to Resolution*, 3rd ed. (Lanham, MD: Rowman & Littlefield, 2007), 252.

28. Louis Kriesberg, "The Conflict Resolution Field: Origins, Growth, and Differentiation," in *Peacemaking in International Conflict: Methods and Techniques*, ed. I. William Zartman (Washington, DC: United States Institute of Peace, 2007), 38.

29. Fisher and Keashly, "The Potential Complementarity of Mediation and Consultation within a Contingency Model of Third Party Intervention."

30. Fisher, "Developing the Field of Interactive Conflict Resolution: Issues in Training, Funding and Institutionalization."

CHAPTER 44

Challenges in Peacemaking: External Interventions

Louis Kriesberg

Interventions to end wars are now more frequent and more diverse than they were in the years of the cold war. During the cold war, the United States and its allies and the Soviet Union and its allies often supported opposing sides in civil and international wars, contributing resources to help the side each aided to end the war in victory. After the cold war, such interventions decreased, which helped explain the decline in wars around the world (Gleditsch 2008; Harbom and Wallensteen 2010; Human Security Centre 2005). Furthermore, interventions directly aimed to make peace between antagonists greatly expanded, partly due to increased United Nations (UN) peace work made possible by the end of the cold war. These peacemaking interventions, together with many other global developments, also contributed to the decline in wars in the 1990s. The expansion of external peacemaking efforts probably also helps explain why civil wars are now more likely than in the past to end in negotiated settlements rather than unilateral impositions. However, negotiated endings are less likely to last than are imposed endings. Indeed, nearly 40 percent of negotiated agreements fail within five years (Harbom, Högbladh, and Wallensteen 2006). This indicates the importance of the qualities of the peace that is reached and how it is then sustained.

In this chapter, I first discuss the variety of peacemaker interveners in large-scale violent conflicts or oppressive relationships and the diverse kinds of peacemaking interventions made in such conflicts. Then, I examine a few peacemaking interventions to illustrate how they can contribute to the transformation and ending of large-scale violent conflicts or societal oppression. Finally, I examine the obstacles to effective peacemaking interventions and how the obstacles may be overcome.

Before proceeding, some observations should be made about the nature of the peacemaking stage of conflict. As discussed in other chapters, peacemaking often refers to efforts to resolve violent conflicts by negotiation, mediation, arbitration, reconciliation, and other processes. It is often used in distinction to an earlier stage of efforts to prevent violent escalation and a later stage of peacebuilding to sustain peace.

In this chapter, I discuss peacemaking very broadly to refer to a stage of conflict resolution in which adversaries, with or without interveners, act to help transform a violent or otherwise destructive conflict into one entering the peacebuilding stage. That usage does not reflect the wide range and variety of peacemaking actions. The very idea of peace ranges from the absence of large-scale direct physical violence, negative peace, to various forms of positive peace, which vary from minimal structural violence (small differences in life chances among large categories of people) to relatively harmonious societal functioning. I usually will refer to peace within or between societies as marked by low levels of direct physical violence and in which conflicts are managed constructively.

I also emphasize that the escalation prevention, peacemaking, and peacebuilding conflict stages overlap each other. An action in one stage often also affects the developments in the next stage. Thus, a peacemaking intervention to foster reconciliation between adversaries may be part of the de-escalation or of the peacebuilding process. Furthermore, different groups on each adversary side may be functioning in a somewhat different location in their conflict's trajectory. Some may be engaged in trying to escalate a conflict while others are trying to de-escalate it. Different kinds of preventive or peacemaking undertakings would be appropriate for those different groups.

Finally, it should be recognized that conflicts are interconnected in many ways, including linked over time and smaller ones nested in larger ones. Consequently, one conflict may be transformed so that it moves from making peace to peacebuilding, while the larger conflict in which that one was embedded does not move very much toward peace. Similarly, one conflict may be resolved while a closely related parallel conflict verging on conflict escalation remains at that stage. For example, the U.S. government at various times has engaged in preventing violent escalations, peacemaking, and peacebuilding actions in the Israeli-Arab set of conflicts. During 1977–1979, the U.S. peacemaking mediation helped bring about a peace treaty between Egypt and Israel, but it had limited impact in transforming the Israeli-Palestinian conflict.

PEACEMAKING INTERVENERS AND INTERVENTIONS

Peacemaking interventions vary greatly and are conducted by numerous kinds of interveners. I focus on peacemaking efforts in large-scale violent conflicts and on interventions by state actors but consider them in the context of other actors and other conflict stages. Particular attention is given to interventions by the U.S. government, because it is such a major intervener.

The increasing number of interveners and scale of their actions is related to the intensifying global economic integration and interdependence, the greater movement of people, and the spreading of shared norms. Thus, norms against perpetrating gross human rights violations are diffusing globally and increasingly accepted as binding. These developments increase the impact of violent conflicts in one place upon larger regions and the increasing need, expectation, and experience of external interventions into large-scale violent conflicts.

Many peacemaking interventions help transform conflicts from destructive warfare to lasting peace, but others escalate or exacerbate a violent conflict (Dayton and Kriesberg 2009). At times, interventions that perpetuate or escalate a conflict are intended to reduce asymmetry or defeat an oppressive party to achieve what the interveners deem a more just outcome. Typically, numerous interventions occur simultaneously and sequentially, in ever-changing combinations. The effectiveness of any constellation of actors and policies depends upon the conditions of a particular conflict at a particular time.

Diverse Interveners

Interveners increasingly include global intergovernmental organizations, such as the United Nations and its numerous components and associated specialized agencies. In addition, intergovernmental organizations are associated with economic issues: the International Monetary Fund, the World Trade Organization, and the World Bank. Regional intergovernmental organizations deal with a great range of economic and political issues—for example, the Organization for Security and Co-operation in Europe, the Organization of American States, and the African Union. This expansion is due in part to the enhanced capacity of the UN to act after the cold war's end. For example, the UN is more active in undertaking mediation missions and in conducting forms of sanctions as well as carrying out peacekeeping operations.

States, individually and in ad hoc coalitions, also act to stop mass violence within and between countries. Such actions include various forms of mediation, from facilitating meetings between the antagonists to largely imposing an outcome. They also take the form of imposing economic sanctions or bans on the sale of military weapons. Once the fighting has lessened or largely ended, the peacemaking actions may relate to reaching peace agreements and managing the transition to establishing stable institutions. Many of these actions are carried out in consort with several other governments, often under the aegis of the United Nations or other international governmental organizations.

A wide diversity of not-for-profit international nongovernmental organizations (INGOs) continue to grow in number, size, and functions relating to mitigating and transforming large-scale violent conflicts (Dunn and Kriesberg 2002; Smith, Chatfield, and Pagnucco 1997). They include many organizations providing humanitarian assistance for refugees from wars and organizations acting to protect the human rights of persecuted ethnic, religious, or political groups. In addition, some INGOs provide conflict-resolution services, including mediation and training in negotiation skills as well as furthering reconciliation between former antagonists. Still other INGOs intervene as aids to one side in a violent conflict, providing arms, fighters, or money; they may do so because they share religious, ethnic, or ideological identities or they do so as advocates of human rights or the well-being of refugees, women, or oppressed peoples.

For-profit nongovernmental organizations also play important intervener roles in ways that advance, but sometimes undercut, peacemaking. They include transnational corporations, banks, and mercenary organizations. They often are allied with powerful local groups, buttressing their local dominance. Their roles in conflict transformation warrant more attention than they receive.

Finally, external peacemaking interveners include individuals and small groups advocating for peace and nonviolence and major foundations aiding in economic development and overcoming major diseases. They also include leaders and engaged persons who are part of transnational social movements such as the movement to foster human rights, women's rights, and indigenous peoples' rights and to counter threats to the environment (Smith and Johnston 2002). Organizations associated with religious communities are also active in providing services that may contribute to peacemaking. In addition, diaspora communities are growing in importance in the ongoing cultural and political lives of their countries of residence and of their previous homelands, some of which can also contribute to peacemaking. The magnitude and diversity of INGOs, private for-profit organizations, and advocacy organizations is not conveyed by gathering them together under the name *nongovernmental organization*.

Diverse Interventions

The kinds of peacemaking interventions that occur contemporaneously vary greatly in kind, magnitude, and duration (Stedman, Rothchild, and Cousens 2002). They include providing humanitarian aid for refugees; various forms of mediation, training, and consultation to improve the functioning of political institutions, monitoring the terms of an agreement; and assistance in economic development. Clearly, different actors are able and likely to carry out a particular set of actions but not others. Governments are relatively likely to conduct peacemaking interventions that emphasize state building and security concerns. Their interventions often entail choosing sides in a conflict. This is notable in the conceptualization of disarmament, demobilization, and reintegration. This often presumes the problem is to manage the militant groups that had challenged a government.

Nonintervention is also a policy choice. Indeed, the lack of international peacemaking interventions in countries where mass murders and genocides may be occurring has become widely condemned. For example, this is the case for the Darfur region in the Sudan (O'Fahey 2004). As will be discussed later in this chapter, the international legal norms and practices about military interventions to stop genocide are increasingly debated. Back in January 1979, when Vietnam invaded Cambodia and ended the genocide and terror that the Khmer Rouge was perpetrating, the UN Security Council condemned the invasion and demanded the withdrawal of Vietnamese military forces. As new norms are coming into force, new dilemmas are added about what kinds of interventions under what auspices in which circumstances are legitimate.

From a constructive conflict perspective, peacemaking would benefit from greater attention to the needs of all primary stakeholders and to the use of nonviolent and noncoercive inducements. Popular attention to positive sanctions has recently been spurred by the discussions of the utility of soft power and of smart power (Armitage and Nye 2007; Nye 2004).

The end of the cold war and the dissolution of the Soviet Union produced rapid changes in the countries of Eastern Europe and in the countries of the former Soviet Union. These great changes were remarkably peaceful, considering the potentialities for violent escalations. The Organization for Security and Co-operation in Europe intervened in ways that helped avoid violent escalation. Its high commissioner on national minorities (HCNM) had the authority to intervene at the earliest possible stage in response to a crisis related to national minority issues that threatened international peace. Max van der Stoel, as the first HCNM, 1993–2001, helped avoid escalating conflicts and resolve them consistent with international norms. For example, this was achieved regarding the language and education rights of the Hungarian minority in Romania and the citizenship rights of ethnic Russians in the newly independent Estonia (Möller 2006). The provision of basic human rights for all citizens was required to receive the benefits of good economic relations with the Western European countries and membership in Western intergovernmental organizations. Such peacemaking actions also help reduce conflict asymmetries (Kriesberg 2009; Mitchell 1995).

Positive inducements in the form of rewards for conduct desired by the interveners can also be covert, as when governments secretly provide funding for cooperative behavior from officials in other countries or from leaders of nongovernmental organizations (NGOs) who are challenging their government. This may occur when interveners support changing the regime that they and substantial numbers of the society regard as oppressive. This sometimes has occurred in the transformations away from highly authoritarian governments in Eastern Europe following the dissolution of the Soviet Union.

The goals of peacemaking interventions differ in several ways, including the duration being considered, the interests being served, and the amount of change being sought. I consider the varying reasons for external interventions that may be important for the diverse members of each intervening party. There is always some mixture of internal reasons with concern for the people being assisted in peacemaking.

Peacemaking has expanded greatly in recent decades, significantly in conducting track-two activities. Some track-two processes may be viewed as functioning semiexternally, in the sense that a conflict is formally conducted by officials representing the adversaries and the track-two actions are taken by nonofficials from the opposing sides (Agha et al. 2003). In the Israeli-Palestinian conflict, many track-two undertakings have been conducted by former government figures, academics, or persons in other spheres of work. Various external interveners are often combined, as in the instance of Norwegian government officials assisting semiofficial track-two negotiations during the Oslo peace process (Beilin 1999). Many conflict-resolution nongovernmental organizations cooperate with governments to promote good governance, political transparency, and reconciliation in the course of conflict transformation. From the perspective of many nonurban, poorly educated, and impoverished people, however, these may not be attentive to their greatest felt needs. The interveners and the relatively deprived people might well be better served by building infrastructure and economically productive capacities.

Illustrative Cases of Intervention

Successful peacemaking largely depends upon the conduct of the adversaries themselves and other people in their local area. They are not passive compliers to external interveners' directives. With due attention to the local conditions, interveners often make positive contributions to constructive conflict transformations. But sometimes the initial successes are short-lived and disappointing (Paris 2004). Moreover, international interveners often are ineffective and raise the costs of peacemaking; sometimes their efforts are even counterproductive for those they would assist and for themselves. Generally, the consequences are mixed, with varying costs and benefits for different elements engaged in the conflict. I briefly note a few cases in which external intervention aided conflict transformation and peacemaking or failed significantly to do so.

The transformation of the civil war in Mozambique is a celebrated case. Although the combatants in the war deserve considerable credit for its largely successful transformation, in the late 1980s and early 1990s, the international intervention was very helpful (Bartoli, Civico, and Gianturco 2009). The Community of Sant'Egidio, a private Catholic organization based in Rome with a long history of providing humanitarian aid in Mozambique, began to facilitate negotiations between the FRELIMO-controlled government and the militant resistance, RENAMO. The talks helped transform each side so that they could form new shared institutions and build a relatively peaceful Mozambique.

In the late 1980s, the civil wars that had long ravaged Central American countries—particularly Guatemala, Nicaragua, and El Salvador—began moving toward peace. Oscar Arias, former president of Costa Rica, brought together the heads of the five Central American countries. Meeting in Esquipulos, Guatemala, they reached an accord that provided a framework for peacemaking. The accord included three components providing for ending the civil wars, promoting democracy, and fostering economic integration. The components were to be implemented simultaneously according to a fixed time schedule, which was negotiated in each of the countries suffering a civil war. For example, the government of El Salvador, dominated by military and economic elites, was controlled by the Nationalist Republican Alliance. The Farabundo Martí para la Liberación Nacional (FMLN) militarily challenged the government. After more than 12 years of armed struggle, costing more than 75,000 lives, peace settlement negotiations began in 1989. The Esquipulos Agreement provided a context for the negotiations, which were assisted by UN mediators, and a peace agreement between the government of El Salvador and the FMLN was signed in 1992. According to the agreement, the armed forces would be reduced in numbers and reorganized, the FMLN would demobilize, and former combatants of both parties would be given preference to receive state-owned land for farming. Moreover, free elections would be held, and institutions to protect human rights were to be established.

The peace agreements ending the civil wars in El Salvador, Guatemala, and Nicaragua have not ended structural violence in those countries. Many of the conditions that underlay the civil wars persist, but the political processes have functioned well enough so that the civil wars have not recurred (Paris 2004). Little progress may have been made toward positive peace, but negative peace has been substantially attained, aided by a combination of interventions by leading political figures and national and international governmental actors.

The many attempts by the U.S. government to mediate the Israeli-Arab conflict and resolve it demonstrate some of the possibilities and difficulties in external peacemaking efforts (Kriesberg 2001). For example, after the October 1973 war of Egypt and Syria versus Israel, U.S. secretary of state Henry Kissinger mediated by shuttling between capitals to reach partial settlements between the Israeli and Egyptian governments and between the Israeli and Syrian governments. Kissinger, believing a comprehensive settlement was not then possible, pursued a step-by-step peacemaking strategy. The adversaries negotiated disengagements of their military forces, and Israel withdrew from some of the Sinai that it occupied as a result of the war (Rubin 1981). Kissinger helped construct the formulas for the settlements and promised U.S. resources that would help ensure their implementation while minimizing the risks if an opposing side violated the agreement. Even the powerful U.S. government, however, could not impose a settlement; its mediation efforts were constrained by the incompatible requirements deemed necessary by the leaders of the conflicting sides.

President Jimmy Carter attempted to mediate a comprehensive settlement of the Arab-Israeli conflicts but was unable to even convene a multilateral peace conference. The Egyptian president, Anwar el-Sadat, doubted that any peace agreements could come from such a conference. Instead, he made the astounding gesture of going to Jerusalem in November 1977, intending to break the psychological barriers preventing peace (el-Sadat 1978). The negotiations that followed foundered, and in 1978, President Carter invited President el-Sadat and a small Egyptian delegation and Prime Minister Begin and a small Israeli delegation to Camp David. Working in seclusion for 13 days, President Carter with a few U.S. officials mediated two agreements (Quandt 1986). One was the basis for the 1979 Egyptian-Israeli peace treaty and the other was intended to provide the basis for negotiations about the political status of the Palestinians in the Israeli-occupied territories. The mediation blended traditional with problem-solving mediation methods, and provided significant sweeteners to make the treaty between Israel and Egypt palatable to the two governments. U.S. mediation, however, was unable to make progress on reaching any agreement between Israel and the Palestinians.

Direct negotiations between Israeli and Palestinian officials had to await many changes within Israeli and Palestinian societies, in their relationship, and in the global context. Those changes included the Middle East Peace Conference, held in Madrid in October 1991, where negotiations were initiated

between Israeli officials and Palestinians approved by the Palestine Liberation Organization (PLO), albeit indirectly and within parameters set by Israel.
That conference was convened by the U.S. government following its success in
leading a broad coalition of forces to free Kuwait from the Iraqi invasion and
incorporation of Kuwait.

Those Israeli-Palestinian negotiations, despite U.S. efforts, floundered. A
breakthrough for direct negotiations between the PLO and Israeli officials
began in January 1993, with a meeting between two Israeli private citizens
with two PLO officials. The initial meeting was arranged by a Norwegian citizen and then they were facilitated by the Norwegian foreign ministry, in secrecy, at a location near Oslo. As progress was made, officials from the Israeli
government entered the negotiations. A formula for a Declaration of Principles was agreed upon, and it was announced in September 1993 in Washington, DC, with President Bill Clinton presiding over the event. With the mutual
recognition of the State of Israel and of the PLO, the Oslo peace process was
underway.

Slowly, and increasingly lagging behind the agreed-upon time schedule
for next steps, some progress was made. In May 1994, the Cairo Agreement
for Palestinian self-rule in Gaza and Jericho was announced. Belatedly, elections for the Palestinian Authority (PA) were held in January 1996, and Arafat was elected president. In September 1995, Israel and the PLO signed an
interim agreement to transfer control of major Palestinian populated areas in
the occupied territories to the PA. But few actions were taken to implement
the agreement. The U.S. government engaged intensively in mediation efforts,
and, finally, in October 1998, an agreement was reached between the Palestinian Authority and the Israeli government, led by Netanyahu. The agreement, known as the Wye River Memorandum, detailed steps to implement the
1995 interim agreement. A portion of the territories stipulated to be transferred
from Israeli control to Palestinian control was done, but progress again was
stopped as the Israeli government charged that the PA failed to take strong
measures to halt terrorist attacks against Israelis.

In the May 1999 Israeli elections, Ehud Barak, leader of the Labor Party,
defeated Netanyahu by a large margin. Barak, in his election campaign, had
promised to withdraw Israeli military forces from southern Lebanon, and that
lent priority to seeking a peace agreement with Syria. Barak believed that was
possible in part because of prior diplomacy, including track-two diplomacy
conducted in 1998 by Ronald Lauder, a U.S. businessman (Ross 2004). U.S. officials, including President Clinton, Secretary of State Albright, and Middle
East Envoy Dennis Ross, engaged in intensive, secret mediation between the
Syrian and Israeli governments. At various moments, a deal seemed very close
to being consummated, but at a meeting including President Clinton and Syrian President Hafez-al-Asad, in March 2000, Asad indicated his lack of interest then in the peace agreement.[1] The mediation had not succeeded in the brief
periods when favorable conditions were aligned.

While Israel gave priority to the negotiations with Syria, negotiations with
the PA were sustained. In September 1999, Barak and Arafat agreed to revise
and revive the Wye River Memorandum's terms. Following the collapse of the

Israeli-Syrian negotiations, Barak soon proposed to move directly to negotiations for a comprehensive final agreement. When those negotiations became stalemated, Barak sought a summit conference with Arafat and with President Clinton's participation. Clinton invited Arafat and Barak to a conference to negotiate a final status agreement, beginning July 11, 2010, at Camp David. The conference ended on July 25 without reaching any agreement. In September, the Intifada II erupted with violence, and Israeli military forces tried to militarily suppress it. The Oslo peace process was over. In the Israeli elections in February 2001, Ariel Sharon was elected prime minister of Israel.

Diverse arguments have been made to explain what went wrong (Pressman 2003). For purposes of this chapter, it suffices to say that the failure of the Oslo process may be seen as a failure of the necessary peacebuilding work by the adversaries and the interveners, at the same time that peacemaking efforts were ongoing and incomplete. In retrospect, the peacemaking interventions were not adequate to overcome the substantial differences in the negotiation policies of the Palestinians and of the Israelis.

The international peacemaking interventions related to the breakup of Yugoslavia in the 1990s are generally regarded as having been belated and inadequate. Clearly, they failed to prevent and then to stop extremely brutal warfare. Indeed, at times they arguably exacerbated the disastrous wars (Gibbs 2009). For example, consider the U.S.-led North Atlantic Treaty Organization (NATO) bombing of Serbia to comply with demands to change Serbian policies regarding Kosovo and make peace there. President Obama, in his December 2009 speech in Oslo accepting the Nobel Peace Prize, praised the U.S. intervention relating to Kosovo. But in actuality, much happened that was not praiseworthy. On March 24, 1999, NATO planes, 70 percent U.S. aircraft, began bombing operations in Serbia and Kosovo. This was justified in terms of a humanitarian emergency, but it was undertaken without UN authorization and the result was a humanitarian calamity. Serbian repression and ethnic cleansing of ethnic Albanians in Kosovo was unleashed; in the course of the war, 850,000 ethnic Albanians (half of the population) were driven out of Kosovo. What was supposed to be a short war to bring peace went on with escalating bombing until June 10. The terms of the settlement to end the war were hardly different than those Serbia was ready to accept at the February 1999 conference about Kosovo meeting in Rambouillet, near Paris. What was unacceptable to Slobodan Milosevic at that time was the provision that NATO troops would have the authority to move anywhere in Serbia. There is evidence that the U.S. government wanted a Serbian rejection so that NATO military action could ensue, demonstrating the capacity and value of NATO.[2]

The U.S. policy in Afghanistan went through many stages following the Soviet invasion of Afghanistan in 1979. At the outset, there was no grand goal, and the Central Intelligence Agency objective of damaging the Soviet Union, paying back for U.S. losses in Vietnam, was the guiding directive on the ground (Coll 2004). The Soviet Union was defeated in Afghanistan, but the U.S. officials' support of radical Islamic militants and their short-sighted goals resulted in severely damaging long-term U.S. interests. After the September 11, 2001, attacks by al Qaeda, a wide array of goals and policies were announced and pursued, most of which were badly conceived and executed. The follow-up after the initial quick defeat of the Taliban regime and overrunning al Qaeda camps might have been more successful with more limited goals. At first, U.S. actions made space for the UN and local actors to be actively engaged in state building and U.S. military activities focused on al Qaeda. But soon the fight became more narrowly conducted by the U.S. government and more militarized. Goals expanded while resources were drawn off to fight in Iraq, and the situation in Afghanistan deteriorated.

The U.S.-led invasion of Iraq in 2003 was portrayed in many different ways by President George W. Bush and his associates. Sometimes it was explained as part of the war the United States was fighting against terrorism. Sometimes it was justified in terms of preventing future wars that Iraq would initiate against the United States and other countries. Other government leaders argued the United States was ending an oppressive regime, a kind of peacemaking. Once Saddam was overthrown, the United States was engaged in what some officials and analysts claimed was peacebuilding or nation building.

In regard to peacemaking in Iraq, President Bush and his closest associates set grandiose objectives that were pursued arrogantly, with little attention to how they might be realistically attained (Kriesberg 2007b). The U.S. leaders' hopes of state building in Iraq were soon dashed, but the realities were denied for years. Greed, incompetence, blinding ideology, and hubris produced a disaster for the United States and worse for the people of Iraq (Beinart 2010; Diamond 2005).

ASSESSING PEACEMAKING INTERVENTIONS

To assess how external interventions sometimes succeed in various ways and sometimes fail in other ways to help de-escalate and overcome violent conflicts, it is useful to understand what is needed so that external interventions do help peaceful conflict transformation (Kriesberg 2007a). A comprehensive analysis of a particular conflict should be made by potential interveners prior to choosing an intervention option; that analysis should give attention to the fluidity as well as the rigidity of the conflict conditions. Conflicts change over time, moving through stages of escalation and de-escalation, settlements and implementation. However, different actors move at different speeds, and larger or smaller backward steps occur at each stage.

Conflict Analysis

A comprehensive analysis encompasses several components. First, the major parties in a conflict need to be identified, recognizing their internal heterogeneity and the varying conflict engagement by the diverse components of each party. Oversimplifying reifications of the contending sides should be avoided. Too often adversaries are viewed as homogeneous, and the internal differences are given scant consideration. Thus, attention should be given to what is sometimes derogatively called "spoilers of peace"; these are groups who commit acts that may disrupt major official peace negotiations. They do this to modify the terms of the coming agreement or to prevent its conclusion or implementation, which they regard as misguided.

Second, the salient issues in contention and also the underlying concerns need to be recognized, such as one contending party having power over another or one having illegitimate control of resources. At the same time, shared interests, values, and identities should be identified and given prominence.

Third, the structural relations and asymmetries among the parties in a conflict warrant examination. They relate to demography, economic resources, political power, coercive resources, normative claims, and other factors. Conflicts vary in the degree to which they may be characterized by asymmetries, but it should be stressed that conflict asymmetries change over time, and certain changes toward greater symmetry are often conducive to constructive conflict transformation and peacebuilding (Kriesberg 2009; Mitchell 1995).

Fourth, the contemporary and historical emotional and subjective relations among the adversaries should be examined, including empathy as well as past atrocities and ongoing feelings of fear and mistrust. Again, it should be recognized that such feelings and beliefs about the past and future are malleable and they shift in salience, depending on conditions and leaders.

Finally, the analysis by protagonists should be extended to include the probable conflict interveners and their likely actions. Would-be external interveners should undertake self-reflective analyses to minimize inopportune and counterproductive policies and maximize choosing and implementing constructive transformative policies.

Changes Needed for Sustainable Peace

Two broad kinds of changes are needed to move toward a lasting peaceful accommodation. One is to reduce the grievances by improving conditions or even raising the prospects for improvement. The other is to enhance the ability of the society members, and their institutions of governance, to transform the handling of conflicts so it is deemed legitimate and equitable.

Reducing the sense of grievance is a basic requirement for peacemaking. This may entail reducing inequities, some degree of reconciliation, and assurance of physical security (Bar-Siman-Tov 2003). It also entails increasing the realities and the perceptions of common interests and values. For example, this may be to protect basic human rights for individuals and collectivities.

All grievances cannot be ended entirely in any country; therefore, societal and governmental institutions and practices are needed to settle disputes legitimately. Generally, peacemaking entails strengthening societal governance and developing effective means of conducting conflicts without recourse to violence. Numerous arrangements have been discussed to accomplish this. Many methods relate to political institutions, including elections and rules for political parties (Lyons 2005). Agreements ending violent struggles may effectively ensure some degree of power sharing among the major contenders, at least for some period of time. The task, which can take a very long time, is to develop ways for the government institutions to be resilient and responsive to societal needs.

MANAGING OBSTACLES TO
CONSTRUCTIVE PEACEMAKING

Three interconnected obstacles to peacemaking warrant attention (Richmond 2004). First, certain kinds of interests that interveners have for their interventions can impair effective peacemaking undertakings. Second, reliance on certain ways of thinking about the conflict and transforming it can lead the interveners astray and obstruct peacemaking. Third, particular structural conditions relating to the conflict and its context hamper intervention being useful for peacemaking. Various strategies can be employed to reduce or overcome these obstacles.

The Interveners' Interests

A major set of obstacles to effective peacemaking interventions are related to the reality that external interveners generally have interests in the conflict, which can hamper constructive peacemaking. Interveners are rarely disinterested outsiders. When their stake is large, they are likely to be considered parties to the conflict. For example, recall the complex roles of the U.S. government in the Vietnam War and also the roles of the Chinese and the Soviet governments in that war. Moreover, the stakes are diverse as different elements in the intervening entity have different concerns about the conflict.

Interveners are particular persons who can commit a government or some agency within it or a nongovernmental organization to try to affect the course of the conflict. Some interests may be held by those persons themselves, while other interests are held by the constituents or segments of the constituency. In the latter case, the leaders with authority may decide that such interests within their constituencies should be given great weight. This may be in response to diaspora communities, corporate leaders in particular industries, or particular agencies of government.

Such internally guided interventions can produce inappropriate and ineffective actions for various reasons. They may result in too little attention to the complex realities of the countries where peacemaking intervention may be undertaken. Particular interest groups may encourage foreign policies that serve to meet their own concerns and ignore broader considerations. They may raise the salience of particular issues and bits of evidence. On the other hand, some internal groups may provide information and considerations that contribute to appropriate interventions.

One way to overcome some of the risks of overly self-serving interventions is for those who contemplate intervention to engage in self-examination and self-reflection. It is useful to think about the possible mistakes that can result from giving too much weight to internal considerations and from neglecting to appreciate the realities of the conflict in which peacemaking intervention may be undertaken.

A more fundamental way to overcome overly self-serving interventions is to internationalize them. Of course, this was crucial in establishing the UN and the rules regarding international intervention, which are embodied in the

Security Council. Considerable international consensus is necessary to authorize significant interventions.

Recent international developments related to the idea of the responsibility to protect (R2P) are responses to the lack of interventions when needed and their inadequacies when undertaken (Hall 2010; Mills and O'Driscoll 2010). They are consistent with the previous points, and locate them in a comprehensive framing for effective peacemaking intervention. The heated debates around the world about whether and how to intervene while mass atrocities were underway during the wars in the former Yugoslavia propelled action to reach consensus about the policies that should be undertaken to deal with such circumstances. UN Secretary-General Kofi Annan, addressing the General Assembly in 1999 and in 2000, called for consensus in the international community about not allowing gross violations of human rights and not assaulting state sovereignty. In September 2000, the government of Canada, joined by major foundations, announced the establishment of the International Commission on Intervention and State Sovereignty.

The commission, co-chaired by Gareth Evans and Mohamed Sahnoun, released its report on September 30, 2001, enunciating and analyzing several core principles.[3] The two basic principles are: (1) "State sovereignty implies responsibility and the primary responsibility for the protection of its people lies with the state itself." (2) "Where a population is suffering serious harm, as a result of internal war, insurgency, repression or state failure, and the state in question is unwilling or unable to halt or avert it, the principle of non-intervention yields to the international responsibility to protect." These basic principles are founded on provisions of the UN charter, legal obligations under international and national laws, developing state practice, and the obligations inherent in the concept of sovereignty.

The responsibility to protect embraces three elements: (1) the responsibility to prevent the kind of harms previously identified by addressing root causes and direct causes of those harms, (2) the responsibility to respond to the situations of compelling need appropriately, and (3) the responsibility to rebuild. The responsibility to prevent should have the highest priority. Military intervention should be the last resort and be of the minimal amount needed to reach the objective. Security Council authorization should be sought in all cases, and if the Security Council does not authorize action, the General Assembly may be asked to consider the proposal.

The standing of the idea that the international community has a responsibility to protect human populations under the circumstances and in the manner prescribed in the report has speedily grown (von Schorlemer 2007). R2P was recognized at the September 2005 United Nations World Summit by the world's heads of state and governments.[4]

Much more progress is needed to strengthen the normative and institutional character of R2P to improve peacemaking interventions. An international coalition of NGOs is engaged in doing this (http://responsibilitytoprotect.org). Furthermore, it is important for the peoples of the world to accept responsibility to protect themselves and each other against genocide and gross violations of human rights and to ensure that their governments so act.

Inappropriate Theorizing

A major problem in external peacemaking intervention is that it is often strongly guided by inadequate yet prevailing ways of thinking among the persons directing the intervention. These ways of thinking, which derive from cultural and ideological premises, shape beliefs about reality and values about preferences. This was manifested most strikingly and disastrously by U.S. policy during George W. Bush's administration, but it has been evident in other U.S. administrations and in many other countries. One major set of contemporary beliefs evident in the United States relates to the presumed universally correct societal arrangement of the U.S. form of political democracy and of free-market capitalism.

The problem of achieving peace settlements that are based on transforming societies and yielding a stable peace is a global challenge (Boulding 1978; Kacowicz et al. 2000). In seeking to achieve such outcomes, external interveners sometimes set overly ambitious goals, which then are counterproductive. The U.S. experience in Afghanistan and Iraq during the administrations of George W. Bush is increasingly held up by many observers as examples of such overreaching. The terms *nation building* and *state building* often are used to justify policies of imposition of external solutions to societal problems. These concepts can take forms that hamper effective peacemaking intervention.

Nation building typically has been used in the past to refer to the consolidation of a shared identity as a people manifested in the conviction of members of a collectivity that they have a shared ethnicity with a common origin and a shared destiny (Smith 1991). This is an expression of ethno-nationalism and is exclusive. Nationalism, however, may also be based on people living in a territory with equal and shared political rights and allegiance to similar political procedures. This is civic nationalism, which is inclusive and not based on common ethnic ancestry.

Nation building has taken on additional meanings and connotations since the end of the cold war. Currently, it often refers to external efforts to stabilize and reconstruct societies after wars or state failures. As described in a Rand report, nation building involves using armed force as part of a broader effort to foster political and economic reforms conducive to peace (Dobbins et al. 2007). This broader effort includes promoting security, humanitarian relief, effective governance, democratization, and economic development.

State building in the past has referred to establishing political territorial entities in Europe and on the power enforcement by the government in society (Tilly 1975). The power enforcement depends upon specialized personnel and enduring institutions with control over territory, in which they have the monopoly of legitimate violence. In recent years, analysts of the state have stressed short-term state-building processes in countries with failed or fragile systems of governance. Recently, as articulated in a report of the Organisation for Economic Co-Operation and Development (2008, 7), the goal of international engagement in fragile states is the building of "effective, legitimate and resilient states."

The concept of peacemaking had its origins in the peace studies field and stressed more than the absence of wars, which is designated as negative peace. Many workers in the field stress the need to strive for positive peace, overcoming structural violence (Galtung 1969). Structural violence refers to the societal circumstances in which categories of people suffer grave diminishments in basic living conditions that are available to many others in the society. Numerous works examine the complex issues relating to building sustainable peace (Reychler and Paffenholz 2001; Schmelzle and Fisher 2009; Zelizer and Rubinstein 2009). Persons engaged in peacemaking in this tradition tend to give significant attention to people at the grassroots and subelites to basic human needs, cultural diversity, and long-term conflict transformation.

Nation building, state building, and peacemaking occur within societies largely by the actions of the members of those societies. External intervention can help but also can hamper those developments in varying degrees. In focusing on external intervention here, it should be recognized that the external actors frequently view peacemaking as a step toward nation building, state building, and peacebuilding to incorporate their own preferred values and conditions. Currently, more or less explicitly, many international interveners assert that they are trying to advance democracy, human rights, and free-market capitalism, often very narrowly conceived. In addition, many of the intervening governmental actors support the establishment of governments that are friendly to them and not to their adversaries. As noted earlier in this chapter, such self-serving considerations by external actors profoundly affect whether and how they intervene and also the consequences of their interventions.

Peacemaking interventions, particularly by governments, also are hampered by reliance on various elements of conventional thinking in both goals and in means. The goals too often are formulated in terms of clichés about free markets and democracy and presumed universal standards. The methods tend to place great reliance on coercion, including especially the use of military force, even in situations ill-suited for it.

A comprehensive constructive approach, incorporating ideas and practices from the conflict resolution, peace studies, and conflict transformation fields, can provide a wider array of methods to advance peacemaking. This approach suggests new ways of thinking about the goals and the means for peacemaking. The approach gives attention to the concerns of multiple stakeholders and the heterogeneity within various actors. It emphasizes nonviolent and even noncoercive inducements. In choosing policies applying this approach, long-term as well as immediate consequences of various options are taken into account. A few suggestions are proffered in the next section about ways to increase the chances of choosing goals and means that are relatively constructive.

Considerable discussion has begun regarding the applicability of international law for nonconventional warfare (Schmitt 2007). Presently, wars usually are not waged between states but between a state and nonstate organizations, but international law is generally formulated in terms of interstate conduct. Discussions are growing about creating new international laws about acceptable conduct in violent conflicts involving nonstate actors rather than relying on existing national and international laws. These matters are unsettled, with many international norms being widely violated.

Some gains have been made by expanding the rules limiting the way any military actions may be conducted. That expansion can help contain the damage from civil as well as international wars. This has been achieved in good measure by efforts of nongovernmental organizations, as exemplified by establishing prohibitions against the use of land mines and against children serving in armed forces.[5] Such prohibitions can affect the behavior of nongovernmental militants as well as state military forces as the militants seek legitimacy.[6]

Structural Problems

Many structural issues affect the undertaking of peacemaking interventions and the quality of the interventions. The issues pertain to the nature of the conflict and its context and to the constraints and capacities of the interveners. Violent conflicts are rarely between purely good and bad sides, since members of each side will usually fight on what they regard as good moral grounds and yet varying numbers of them commit self-aggrandizing actions and commit atrocities against their opponents. The interveners, as already discussed, have many internal factors affecting whether and how they intervene that shape how effective the interventions will be.

Without examining the various structural problems challenging the utility of peacemaking interventions, some general considerations will be discussed that help overcome the challenging problems. Some problems may be overcome by changing the organizational orientation of the external interventions. For more effective external intervention, greater attention should be given to the local people's highest priorities. Activities that improve the circumstances of their impoverished lives might well be accompanied with activities that enhance governance and civil society functioning. For example, establishing local cooperatives to handle local service and production functions would also foster conflict resolution capabilities. In large construction and production undertakings, trade union organizations should be promoted since they can help build a strong civil society.

Expanding NGO capacities would help improve peacemaking interventions. This expansion should involve means more than increasing the number and size of transnational organizations. Coalitions and working alliances among several nongovernmental organizations could enable them to undertake and sustain larger projects. Ensuring local autonomy in many of the transnational nongovernmental organizations will help maintain knowledge about and experience with local actors. Greater financial resources and organizational autonomy would obviously be advantageous, and greater variety of income sources should be secured.

Changes in governmental structures and missions would help in conducting more effective peacemaking operations. A reduction in military expenditures and an increase in external expenditures for humanitarian, development, and civil society assistance could help increase the capacity for transforming conflicts and making peace. That change in the balance of military and nonmilitary capacities would make it less likely for governments to resort to military force believing there is no other ready option.

The multiplicity of interveners in many cases produces unwanted consequences, as when they compete with each other, are played off against each other by local actors, or unintentionally undercut each other's peacemaking efforts. The growing attention to these issues has identified mechanisms that minimize undesired consequences (Nan and Strimling 2006). At one extreme, the mechanism is simply for organizations with a broad shared objective to have regular meetings at which they exchange information about their specific activities. At the other extreme, one organization may be given the leadership to directly coordinate the relevant activities of other organizations. In addition, many ad hoc arrangements may be made to sequence the work of different organizations or for them to cooperate on specific peacemaking projects.

Finally, new transnational institutional structures would help overcome the hazards of traditional thinking and the self-serving character of much peacemaking work. More peacemaking undertakings might be associated with UN agencies and organized on a regional basis. The people working in these peacemaking organizations might include youths serving for brief periods and also persons engaged for many years in a few countries, learning the cultures and needs of people where they live and work. These peacemakers would work closely with local people, learning how they live and helping them do what they are striving to do to make their lives better for themselves, their families, and their countries.

CONCLUSIONS

Good intentions do not ensure good conduct and outcomes. Those who are to be the beneficiary of the good intentions may be too narrowly defined so that a great many people are severely harmed. Furthermore, for many of the reasons discussed in this chapter, the actual consequences of peacemaking interventions in terrible conflicts are too often disappointing. They are frequently ineffective and many times counterproductive, causing widespread injury. And yet, in so many circumstances interventions are greatly needed (Ury 2000).

Intervening constructively requires good analyses of the problems that require solutions, including understanding their sources and consequences as well as assessing what policies might overcome those problems. In addition, attention needs to be given to the local capabilities that can contribute to the solutions as well as those capabilities that support undesired solutions. Then, careful assessments need to be made of what contributions various external interveners realistically can make. It is impossible to have all the information and knowledge of relevant social processes to accurately make all such assessments. Yet thoughtful assessments can help guide actors to pursue policies that are likely to be somewhat more effective and not be counterproductive.

External peacemaking interventions are likely to become ever more frequent with the growing integration of the world. This analysis should make it clear that no single entity can or should be the universal intervener. Many different kinds of interventions are appropriate for diverse conflicts and stages of conflicts, and they are best undertaken by interveners with particular kinds of capabilities. Consequently, collaboration and cooperation among different peacemaking interveners is crucial for the best outcomes.

Various potential peacemakers should enhance standby capacities for intervention in conflicts of particular kinds and at different conflict stages. Regrettably, at present in most countries, the only major standby capacities are those within the military forces, and therefore they are called upon for various kinds of interventions, even when they are not the most appropriate interveners.

More attention needs to be given to these issues by researchers and by governmental and nongovernmental practicing interveners. More reflection is needed before and after peacebuilding interventions are undertaken to improve policy making and avoid being more harmful than beneficial. Transforming large-scale violent conflicts and making peace is necessarily a long process. External peacemaking interventions can contribute to that process over the long term. Recognizing that time perspective is challenging, but it can also be reassuring.

NOTES

An earlier draft of some of these ideas was presented at the conference on External Intervention in State and Nation Building in Conflict Situations, hosted by the Walter Lebach Institute for Jewish Arab Co-existence at Tel Aviv University, January 12, 2010. I benefited from the discussion of the paper at the conference. I want to thank Bruce W. Dayton, Azra Hromadizic, and William Banks for their comments and suggestions for this chapter.

1. Asad was seriously ill and focused on arranging his son's succession to the presidency of Syria.

2. John Gilbert, who was the chief of intelligence for the United Kingdom defense minister, observed of the Contact Group negotiators: "I think certain people were spoiling for a fight in NATO; . . . we were at a point when some people thought something had to be done [against Serbia], so you just provoked a fight." David N. Gibbs, 2009. *First Do No Harm: Humanitarian Intervention and the Destruction of Yugoslavia.* Nashville, TN: Vanderbilt University Press, p. 190.

3. The report can be downloaded at http://www.responsibilitytoprotect.org/index.php/publications.

4. In 2007, Secretary-General Ban Ki-moon appointed Francis Deng to be special representative of the secretary general, at the under-secretary-general level, and he appointed Edward Luck as a special adviser, working together on the responsibility to protect.

5. The Ottawa Treaty (Convention on the Prohibition of the Use, Stockpiling, Production and Transfer of Anti-Personnel Mines and on Their Destruction) came into force in 1999, largely as the result of leadership of the Canadian government and of the International Campaign to Ban Landmines.

The Optional Protocol to the Convention on the Rights of the Child on the involvement of children in armed conflict, a UN treaty, entered into force in 2002. Major nongovernmental organizations formed the Coalition to Stop the Use of Child Soldiers in May 1998, which mobilized support for the Protocol and continues to work for its full compliance.

6. Jo Becker, advocacy director of the Children's Rights Division at Human Rights Watch, working to advance the prohibition against child solders, reports some instances of this conduct. Presentation at Syracuse University, September 21, 2010.

REFERENCES

Agha, Hussein, Shai Feldman, Ahmad Khalidi, and Zeev Schiff. 2003. *Track-II Diplomacy: Lessons from the Middle East.* Cambridge, MA: MIT Press.

Armitage, Richard L., and Joseph S. Nye Jr. 2007. "A Smarter More Secure America." Washington, DC: Center for Strategic and International Studies.

Bar-Siman-Tov, Yaacov, ed. 2003. *From Conflict Resolution to Reconciliation.* Oxford, UK: Oxford University Press.

Bartoli, Andrea, Aldo Civico, and Leone Gianturco. 2009. "Mozambique—Renamo." In *Conflict Transformation and Peacebuilding,* edited by Bruce W. Dayton and Louis Kriesberg (pp. 140–155). London and New York: Routledge.

Beilin, Yossi. 1999. *Touching Peace: From the Oslo Accord to a Final Agreement.* London: Weidenfeld & Nicolson.

Beinart, Peter. 2010. *The Icarus Syndrome: A History of American Hubris.* New York: Harper.

Boulding, Kenneth E. 1978. *Stable Peace.* Austin: University of Texas Press.

Coll, Steve. 2004. *Ghost Wars: The Secret History of the CIA, Afghanistan, and bin Laden, from the Soviet Invasion to September 10, 2001.* New York: Penguin Press.

Dayton, Bruce W., and Louis Kriesberg, eds. 2009. *Conflict Transformation and Peacebuilding: Moving from Violence to Sustainable Peace.* Oxford, UK: Routledge.

Diamond, Larry. 2005. *Squandered Victory.* New York: Henry Holt.

Dobbins, James, Seth G. Jones, Keith Crane, and Beth Cole DeGrasse. 2007. *The Beginner's Guide to Nation-Building.* Santa Monica, CA: RAND Corporation.

Dunn, Larry, and Louis Kriesberg. 2002. "Mediating Intermediaries: Expanding Roles of Transnational Organizations." In *Studies in International Mediation: Essays in Honour of Jeffrey Z. Rubin,* edited by Jacob Bercovitch (pp. 194–212). London and New York: Palgrave Macmillan.

el-Sadat, Anwar. 1978. *In Search of Identity: An Autobiography.* New York: Harper & Row.

Galtung, Johan. 1969. "Violence, Peace, and Peace Research." *Journal of Peace Research* 3 (3):168.

Gibbs, David N. 2009. *First Do No Harm: Humanitarian Intervention and the Destruction of Yugoslavia.* Nashville, TN: Vanderbilt University Press.

Gleditsch, Nils Petter. 2008. "The Liberal Moment Fifteen Years On." *International Studies Quarterly* 52 (4):691–712.

Hall, B. Welling. 2010. "International Law and the Responsibility to Protect." In *The International Studies Encyclopedia,* edited by Robert A. Denemark. Blackwell Reference Online, http://www.isacompendium.com/subscriber/tocnode?id=g9781444336597_chunk_g978144433659711_ss1–32.

Harbom, Lotta, and Peter Wallensteen. 2010. "Armed Conflicts, 1946–2009." *Journal of Peace Research* 47 (4) (July):501–509.

Harbom, Lotta, Stina Högbladh, and Peter Wallensteen. 2006. "Armed Conflict and Peace Agreements." *Journal of Peace Research* 43 (5):617–613.

Human Security Centre. 2005. *Human Security Report 2005.* New York: Oxford University Press.

Kacowicz, Arie M., Yaacov Bar-Siman Tov, Ole Elgstrom, and Magnus Jerneck, eds. 2000. *Stable Peace among Nations.* Lanham, MD: Rowman & Littlefield.

Kriesberg, Louis. 2001. "Mediation and the Transformation of the Israeli-Palestinian Conflict." *Journal of Peace Research* 38 (3):373–392.

Kriesberg, Louis. 2007a. *Constructive Conflicts: From Escalation to Resolution*, 3rd ed. Lanham, MD: Rowman & Littlefield.

Kriesberg, Louis. 2007b. "Long Peace or Long War: A Conflict Resolution Perspective." *Negotiation Journal* 23 (2):97–116.

Kriesberg, Louis. 2009. "Changing Conflict Asymmetries Constructively." *Dynamics of Asymmetric Conflict* 2 (1) (March):4–22.

Lyons, Terrence. 2005. *Demilitarizing Politics: Elections on the Uncertain Road to Peace.* Boulder, CO: Lynne Rienner.

Mills, Kurt, and Cian O'Driscoll. 2010. "From Humanitarian Intervention to the Responsibility to Protect." In *The International Studies Encyclopedia*, edited by Robert A. Denemark. Blackwell Reference Online, http://www.isacompendium.com/subscriber/tocnode?id=g9781444336597_chunk_g97814443365978_ss1–28.

Mitchell, Christopher R. 1995. "Asymmetry and Strategies of Regional Conflict Reduction." In *Cooperative Security: Reducing Third World Wars*, edited by I. William Zartman and Victor A. Kremenyuk (pp. 25–57). Syracuse, NY: Syracuse University Press.

Möller, Frank. 2006. *Thinking Peaceful Change: Baltic Security Policies and Security Community Building.* Syracuse, NY: Syracuse University Press.

Nan, Susan Allen, and Andrea Strimling. 2006. "Coordination in Conflict Prevention, Conflict Resolution and Peacebuilding." *International Negotiation* 11 (1):1–6.

Nye, Joseph S. Jr. 2004. *Soft Power: The Means to Success in World Politics.* New York: Public Affairs.

O'Fahey, Rex Sean. 2004. "Environmental Degradation as a Cause of Conflict in Darfur." In *Conference Proceedings*, edited by Rex Sean O'Fahey (pp. 1–112). Khartoum, Sudan: University for Peace.

Organisation for Economic Co-operation and Development, 2008, *Concepts and Dilemmas of State Building in Fragile Situations: From Fragility to Resilience*, http://www.oecd.org/dataoecd/59/51/41100930.pdf.

Paris, Roland. 2004. *At War's End: Building Peace after Civil Conflict.* Cambridge: Cambridge University Press.

Pressman, Jeremy. 2003. "Visions in Collision: What Happened at Camp David and Taba?" *International Security* 28(2):5–43.

Quandt, William B. 1986. *Camp David.* Washington, DC: Brookings Institution.

Reychler, Luc, and Thania Paffenholz. 2001. *Peacebuilding: A Field Guide.* Boulder, CO Lynne Rienner.

Richmond, Oliver P. 2004. "The Globalization of Responses to Conflict and the Peacebuilding Consensus." *Cooperation and Conflict* 39 (2):129–150.

Ross, Dennis. 2004. *The Missing Peace: The Inside Story of the Fight for Middle East Peace.* New York: Farrar, Straus and Giroux.

Rubin, Jeffrey Z., ed. 1981. *Dynamics of Third Party Intervention: Kissinger in the Middle East.* New York: Praeger.

Schmelzle, Beatrix, and Martina Fisher, eds. 2009. *Peacebuilding at a Crossroads? Dilemmas and Paths for Another Generation.* Berlin: Berghof Research Center for Constructive Conflict Management.

Schmitt, Michael N. 2007. "21st Century Conflict: Can the Law Survive." *Melbourne Journal of International Law* 8:443–476.

Smith, Anthony. 1991. *National Identity.* Reno: University of Nevada Press.

Smith, Jackie, and Hank Johnston, eds. 2002. *Globalization and Resistance: Transnational Dimensions of Social Movements.* Lanham, MD: Rowman & Littlefield.

Smith, Jackie, Charles Chatfield, and Ron Pagnucco, eds. 1997. *Transnational Social Movements and Global Politics: Solidarity beyond the State.* Syracuse, NY: Syracuse University Press.

Stedman, Stephen John, Donald Rothchild, and Elizabeth M. Cousens, eds. 2002. *Ending Civil Wars: The Implementation of Peace Agreements.* Boulder, CO: Lynne Rienner.

Tilly, Charles, ed. 1975. *The Formation of National States in Western Europe.* Princeton, NJ: Princeton University Press.

Ury, William. 2000. *The Third Side.* New York: Penguin.

von Schorlemer, Sabine. 2007. "The Responsibility to Protect as an Element of Peace." *Policy Paper 28* (pp. 1–12). Bonn, Germany: Development and Peace Foundation.

Zelizer, Craig, and Robert A. Rubinstein, eds. 2009. *Peacebuilding: Creating the Structure and Capacity for Peace.* West Hartford, CT: Kumarian.

CHAPTER 45

The South African Peace Process: An Urgency Theory Analysis

Dean Pruitt

Traditionally in South Africa, whites totally dominated nonwhites (blacks, coloureds, and Indians[1]) and relegated them (especially the black majority) to an extraordinarily inferior economic and social position. This tradition was codified and intensified after 1948 by a series of apartheid laws that (a) physically separated the races, forcing many nonwhites to give up their homes; (b) required all nonwhites to carry identification cards ("passes"); (c) required nonwhites to gain permission to move from rural to urban areas; (d) prohibited marriage and sexual relations between the races; (e) severely limited educational and occupational opportunities for nonwhites; and (f) eventually stripped all blacks of their South African citizenship and made them citizens of rural and impoverished homelands (Welsh 2009).

Many anti-apartheid organizations developed during the 20th century, but the African National Congress (ANC) became predominant and will be the main one discussed here.[2] Early protests involved petitions and small manifestations, but the movement mushroomed over time—with larger nonviolent demonstrations in the 1950s—until the Sharpeville Massacre of 1960, in which the government killed 69 people who were demonstrating against the pass laws. At that time, the ANC leaders decided that nonviolent protest was ineffective, and they organized a guerrilla resistance, Umkhonto we Sizwe (commonly called MK), which mainly attacked physical structures. In reaction, the government sentenced a number of opposition leaders to life imprisonment—including Nelson Mandela, a prominent ANC lawyer and the organizer of MK, whose imprisonment lasted more than 27 years (Mandela 1994). Other opposition leaders fled abroad, eventually establishing ANC headquarters in Lusaka, Zambia, under the leadership of Oliver Tambo.

A major aim of apartheid was to limit the number of nonwhites in urban regions, but this was not possible because of the need for nonwhite labor. Nonwhites poured into segregated townships close to the main cities. Anti-government strikes and demonstrations continued, culminating in a large-scale countrywide township uprising in 1976–1977. This uprising was put down, and the protest movement appeared to be crushed. But in reality a new organizational effort was underway, culminating in the 1983 founding of the United Democratic Front (UDF). This was "a loose association of some six hundred community groups, trade unions and churches . . . [which] openly identified with the banned ANC and its imprisoned and exiled leadership" (Sisk 1995, p. 64).

Between 1984 and 1987, there was another township-based uprising which dwarfed the earlier ones. This consisted of protest meetings, marches, and demonstrations; rent, school, and consumer boycotts; riots, and citizen take-overs of several of the townships (Lodge and Nasson 1991; O'Malley 2007; Welsh 2009). There were many violent incidents, including the execution of hundreds of supposed government collaborators (Sisk 1995; Welsh 2009).

The uprising started in a march to protest rent increases in the Sebokeng Townships, which resulted in the death of 14 demonstrators at the hands of the police (Welsh 2009); and it quickly spread around the country under UDF leadership (Sparks 1995; Welsh 2009). It was complemented by a long series of strikes by another large new anti-apartheid organization, the Congress of South African Trade Unions (COSATU) (O'Malley 2007). The ANC and MK also contributed by calling for residents to make the townships ungovernable and by exploding more bombs (O'Malley 2007).

The government responded by declaring a state of emergency, arresting more than 30,000 demonstrators and killing more than 3,000 (Lieberfeld 1999). This resulted in a lull in 1988, but the uprising began to rebuild in 1989 under the leadership of the Mass Democratic Movement (MDM), an alliance of UDF and COSATU (Lodge and Nasson 1991).

In the late 1970s and early 1980s, the government under its prime minister and later president, P. W. Botha, had made a series of concessions to the nonwhite majority in an effort to stem the disorder. For example, nonwhite schools were improved, businesses and home ownership encouraged, and limited self-government brought to the townships. A 1983 constitutional revision set up a tricameral parliament with separate houses for the coloureds and the Indians; and, in an effort to divide the ANC, the government offered to release Mandela if he would renounce violence (Harvey 2001; Welsh 2009). None of these measures had much impact on the gathering storm. Most of the coloureds and Indians boycotted the election to the new parliament (Clark and Worger 2004), and Mandela turned down the offer (Mandela 1994). However, instituting these measures led to a split in the dominant white National Party (NP). A new Conservative Party was created in 1982, which was dedicated to restoring apartheid in its earlier, more extreme form (Welsh 2009).

The government's apartheid policies and heavy repression of demonstrators produced a backlash of condemnation and pressure from the outer world. After the events in the 1976–1977 period, an arms embargo was ordered by the United Nations, and South African business began to experience difficulty raising money. By 1986, a full-scale Western sanctions movement was in place, culminating in the Comprehensive Anti-Apartheid Act, which was passed by the U.S. Congress over President Ronald Reagan's veto (Lieberfeld 1999). This act demanded the release of Mandela, the abolition of apartheid, and negotiation to establish a nonracial democracy. The sanctions produced a financial crisis and "contributed significantly to [an] assault on the psyche of white South Africans" (Waldmeir 1998, 57). Their government had "lost international legitimacy and brought pariah status on itself and its own banishment from the world community, and the cost for all these shortcomings was steadily mounting beyond the country's economic capacity" (Zartman 1995, 148).

In the late 1980s, pessimistic long-range thinking developed in the minds of an increasing number of Afrikaner[3] leaders, the people who controlled the National Party, which formed the government. Though by 1988, they had been able to contain three revolts, the conviction grew that their long-term prospects were dim. Many of them began to worry that the next revolt would be unmanageable, destroying, perhaps forever, their privileged way of life (Waldmeir 1998).

The crisis produced by the uprisings, the sanctions, and pessimism about the future was particularly difficult because the only real alternative—negotiating a new government with leaders of the nonwhite majority—challenged the deeply imbedded apartheid tradition and also seemed very risky. The blacks, in particular, were seen as poorly educated and as lazy, dumb, and criminal (du Plessis 2001)—hardly the kind of people you would want in government. Furthermore, there were negative images of the ANC leaders as "wild-eyed terrorists [not as] reasonable men" (Mandela 1994, 546) and as communists who would abolish private ownership and might act as a fifth column for the Soviet Union (Lieberfeld 2007; Waldmeir 1998). Whites were also reluctant to negotiate with an organization that continued to advocate violence, and they feared that a majority government would trample on white rights and seek revenge for prior injustices (Lieberfeld 1999). All of these concerns meant that the thoughtful white elite faced a severe dilemma, a choice between two perceived evils.

Such a dilemma calls for information gathering to judge whether fears about the adversary are accurate and whether a deal is possible—and this is what happened in the latter half of the 1980s. It occurred in two tracks—citizen contacts with the exiled ANC leadership, which started in 1985, and government contacts with prisoner Mandela, which started in 1987. In these contacts, the ANC leaders did their best to counteract white stereotypes. They successfully portrayed themselves as sober, intelligent, and well-educated men who treasured their South African identity and wished to build a society in which all people would participate in an equal-status democracy. While criticizing government policies and demanding equal political rights, they showed respect for Afrikaner culture and traditions and seemed to lack vindictiveness. They maintained that their enemy was apartheid, not the white man (Lieberfeld 2002; Waldmeir 1998).

The early meetings with the ANC exiles were between delegations of white South African citizens (and an occasional opposition legislator) and delegations of ANC leaders headed by Thabo Mbeki, a member of Tambo's inner circle who was in charge of contact with the outer world (Gevisser 2009). The results of these meetings were publicized in South Africa and appear to have "built [among whites] a reservoir of latent readiness to accept the ANC as a legitimate participant in a negotiated settlement" (Lieberfeld 2002, 368).

The next step in this track was a series of 12 secret meetings between ANC leaders led by Mbeki and highly placed Afrikaner citizens, some of whom reported back to government officials and to leaders of the Broederbond, an organization of the Afrikaner social and economic elite. These meetings spanned the period between 1987 and 1990 and mainly took place at the Mells Park estate in England.[4] Most of the issues later covered in the formal negotiations were discussed in these meetings (Lieberfeld 2007). Much time was spent reassuring the Afrikaners about the effect of future majority rule on their community. As the meetings progressed, they increasingly resembled prenegotiation, and substantive agreements were occasionally reached (Harvey 2001).

Toward the end of these meetings, in 1989, the ANC published a moderate position paper, the Harare Declaration, calling for negotiation of a new South African constitution based on the principles of equality and democracy. This declaration stated the conditions under which the ANC would negotiate and some of the stages the negotiation should take. Knowledge gained at the Mells Park meetings helped shape this document (Sparks 1995), which was mainly drafted by Tambo and Mbeki (Gevisser 2009).

The contact with Mandela involved nearly 50 secret meetings with government officials, beginning with Kobie Coetsee, the minister of justice; moving on to Niel Barnard, the powerful head of the National Intelligence Service; and culminating in South African president, P. W. Botha, and his successor, F. W. de Klerk. Mandela's aim in these meetings was to foster negotiation between the government and the ANC leadership. He spent a lot of time recounting the history of the ANC and its demand for majority rule and explaining why it had turned to violence. The government officials indicated their concern that white rights would be trampled under majority rule, voiced alarm about communist domination of the ANC, and called for the ANC to renounce violence. Mandela responded that he "was concerned that the white minority feel a sense of security in any new South Africa," that "whites were Africans as well," and that "in any future dispensation the majority would need the minority" (Mandela 1994, 528 and 539). He said that the ANC was not dominated by communists but had been allied with the South African Communist Party for decades and would not drop this alliance—also that the ANC would not renounce violence until the government stopped its violent campaign against his people. However, he added that ANC violence "could never be the ultimate solution" (Mandela 1994, 528).

In 1989, there was a change of leadership in the heavily conflicted National Party. The cabinet asked Botha to resign, and de Klerk was soon elected president. This provided an opportunity for new thinking about what to do about the unfolding crisis. Finally, on February 2, 1990, de Klerk announced to a surprised world that he would legalize the ANC, the South African Communist Party, and other protest groups; release all political prisoners, including Mandela; and begin negotiation of "a new, democratic constitution [producing] universal franchise."[5] Thoughtful whites who saw the need for a drastic change in policy applauded these moves, but there were many vigorous opponents.

Just after de Klerk's announcement, Mbeki and other ANC leaders traveled to Lucerne, Switzerland, to meet officials of the National Intelligence Service to discuss how to free political prisoners, repatriate ANC leaders in exile, and compose the initial negotiation teams (Harvey 2001; Sparks 1995). Formal prenegotiation between Mandela and de Klerk started in May 1990, and the ANC declared a ceasefire shortly thereafter.

Two formal multiparty negotiation sessions, called CODESA, ensued in 1991 and 1992. Neither produced a definitive agreement, though apartheid was being rapidly dismantled by the government. The main unresolved issues concerned how to protect white rights and prerogatives in a majority government. When progress in these meetings flagged, the ANC and its allies withdrew and organized mass demonstrations to put pressure on the whites. Nevertheless, the two sides were inching toward agreement in secret, backchannel meetings, and a final agreement was reached by a new Multi-Party Negotiation Forum in November 1993—with concessions made by both the ANC and the NP, which spoke for the government. This was followed by a one-person-one-vote election in April 1994, which led to an ANC-dominated government with Mandela as president. De Klerk was second vice-president, and whites controlled four ministries, but it was agreed that this minimal power sharing would only last five years (Welsh 2009). The final constitution that was produced shortly after that time persists to this day, and the overseas sanctions are gone.

URGENCY THEORY

How to explain the dramatic transition from intractable conflict to serious negotiation in a period of five years? The most prominent theory about this kind of transition, Zartman's (1989, 2000a) *ripeness theory*, has been successfully used to understand much of what happened (Sisk 1995; Zartman 1995a). That theory specifies two necessary, though not sufficient, conditions for the initiation of negotiation in conflict situations where two parties are trying to defeat each other:

- The decision makers on both sides see themselves as in a "mutually hurting stalemate," where neither can defeat the other and both have unacceptable costs. A "recent or impending catastrophe" can add impetus to such a stalemate.
- The decision makers see a way out, that is, they foresee that a "negotiated solution is possible for the searching and that the other party shares that sense and the willingness to search too" (Zartman 2000a, 228).

Zartman (2000a) adds that his theory is also useful for understanding the continuation of negotiation once it has started: "The perception of ripeness must continue during negotiation if the parties are not to reevaluate their positions and drop out" (242).

I have developed an extension of ripeness theory, *urgency theory*, which explains additional features of the South African peace process and other historical peace processes as well. This theory is a further development of some of my earlier ideas about readiness for negotiation (Pruitt 1997, 2005).

Urgency Theory is Distinctive in Four Ways

1. It looks separately at the development of ripeness on the two sides of a conflict. Zartman (2000) agrees that the sides often differ in the processes involved in moving toward ripeness, but these differences are not part of his formal theory. The term *readiness* refers to either side's willingness to enter negotiation.

2. It views readiness, and all of its antecedents as variables. Zartman (2000a) acknowledges the importance of variables when he speaks of a "deadlock [that is] painful to both [parties], *although not necessarily in equal degrees*" (228, emphasis added). But most of his writing deals with states rather than variables.

3. It sorts Zartman's antecedents of ripeness into three variables rather than two:

   - Pessimism about winning the conflict at acceptable cost, which is closely related to perceived stalemate. The cost in this definition would result from escalating the conflict in search of victory, not from continuing at the current level of escalation, which is an element of urgency.

   - Perceived urgency to escape the conflict—a variable that grows larger: (a) the greater the ongoing cost of the conflict, (b) the greater the ongoing risk of a future catastrophe weighted by the probable size of that catastrophe, and (c) the closer a deadline at which a catastrophe is likely to occur weighted by the probable size of that catastrophe. A party that experiences an acute sense of urgency is said to be in crisis, in Hopmann's (1998) sense that high priority goals are threatened and the threat is believed to increase over time.[6] For simplicity, the term *urgency* will substitute for *perceived urgency to escape the conflict* in the rest of this chapter. Urgency will be discussed in greater detail later in the chapter.

   - Optimism about the outcome of negotiation, which is a restatement of perceived way out as a variable pertaining to each side separately. Optimism has two components:
     - Belief that the negotiators on the other side and the people they represent have the capacity to alleviate costs and risks.
     - Belief that the negotiators on the other side and the people they represent are willing to do so at an acceptable price.

   The first and third of these variables are gating variables that allow but do not demand certain actions. Pessimism about winning allows escaping the conflict, and optimism about the outcome of negotiation allows movement toward negotiation. Urgency, on the other hand, is a dynamic variable that encourages action when a gate is open. It encourages efforts to escape the conflict to the extent that there is pessimism about winning and efforts to move toward negotiation to the extent that there is optimism about the outcome of negotiation.

Optimism about the outcome of negotiation is compensatory to the other two variables. There must be some degree of all three variables to get negotiation going. But the greater the optimism, the less important it is to believe that the conflict cannot be won or that continuing the conflict will produce significant costs or risks.[7]

4. Urgency theory views movement toward negotiation as a gradual approach that is regulated by level of optimism about the outcome of negotiation. In severe conflict, there are many risks associated with proposing or entering negotiation, including conferring legitimacy on the adversary, being seen as weak in the eyes of the opponent or one's constituents, undermining the commitment of one's fighting forces, and becoming embarrassed if the negotiation does not bear fruit. Hence, leaders who feel urgency about ending the conflict and recognize that negotiation is the only solution will nevertheless move cautiously at first, approaching direct negotiation through stages as their optimism grows (Pruitt 2011a).

   Two earlier case studies illustrate this progression of stages. The series of events that led to the establishment of the Palestinian State in the Middle East (Pruitt 1997) started with track-one-and-a-half diplomacy, where third-level officials of the Palestine Liberation Organization (PLO) talked with private Israeli citizens who were in touch with their government. It moved on to back-channel talks in which these PLO officials talked with third-level Israeli officials, and then to a conversation between the foreign ministers of Israel and the PLO with the top leaders tuning in. It was only when the foreign ministers had reached agreement that the top leaders met to sign it.

   The second case is the Northern Ireland peace process (Pruitt 2007b), which started with an exchange of conciliatory signals between Gerry Adams, who was the head of Sinn Fein (the political wing of the Irish Republican Army or IRA), and the British secretary of state (governor) for Northern Ireland. They then moved on to secret intermediation, in which Adams talked with moderate Irish leaders who communicated with the British government, and finally to publicized negotiations between the two sides.

MORE ABOUT THE CAUSES AND CONSEQUENCES OF URGENCY

Urgency is the key concept in the theory just described. It provides the impetus to explore and enter negotiation, to stay in the negotiation, and—as shown in laboratory experiments on negotiation—to speed up concession making (Pruitt 1981). There are many sources of urgency, and they have different implications for the course and outcome of the conflict.

- A common source of urgency is the cost and risk of engaging in conflict—lives and property lost in battle, the danger of a disastrous future escalation. If the leaders on both sides become pessimistic about winning the conflict and this is the main source of urgency, they can sometimes escape the conflict without negotiation. They may enter what Zartman (2006) calls an S^5 situation—a "soft stable self-serving stalemate . . . where the two sides continue in a de facto partition, punctuated by flashes of violence, and learn to live with it and even enjoy it" (255). An example would be the 2010 stalemate between Israel and

Hezbollah. However, if either party's urgency is due to other sources, the S^5 route is not available, and a negotiated settlement becomes the only way out of the conflict.

- A second source of urgency, the plight of one's constituents, is experienced when leaders who are dedicated to the welfare of a disadvantaged group become pessimistic about winning. An S^5 solution does not relieve such urgency because it does not improve the welfare of their constituents. Hence, they are likely to continue fighting, if possible, while cautiously exploring the prospects for negotiation. This happened in Northern Ireland, where Gerry Adams and his close associates began secret communication with the British government while the IRA fought on. The British government would probably have been satisfied with an S^5 solution in which the IRA diminished its attacks and the conflict mellowed. But this solution was not available, because the IRA was fighting for a substantial cause and required a structural solution before it would stop fighting. This kind of urgency is a function of leader identification with the plight of their constituents and the extent of this plight.

- A third source of urgency is pressure to prepare for or enter negotiation by third parties who are alarmed or inconvenienced by the conflict. Examples of such third parties are allies who are getting tired of supporting a fighting force. Allies are particularly likely to apply pressure if there is reason for optimism about finding a reasonable solution, as when Robert Mugabe's allies pushed him into signing an agreement that ended the Zimbabwe War (Stedman 1991). Urgency will be greater the more important the third party and the heavier its pressure.

- A fourth source of urgency is fear that militant leaders will gain power on one's own or the other side. Examples of such leaders are military officers—who gain prominence during fighting—and hardline politicians who may be elected with the promise of increasing pressure on the adversary. Such a development is an obvious catastrophe for the leaders who are displaced. But it may also be so viewed by leaders on the other side if they hope to move toward settlement.

- A fifth and final source of urgency is the perception that time favors the other side. Even if both sides recognize that they cannot win, competition for advantage is likely to continue; and if the other side is better at this competition, one's bargaining strength will decrease over time. This makes it urgent to reach agreement soon. The more effective the other party's competitive moves, the greater the urgency

By viewing urgency as a variable, it becomes possible to talk about different levels of urgency on the two sides of a conflict. The party with the greater urgency—whatever the source—will have lower bargaining strength and, hence, will make larger concessions to get negotiation going and to reach agreement.

WHY THE WHITES NEGOTIATED: AN URGENCY THEORY ANALYSIS

After 1984, a sense of crisis—that is, severe urgency to escape from the conflict—began to sweep across the white elite community in South Africa. There were four main problems, with associated costs. One was the township uprisings and industrial strikes. Many of the townships became ungovernable and major industries were often shut down. The second was international sanctions, the most devastating of which was the withholding of capital transfers. The third was the economic decline brought on by the first two problems. The fourth was attacks by MK. These killed few people and did not have a large economic impact, but they were important because they gave impetus to the township uprisings (O'Malley 2007).

For many thoughtful whites, including members of the Afrikaner elite and government officials, this sense of urgency was enhanced by the perceived risk of a still larger uprising that could overwhelm the white minority in the not-too-distant future. Thus, Sisk (1995) remarks, "Each successive period of resistance—1952, 1960, 1976–77, 1984–88—was more intense and widespread, and the regime's efforts to contain revolution through repression were less and less successful. . . . How long before another round of violence and repression would begin? And if it began, how long would it last and how many lives would be lost? And the next time, would the state have the capacity to contain it? These thoughts were foremost in the minds of the NP leaders" (61, 64–65). When demonstrations began again in 1989, these fears must have intensified.

Implicit in the anxiety about a devastating future revolt were pessimism about ultimately winning the conflict and a perception that time favored the other side. The latter suggested that delaying negotiation would produce a worse agreement for the whites, a point implied by de Klerk when he said shortly after his February 2, 1990, speech, "We did not wait until the position of power dominance turned against us before we decided to negotiate" (quoted in Sisk 1995, 84). For many leaders of the governing National Party, the continued disorder created another threat—that white backlash would further strengthen the Conservative Party to the point of destroying the NP's majority (Harvey 2001). It became increasingly clear that the government would have to negotiate with nonwhite leaders soon.

This negotiation had to be with Mandela and the rest of the ANC, because only they could alleviate the major costs and risks for the white community. The ANC was widely supported by the nonwhite community (Lieberfeld 2005), and Mandela was famous in his own country and around the world (Welsh 2009). Hence, they were unique in their ability to control the township residents and persuade the world to discontinue its sanctions. Furthermore, the many unofficial meetings with leaders of the ANC had encouraged optimism that an agreement was possible at an acceptable price. Thus, Welsh (2009) writes about these meetings, "These encounters . . . strengthen[ed] support for the principle of negotiating with the ANC, now increasingly accepted as inevitable among sections of the Afrikaner elite" (354). The Harare Declaration, with its endorsement of negotiation and failure to mention the people's war, must have produced added optimism.

However, as Welsh (2009) also notes, "Grassroots white opinion . . . remained generally hostile" (354). The crisis and its solution was mainly in the minds of people at the top of white society. Even at that level, there were many dissenters, among them President Botha, who had surrounded himself with hardliners in the security community.

By 1989, the elite sentiment for negotiation had grown so strong that Botha was pushed out of office and the hardliners demoted in their influence. De Klerk, Botha's replacement, was not at first committed to negotiation. But he quickly concluded that it was the only possible solution to the crisis, which would deepen if it did not start soon. He also faced pressure to negotiate from several European leaders and leaders of the African frontline states (Sparks 1995). So he met the most important ANC preconditions for negotiation—legalizing the ANC and related organizations and freeing political prisoners—and called for negotiation, which began soon thereafter.

Two other elements of the situation in 1989 to 1990 reduced the perceived risk of agreement with the ANC and hence contributed to optimism about negotiation: the decline of the Soviet Union and the negotiated agreements that removed Cuban troops from Angola and gave Namibia its independence. Earlier, many whites had feared that the ANC was a tool of the Soviet Union and would foster that country's interests if admitted to the government. But with the Cuban troops gone and Soviet power sharply eroding, concern about the "red menace" largely disappeared (Waldmeir 1998). The Namibian agreement showed that it was possible to negotiate a reasonable agreement with African leaders who were comparable to those at the head of the ANC (Welsh 2009).

WHY THE ANC NEGOTIATED: AN URGENCY THEORY ANALYSIS

Mandela

Mandela's rationale for seeking negotiation is well modeled by urgency theory. In 1985, while still a prisoner, he sent a letter to Coetsee, who had just been appointed minister of justice, proposing "a meeting to discuss talks between the ANC and the government" (Mandela 1994, 523). He was motivated in part by a perception that the anti-apartheid forces could not win at acceptable cost. He writes, "It was clear to me that a military victory was a distant if not impossible dream" and the effort would cost "thousands if not millions of lives" (525). Furthermore, there was a strong element of urgency: "If we did not start a dialogue soon, both sides would be plunged into a dark night of oppression, violence, and war" (525). This was enough to start him exploring the possibility of negotiation.

Soon thereafter, he was taken to hospital for prostate surgery and, while there, received a courtesy visit from Coetsee. He interpreted this as a signal that the government was also concerned about the danger of a race war—a basis for optimism. "They must have known this as well. It was time to talk" (525). According to Mandela's autobiography, he was right about this inference. When the secret talks started in 1987, they concerned such topics as the ANC's preconditions for negotiation and what would be done to protect white rights in an ANC-led state. Actually, only part of the government was interested in negotiation, but the people he mainly talked with—Coetsee and Barnard—were in that part.

THE ANC EXILES

The path toward negotiation was rather different for the exiles who ran the ANC in Lusaka. A resolution that was adopted in 1985 strongly endorsed a "people's war" to overthrow the white regime (Sisk 1995). Yet a scant four years later, the Harare Declaration mainly talked about negotiation and said nothing about a people's war. What accounts for this dramatic transformation?

From its earliest times, the ANC had always favored a democratic, equal-status state, including people of all races. This was embodied in the organization's most sacred document, its 1955 Freedom Charter.[8] Equal status implies that differences should be settled consensually, and the ANC had traditionally "left the door open to negotiation" (O'Malley 2007, 252). Willingness to negotiate is briefly mentioned in an otherwise bellicose 1985 statement by Tambo, the ANC president who was speaking for the ANC's National Executive Committee. He said that "no revolutionary movement can be against negotiations in principle," but he viewed them as infeasible because "this regime is not interested in a just solution of the South African question" (Tambo 1987, 161). That statement implies that, for Tambo and likeminded ANC leaders, the people's war was designed to force the government to negotiate a new order. This conclusion is reinforced by George Bizos (2007), one of Mandela's lawyers, who reports that, in 1985, Tambo told him in private that, "ever since the 1950s the ANC's policy had been to bring the government to the negotiation table" (420) and that he fully supported Mandela's efforts to start talks with the government.

Though Mandela was pushing negotiation and Tambo was pushing people's war, there was probably little difference in their basic outlook. Tambo subsequently supported Mandela's talks, even when some militant UDF and ANC leaders accused Mandela of selling out (O'Malley, 2007). Likewise, Mandela (2007) later wrote that he was in full accord with the "four pillars of the struggle . . . mass mobilization and action, building a sustainable political underground, building MK and developing the armed struggle, and international action to isolate apartheid South Africa" (10), which were the basic elements of Tambo's strategy.

This looks like an unplanned but mutually acceptable division of labor in a bad-cop/good- cop strategy. In this strategy, one member of a team (the bad cop) threatens and harasses the adversary while another team member (the good cop) is friendly with the adversary and provides assurances of the rewards that will result from making the required concessions. Tambo, the bad cop, had the job of creating a crisis that would force the government to seriously consider negotiation; and Mandela, the good cop, had the job of encouraging government optimism about the outcome of such negotiation. Mandela, in prison, could hardly command the troops, as in the past, but he could secretly meet government officials, so he had the good cop job. All of this suggests that both men realized the urgency of moving to negotiation, but they approached this challenge in different but complementary ways.

The bad-cop/good-cop strategy uses the elements of urgency theory (and its parent, ripeness theory) to manipulate the other side. The job of the bad cop is to show the other side that it cannot win the conflict, which should be urgently abandoned. The job of the good cop is to make the other side optimistic about reaching a negotiated agreement without sacrificing its most basic interests. The bad-cop/good-cop strategy is a powerful one, as shown in the psychological laboratory (Hilty and Carnevale 1993) and often in history.

Tambo became more directly involved in good-cop activity—optimism building—when he authorized Mbeki to hold friendly talks with white South African delegations. The broader ANC leadership had approved these talks with the thought of trying to win the delegates over to the ANC position (Lieberfeld 2005). But as the talks continued and as Mandela began his meetings, it became clear that there was a growing white sentiment for negotiation at some of the highest levels of Afrikanerdom (Welsh 2009). This suggested to Tambo, in 1997, that the ANC should prepare for negotiation in case the government should suddenly propose it. According to Welsh (2009), he worried that the ANC's allies might force his organization to accept such a proposal, recalling that this had happened to Rhodesian rebel leader Robert Mugabe when the British proposed negotiation in 1979. So he asked Mbeki to find a way to talk with powerful Afrikaners. The result was the Mells Park meetings, which further strengthened optimism about negotiation on both sides.

Eventually, in 1989, there was outside pressure on the ANC to adopt a strategy that would lead to negotiation. This came "from major Western governments . . . the frontline states, [and] the ANC's major backer, the Soviet Union" (Welsh 2009, 371). According to O'Malley (2007), this pressure became so strong that Tambo began to worry that some other individual or group—for example, Prime Minister Margaret Thatcher of Great Britain—would seize the initiative and try to structure South Africa's political future. Instead, he wanted the ANC to "take charge of what needs to be done in our country" (315)—to maintain the moral high ground that it enjoyed and avoid being pushed into an unfavorable agreement. The result was the Harare Declaration, which moved both sides even closer to negotiation.

Though the top leaders of the ANC were preparing for negotiation in 1989, some secondary leaders and rank-and-file members—especially those associated with MK—were still plumping for violent overthrow of the white government. These differences may paradoxically have produced another element of urgency for the top ANC leadership once negotiation seemed a serious possibility. According to Harvey (2001), "Tambo and Mbeki were increasingly concerned that control of the movement might slip into the hands of the young radicals, which was a powerful incentive for them not to allow South Africa to drift into civil war" (111).

WHITE VERSUS ANC URGENCY: A COMPARISON

In early 1990, both sides became committed to negotiation. Clearly, this was the outcome of a mutual hurting stalemate as asserted by Sisk (1995) and

Zartman (1995a). In urgency theory terms, the top leaders on both sides became pessimistic about winning at acceptable cost and began to share a sense of urgency to escape the conflict.[9] But it would be hard to argue that urgency was equal on the two sides, as implied by Sisk (1995), when he speaks of a "roughly equal . . . balance" (74) and by Welsh (2009), when he says that "When the (negotiation) process started in 1990 the NP and the ANC . . . had a rough parity of bargaining resources" (487–488).

White elites, including the new president and most of his cabinet, were in a real crisis in 1989 and thereafter. Ending the conflict was an extremely urgent matter. The government's main strategy, police enforcement of the apartheid laws, was a failure. There were thousands of political prisoners, yet strikes, boycotts, and nonpayment of township rents continued unabated (Clark and Worger 2004), and heavier action was beginning again. Powerful outside pressures to end the conflict had taken the concrete form of sanctions, which had all but stopped economic growth. Furthermore, when thoughtful whites looked ahead, they saw a strong possibility that the next revolt would overwhelm the white security forces, causing whites to fall from comfortable affluence to abject misery, a very great distance.

ANC leaders also felt some urgency. They and their constituents were hurting from the conflict, and they knew that a race war would be a lot more painful. There were also outside pressures to end the conflict, which would probably intensify if the ANC refused the government's offer of negotiation; and there was a danger, similar to that faced by the whites, that extremists would become more powerful if the conflict continued.

However, elements of the situation made it much less urgent for the ANC to find a way out of the conflict than for the white elites. Nonwhites and the ANC held the moral high ground—the outside world was supporting them and punishing the whites. Also, time was working in their favor and against the whites, in the sense that their strategy of township revolts and frequent strikes was, on the whole, successful. The existence of large new ANC allies, UDF and COSATU, meant that the nonwhite population was much better organized than ever before and hence could be mobilized repeatedly in the foreseeable future. In light of this potential for mobilization, their 10-to-1 population advantage over the whites made a big difference. Furthermore, the ANC's constituents did not have so far to fall if a race war occurred because they were already on the bottom. Their catastrophe would not be as great as for the whites, whose affluent and protected way of life would not survive.

This asymmetry, this difference in urgency, suggests that by 1989 to 1990, the whites were in a far weaker bargaining position than the nonwhites, despite their advantage in fire power, wealth, and control of the government. This weakness helps explain why they made so many large and wrenching concessions in contrast to the ANC.

The most astonishing concessions were made by de Klerk in his February 2, 1990, speech before the negotiation began. Admitting the ANC to equal-status negotiations represented an extraordinary departure from the centuries of extreme white dominance, the legal codification and doctrinal justification of apartheid, and the belief in black inferiority. It is true that this concession was the culmination of a gradual process over the prior five years, but that makes it no less of a concession. In exchange, the ANC only agreed to negotiate, which had been the goal of its top leadership all along. Another major de Klerk concession was legitimizing the ANC without requiring public renunciation of violence or even a formal MK ceasefire. Failing to insist on these preconditions would have been unthinkable a year earlier.[10] Still another big concession was to legitimize mass demonstrations led by the ANC while delegitimizing government resistance in the form of shooting or arresting demonstrators. This altered the balance of coercive power away from the government, though some irregular police personnel continued to use force covertly.

The NP under de Klerk made other major concessions during the negotiation. It agreed to the ANC's main demand to hold one-person-one-vote elections, though this practically assured that nonwhites would end up running the government. It abandoned efforts to establish permanent power sharing and agreed to a limited five-year participation in the new government (Welsh 2009). In 1992, after the ANC had withdrawn from CODESA and launched mass demonstrations, de Klerk met with Mandela and agreed to demands that separated him from his only substantial black ally, the Zulu-based Inkatha, and released political prisoners who had committed crimes (Welsh 2009). Another major NP concession was abandoning a proposal for a highly decentralized federal system in which regions such as that housing Inkatha would be largely independent of the central government. Instead, the NP accepted an ANC proposal for limited regional powers that could be overridden by central government policies (Welsh 2009).

The ANC did make some concessions in the end—most notably, allowing a limited coalition government in the first five years after the election; leaving industry in white hands; allowing white attrition by retirement in the civil service, police, and the army; and giving local regions a measure of self-government. However, the first concession was not very large, being confined to a limited period of time. And the ANC became convinced, as they looked at the larger picture, that the second to fourth concessions were in their own best interest (Welsh 2009). Though it was a big concession from previous positions, leaving industry in white hands avoided disrupting the economy and alienating the foreign investors that were so important for that economy. The ANC recognized that this concession would give them access to resources they would later need to govern effectively. The other two concessions satisfied constituencies that would otherwise have opposed the final agreement and could have destroyed it. All four of these concessions helped build a broad central coalition of groups that either favored or could live with the final agreement, greatly increasing the likelihood that the agreement would endure.[11]

Of the relative strength of the two parties during the negotiation, Zartman (1995a) says, "The National Party made the largest concessions" (168). Welsh (2009) agrees: "The fundamental trend of the negotiations was that the NP's bargaining power had declined to the extent that [in 1993] it had to abandon some of its earlier proposals, receiving few concessions in return" (487). In addition to the ANC's new capacity for legitimate mass demonstrations,

Welsh attributes this decline to the previously negotiated April 1994 deadline for elections, an additional source of urgency as that deadline approached. Trying to put off that deadline would probably have cost the NP its working relationship with the ANC and could well have produced a massive non-white backlash. In a newspaper article that appeared just before the November agreement, two anonymous NP negotiators were quoted as saying, "[The NP] was bargaining from such a weakened position that it could achieve no more" and "[The task of the government negotiators was] to sell off the family silver as gracefully as possible" (Welsh 2009, 508).

STAGES IN THE MOVEMENT TO DIRECT NEGOTIATION

An overview of the talks preceding the opening of formal negotiation reveals a similar pattern of stages to that seen in the earlier two cases. The talks began cautiously and became more direct as time went on. Directness refers to closeness to the top leadership on both sides. It is measured in two overlapping ways: (a) the rank in the governing elite of the senior representative on each side and (b) the number of intermediaries between the senior representative and the top leader on each side. There were two series of talks before the release of Mandela: (a) between ANC leaders in exile, led by Mbeki, and various representatives of the white community and (b) between Mandela and various members of the government. Both became more direct over time.

The early talks with the exiles (1995–1997) were track-one-and-a-half meetings, involving officials from the ANC side and private citizens or opposition parliamentarians on the white side. When the Mells Park talks (1997–1990) started, the government became more directly involved, in that the leaders of the white delegation reported to high government officials. I call these *linked* track-one-and-a-half meetings. Even greater directness was achieved in 1990, when Mbeki met with National Intelligence Service officials, in what can be considered back-channel talks.

Mandela's secret talks were all linked track-one-and-a-half meetings in that Mandela did not speak as a representative of the ANC but was occasionally in touch with Tambo through intermediaries (Bizos 2007; O'Malley 2007). However, they also became more direct over time in that they moved closer and closer to the center of white power. Mandela started talking with Coetsee, a member of Botha's cabinet; then moved on to Barnard, who was closer to the president; and finally to both presidents, Botha and de Klerk. This series ended in 1990 with fully direct talks between the two organizations, represented by de Klerk as head of the government and Mandela as de facto leader of the ANC after Tambo's stroke (Lodge 2006).

SUMMARY AND CONCLUSIONS

The goal of the larger Comparative Peace Processes project, which includes the South African case among others, is to develop new theory about the processes by which intractable conflicts are solved. Urgency theory was developed from this and other cases and seems to fit this case well. The theory specifies three variables that contribute to a party's readiness for negotiation: pessimism about winning the conflict at acceptable cost, perceived urgency to escape the conflict, and optimism about the outcome of negotiation.

Urgency theory helps understand each side's movement toward negotiation during the crisis in the late 1980s—the largest racial conflict in South African history. On the white side: (1) An increasing number of white elites, including prominent Afrikaners and government officials, became convinced that they could not defeat the dissidents and restore apartheid. (2) They felt increasing urgency about stopping the conflict because of the sanctions, the declining economy, and the growing fear that the security forces would be overwhelmed in the next uprising. The nonwhites had a stronger strategy and more powerful allies, which meant that the whites held an ever-weakening bargaining hand. (3) The whites felt increasingly optimistic about negotiating with the ANC, which (a) seemed capable of controlling the protest and persuading the international community to lift the sanctions; and (b) seemed willing to do so at a high but acceptable price. The latter conclusion was based on meetings between white delegations and ANC leaders in exile, conversations between Mandela and government officials, and the Harare Declaration.

On the ANC side, Mandela became convinced that nonwhites could not win at an acceptable cost and that a devastating race war was around the corner. He interpreted Coetsee's visit to his hospital room as an optimistic signal of government interest in finding a negotiated settlement. His optimism must have risen when he began to talk with the government and again when he was admitted to audiences with Botha and de Klerk.

In 1985, the ANC exiles endorsed a people's war that would make the townships ungovernable. While some ANC cadres envisioned a fight to the finish, their top leader, Oliver Tambo, and likeminded companions, apparently saw this war as a way to turn the whites toward negotiation. Somewhat later, he became aware of a growing white sentiment for negotiation, which convinced him of the need to meet prominent Afrikaners so as to be prepared if negotiation was actually proposed. This led to the Mells Park meetings, which created further optimism about the possibility of successful negotiation. By 1989, three new elements of urgency had entered the picture. One was pressure for negotiation from outside supporters, especially the Soviet Union. The second was fear that some other individual or group would try to structure an agreement, leaving the ANC out of the planning. The third was fear that if the conflict continued too long, militant forces within the ANC might take over, making negotiation impossible. The result was a pivotal document, the Harare Declaration, calling for the negotiation of a new South African constitution that would produce fully democratic elections.

These events were followed by a major speech by de Klerk legalizing the ANC and other anti-apartheid parties; freeing many political prisoners, including Mandela; and proposing negotiation. Formal talks between de Klerk and Mandela began soon thereafter, leading, after many ups and downs, to an agreement that involved concessions from both sides, though not in equal measure.

It seems clear that urgency was considerably greater for the whites than for the nonwhites. This unevenness probably explains why the government made so many wrenching concessions, both before and during the negotiation, and the ANC so few.

Urgency theory also holds that, in severe conflict, movement toward negotiation is a gradual process that yields increasingly direct talks as optimism increases. In support of this proposition, several prenegotiation stages were found in the South African case. The talks went from track-one-and-a-half meetings to linked track-one-and-a-half meetings, to back-channel meetings involving increasingly higher officials, and finally to meetings between the heads of the two organizations, Mandela and de Klerk.

Urgency theory, and ripeness theory as well, provide an explanation for the frequent success of the bad-cop/good-cop strategy. The bad cop encourages the adversary to believe that it cannot win and that it is urgent to end the conflict—that is, the bad cop encourages a sense of hurting stalemate. The good cop encourages optimism about the outcome of a settlement in which the adversary makes the required concessions. This strategy was enacted by the ANC, with Tambo and most of the ANC leadership playing the role of bad cop—encouraging the township rebellions—while Mandela and Mbeki (at Mells Park) played the role of good cop—helping work out a preliminary agreement in which the white government made the ANC's required concessions while not losing its shirt.

While urgency theory is an offspring of ripeness theory, it is also distinctive in its analysis of each side separately, its emphasis on variables rather than states, and its tripartite distinction between pessimism about winning, perceived urgency to escape the conflict, and optimism about the outcome of negotiation. Making optimism a variable allows understanding the stages that are often found as parties in a mutually hurting stalemate (both doubtful about winning, both feeling some urgency about escaping the conflict) move gradually toward direct contact. Making urgency a variable allows for the possibility that (a) urgency may grow, as it did for both sides in this conflict; and (b) parties in a mutually hurting stalemate may nevertheless differ in bargaining strength, such that one of them substantially outpoints the other in the prenegotiation and negotiation phases. By 1989, the nonwhites had become the stronger side.

The latter suggests a possible defect, not in ripeness theory but in the way it is frequently applied: the assumption that the parties must be of comparable strength for a hurting stalemate to occur. In the South African case, there was a mutual hurting stalemate, in which the key leaders on both sides concluded that they could not beat each other at acceptable cost and that ongoing costs and risks were large enough to warrant trying to settle the conflict. This and growing optimism caused them to enter negotiation, stay in it (back channels were usually at work during breaks in the formal negotiation), and pull back from the brink when there was danger of runaway escalation. Yet the two sides differed in bargaining strength as a result of (a) the vast inequality in population size; (b) the emergence of the UDF and COSATU, which were able to mobilized large segments of the nonwhite population; (c) white fears that their superior *physical* force would be insufficient in the next big confrontation; (d) the ever-increasing international isolation and sanctions against the whites; and (e) the fact that whites had much further to fall in a race war than did blacks. This created a crisis for the whites, a level of urgency that could only be remedied by wrenching and often unreciprocated concessions.

The fit between our case and urgency theory does not prove the validity of that theory. Indeed, part of the inspiration for that theory was the case itself. Validation requires testing whether urgency theory helps understand other cases not yet examined. In testing that theory—indeed any theory—against subsequent cases, one is sure to find boundary conditions beyond which it is not useful. Discovering and understanding such boundary conditions is a further element of theory building and hence should be welcomed.

ACKNOWLEDGMENTS

I wish to thank Samantha Levine for her early help with the literature, Christopher Mitchell for his comments on an earlier draft, and Daniel Lieberfeld for his comments on two earlier drafts.

NOTES

1. Blacks make up 79.4 percent of the South African population; coloureds, descents of the no-longer-existent Khoisan tribes of the Cape who intermarried with whites, make up 8.8 percent; Indians and other Asians make up 2.6 percent; and whites make up 9.2 percent. In 2010 the population stood at 50 million people (see http://www.southafrica.info/about/people/population.htm).

2. The ANC was a multiracial organization with blacks, Indians, and whites in leadership positions.

3. There are two main white groups in South Africa. About 60 percent are Afrikaners, who mainly descend from Dutch settlers, and 40 percent are English-speakers, who mainly descend from English settlers and immigrants from other European countries. The main language of the Afrikaners is Afrikaans, a derivative of Dutch.

4. A 2009 movie dramatizes these meetings: *Endgame*, staring William Hurt.

5. This speech can be read at www.disa.ukzn.ac.za/index.php?option=com_displaydc&recordID=spe19900202.026.021.000.

6. Urgency plays a central role in a rival theory of ripeness. Haass (1990) writes that, "The most important [essential of ripeness] is that parties must conclude that in the absence of an agreement, *time does not work in their favor*" (27; emphasis added).

7. This is implied by Mitchell's (1995) hypothesis that attraction to negotiation often lies in the parties' "belief that . . . they would win more cheaply . . . (than by) coercive means" (45).

8. The Freedom Charter can be read at www.waado.org/NigerDelta/Documents/ConstitutionalDocuments/ANCFreedomCharter.html.

9. At the end of 1989, Alfred Nzo, the ANC's acting president after Tambo's stroke, acknowledged "that we do not have the capacity to intensify the armed struggle in any meaningful way" (Lodge 2006, 171).

10. The ANC announced a ceasefire on August 7, 2000, seven months after de Klerk's speech (Lodge 2006).

11. For central coalition theory, see Pruitt (2005, 2007b).

CHAPTER 46

Peacemaking through Mediation: The Swiss FDFA in Israel-Palestine, Sudan, and Guatemala

Simon J. A. Mason

The aim of this chapter is to show the potential of mediation as a peacemaking approach by learning from three cases in which the Swiss Federal Department of Foreign Affairs (FDFA) was involved: Israel-Palestine, Sudan North-South, and Guatemala.[1] The cases were chosen for their geographic diversity and because they illustrate different tracks and phases of a peace process. To assess the cases, we examine four questions: who? (actors), when? (phases), what? (topics), and how? (methodology). These four dimensions are introduced and then are used to analyze the three cases. The chapter concludes with nine lessons from the cases regarding some of the ongoing challenges faced by peacemakers.

WHO? MULTIACTOR APPROACH

A multiactor approach means both a multitrack approach[2] involving various conflict actors from the state level to the grassroots level and a multimediator approach. One can distinguish the following third parties: international organizations (e.g., the United Nations [UN][3]); regional and subregional organizations (e.g., the European Union or the African Union, the Intergovernmental Authority on Development); states, which consist of large powers such as China and the United States, neighboring states to a conflict such as South Africa and Turkey, and small states such as Norway and Switzerland; nongovernmental organizations (NGOs), which include local or regional NGOs (e.g., Serapaz, the African Center for the Constructive Resolution of Disputes[4]); international NGOs (e.g., Sant'Egidio, Center for Humanitarian

Dialogue, Crisis Management Initiative, Carter Center[5]); and personalities (e.g., Nelson Mandela, Jimmy Carter, Kofi Annan, Martti Ahtisaari).

Due to the complexity of peace processes, information exchange, coordination, and cooperation between third parties are essential, especially if they do not want to be manipulated by the conflict parties. There is a golden rule that once a process has started and is working, no other third party should start a competing process. For there is always the danger that parties start window-shopping, looking for better mediators and processes. Yet this impedes or even blocks the work on the main process track. Third-party coordination also requires careful assessment of the comparative advantages of the various third parties—which differ from case to case. NGOs, for example, may be more flexible and therefore may find it easier to access armed nonstate actors, especially in preliminary stages of a peace process (talks about talks) or in countries where the government does not want international involvement. From a government's point of view, it is easiest to get rid of an NGO, somewhat harder but still possible to get rid of another mediating state if it is small, but quite difficult to get rid of a powerful state or an organization like the UN once it has become involved. This is why NGOs may be a first entry point, even if they often have less legitimacy and fewer resources. For the same reason, the UN may not be welcomed in as a mediator during the negotiation process in some conflicts—such as in Nepal or Sri Lanka—because the respective government does not want the international focus of the UN but regards the problem as an internal affair. Nevertheless, Nepal still welcomed the UN for the implementation phase, because it needed the resources the UN could offer. The UN has resources for implementing peace agreements that no other organization can muster, typically making it the key actor in the implementation phase. Thus, different mediators have different comparative advantages; the challenge is how to get them to collaborate and how to avoid the negative aspects of competition.

WHEN? MULTIPHASE APPROACH

The peace process can be distinguished into four phases[6]: First, in the phase of *informal talks* or prenegotiations, a mediator may be in contact with the conflict parties over years or even decades—building trust, getting to understand the issues at stake, exploring under what conditions talks or talks about talks are possible.[7] Second, in the *talks about the talks,* or prenegotiation phase, parties want to negotiate but have not agreed on goal, venue, frequency, and participation. This phase is important to clarify the framework for the negotiations. Often preconditions for negotiations are brought up by the parties. In this case, the mediator may try and convince them to discuss their preconditions together at the table rather than hinder the initiation of direct contacts. Third, in the *negotiation phase,* parties enter a process of joint decision making aimed at signing a peace agreement. This phase can roughly be differentiated into an emotional phase, where the parties are not negotiating but are ventilating positions and emotions, and then over time it shifts into a more substantive phase, where the parties are actually negotiating together on how to deal with the issues. The mediator sits in the same room with the conflict parties, or shuttles between them, and structures and facilitates the process—for example, by collecting issues, setting the agenda, working through the issues, drafting mutually acceptable proposals, and making sure the relevant topics are addressed.[8] Fourth, in the *implementation phase*, or post-agreement phase, some mediation may still have to be done, because many issues may arise that have not been dealt with sufficiently in the peace agreement. The question is who does this mediation. Often it can be done by the implementation team or someone designated by them as it often concerns very concrete issues.

WHAT? MULTITOPIC APPROACH

The multitopic approach consists of being aware of the diverse topics that need to be addressed in a peace process and ensuring that they are coordinated, making best use of the links between the topics. These topics[9] include *security* (e.g., the disarmament, demobilization, and reintegration of former fighters [DDR], *security sector reform* (SSR), i.e., the reform of the police and military forces), *justice and human rights* (e.g., transitional justice, dealing with the past [DwP], international and local laws and standards, protection of victims, reform of the judicial system), *state and institution building* (e.g., power sharing, transitional arrangements, constitutional reform, elections), *economy and environment* (e.g., wealth sharing, investment, business, sustainable development), and *social and cultural aspects* (e.g., gender, culture, religion, and media).

Two examples of topics illustrate the need for better linkages: a DDR process is essential for disarming former combatants and reintegrating them into the state army or society by giving them economic and social opportunities. A DwP process is also essential to rehabilitate victims of the conflict in society and to avoid impunity for serious crimes (e.g., by following the Joinet principles: the right to know, the right to justice, to reparations, and the guarantee of no repetition).[10] So both the combatants and the victims need to be reintegrated into the same society, which needs to provide the economic, political, legal, and social framework for these processes. Rather than focusing on DDR and DwP as separate topics, the commonalities and links need to be made clear so that efforts work in the same overall direction.

HOW? METHODOLOGY

Two dimensions of mediation methodology are important: *micro-skills* and *process design*. The more operative micro-level skills involve how to communicate with and between the parties, how to get them to engage, how to structure the meetings, and how to draft documents. Although there is an ongoing debate about facilitative, formulative, or directive mediation,[11] most mediators will use a mix, and this will be shaped by the needs of the process rather than by the school the mediator comes from. Second, on a more strategic level, mediators design the process in a longer-term time frame. The main principle of process design is that *the nature of the conflict shapes the nature of the process.*[12] Mediators must therefore understand the nature of the conflict before trying to shape a process for dealing with it. Generally, there is also not one and only process design but rather a main path and then alternative paths depending on how things develop. A key issue that must be considered is the inclusivity of the process—that is, which actors sit at the table. In some cases, past elections may be an indication of a party's strength (e.g., in the Burundi Arusha process); in other cases, the parties at the table may be militarily the most powerful actors, even if their democratic legitimacy is unclear. Generally, mediators will try to get all relevant actors to the table. Yet questions about who is relevant and whether the key actors agree to having other actors on board can be stumbling blocks. Even if an actor is not at the table, parallel process can be created to keep them informed, consult their views, and possibly get them on board later on. If a process is not inclusive enough, it lacks legitimacy. If it becomes inclusive by adding more and more actors, however, it can become unmanageable. Thus, inclusivity remains one of the key dilemmas of a mediator and one over which he or she only has limited influence. For example, how should internally displaced people and refugees who had to leave their homes many years ago and whose properties have been seized by others be included in the peace process, or at least consulted in some form in a parallel process?

Once the goal of the process and participation is clear, mediators can suggest how to combine various formats—for example, how to use the plenary, the committee level, and working groups and how to work the topics in parallel or in sequence. No format is definite, and it might change as the negotiations advance. This depends on the efficiency of the method and what the content is. Part of process design is also to see how the process is linked to the context, which is also changing during the negotiations. Mediators are continually looking for new methods to keep the ball rolling. The lead mediator, for example, may spend time meeting with heads of states of neighboring states to get their support for the process before the process hits troubled waters.

THREE CASE STUDIES

Mediation can be used in different phases, on different tracks, and involving different topics. Based on the experience of the Swiss FDFA, this part of the chapter examines cases illustrating how mediation can be used. The Swiss FDFA has been involved in approximately 30 peace processes in over 20 countries in the last decade. Most of the Swiss FDFA's engagements focused on the track one level (e.g., Indonesia, Colombia, Cyprus, Georgia, Macedonia, Middle East, Nepal, North Uganda, Sir Lanka, Sudan, Burundi, and Western Sahara) and mostly in the prenegotiation and negotiation phases. The track-one focus is due to the mandate of the Swiss FDFA, outlined in the Bill to the Parliament,[13] which is based on the Swiss constitution, which stipulates that "The Confederation shall promote . . . the peaceful co-existence of peoples." There were, however, also some track one and a half cases (Georgia, Israel-Palestine, and Israel-Syria[14]) and some multitrack engagements (e.g., Guatemala, Middle East, Sri Lanka, and Sudan). Most of these efforts required many years of engagement with more than one mediator/expert involved. Generally, the Swiss FDFA is directly involved with its own ambassadors, diplomats, mediators, and topical experts (e.g., constitutional or power-sharing experts), but in some cases (e.g., Georgia track one and a half effort of Conciliation Resources and Berghof, or the Sri Lanka multitrack effort of Berghof Peace Support), it was mainly funding a third-party NGO. Besides being directly involved in mediation activities, Switzerland also supports key mediation actors such as the UN and its regional organizations with funds and expertise, especially the Mediation Support Unit of the UN Department of Political Affairs.[15]

In some conflict countries or regions (Colombia, Balkans, Great Lakes, Middle East, Nepal, Sri Lanka, and Sudan), Switzerland is also engaged with a broad range of conflict transformation programs. These programs are co-ordinated by peacebuilding advisors on the spot (in cases where multitrack and long-term peacebuilding efforts are undertaken) or by special envoys in Berne (often in cases where a track one process needs high-level advice as well as coordination with Swiss policy in Bern). These programs include the promotion of dialogue between the parties, monitoring and protection of human rights, capacity building for various segments of the society, reform of the security system, support of the civil society, and dealing with the past.

CASE STUDY 1: PRENEGOTIATIONS PHASE: GENEVA INITIATIVE REGARDING ISRAEL-PALESTINE

This case is selected to illustrate how a peace process can be pushed ahead on a track one and a half level when the formal official peace process is blocked. Despite the limitations of such a process, ideas can be generated that influence the formal process.

BACKGROUND

The Israel-Palestine conflict goes back to a clash between an indigenous, largely Arab-Muslim, population and modern Zionist settlers, who had historical and religious ties dating back to biblical times and were aiming to create their return to what they considered to be their ancient homeland and reconstitute themselves as a nation. In the 1920s and 1930s and then mainly after the Holocaust, during which 6 million Jews were murdered by the Nazi regime and their collaborators, Jews emigrated in large numbers to Palestine. After the UN partition plan of Palestine was rejected by the Palestinians and Arab states, Israel declared its independence in 1948. Within hours of this declaration, a war ignited between Israel on the one hand and Egypt, Jordan, Syria, Lebanon, and Iraq on the other. In the course of the war and the succeeding years, hundreds of thousands of Palestinians fled or were expelled from their homes, becoming refugees in Gaza, the West Bank, Egypt, Jordan, Syria, Lebanon, and other countries. The Six-Day War of June 1967—fought between Israel and the neighboring states of Egypt, Jordan, and Syria—resulted in Israel's occupation of the Sinai Peninsula,

West Bank, East Jerusalem, the Golan Heights, and Gaza Strip—territories containing the heartland of the Palestinian population.

While the dominant pattern of Israeli-Arab-Palestinian relations since 1948 has been one of wars and uprisings, there have also been hesitant and partial steps forward on the diplomatic front. In 1979, Egypt and Israel signed a peace treaty based on U.S.-mediated understandings at Camp David. In 1994, Israel and Jordan signed a peace treaty, normalizing relations between the two countries. Nevertheless, in the last decade since 2000, around 1,000 Israeli deaths have resulted mostly from suicide bombing against innocent civilians, and approximately 6,500 Palestinian were killed by Israeli actions that some in the international community saw as disproportionate, others called war crimes.

In 2000, Bill Clinton put forth his parameters for peace between Israel-Palestine after a disastrous failure of a summit between Yasser Arafat and Ehud Barak at Camp David and just before leaving office. At the time, President Clinton told both parties: "These are my ideas. If they are not accepted, they are not just off the table, they also go with me when I leave the office."[16] This is what happened when he left office in November 2000. Nevertheless, talks between Israelis and Palestinians continued in Taba on the Sinai Peninsula from January 21–27, 2001, but were discontinued as a result of the upcoming Israeli elections. The Taba talks aimed at reaching the "final status" negotiations to end the Israel-Palestine conflict; the negotiations came close to reaching a final settlement but ultimately failed to achieve their goals.

OVERVIEW

The Geneva Initiative goes back to the initiative of Yasser Abed Rabbo[17] and Yossi Beilin,[18] who wanted to complete the work begun in Taba during the peace talks in January 2001. Alexis Keller, lecturer at the University of Geneva, invited Beilin to a conference on "Just Peace" in October 2001. In an informal talk on the sidelines of the conference, Keller offered Beilin financial support for their project. The Swiss government only became directly involved later on, when Alexis Keller and Rob Malley[19] asked the Swiss representation in Ramallah for logistical help. Out of this initial support, Switzerland became the main backer of the Geneva Initiative. Switzerland was the choice of the conflict parties, because it had no historical involvement in the region that might complicate the process; it was independent and not a member of a super-structure such as the European Union (the European Union declined to respond to the request). Switzerland's role consisted of financial and logistical support by helping with the organization and providing the infrastructure, but it had no influence on the content. On the Israeli side, the talks involved former officials, and on the Palestinian side, officials from the PLO participated. The outcome of the Geneva Initiative was a document entitled "The Geneva Accord, A Model Israeli-Palestinian Peace Agreement."[20] After presenting the accord to the wider public, Switzerland continued to support the dissemination of the content of the accord and its key messages. In the last years, Switzerland supported the parties in the elaboration of the GI-Annexes, which were solutions for specific topics such as Jerusalem, refugees, water, environment, and the economy.

WHAT?

The Geneva Accords of 2003 was a model agreement that aimed to end the conflict and end all claims. It consisted of a mutual recognition of Israeli and Palestinian rights to two separate states, with a final agreed-upon border. Large settlement blocks and most of the settlers were annexed to Israel as part of a one-to-one land swap. The agreement included recognition of the Jewish neighborhoods in Jerusalem as the Israeli capital and recognition of the Arab neighborhoods of Jerusalem as the Palestinian capital. The Palestinian state was to be a demilitarized state, and there was agreement for a comprehensive and complete Palestinian commitment to fighting terrorism and incitement. There was a comprehensive solution to the refugee problem, yet the right of return was addressed in a way that many Palestinians found unsatisfactory. The implementation was to be overseen by an international verification group.[21]

WHEN, WHO, AND HOW?

Methodologically, the GI is a typical track one and a half effort involving officials and nonofficials, all of whom participated in their personal capacity. It is an example of a creative approach in a failed postnegotiation or expectant prenegotiation phase, based on a demand by the elites of the conflict parties. On the negative side, the GI is not inclusive of some central actors, such as the government of Israel or religious actors on both sides. Hamas, a key actor on the Palestinian side, as the 2006 elections showed, was not represented in any way, because the preconditions[22] for negotiations as set by Israel—and supported by the United States, the European Union, the United Nations, and Russia—are blocking a wider inclusivity of key actors in the peace process. The Geneva Initiative is rather a process of liberal elites on both sides talking with each other, and it still reaches only a small segment of the society.[23] The process is also content oriented, showing an example or blueprint of what the solution could look like. For negotiations coming afterward, blueprint peace agreements can also be an impediment and not just a source of inspiration, especially if negotiators do not want to be associated with the GI process. The actors in the GI process were also skeptically viewed by the wider Israeli and Palestinian constituency, because they were mainly politicians but not part of the government, at least on the Israeli side. On the Palestinian side, there were close links to the acting government. A key challenge of such track one and a half processes is, therefore, how it can be linked to the government on both sides. If it is not linked, or only weakly linked, its impact is often minimal. Many mediators, therefore, argue for keeping the government informed and seeking an implicit, if not explicit, go-ahead.

On the positive side, the achievement of the GI accord is to show that both sides could make concessions and that a negotiated agreement is possible in a final status shape, something that had never been done before. This way it provides hope in a context where hope is often lacking. The accord is an important reference document for future peace agreements. The GI also breaks some of the long-standing taboo questions—for example, the return of Palestinian refugees—thereby enabling a debate on key issues. The GI also contributed to the unilateral withdrawal from Gaza in 2005, because Prime Minister Ariel Sharon was worried that international pressure would mount if he did not take a decisive step. Nevertheless, the unilateral withdrawal from Gaza did not lead to peace. Stiff economic sanctions have been in place, stopping imports into Gaza.

CASE STUDY 2: ALL PHASES: SUDAN NORTH-SOUTH

The Swiss engagement in Sudan is one of the longest (since 1994) and broadest engagements of the Swiss FDFA, involving numerous tracks and all phases of a peace process. Many third parties were involved, showing how third-party cooperation is possible and essential in peacemaking.

BACKGROUND

In the second civil war between north and south Sudan from 1983 to 2005, more than 4 million people were displaced, 600,000 refugees left the country, and more than 2 million people lost their lives, either directly through the fighting or indirectly from other consequences of the war, such as famine and disease. Among the root causes of the conflicts in the Sudan was the already-existing historical and racial discrimination of the south by the north before independence in 1956. Tensions between the center and the periphery were a consequence of disparate socio-economic and political development between the north and central Sudan on the one hand and south Sudan and other regions (e.g., Beja in the east and Darfur in the west) on the other hand. The Sudan People's Liberation Movement/Army (SPLM/A) in the south and the government of Sudan (GoS), dominated by the National Islamic Front/National Congress Party (NIF/NCP) in the north were the main parties involved in the negotiations. The main issues involved the relationship between religion and state, wealth and power sharing, the three contested areas (Blue Nile Hills, Abyei, and Nuba Mountains), and security issues.[24]

OVERVIEW

The Swiss FDFA became involved because Josef Bucher, the then Swiss ambassador to Libya, had close contacts with the Sudanese ambassador, who approached him with the request for Swiss assistance to facilitate talks between the SPLM/A in the south of Sudan and the government of Sudan. This led to intensive contacts over the years with both sides of the conflict from about 1994 to 2002 in a prenegotiation mode. In 2002, Ambassador Bucher mediated the negotiations on the Nuba Mountains ceasefire agreement in Switzerland. Three years later, the Comprehensive Peace Agreement between the north and the south was signed in 2005. The Swiss FDFA was also involved in various efforts after the signing of the Comprehensive Peace Agreement (CPA) to promote peace in Sudan.[25]

SUPPORTING PEACE STRUCTURES IN THE SOUTH

As part of the contacts with the south Sudanese, the Swiss FDFA supported a House of Nationalities project, which aimed to facilitate the development of forums for tribal leaders to deal with intertribal tensions.[26] Intertribal south-south conflicts led to tens of thousands of deaths during the north-south war. From the beginning in 2000, the project aimed to support southern Sudan in anticipation of the day of peace with the north. The logic was that, without governance structures in the south, the elites in the south and the north could easily divide and rule by exploiting the latent intertribal tensions in the south. The informal nature of politics in fragile states calls for responses that build on these structures and develop them rather than imposing models of Western democratic institutions.[27] Since the signing of the Comprehensive Peace Agreement in 2005, this project was adapted to take into consideration the developing institutions and laws of the government of South Sudan—for example, in the context of the 2009 Council of Traditional Leaders Authority workshop.[28]

NUBA CEASEFIRE AGREEMENT

Besides support of governance structures in the south, the contacts between the Swiss FDFA and the Sudanese in both the north and south led to negotiations of the Nuba Mountains ceasefire agreement in January 2002. Under pressure from the United States (especially after 9/11, because Osama bin Laden had lived in Sudan in the 1990s), the SPLM/A and the GoS came to the table as a show of goodwill. The negotiations took place at Bürgenstock in Switzerland and lasted six days, mediated by a U.S.-Swiss team.[29] The mediation team consisted of members from the United States and Switzerland, including officers, legal advisors, and diplomats. The process started by dealing with procedural questions. It was agreed to avoid direct contacts between the two conflict parties at first, and rather to have separate parallel meetings—the one side dealing with the military questions, the other with political and legal questions, and then changing over. The following days were spent in clarifying where the military forces were positioned and specifying the various perspectives regarding an international monitoring commission. There was a disagreement about how to proceed: the GoS wanted to sign a general ceasefire immediately and deal with the details later on the ground. The Swiss-U.S. team, however, did not go along with this proposal, because the main difficulty is precisely in the details. The Swiss-U.S. team, therefore, came up with a concrete proposal about where the various troops should be pulled back to. Although the proposal was initially received with shock by both the GoS and the SPLM/A, it allowed for progress, as the parties started to work jointly on correcting the proposal. Details were discussed and clarified until the final version was put together at 7:00 A.M. on the sixth day.[30] Methodologically, it is interesting to see how presenting a mediators' document is a delicate step, but sometimes useful to push the process forward. The key is that the document be based on an in-depth understanding of the actors' views and interests. Furthermore, it must be made very clear that it is not set in stone; rather, it must be changed and adapted by the parties so that they make it their own.

IGAD-LED PEACE PROCESS

After the Nuba Mountains ceasefire, new life was breathed into the Intergovernmental Authority on Development (IGAD)[31] peace process that had been going on for years. Kenyan General Lazaro Sumbeiywo[32] was the lead mediator of this process, providing legitimacy and moral authority, choosing the members of the mediation team, and keeping all the threads together. Nicolas "Fink" Haysom, a South African, and Julian T. Hottinger of the Swiss FDFA were mediators on the IGAD mediation team who dealt with the daily nuts and bolts of the process. Hottinger had also been a member of the Bürgenstock mediation team. The IGAD process was supported by the United Kingdom, the United States, and Norway, heavily funded by the European Union. The IGAD process took nearly three years of practically continuous negotiations. It was much more complicated than the Nuba Mountains ceasefire negotiations, because it entailed diverse political questions. These political details generally can be negotiated only if the parties have a common goal and a clear framework agreement before they begin the negotiations. This is well illustrated in the case of the Sudan north-south process: The GoS and SPLM/A signed the Machakos protocol on July 20, 2002, and it provided the goal and framework to structure the negotiations in the subsequent years. An interesting procedural aspect of the process was that the agreement was negotiated protocol for protocol, signing each one once it had been negotiated.[33] While this was the wish of the parties, it proved challenging to the process, because it meant that no trade-offs between protocols could be made once they had been signed.

WHAT?

Some of the issues addressed in the 260-page Comprehensive Peace Agreement,[34] signed in January 2005, were security (armed forces, DDR, SSR), territorial questions, power-sharing issues (interim government, asymmetrical federal structure), wealth sharing (oil), and human rights. The cornerstone of the agreement was the accord to give privilege to unity of the country, but with the possibility of consulting the southern Sudanese via a referendum on the possibility of separating, and thereby for the south to become an independent state. In January 2011, close to 90 percent of the people of southern Sudan voted, and on July 9, 2011 South Sudan became independent.[35]

WHEN AND HOW?

The CPA process covered all phases: prenegotiations (1990s–2002), negotiations (2002–2005), and implementation (2005–2011). From a methodological point of view, one of the main tasks of the mediators, besides structuring the process, is to listen and facilitate the dialogue. Through dialogue, the parties begin to realize that what they thought about the other side was not exactly correct.

As we begin to change our views of the other side, space is created for us to adapt our own position. This takes time but can lead to joint collaboration in the form of a peace agreement, as happened with the Comprehensive Peace Agreement. The Sudan north-south negotiations were an example of the use of facilitative, formulative, and directive mediation, where approaches involving both pressure and dialogue were combined. Without some degree of pressure, it is very unlikely that the parties would ever have come to the negotiation table and to a peace accord. The case shows that, while dialogue and pressure are complementary, it is often useful to split the roles of the parties exerting pressure and facilitating, respectively. In the Nuba Mountains ceasefire negotiations, pressure and dialogue were combined in the U.S.-Swiss mediation team, with the United States exerting the pressure, and the Swiss having built up dialogue over the years. In the CPA process, one way the mediation team helped to level the ground between the parties on a knowledge level was to organize workshops where international experts briefed both parties on key issues (e.g., oil economics), creating the needed knowledge to negotiate these complex questions. The Sudan case is perhaps one of the first Swiss mediation engagements where a multitrack, multiphase, and multitopic approach was adopted—an approach that was developed over a period of more than 13 years, highlighting the need for patience and perseverance.[36]

The CPA was successful in ending the war now for six years—yet Sudan is still far from peace. The conflict in Darfur was not addressed in the CPA, because the IGAD mandate was limited to dealing with the north-south conflict along the 1956 north-south border. The implementation of the agreement has proven to be very difficult, and armed conflicts in the south erupted in the last years. Peace agreements are imperfect agreements. They should be seen as a stepping-stone to a more peaceful form of dealing with conflicts rather than an ultimate solution.

CASE STUDY 3: POST–PEACE AGREEMENT PHASE: GUATEMALA

The peacemaking engagement of the Swiss FDFA in Guatemala in 2003, seven years after the signing of a peace agreement in 1996, gives some idea of what mediative approaches may look like in the implementation phase. Mediation in this context is very different; it is a facilitated process with multiple local and international third parties seeking to bring civil society and the government to work on specific issues that were not fully or clearly enough addressed in the peace agreement.

BACKGROUND

The roots of the Guatemalan conflict go back generations, originating in the practice of the colonial and republican governments to divide up indigenous people's land to reward the loyalty of their supporters. Besides land, key factors in the Guatemalan civil war were the marginalization of the indigenous population, the exclusive political organization of the government, and the lack of checks and balances on the state security apparatus. Guatemala was also caught up in regional tensions; for example, the CIA orchestrated an over-throw of the democratically elected reformist Jacobo Arbenz in 1954. During more than three decades of war, between 1960 and 1996, it is estimated that 180,000 people were killed, 40,000 people "disappeared," and 100,000 people sought refuge in Mexico.[37] In 1996, the Guatemalan government and the rebel army, the Unidad Revolucionaria Nacional Guatemalteca, signed a peace agreement ending a war that had lasted 36 years.[38]

OVERVIEW

The 1996 agreement[39] came out of a process where civil society and business actors had an indirect input into the negotiation process. Nevertheless, the political will to implement the agreement was not sufficient, and the government negotiating the agreement was not the same one as the government implementing it. In 1999, a referendum was held on integrating aspects of the 1996 peace agreement into the constitution. This proposal was rejected by 78 percent of the voting population. Due to the lack of political will, the international community de facto took over and replaced the local actors in creating and pushing forward the process. This approach had severe limitations. Years later, the compensation program for victims became a key point of polarization.

In 2003, the Swiss FDFA became involved, and its peacebuilding advisor, Mô Bleeker, was asked to support talks among local actors who strongly and vehemently opposed each other on how to set up a victim compensation program. Bleeker met with numerous governmental and NGO representatives and offered to work with them in a conflict transformative manner. A support group called *Gadres* was established; the group consisted of international organizations (United Nations Development Programme, Deutsche Gesellschaft für Technische Zusammenarbeit [GTZ], etc.) and local NGOs that were still viewed as being impartial.

WHO, WHAT, AND HOW?

The Gadres first worked separately with the government and elements of the civil society before bringing them together. Each step was transparently communicated, and great weight was given to the establishment of clear guidelines for these talks. Among these criteria were the following: First, the process would not include chaotic talk and mutual blame; rather, a mediation space would be provided for all parties to talk with each other, by setting clear rules about when and how to speak, clearly indicating the aim, roles, and final product. Second, the process would be facilitated by a multipartial third party. Third, both technical training (e.g., on what a compensation fund is and what it requires, options to shape it) and facilitation to bring the people together would be used—yet the two tasks would not be carried out by the same representatives of a third party (clear role division). The methodology therefore consisted of combining technical expertise with process expertise. Workshops were organized with experts of compensation programs and reconciliation strategies to increase the knowledge about the topic. On the process level, a dozen special meetings were organized by the Gadres to assess the wide range of needs, difficulties, and commonalities. These events were carried out separately by government and civil society organizations. The result was an assessment of the main problems, opportunities, and proposed solutions on both sides. Only after civil society on the one side and the government on the other side had clarified their internal differences could a meeting across sides be beneficial. The results of these two independent processes provided the basis for meetings between the civil society and the government. The Gadres were asked to mediate regularly between government and civil societies about specific topics and to offer technical support to both parties so that they would be better prepared to negotiate how to set up the compensation commission and the design of the compensation program.

Methodologically, the case shows the potential of using mediation in the post–peace agreement phase; in situations where the political process is blocked, society remains deeply divided and specific issues had not been negotiated clearly enough in the peace agreement. It shows how third-party coordination was carried out in the form of a facilitation team (along the lines of a co-mediation model) combining internal and external third parties. The facilitation helped to move ahead in a situation in which the international community had unsuccessfully tried to apply pressure—for example, via financial incentives. This case also shows how technical expertise—for example, on compensation issues—needs to be complemented with facilitation expertise. The Gadres-led process did not solve the victim compensation question in Guatemala, because the divisions within the civil society regarding this question were so deep. Nevertheless, it did clarify issues and bring the negotiations a step forward. The process also illustrated how negotiations between the elites of a government and civil society are more solid if they are built on processes that combine track-one, track-two, and track-three actors.

LESSONS

What have we learned from these three case studies about the potential and limits of mediation, as well as what mediators can do to address some of the proximate and contextual challenges in peacemaking? The first five lessons are of a proximate nature, and the last four lessons are of a contextual nature:

- *Actors use violence—but they are limited by it and may want to test negotiations.* The conflict actors' ambivalence toward peace is one of the key challenges to peacemaking, but it also presents an opportunity. For some conflict actors, peace means less power, less status, loss of their fighter's identity, no income, or imprisonment. For other conflict actors, the incentive of peace is to gain political power and to become part of the new government. As violence continues, even those actors who originally benefited from it may begin to feel its limitations. The war economy or the economy in a war situation, for example, cannot grow above a certain level, thus creating an economic incentive to build peace.[40] The oil industry in Sudan, for instance, was always threatened by the fighting and could flourish and attract greater investment after the peace agreement of 2005. Furthermore, it may become clearer over time that military victory is unrealistic.[41] This was the case in both Sudan and Guatemala. Thus, actors in a conflict may feel the limits of the ongoing armed conflict and want to test negotiations as an alternative way to get what they are seeking. To support such considerations, mediators need to place greater priority on the question of, "For me as an actor in the conflict, what is in peace for me, what is my personal peace dividend?" If parties do not see what is in the peace for them, they will be against it.

- *It takes time and a structured process to build trust and a common understanding.* The essential idea of bringing parties together in a negotiation process is to expand their perceptions of the problem and build common understanding and trust by working on the same issues. Once the issues are seen differently, the will for a peaceful solution may increase. Sometimes mediators negotiate with the present generation for future generations. The aim is to say: "This generation is lost, but maybe in subsequent generations things will be different." Especially in these cases, a peace process will only work once the parties have agreed on some joint vision, some common goal. Once that exists, the negotiations can then hash out how to get there in a mutually acceptable manner. Time is a key factor in these considerations, because the conflict and a peace process evolves over time.

- *Different ways of leveling the power asymmetry: reconciliation of parties within themselves, knowledge-building workshops, and the use of external pressure.* If the power asymmetry is too large, negotiations are difficult. The Israel-Palestine case indicates such a situation, especially because Israel has a strong U.S. backing. Even here, however, the asymmetry can be partially leveled, for example, by fostering inter-Palestinian and inter-Israeli reconciliation as a first step to Israel-Palestine negotiations. The Israel-Palestine negotiations have often broken down because the different factions within the parties were not pulling in the same direction.[42] As there are different forms of power, there are also different ways of trying to level the ground. The knowledge asymmetry between parties can be partially leveled through workshops and training, as occurred in Guatemala with the civil society actors on the technical dimensions of a compensation fund. In Sudan, the issues negotiated were extremely complex, with asymmetric knowledge between the parties; thus, workshops were needed to level the ground before the issue could be negotiated. Sudan also illustrates how external pressure from the United States toward the government of Sudan after 9/11 helped to bring the parties to the table.

- *Inclusivity can be partly increased through parallel formats. Peace agreements are imperfect, yet often key stepping-stones to state institutions with greater democratic legitimacy.* Even if a process is not fully inclusive of all relevant actors, mediators can help to establish parallel processes or formats so that key actors are kept informed and consulted, and they may even be brought on board in the main process at a later stage. Nevertheless, a peace agreement is always an imperfect document that lacks democratic legitimacy. The actors at the negotiation table are often there due to their military power and not because they were democratically elected. Yet the aim of a peace process is to find a minimal agreement that the parties can live with. This is a step better than ongoing violent conflict. The idea is to build into the peace agreement institutions and mechanisms for the transitional phase, which will lead to a broader public participation to ensure a broader political ownership and to a normal democratic political system over time. Moreover, due to the imperfection of peace agreements, a peace process needs to be supported long after the negotiations have finished.

- *Mediation is also useful in the implementation phase.* The case of Guatemala shows how mediation in the postagreement phase may support the renegotiation of issues of the peace agreement if these were not sufficiently addressed in the original agreement or if the wrong actors were at the table negotiating them, so that they do not represent broad enough constituencies. Many mediators, however, argue for trying to build peace incrementally, building trust through the process rather than placing too high expectations on the actual peace agreement. Once the agreement is signed, it is often much harder and more delicate to reopen issues, as the entire deal may break down.[43] So a clear distinction has to be made between renegotiating fundamentals of the peace agreement and fine-tuning details that were left unclear.

- *Minimal consensus of global and regional actors is needed to allow a process to work.* The Sudan process could only begin once there was a minimal consensus of the neighboring (IGAD member) states that a solution had to be found. Once this consensus was backed by the United States, the negotiations took off. In other cases—such as Somalia or Darfur—such a regional or global consensus is missing so far, so that the parties may meet and talk, but the disruptive elements overpower the chances for a successful process. In the case of Israel-Palestine, the Arab Peace Initiative was a positive sign of how neighboring Arab states could see a minimal consensus, which could have helped to integrate the bilateral process with a regional one. Thereby, it could have breathed new life into the peace process, had it been taken up and used.[44]

- *The right balance between pressure and dialogue is characterized by a situation where actors are respected, some space is given to their need for autonomy, yet movement is still made toward a mutually acceptable outcome.* In the case of Sudan, external pressure (by the United States) combined with dialogue was needed to bring the parties to negotiate. Furthermore, the UN, with its 10,000-soldier, "boots on the ground," was central for the implementation of the Sudan Comprehensive Peace Agreement in the United Nations Mission in Sudan. Especially in the implementation phase, external pressure is often vital. Yet pressure is only effective in fostering negotiations or the implementation of a peace agreement if it can be retracted progressively as the parties make progress. If pressure cannot be retracted, like toothpaste once squashed cannot be sucked back into the tube, parties will not react to it by engaging in negotiations.[45] Threats of pressure in the forms of deadlines that are not adhered to have no effect.[46] Besides the appropriate use of pressure, however, building trust through dialogue is essential. Through the many years of prenegotiations and the three-year-long Sudan negotiation process, trust could be built through the efforts of the mediators and the structure of the process, and a mutually acceptable outcome could be found. This is also why the use of pressure is not the task of the mediator, because it could negatively influence the mediator's impartiality and credibility.

- *Getting actors, who do not list armed nonstate actors as terrorists, to talk with them.* The United States and the European Union have compiled lists of armed nonstate actors (ANSAs) that are considered to be terrorist organizations—for example, Hamas in the Middle East and the Liberation Tigers of Tamil Eelam in Sri Lanka. The logic of these lists is to say more or less the following: "Parties will misbehave and do the worst to attract attention and come in strong at the negotiation table. So for this not to happen there is an invisible line that is drawn, and if you go beyond that line, we will not negotiate with you because you have done the unacceptable. Furthermore, in certain cases, violence might be used to get rid of you."[47] This logic is not the logic of a mediator, but it is an argument that exists and that mediators have to deal with. The lists aim to isolate actors from finances and contacts with the outside world. The lists often make it extremely difficult for mediators to talk to such actors and, in some cases, impede communication, yet mediators have to deal with all relevant actors if they want to make peace. In the case of the Geneva Initiative between Israel and Palestine, the nonofficial dialogue helped to develop ideas and provide hope in a situation where the official negotiations were stuck. Yet key actors that are relevant to peace, like Hamas, were sidelined by the international community, even if its democratic legitimacy was recognized. From a mediator's point of view, isolation tends to support the extremists; dialogue tends to support the development of political space. One way around this dilemma is to get countries such as Norway or Switzerland, who do not have lists of terrorist organizations, to speak with armed nonstate actors, something the United States and European Union countries cannot do. Both in Nepal (see the contribution in volume 1 by Günther Baechler on this process) and in Sri Lanka, the United States was interested in hearing more about actors such as the Maoists and the Tamil Tigers, even if it could not talk directly to them. Thus, from a mediation perspective, the pros and cons of terrorist lists should be reevaluated and the delisting of actors should be made easier.[48]

- *Communication and coordination of third parties.* Groups of friends and contact groups[49] on the state and donor level and joint facilitation or mediation teams on the operational level are some of the ways in which mediators can improve third-party coordination by informing and coordinating various initiatives. The Gadres in Guatemala illustrate how this can work on an operational level. In the case of Sudan, IGAD represented the regional neighbors and the lead mediator, which had international experts as well as the coordinated backing of the United States, United Kingdom, and Norway. With this coordinated approach, it was possible to prevent competing processes from being started that would have been detrimental to the main track.

CONCLUSIONS

Peacemaking is challenging, yet mediation has ways and means to respond to these challenges. Even if mediation is no magic method that leads quickly to peace, it can help societies move a step closer in the direction of dealing with conflicts in a nonviolent manner. The peace processes of Israel-Palestine, Sudan, and Guatemala illustrate some of the ways mediators responded to the specific challenges of the various conflicts. The pros and cons of the various options change from case to case, calling for in-depth analysis before action is taken. The ultimate criterion to assess the various mediation options is the principle of not making things worse. Indeed, the assessment of which approach will not do more harm is the toughest question of all. Nevertheless, even if it is hard to find a clear answer to this question, it should not paralyze all action. A carefully calculated risk is worth taking if there is a chance for mediators to help parties realize what is in peace for them, and thereby alleviate the suffering of the wider population.

ACKNOWLEDGMENTS AND DISCLAIMER

Thanks to the financial support of the Mediation Support Project, a joint project of the Center for Security Studies, ETH Zurich, and swisspeace Bern, funded by the Swiss Federal Department of Foreign Affairs (www.peace mediation.org). Special thanks for the very helpful comments and input from Murezi Michael, Mô Bleeker, Julian T. Hottinger (Swiss FDFA), and Matthias Siegfried (Mediation Support Project, swisspeace Bern). All mistakes and biased interpretations remain the responsibility of the author alone.

NOTES

1. The chapter is based on interviews with mediators and peacebuilding advisors. The methodology is described in Simon Mason and Matthias Siegfried, "Debriefing Mediators to Learn from Their Experiences," United States Institute of Peace, Center for Security Studies, ETH Zurich, swisspeace, 2010. Online http://www.peace mediation.ch/resources/documents/PMT_Debriefing_Mediators.pdf.

2. Track one refers to processes in which the top leaders of both conflict parties are engaged with each other (i.e., representatives of the government and commanders of armed nonstate actors). In track-one-and-a-half processes, the top leadership of only one conflict party is engaged in the peace process, or both leaderships are involved but in an informal setting and in their personal capacity. In track-two activities, influential elites and decision makers (e.g., civil society representatives, religious leaders, members of the business community) are involved but not the top leadership of the conflict parties. In track-three activities, grassroots actors are involved. In multi-track activities, multiple actors from at least two tracks are involved. Joseph Montville, "The Arrow and the Olive Branch: A Case for Track Two Diplomacy," in *Conflict Resolution: Track Two Diplomacy*, ed. J. McDonald and D. Bendahmane (Washington, DC: Foreign Service Institute, U.S. Department of State, 1987). See also Susan Allen Nan, "Track One-and-a-Half Diplomacy: Contributions to Georgian-South Ossetian Peacemaking," in *Paving the Way: Contributions of Interactive Conflict Resolution to Peacemaking*, ed. Ronald J. Fisher (Lanham, MD: Lexington Books, 2005).

3. See http://peacemaker.unlb.org.

4. See http://www.serapaz.org.mx/ and http://www.acordinternational.org/.

5. See http://www.santegidio.org, http://www.hdcentre.org/, http://www.cmi.fi/, and http://www.cartercenter.org/.

6. These phases were distinguished by Julian Thomas Hottinger, Peace Mediation Course 2010, Hotel Oberhofen, www.peacemediation.ch.

7. Julian Thomas Hottinger, "Auf das achten, was nicht gesagt wird," in *Schweiz Global*, vol. 4 (2005), 32f.

8. See Simon Mason, "Learning from the Swiss Mediation and Facilitation Experiences in Sudan," Working paper, Mediation Support Project (Zurich: Center for Security Studies, ETH Zurich & swisspeace, 2007), http://www.isn.ethz.ch/news/dos

sier/mediation/pubs/pub.cfm; German version: Simon Mason, "Lehren aus den Schweizer Mediations- und Fazilitationsdiensten im Sudan," in *Bulletin zur schweizerischen Sicherheitspolitik*, ed. Andreas Wenger and Victor Mauer (Zurich: Center for Security Studies, ETH Zurich, 2006).

9. For an overview of topics and a collection of related links and documents, see the online dossier "Mediation and Facilitation in Peace Processes" at http://www.isn.ethz.ch.

10. Jonathan Sisson (ed.), *Dealing with the Past in Post-Conflict Societies: Ten Years after the Peace Accords—in Guatemala and Bosnia-Herzegovina* (Bern: swisspeace Annual Conference 2006, September 2007), http://www.swisspeace.ch/; Mô Bleeker and Jonathan Sisson, eds., "Dealing with the Past: Critical Issues, Lesson Learned, and Challenges for Future Swiss Policy," Bern: swisspeace working paper, Koff Series, 2004, http://www.swisspeace.org/publications/wp/KOFF_DealingWithThePast.pdf.

11. Mediation is defined here as a structured process, where a third party accepted by the actors in a conflict supports them in their negotiations and conflict transformation. Facilitative mediation, or neutral low-powered mediation, is less directive, bringing the parties together, possibly supporting and structuring the communication, but not using much power. In formulative mediation, mediators help the parties draft parts of the peace agreement, always under the understanding that they have the final word on content. In directive, manipulative, or power mediation, more pressure is used, the process being strongly controlled by the mediators.

12. Hottinger, Peace Mediation Course.

13. Bill to Parliament concerning the continuation of measures relating to civilian peacebuilding and the promotion of human rights, presented June 15, 2007. English summary at http://www.eda.admin.ch.

14. Nicolas Lang, "'Syriens Bekenntnis zum Frieden ist glaubwürdiger geworden' / Sonderbotschafter Nicolas Lang blickt auf acht Jahre Friedensdiplomatie im Nahen Osten zurück," *Neue Zürcher Zeitung* no. 18 (April 17, 2007): 13.

15. See the website hosted by the United Nations Mediation Support Unit: http://peacemaker.unlb.org/index1.php.

16. The Clinton Parameters, December 23, 2000 http://www.ipcri.org/files/clinton-parameters.html; http://www.ipcri.org/files/clinton-parameters.html.

17. Former head of the Palestinian Authority's negotiating team on final status talks, who resigned in May 2000.

18. Former minister of justice under Ehud Barak.

19. Clinton's special advisor for the Israel-Palestine negotiations between 1998 and January 2001.

20. See http://www.geneva-accord.org/.

21. http://www.geneva-accord.org/mainmenu/summary

22. Renounce violence, recognize Israel, accept past peace agreements.

23. Simon Mason and Moncef Kartas, eds., *Transforming Conflicts with Religious Dimensions, Methodologies and Practical Experiences*. Geneva, Zurich, 2010. Graduate Institute Geneva, Center for Security Studies, ETH Zurich, Swiss FDFA.

24. Background paragraph from Simon J. A. Mason. Sudan, North-South Comprehensive Peace Agreement. 2008. In *Unpacking the Mystery of Mediation in African Peace Processes*. Zurich: Mediation Support Project, Center for Security Studies, ETH Zurich and swisspeace. www.peacemediation.ch.

25. Simon J. A. Mason and David Lanz, *Towards a Swiss "Whole of Government" Approach in Sudan: 2005–2008*, Swiss Background Paper 3C Conference 2009 (Zurich: Center for Security Studies and swisspeace, March 2009), http://www.peacemediation.ch/resources/documents/Swiss-WGA-in-Sudan-18Mar09.pdf. For more recent Swiss support, see "Der Südsudan lässt sich von der Schweiz beraten," *Echo der Zeit*,

January 8, 2011, http://www.drs.ch/www/de/drs/sendungen/echo-der-zeit/de/drs/sendungen/echo-der-zeit/2646.bt10164320.html.

26. Another project supported by the Swiss FDFA was work with the south Sudanese diaspora. See http://www.gurtong.net.

27. Josef Bucher, "A Holistic Approach for Promoting the Rule of Law," Human Rights and Human Welfare Working Paper no. 49, http://www.du.edu/korbel/hrhw/workingpapers/2008/49-bucher-2008.pdf. See also Conradin Perner, "Kwacak woros interner Arbeitsbericht über den Aufbau eines 'House of Nationalities' im Südsudan und in den Nuba Bergen," Januar-Oktober 2005, Unpublished; www.houseofnationalities.org; and Mason and Lanz, *Towards a Swiss "Whole of Government" Approach*.

28. *Council of Traditional Authority Leaders* (COTAL) Workshop: *Organised by the Local Government Board (LGB) of the Government of Southern Sudan (GoSS) with the support of the Federal Department of Foreign Affairs of Switzerland (FDFA)*. Report, December 2–4, 2009. http://www.houseofnationalities.org/pdf/COTAL_.pdf.

29. Josef Bucher, "Eine Nische für den Frieden," in *Helvetia im Aussendienst: Was Schweizer in der Welt bewegen*, ed. Jürg Altwegg (Zurich and Vienna: Nagel & Kimche, 2004).

30. Bucher, "Eine Nische für den Frieden." Mason "Learning from the Swiss Mediation and Facilitation Experiences in Sudan."

31. A regional organization consisting of six countries in the Horn of Africa: Djibouti, Eritrea, Ethiopia, Kenya, Somalia, Sudan, and Uganda. See http://www.igad.org/.

32. For more on Lazaro Sumbeiywo, see Lazaro Sumbeiywo, To Be a Negotiator: Strategies and Tactics (Zurich: Center for Security Studies, ETH Zurich, and swisspeace, 2009), http://www.peacemediation.ch/resources/documents/negotiator.pdf. See also Waithaka Waihenya, *The Mediator: General Lazaro Sumbeiywo and the Southern Sudan Peace Process* (Nairobi: East African Educational Publishers, 2006); and Martin Harriet, *Kings of Peace, Pawns of War* (London: Continuum International, 2006).

33. The protocol of Machakos: July 20, 2002. The protocol on security arrangements: September 25, 2003. The protocol on wealth sharing: January 7, 2004. The protocol on power sharing: May 26, 2004. The protocol on the resolution of conflict in southern Kordofan/Nuba Mountains and the Blue Nile States: May 26, 2004. The protocol on the resolution of conflict in Abyie: May 26, 2004. United Nations Mission in Sudan, http://unmis.unmissions.org/Default.aspx?tabid=515.

34. Sudan Comprehensive Peace Agreement, http://www.unmis.org/English/cpa.htm.

35. Peter Martell, "South Sudanese Celebrate their Divorce," *BBC News*, http://www.bbc.co.uk/news/world-africa-14091903.

36. Mason, "Learning from the Swiss Mediation and Facilitation Experiences in Sudan. Johan Brosché, *Sharing Power—Enabling Peace? Evaluating Sudan's Comprehensive Peace Agreement 2005* (Uppsala, Sweden: Department of Peace and Conflict Research, Uppsala University, 2009). Mark Simmons and Peter Dixon, eds., *Peace by Piece: Addressing Sudan's Conflicts* (London: Conciliation Resources, 2006).

37. P. Costello, "Historical Background," in *Negotiating Rights: The Guatemalan Peace Process*, ed. J. Armon, R. Sieder and R. Wilson (London: Conciliation Resources, issue 2, 1997).

38. "Negotiating Rights: The Guatemalan Peace Process," *Conciliation Resources*, issue 2 (1997).

39. Guatemala Peace Agreement, United States Institute of Peace, http://www.usip.org/library/pa/guatemala/pa_guatemala.html. See also *The Guatemala Peace Agreements* (Geneva: United Nations, Department of Public Information, 1998).

40. D. Sguaitamatti, A. Iff, R. Aluri, and S. Mason, *Peace Mediation Essentials: Business Actors in Mediation Processes* (Zurich: Mediation Support Project, Center for Security Studies, ETH Zurich and swisspeace, Bern, 2010). See also Achim Wennmann, *Money Matters: The Economic Dimensions of Peace Mediation.* PSIS Occasional Paper no. 4 (Geneva: Graduate Institute of International Studies, 2007).

41. Zartman's ripeness theory posits that negotiations can begin when the parties have the perception of a mutually hurting stalemate, feel a catastrophe is impeding or has been narrowly avoided, and they have the perception that there is a way out. I. William Zartman, "Ripeness," in *Beyond Intractability,* ed. Guy Burgess and Heidi Burgess (Boulder, CO: Conflict Research Consortium, University of Colorado, August 2003), http://www.beyondintractability.org/essay/ripeness/.

42. Yossi Alpher, "The Palestinian Question has been the Specific Catalyst of the Downfall of Every Governing Israeli Coalition for the past Twenty Years," in *The Future of the Israeli-Palestinian Conflict Critical Trends Affecting Israel.* USIP special report 149, Sept. 2005.

43. Jean Arnault, "Good Agreement? Bad Agreement? An Implementation Perspective." Center of International Studies, Princeton University. http://id.cdint.org/content/documents/Good_Agreement_Bad_Agreement.pdf

44. Mohammed S. Dajani Daoudi, *Wasatia The Spirit of Islam* (Jerusalem: Wasatia Publishing, 2009).

45. Thus, legal means make sense to prevent future atrocities or other actors from committing similar atrocities but are probably limited as a tool in bringing parties to the table if the legal procedure cannot be retracted.

46. See the failed deadline diplomacy in the Darfur peace process. Laurie Nathan, "No Ownership, No Peace: The Darfur Peace Agreement," Working paper no. 5 (London: London School of Economics, Crisis States Research Centre, 2006).

47. Lakhdar Barhimi explains the mediation logic as follows: "If you accept these kinds of jobs, you go and mediate between warlords, faction leaders, bandits, all sorts of people, people whom the human rights purists want to see hang. What I tell them is 'Let me finish, and then go ahead and hang them.'" He was also asked if he would talk to Osama bin Laden. "If I were to mediate between Al Qaeda and the United States, I suppose I would have to. But we are not there yet, are we? And Osama would refuse to talk to me, you have to remember that." Harriet Martin, *Kings of Peace, Pawns of War: The Untold Story of Peace-Making* (London: Continuum International Publishing Group, 2006), 25–26.

48. Oliver Wils and Véronique Dudouet, "Berghof: Challenges Facing Peacebuilders Engaging with Listed Groups," *Charity and Security Network,* June 17, 2010, http://www.charityandsecurity.org/background/Berghof_Challenges_Facing_Peace builders_Enagaging_Listed_Groups.

49. Therese Whitfield, *Working with Groups of Friends,* The Peacemaker's Toolkit Series (Washington, DC: United States Institute of Peace, 2010), www.usip.org.

CHAPTER 47

Attending to Unfinished Business in Peacemaking: Preliminary Findings from the Reflecting on Peace Practice Project

Peter Woodrow and Diana Chigas

The question of how to improve and measure the impact of peacebuilding and conflict transformation work has been the subject of much discussion and debate over the last decade. It is difficult to assess the contribution to "peace writ large," as the Reflecting on Peace Practice Project (RPP) has described the larger peace beyond the immediate confines of a project or program. Most peacebuilding programs are discrete efforts aimed at affecting one (often small) piece of the puzzle, and no one effort can do everything. As two practitioners have noted, "Peace requires that many people work at many levels in different ways, and, with all this work, you cannot tell who is responsible for what."[1] In the face of this complexity, practitioners often assume that "[a]ll of our good efforts must be adding up. With so much good stuff happening, the effects will become clear someday."[2]

The evidence gathered by RPP from 1999 to 2003 in a collaborative examination of actual experiences with peacemaking and peacebuilding,[3] suggested that, although many people do, indeed, work at many levels, conducting good programs at each level, these programs did not automatically "add up" to peace. In other words, the potential of these multiple efforts was not being realized fully.[4] RPP found that peacebuilding programs that were effective in contributing to peace writ large addressed key factors driving the conflict and established a variety of linkages.[5]

The initial findings of RPP, however, yielded less evidence regarding the cumulative effects of multiple peacemaking and peacebuilding efforts in a single conflict zone. And while the field has learned much about how to improve and assess impacts in the last 10 years, most research (including the initial phase of RPP) has focused on single projects or programs—or, as donors have done in undertaking joint evaluations, on the cumulative effects of a limited number of externally funded programs. The question of how and when multiple attempts to promote peace add up to significant progress toward sustainable peace write large" remains largely unanswered.[6] What, for example, constitutes a good or effective linkage? The earlier RPP process found that peace efforts in which there were stronger linkages were more effective—but there was insufficient evidence to determine how linkages work and which kinds might be more important than others. How can micro and macro levels, and bottom-up and top-down efforts be linked to improve the cumulative effects of all programs? Many practitioners are uneasy with the emphasis on peace writ large as a standard, because it is often difficult to determine how small, grassroots initiatives can be linked to impacts at the macro level.

This chapter discusses some preliminary findings from a new effort by RPP, undertaken in 2008, on "Understanding Cumulative Impacts." The new cumulative cases were designed to explore how specific societies and peace processes had managed to make progress toward peace—that is, how the process added up and whether and how linkages contributed to progress. RPP commissioned 16 cumulative impact case studies, focused on such diverse countries as South Africa, Tajikistan, Cambodia, and the Solomon Islands, to examine what made progress possible and, in the cases where progress was not sustained or was reversed, how the efforts ultimately failed to add up.[7] The information for the RPP case studies was gathered mainly through interviews with a variety of people in each setting. These concentrated on well-informed people of all types, reaching, whenever possible, beyond urban centers and capital cities. The interviews were open-ended, guided by a set of broad questions: the nature of the conflict, key moments of shift toward peace, identification of any progress made, explanations of why and how that happened, and remaining issues in the peace process. In most instances, the conversations did not focus primarily on peace programming—at least not initially. Rather, the inquiry was about the shape and direction of the overall peace process and comprehension of it.

As of this writing, all but one of the case studies in this series have been finalized, and initial analytical processes have started. Four consultations among case authors, practitioners, and donors regarding the case material have helped to identify several emerging themes that will be discussed and refined further in a series of feedback workshops to be held around the world.

INITIAL FINDINGS AND ISSUES

A number of issues have emerged as relevant to cumulative impacts from the initial case discussions and examination of the case materials. The role of civil society, both local and international, and the roles and relationships of outsiders to insiders have been important issues of debate in the peacebuilding field and have emerged as important dimensions of adding up. Yet no clear typology of effective roles has emerged to date; the roles of these actors have varied from context to context. Their effectiveness appears to depend on their ability to address the key drivers and actors in the context and to establish linkages with other efforts, levels, and sectors. In three of the cases, there was little or no continued gains toward peace, and peace was considered to be at risk in another five or six cases.

In those cases where significant progress toward peace was achieved, its sustainability depended to some extent also on the ability of key actors to shift their roles and develop new strategies, organizational structures, and approaches to deal with unfinished business. Such unfinished business consists of issues, problems, or conflicts that were not resolved in the peace agreement, or events that constituted progress but were considered to need additional attention in order to achieve a deeper or more sustained peace. These points will be greatly expanded once the case analysis and feedback workshops are completed. In the balance of this chapter, we will address these two aspects of adding up and creating momentum for peace: linkages and unfinished business.

LINKAGES AND DISCONNECTS AMONG TRACK ONE, TRACK TWO, AND TRACK THREE

The earlier RPP process found that it is important to link strategies that engage the larger population with efforts that focus on key decision makers.[8] In RPP terms, we call this linking *more people* and *key people* strategies. For instance, if negotiations among political elites are never connected with processes that consult with civil society, the resulting peace accord is less likely to be sustained. The process also found that efforts to transform attitudes, small group relationships, and skills (individual-personal level changes) are significant to the broader peace only if they are translated into action at the socio-political level or within the public, political, or institutional sphere.[9] For instance, a vast amount of training and individual transformation work has taken place in Mindanao, yet this work has not resulted in positive effects on political processes or on local dynamics of power and violence.

The cumulative impact case studies of peacebuilding have reinforced these findings and underlined the importance of linkages in helping efforts to add up. Vertical linkages across tracks or levels (e.g., tracks one, two, and three) appear to be particularly important in enhancing the cumulative effectiveness of peacebuilding work. The nature of the linkages varied. Effective vertical linkages included a wide range: churches working in a coherent way at different levels based on a shared theory of change in Mozambique; communication initiatives in South Africa that made people feel part of the process; and broad-based European Union and government agency funding for community-based initiatives integrated into the peace process in Northern Ireland. Yet the similar connections these mechanisms created between the official track-one process and other levels and constituencies contributed to the impacts of the efforts at all levels. By contrast, in places where peace processes have stalled—such as Cyprus, Sri Lanka, Israel-Palestine, and Mindanao—there appeared to be a near-complete disconnect between track one and other levels (especially local communities at track three), and many attributed the lack of progress to this absence of linkage.

Horizontal linkages across peace efforts in different sectors or with different constituencies, and conceptual linkage, in which groups come to understand how their efforts are connected conceptually, such as in a policy framework or a shared vision, also appear to enhance cumulative impacts. Coalitions and movements for peace bringing different groups together to advocate for change based on shared goals, common interests, or a shared vision were effective in the Philippines, in Nepal (where the 2006 People's Movement came together against the king), and in northern Cyprus (where the This Country Is Ours movement successfully mobilized a favorable vote on the United Nations–proposed peace agreement). Similarly, in Northern Ireland, different initiatives to address the same issue—such as discrimination—in different ways in different sectors and with different constituencies converged to generate broader impact.

Significantly, the cases suggest that many of the mechanisms practitioners currently use to create linkages are not sufficient in themselves, even if they facilitate or promote linkages. Such efforts include coordination mechanisms, relationship building, communication among agencies or among groups, work with "middle out" actors and undertaking work at different levels of society.[10] Effective efforts must also deal with and prevent detractors from linkage, such as proliferation of groups, competition for funds, ignorance of what others are doing, or government suppression.

ADDRESSING OR NEGLECTING UNFINISHED BUSINESS: AN IMPORTANT FACTOR FOR ADDING UP?

Of the 15 cases completed, four—Cyprus, Israel/Palestine, Sri Lanka, and Kosovo—involved situations in which there had been progress followed by reversals, setbacks, or failure of peace efforts. In the remaining 11 instances,[11] a peace agreement of some sort was signed among the contending parties or a peacekeeping operation deployed, and violence significantly abated. We will examine the preliminary conclusions emerging from those 11, each of them a post-conflict or, more accurately, a post-violence setting.[12]

The Nature of Unfinished Business

We found 20 types of unfinished business that were identified in more than one case. There are few surprises, as these are issues one would naturally expect in a postwar setting, and many will take many years to resolve. The question is whether these factors are being addressed at all or adequately—and whether some of them represent significant threats of a relapse into violence.[13]

Table 47.1 lists the issues of unfinished business that were found, categorized in several major domains: political, social fabric, security, justice, and economic. Seven of the issues concern various aspects of political struggle, four relate to social fabric, three involve justice, and two are in the economic sphere. The chart also identifies the number of cases where each issue was raised.[14] One issue, institutional dysfunction, was identified explicitly in only five cases. However, general knowledge of these conflict zones would suggest that this is probably a more widespread concern, even if it was not mentioned in those specific terms.

Table 47.1
Unfinished Business Categories and Occurrence in Cases

		Number of Cases
	Political Domain	
1.	Governance, democracy, rule of law	10
2.	Structural inequalities, power struggles, political culture	10
3.	Exclusionary policies and practices	7
4.	Corruption and impunity	7
5.	Indigenous and minority rights, identity, land, and traditions	7
6.	Peace agreements and laws versus implementation	4
7.	Inclusion and exclusion of groups from peace processes, spoilers	2
8.	Institutional dysfunction	5?
	Social Fabric Domain	
9.	Need for improved intergroup relations	9
10.	Sense of national identity, unity, vision	5
11.	Dealing with the past, reconciliation	8
12.	Need for deeper dialogue (local or national)	7
	Security Domain	
13.	Incomplete or unfair DDR, SSR, small arms	8
14.	Stability prioritized over peace and justice	4
15.	Dependence on external forces and roles	4
	Justice Domain	
16.	Human rights abuses	4
17.	Transitional justice and impunity	5
18.	Judicial reform and strengthening	5
	Economic Domain	
19.	Equitable development, distribution of benefits, resource management	11
20.	Specific disputes over land, returns	8

Among the top five categories of unfinished business are inequitable economic development, distribution of benefits, and resource management (11 instances); governance, democracy, and rule of law (10); structural inequalities and power struggles (10); the need for improved intergroup relations (9); and incomplete or unfair Disarmament, Demobilisation and Reintegration (DDR) or Security Sector Reform (SSR) processes and persistence of small arms (8). Dealing with the past and reconciling specific disputes over land and returns also were considered to be important unfinished business in 8 of the cases.

All of these are familiar themes in postwar peacebuilding. In many ways, RPP's findings confirm the post-conflict peacebuilding agenda that international agencies have supported since the 1990s. However, the nature of the issues within each category and the persistence of unfinished business long after the initial post-conflict agenda is implemented suggest that reconsideration of strategies and approaches may be necessary. Some cases show a greater number and density of issues (see Table 47.2 at the end of this chapter, showing which issues were found in which cases). Liberia, for example, shows 18 of the 20 issues and Burundi 17. In Northern Ireland, our sources identify 11 and in South Africa only 7. Tajikistan exhibits 16 issues, Haiti 3, and Aceh 10. While we would not claim this to be yet another index of fragility, the density of unfinished business issues in a single conflict zone may represent an indicator of vulnerability to renewed violence over time. In situations such as Tajikistan, Burundi, and Liberia, where international attention and assistance has been declining as time has elapsed, since the peace agreement and violence has remained minimal, this may suggest both an urgency and an agenda for conflict prevention. On the other hand, it would be necessary to delve further into each situation to judge the seriousness of the concern or issue to determine with any confidence which issues constitute real threats of future violence. In addition, the nature of the specific issues within each familiar category may suggest that a shift of emphasis in longer-term postagreement agendas is needed.

Issues in the Political Domain: Governance, Democracy, and Power

Concern regarding governance was extremely widespread, encountered in 10 of the 11 cases. Again, this is not surprising, as improvements in government effectiveness, delivery of services, and responsiveness to the needs and concerns of citizens remains a key challenge in most of the developing world. In almost all cases, the concern regarding governance and democracy occurred in connection with the issue of structural inequalities and power struggles. Looking beyond the broad title to the specific issues, the concerns regarding governance and power involve deeply held values and practices embedded in the political culture of these societies. Thus, in Mindanao, interviewees noted the need for changes in the autocratic—even feudal—systems of local dynasties that dominate politics, often in collaboration with central government powers in Manila. Similar language is used in Mozambique to describe a zero-sum mindset in which political parties vie for total control over the state to perpetuate the entrenched patron-client system. The underlying patron-client (or "big man") model of governance is also seen as problematic in Liberia. Increasingly successful efforts at one-party capture of the state are found in Mozambique, Cambodia, and Tajikistan.

Centralization of the state is seen as problematic in Tajikistan, Liberia, Mindanao, and Haiti. In Tajikistan, control of the state by a powerful clan from one region and lack of devolution of administrative power to other areas are elements of ongoing conflict and are connected with disparities in access to economic resources. In contrast to most of the other cases, the divide in Haiti is largely along class lines, describing tensions between privileged urban elites who have traditionally controlled government and the broad mass of the population who remain desperately poor. The election of Aristide as a champion of the disenfranchised majority resulted twice in his ouster by a fearful elite class. In some cases, the problems of governance are traced back to the colonial legacy and inadequate preparation for administration of a modern state—as in Burundi, Mozambique, and the Solomons—or rapid dissolution of a previous regime—as in Tajikistan.

In South Africa and Northern Ireland, the governance issues were somewhat different, and there is a sense that the peace process is irreversible in those countries. In contrast to the other cases, new regimes in those settings inherited functioning and relatively efficient state structures, where the question was only which groups would control them. Interestingly, the 20 issues of unfinished business were less prevalent in South Africa. And, while some issues were present in Northern Ireland, they were seen to be acknowledged and in the process of being addressed (and thus of less immediate concern). These societies are certainly not free from problems associated with conflict, but they are not plagued with the number and depth of issues faced by people and their leaders in the other cases. Nevertheless, in Northern Ireland, there is some perception that parties gain from emphasizing sectarian identities and claiming that the peace agreements constitute sellouts of their constituencies, particularly in difficult economic times.[15]

In the political realm, serious concerns arise when the issues of democratic governance and political culture—long-term development issues—are coupled with claims of corruption, exclusionary policies and practices (based on religion, ethnicity, class, or geography/region), indigenous or minority rights, and failures to implement peace agreements. These trends in postwar settings are particularly disturbing when these factors constitute in whole or in part the original reasons for the war and violence. In other words, the causes of the conflict persist, despite years, sometimes decades, of fighting and concerted efforts to establish peace, often supported by enormous amounts of international assistance.

Burundi is an apt illustration. The ruling party did not participate in the peace process and feels no commitment to implementing the Arusha Accords (issue 7 in Table 47.1). They have been systematically undermining their political opponents and committing what many see as human rights abuses, despite considerable international pressure (issues 3 and 16). In fact, they are perceived as treating their election victory as equivalent to a military triumph and license to exclude others and engage in widespread corrupt practices (issue 4). While these are not unusual problems, given Burundi's history, the fact that they are not openly acknowledged as problems leaves little political space for raising these issues, much less addressing them. Thus, the fragile peace in Burundi appears threatened by the persistence of unfinished business from a long legacy of violence.

Issues in the Social Fabric Domain

The social fabric domain involves intergroup relations, perceptions and attitudes, social norms, and the degree to which people embrace a national identity, feel a sense of unity, and support a common vision of the future. In 9 of the 11 cases, intergroup relations were identified as problematic and in need of additional efforts. This issue was often coupled with calls for more effective efforts to deal with the past and to promote reconciliation—or for more general dialogue as a means for improving communication, creating mutual understanding, and developing a better modus vivendi.

By itself, the presence of unfinished business in the social fabric domain was not sufficient to undermine the peacebuilding process. However, coupled with the absence of (or need for) deeper dialogue and/or the presence of unfinished business in the political or economic domain, these issues become more serious. There appears to be an expectation that issues related to intergroup relations, national identity, and dealing with the past are long-term issues not solved in months or a few years. In this regard, it is instructive to point out—briefly—the massive efforts to break down hostilities and build a sense of unity in Europe in the wake of two world wars, especially between France and Germany. A wide array of efforts, including student exchanges, paired cities, and artist exchanges were organized for 30 or 40 years after 1945, to the point that young people in those two countries now have difficulty understanding the depths of animosity experienced by their parents and grandparents. Contending groups cannot be expected to reverse years of hostility and even mutual massacres after a few short years or a few joint workshops. However, clear commitments and visible efforts to improve relations will provide a sense of progress in this domain sufficient to prevent unfinished business in this area from undermining momentum toward peace.

In some cases, the need for dialogue was in relation to quite specific groups. For example, in Mozambique, there was a need for discussions between elected leaders and key representatives of ex-combatant groups to resolve a series of aggravating issues that threaten the peace (connected to issue 13 regarding incomplete or unfair DDR processes). In other areas, the necessity for dialogue had a broader sense. In Haiti, dialogue across social classes is totally missing, so that fundamentals of the conflict remain unaddressed. In Burundi, exchanges between the government and opposition political parties are needed. In Tajikistan, dialogue is needed to address elements of the peace agreement, such as amnesty, that have not been implemented, and a broad set of issues remain unaddressed, since the National Dialogue Project has fallen apart without ongoing support from the international community.

In the Solomon Islands and Tajikistan, the very nature of the nation or national identity was in question, as were issues regarding a shared vision of the future, which was also an issue in Liberia and Haiti. In some cases, interviewees felt that dialogue among key groups was needed; in others, they felt that stronger leadership could offer a more compelling vision to promote unity and further progress toward sustainable peace.

Issues in the Security Domain

The most salient issue in the security domain involved incomplete or unfair DDR processes—often coupled with issues regarding security sector reform (integration of armed forces, professionalization of the police, depoliticization of the military, etc.). In 8 of the 11 cases, there were serious concerns with poor treatment of ex-combatants, persistent unemployment, and unfair distribution of payments. In Aceh, former rebel soldiers were not receiving payments in an even-handed manner, and some forces loyal to the government were not acknowledged in the peace accord but received payments nonetheless, fueling tensions among the population. The persistence of the Armed Men of RENAMO in Mozambique represented a clear threat to security, and former combatants were blocked from obtaining amnesty in Tajikistan. While ex-combatant issues do not represent long-term structural problems, they do constitute short- and intermediate-term threats, as, in many cases, former soldiers retain access to small arms and loyalty to their former commanders, a persistent threat in Liberia, for instance.

In several places, local populations felt dependent on the presence of international peacekeeping forces and feared that the security situation would deteriorate if those forces withdrew. In Haiti, interviewees appreciated the small gains in security provided by United Nations troops but indicated that chaos would return if those forces withdrew. In the Solomon Islands, there were ambivalent feelings about the role of the regional peacekeeping force, RAMSI, but people also felt that their departure would bring a resurgence of violence. Similar sentiments were expressed in Liberia, where the army and police have been completely rebuilt from nothing, but their ability to keep the peace is still in question.

Issues in the Economic Domain

Most of the issues raised in the economic realm concerned horizontal inequalities, not the absolute levels of poverty. Interviewees pointed to questions about how economic benefits and international aid are distributed. Others identified issues regarding who has access to resources and how disputes are resolved, particularly those over land. Again, while it appears that people are generally concerned about the persistence of poverty, at the same time, they primarily want assurance that progress is being made and that the system is addressing issues of equity. Here there is a clear connection to government decision making and repeated claims of exclusion, as well as perceptions of corruption and diversion of regular government revenues and development funds.

At times, economic issues lie at the heart of the conflict, such as in the Solomon Islands, where years of favoritism toward people from Malaita (in terms of government and security sector jobs), as well as transmigration policies, have caused the people of Guadalcanal to build a sense of grievance that led eventually to violence. Certainly, economic issues drive much of the conflict dynamics in Haiti, as already noted. In Aceh, local people have long resented the flow of oil and natural gas revenues derived from Acehnese resources into central government coffers, while they have seen relatively few benefits.

The case evidence seems to suggest that economic issues are not of significant concern by themselves. Rather, only when issues of poverty are coupled with political decision making and structural inequalities do they become a threat to the peace. In fact, as we examine the cases further, we will need to resolve contradictory evidence. For instance, in two of the cases, Sri Lanka and Cyprus, there was considerable economic progress made—by some groups—in the midst of conflict. Here again, the answer may lie in the differential gains and the perceptions of government policies rather than absolute levels of poverty. The cases also suggest that economic factors may serve as a motivator, given expectations of a peace dividend or economic prosperity (or fear of something worse). But economic progress does not seem to be correlated with progress in the peace process—that is, it does not appear to contribute to adding up. This may be because many of the economic programs, such as youth employment, DDR, or ex-combatant training, are not sufficiently comprehensive or linked with other efforts, or they do not attain the scale needed to produce real transformation. At the same time, economic factors were the most often cited as unfinished business, suggesting that unrealized expectations in this domain in a post-agreement period, especially if mobilized politically, could become quite destabilizing.

The Significance of Unfinished Business

In most of the case studies, the unfinished business represents key conflict factors that were not being addressed—or were being addressed inadequately. However, unfinished business has not caused fragility in the peace process in all cases. RPP's preliminary findings suggest that the number, severity, and diversity or a combination of issues of unfinished business prevent adding up to more sustainable peace. The prevalence and persistence of deep issues of political culture and governance suggest that the transformational impact of peacebuilding interventions has been limited with regard to the issues that matter the most for sustainable peace. The vast amounts of money, technical assistance, and programming have not substantially touched the most important issues of political culture and concentration of power. This unfinished business, coupled with effects of exclusion and unfair distribution of resources, appears to form the primary concern of peace proponents in the majority of case studies in the RPP process.

Perhaps more important is the failure to acknowledge the unfinished business or denial of its importance. Where progress has been accompanied by an open recognition or identification of unfinished business and a process for addressing it, it has not undermined further momentum. Where, for example, the new government or regime has not been connected with the old system and has a clear commitment to pursue change, such as in South Africa, Northern Ireland, the Solomon Islands, and Liberia, peace processes at all levels have continued to add up despite the unfinished business. The post-apartheid government in South Africa is intent on dismantling all of the institutions, policies, and practices that entrenched white privilege there. While there are complaints regarding the slowness of economic progress for large numbers of people, there is no doubt that changes have occurred, from the constitution to specific policies to the reallocation of government resources. Similarly, in Northern Ireland, people describe the peace process as irreversible, even though concerns linger over groups that remain ready to undertake violence to pursue their goals. In the Solomon Islands, the issues were openly acknowledged, and concerted local and international efforts were underway. There, the international community's efforts were concentrated on national-level government institutions in a significant state-building enterprise, while local community and church organizations (often with international support) were working from the ground up on issues of reconciliation and dialogue. Although there were critiques about the disconnect between these two types of efforts and the slow pace of progress, nevertheless, there was appreciation for the fact that the fundamental issues were recognized and addressed.

Liberia is a more mixed picture. The elected government has been quite willing to acknowledge the problematic nature of the regimes from the 1980s onward, as presented clearly in government documents, including the Poverty Reduction Strategy. At the same time, it has been reluctant to deal with long-term issues of power and privilege associated with the dominance of Americo-Liberians over all other local tribes since the 19th-century establishment of the nation. The persistent marginalization of rural areas over Monrovia and the relative neglect of other tribes remain points of contention. To quote the case study:

> Many interviewees, apart from those subjective assessments of the current situation in Liberia, stressed that they found the conditions in post-war Liberia to resemble pre-war Liberia and that the root causes of the war had not been properly addressed. One observer noted that the fact that many people were "disgruntled and marginalized" had not changed. Widespread poverty, underdevelopment, exclusion of parts of the country and the marginalization of parts of the population were all cited as root causes of the conflict that have largely remained unchanged. According to those interviewed, most development remains focused on Monrovia at the expense of the countryside, and "resources are not being distributed as they should be." The government is seen to take action mainly for its own benefit or for the benefit of the rich. One informant summed it up as follows: "Those who were wealthy sent their kids abroad and they are coming back now and get all the good jobs. Corruption and lack of opportunities [continue], just like in the history of our country."[16]

These four are the exceptions; the other seven cases exhibit persistent, sometimes deliberate, blindness to the existence or the severity of the unfinished business. As a result, they exhibit a greater sense of vulnerability to a return to violence and a more negative perception of the accomplishments of the peace process. As suggested, some of the unfinished business issues represent normal issues of institutional, social, and economic development, but it is the *combination, density, and severity* of issues that represent the threat to sustained peace, especially when attention to these factors is suppressed. The persistence of these issues, in some cases more than 10 years after a peace agreement, suggests that a renewed agenda for peacebuilding is needed. Thus, Tajikistan is confronted by discontent from the subregions of the country that are systematically excluded from power, decision making, and access to resources; persistent claims of corruption and favoritism; a series of unresolved issues in the formal peace agreements and current policy debates; and claims of discriminatory practices in relation to ex-combatants and government positions. While the population seems content, for the moment, to trade assurance of security for progress in more open governance, it is unclear how long this will last.

The Haiti case study makes a strong argument that the fundamental issues that drive conflict in the country are neither acknowledged nor addressed. In fact, the ruling elites appear to operate out of deep fear of the general population; they concentrate on maintaining control over the security situation, at least to contain localized violence in poor neighborhoods. Repeated attempts to achieve change nonviolently through the ballot box have failed, as the power elites have rejected the results and ousted the champions of change. The question in Haiti is whether the current stalemate, overseen by United Nations peacekeepers, can last—and whether the strategy of ignoring the more fundamental problems can succeed in the long run or whether violence will continue to erupt periodically.

CONCLUSION: DO PEACE EFFORTS ADD UP?

The original reason for commissioning these cumulative case studies was to address several questions: How do various peace efforts add up to sustained peace for a whole society? Are the efforts undertaken in these postviolence settings sufficient to prevent a relapse into violence over time? This chapter has examined one dimension of the issue: the nature and role of unfinished business.

There is no debate about the fact that the effects of war and violence persist long after a ceasefire, a peace accord, a new constitution, and a first peaceful election take place. It would appear that the international community generally feels that its job is done once those basic steps have been taken and that the longer-term work of addressing the lingering problems should be incorporated into normal development processes. However, the evidence suggests that national governments and their international partners (donor governments, United Nations agencies, even international nongovernmental organizations) (a) seldom acknowledge the very existence of the issues identified in these settings—even when those issues are significant and unmistakable; and (b) even when they do recognize the issues, fail to devote adequate resources to address them at a realistic scale and depth. Mechanisms like the United

Nations Peacebuilding Commission and Fund (PBF) allocate relatively small amounts of money to post-conflict peacebuilding in relation to the scale of the problem and the resources made available for other kinds of assistance. Also, so far, the process for identifying the priority needs of the countries receiving PBF funds has failed in most cases to focus on the real drivers of conflict. Instead, funds have been allocated to the priority projects of implementing United Nations agencies or to the priorities of the governments in power, which are seldom committed to addressing the real conflict issues. The Peacebuilding Commission is only an example; other donors have also taken a superficial approach to the issue of consolidating peace in postwar settings.

The RPP case studies were not focused exclusively on the question of unfinished business. Thus, none of the cases should be considered definitive analyses of the salient issues that demand attention. Nevertheless, interviewees in every situation were quite forthcoming about the changes they saw as needed to consolidate peace. This experience suggests that it is not difficult to identify key priorities in terms of the unfinished business. Once such issues are identified, the subsequent challenge is devising effective strategies for addressing them and mobilizing the will and resources to implement programs of change over the long haul.

NOTES

1. Mary B. Anderson and Lara Olson, *Confronting War: Critical Lessons for Peace Practitioners* (Cambridge, MA: Collaborative Learning Projects (CDA), 2003), 6.

2. Ibid.

3. An initial set of 26 case studies conducted all over the world and on many types of peace work, together with 35 consultations and feedback workshops at which the emerging themes, issues, and patterns were discussed and refined by practitioners, policy makers, donors, and academics resulted in the publication of *Confronting War.*

4. Anderson and Olson, *Confronting War.*

5. Anderson and Olson, *Confronting War.*

6. *Peace writ large*, a term introduced in *Confronting War*, refers to larger, societal-level peace—that is, beyond the level of individuals or communities.

7. The full list of case studies includes South Africa, Northern Ireland, Burundi, Liberia, Mozambique, Kosovo (from an earlier study), Cyprus, Israel/Palestine, Sri Lanka, Tajikistan, Cambodia, Aceh, Mindanao, Solomon Islands, Haiti, and Guatemala. These are available on the CDA website: http://www.cdainc.com/ Click on Reflecting on Peace Practice, then on Project Documents, and then Case Studies/Field Visits. As of this writing, the Guatemala case was not complete.

8. See M. B. Anderson, and L. Olson. *Confronting War: Critical Lessons for Peace Practitioners* (Cambridge, MA: CDA, 2003).

9. Ibid.

10. John Lederach, *Building Peace: Sustainable Reconciliation in Divided Societies* (Washington, DC: United States Institute of Peace Press, 1997).

11. Excluding Guatemala, which is not finished. Haiti is a special case, since there was no real civil war there but chronic violence and periodic instances of large-scale killings.

12. The international community uses the term *post-conflict* to describe countries that have achieved a cessation of active warfare and, in most cases, signed a peace

agreement. In almost all cases, as we shall see, the "conflict" continues in important ways.

13. The cases studies on Northern Ireland and South Africa did not include much information on unfinished business, because these were among the first cases completed, and this specific topic was not included in the original terms of reference for case researchers and writers. Therefore, we have asked people familiar with the situation in those two situations (including the case authors) to identify what they see as the unfinished business, intending to seek further confirmation of their estimates in the next months.

14 This is not a calculation of the number of interviewees that raised the issue in each case. The qualitative interview information does not permit such quantitative analysis.

15. Correspondence with the case authors.

16. Christof Kurz, "Peacebuilding in Liberia," Reflecting on Peace Practice Project, CDA Collaborative Learning Projects, 2010, p. 41.

Table 47.2
Categories and Issues of Unfinished Business in RPP Cumulative Case Studies

	Aceh	Burundi	Cam-bodia	Haiti	Liberia	Mindanao	Mozam-bique	North-ern Ireland	Solo-mon Islands	South Africa	Tajik-istan	Number of Cases
Political Domain												
1. Poor governance, democracy, rule of law	X	X	X	X	X	X	X	X	X		X	10
2. Structural inequalities, power struggles		X	X	X	X	X	X	X	X	X	X	10
3. Exclusionary policies and practices	X	X		X	X		X	X			X	7
4. Corruption and impunity		X	X	X	X	X	X				X	7

(Continued)

Table 47.2 (Continued)

	Aceh	Burundi	Cambodia	Haiti	Liberia	Mindanao	Mozambique	Northern Ireland	Solomon Islands	South Africa	Tajikistan	Number of Cases
5. Threat to indigenous and minority rights, identity, land, and traditions	X	X	X		X	X				X	X	7
6. Peace agreements and laws versus implementation	X	X	X								X	4
7. Inclusion and exclusion from peace processes, spoilers		X						X				2

8. Institutional dysfunction		X	X	X		X	X		X	5?
Social Fabric Domain										
9. Need for improved inter-group relations	X	X	X	X	X	X	X		X	9
10. Lack of a sense of national identity, unity, vision	X	X	X	X		X	X		X	5
11. Inadequate dealing with the past, reconciliation	X	X	X	X		X	X	X	X	8
12. Need for deeper dialogue (local or national)	X	X	X	X	X	X	X		X	7

(Continued)

Table 47.2 (Continued)

	Aceh	Burundi	Cambodia	Haiti	Liberia	Mindanao	Mozambique	Northern Ireland	Solomon Islands	South Africa	Tajikistan	Number of Cases
Security Domain												
13. Incomplete or unfair DDR, SSR, small arms	X	X	X	X	X	X	X				X	8
14. Stability prioritized over peace and justice			X	X	X						X	4
15. Dependence on external forces and roles	X			X	X				X			4
Justice Domain												
16. Human rights abuses	X	X				X					X	4

778

The following table is rotated on the page. It is reconstructed below in normal reading orientation. Columns represent individual cases; the final column gives the total ("Number of issues per case" appears as the last row giving the per-case totals).

	1	2	3	4	5	6	7	8	9	10	11	Total
17. Incomplete transitional justice and impunity		X	X		X	X		X			X	5
18. Need for judicial reform and strengthening		X		X	X	X	X	X				5
Economic Domain												
19. Inequitable development, distribution of benefits, resource management, unemployment	X	X	X	X	X	X	X	X	X	X	X	11
20. Specific disputes over land, returns	X	X	X		X	X	X	X	X	X	X	8
Number of issues per case	10	17	11	13	18	8	10	11	9	7	16	

779

CHAPTER 48

The Dialogic Subject

Ranabir Samaddar

A federal vision of society based on intersecting autonomies is not only a different spatial vision of the world we inhabit but of democracy as well. Such a process is not conflict-free. It requires daily negotiations, daily plebiscite—in one word, *dialogue.* The figure of the subject I am invoking in this chapter is not the transcendental subject of Kant, who moves by practical reason and hence unites with others as a mark of reasonableness; my figure is that of a dialogic subject. In tracing the emergence of the dialogic subject, we must be aware of the contentious time we are passing through. The diversities constitute opportunities for convergence and cooperation, but, as concrete phenomena, they stay in asymmetrical relationships. These contentions will be and are marked by rival claims, collective assertions, violence, governmental controls over society, and wealth and pomp on one hand and want and desire on the other. This world is too physical to be thought of as a clean space of convergence and cooperation. Dialogues are, therefore, as I remarked in *The Politics of Dialogue* (Samaddar 2004), contested conversations. Beneath each dialogue, one can hear the echo of the clash of voices, interests, passions, and powers.

Dialogue means conversing through these contentions—that is, daily bargaining, a plebiscitary, federal society. It is only in this sense that we can think of a dialogic subject. The presence of such a subject indicates the need for a continuous exchange of our experiences of the physicality of our lives, our ways of thinking, and our passions and dreams. The ways in which we eat, or live, strive for resources to eat and live, sleep, rear families, think, write, turn the disparate "I"s into a "we," our hate and love objects, and our imagined futures already constitute the night sky of seemingly stationary stars pulling each into each other's direction. This is a physically constituted world, yet it appears dreamy, surreal. In that world of physical existences, friendship has been the key word from ancient times. Friendship, and not destructive close-ness through integration, is the key political concept. To that dialogic moment we are all pushing ourselves as subjects.

DIALOGUE AS THE CONTINUUM OF WAR AND PEACE

As they were in the ancient days of the *Mahabharata*, the dialogic practices of our time are conditioned by the political history of war and peace that accompanies these practices. War and peace influence the dynamics of the dia-logic self, because democracy by itself is parched on our destiny of war and peace. Democracy and war-peace are the two continuous themes marking the emergence of the dialogic subject today. By *today*, I mean conditions of our present existence—namely, our dialogic practices in the milieu of some wars, fragile peace, endemic and structural violence, and a pervasive condition of no war–no peace.

There is another reason why we should turn our attention to the issue of the dialogic subject. After all, modernity, along with its many gifts, has given us the complex of the no war–no peace situation, which, from the time of Ma-chiavelli and, more particularly, Kant, has been marked as one of strategic ambiguity, where and when the politics of carrying out the policies of one situation (war/peace) through the politics of its reverse situation (peace/war) is mapped out. This situation is one of hybridity, claustrophobia, and an all-pervasive desire to come out or break clean of this situation. Dialogues are the marks of this hybrid condition. Plural dialogues not only mean dialogues at several levels; they also indicate the signs of a capillary (diffused) situation of power, resistance, and contested conversations in politics. In itself no virtue, dialogue in all its complexities therefore has to be analyzed as a pointer to how war and power grow out of each other, how dialogue may lead to war, and how plural dialogues may lead to accommodation, reconciliation, and peace.

The persistence of the dialogic situation as a mark of ambiguity forces us to face the question, Can we escape the binary of war and peace and thus avoid the exclusivist discourse of either militarism or banal pacifism? In other words, can we bring to light the alterability and mutuality of the conditions of war and peace so that we can think of the conditions of justice, dialogue, and therefore sustainable peace?

To make sense of the emergence of the dialogic subject in the modern post-colonial world, we have to study the narratives of contentious situations of dialogue, which are open ended and suggest alternative possibilities—possibilities that at first sight had seemed closed. Studies of dialogue sit at the heart of peace studies. My argument in replacing the peace-seeking subject with the dialogic subject—thereby opening up the aporia of a war/peace bi-nary—is, however, not only methodological. The argument is also existential. The challenge to the state from within and without is now on a new ground, which has the advantage of forcing the most reluctant power to converse and communicate. As if the message from those who yearn for justice is, *we are not out to destroy the world; all we want is justice, speak to us, give us political recognition.* Such a notion of dialogic justice can cross the limits of retributive justice by suggesting restorative possibilities. In terms of political technique, it inverts the moral fabric of the reasons of the state with reasons of dialogue. It replaces the state agenda with the agenda of expanding political community, violence with accommodation, revenge with reconciliation, and rights with justice. We are living in a world of binaries, and the dialogic position has to work on the antagonisms of such irreconcilables as state/community, universalism/particularism, globality/territoriality, nationalism/global morality, citizenship/alienhood, and destruction/peace. The reworked positions arrived at through dialogic procedures are often predicated by contingencies of the time and therefore cannot guarantee permanence. Yet what is crucial about this contingency is that the dialogic position forces the mainstream positions to rework themselves. But this also means that the dialogic subject will always call for what is known as the ethos of permanent plebiscite. The dialogic journey is therefore permanent, with which a state-centric view (on war or peace) finds it hard to agree.

It is not that liberal theorists are unaware of the place of dialogue in a situation marked by binaries. For instance, Rawls spoke of "laws of peoples,"[1] where his enterprise was to get over in the interest of peace the distinction between what he thought to be authoritarian polities and liberal polities. Communitarians in the same vein have tried to reconcile abstract and apparently rootless individualism with community identity, and hence group emotions, sentiments, and loyalties. If nationalism and ethnic allegiances are producing appalling bloodshed and devastation, they argue that, in the interest of multicultural harmony based on group rights, an alternative form of loyalty and harmony has to be theorized that will be compatible with universal norms and yet capable of attracting people of a particular territory.[2] Jürgen Habermas also suggests a dialogic strategy when he advocates constitutional patriotism to "fight nationalism on its own ground."[3] All of these revisionist exercises contain an attempt to reconcile morality and the facts of life through dialogic tropes—dialogues between the contradictory features in place of treating them as antinomies. Yet, noticeable in all these attempts is a remarkable silence about the question of power.

It is necessary to move away from such a synthetic version of dialogic politics. If we have to see dialogue in the context of the incipient forms of justice and democracy, we must also begin viewing it in the context of power, whose one form is the institutional management of conflicts, which has now become a feature of the dialogic game.

The need to disentangle the story of alternative possibilities of dialogue and reconciliation from ruling accounts of management of contentious events is now greater in the context of what has been described as the "dangerous liaison" between globalization and the current discourse of democracy and development.[4] This discourse is also a reflection of the strong connection between war and development. Michel Foucault, in one of his last writings, had remarked,

The French Revolution gives the signal for the great national wars of our days, involving national armies and meeting their conclusion or their climax in huge mass slaughters. I think that you can see a similar phenomenon during the Second World War. In all history it would be hard to find such butchery as in World War II, and it is precisely this period, this moment, when the great welfare, public health, and medical assistance programs were instigated. The Beveridge program has been, if not conceived, at least published at this very moment. One could symbolize such coincidence by a slogan: Go get slaughtered and we promise you a long and pleasant life. Life insurance is connected with a death command.[5]

The dramatic improvements in the technology of rule have come in the wake of global developments in technologies of social administration, which base themselves on the increasing capacity to govern and have nothing to do with dialogic politics. Ivan Ivekovic, the Balkan political analyst, in an essay on different stages of social structures of accumulation, has shown how development has induced underdevelopment; the inadequate resolution of the peasant question has provoked neo-patriarchal clan wars, and the institutional dynamics of accumulation today faces three traps: the Malthusian trap, the technology trap, and the ecological trap. The severity of these traps is compounded by the illusion that, while keeping huge sections of the population at subsistence level (the level itself is revised from time to time), accumulation can continue unhindered on the basis of institutional management of these three issues of population, technology, and environment.[6] Ivekovic also shows how patriarchy, neo-patriarchal convulsions, and political violence are linked in this process.

Besides the well-known factors such as inequitable access to land reforms, patriarchal residues after "modernization" with its attending features of urbanization and migration, and the production of déclassé elements in such modern society,[7] Ivekovic draws attention to the crucial development of neo-patriarchy—that is, "patriarchy distorted by modernization." Therefore, we have one on hand what Valentine Moghadam calls the classic patriarchy, which is, where "the senior man has authority over everyone else in the family, including younger men and women subject to distinct forms of control," and the "key to the reproduction of classic patriarchy lies in operations of the patriarchy-extended household, which is also commonly associated with the reproduction of the peasantry in agrarian societies."[8] On the other hand, today we have a situation, where, with new technology and new processes of accumulation, the household mode of production faces grave threat. Poorly paid family labor and the eternally marginal existence of the household unit in the world of advanced capitalist production produce neo-patriarchy, where women are compelled to be the lowest-paid labor in the household to maintain the house as an economic unit.

The family organization of survival and work and the patrilinear mode of appropriation are now the direct result of globalization, where guest workers, family workers, marginalized peasant groups, small producing units, operatives in the service sector, and various categories of "frontier workers" (a phrase used to denote migrant workers in Europe) have to survive by constantly negotiating globalization. Women form the core of the "surplus army" now employable, now unemployable, but always the underclass of the present age. States are being re-formed, reorganized, regrouped, and re-arranged on the basis of neo-patriarchy not only in an economic sense, but directly politically. Women symbolize most the phenomenon of citizen-alien, the insider-outsider, and the worker-family keeper. Eternally moving from their own homes to another, across families, villages, towns, and then inter-national boundaries, they are not only the unhomed but are crucial in hom-ing the modern state in an age of globalization.

Neither realists and neo-realists nor moralists have looked into the funda-mental phenomenon in international politics—the role of women in the re-organization of the world power structure today. It should not astonish us, therefore, that the demands of dialogue and the desire to transcend the lan-guage of rights with a language of justice, propelled by women's desire ev-erywhere for dignity and recognition (for example, in South Africa, Bosnia, Palestine, Guatemala, Chile, and South Asia), have not been theorized. Almost everywhere massive numbers of women are confronting dominant power structures with demands for dialogue on all contested issues. One of the aims of critical theory of peace is to acknowledge the massive existence of women as subjects of world politics today. To do so will be to take one more step away from the futile language of conflict moderation toward one of dialogue, justice, and peace.

In the 20th century, the connection of war with development signaled an all-enveloping and all-consuming notion of gain. International relations the-ory failed to understand the impact of developmental strategy connected with militarism and war on patterns of dialogue, because such strategy was im-mersed in the neo-classical theory of utility and gain. Thus, it had nothing to offer as insight on the dynamics of dialogue, an enduring feature of world re-lations in the second half of the 20th century. It had no answer to the following posers: What does the mediating agency of dialogue speak of the war-peace continuum that it straddles? More important, is dialogue reducible to a status of being the language of negotiation? All that the international relations theory could do was to explicate various scenarios of bargaining in terms of rational choices. Thus, its own explanation of the dynamics of dialogue in terms of comparison of utilities, the Pareto optimality, distributive bargaining, and in-tegrative bargaining was of no relevance to the historical situation developing, particularly in the postcolonial world, amid cold war, neo-colonialism, proxy wars, irreducible poverty, great power domination, and an increasingly global but fragmented scenario.

The theory of rational bargaining tells us that each party has stable prefer-ences, which are arranged along a single line of homogeneous dimension util-ity. The theory, of course, acknowledges that, although "the bargainers (may) differ in their stockpiles of utility so that one is far wealthier than the other, this will have no impact on their evaluation of further units of utility, [and] an additional unit will not be more valuable to the poor bargainer than to the wealthy one."[9] Thus, notions of justice, independence, equality, reparations, and human rights were not considered as calculable units of utility; yet these have persistently influenced the fates of attrition, coexistence, and peace and have provoked major demands for dialogue. We can follow the question further. For example, what if parties do not have stable preferences either due to information deficiencies or changing perceptions because these parties as new states and nations are in that seemingly endless twilight zone of transition?[10]

While conflict theorists will put these issues to "limited perceptual capabilities of bargainers in actual conflicts" and "goals comprised of independent, and even conflicting constraints as opposed to homogenous utilities (that) cause some of the difficulties,"[11] the post-colonial experiences lead us to factors such as ideologies, values, and group ethos. These factors suggest that the dialogic subject cannot be conflated with the bargaining subject, who remains motivated by a theory of calculus of marginal utility or gain. If we have to step beyond the theory of bargaining in our effort to understand the politics of dialogue, the key to such understanding is a rigorous probe into the war-peace and conflict-peace continuums.[12]

Most of the time, we think that restoration of constitutional culture is the way to reinforce dialogic politics. But we may ask: Will such a restoration be enough to guarantee new dialogic practices and allow the latter a broader site? Going by the indications available now, we can see that not only constitutions everywhere are failing to be effective conflict-resolution mechanisms; they are at times, and on the contrary, exacerbating the conflicts. In the case of India, this is most evident in Kashmir. If the conflict is over the constitution, then it becomes difficult when a constitution in question demands that the society has to acknowledge the constitution as the supreme political voice and starts presiding on avenues and processes of dialogue. In any case, as the saying goes, *inter arma silent leges*—in times of war, the laws are silent. And not only the present juridical situation is shaken in the wake of national, social, and political wars; even the formation of future laws for the purpose of codified rules of negotiation of differences are also suspended. In such a context, a public discourse of constitutional democracy has to answer, in the first place, how this public is constituted and how this discourse of democracy will respond to an alternative philosophy of conversations.[13]

To conduct a concrete analysis of the great failure of constitutional democracy in moderating conflicts, it is necessary to abandon the centrality of sovereignty in the study of war and peace. The theory of sovereignty lends a centralized form to power, ignoring the myriad ways power forms to dominate and suppress people and turn subjects into victims. For instance, the Indian Constituent Assembly debates were clear as to how power was being formed. Groups, classes, estates, and rebellious nationalities were not fighting each other to death. "War of all against all" was, in fact, suspended in favor of "measuring of all against all" to found the commonwealth. The constitution is a record of a will to compose various forms of power and of the postponement of that final fight, because society had to be run, citizens had to be ruled, and therefore the act of suspending bellicosity was scripted in the political document (the classic no war–no peace document).

In such context, a constitution helps conversations for reconciliation and peace but is never the principal dialogic site, simply because it does not encode what will be called sovereign power. Dialogue undermines the fiction of a monolithic institutionalization of power. Beneath the compact text of a constitution, one does not have to stretch ears far to hear the drum of wars of all kinds (caste, ethnic, religious, class), the violence, passions, enmities, revenges, strains of illusive peace, desperate truce, reconciling acts, precarious friendships promising both war and peace, and, finally, the tensions that cut social body, the decisive battles for which all are preparing. Sovereignty is not the explanatory principle here. Its role is to provide an image in which processes of war appear to be under control, processes of peace appear as harmless enough so as not to consume every organ with the fire of justice. Constitution and the fiction that it has given birth to and goes by the name of sovereignty aspires for the juridical-philosophical universality that lawmakers and philosophers have always dreamed of and aspired for—the position between adversaries, the position of the center and yet above the adversaries, the agency that imposes the armistice, the order that brings reconciliation. Dialogue poses before such a politics questions about ways of power, the visible brutality of law, and possibilities of imagining new ways of conversation. In this relational context, new ideas of rights and justice are emerging; they form the terrain where new dialogic acts are shaping up, old divides are being interrogated, and quotidian conversation wrestles with the exceptional. These conversations show at times dialogue as strategy of rule and at times the terrain of justice, rights, and peace. In all senses, thus, dialogue is not just a way to end war but a way in which we want the world to be governed.

There is also the question of risk in dialogue, which highlights the complex relation of dialogue to the art of governing because of the different ways of truth telling inherent in the dialogue game.

DIALOGUE AND RISK

In September 2010, something common happened in two Indian states, Kashmir and West Bengal, specifically Srinagar and Kolkata. One case was reported in detail in various news columns and on television screens and the other was largely ignored, but both happened in the wake of militancy. In West Bengal, the insurgents were the Maoists; in Kashmir, the stone-throwing hundreds were the angry youth demanding *azadi*. Both were situations of truth telling marked by different postures of sovereign power, pregnant with different possibilities, and characterized by different ways of articulating politics.

In Kashmir, a large team of politicians and legislators led by the union home minister visited Srinagar in the wake of more than a hundred deaths at the hands of security forces in civil agitations in the last three months. Some of the team members went to the homes of the political leaders of the valley and said that they had come to meet the people of Srinagar and the valley, share their anguish and loss, and find out through dialogue a way toward a solution to the Kashmir issue. In the other case, in West Bengal, in the wide expanse of the southwestern part of the state called the Junglemahals, where a large number of people died in the last few months, the chief minister in a public meeting had remarked in exasperation that he knew he would have to talk with the

Maoists, but whom would he talk to? These remarks came from him after the villagers led by the Maoists started successfully resisting the ruling party's efforts to return to the contested area and rule people there in the business-as-usual style. The chief minister further said that he knew that police and army measures could not be effective in the long run and that dialogue would have to commence, but, because the Maoists were believers of violence and revenge, how could the government start a conversation? By implication, he was saying that, since the Maoists were not amenable to the government's reasoning, there was no point in talking to them; the operations had to continue. In the case of Kashmir, the government was saying that all draconian restrictions would remain in place, but some boys could be released from jail, and each killing by a police officer, a paramilitary, or army personnel would fetch a half million rupees from the sovereign power as compensation for the family members of the victim. Henceforth, tickets of death command the government conveyed would be signed with soft gestures. Killings will be accompanied by promises of new life.

Noticeable in both cases is the ambiguous way of telling the truth in situations of civil war. In West Bengal, the chief minister was admitting that he was finding it difficult to fight a shadowy foe whose rules of engagement, publicity, talks, and battle are different from those of the sovereign power. He knew how to kill through due process, proper procedure, notifying appropriately the deployment of paramilitary forces, and detention without trial. But he did not know how to invoke rules of democracy when the chains of command of the enemy and its style were not conforming to his rules—that is, the sovereign's rules. But here also he was telling a half-truth, because the Maoists had, on several occasions in the past, proposed talks and suggested modes, and, at the end, only its emissaries had been killed by the government forces. The chief minister knew all this; still, why was he urging the Maoists to be more visible—to talk or allow his counterinsurgency forces to eliminate in the process whoever would surface?[14]

Both gestures show that the sovereign power wants to talk, because rule otherwise is becoming difficult. Governing unruly populations is a nightmare for all sovereigns. Yet, how can the sovereign talk? What will it require to invoke the truth that suppression has failed and politics must be conducted in a *political way*—which means in a nonsuppressive way? Hundreds of deaths, a thousand deaths, many thousand deaths, extreme unpopularity, complete boycott by civilian population, wise counsel, election results—what will the sovereign power need to invoke or accept the truth?

Clearly, accepting such a position entails risk for the sovereign. Loss of legitimacy, credibility, and breakdown of command are some of the usual risks. Greater risk, the sovereign thinks, is a loss or diminishing or reduction of sovereignty. In the recent half-hearted visit by the legislators from Delhi to Kashmir or the West Bengal chief minister's remark of despair, the early signs of truth come out: the truth of the fear of loss of legitimacy, of failure of war mode of governance, of the incapacity of the government to dialogue, of the sovereign's inability to run the polity in a permanent dialogic mode, accepting as ethics of governance a notion of permanent plebiscite on the quality of those who rule.

For the citizens, telling truth is easier. They do it all the time—through votes, at times with hands, at times with feet. They converge, congregate, shout, speak, proceed, charter, mumble, gossip, throw stones, farce, satire, publish, and commit occasional acts of violence. But it is difficult for the sovereign to tell the truth, because the sovereign is tied to a structure of power. Therefore, only in a structured manner truth comes out of the sovereign source, the truth of its failure or the truth that it wants to talk about because it is finding the task of governing increasingly difficult. The result is that, even in a lowly magistrate's office, claims or assertions of truth are made, enacted, and accepted in a bizarre way.

But truth telling, however programmed, may have unintended consequences. That is where the biggest risk lies for the sovereign. For instance, in response to the West Bengal chief minister's remark, the Maoists may say, *here is our signal, here is the letter, here is what we want to talk about, and let us begin.* This happened in the past, and that may increase the confusion. It may increase the pressure on the government. Or the rebel leaders in Kashmir may say, *we do not want money for deaths but unconditional release of all prisoners, punishment of the guilty, and a time-bound general inquiry (let it be a national inquiry) into what had happened in the last three months in the valley.* Or think what happens when the armed forces admit the truth that, with the usual rules of accountability for their actions, they cannot do what they are asked to do. In other words, what can be the unpredictable outcome when the sovereign cannot explain why it chooses to kill? What can be the consequences of such an admission of truth? What will erupt out of these acts of truth telling? We must understand the open-ended nature of such a war-politics continuum when it plays out in popular politics.

Or to give one last pair of instances, what is the signal when from the same delegation to Kashmir two sorts of voices come out: one saying, *we (Indians) must not placate them, the Kashmiris, and hence there was no point in showing them gestures by going to their houses;* the other saying, *we cannot do anything now, at least let us visit them?* Or, in West Bengal, when the sovereign admits that it cannot meet the demands of recalcitrant people and hence must offer money to those who want to turn approvers. These were all time-honored ways of colonial government's truth-telling ways—to offer compromises, to backtrack—so that rule could continue. In popular politics, truth has a way of claiming its price. It compels persons, institutions, and forces to attach to the truth that has been spoken. Also, truth telling in popular politics has an open-ended nature in terms of consequences. Those who study popular politics must take these signs seriously, not the least because they are of consequence to a politics of peace.

We can now summarize the historical lessons of the dialogic acts. First, these acts are played out and unfold in a constituted space of two interfacing series—politics-war and war-politics. Second, dialogue suggests some kind of unrestrained speech (no longer restrained by war), which claims to tell a specific kind of truth. Third, this truth, which is dialogic truth, is contingent, provisional, and interactive and faces other truths that are either marked by absolute proclamations or institutional rigidities. Fourth, because of its provisional nature, dialogue opens up a closed situation with at times unpredictable consequences. Fifth, because this truth is contingent, it carries risk. Sixth, with this risk of truth telling, the dialogist carries a responsibility exactly in the same way a general opting for war carries the responsibility of winning the war. Seventh, and finally, the relationship between war, state making, dialogue, and democracy is a complex one.

Dialogue offers a particular theory of knowledge of social conversation in the wake of war that threatens to replace the institutional mode of governance. Even within the war mode of politics, contentious conversations take place, and their traces can be found out with meticulous research. The art of governing can learn much from such research.

THE PRACTITIONER OF DIALOGUE AND CONSIDERATIONS OF JUSTICE

The practitioner of dialogic situation is located in a difficult position. A dialogic position is one of taking a deliberative position to talk and to engage through talk. It is thus a willful position. It implies that it is faced with other positions such as warlike, monologue, deadlock, and so on. A dialogic position presumes the existence of the other, concedes legitimacy (at least partial) to the other, and is based on the principle of making an opening through conversational strategies. This also can be singular in character, but basically the dialogic position implies plurality, conceding that there is more than one actor, one issue, one way out, and one level. Clearly, then, dialoguing is an art.

Here is a dilemma. The practitioner of a dialogic situation is not a spontaneous dialogist meeting his or her interlocutor on the way to the market, or in the office, or in a club, or in an association, or suddenly in the parliamentary chamber. She or he is a dialogist by design. The dialogist is moved by an effort, often has an agenda, has a program, and, above all, is bound by choice to continuing the dialogue in a democratic manner. Although this, too, is an open-ended situation, the practitioner through design, program, and aim, may have closed it as much as possible, although this does not mean that she or he is not flexible or that he or she does not want the dialogue to continue in a flexible manner. Yet there is a difference between being open ended and flexible. The practitioner wants to be goal oriented while remaining flexible. Worldwide experiences of dialogues convey the difficulty of the task. Clearly, the challenge is to become the conversationalist of the everyday situation, retain the plasticity of the situation, yet turn the situation and the art of conversation to the goal of peace and reconciliation.

How does one put concepts to practice? What role can the dialogue practitioner play? What is a dialogic approach? How does one explore its possibility? And, most importantly, what is the critical element that dialogue carries in deliberation? Because the practice of dialogue is at the same time an account of its goals and methods, dialogue is an art whose aesthetic component we can appreciate but which we cannot reduce to a few scientific principles. The fine part of a dialogic exercise is that dialogue is not merely a situation, goal, or technique; it is like a medium that is its own message. In other words, its goal, method, design, and location are all determined dialogically and not unilaterally.

What adds sustainability of dialogue? And why is sustainability necessary? First, since dialogic situations carry several possibilities, we need to sustain dialogue to carry it to a democratic outcome. Second, dialogic actors are socially constituted beings and not conversationalists engaged in a senate meeting or aristocrats meeting in a Roman bathhouse or a luxurious parlor away from the street noises—though some dialogues are indeed held in that manner. Think of an industrial bargaining situation, where the trade union leaders can go into the bosses' room to negotiate and may even arrive at some agreement; but they are aware that the workers are standing outside, that the rank and file is waiting to hear from them, and a false move may destroy their credibility. Staged dialogues aim at removing reality from the dialogue scene, which is why we need to keep in mind that the dialogic actors are socially constituted beings, they are agents of collective interests; and, while reality pushes them across group divides to dialogue, dialogue requires continuity. In that sense, dialogism is at times avant gardism—from everyday conversation to sustained dialogue is the process where the art of sticking to conversational mode is at play. For all these reasons, the impediments to dialogue or the impediments inherent in dialogue are severe. Dialogue is contested conversation. Dialogue is never without power configuration. There is no dialogic situation without its power matrix. Thus, dialogues are contested, conflictive, and open ended in the sense that, until the last moment, no one is sure of the outcome. In other words, they are historically contingent.

Thus, in the instance of Nepal, the dialogues between the governmental team and the Maoist team, or the ones between the seven-member parliamentary party alliance and the Maoists determined or influenced the outcome of other dialogues, changing the face of the country permanently. The monarchy ended, the Constituent Assembly began, and these two developments in turn threw the previously agreed-upon structure of the dialogue wide open. Dialogue, in this case, has depended clearly on the extent of interface between two visions, their meetings and conflicts, and truly became a case of contested conversation. This is what I meant by historical contingency. One way out could be to lead the dialogists to do an audit of history, attempting to gain a consensus about a historical understanding of the reason and the genesis of dialogue. One can also term it as a *genealogical understanding of dialogue.*

A dialogic regime is like a truth regime, which means that there is no time-cutting, place-cutting, or location-cutting truth principle, but truth is determined contingently, as an outcome of certain discourses and institutional practices, where the power principle is as important as the knowledge principle. Indeed, knowledge would contribute to power. Truth is thus always in relation. Similarly, a dialogic regime means the order set by given discourses, institutions, and structures of power. These discourses, institutions, and structures tell us to talk, or not to talk; they tell us how much to talk and the limits we must not cross; and they shape our mind, agenda, and the public sphere of conversation. They also cause hierarchies of dialogue. We are familiar with summit talks, parliamentary talks, party-level talks, dialogues of statesmen, public talks, talks of citizens, interest group meetings, rival army commanders' meetings, and arms control talks. Yet do they reduce chances of war? Not always. They establish a hierarchical order of dialogues whereby a lot of domestication takes place, and a regime of dialogues is established whereby dangerous talks are banished.

This is where we must proceed a little more and push the dialogic argument further. What is dangerous dialogue? When the underprivileged demand talks for justice; when victims of war demand talks for peace; when men and women long suffering from human rights abuses demand talks for restoration for dignity, for new constitution, and for new ethical principles—then the talks become dangerous. It appears to the rich, powerful, dominant, hegemonic, and the big that the wretched are ganging up and that their demand for talks are not talks but conspiracies. In all these cases, justice is the yardstick. What is the aim? What do they want to achieve vis-à-vis the rulers, possessors, and the mighty? Here we have to grasp the significance of dialogic justice.

Dialogic justice links justice to dialogue and sees in the process of dialogue the promise of justice. That promise must be, by and large, met if we want that society to stick to a dialogic path. Dialogue does not assure maximal justice, but it has to ensure minimal justice. Maximal justice is programmatic, which may differ from actor to actor or from context to context. But minimal justice is historically arrived at.[15] To arrive historically is to arrive through contestation, bargaining, negotiations, truth conflicts, and truth games. Dialogues, in this sense, are the weapons of the weak who demand talks for justice. Thus, minimal justice must ensure through dialogues (a) recognition of past injustices; (b) some amount of compensation, restoration, and restitution; (c) that such instances will not recur and hence joint custodianship of the process of restitution; and, finally, (d) innovations in methods and institutions so that society and relations can take a new turn.

We can now make a new meaning of the word *dialogue* with the help of affirmations, confirmations, revisions, and additions to the old concept of dialogue as conversation. The following points can be made about dialogic understanding:

- Democratic dialogue means plurality of actors, themes, and levels. A democratic dialogue is multilevel and a more complicated game. It means allowing the dialogic situation to inhere and absorb conflict and conflictive positions.
- Democratic dialogue is based on contested conversations.
- It is the weapon of the weak.
- It aims at providing minimal justice.
- It hastens the process of collective claim making.
- It never assures or assumes permanent solutions; it is like a daily plebiscite.
- Finally, it makes society dialogic as the everyday habit.

These seven principles suggest a new (or enriched) meaning of democracy. In plain language, it says that only with dialogues relations are democratized. There can be no democracy without dialogues. And, to strengthen the point, dialogues are incessant; there is no end to dialogues. As deep and as wide as relations, dialogues are like flight paths of beings, they configure a new topos of relations, existences, and resistances. They indicate how political subjects make moves, to stress the point, in many cases, how a political subject emerges through embarking on the dialogic path. Dialogue has been one of the historical tools of making a political society. Dialogues among sections help setting goals, norms, mores, and a unity called the political society, though dialogues refuse to be compliant to this society. They make and remake it.

NOTES

1. John Rawls, "Laws of Peoples," in Samuel Freeman (ed.), *Collected Papers of John Rawls* (Cambridge, MA: Harvard University Press, 1999).

2. Charles Taylor, "Why Democracy Needs Patriotism," in Martha C. Nussbaum et al. (eds.), *For Love of Country—Debating the Limits of Patriotism* (Boston: Beacon Press, 1996); Charles Taylor, "Cross-purposes—The Liberal Communitarian Debate," in Nancy L. Rosenblum (ed.), *Liberalism and the Moral Life* (Cambridge, MA: Harvard University Press, 1989). See also in this context Alasdair MacIntyre, "Is Patriotism a Virtue?" E. H. Lindley Memorial Lecture (Lawrence: University Press of Kansas, 1984). For a critical summary of the views, see Margaret Canovan, "Patriotism Is Not Enough," *British Journal of Political Science* 30 (2000): 413–432.

3. Jürgen Habermas, "Citizenship and National Identity," in *Between Facts and Norms—Contributions to a Discourse Theory of Law and Democracy* (Cambridge, MA: MIT Press, 1996), appendix 2.

4. The democratic theorist Claude Ake calls the current interface of globalization and democracy one of "dangerous liaisons" in "Dangerous Liaisons: The Interface of Globalization and Democracy," in Axel Hadenius (ed.), *Democracy's Victory and Crisis* (Cambridge: Cambridge University Press, 1997), 282–296.

5. Michel Foucault, "The Political Technology of Individuals," in *Technologies of the Self—A Seminar with Michel Foucault* (Amherst: University of Massachusetts Press, 1988), 160.

6. Ivan Ivekovic, "Contemporary Ethnic Conflicts in a Comparative Perspective," in Ursula Oswald-Spring (ed.), *Peace Studies from a Global Perspective* (Delhi, India: Madhyam Books, 1999), pp. 186–251.

7. On the relation between new ethnicity and masculinity, brought out so vividly by, among others, the Balkan wars, see Cynthia Enloe, "All the Men Are Militias, All the Women Are Victims—The Politics of Masculinity and Femininity in Nationalist Wars," in Lois Ann Lorentzen and Jennifer Turpin (eds.), *The Women and War Reader* (New York: New York University Press, 1998), 50–62.

8. Valentine Moghadam, *Modernizing Women: Gender and Social Change in the Middle East* (Cairo: American University in Cairo Press, 1993), 104.

9. Charles Lockhart, *Bargaining in International Conflicts* (New York: Columbia University Press, 1979), 5.

10. In fact, Lockhart cites the work of Prichard Walton and Robert Mckersie, *A Behavioral Theory of Labor Negotiations: An Analysis of Social Interaction System* (New York: McGraw-Hill, 1965), to show how rational bargaining leading to expectations of "distributive bargaining" (division of spoils) or "integrative bargaining" (upgrading of common interest) are prevented by intraparty disagreements that make "commitments fuzzy and hinder integrative bargaining," thus making "attitudinal structuring" (influencing perceptions of the opponent)—one of the main goals of bargaining—almost impossible. See Lockhart, *Bargaining in International Conflicts*, 13–15.

11. Lockhart, *Bargaining in International Conflicts*, 43.

12. In Ranabir Samaddar, *A Biography of the Indian Nation* (New Delhi: Sage, 2001), chapter 8, I discuss two instances of how bargaining becomes the form of contradictory and yet complementary processes of relations between post-colonial nations marked by the war-peace continuum. Irving Louis Horowitz (1957) long ago had shown how, in philosophical and social thought, the continuum had been an important object of inquiry. See his *War and Peace in Contemporary Social and Philosophical Theory* (London: Souvenir Press, 1973).

13. The African political scientist Julius Ihonvhere notes the rise of new constitutionalism in several countries of Africa. He describes how earlier, even if states had constitutions, the leaders whom he calls "the big man" did not care for these constitutions or were simply ignorant of the existence of such basic laws. There was no popular deliberation, and constitution was irrelevant to the social and political conflicts and turmoil in the country. He then describes how, in many of these countries, new rules are being forged through popular deliberations, or at least popular coalitions are trying to formulate new basic laws, moved by experiences of conflicts and wars. Julius O. Ihonvhere, *Towards the New Constitutionalism in Africa* (London: Centre for Democracy and Development, 2000); also his lecture "Engaging the Leviathan: Constitutionalism and the New Politics in Africa," Annual Minority Rights Address, organized by the International Centre for Ethnic Studies (Colombo), Geneva, May 18, 2001.

14. One can note in passing that the Maoists over time would probably find ways to talk, dialogue, and forge a policy of just reconciliation. They will know how urgent such need is, or only they can tell how urgently they have realized it, because they will suffer most due to a lack of appropriate peace politics—as people in Kashmir have paid a heavy price because their rebels had no appropriate peace strategy to achieve minimal justice or maximally what they want through war.

15. This is the reason why I have suggested elsewhere that past histories of failed and successful dialogues in various contexts should be studied. For reference, one can see how Michael Walzer, in *Spheres of Justice* (New York: Basic Books, 1983), uses the instances of Greek dialogues to illustrate his idea of justice or Indian nationalist political thinkers have used the *Mahabharata*.

Postscript

Zachariah Cherian Mampilly

We are constantly making war and making peace, often simultaneously. It sometimes seems as though we do little else. From the dawn of humanity war and peace have remained powerful drivers of our social reality. Even among our closest relatives in the animal kingdom we can witness analogous behavior. War and peace bring us together and tear us apart. They give our lives meaning. They demonstrate the extraordinary capacity of human potential, as well as the nadir of our baser selves. Indeed, it is precisely in the depths of the most heinous brutalities that we witness the pinnacle of humanity's capacity to make peace. A world without either is merely a phantasm, devoid of meaning itself. Wars for peace and peace from war. How else can it be?

But before there was war and before there was peace, there was survival. The human ability to endure even in the face of tremendous odds is extraordinary. A prince reduced to a pauper can still find ways to survive, even if never confronted with basic challenges before. We are survivors first, warriors and peacemakers second. We move on in the face of death and destruction, in the face of loss and sorrow. We adapt and sometimes, we thrive.

Within this human desire for survival is the core elements of both peacemaking and war-making. As innately social activities concerned with the reproduction and enhancement of human life, they are progeny of the same mother, encompassing many comparable dynamics. How we choose to ensure our own survival and that of our children represents the defining dilemma of our social reality. In this way, war-makers and peacemakers are driven by the same preoccupation with continuity, although they differ in their conception of how best this is achieved.

These thoughts struck me during a visit to an area of the world where the struggle for survival is visible in its starkest manifestations—Sudan, Africa's largest country, and for too long, one of its most troubled. In January 2011, I had the privilege of bearing witness to the historic referendum through which South Sudanese elected to detach their Texas-size portion to begin the thorny process of creating their own independent homeland. A victory that came at great cost by any measure, South Sudan endured almost 50 years of war and over 2 million dead on its way to nationhood. The referendum itself capped a 6-year long transition process fraught with difficulty at every step, including the tragic death of the independence leader John Garang barely six months after the signing of a comprehensive peace agreement. Despite such formidable obstacles, the world's newest country defied naysayers who doubted the possibility that a nonviolent process could finally claim dignity and peace for a long-suffering population.

A month later in neighboring Egypt, a wave of nonviolent revolutions that began in Tunisia swept through. After several hundred protesters were killed at the hands of brutal government thugs, Egyptian protesters declared victory as the dictatorship of Hosni Mobarak came to an ignominious end. Contrary to depictions of the North African protests as spontaneous outbreaks of anger, these movements were the product of patient and brave youth organizers, such as the April 6 Youth Movement in Egypt. Influenced by youth activists from around the world, including South Africa's anti-apartheid struggle and the Otpor! movement in Serbia, protesters deployed nonviolent strategies developed by Mahatma Gandhi and popularized by an American expert on nonviolence, Gene Sharp, forging connections across generations and continents. Although still in motion at the time this volume went to press, the events unfolding in North Africa and West Asia have fundamentally reordered their societies, challenging analysts who assumed that cultural forces rendered "Arab democracy" a contradiction in terms.

Egypt and Sudan, two societies tied together for millennia, both rightly famed for their contributions to human progress, are again demonstrating the potency of the continual human yearning for a life without violence. Through two very different routes—one a decades long military struggle culminating in a peaceful election and the other a largely nonviolent effort—activists in Egypt and South Sudan represent the potential of humans as peacemakers. Whether the hidden oppression of a brutal regime prized for its stability or the debilitating military machine of an international pariah, both societies have demonstrated that the weapon of the oppressor need not become the tool of the oppressed, opting instead for nonviolent protests or patiently waiting in line to cast a vote. Though South Sudan and Egypt still face many challenges, the experiences of both remind us that peaceful actions are effective in resisting oppressive systems, and remain central to building stable societies.

As I spoke to South Sudanese during the referendum I was struck by their optimism, even if it was coupled with a wariness of succumbing to another round of bloodletting. Poised at the precipice of a new and independent homeland, it was impossible for many to forget the devastation of three decades of war that had brought this chance for peace. Nor was it possible to ignore the serious threats to stability that remained. In their struggle for survival, they had covered the spectrum of war-making and peacemaking. But regardless of what the future holds, there is little doubt that most South Sudanese preferred to resolve their problems through peaceful actions over more violent means.

Among many other noteworthy failings arising from these extraordinary developments was the incapacity of most in the scholarly and policy community to predict the events that unfolded. Instead, most argued, often forcefully, that a peaceful referendum in Sudan would never go forward,[1] and that change in Egypt would only arrive incrementally, or through violence.[2] Part of this shortcoming is attributable to a problematic assumption at the core of the conflict resolution field, that is, that we must focus on violence in order to understand peace. However, a narrow emphasis on violence could not explain the largely peaceful events in Sudan and Egypt that unfolded in early 2011. Instead, scholars and policy analysts were left scratching their heads at how they so thoroughly misinterpreted events.

As a scholar of rebellion, I can attest to the institutional bias that positions studies of war-making as both more necessary and more rigorous than studies of peacemaking. Benefitting from this bias, scholars have fruitfully dissected war-making across the human experience, from the earliest conflicts among hunters and gatherers to the large-scale military conflicts that defined the 20th century. They have demonstrated how techniques of warfare traveled across continents: gunpowder moving from China to Europe and on throughout the rest of the world; guerrilla strategies evolving in the New World and migrating to irregular conflicts in every corner of the globe; suicide vests emerging in the battlefields of Sri Lanka and wreaking havoc in Palestine, Chechnya, and beyond. And importantly, they have shown how warfare transforms political and economic realities, promoting state building or encouraging economic growth on the one hand, while leaving destruction and misery in its wake on the other.

Although it may be a natural proclivity to try and understand the behavior of those engaged in the most heinous acts, it is important to remember that even in situations of mass violence, most people, most of the time, interact in nonviolent ways. This is not only an intuitive observation but a finding with wide social scientific support.

In these volumes, the authors probe facets of peacemaking with the same attention generally devoted to the study of war-making. Studying peacemaking has value both intellectually and practically. At a minimum, a focus on peacemaking provides the intellectual framework and analytical rigor necessary to understand key events unfolding across the globe during a period of intense economic and political flux. In addition, a focus on peacemaking provides practical utility for peacemakers, offering various philosophies, strategies, and interpretations to help respond to outbreaks of violence or prevent conflicts from turning violent in the first place. Studying peacemaking provides archetypes through which would-be peacemakers can envision nonviolent approaches to resolve their own troubles.

The two volumes you have before you take up the call to expand our understanding of peacemaking. Contributors make several important advances to the study of peacemaking in specific and the field of conflict resolution in general. First, at a conceptual level, they reject the portrayal of peacemaking as simply a technical process shoehorned between preventive diplomacy and peacekeeping in the conflict resolution continuum. Second, peacemaking is understood as an organic process, emerging from human practice that draws on longstanding knowledge embedded deep within humanity. And finally, they broaden the tent for how we study peacemaking by tearing down the formal barriers that exclude contributions from peacemakers drawing on alternate traditions as well as those who labor to make peace without recognition from formal institutions.

Contributors upend the notion that peacemaking can be confined to a single step within the technical continuum of conflict resolution. Instead, they suggest that peacemaking is in fact the central concern of conflict resolution as a field. Rather than a discrete process, then, peacemaking subsumes peacebuilding by rejecting the notion of a clear end to conflict simply at the moment in which fighting ceases. Peacemaking may even subsume preventive diplomacy and peacekeeping, if we accept that making peace must be both a holistic and continual process, as contributors to this volume argue. The point is not to deemphasize the conceptual clarity such a division of conflict resolution may provide. Rather, it is to foreground the artificiality of these divisions and recognize that peacemaking and other conflict resolution steps are always "mutually complementary and function in parallel" as Timothy Murithi notes in his contribution.

Relatedly, contributors reject the notion that peace is merely an objective social or political condition. Instead, they emphasize its subjective dimension, the necessity of first creating a collective understanding of peace that can only then be made through struggle. As such, understanding violence or peace must emerge organically by grasping the local contexts produced by the actions of countless individuals. Recognizing this reality implies that, for the concerned student, it is essential to reject approaches that divorce peacemaking (and war-making) from the social reality from which it emerges.

More importantly, it requires recognition that war and peace, for all the very real suffering and very real joys, are imagined states that exist on a continuum. Contributors to these volumes contend that a state of peace requires not simply the end of active conflict, but also the emergence of a positive peace given meaning and form by those who seek to bring it into existence. The existence of positive peace necessitates a constant reordering of society along principles of equity and justice for all achieved through a perpetual process of peacemaking. Such a subjective notion of peace recognizes that people coexist as social beings, as members of a community, despite the lines that may divide them, jointly constructing the world in which they live.

Finally, these volumes include analyses of peacemaking that encompass a similar breadth of approaches and perspectives as those found in studies of war, particularly in regards to ideological and disciplinary traditions, cultural and national backgrounds of the contributors, and, of course, in regards to the focus of the analyses themselves. Importantly, the chapters offered in these volumes range across analytical and narrative modes, providing both structural analyses of the macro level conditions that foster war or peace, as well as taking an intimate look inside the behavior of individual peacemakers. Contributors also reject the secularizing and westernizing tendencies of some peacemaking analyses, purposefully recognizing and interrogating the cultural and religious domains as crucial arenas for analysis.

Of course, in the end, there is nothing inevitable about the decisions individuals make that lead to war or peace. Nor are there fixed social laws that determine why some conflicts are resolved peacefully, whereas others descend into violent conflagrations. And, of course, there is no fundamental cultural characteristic or institutional arrangement that can predict violence or peace. The best we can do as a community of concerned scholars and activists is to recognize that the time is ripe for a more sustained research agenda and dialogue around peacemaking. As such, our real intention with these volumes has always been to open up the conversation. Welcome.

NOTES

1. For just one example, Nicholas Kristof wrote a histrionic op-ed in the September 29, 2010 edition of the *New York Times* titled "Chronicle of a Genocide Foretold." In the essay, he predicted, wrongly, that the referendum would be tainted by "widespread irregularities" followed by an invasion of the region by the national army ultimately culminating in a genocide. In fact, the referendum moved forward peacefully, and Sudan's president promised to recognize an independent South Sudan. Article accessed February 20, 2011, from http://www.nytimes.com/2010/09/30/opinion/30kristof.html.

2. Most Egyptian analysts focused their attention on the activities of the Muslim Brotherhood, assuming, incorrectly, that it would be the key driver of any social transformation that might occur. Almost none predicted that the truly revolutionary force in Egyptian society rested with the educated youth.

Bibliography

Abrams, I. R. 1983. Kinship and Descent, Part 1. *The Faces of Culture* series. Arlington, VA: Public Broadcasting Service.

Abu-Nimer, M. 1996. Conflict Resolution Approaches. *American Journal of Economics and Sociology* 55, no. 1: 35–52.

Abu-Nimer, M. 2001a. Conflict Resolution, Culture and Religion: Toward a Training Model for Interreligious Peacebuilding. *Journal of Peace Research* 38, no. 6: 685–704.

Abu-Nimer, M. 2001b. *Reconciliation, Justice, and Coexistence: Theory and Practice.* Lanham, MD: Lexington Books.

Abu-Nimer, M. 2003. *Nonviolence and Peace Building in Islam: Theory and Practice.* Gainesville: University of Florida.

Abusharaf, R. M. 2010. Debating Darfur in the World. *The ANNALS of the American Academy of Political and Social Science* 632, no. 1: 67–85.

Ackerman, P. and J. DuVall. 2001. *A Force More Powerful: A Century of Non-Violent Conflict.* New York: Palgrave MacMillan.

Ackerman, P. and J. DuVall. 2006. Strategic Nonviolence: The Right to Rise Up: People Power and the Virtues of Civic Disruption. *Fletcher Forum of World Affairs* 30: 33–221.

Adams, R. 2000. Loving Mimesis and Girard's "Scapegoat of the Text": A Creative Reassessment of Mimetic Desire. In *Violence Renounced: René Girard, Biblical Studies, and Peacemaking,* ed. W. Swartley, 4:277–307. Telford, PA: Pandora Press.

Adebajo, A. 2002. *Building Peace in West Africa: Liberia, Sierra Leone, and Guinea-Bissau.* Boulder, CO: Lynne Rienner.

Adebajo, A., and C. Landsberg. 2003. South Africa and Nigeria as Regional Hegemons. In *From Cape to Congo: Southern Africa's Evolving Security Challenges,* eds. M. Baregu and C. Landsberg, 171–204. Boulder, CO: Lynne Rienner.

Afolabi, B. T. 2009. Peacemaking in the ECOWAS Region: Challenges and Prospects. *Conflict Trends* no. 2: 24–30.

Agha, H., S. Feldman, A. Khalidi, and Z. Schiff. 2004. *Track-II Diplomacy: Lessons from the Middle East.* Cambridge, MA: The MIT Press.

Aguswandi, and J. Large, eds. 2008. *Re-Configuring Politics: The Indonesia-Aceh Peace Process.* London: Conciliation Resources.

Ahmed, S., and D. M. Potter. 2006. *NGOs in International Politics.* Sterling, VA: Kumarian Press.

Akashi, Y. 1995. The Limits of UN Diplomacy and the Future of Conflict Mediation. *Survival* 37, no. 4: 83–98.

Ake, C. 1991. Rethinking African Democracy. *Journal of Democracy* 2, no. 1: 32–44.

Ake, C. 1997. Dangerous Liaisons: The Interface of Globalization and Democracy. In *Democracy's Victory and Crisis,* ed. A. Hadenius. Vol. 290. Cambridge: Cambridge University Press.

Alexander L. G., and J. E. Holl. 1997. *The Warning-Response Problem and Missed Opportunities in Preventive Diplomacy.* A Report to the Carnegie Commission on Preventing Deadly Conflict. Washington, DC: Carnegie Commission on Preventing Deadly Conflict.

Ali Abu Awwad interview. *Just Vision.* http://www.justvision.org/portrait/76100/interview.

Alim, H. S. 2006. *Roc the Mic Right: The Language of Hip Hop Culture.* New York: Routledge.

Allison, R. 2004. Regionalism, Regional Structures and Security Management in Central Asia. *International Affairs* 80, no. 3: 463–483.

Alvord, S. H., L. D. Brown, and C. W. Letts. 2004. Social Entrepreneurship and Societal Transformation: An Exploratory Study. *The Journal of Applied Behavioral Science* 40, no. 3: 260–282.

Amnesty International. 2008. *Myanmar Ethnic Group Faces Crimes Against Humanity.* http://www.amnesty.org/en/news-and-updates/report/myanmar-ethnic-group-faces-crimes-against-humanity-20080605.

Anahit Shirinyan. 2010. Shut up! The Enemy Might Hear You! June 1. http://caucasusedition.net/blog/shut-up-the-enemy-might-hear-you/.

Anderlini, S. N. 2000. *Women at the Peace Table: Making a Difference.* New York: United Nations Development Fund for Women. http://www.unifem.org/materials/item_detail.php?ProductID=15.

Anderlini, S. N. 2007. *Women Building Peace: What They Do, Why It Matters.* London: Rienner.

Anderson, M. B. 1996. Humanitarian NGOs in Conflict Intervention. In *Managing Global Chaos: Sources of and Responses to International Conflict,* ed. Chester A. Crocker, Fen Osler Hampson, and Pamela Aall, 343–354. Washington, DC: United States Institute of Peace Press.

Anderson, M. B. 1999. *Do No Harm: How Aid Can Support Peace—or War.* Boulder, CO: Lynne Rienner.

Anderson, M. B., and L. Olson. 2003. *Confronting War: Critical Lessons for Peace Practitioners.* Cambridge, MA: CDA.

Annan, K. 1999. Two Concepts of Sovereignty. *The Economist,* September 20.

Annan, K. 2000. *We the Peoples: The Role of the United Nations in the 21st Century.* New York: United Nations Department of Public Information. http://www.un.org/millennium/sg/report/.

Appiah-Mensah, S. 2006. *Monitoring Fragile Ceasefires: The Challenges and Dilemmas of the Role of AMIS.* Institute for International Studies Paper, 127.

Appleby, R. S. 1998. Religion and Global Affairs: Religious "Militants for Peace." *SAIS Review* 18, no. 2: 38–44.

Arendt, H. 1969. Reflections on Violence. *Journal of International Affairs* 23, no. 1: 1–35.

Arendt, H. 1972. *Crises of the Republic: Lying in Politics, Civil Disobedience on Violence, Thoughts on Politics, and Revolution.* New York: Mariner Books.

Aristotle. 2009. *Nicomachean Ethics.* Revised edition. Cambridge, MA: Oxford University Press.

Armitage, R. L., and J. S. Nye, Jr. 2007. *A Smarter, More Secure America.* Washington, DC: Center for Strategic and International Studies.

Arnault, J. 2001. *Good Agreement, Bad Agreement? An Implementation Perspective.* Occasional Paper. Center of International Studies, Princeton University.

Arnold, D. 2001. *Gandhi: Profiles in Power.* London: Pearson Education.

Arnson, C., J. and T. Whitfield. 2005. Third Parties and Intractable Conflicts. In *Grasping the Nettle: Analyzing Cases of Intractable Conflict,* ed. Chester A. Crocker, Fen Osler Hampson, and Pamela Aall. Washington, DC: U.S. Institute of Peace Press.

Arthur, P. 2009. How "Transitions" Reshaped Human Rights: A Conceptual History of Transitional Justice. *Human Rights Quarterly* 31, no. 2: 321–367.

Ashoka: Innovators for the Public. 2000. *Selecting Leading Social Entrepreneurs.* Arlington: Ashoka.

Aslan, R. 2006. *No god but God: The Origins, Evolution, and Future of Islam.* New York: Random House.

Assefa, H. 2001. Coexistence and Reconciliation in the Northern Region of Ghana. In *Reconciliation, Justice, and Coexistence: Theory and Practice.* Lanham, MD: Lexington Books.

Assefa, H., and G. Wachira. 1996. *Peacemaking and Democratization in Africa.* Nairobi: East African Educational Publishers.

Augsberger, D. 1992. *Conflict Mediation Across Cultures.* Louisville, KY: Westminster John Knox.

Aureli, F., M. Cords, and C. P. Van Schaik. 2002. Conflict Resolution Following Aggression in Gregarious Animals: A Predictive Framework. *Animal Behaviour* 64, no. 3: 325–343.

Avruch, K. 1998. *Culture and Conflict Resolution.* Washington, DC: United States Institute of Peace Press.

Axelrod, R. M. 1984. *The Evolution of Cooperation.* New York: Basic Books.

Axelrod, R. M., and R. O. Keohane. 1985. Achieving Cooperation Under Anarchy: Strategies and Institutions. *World Politics* 38, no. 1: 226–254.

Ayed M. n.d. Interview. http://electronicintifada.net/v2/article11608.shtml.

Azar, E. E. 1990. *The Management of Protracted Social Conflict: Theory and Cases.* Dartmouth, UK: Dartmouth Publishing.

Azar, E. E., P. Jureidini, and R. McLaurin. 1978. Protracted Social Conflict; Theory and Practice in the Middle East. *Journal of Palestine Studies* 8, no. 1: 41–60.

Bacha, J. 2010. *Budrus.* JustVision. http://www.justvision.org/en/budrus.

Badescu, C. G., and T. G. Weiss. 2010. Misrepresenting R2P and Advancing Norms: An Alternative Spiral? *International Studies Perspectives* 11: 354–74.

Bailey, S. D. 1977. Cease-Fires, Truces, and Armistices in the Practice of the UN Security Council. *American Journal of International Law* 71, no. 3: 461–473.

Balachandra, L., F. Barrett, H. Bellman, C. Fisher, and L. Susskind. 2005. Improvisation and Mediation: Balancing Acts. *Negotiation Journal* 21, no. 4: 425–434.

Baldwin, L. V., C. Carso, R. Burrow Jr., B. Holmes, and S. Holmes Winfield, eds. 2002. *The Legacy of Martin Luther King, Jr.: The Boundaries of Law, Politics, and Religion.* Notre Dame, IN: University of Notre Dame Press.

Balibar, E. 1998. *Spinoza and Politics.* London: Verso Books.

Ball, T. 1987. Deadly Hermeneutics; Or, Sinn and the Social Scientist. In *Idioms of Inquiry: Critique and Renewal in Political Science,* ed. T. Ball. New York: State University of New York Press.

Banks, J. A. 2004. Multicultural Education: Historical Developments, Dimensions, and Practice. In Handbook of Research on Multicultural Education, ed. James A. Banks and Cherry A. McGee Banks, 3–29. 2nd ed. San Francisco: Jossey-Bass.

Bar-On, D. 2008. *The Others within Us: Constructing Jewish-Israeli Identity.* Cambridge: Cambridge University Press.

Bar-Siman-Tov, Y., ed. 2004. *From Conflict Resolution to Reconciliation.* Oxford: Oxford University Press.

Bar-Tal, D. 2000. From Intractable Conflict Through Conflict Resolution To Reconciliation: Psychological Analysis. *Political Psychology* 21, no. 2: 351–365.

Bar-Tal, D. 2007. Sociopsychological Foundations of Intractable Conflicts. *American Behavioral Scientist* 50, no. 11: 1430–1453.

Barak, O. 2005. The Failure of the Israeli–Palestinian Peace Process, 1993–2000. *Journal of Peace Research* 42, no. 6: 719–736.

Barltrop, R. 2008a. *The Negotiation of Security Issues in the Burundi Peace Talks.* Negotiating Disarmament Country Study. Geneva: Centre for Humanitarian Dialogue.

Barltrop, R. 2008b. *The Negotiation of Security Issues in Sudan's Comprehensive Peace Agreement.* Negotiating Disarmament Country Study. Geneva: Centre for Humanitarian Dialogue.

Barnes, C. 2009a. Civil Society and Peacebuilding: Mapping Functions in Working for Peace. *The International Spectator* 44, no. 1: 131–147.

Barnes, C. 2002b. Democratizing Peacemaking Processes: Strategies and Dilemmas for Public Participation. "Owning the Process: Public Participation in Peacemaking." *Accord: An International Review of Peace Initiatives* 13: 6–12.

Bartoli, A. 1999. Providing Space for Change in Mozambique. In *Transforming Violence: Linking Local and Global Peacemaking,* ed. Robert Herr and Judy Zimmerman Herr, 190–202. Scottdale, PA: Herald Press.

Bartoli, A. 2001. Forgiveness and Reconciliation in the Mozambique Peace Process. In *Forgiveness and Reconciliation,* ed. Raymond G. Helmick and Rodney L. Petersen. West Conshohocken, PA: Templeton Foundation Press.

Bartoli, A. 2005. Learning from the Mozambique Process: The Role of the Community of Sant' Egidio. In *Paving the Way: Contributions of Interactive Conflict Resolution to Peacemaking,* ed. R. J. Fisher. Lanham, MD: Lexington Books.

Bartoli, A., A. Civico, and L. Gianturco. 2009. Mozambique—Renamo. In *Conflict Transformation and Peacebuilding,* ed. Bruce W. Dayton and Louis Kriesberg, 140–155. London and New York: Routledge.

Bartoli, A., L. Bui-Wrzosinska, and A. Nowak. 2010. Peace Is in Movement: A Dynamical-Systems Perspective on the Emergence of Peace in Mozambique. *Peace and Conflict: Journal of Peace Psychology* 16, no. 2: 211–230.

Bartoli, A., and P. Coleman. 2003. Dealing with Extremists. In *Beyond Intractability,* ed. Guy Burgess and Heidi Burgess. Boulder, CO: Conflict Research Consortium, University of Colorado.

Battle, M. 1997. *Reconciliation: The Ubuntu Theology of Desmond Tutu.* Cleveland: The Pilgrim Press.

Beardley, K. 2008. Agreement without Peace? International Mediation and Time Inconsistency Problems. *American Journal of Political Science* 52, no. 4: 723–740.

Beauregard, M., and D. O'Leary. 2007. *The Spiritual Brain.* New York: HarperCollins.

Beilin, Y. 1999. *Touching Peace: From the Oslo Accord to a Final Agreement.* London: Weidenfeld & Nicolson.

Beinart, P. 2010. *The Icarus Syndrome: A History of American Hubris.* New York: Harper.

Bekoe, D. 2008. *Kenya: Setting the Stage for Durable Peace?* Washington, DC: U.S. Institute of Peace.

Bell, C. 2006. *Negotiating Justice?: Human Rights and Peace Agreements: Summary.* Geneva: International Council on Human Rights.

Bellamy, A. J. 2009. *Responsibility to Protect: The Global Effort to end Mass Atrocities.* Cambridge, UK: Polity Press.

Beller, K., and H. Chase. 2008. *Great Peacemakers: True Stories from around the World.* Sedona, AZ: LTS Press.

Belloni, R. 2008. Civil Society in War-to-Democracy Transitions. In *From War to Democracy: Dilemmas of Peacebuilding,* ed. Anna Jarstad and Timothy D. Sisk, 182–210. Cambridge: Cambridge University Press.

Bercovitch, J. 1991. International Mediation and Dispute Settlement: Evaluating the Conditions for Successful Mediation. *Negotiation Journal 7,* no. 1: 17–30.

Bercovitch, J. 1996. *Resolving International Conflicts: The Theory and Practice of Mediation.* Boulder, CO: Lynne Rienner.

Bercovitch, J. 2005. Mediation in the Most Resistant Cases. In *Grasping the Nettle: Analyzing Cases of Intractable Conflict,* ed. Chester A. Crocker, Fen Osler Hampson, and Pamela Aall, 99–122. Washington, DC: United States Institute of Peace.

Bercovitch, J., ed. 2002. *Studies in International Mediation: Essays in Honor of Jeffrey Z. Rubin.* New York: Palgrave Macmillan.

Bercovitch, J., K. Kressel, and D. G. Pruitt. 1989. International Dispute Mediation: A Comparative Empirical Analysis. In *Mediation Research: The Process and Effectiveness of Third Party Intervention,* 53–67. San Francisco: Jossey-Bass.

Bercovitch, J., and S. S. Gartner. 2006. Is There Method in the Madness of Mediation? Some Lessons for Mediators from Quantitative Studies of Mediation. *International Interactions 32,* no. 4: 329–354.

Bertelsmann S. 2009. *Sustainable Governance Indicators: Policy Performance and Executive Capacity in the OECD.* Gütersloh, Germany: Bertelsmann Foundation.

Bilimoria, P., J. Prabhu, R. M. Sharma, and J. Prabhu, eds. 2007. Gandhi, Empire, and a Culture of Peace. In *Indian ethics: classical traditions and contemporary challenges.* Aldershot, UK: Ashgate.

Bizos, G. 2007. *Odyssey to Freedom.* Houghton, South Africa: Random House.

Block, T. 2010. *Shalom-Salam: A Story of a Mystical Fraternity.* Louisville, KY: Fons Vitae.

Bloomfield, D., T. Barnes, and L. Huyse. 2003. *Reconciliation After Violent Conflict: A Handbook.* Stockholm: International Institute for Democracy and Electoral Assistance.

Bøås, M., R. Lotsberg, and J. L. Ndizeye. 2009. *The International Conference on the Great Lakes Region—Review of the Norwegian Support to the ICGLR.* Oslo, Norway: Norwegian Agency for Development, (NORAD), June. http://www.norad.no/en/Tools+and+publications/Publications/Publication+Page?key=131851

Boehm, C. 1987. *Blood Revenge: The Enactment and Management of Conflict in Montenegro and Other Tribal Societies.* Philadelphia: University of Pennsylvania Press.

Bohm, D. 1981. *Wholeness and the Implicate Order.* New York: Routledge.

Bohm, D. 1997. *On Dialogue.* London, New York: Routledge.

Bohm, D. 2004. *On Dialogue,* 2nd ed. New York: Routledge.

Bole, W., D. Christiansen, and R. Hennemeyer. 2004. *Forgiveness in International Politics: An Alternative Road to Peace.* Washington, DC: United States Conference of Catholic Bishops.

Bolen, D. 2009. *Reconciling Paths: Ecumenical Learning, Conversing and Deepening Fundamental Human Experiences*. Regina, SK: Campion College at the University of Regina.

Bombande, E. 2007. Ghana: Developing an Institutional Framework for Sustainable Peace—UN, Government and Civil Society Collaboration for Conflict Prevention. In *GPPAC Issue Paper*. http://www.gppac.net/uploads/File/programmes/ Interaction%20and%20Advocacy/Issue%20Paper%204%20December%202007 %20Gov-CSO%20Cooperation.pdf.

Bonini, R. 2008. *Peace in Guatemala. I colloqui segreti tra il governo e la guerriglia e gli storici accordi di pace*. Milan: Guerini e Associati.

Borer, T. A. 2001. *Reconciliation in South Africa: Defining Success*. Working paper: CIAO. afile:///Users/sara/Library/Mail%20Downloads/reconciliation%20lit%20re view/borer_Reconciliation%20in%20South%20Africa:%20Defining%20Success. html.

Bornstein, D. 1998. Changing the World on a Shoestring. *The Atlantic Monthly* 281: 34–39.

Bornstein, D. 2004. *How to Change the World: Social Entrepreneurs and the Power of New Ideas*. New York: Oxford University Press.

Borris, E. R. 2003. *The Healing Power of Forgiveness*. Occasional Paper Number 10. Institute for Multi-Track Diplomacy, October.

Boshoff, H., J. M. Gasana, and R. Cornwell. 2009. Burundi: The End of the Tunnel? *ISS Situation Report*. Pretoria, South Africa: Institute of Security Studies.

Boulding, K. E. 1978. *Stable Peace*. Austin: University of Texas Press.

Boulding, K. E. 1990. *Three Faces of Power*. Newbury Park, CA: Sage Publications.

Boutros-Ghali, B. 1992. *An Agenda for Peace: Preventive Diplomacy, Peacemaking and Peace-keeping: Report of the Secretary-General Pursuant to the Statement Adopted by the Summit Meeting of the Security Council on 31 January 1992*. A/47/277-S/ 24111. New York: United Nations. http://www.un.org/Docs/SG/agpeace. html.

Bowker, J. 2008. *Conflict and Reconciliation: The Contribution of Religions*. Toronto, ON: The Key Publishing House.

Brauer, J., J. T. Marlin, and L. Routledge. 2009. *Defining Peace Industries and Calculating the Potential Size of a Peace Gross World Product by Country and by Economic Sector*. Sydney: Institute for Economics and Peace.

Brickhill, J. 2007. *Protecting Civilians through Peace Agreements: Challenges and Lessons of the Darfur Peace Agreement*. ISS Paper 138 presented at the Institute for Security Studies, Pretoria, South Africa.

Brinckerhoff, P. C. 2000. *Social Entrepreneurship. The Art of Mission-based Venture Development*. New York: John Wiley & Sons.

Brooks, E. B. 2007. Warring States Workgroup. Online posting at wsw@yahoogroups. com, December 6.

Brooks, E. B., and A. T. Brooks. 1997. Intellectual Dynamics of the Warring States Period. *Studies in Chinese History* 7: 1–32.

Brooks, E. B., and A. T. Brooks. 2001. The Nature and Historical Context of the Mencius. In *Mencius: Contexts and Interpretations*, ed. Alan K. L. Chan, 242–281. Honolulu: University of Hawaii Press.

Brooks, E. B., and A. T. Brooks. 2010. *The Emergence of China: From Confucius to the Empire*. Warring States Project, September 30.

Brotherton, D. C. 1997. Old Heads Tell Their Stories: From Street Gangs to Street Organizations in New York City. *Journal of Free Inquiry in Creative Sociology* 27, no. 1: 1–15. (Reprinted in special journal edition 28, no. 1, 2001).

Brounéus, K. 2010. The Trauma of Truth Telling: Effects of Witnessing in the Rwandan Gacaca Courts on Psychological Health. *Journal of Conflict Resolution* 54, no. 3: 408–437.

Brown, A., and K. Poremski. 2005. *Roads to Reconciliation: Conflict and Dialogue in the Twenty-First Century*. London: M. E. Sharpe.

Brown, J. M. 1989. *Gandhi: Prisoner of Hope*. New Haven, CT: Yale University Press.

Brown, S., and L. M. Parsons. 2008. The Neuroscience of Dance. *Scientific American* 299, no. 1: 78–83.

Bruner, J. 1990. *Acts of Meaning: Four Lectures on Mind and Culture*. Cambridge, MA: Harvard University Press.

Brzeziński, Z. 1993. *Out of Control: Global Turmoil on the Eve of the Twenty-first Century*. New York: Collier books.

Buber, M. and J. L. Magnes. 1939. *Two Letters to Gandhi*. Jerusalem: Rubin Mass.

Bull, H. 2002. *The Anarchical Society: A Study of Order in World Politics*. New York: Columbia University Press.

Burton, J. W. 1969. *Conflict & Communication: The Use of Controlled Communication in International Relations*. London: Macmillan.

Burton, J. W. 1987. *Resolving Deep-Rooted Conflict: A Handbook*. Lanham, MD: University Press of America.

Burton, J. W. 1988. *Conflict Resolution as a Political System*. Arlington, VA: George Mason University Institute for Conflict Analysis and Resolution.

Burton, J. W. 1990. *Conflict: Human Needs Theory*. New York: Macmillan.

Butterfield, H. 1957. *The Origins of Modern Science*. New York: Macmillan/Free Press.

Byers, M. 2005. *High Ground Lost on UN's Responsibility to Protect*. Winnipeg: Winnipeg Free Press.

Call, C. T., and E. M. Cousens. 2008. Ending Wars and Building Peace: International Responses to War-Torn Societies. *International Studies Perspectives* 9, no. 1: 1–21.

Campbell, D. 1999. Searching for Responsibility / Community in International Relations. In *Moral Spaces: Rethinking Ethics and World Politics*, ed. M. J Shapiro and Daniel Warner. Minneapolis: University of Minnesota Press.

Cannata, M. J. 2009. Achieving Peace in the Streets: How Legislative Efforts Fail in Combating Gang Violence in Comparison to Successful Local Community-Based Initiatives. *New England Journal on Criminal and Civil Confinement* 35: 243–289.

Canovan, M. 2000. Patriotism is not Enough. *British Journal of Political Science* 30, no. 3: 413–432.

Carayannis, T. 2009. *Challenge of Building Sustainable Peace in the DRC*. Background Paper. Geneva: Centre for Humanitarian Dialogue.

Card, C. 1972. On Mercy. *The Philosophical Review* 81, no. 2: 182–207.

Carment, D., and A. Schnabel. 2004. *Conflict Prevention from Rhetoric to Reality: Opportunities and Innovations*. Lanham, MD: Lexington Books.

Carter, A., and G. Stokes. 1998. *Liberal Democracy and Its Critics*. Cambridge, MA: Polity Press.

Caso, A. 1983. El Pueblo del Sol. In *De Teotihuacán a Los Aztecas: Antología de Fuentes e Interpretaciones Históricas*, ed. Miguel León-Portilla, 518–520. Mexico: Universidad Autónoma de México.

Caucasus Conflict Voices. *Global Voices*. http://globalvoicesonline.org/specialcoverage/caucasus-conflict-voices/.

The Caucasus NGO Forum. http://groups.yahoo.com/group/Caucasus_Forum/.

Cavalli-Sforza, L. L., P. Menozzi, and A. Piazza. 1994. *The History and Geography of Human Genes*. Princeton, NJ: Princeton University Press.

Center for International Cooperation. 2009. *Annual Review of Global Peace Operations*. New York.

Center for Islamic Pluralism. 2008. *Black America, Prisons and Radical Islam: A Report*. Washington, DC: Center for Islamic Pluralism.

Center for Research and Dialogue, and Interpeace. 2009. The History of Mediation in Somalia Since 1988. http://www.interpeace.org/index.php/Publications/Pub lications.html.

Centre for Humanitarian Dialogue. 2009. *Mediation for Peace 1999–2009*. http://www. hdcentre.org/publications/mediation-peace-1999-2009-part-1-18mb.

Chan, A. K. 2002. *Mencius: Contexts and Interpretations*. Honolulu: University of Hawaii Press.

Charmaz, K. 1995. Grounded Theory. In *Rethinking Methods in Psychology*, ed. J. A. Smith, R. Harré, and L. Van Langenhove. Thousand Oaks, CA: Sage Publications.

Chatman, S. B. 1980. *Story and Discourse: Narrative Structure in Fiction and Film*. Ithaca, NY: Cornell University Press.

Chatterjee, P. 1986. *Nationalist Thought and the Colonial World: A Derivative Discourse*. Delhi: Oxford University Press.

Chayes, A., and M. Minow, eds. 2003. *Imagine Coexistence: Restoring Humanity After Violent Ethnic Conflict*. San Francisco: Jossey-Bass.

Cherrer, C. P. 2002. *Genocide and Crisis in Central Africa: Conflict Roots, Mass Violence, and Regional War*. Westport, CT: Praeger.

Chomsky, N. 1978. An Exception to the Rules. *Inquiry* 17: 23–27.

Chrétien, J. P. 1985. Hutu et Tutsi au da et au Burundi. In *Au coeur de l'ethnie: Ethnie, tribalism et état en Afrique*, ed. Jean-Loup Amselle and Elikia M'Bokolo, 129–165. Paris: Editions de la Découverte.

Cingranelli, D. L. 2010. The Cingranelli-Richards (CIRI) Human Rights Dataset. *Human Rights Quarterly* 32, no. 2: 401–424.

Claes, J. 2012 (forthcoming). Protecting Civilians from Mass Atrocities: Meeting the Challenge of R2P Rejectionism. *Global Responsibility to Protect*.

Clapham, C. 1996. *Africa and the International System*. Cambridge: Cambridge University Press.

Clark, N. L. and Worger, W. H. 2004. *South Africa: The Rise and Fall of Apartheid*. Harlow, England: Pearson Longman.

Cleary, E. L. 1997. The Brazilian Catholic Church and Church-State Relations: Nation-Building. *Journal of Church & State* 39, no. 2: 253.

Clement, G. 1996. *Care, Autonomy, and Justice: Feminism and the Ethics of Care*. Boulder, CO: Westview.

Cliffe, L. n.d. *The Sudan-IGAD Peace Process: Signposts for the Way Forward*. Occasional Paper. African Security Analysis Programme. Pretoria, South Africa: Institute for Security Studies.

Cliffe, L. 1999. Regional Dimensions of Conflict in the Horn of Africa. *Third World Quarterly* 20, no. 1: 89–111.

Cobb, S. 2006. Developmental Approach to Turning Points: Irony as an Ethics for Negotiation Pragmatics. *Harvard Negotiation Law Review* 11, no. 147: 147–197.

Cobb, S. 2010. Stabilizing Violence: Structural Complexity and Moral Transparency in Penalty Phase Narratives. *Narrative Inquiry* 20, no. 2: 296–324.

Coghlam, B. 2009. *Mortality in the Democratic Republic of Congo, An Ongoing Crisis*. International Rescue Committee. http://www.rescue.org/special-reports/congo-forgotten-crisis.

Cohen, M. 2003. Marc Gopin. Between Eden and Armageddon: The Future of World Religions, Violence, and Peacemaking. New York: Oxford University Press, 2000. viii, 312 pp. *Association of Jewish Studies (AJS) Review* 27, no. 1: 155–157. http://journals.cambridge.org/action/displayAbstract?fromPage=online& aid=214368.

Coleman, I. 2010. *Paradise Beneath Her Feet: How Women Are Transforming the Middle East*. New York: Random House.

Coleman, P. T. 2003. Characteristics of Protracted, Intractable Conflict: Toward the Development of a Meta-framework-I. *Peace and Conflict: Journal of Peace Psychology* 9, no. 1: 1–37.

Coleman, P. T. 2006. Conflict, Complexity, and Change: A Meta-Framework for Addressing Protracted, Intractable Conflicts—III. *Peace and Conflict: Journal of Peace Psychology* 12, no. 4: 325–348.

Coleman, P. T., L. Bui-Wrzosinska, R. Vallacher, and A. Nowak. 2006. Approaching Protracted Conflicts as Dynamical Systems: Guidelines and Methods for Intervention. In *The Negotiator's Fieldbook*, ed. A. Schneider and C. Honeyman, 61–74. Chicago: American Bar Association Books.

Coleman, P. T., R. Vallacher, A. Nowak, and L. Bui-Wrzosinska. 2007. Intractable Conflict as an Attractor: Presenting a Dynamical Model of Conflict, Escalation, and Intractability. *American Behavioral Scientist* 50, no. 11: 1454–1475.

Coll, S. 2004. *Ghost Wars: The Secret History of the CIA, Afghanistan, and bin Laden, from the Soviet Invasion to September 10, 2001*. New York: The Penguin Press.

Collected Works of Mahatma Gandhi Online. Vol. 10. http://www.gandhiserve.org/ cwmg/cwmg.html.

Collected Works of Mahatma Gandhi Online. Vol. 68. http://www.gandhiserve.org/ cwmg/cwmg.html.

Colletta, N. J. 2006. Citizen Security—The Role of NGOs and Broader Civil Society in Ceasefire Monitoring: Lessons from Mindanao. *Journal of Peacebuilding & Development* 2, no. 3: 21–34.

Colletta, N. J., and M. L. Cullen. 2000. *Violent Conflict and the Transformation of Social Capital: Lessons from Cambodia, Rwanda, Guatemala, and Somalia*. Washington, DC: World Bank Publications.

Colletta, N. J. 2004a. *Draft (Jan. 7, 2005)—Enabling Security Sector Reform: NGO and Civil Society Engagement in Ceasefire Monitoring in Aceh (Indonesia) and Mindanao (Philippines)*. New York: International Peace Academy.

Colletta, N. J. 2004b. *Draft (Nov. 29, 2004)—The Role of NGOs and Civil Society in Security Sector Reform: The Center for Humanitarian Dialogue and the Bantay Ceasefire: NGO and Civil Society Engagement in Ceasefire Monitoring in Aceh (Indonesia) and Mindanao (Philippines)*. West Point: Authors' Meeting, December 9.

Colletta, N. J. 2007. Unpublished Field Notes from Nepal DDR Mediation, January.

Collier, P. 2003. *Breaking the Conflict Trap: Civil War and Development Policy*. Washington, DC: A World Bank Publication.

Conciliation Resources. n.d. Breaking Down Barriers through Film. *Dialogue through Film Project*. http://www.c-r.org/our-work/caucasus/dialogue_through_film.php.

Conciliation Resources. n.d. Unbiased Media Coverage of Armenia-Azerbaijan Relations Project. *Armenia—Azerbaijan Media Bias Project*. http://www.epfound.am/ index.php?article_id=260&clang=0.

Conciliation Resources. n.d. Whose Peace Is it Anyway? Connecting Somali and International Peacemaking. *Policy Brief*. http://www.c-r.org/our-work/accord/so malia/somali-led-peace.php.

Conciliation Resources. 2002. *Protracted Conflict, Elusive Peace: Initiatives to End the Violence in Northern Uganda.* London: Accord—International Review of Peace Initiatives.

Conciliation Resources. 2008. *Policy Brief: Incentives, Sanctions and Conditionality in Peace-making 2008.* http://www.c-r.org/our-work/influencing-policy/incentives-policy-briefing.php.

Conciliation Resources. 2009a. *Policy Brief: Choosing to Engage: Armed Groups and Peace Processes.* http://www.c-r.org/our-work/influencing-policy/engaging-groups-policy-briefing.php.

Conciliation Resources. 2009b. *Policy Brief: Ending War: The Need for Peace Process Support Strategies.* http://www.c-r.org/our-work/influencing-policy/peace-process-support-strategies.php.

Confucius. 1979. *The Analects.* Trans. C. Lau. New York: Penguin Books.

Constitutive Act of the African Union adopted by the Thirty-Sixth Ordinary Session of the Assembly of Heads of State and Government on 11 July, 2000, Lome, Togo. http://www.africa-union.org/root/au/aboutau/constitutive_act_en.htm.

Conover, T. 2000. *Newjack: Guarding Sing Sing.* New York: Random House.

Conway, L. G., P. Suedfeld, and P. E. Tetlock. 2001. Integrative Complexity and Political Decisions that Lead to War or Peace. In *Peace, Conflict, and Violence: Peace Psychology for the 21st century,* ed. D. Christie, R. V. Wagner, and D.D.N. Winter, 66–75. Upper Saddle River, NJ: Prentice Hall.

Cooper, R., and M. Berdal. 1993. Outside Intervention in Ethnic Conflicts. *Survival* 35, no. 1: 118–142.

Coser, L. A. 1956. *The Functions of Social Conflict.* New York: The Free Press.

Cowell, F. 2009. *Measuring Inequality.* London: Oxford University Press.

crazy_patriot. n.d. The Truth is Next to You . . . Just Look Into It's Eyes . . . http://crazy-patriot.livejournal.com/.

Crocker, C., F. Osler Hampson, and P. Aall, eds. 1999. *Herding Cats: Multiparty Mediation in a Complex World.* Washington DC: United States Institute of Peace Press.

Crowther, S. 2001. *The Role of NGOs, Local and International in Post-War Peacebuilding.* Committee for Conflict Transformation Support. Newsletter 15, Winter. http://www.c-r.org/ccts/ccts15/index.htm.

Csikszentmihalyi, M. 1996. *Creativity: Flow and the Psychology of Discovery and Invention.* New York: HarperCollins.

Cummings, G. 1993. Black Theology and Latin American Theology. In *New Visions for the Americas: Religious Engagement and Social Transformation,* ed. David Batstone, 215–229. Minneapolis: Fortress.

Cummings, S., D. J. Monti, and D. Vigil, eds. 1993. The Established Gang. In *Gangs: The Origins and Impact of Contemporary Youth Gangs in the United States.* Albany: State University of New York Press.

Curle, A. 1971. *Making Peace.* London: Tavistock Publications.

Curle, A. 1986. *In the Middle: Non-Official Mediation in Violent Situations.* New York: St. Martins Press.

Curle, A. 1990. *Tools for Transformation: A Personal Study.* Stroud, UK: Hawthorn Press.

Curle, A., and S. Elworthy. 1995. *Another Way: Positive Response to Contemporary Violence.* Oxford, UK: Jon Carpenter.

Curry, G. D., and S. H. Decker. 1996. Understanding and Responding to Gangs in an Emerging Gang Problem Context. *Valparaiso University Law Review* 31: 523.

Dalton, D. 1993. *Mahatma Gandhi: Nonviolent Power in Action.* New York: Columbia University Press.

Daly, E., and J. Sarkin. 2007. *Reconciliation in Divided Societies: Finding Common Ground.* Philadelphia: University of Pennsylvania Press.

D'Amico, L. C., and R. A. Rubinstein. 1999. Cultural Considerations when "Setting" the Negotiation Table. *Negotiation Journal* 15, no. 4: 389–395.

Dannin, R. 2002. *Black Pilgrimage to Islam.* Cambridge, MA: Oxford University Press.

Darby, J. 2001. *The Effects of Violence on Peace Processes.* Washington, DC: USIP Press.

Darwin, C. 1998 [1971]. *The Descent of Man.* New York: Prometheus Books.

Dassin, J. 1998. *Torture in Brazil: A Shocking Report on the Pervasive use of Torture by Brazilian Military Governments, 1964–1979.* Austin: University of Texas Press.

Davidson, B. 1992. *The Black Man's Burden: Africa and the Curse of the Nation-state.* London: James Currey.

Davie, M. R. 1929. *The Evolution of War: A Study of its Role in Early Societies.* New Haven, CT: Yale University Press.

Davies, M. 2008. A Foreword. In *A World of Gangs: Armed Young Men and Gangsta Culture,* ed. John M. Hagedorn. Minneapolis: University of Minnesota Press.

Dayton, B. W. 2009. Useful but Insufficient: Intermediaries in Peacebuilding. In *Conflict Transformation and Peacebuilding,* ed. Bruce W. Dayton and Louis Kriesberg, 61–73. New York: Routledge.

Dayton, B. W., and L. Kriesberg. 2009. *Conflict Transformation and Peacebuilding: Moving From Violence to Sustainable Peace.* Oxford, UK: Cambridge University Press.

De Chardin, P. T., J. Huxley, and B. Wall. 1959. *The Phenomenon of Man.* Vol. 5. London: William Collins Sons.

Dees, J. G. 1998. The Meaning of "Social Entrepreneurship." Kauffman Center for Entrepreneurial Leadership, October 31. http://www.fntc.info/files/documents/The%20meaning%20of%20Social%20Entreneurship.pdf.

De Gruchy, J. W. 2002. *Reconciliation: Restoring Justice.* Minneapolis: Fortress Press.

DeMars, W. 2004. *Dancing in the Dark: NGOs and States in Former Yugoslavia.* Paper presented at the 45th Annual International Studies Association (ISA) Convention. Montreal, Quebec, Canada. March 17–20, 2004.

Dennis, M. 1993. *Cultivating a Landscape of Peace: Iroquois-European Encounters in Seventeenth-Century America.* Ithaca, NY: Cornell University Press.

Dentan, R. K. 1968. *The Semai: A Non-Violent People of Malaya.* New York: Holt, Reinhart and Winston.

Department for International Development. 2000. *Access to Justice in Sub-Saharan Africa: The Role of Traditional and Informal Justice Systems.* London: DFID.

DeRouen, K., and J. Bercovitch. Forthcoming. Enduring Internal Rivalries: A New Framework for the Analysis of Civil Wars. *Journal of Peace Research.*

Derrig, R. A., and H. I. Weisberg. 2004. Determinants of Total Compensation for Auto Bodily Injury Liability Under No-Fault: Investigation, Negotiation and the Suspicion of Fraud. *Insurance and Risk Management-Montreal* 71, no. 4: 633–662.

Des Forges, A. 1999. *Leave None to Tell the Story.* New York: Human Rights Watch.

De Soto, A. 1999. Ending Violent Conflict in El Salvador. In *Herding Cats: Multiparty Mediation in a Complex World,* 349–385. Washington, DC: USIP.

Deutsch, K. W. and R. Merritt. 1665. Effects of Events on National and International Images. In *International Behaviour; A Social-Psychological Reader,* ed. H. C. Kelman, chapter 5. New York: Holt, Rhinehart & Winston.

Deutsch, M. 1973a. Conflicts: Productive and Destructive. In *Conflict Resolution through Communication,* ed. F. E. Jandt, 155–197. New York: Harper & Row.

Deutsch, M. 1973b. The Resolution of Conflict. *American Behavioral Scientist* 17, no. 2: 248.

Deutsch, M. 1973c. *The Resolution of Conflict; Constructive and Destructive Processes*. New Haven, CT: Yale University Press.

Deutsch, M. 1994. Constructive Conflict Resolution: Principles, Training, and Research. *Journal of Social Issues* 50, no. 1: 13–32.

Deutsch, M., and Peter T. Coleman. 2000. *The Handbook of Conflict Resolution: Theory and Practice*. San Francisco: Jossey-Bass.

de Waal, F.B.M. 1990. *Peacemaking among Primates*. Cambridge, MA: Harvard University Press.

de Waal, F.B.M. 2000. Primates: A Natural Heritage of Conflict Resolution. *Science* 289, no. 5479: 586–590.

de Waal, F.B.M. 2004a. Evolutionary Ethics, Aggression and Violence: Lessons from Primate Research. *Journal of Law, Medicine and Ethics* 32: 18–23.

de Waal, F.B.M. 2004b. Peace Lessons From an Unlikely Source. *PLoS Biology* 2, no. 4 (April): 434–436.

de Waal, F.B.M. 2009. *The Age of Empathy: Nature's Lessons for a Kinder Society*. New York: Harmony Books.

de Waal, F.B.M., and M. Suchak. 2010. Prosocial Primates: Selfish and Unselfish Motivations. *Philosophical Transactions of the Royal Society B: Biological Sciences* 365, no. 1553: 2711.

Dewi Fortuna, A. 1999. The Habibie Presidency. In *Post Soeharto Indonesia: Renewal or Chaos?* ed. G. Forrester, 33–47. Singapore: Institute of Southeast Asian Studies.

Diamond, J. 1997. *Guns, Germs and Steel: The Fates of Human Societies*. New York: W. W. Norton.

Diamond, L. 2005. *Squandered Victory*. New York: Henry Holt.

Diamond, L., and J. McDonald. 1991. *Multi-Track Diplomacy: A Systems Guide and Analysis*. Grinnell: Iowa Peace Institute.

Diamond, L., and J. W. McDonald. 1996a. *Multi-Track Diplomacy: A Systems Approach to Peace*. Sterling, VA: Kumarian Press.

Diamond, L., and J. McDonald. 1996b. What is Multi-Track Diplomacy? In *Multi-Track Diplomacy: A Systems Approach to Peace*. Sterling, VA: Kumarian Press. http://www.imtd.org/at-a-glance/mission/working-methods/what-is-multi-track-diplomacy/.

Dingwaney, A., and C. Maier, eds. 1996. *Between Languages and Cultures*. Delhi: Oxford University Press.

Dobbins, J., S. G. Jones, K. Crane, and B. Cole DeGrasse. 2007. *The Beginner's Guide to Nation-Building*. Santa Monica, CA: RAND.

Dorner, D. 1996. *The Logic of Failure: Why Things Go Wrong and what We can Do to Make Them Right*. New York: Holt.

Dowdney, L. 2006. *Neither War nor Peace: International Comparisons of Children and Youth in Organised Armed Violence*. Rio de Janeiro: 7Letras.

Doxtader, E. 2008. *With Faith in the Work of Words: The Beginnings of Reconciliation in South Africa, 1985–1995*. East Lansing: Michigan State University.

Doyle, M. W. 1997. *Ways of War and Peace*. New York: W. W. Norton.

Doyle, M. W, and N. Sambanis. 2000. International Peacebuilding: A Theoretical and Quantitative Analysis. *American Political Science Review* 94, no. 4: 779–801.

Drayton, W. 2002. The Citizen Sector: Becoming as Entrepreneurial and Competitive as Business. *California Management Review* 44, no. 3: 120–132.

Drayton, W. 2005. Where the Real Power Lies. *Alliance* 10, no. 1: 29–30.

DRC Mapping Human Rights Violations 1993–2003. Office of the High Commissioner on Human Rights. http://www.ohchr.org/Documents/Countries/ZR/DRC_MAPPING_REPORT_FINAL_EN.pdf.

Dress, T. P. 2005. *Designing a Peacebuilding Infrastructure: Taking a Systems Approach to the Prevention of Deadly Conflict.* Development Dossiers by UN NGLS.

Dubey, A. 2002. *Domestic Institutions and the Duration of Civil War Settlements.* Paper read at International Studies Association, March 24–27, 2002, New Orleans.

Dumper, M., and B. E. Stanley. 2007. *Cities of the Middle East and North Africa: A Historical Encyclopedia.* Santa Barbara, CA: ABC-Clio.

Dunn, L., and L. Kriesberg. 2002. Mediating Intermediaries: Expanding Roles of Transnational Organizations. In *Studies in International Mediation: Essays in Honour of Jeffrey Z. Rubin,* ed. Jacob Bercovitch, 194–212. London and New York: Palgrave MacMillan.

Durand, J. D. 2005. *L'esprit d'Assise.* Paris: Cerf.

Easton, C. 1976. *The Search for Sam Goldwyn.* New York: William Morrow.

Easton, D. 1965. *A Framework for Political Analysis.* Vol. 1. Englewood Cliffs, NJ: Prentice-Hall.

Easwaran, E. 1984. *A Man to Match His Mountains: Badshah Khan, Nonviolent Soldier of Islam.* Tomales, CA: Nilgiri Press.

Economist Intelligence Unit. 2008. *Index of Democracy.*

ECOWAS. 1994. *Protocol Relating to the Community Parliament,* REV. 3 of 6. August.

ECOWAS. 1998. Moratorium on the Importation, Exportation and Manufacture of Light Weapons in West Africa, Abuja, October, 31.

ECOWAS. 2000. ECOWAS Press Release No. 97/2000. November 20.

ECOWAS Secretariat. 2001. Status of Implementation of the Protocol Relating to the Mechanism for Conflict Prevention, Resolution and Management, Peacekeeping and Security. Abuja, June.

Edwards, M., and D. Hulme. 1996. *Beyond the Magic Bullet: NGO Performance and Accountability in the Post-Cold War World.* West Hartford, CT: Kumarian Press.

El-Affendi, A. 2001. The Impasse in the IGAD Peace Process for Sudan: The Limits of Regional Peacemaking? *African Affairs* 100, no. 401: 581–599.

Encounter Points. 2006. www.justvision.org.

Endicott, K. M., and K. L. Endicott. 2008. *The Headman Was a Woman.* Long Grove, IL: Waveland Press.

Enloe, C. 1998. All the Men are in the Militias, all the Women are Victims: The Politics of Masculinity and Femininity in Nationalist Wars. In *The Women and War Reader,* ed. Lois Ann Lorentzen and Jennifer Turpin, 50–62. New York: New York University Press.

Ertel, D. 2004. Getting Past Yes. *Harvard Business Review,* November: 60–68.

European Centre for Conflict Prevention. 1999. *People Building Peace: 35 Inspiring Stories from Around the World.* Utrecht: European Centre for Conflict Prevention.

European Parliament. 2009. *European Parliament Resolution of 15 January 2009 on Srebrenica.* http://www.europarl.europa.eu/sides/getDoc.do?type=TA&reference=P6-TA-2009–0028&language=EN.

Evans, G. 2005. The Reform of the United Nation. Presented at the Welt am Sontag/BDLI Forum on Reassurance at a Time of Insecurity, October 24, Berlin, Germany.

Evans, G. 2008. *The Responsibility to Protect, Ending Mass Atrocity Crimes Once and For All.* Washington, DC: Brookings Institution.

Executive Secretariat. 2001. Protocol on Democracy and Good Governance Supplementary to the Protocol Relating to the Mechanism for Conflict Prevention, Management, Resolution, Peacekeeping and Security. Dakar, December.

Facebook page of the Azerbaijani Film Festival. http://www.facebook.com/event.php?eid=118393321556010&index=1.

Facebook pages. http://www.facebook.com/home.php?sk=group_170382072987 153. See also http://www.facebook.com/pages/I-HATE-ARMENIA/251917412 515?v=wall.

Facilitation of Dialogue Processes and Mediation Efforts. 2010. Concept Note presented at the Folke Bernadotte Academy. May 20, Sando, Sweden.

Fairbank, J. K. 1974. Introduction: Varieties of the Chinese Military Experience. In *Chinese Ways in Warfare*, ed. F. A. Kierman, J. K. Fairbank, and E. L. Dreyer, 1–26. Cambridge, MA: Harvard University Press.

Fairbank, J. K., and Tung-tse Chu, eds. 1968. *The Chinese World Order: Traditional China's Foreign Relations*. Cambridge, MA: Harvard University Press.

Falk, R. 1978. The Moral Argument as Apologia. *The Nation* 25: 341–343.

Falk, R. A., and S. S. Kim. 1980. *The War System: An Interdisciplinary Approach*. Boulder, CO: Westview Press.

Fanon, F., and R. Philcox. 2004. *The Wretched of the Earth*. New York; Grove Press.

Fanta, E. 2009. *The Capacity of African Regional Organizations in Peace and Security*. Paper presented at the ERD Workshop: Transforming Political Structures: Security, Institutions, and Regional Integration Mechanisms, Florence, April.

Feil, S. R. 1998. *Preventing Genocide: How the Early Use of Force Might Have Succeeded in Rwanda*. New York: Carnegie Corporation.

Fellner, J. 2006. A Corrections Quandary: Mental Illness and Prison Rules. *Harvard Civil Rights-Civil Liberties Law Review* 41: 391.

Feng, H. 2007. *Chinese Strategic Culture and Foreign Policy Decision-Making: Confucianism, Leadership and War*. New York: Routledge.

Ferguson, B. 2000. The Causes and Origins of "Primitive Warfare" on Evolved Motivations for War. *Anthropological Quarterly* 73, no. 3 (July): 150–164.

Ferrer, J. N. 2002. *Revisioning Transpersonal Theory: A Participatory Vision of Human Spirituality*. Albany: State University of New York Press.

Firestone, R. 2010. The Ground Zero-Sum Game. *Religious Dispatches* August 23. http://www.religiondispatches.org/archive/atheologies/3176/the_ground_zero-sum_game__.

Fisas Armengol, V. 2010. *Ceasefire! Handbook of Peace Processes*. Barcelona: Escola de Cultura de Pau, Universitar Autonoma de Barcelona.

Fischer, R., and K. Hanke. 2009. Are Societal Values Linked to Global Peace and Conflict? *Peace and Conflict: Journal of Peace Psychology* 15, no. 3: 227–248.

Fisher, R., W. Ury, and B. Patton. 1991. *Getting to Yes: Negotiating Agreement without Giving In*, 2nd ed. New York: Penguin Books.

Fisher, R. J. 1990. *The Social Psychology of Intergroup and International Conflict Resolution*. New York: Springer-Verlag Publishing.

Fisher, R. J. 1997. *Interactive Conflict Resolution*. Syracuse, NY: Syracuse University Press.

Fisher, R. J. 2007. Assessing the Contingency Model of Third-Party Intervention in Successful Cases of Prenegotiation. *Journal of Peace Research* 44, no. 3: 311–329.

Fisher, R. J., ed. 2005. *Paving the Way: Contributions of Interactive Conflict Resolution to Peacemaking*. Lanham, MD: Lexington Books.

Fisher, W. R. 1987. *Human Communication as Narration: Toward a Philosophy of Reason, Value, and Action*. Vol. 201. Columbia: University of South Carolina Press.

Fitzduff, M., and C. Church. 2004. *NGOs at the Table: Strategies for Influencing Policies in Areas of Conflict.* Lanham, MD: Rowman & Littlefield.

Flack, J. C., F.B.M. de Waal, and D. C. Krakauer. 2005. Social Structure, Robustness, and Policing Cost in a Cognitively Sophisticated Species. *The American Naturalist* 165, no. 5: 126–139.

Flanagan, K., and P. C. Jupp. 2007. *A Sociology of Spirituality.* Aldershot, UK: Ashgate.

Fletcher, A. C., and F. La Flesche. 1911. The Omaha Tribe. *Annual Reports of the Bureau of American Ethnology* 27: 17–642.

Fong, R. S., and S. Buentello. 1991. The Detection of Prison Gang Development: An Empirical Assessment. *Federal Probation* 55, no. 1: 66–69.

Forsythe, D. P. 1977. United Nations Peacemaking. *Proceedings of the Academy of Political Science* 32, no. 4: 206–220.

Fortna, V. P. 2004a. Does Peacekeeping Keep Peace? International Intervention and the Duration of Peace after Civil War. *International Studies Quarterly* 48, no. 2: 269–292.

Fortna, V. P. 2004b. *Peace Time: Cease-fire Agreements and the Durability of Peace.* Oxford: Princeton University Press.

Fortna, V. P. 2004c. Data Notes: The Cease-Fire Data Set. In *Peace Time—Cease-Fire Agreements and the Durability of Peace,* ed. V. P. Fortna, 219–222. Princeton, NJ: Princeton University Press.

Fortna, V. P. 2008a. Data Notes. In *Does Peacekeeping Work? Shaping Belligerents' Choices After Civil Wars,* ed. V. P. Fortna, 181–186. Princeton, NJ: Princeton University Press.

Fortna, V. P. 2008b. Peacekeeping and Democratization. In *From War to Democracy: Dilemmas of Peacebuilding,* eds. A. Jarstad and T. D. Sisk, 39–79. Cambridge, MA: Cambridge University Press.

Foucault, M. 1988. The Political Technology of Individuals. In *Technologies of the Self: A Seminar with Michel Foucault,* ed. L. H. Martin, H. Gutman, and P. H. Hutton, 145–162. Ahmerst: University of Massachusetts Press.

Fox, J. A., and L. D. Brown. 1998. *The Struggle for Accountability: The World Bank, NGOs, and Grassroots Movements.* Cambridge, MA: The MIT Press.

Francesch, M. C., V. F. Armengol, P. G. Amado, M. P. Chevalier, J. M. Royo Aspa, J. U. García, P. U. Arestizábal, A. V. Ariño, and M. V. Ariño. 2010. *Alert 2010: Report on Conflicts, Human Rights and Peacebuilding.* Bellaterra: Escola de Cultura de Pau. http://escolapau.uab.cat/img/programas/alerta/alerta/alerta10i.pdf.

Francis, D. J. 2006. *Uniting Africa: Building Regional Peace and Security Systems.* Aldershot, UK: Ashgate.

Franke, B. 2009. *Security Cooperation in Africa: A Reappraisal.* Boulder, CO: First Forum Press.

Frankl, V. 1984. *Man's Search for Meaning.* New York: Pocket Press.

Frazer Institute. 2009. *Economic Freedom of the World 2009 Annual Report.* Calgary: Frazer Institute.

Freire, P. 1993. *Pedagogy of the Oppressed.* New York: Continuum International Publishing Group.

Freire, P. 2000. *Pedagogy of the Oppressed.* Reprint. New York: Continuum International Publishing Group.

Fremon, C., and T. Brokaw. 2008. *G-Dog and the Homeboys: Father Greg Boyle and the Gangs of East Los Angeles.* Albuquerque: University of New Mexico Press.

Fry, D. P. 2000. Conflict Management in Cross-Cultural Perspective. In *Natural Conflict Resolution,* F. Aureli and F.B.M. de Waal, 334–351. Berkeley: University of California Press.

Fry, D. P. 2007. *Beyond War: The Human Potential for Peace*. Oxford: Oxford University Press.

Fry, D. P. 2009. Anthropological Insights for Creating Non-Warring Social Systems. *Journal of Aggression, Conflict and Peace Research* 1, no. 2: 4–15.

Fukuyama, F. 1993. *The End of History and the Last Man*. New York: Avon Books.

Funk, N. C., and A. A. Said. 1977. *Islam and Peacemaking in the Middle East*. Boulder, CO: Lynne Rienner.

Funk, N. C., and A. A. Said. 2010. Localizing Peace: An Agenda for Sustainable Peacebuilding. *Peace and Conflict Studies* 17, no. 1: 101–143.

Gadamer, H. G., J. Weinsheimer, and D. G. Marshall. 2004. *Truth and Method*. New York: Continuum International.

Galilei, G. 1989. *Two New Sciences, Including Centers of Gravity and Force of Percussion*. Trans. Stillman Drake. Toronto: Wall and Thompson.

Galin, L. 2002. *Egypt: Gods, Myths and Religion*. London: Anness Publishing.

Galtung, J. 1964. A Structural Theory of Aggression. *Journal of Peace Research* 1, no. 2: 95–119.

Galtung, J. 1969. Violence, Peace and Peace Research. *Journal of Peace Research* 6, no. 3: 167–191.

Galtung, J. 1977. *Essays in Methodology: Methodology and Ideology*. Copenhagen: Ejlers.

Galtung, J. 1989. *Solving Conflicts: A Peace Research Perspective*. Honolulu: University of Hawaii Press.

Galtung, J. 1994. *Human Rights in Another Key*. Cambridge, MA: Polity Press.

Galtung, J. 1996. *Peace by Peaceful Means: Peace and Conflict, Development and Civilization*. Thousand Oaks, CA: Sage Publications.

Gandhi, M. 1948. *Autobiography: The Story of my Experiments with Truth*. Translated by M. H. Desai. Washington, DC: Public Affairs Press.

Gandhi, M. 2009. As quoted in Arun Gandhi Shares the Mahatma's Message by Michel W. Potts. *India-West* [San Leandro, California] 27, no. 13: 1.

Gandhi, M. K. 1958. *Collected Works*. 100 vols. New Delhi: Publication Division, Ministry of Information and Broadcasting.

Gandhi, M. K., and V.G.T. Desai. 1938. *Satyagraha in South Africa*. Madras: S. Ganesa.

Gandhi, R. 2006. *Mohandas: A True Story of a Man, his People, and an Empire*. Delhi: Penguin Books.

Ganguly, K. M., trans. 2004. *Mahabharata of Krishna-Dwaipayana Vyasa*. Munshirm Manoharlal Pub Pvt Ltd, January 1. http://www.mahabharataonline.com/translation.

Gardell, M. 1996. *In the Name of Elijah Muhammad: Louis Farrakhan and the Nation of Islam*. Durham, NC: Duke University Press.

Gardner, J., and J. Maier. 1985. *Gilgamesh: Translated from the Sin-Leqi-Unninni Version*. New York: Vintage Books.

Gay, G. 2000. *Culturally Responsive Teaching: Theory, Research, and Practice*. New York: Teachers College Press.

Gay, G. 2004. Curriculum Theory and Multicultural Education. In *Handbook of Research on Multicultural Education*, ed. J. A. Banks and C. A. McGee Banks, 30–49. San Francisco: Jossey-Bass.

Gentile, M. C. 2002. *Social Impact Management and Social Enterprise: Two Sides of the Same Coin or Totally Different Currency*. New York: Aspen Institute for Social Innovation in Business. www.aspeninstitute.org/sites/default/files/content/docs/business%20and%20society%20program/SOCIMPACTSOCENT.PDF.

Gersick, C.J.G. 1991. Revolutionary Change Theories: A Multilevel Exploration of the Punctuated Equilibrium Paradigm. *Academy of Management Review* 16: 10–36.

Gevisser, M. 2009. *A Legacy of Liberation: Thabo Mbeki and the Future of the South African Dream.* Hampshire, England: Palgrave Macmillan.

Gibbs, D. N. 2009. *First Do No Harm: Humanitarian Intervention and the Destruction of Yugoslavia.* Nashville: Vanderbilt University Press.

Gibney, M., L. Cornett, and R. Wood. 2008. Political Terror Scale 1976–2008. http://www.politicalterrorscale.org.

Giffen, A. 2009. Addressing the Doctrinal Deficit: Developing Guidance to Prevent and Respond to Widespread or Systematic Attacks Against Civilians. In *Report from the International Experts Workshop,* 21–24. Washington, DC: The Henry L. Stimson Center.

Girard, R. 1987. *Things Hidden Since the Foundation of the World.* Stanford, CA: Stanford University Press.

Girard, R. 1988. *Violence and the Sacred.* Baltimore: Johns Hopkins University Press.

Girard, R. 1989. *The Scapegoat.* Baltimore: Johns Hopkins University Press.

Girard, R. 1990. *Deceit, Desire and the Novel: Self and Other in Literary Structure.* Trans. Y. Feccero. Baltimore: The Johns Hopkins University Press.

Girard, R. 2000. *A Theatre of Envy: William Shakespeare.* Leominster, UK: Gracewing and Indigo.

Giro, M. 1998. The Community of Saint Egidio and its Peace-making Activities. *The International Spectator* 33, no. 3: 85–100.

Gladwell, M. 2000. *The Tipping Point: How Little Things can Make a big Difference.* Boston: Little, Brown.

Glaser, B. G., and A. L. Strauss. 1967. *The Discovery of Grounded Theory: Strategies for Qualitative Research.* London: Weidenfeld and Nicholson.

Glazer, I. M. 1997. Beyond the Competition of Tears: Black-Jewish Conflict Containment in a New York Neighborhood. In *Cultural Variation in Conflict Resolution: Alternatives to Violence,* ed. D. P. Fry and K. Björkqvist, 9–23. Mahwah, NJ: Lawrence Erlbaum Associates.

Gleick, J. 1987. *Chaos: Making a New Science.* New York: Penguin.

Global Partnership for the Prevention of Armed Conflict. 2010. *Infrastructures for Peace.* Working Paper Series. The Hague: European Centre for Conflict Prevention, March.

Goduka, I., and B. B. Swadener. 1999. *Affirming Unity in Diversity in Education: Healing with Ubuntu.* Johannesburg: Thorold's Africana Books.

Goertz, G., and P. F. Diehl. 1993. Enduring Rivalries: Theoretical Constructs and Empirical Patterns. *International Studies Quarterly* 37: 147–171.

Goitein, S. 2005. *Jews and Arabs: A Concise History.* Mineola, NY: Dover.

Goldschmidt, W. 1994. *Peacemaking and the Institutions of Peace in Tribal Societies.* In *The Anthropology of Peace and Nonviolence,* ed. L. E. Sponsel and T. Gregor, 109–132. Boulder CO: Lynne Rienner.

Goldstein, A. P. 1993. *The Gang Intervention Handbook.* Champaign, IL: Research Press.

Goldstone, J. A., R. H. Bates, D. L. Epstein, T. R. Gurr, M. B. Lustik, M. G. Marshall, J. Ulfelder, and M. Woodward. 2010. A Global Model for Forecasting Political Instability. *American Journal of Political Science* 54, no. 1: 190–208.

Goldstone, R. J. 1996. Justice as a Tool for Peace-Making: Truth Commissions and International Criminal Tribunals. *Journal of International Law and Politics* 28: 485–503.

Goodhand, J. 2006. *Aiding Peace?: The Role of NGOs in Armed Conflict.* Boulder, CO: Lynne Rienner Publishers.

Goodhand, J. 2009. Effective Participation of National Minorities as a Tool for Conflict Prevention. *International Journal of Minority and Group Rights* 16, no. 4: 539–547.

Gopin, M. 2000. *Between Eden and Armageddon: The Future of World Religions, Violence, and Peacemaking.* New York: Oxford University Press.

Gopin, M. 2002. *Holy War, Holy Peace: How Religion can Bring Peace to the Middle East.* New York: Oxford University Press.

Gopin, M. 2009. *To Make the Earth Whole: The Art of Citizen Diplomacy in an Age of Religious Militancy.* Lanham, MD: Rowman & Littlefield.

Government of Uganda. 2003. *Referral of the Situation Concerning the Lord's Resistance Army.* Handed out at the Uganda Human Rights Commission's conference on "The Implications of the ICC Investigations on Human Rights and the Peace Process in Uganda," Kampala, October 5, 2004. Kampala.

Govier, T. 1998. *Social Trust and Human Communities.* Montreal: McGill-Queens University Press.

Granovetter, M. S. 1973. The Strength of Weak Ties. *American Journal of Sociology* 78, no. 6: 1360–1380.

Gregor, T. 1990. Uneasy Peace: Intertribal Relations in Brazil's Upper Xingu. In *The Anthropology of War,* ed. J. Haas, 105–124. Cambridge: Cambridge University Press.

Gregor, T. 1994. Symbols and Rituals of Peace in Brazil's Upper Xingu. In *The Anthropology of Peace and Nonviolence,* ed. L. E. Sponsel and T. Gregor, 241–257. Boulder, CO: Lynne Rienner.

Greig, M. J. 2001. Moments of Opportunity: Recognizing Conditions of Ripeness for International Mediation between Enduring Rivals. *Journal of Conflict Resolution* 45, no. 6: 691–718.

Greig, M. J. 2005. Stepping into the Fray: When Do Mediators Mediate? *American Journal of Political Science* 49, no. 2: 249–266.

Greig, M. J., and P. M. Regan. 2008. When Do They Say Yes? An Analysis of the Willingness to Offer and Accept Mediation in Civil Wars. *International Studies Quarterly* 52, no. 52: 759–781.

Greig, M., and N. Rost. 2005. Which Tools Get Used? A Multidimensional Analysis of Conflict Management within Civil War. Conference presented at the Annual Meeting of the Midwest Political Science Association, April, Chicago.

Griffiths, M. 2005. *Talking of Peace in a Time of Terror: United Nations Mediation and Collective Security.* Geneva: Henri Dunant Centre.

Griffiths, M., and T. Whitfield. 2010. *Mediation Ten Years On: Challenges and Opportunities for Peacemaking.* Geneva, Switzerland: Centre for Humanitarian Dialogue.

Gurr, T. R. 1988. War, Revolution, and the Growth of the Coercive State. *Comparative Political Studies* 21, no. 1: 45.

Gurr, T. R. 1993. *Minorities at Risk: A Global View of Ethnopolitical Conflicts.* Washington, DC: United States Institute of Peace Press.

Gurr, T. R. 2000. *Peoples Versus States: Minorities at Risk in the New Century.* Conflict Resolution collection. Washington, DC: United States Institute of Peace Press.

Haass, R. N. 1990. *Conflicts Unending: The United States and Regional Disputes.* New Haven, CT: Yale University.

Habermas, J. 1998. Citizenship and National Identity. In *Between Facts and Norms: Contributions to a Discourse Theory of Law and Democracy,* 491–516. Cambridge, MA: MIT Press.

Hagedorn, J. M. 2008. *A World of Gangs: Armed Young Men and Gangsta Culture.* Minneapolis: University of Minnesota Press.

Halkin, A. 2006. The Great Fusion. In *Great ages and Ideas of the Jewish People,* ed. L. Schwarz. New York: Random House.

Hall, B. W. 2010. International Law and the Responsibility to Protect. In *The International Studies Encyclopedia,* ed. Robert A. Denemark. Oxford, UK: Blackwell.

http://www.isacompendium.com/subscriber/tocnode?id=g9781444336597_chunk_g978144433659711_ss1–32.

Hallowell, I. 1940. Aggression in Saulteaux Society. *Psychiatry*, 3: 395–407.

Hallowell, I. 1953. Aggression in Saulteaux Society. Reprinted in *Nature, Society and Culture*, 2nd ed., ed. Clyde Kluckhohn, H. A. Murray, and D. M. Schneider, 260–275. New York: Alfred A. Knopf.

Hamieh, C. S., and R. Mac Ginty. 2009. A Very Political Reconstruction: Governance and Reconstruction in Lebanon after the 2006 War. *Disasters* 34, no. 1: 103–123.

Hamm, M. S. 2007. *Terrorist Recruitment in American Correctional Institutions: An Exploratory Study of Non-Traditional Faith Groups Final Report*. Commissioned Report for the U.S. Department of Justice.

Hammonds, K. H. 2005. *A Lever Long Enough to Move the World. Fast Company*. January 1. http://www.fastcompany.com/magazine/90/open_ashoka.html.

Hampson, F. O. 1996. *Nurturing Peace: Why Peace Settlements Succeed or Fail*. Washington, DC: United States Institute of Peace Press.

Hampson, F. O., and D. Malone, eds. 2002. *From Reaction to Conflict Prevention: Opportunities for the UN System*. Boulder, CO: Lynne Rienner Publishers.

Hansson, N. 2003. Peacemaking and Civil Society in Intra-State Conflict in the Post-Cold War Era. PhD diss. Sweden: University of Uppsala.

Harbom, L., E. Melander, and P. Wallensteen. 2008. Dyadic Dimensions of Armed Conflicts, 1946–2007. *Journal of Peace Research* 45, no. 5: 697–710.

Harbom, L., S. Högbladh, and P. Wallensteen. 2006. Armed Conflict and Peace Agreements. *Journal of Peace Research* 43, no. 5: 617–631.

Harré, R., and N. Slocum. 2003. Disputes as Complex Social Events. *Common Knowledge* 9, no. 1: 100–118.

Harré, R. E., and F. E. Moghaddam. 2003. *The Self and Others: Positioning Individuals and Groups in Personal, Political, and Cultural Contexts*. Westport, CT: Praeger.

Harrington, M. 1987. *The Next Left: The History of a Future*. London: IB Tauris.

Hart, B., ed. 2008. *Peacebuilding in Traumatized Societies*. Lanham, MD: University Press of America.

Hart, C.W.M., and A. R. Pilling. 1960. *The Tiwi of North Australia*. New York: Holt, Rinehart & Winston of Canada.

Hart, J. G. 1994. Recent Works in Gandhi Studies. *Philosophy East and West* 44, no. 1: 149–167.

Hartzell, C., M. Hoddie, and D. Rothchild. 2001. Stabilizing the Peace after Civil War: An Investigation of some Key Variables. *International Organization* 55, no. 1: 183–208.

Harvey, R. 2001. *The Fall of Apartheid: The Inside Story from Smuts to Mbeki*. Houndmills, England: Palgrave Macmillan.

Haughton, J. H., and S. R. Khandker. 2009. *Handbook on Poverty and Inequality*. Washington, DC: World Bank Publications.

Hausmann, R., L. D'Andrea Tyson, and S. Zahidi. 2007. *The Global Gender Gap Report 2007*. New York: World Economic Forum.

Hayner, P. 2009. *Negotiating Justice: GUIDANCE for Mediators*. Geneva: Centre for Humanitarian Dialogue.

Haysom, N., and J. Hottinger. 2004. Do's and Don'ts of Sustainable Ceasefire Agreements. Paper initially presented to the IGAD Sudan Peace Process Workshop on Detailed Security Arrangements, Sudan.

Haysom, N., and J. Hottinger. 2010. Do's and Don'ts of Sustainable Ceasefire Agreements. Presentation revised for use by Peace Appeal in Nepal and Sri Lanka.

Healy, S. 2008. Lost Opportunities in the Horn of Africa: How Conflicts Connect and Peace Agreements Unravel. Chatham House Report. London: RIIA.

Healy, S. 2009. Peacemaking in the Midst of War: An Assessment of IGAD's Contribution to Regional Security. Crisis States Working Paper. Series 2. London: CSRC, London School of Economics.

Heinz W., and D. Shah. 1994. Crisis Negotiations Between Unequals: Lessons From a Classic Dialogue. *Negotiation Journal* 10, no. 2: 129–141.

Held, V. 2007. *The Ethics of Care: Personal, Political, Global.* Oxford: Oxford University Press.

Helmick, R. G., and R. L. Petersen. 2002. *Forgiveness and Reconciliation: Religion, Public Policy & Conflict Transformation.* Philadelphia, PA: Templeton.

Helmick, R. G., and R. L. Petersen, eds. 2001. *Forgiveness and Reconciliation: Religion, Public Policy, and Conflict Transformation.* West Conshohocken, PA: Templeton Foundation Press.

Helminiak, D. A. 1998. *Religion and the Human Sciences: An Approach via Spirituality.* Albany: State University of New York Press.

Henderson, M. 1996. *The Forgiveness Factor: Stories of Hope in a World of Conflict.* Salem, OR: Grosvenor Books.

Hercik, J. M. 2004. *Prisoner Reentry, Religion and Research.* Washington, DC: Department of Health and Human Services.

Herman, J. 1997. *Trauma and Recovery.* New York: Basic Books.

Hewitt, J., J. Wilkenfeld, and T. Gurr, eds. 2010. *Peace and Conflict 2010.* Boulder, CO: Paradigm.

Hilty, J. A. and P. J. Carnevale. 1993. Black-Hat/White-Hat Strategy in Bilateral Negotiation. *Organizational Behavior and Human Decision Processes* 55: 444–469.

Hoddie, M., and C. Hartzell. 2005. Power Sharing in Peace Settlements: Initiating the Transition from Civil War. In *Sustainable Peace: Power and Democracy After Civil Wars,* ed. P. Roeder and D. S. Rothchild, 83–106. Ithaca, NY: Cornell University Press.

Hodgson, M.G.S. 1977. *The Venture of Islam, Volume 3: The Gunpowder Empires and Modern Times.* Chicago: University of Chicago Press.

Hoebel, E. A. 1940. The Political Organization and Law-ways of the Comanche Indians. *Memoirs of the American Anthropological Association* 54: 36.

Hofstede, G. H. 2005. *Cultures and Organizations: Software of the Mind,* 2nd ed. New York: McGraw-Hill.

Högbladh, S. 2006. Patterns of Peace Agreements—Presenting new Data on Peace Processes and Peace Agreements. Presented at the 2006 annual meeting of the International Studies Association, March 22, San Diego, CA. http://www.allacademic.com/meta/p_mla_apa_research_citation/0/9/9/1/2/p99120_index.html.

Hollenbach, D. 2010. Humanitarian Intervention. Commonwealth. November 3, 2010. http://www.commonwealmagazine.org/humanitarian-intervention-0.

Homer. 1974. *The Iliad.* Trans. Robert Fitzgerald. New York: Anchor Books/Doubleday.

Hopmann, P. T. 1998. *The Negotiation Process and the Resolution of International Conflicts.* Columbia: University of South Carolina Press.

Horne, A. 2006. *A Savage War of Peace: Algeria 1954–1962.* New York: New York Review of Books Classics.

Horowitz, I. L. 1973. *War and Peace in Contemporary Social and Philosophical Theory.* London: Souvenir Press.

Howell, S. 1988. From Child to Human: Chewong Concepts of Self. In *Acquiring Culture: Cross Cultural Studies in Child Development*, ed. G. Jahoda and I. M. Lewis, 147–168. London: Croom Helm.

Hsiao, K. 1977. Legalism and Autocracy in Traditional China. In *Shang Yang's Reforms and State Control in China*, ed. Yu-ning Li. White Plains, NY: M. E. Sharpe.

Hsu, C. 2005. Entrepreneur for Social Change. *US News & World report*, October 31. http://www.usnews.com/usnews/news/articles/051031/31drayton.htm.

Hui, V. Tin-bor. 2005. *War and State Formation in Ancient China and Early Modern Europe.* New York: Cambridge University Press.

Hui, V. Tin-bor. 2008. How China Was Ruled? *The American Interest* (March/April): 53–67.

Human Rights Council. 2010. Situation of Human Rights in the Democratic Republic of the Congo and the Strengthening of Technical Cooperation and Consultative Services, Resolution 13/22 adopted by the Human Rights Council at Thirteenth session, A/HRC/RES/13/22, New York, April 15.

Human Rights Watch. 2008. *Ballots to Bullets, Organized Political Violence and Kenya's Crisis of Governance,* Online report. March 16. http://www.hrw.org/en/reports/2008/03/16/ballots-bullets.

Human Rights Watch. 2010. *Where Is the Justice? Interethnic Violence in Southern Kyrgyzstan and its Aftermath,* August 16. http://www.hrw.org/en/reports/2010/08/16/where-justice.

Human Security Centre. 2006. *Human Security Brief 2006.* Vancouver: Human Security Centre, University of British Columbia.

Hume, C. R. 1994. *Ending Mozambique's War: The Role of Mediation and Good Offices.* Washington, DC: United States Institute of Peace Press.

Huntington, S. P. 1997. *The Clash of Civilizations and the Remaking of World Order.* New York: Simon and Schuster.

ICISS. 2001. *The Responsibility to Protect.* Report of the International Commission on Intervention and State Sovereignty, December 2001.

Ihonvbere, J. 2000. *Towards a new Constitutionalism in Africa.* London: Centre for Democracy and Development.

Iklé, F. 1971. *Every War Must End.* New York: Columbia University Press.

Iltezam Morrar interview. http://www.justvision.org/portrait/96566/interview.

Impagliazzo, M., and M. Giro. 1997. *Algeria in ostaggio: tra esercito e fondamentalismo, stroria di una pace difficile.* Milan: Guerini.

Ingelaere, B. 2009. "Does the Truth Pass across the Fire without Burning?" Locating the Short Circuit in Rwanda's Gacaca Courts. *The Journal of Modern African Studies* 47, no. 4: 507–528.

Institute for Economics and Peace. 2010. *2010 Global Peace Index: Methodology, Results and Findings.* http://reliefweb.int/sites/reliefweb.int/files/resources/Full_Report_1575.pdf.

International Coalition for the Responsibility to Protect. n.d. *The Crisis in Burma.* http://www.responsibilitytoprotect.org/index.php/crises/crisis-in-burma.

International Coalition for the Responsibility to Protect. n.d. *Crisis in the Democratic Republic of Congo.* http://www.responsibilitytoprotect.org/index.php/crises/crisis-in-drc.

International Commission on Intervention and State Sovereignty (ICISS). 2001. Ottawa: IDRC. XI., 13, 2.

International Commission on Missing Persons. n.d. *Podrinje Identification Project in Tuzla.* http://www.ic-mp.org/.

International Crisis Group (ICG). 2006. *Darfur's Fragile Peace Agreement*. http://www. crisisgroup.org/en/regions/africa/horn-of-africa/sudan/B039-darfurs-frag ile-peace-agreement.aspx.

Interpeace. 2010. Connecting the Dots: Linking Peacemaking to Peacebuilding to Development. Workshop presented at the Interpeace and the Peacebuilding and Stabilization Unit of the Government of the Netherlands, June 8, Geneva.

In Women's Hands. 2010. www.inwomenshands.org.

Irani, G. E., and N. C. Funk. 1998. Rituals of Reconciliation: Arab-Islamic Perspectives. *Arab Studies Quarterly (ASQ)* 20, no. 4: 53–55.

IRIN Weekly Round-up 1. 2000. UN Office for the Coordination of Humanitarian Affairs Integrated Regional Information Network for the Horn of Africa. http:// www.cidi.org/report/6710.

Irvine, A. D. 2009. Russell's Paradox. http://plato.stanford.edu/entries/russell-paradox/.

Islamist Insurgents Assault Mogadishu Airport. 2010. *France 24*, October 9. http:// www.france24.com/en/20100909-islamist-insurgents-assault-mogadishu-air port-somalia.

Ismael, J. S., and W. W. Haddad, eds. 2006. *Barriers to Reconciliation: Case Studies on Iraq and the Palestine-Israel Conflict*. New York: University Press of America.

Ivekovic, I. 1999. Peace Studies from a Global Perspective. In *Peace Studies from a Global Perspective*, ed. U. Oswald-Spring, 186–251. Delhi: Madhyam Books.

Iyamuremye, J. 2006. How Rwanda's Education System let Genocide to Abound. *The New York Times*. http://allafrica.com/stories/printable/200601190104.html.

Iyer, R. N., and W. Spencer. 1973. *The Moral and Political thought of Mahatma Gandhi*. Vol. 2. Oxford: Oxford University Press.

Jack, H. A. 1994. *The Gandhi Reader: A Sourcebook of His Life and Writings*. New York: Grove Press.

Jackson, T. F. 2007. From Civil Rights to Human Rights: Martin Luther King, Jr., and the Struggle for Economic Justice. In *Politics and Culture in Modern America*, ed. M. Kazin, G. Gilmore, and T. J. Sugrue. Philadelphia: University of Pennsylvania Press.

Jafari, S. 2007. Local Religious Peacemakers: An Untapped Resource in U.S. Foreign Policy. *Journal of International Affairs* 61, no. 1: 111–130.

Jeong, Ho-Won. 2000. *Peace and Conflict Studies: An Introduction*. Studies in peace and conflict research. Aldershot, UK: Ashgate.

Jing-shen Tao. 1983. Barbarians or Northerners: Northern Sung Images of the Khitans. In *China among Equals: The Middle Kingdom and its Neighbors, 10th–14th centuries*, ed. M. Rossabi, 66–88. Los Angeles: University of California Press.

Joachim, H. H., and D. A. Rees. 1951. *Aristotle. The Nicomachean Ethics: A Commentary*. Oxford: Clarendon Press.

Johnson, D. W., R. T. Johnson, and D. Tjosvold. 2000. Constructive Controversy: The Value of Intellectual Opposition. In *The Handbook of Conflict Resolution: Theory and Practice*, ed. M. Deutsch and P. T. Coleman, 65–85. San Francisco: Jossey-Bass.

Johnson, D. W., R. T. Johnson, and K. A. Smith. 2000. Constructive Controversy: The Power of Intellectual Conflict. *Change* 32, no. 1: 28–37.

Johnson, J. T. 1975. *Ideology, Reason, and the Limitation Religious and Secular Concepts, 1200–1740*. Princeton, NJ: Princeton University Press.

Johnson, S. 2001. *Emergence: The Connected Lives of Ants, Brains, Cities, and Software*. New York: Scribner.

Johnston, A. I. 1998. *Cultural Realism: Strategic Culture and Grand Strategy in Chinese History*. Princeton, NJ: Princeton University Press.

Johnston, D., and C. Sampson. 1995. *Religion, the Missing Dimension of Statecraft.* New York: Oxford University Press.

Johnston, D. 2003. *Faith-Based Diplomacy: Trumping Realpolitik.* New York: Oxford University Press.

Jolly, R., L. Emmerij, and T. G. Weiss. 2009. *UN Ideas that Changed the World.* Bloomington: Indiana University Press.

Jones, B. D. 2002. The Challenges of Strategic Coordination. In *Ending Civil Wars: The Implementation of Peace Agreements*, ed. S. J. Stedman, D. S. Rothchild, and E. M. Cousens, 89–115. Boulder, CO: Lynne Rienner.

Jones, W., and S. H. Hughes. 2003. Complexity, Conflict Resolution and how the Mind Works. *Conflict Resolution Quarterly* 20: 4–20.

Jordan, L., and P. van Tuijl, eds. 2006. *NGO Accountability: Politics, Principles and Innovations.* London: Earthscan.

Kacoke Madit. 2000. *The Quest for Peace in Northern Uganda.* London: Kacoke Madit.

Kang, D. C. 2010. *East Asia Before the West: Five Centuries of Trade and Tribute.* New York: Columbia University Press.

Kacowicz, A., Y. Bar-Siman, O. Elgstrom, and M. Jerneck, eds. 2000. *Stable Peace Among Nations.* Lanham, MD: Rowman & Littlefield.

Kauffman, S. A. 1995. *At Home in the Universe: The Search for Laws of Self-organization and Complexity.* New York: Oxford University Press.

Kauffman, S. A. 2008. *Reinventing the Sacred: A New View of Science, Reason, and Religion.* New York: Basic Books.

Kaufman, J., K. P. Williams, and K. Williams. 2010. *Women and War: Gender Identity and Activism in Times of Conflict.* Sterling, VA: Kumarian Press.

Kaufmann, D., A. Kraay, and M. Mastruzzi. 2009. *Governance Matters 2009.* Washington, DC: World Bank Publications.

Kayoya, M. 2007. *Entre deux mondes: D'une génération à l'autre.* Bologna, Italy: Grafiche Universal.

Kegan, R. 1982. *The Evolving Self: Problem and Process in Human Development.* Cambridge, MA: Harvard University Press.

Kelman, H. C. 1972. The Problem-Solving Workshop in Conflict Resolution. In *Communication in International Politics*, ed. R. L. Merritt, 168–200. Urbana, IL: University of Illinois Press.

Kelman, H. C. 1995. Contributions of an Unofficial Conflict Resolution Effort to the Israeli-Palestinian Breakthrough. *Negotiation Journal* 11, no. 1: 19.

Kelman, H. C. 1996. The Interactive Problem-Solving Approach. In *Managing Global Chaos: Sources of and Responses to International Conflict*, ed. C. A. Crocker, F. O. Hampson, and P. R. Aall, 501–520. Washington, DC: United States Institute of Peace Press.

Kelman, H. C. 2008. Evaluating the Contributions of Interactive Problem Solving to the Resolution of Ethnonational Conflicts. *Peace and Conflict: Journal of Peace Psychology* 14, no. 1 (January): 29–60.

Kelman, H. C., R. S. Ezekiel, with the collaboration of R. B. Kelman. 1970. *Cross-National Encounters.* San Francisco: Jossey-Bass.

Kelman, H. C., and S. P. Cohen. 1976. The Problem-solving Workshop: A Social-Psychological Contribution to the Resolution of International Conflicts. *Journal of Peace Research* 13, no. 2: 79–90.

Keohane, R. O. 1984. *After Hegemony: Cooperation and Discord in the World Political Economy.* Princeton, NJ: Princeton University Press.

Keohane, R. O., and J. S. Nye. 1977. *Power and Interdependence: World Politics in Transition.* Boston: Little, Brown.

Keohane, R. O., and L. Martin. 1995. The Promise of Institutionalist Theory. *International Security* 20, no. 1: 39–51.

Khadiagala, G. L. 2007. *Meddlers or Mediators? African Intervention in Civil Conflict in Eastern Africa*. Leiden, Netherlands: Brill.

Khadiagalia, G. L. 2008. *Eastern Africa: Security and the Legacy of Fragility*. New York: International Peace Institute.

Khamisa, A. n.d. Bibliography. http://www.azimkhamisa.com/topics/view/17771/.

Khamisa, A. 2006. A Father's Journey from Murder to Forgiveness. *Reclaiming Children and Youth* 15, no. 1: 15–18.

Khamisa, A. N. 2005. *Azim's Bardo—From Murder to Forgiveness—A Father's Journey*. n.p.: ANK Publishing.

Khan, S. R. 2008. *Regional Trade Integration and Conflict Resolution*. New York: Routledge.

Khoza, R. 1994. *Ubuntu: African Humanism*. Occasional Paper. Johannesburg: HSRC.

Kim, S., ed. 2008. *Peace and Reconciliation: In Search of Shared Identity*. Aldershot: Ashgate.

King, M. L. Jr. 1963. *Strength to Love*. Philadelphia: Fortress Press.

King, M. L. Jr. 1964a. Martin Luther King—Nobel Lecture. http://nobelprize.org/nobel_prizes/peace/laureates/1964/king-lecture.html.

King, M. L. Jr., 1964b. *Why We Can't Wait*. New York: Mentor.

King, M. L. Jr., 1986a. Stride Towards Freedom. In *A Testament of Hope: The Essential Writings and Speeches of Martin Luther King, Jr.*, ed. J. M. Washington, 417–490. New York: HarperCollins.

King, M. L. Jr., 1986b. The Trumpet of Conscience. In *A Testament of Hope: The Essential Writings and Speeches of Martin Luther King, Jr*, ed. J. M. Washington, 634–656. New York: HarperCollins.

King, M. L. Jr., 1991. A Testament of Hope. In *A Testament of Hope: The Essential Writings and Speeches of Martin Luther King, Jr*, ed. J. M Washington, 313–330. New York: HarperOne.

King, M. E. 2005. What Difference Does it Make? Gender as a Tool in Building Peace. In *Gender and Peace Building in Africa*, ed. D. Rodriguez and E. Natukunda-Togboa, 27–50. Ciudad Colon, Costa Rica: University of Peace.

King, M. L. Jr., C. S. King, and V. Harding. 1968. *Where do We Go from Here: Chaos or Community?* Boston: Beacon Press.

King, M. E. 2007. *A Quiet Revolution: The First Palestinian Intifada and Nonviolent Resistance*. New York: Nation Books.

King, U. 2008. *The Search for Spirituality: Our Global Quest for a Spiritual Life*. New York: BlueBridge.

Kiser, J. W. 2008. *Commander of the Faithful: The Life and Times of Emir Abd el-Kader*. Rhinebeck, New York: Monkfish.

Kishtainy, K. 1990. Violent and Nonviolent Struggle in Arab History. In *Arab Nonviolent Political Struggle in the Middle East*, ed. R. Crow, P. Grant, and S. I. Ibrahim, 9–24. Boulder, CO: Lynne Rienner Publishers.

Kister, M., ed. 1972. Haddithu 'Bani Isra'il wa-la Haraja: A Study of an Early Tradition. In *Israel Oriental Studies II*. Piscataway, NJ: Transaction Publishers.

Klaiber, J. L. 1998. *The Church, Dictatorships, and Democracy in Latin America*. Maryknoll, NY: Orbis Books.

Klein, M. W. 1995. *The American Street Gang*. New York: Oxford University Press.

Koch, K. F., S. Altorki, A. Arno, and L. Hickson. 1977. Ritual Reconciliation and the Obviation of Grievances: A Comparative Study in the Ethnography of Law. *Ethnology* 16, no. 3: 269–283.

Kontos, L., D. Brotherton, and L. Barrios. 2003. *Gangs and Society: Alternative Perspectives*. New York: Columbia University Press.

Kordas, A. 2000. Losing My Religion: Controlling Gang Violence through Limitations on Freedom of Expression. *Boston University Law Review* 80: 1451–1492. http:// heinonline.org/HOL/Page?handle=hein.journals/bulr80&id=1469&div=&col lection=journals.

Kouchner, B. 2008. Violence in Kenya. *France Diplomatie,* January 31.

Kouchner, B., and M. Bettati. 1987. *Le Devoir D'ingerence: Peut-on les Laisser Mourir?* Paris: Denoel.

Kramer, M. R. 2005. *Measuring Innovation. Evaluation in the Field of Social Entrepreneurship.* The Skoll Foundation. http://www.foundationstrategy.com/documents/ Measuring%20Innovation.pdf.

Kriesberg, L. 1992. *International Conflict Resolution: The U.S.-USSR and Middle East Cases.* New Haven, CT: Yale University Press.

Kriesberg, L. 2005. Nature, Dynamics, and Phases of Intractability. In *Grasping the Nettle: Analyzing Cases of Intractable Conflict,* ed. C. A. Crocker, F. O. Hampson, and P. Aall, 65–98. Washington, DC: United States Institute of Peace.

Kriesberg, L. 2007a. *Constructive Conflicts: From Escalation to Resolution,* 3rd ed. Lanham, MD: Rowman & Littlefield.

Kriesberg, L. 2007b. Long Peace or Long War: A Conflict Resolution Perspective. *Negotiation Journal* 23, no. 2: 97–116.

Kriesberg, L. 2009. Changing Conflict Asymmetries Constructively. *Dynamics of Asymmetric Conflict* 2, no. 1 (March): 4–22.

Krishna, S. 1999. *Postcolonial Insecurities: India, Sri Lanka, and the Question of Nationhood.* Minneapolis: University of Minnesota Press.

Krugman, P. R. 1999. *The Return of Depression Economics.* New York: Penguin Press.

Kruz, C. 2010. *Peacebuilding in Liberia.* Reflecting on Peace Practice Project, CDA Collaborative Learning Projects.

Kupers, T. A., and H. Toch. 1999. *Prison Madness: The Mental Health Crisis behind Bars and what We must Do about it.* San Francisco: Jossey-Bass.

Kut, G. n.d. *Kenya: Towards the National Policy on Peacebuilding and Conflict Management.* GPPAC Issue Paper on Joint Action for Prevention: Civil Society and Government Cooperation on Conflict Prevention and Peacebuilding. http://www. gppac.net/page.php?id=1889.

Kutsukake, N. 2009. Complexity, Dynamics and Diversity of Sociality in Group-living Mammals. *Ecological Research* 24, no. 3: 521–531.

Kydd, A. 2003. Which Side Are You On? Bias, Credibility, and Mediation. *American Journal of Political Science* 47, no. 4: 597–611.

Kymlicka, W., ed. 2008. *Politics of Reconciliation in Multicultural Societies.* Oxford: Oxford University Press.

Lacina, B. 2006. *Analysis of Uppsala War Terminations Data.* Memo. Uppsala, Sweden: Human Security Centre, August.

LaFayette, B., and D. C. Jehnsen. 1995. *The Briefing Booklet: An Orientation to the Kingian Nonviolence Conflict Reconciliation Program & The Leaders Manual—A Structured Guide and Introduction to Kingian Nonviolence: The Philosophy and Methodology.* Galena, OH: IHRR Publications.

Lagerspetz, O. 1998. *Trust: The Tacit Demand.* Dordrecht: Klower Academic Publishers.

Large, J., and Aguswandi, eds. 2008. Reconfiguring Politics: The Indonesia—Aceh Peace Process. *Conciliation Resource.* http://www.c-r.org/our-work/accord/ aceh/contents.php.

Larke, B. 2009. ". . . And the Truth Shall Set You Free": Confessional Trade-Offs and Community Reconciliation in East Timor. Asian Journal of Social Science 37, no. 4: 646–676.

Latané, B., and A. Nowak. 1994. Attitudes as Catastrophes: From Dimensions to Categories with Increasing Involvement. In *Dynamical Systems in Social Psychology*,
ed. R. R. Vallacher and A. Nowak, 219–249. San Diego: Academic Press.

Lau, D. C. 2003. *Mencius*. Hong Kong: Chinese University Press.

Lau, Nap-yin. 2000. Waging War for Peace? The Peace Accord between the Song and
the Liao in AD 1005. In *Warfare in Chinese history*, ed. H. J. Van de Ven, 180–221.
Leiden, the Netherlands: Brill.

Leadbeater, C. 1997. *The Rise of the Social Entrepreneur*. London: Demos.

LeBaron, M., and N. Alexander. 2010. Exporting Mediation Through Roleplays:
Intercultural Considerations in Knowledge Transfer, *International and Re-
gional Perspectives on Cross-Cultural Mediation* 5. Studien zur interkulturellen
Mediation.

Lederach, J. P. 1995. *Preparing for Peace: Conflict Transformation across Cultures*. Syracuse:
Syracuse University Press.

Lederach, J. P. 1996. *Preparing for Peace. Conflict Transformation across Cultures*. Syracuse,
NY: Syracuse University Press.

Lederach, J. P. 1997. *Building Peace: Sustainable Reconciliation in Divided Societies*. Washington, DC: United States Institute of Peace Press.

Lederach, J. P. 2003. *The Little Book of Conflict Transformation*. Intercourse, PA: Good
Books.

Lederach, J. P. 2005. *The Moral Imagination: The Art and Soul of Building Peace*. New
York: Oxford University Press.

Lederach, J. P. 2010. *The Moral Imagination: The Art and Soul of Building Peace*. Reprint.
New York: Oxford University Press.

Lederach, J. P., and A. J. Lederach. 2010. *When Blood and Bones Cry Out: Journeys through
the Soundscape of Healing and Reconciliation*. St. Lucia: University of Queensland
Press.

Leebaw, B. A. 2008. The Irreconcilable Goals of Transitional Justice. *Human Rights
Quarterly* 30, no. 1: 95–118.

Lemarchand, R. 1994. *Burundi: Ethnocide as Discourse and Practice*. New York: Woodrow
Wilson Center Press and Cambridge University Press.

Lemarchand, R. 2009. *The Dynamics of Violence in Central Africa*. Philadelphia: University of Pennsylvania.

Lerche, C. O. 2000. Truth Commissions and National Reconciliation: Some Reflections
on Theory and Practice. *Peace and Conflict Studies* 7, no. 1: 1.

Levi, P. 1989. *The Drowned and the Saved*. New York: Vintage Books.

Levine, R. A., and D. T. Campbell. 1972. *Ethnocentrism: Theories of Conflict, Ethnic Attitudes and Group Behavior*. New York: Wiley

Levy, J. S. 1989. The Diversionary Theory of War: A Critique. In *Handbook of war studies*,
ed. M. Midlarsky, 259–288. London: Unwin Hyman.

Lewis, B. 1984. *The Jews of Islam*. Princeton, NJ: Princeton University Press.

Lewis, M. E. 1990. *Sanctioned Violence in early China*. Albany: State University of New
York Press.

Leydesdorff, S. 2007. Stories from No Land: The Women of Srebrenica Speak Out.
Human Rights Review 8, no. 3: 187–198.

Licklider, R. 1995. The Consequences of Negotiated Settlements in Civil Wars,
1945–1993. *American Political Science Review* 89, no. 3: 681–690.

Lieberfeld, D. 1999. *Talking with the Enemy: Negotiation and Threat Perception in South
Africa and Israel/Palestine*. Westport, CT: Praeger.

Lieberfeld, D. 2002. Evaluating the Contributions of Track-Two Diplomacy to Conflict
Termination in South Africa, 1984–90. *Journal of Peace Research* 39: 355–372.

Lieberfeld, D. 2005. Contributions of a Semi-Official Prenegotiation Initiative in South Africa: Afrikaner-ANC Meetings in England, 1987–1990. In *Paving the Way*, ed. R. J. Fisher, 105–125. Lanham, MD: Lexington Books.

Lieberfeld, D. 2007. Promoting Tractability in South Africa and Israel/Palestine: The Role of Semiofficial Meetings. *American Behavioral Scientist* 50: 1542–1562.

The Limits of the Liberal Peace—A Mediator's View. 2006. Background Paper. Oslo Forum 06. www.hdcentre.org/files/TheLimitsoftheLiberalPeace.pdf.

Lindberg, S. I. 2006. *Democracy and Elections in Africa.* Baltimore, MD: Johns Hopkins University Press.

Lindgren, M., P. Wallensteen, and H. Grusell. 2010. *Meeting the Challenges to International Mediation.* Uppsala, Sweden: Uppsala University, Department of Peace and Conflict Research, UCDP Report 7.

Lindner, E. 2006. *Making Enemies: Humiliation and International Conflict.* Westport, CT: Praeger.

Lipson, C. 1991. Why Are some International Agreements Informal? *International Organization* 45: 495–538.

Litchfield, J. 1999. *Inequality: Methods and Tools.* Washington, DC: World Bank Publications.

Little, D., ed. 2007. *Peacemakers in Action: Profiles of Religion in Conflict Resolution.* Cambridge: Cambridge University Press.

Littleton, C. S. 2002. *Mythology: The Illustrated Anthology of World Myth and Storytelling.* London: Duncan Baird Publishers.

Lockhart, C. 1979. *Bargaining in International Conflicts.* New York: Columbia University Press.

Lodge, T. 2006. *Mandela: A Critical Life.* Oxford, England: Oxford University Press.

Lodge, T., and Nasson, B. 1991. *All, Here, and Now: Black Politics in South Africa in the 1980s.* New York: Ford Foundation & Foreign Policy Association.

Lonergan, B. 1957. *Insight: An Essay in Human Understanding.* London: Longman's Green.

Lonergan, B. 1972. *Method in Theology.* New York: Herder and Herder.

Lonergan, B. 1974. *Insight: A Study of Human Understanding.* San Francisco: Harper and Row.

Lonergan, B. 1985a. Aristotle's Posterior Analytic, "Aquinas Today: Tradition and Innovation". In *A Third Collection: Papers by Bernard J. F. Lonergan, S. J.,* ed. Frederick E. Crowe, 41–44. New York: Paulist Press.

Lonergan, B. 1985b. Method: Trend and Variations. In *A Third Collection: Papers by Bernard J. F. Lonergan, S. J.,* ed. Frederick E. Crowe, 13–22. New York: Paulist Press.

Lonergan, B. 1985c. The Ongoing Genesis of Methods. In *A Third Collection: Papers by Bernard J. F. Lonergan, S. J.,* ed. Frederick E. Crowe, 146–165. New York: Paulist Press.

Lonergan, B. 1985d. A Post-Hegelian Philosophy of Religion. In *A Third Collection: Papers by Bernard J. F. Lonergan, S. J.,* ed. F. E. Crowe, 205. New York: Paulist Press.

Long, W., and P. Brecke. 2003. *War and Reconciliation: Reason and Emotion in Conflict Resolution.* Cambridge, MA: The MIT Press.

Los Angeles City Council's Ad Hoc Committee on Gang Violence and Youth Development. 2008. *The Community Engagement Advisory Committee's Community-Based Gang Intervention Model: Definition and Structure.* http://www.westernjustice.org/documents/GangInterventionModel.pdf.

Lu, Xun. 1990. *Diary of a Madman and Other Stories.* Trans. William A. Lyell. Honolulu: University of Hawaii Press.

Luck, E. C. 2010. The Responsibility to Protect: Growing Pains or Early Promise? *Ethics and International Affairs* 24, no. 4: 349–365.

Lund, M. S. 1996. *Preventing Violent Conflicts: A Strategy for Preventive Diplomacy.* Washington, DC: United States Institute of Peace Press.

Lyons, T. 2005. *Demilitarizing Politics: Elections on the Uncertain Road to Peace.* Boulder, CO: Lynne Rienner.

MacIntyre, A. 1984. Is Patriotism a Virtue? The EH Lindley Memorial Lecture, University of Kansas, Lawrence.

Mack, A. 2007. *Global Patterns of Political Violence.* Working Paper. New York: International Peace Academy.

Mack, A., and Z. Nielsen. 2009. *Human Security Report: The Shrinking Costs of War.* Human Security Report. Vancouver, BC: Human Security Report Project. http://www.humansecuritygateway.com/documents/HSRP_ShrinkingCostsOfWar.pdf.

Mair, J., J. Robinson, and K. Hockerts. 2006. Introduction. In *Social Entrepreneurship,* ed. J. Mair, J. Robinson, and K. Hockerts, 1–13. New York: Palgrave MacMillan.

Major Episodes of Political Violence, 1946–2009, Dataset Posted on the Center for Systemic Peace website. www.systemicpeace.org/inscr/inscr.htm.

Makoba, Johnson W., and E. Ndura. 2006. The Roots of Contemporary Ethnic Conflict and Violence in Burundi. In *Perspectives on Contemporary Ethnic Conflict: Primal Violence or the Politics of Conviction?,* ed. Santosh C. Saha, 295–310. Lanham, MD: Lexington Books.

Malan, J. 1997. *Conflict Resolution Wisdom from Africa.* Durban: Accord.

Malhotra, D., and M. H. Bazerman. 2007. Investigative Negotiation. *Harvard Business Review* 85, no. 9: 72.

Mamdani, M. 2001. *When Victims become Killers: Colonialism, Nativism, and the Genocide in Rwanda.* Princeton, NJ: Princeton University Press.

Mandela, N. 1994. *Long Walk to Freedom.* New York: Little Brown.

Mandela, N. 2007. Foreword. In *Shades of Difference: Mac Maharaj and the Struggle for South Africa,* ed. P. O'Malley, 1–20. New York: Penguin.

Manning, C. 2007. Interim Governments and the Construction of Political Elites. In *Interim Governments: Institutional Bridges to Peace and Democracy?,* ed. K. Guttieri and J. Piombo, 53–72. Washington, DC: United States Institute of Peace Press.

A Manual on Kingian Nonviolence. n.d. The Martin Luther King, Jr. Center for Nonviolent Social Change, Inc.

Maoz, I. 2000a. An Experiment in Peace: Reconciliation-aimed Workshops of Jewish-Israeli and Palestinian Youth. *Journal of Peace Research* 37, no. 6: 721–737.

Maoz, I. 2000b. Social Psychology of Intergroup Reconciliation: From Violent Conflict to Peaceful Co-Existence. *Journal of Peace Research* 37, no. 6: 721–737.

Mapendere, J., and J. Neu. 2009. *Supporting Eminent Persons as Mediators.* United Nations Department of Political Affairs Draft Operational Guidance Note. New York: United Nations.

Maphisa, S. 1994. Man in Constant Search of Ubuntu—A Dramatist's Obsession. Unpublished conference paper presented at the Ubuntu Conference (AIDSA). Pietermaritzburg, University of Natal.

Marks, S. C. 2000. *Ubuntu, Spirit of Africa: Example for the World.* Washington, DC: United States Institute of Peace Press.

Marsh, J. 1988. *Post-Cartesian Meditations: An Essay in Dialectical Phenomenology.* New York: Fordham University Press.

Marshall, C. D. 2001. *Beyond Retribution: A New Testament Vision for Justice, Crime, and Punishment*. Grand Rapids, MI: Wm. B. Eerdmans.

Marshall, M. G. 1999. *Third World War: System, Process, and Conflict Dynamics*. Lanham, MD: Rowman & Littlefield.

Marshall, M. G., and B. R. Cole. 2009. Global Report 2009: Conflict, Governance, and State Fragility. Center for Global Policy. http://www.humansecuritygateway.com/documents/CSP_GlobalReport2009_ConflictGovernanceStateFragility.pdf.

Marshall, M. G. 2008. *A Macro-Comparative Analysis of the Problem of Factionalism in Emerging Democracies*. Paper delivered at the 2008 Annual Meeting of the American Political Science Association in Boston, August 29.

Marshall, M. G., and B. R. Cole. 2010. *State Fragility Index and Matrix 2009*. www.systemicpeace.org/SFImatrix2009c.pdf.

Maruyama, M. 1963. The Second Cybernetics: Deviation Amplifying Mutual Causal Processes. *American Scientist* 51: 164–179.

Maruyama, M. 1982. Mindscapes, Management, Business Policy, and Public Policy. *Academy of Management Review* 7: 612–619.

Martin, H. 2006. *Kings of Peace, Pawns of War: The Untold Story of Peace-Making*. London: Continuum.

Martin, M. 2007. *Intervening at the Inflection Point*. UBS Philanthropy Services Viewpoints. http://www.acumenfund.org/uploads/assets/documents/Viewpoints%202007%20-%20UBS_3GnYUiZ5.pdf.

Martin, R. L., and Osberg, S. 2007. Social Entrepreneurship: The Case for Definition. *Stanford Social Innovation Review* Spring: 29–39.

Masina, N. 2000. Xhosa Practices of Ubuntu for South Africa. In *Traditional Cures for Modern Conflicts: African Conflict "Medicine,"* ed. I. W. Zartman, 169–182. Boulder, CO: Lynne Rienner.

Mathews, D. 2001. *War Prevention Works: 50 Stories of People Resolving Conflict*. Oxford: Oxford Research Group.

Mattes, M., and B. Savun. 2009. Fostering Peace after Civil War: Commitment Problems and Agreement Design. *International Studies Quarterly* 53, no. 3: 737–759.

Maxson, C. L., K. Hennigan, D. Sloane, and K. A. Kolnick. 2004. *Can Civil Gang Injunctions Change Communities? A Community Assessment of the Impact of Civil Gang Injunctions*. Irvine: University of California, School of Social Ecology.

McCarthy, M. 1989. *The Crisis in Philosophy*. New York: SUNY Press.

McCartney, C. 1999. *Striking a Balance: The Northern Ireland Peace Process*. Accord, Issue 8. Conciliation Resources. http://www.c-r.org/our-work/accord/northern-ireland/index.php.

McDonald, J. W. 1991. Further Exploration of Track Two Diplomacy. In *Timing the De-Escalation of International Conflicts*, ed. Louis Kriesberg and Stuart J Thorson, 201–220. Syracuse studies on peace and conflict resolution. Syracuse, NY: Syracuse University Press.

McDonald, J. W. 2003. Multi-Track Diplomacy. In *Beyond Intractability*, ed. G. Burgess and H. Burgess. Boulder, CO: Conflict Research Consortium, University of Colorado. http://www.beyondintractability.org/essay/multi-track_diplomacy/?nid=1332.

McDonald, J. W., and D. B. Bendahmane. 1987. *Conflict Resolution: Track Two Diplomacy*. Washington, DC: Foreign Service Institute, U.S. Dept. of State.

McGonegal, J. 2009. *Imagining Justice: The Politics of Postcolonial Forgiveness and Reconciliation*. Montreal: McGill-Queen's University Press.

McGuigan, R. 2006. *How Do Evolving Deep Structures of Consciousness Impact the Dis-putant's Creation of Meaning in a Conflict?* Cincinnati, OH: Union Institute and University.

McHugh, G. 2010. Integrate Human Rights and Interests of IDPs in the Peace Agreement. In *The Peacemaker's Toolkit Series*, ed. Heather Coyne and Nigel Quinney, 51–65. Washington, DC: United States Institute of Peace Press. http://www. usip.org/files/resources/USIP_PMT_Bern_IDP.pdf.

McHugh, G., and M. Bessler. 2006a. *Guidelines on Humanitarian Negotiations with Armed Groups.* New York: United Nations.

McHugh, G., and M. Bessler. 2006b. *Humanitarian Negotiations with Armed Groups: A Manual for Practitioners.* New York: United Nations.

McIntyre, J. 2010. Interview: Budrus "Built a Model of Civil Resistance." November 4. http://electronicintifada.net/v2/article11608.shtml.

McKenzie, D. 2004. *Measuring Inequality with Asset Indicators.* Stanford, CA: Stanford University Press.

Mearsheimer, J. J. 1995. The False Promise of International Institutions. *International Security* 19, no. 3: 5–49.

Mediation Support Unit. 2010a. *Decision-Making Procedures in Ceasefire Implementation Mechanisms.* Think Piece on Darfur Mediation. New York: United Nations, June 12.

Mediation Support Unit. 2010b. *Partial Ceasefire Agreements.* Think Piece on Darfur Mediation. New York: United Nations, June 25.

Meggitt, M. J. 1977. *Blood Is Their Argument: Warfare among the Mae Enga Tribesmen of the New Guinea Highlands.* Mountain View, CA: Mayfield.

Melander, E. 2001. The Nagorno-Karabakh Conflict Revisited: Was the War Inevitable? *Journal of Cold War Studies* 3, no. 2: 48–75.

Melander, E., F. Möller, and M. Öberg. 2009. Managing Intrastate Low-Intensity Armed Conflict 1993–2004: A New Dataset. *International Interactions* 35, no. 2: 1–28.

Melber, H. 2004. Regional Cooperation: What Future for SADC? *Pambazuka* 180, October 28. http://pambazuka.org/en/category/features/25380.

Melchin, K. R., and C. A. Picard. 2008. *Transforming Conflict through Insight.* Toronto: University of Toronto Press.

Melin, M. and I. Svensson. 2009. Incentives for Talking: Acceptance of Mediation in International and Civil Wars. *International Interactions* 35, no. 3: 249–271.

Memorial. 2009. *An Appeal of a Systematically Exterminated People.* August 15. http:// www.war-memorial.net/mem_det.asp?ID=62.

Mendelson, S. E., and J. K. Glenn. 2002. *The Power and Limits of NGOs: A Critical Look at Building Democracy in Eastern Europe and Eurasia.* New York: Columbia University Press.

Merikallio, K. 2006. *Making Peace: Ahtisaari and Aceh.* Helsinki, Finland: WS Bookwell Oy.

Mesquita, B. B. de. 1983. *The War Trap.* New Haven, CT: Yale University Press.

Meyer, C. O. 2010. Recasting the Warning-Response Problem: Persuasion and Preventive Policy. *International Studies Review* 12: 556–578.

Miall, H. 2004. Conflict Transformation: A Multi-Dimensional Task. In *Transforming Ethnopolitical Conflict: The Berghof Handbook*, ed. A. Austin, M. Fischer, and N. Ropers, 67–89. Wiesbaden, Germany: VS Verlag.

Michel, T. F. 2010. *A Christian View of Islam.* New York: Orbis Books.

Mikkelsen, T. S., L. W. Hillier, E. E. Eichler, M. C. Zody, D. B. Jaffe, S. P. Yang, W. Enard, et al. 2005. Initial Sequence of the Chimpanzee Genome and Comparison with the Human Genome. *Nature* 437: 69–87.

Miklikowska, M., and D. P. Fry. 2010. Values for Peace: Ethnographic Lessons From the Semai of Malaysia and the Mardu of Australia. *Beliefs and Values* 2, no. 2: 124–137.

Mills, K., and C. O'Driscoll. 2010. From Humanitarian Intervention to the Responsibility to Protect. In *The International Studies Encyclopedia,* ed. R. A. Denemark, 2532–2552. London: Blackwell.

Ministry of Interior. 2006. National Architecture for Peace in Ghana. http:www.gppac. net/page.php?id=1#par2544,

Minow, M. 1998. *Between Vengeance and Forgiveness: Facing History after Genocide and Mass Violence.* Boston: Beacon Press.

Mitchell, C. (Forthcoming). Causing Conflicts to Continue. In *Value Conflicts and Intercultural Dialogue,* ed. Johanna Seibt and Jaspar Garsdal. Oxford: Oxford University Press.

Mitchell, C. 1995. The Right Moment: Notes on Four Models of "Ripeness." *Paradigms* 9: 38–52.

Mitchell, C. 2001. *Gestures of Conciliation.* Houndsmill, UK: Palgrave/Macmillan.

Mitchell, C. 2006. Conflict, Social Change and Conflict Resolution; An Enquiry. In *Social Change and Conflict Transformation,* ed. David Bloomfied et al., 13–36. Berlin: Berghof Research Center.

Mitchell, C. R. 1981a. *Peacemaking and the Consultant's Role.* New York: Gower Nichols.

Mitchell, C. R. 1981b. *The Structure of International Conflict.* New York: St. Martin's Press.

Mitchell, C. R. 1993. The Process and Stages of Mediation. In *Making War and Waging Peace: Foreign Intervention in Africa,* ed. D. Smock, 139–160. Washington, DC: U.S. Institute of Peace Press.

Mitchell, C. R. 2000. *Gestures of Conciliation: Factors Contributing to Successful Olive Branches.* New York: Macmillan Press.

Mitchell, C. R., I. W. Zartman, and A. Kremenyuk. 1995. Asymmetry and Strategies of Regional Conflict Reduction. In *Cooperative Security: Reducing Third World Wars,* 25–57. Syracuse, NY: Syracuse University Press.

Mitchell, C. R., and M. Banks. 1996. *Handbook of Conflict Resolution: The Analytical Problem Solving Approach.* New York: Pinter.

Moghadam, V. M. 1993. *Modernizing Women: Gender and Social Change in the Middle East.* Cairo: The American University in Cairo Press.

Möller, F. 2006. *Thinking Peaceful Change: Baltic Security Policies and Security Community Building.* Syracuse, NY: Syracuse University Press.

Möller, F. 2010. *Identifying Conflict Prevention Measures: Comparing Two Approaches.* UCDP Paper 5. Uppsala University: Department of Peace and Conflict Research.

Montesquieu, C. 1748. *The Spirit of the Laws.* Cambridge: Cambridge University Press.

Montville, J. V. 1987. The Arrow and the Olive Branch: The Case for Track Two Diplomacy. In *Conflict Resolution: Track Two Diplomacy,* ed. J. W. McDonald and D. B. Bendahmane, 5–20. Washington DC: Foreign Service Institute, Department of State.

Moore, S. 2008. *Military Chaplains as Agents of Peace: The Theology and Praxis of Reconciliation in Stability Operations.* PhD diss., Saint Paul University, Ottawa, Canada.

More, S., and H. Boshoff. 2008. *Reinforcing Efforts to Seize the Fleeting Window of Opportunity in North Kivu (Summary).* CRU Policy Brief. The Hague: The Clingendael Institute, November 2.

Morgan, G. 1997. *Images of Organization.* London: Sage.

Morozzo Della Rocca, R. 2003. *Mozambique: Achieving Peace in Africa.* Washington, DC: Georgetown University Press.

Morozzo Della Rocca, R. 2010. *Fare pace. La Comunità di Sant'Egidio negli scenari internazionali.* Rome: Leonardo.

Morozzo Della Rocca, R., and M. Giro. 1997. *Algeria in ostaggio. Tra esercito e fondamentalismo, storia di una pace difficile.* Milan: Guerini e Associati.

Moses, G. 1997. *Revolution of Conscience: Martin Luther King, Jr., and the Philosophy of Nonviolence.* New York and London: The Guilford Press.

Moynahan, B. 2004. *The Faith: A History of Christianity.* New York: Doubleday.

Murithi, T. 2006. Practical Peacemaking Wisdom from Africa: Reflections on Ubuntu. *Journal of Pan African Studies* 1, no. 4: 25–37.

Murithi, T., and D. Pain. 1999. *African Principles of Conflict Resolution and Reconciliation.* Addis Ababa, Ethiopia: Shebelle Publishing House.

Murithi, T., and P. Murphy-Ives. 2007. Under the Acacia: Mediation and the Dilemma of Inclusion. In *Conflict Mediation in Africa: Challenges and Opportunities,* ed. K. Papagianni, 77–84. Geneva: Centre for Humanitarian Dialogue.

Murphy, J. G., and J. Hampton. 1990. *Forgiveness and Mercy.* Cambridge: Cambridge University Press.

Museveni Wants to Hunt LRA in Congo. 2006. *New Vision,* June 19. http://www.newvision.co.ug/D/8/13/504856.

Möller, F. 2010. Identifying Conflict Prevention Measures: Comparing Two Approaches, UCDP Paper 5. Uppsala University: Department of Peace and Conflict Research.

Nadler, A., T. Malloy, and J. D. Fisher. 2008. *Social Psychology of Intergroup Reconciliation: From Violent Conflict to Peaceful Co-Existence.* New York: Oxford University Press.

Nan, S. Allen. 2008. Conflict Resolution in a Network Society. *International Negotiation* 13, no. 1: 111–131.

Nandy, A. 2001. Defining a New Cosmopolitanism: Towards a Dialogue of Asian Cultures. *Identité, culture et politique* 2, no. 1: 46.

Nathan, L. 2006a. *No Ownership, no Peace: The Darfur Peace Agreement.* Crisis States Working Papers Series No. 2. London: Crisis States Research Centre.

Nathan, L. 2006b. SADC's Uncommon Approach to Common Security, 1992–2003. *Journal of Southern African Studies* 32, no. 3: 605–622.

Nathan, L. 2008. *Anti-Imperialism Trumps Human Rights: South Africa's Approach to the Darfur Conflict.* Working Paper. Series 2. London: Crisis States Research Centre, LSE.

Nathan, L. 2010. The African Union and Regional Organisations in Africa: Communities of Insecurity. *African Security Review* 19, no. 2: 106–113.

National Science Foundation. 2005. *New Clues Add 40,000 Years to Age of Human Species.* Press Release 05–024. February 16. http://www.nsf.gov/news/news_summ.jsp?cntn_id=102968.

Ndikumana, L. 2005. Distributional Conflict, the State and Peace Building in Burundi. *The Round Table* 94, no. 381: 413–427.

Ndura-Ouédraogo, E. 2006a. The Role of Cultural Competence in the Creation of a Culture of Nonviolence. *Culture of Peace Online Journal* 2, no. 1: 39–48.

Ndura-Ouédraogo, E. 2006b. Western Education and African Cultural Identity in the Great Lakes Region of Africa: A Case of Failed Globalization. *Peace and Change* 31, no. 1: 90–101.

Ndura-Ouédraogo, E. 2007. Calling Institutions of Higher Education to Join the Quest for Social Justice and Peace. *Harvard Educational Review* 77, no. 3: 345–350.

Ndura-Ouédraogo, E. 2009a. Grassroots Voices of Hope: Educators' and Students' Perspectives on Educating for Peace in Post-conflict Burundi. In *Peace Education in Conflict and Post-conflict Societies: Comparative Perspectives,* ed. C. McGlynn, Z. Bekerman, and M. Zembylas, 27–41. New York: Macmillan.

Ndura-Ouédraogo, E. 2009b. The Role of Education in Peace-building in the African Great Lakes Region: Educators' Perspectives. *Journal of Peace Education* 6, no. 1: 37–49.

Ndura-Ouédraogo, E. 2011. Building a Foundation for Sustainable Peace in Burundi: A Transformative Multicultural Education Approach. In *Seeds Bearing Fruit: Pan-African Peace Action for the Twenty-First Century*, ed. E. Ndura-Ouédraogo, M. Meyer, and J. Atiri, 3–18. Trenton, NJ: Africa World Press, Inc.

Ndura-Ouédraogo, E., and J. W. Makoba. 2008. Education for Social Change in Burundi and Rwanda: Creating a National Identity beyond the Politics of Identity. In *Ethnicity and Sociopolitical Change in Africa and other Developing Countries: A Constructive Discourse in State Building*, ed. S. C. Saha, 59–76. Lanham, MD: Lexington Books.

Ndura-Ouédraogo, E., and M. Meyer. 2009. *Linking NAME and PJSA to Reach new Heights in the Quest for Social Justice and Peace*. Paper presented at National Association for Multicultural Education 19th Annual International Conference, October 28–November 1. Denver, Colorado.

Ndura-Ouédraogo, E., M. Meyer, and J. Atiri, eds. 2011. *Seeds Bearing Fruit: Pan-African Peace Action for the Twenty-First Century*. Trenton, NJ: Africa World Press.

Ndura-Ouédraogo, E., and S. Lafer. 2004. Exploring the Self and the Other: Achieving the Empathic Goals of Teacher Preparation through Multicultural Education. *Electronic Magazine of Multicultural Education* 6, no. 1. http://www.eastern.edu/publications/emme/2004spring/index.html.

Nehru, J. 1947. *Jawaharlal Nehru, an Autobiography: With Musings on Recent Events in India*. London: Bodley Head.

Nelson, H. L. 2001. *Damaged Identities, Narrative Repair*. Ithaca, NY: Cornell University Press.

Nelson, J. 2000. *The Business of Peace*. Prince of Wales Business Leaders Forum. London. www.pwblf.org.

Nelson, R. E. 1989. The Strength of Strong Ties: Social Networks and Intergroup Conflict in Organizations. *The Academy of Management Journal* 32, no. 2 (June 1): 377–401. doi:10.2307/256367. http://www.jstor.org/stable/256367.

Newman, L. 2010. *Repentance: The Meaning and Practice of Teshuvah*. Woodstock, NY: Jewish Lights Publishing.

Ngoma, N. 2004. SADC's Mutual Defence Pact: A Final Move to a Security Community? *The Round Table* 93, no. 375: 411–423.

Ngugi wa Thiong'o. 1986. *Decolonising the Mind: The Politics of Language in African Literature*. Nairobi, Kenya: East African Educational Publishers.

Ngugi wa Thiong'o. 1993. *Moving the Centre: The Struggle for Cultural Freedoms*. Nairobi, London: East African Educational Publishers.

Nhema, A. G., A. Nhema, and P. T. Zeleza. 2008. *The Resolution of African Conflicts: The Management of Conflict Resolution & Post-conflict Reconstruction*. Oxford: James Currey.

Nieto, S. 2000. Placing Equity Front and Center: Some Thoughts on Transforming Teacher Education for a New Century. *Journal of Teacher Education* 51, no. 3: 180–187.

Nieto, S. 2004. *Affirming Diversity: The Sociopolitical Context of Multicultural Education*, 4th ed. Boston: Pearson.

Nilsson, D. 2008. Partial Peace: Rebel Groups Inside and Outside of Civil War Settlements. *Journal of Peace Research* 45, no. 4: 479.

Nilsson, D. 2010. Turning Weakness into Strength: Military Capabilities, Multiple Rebel Groups and Negotiated Settlements. *Conflict Management and*

Peace Science 27, no. 3 (6): 253–271. http://cmp.sagepub.com/cgi/doi/10.1177/0738894210366512.

Nobles, M. 2008. *The Politics of Official Apologies*. Cambridge: Cambridge University Press.

Nonviolent Peace force (NPF). 2009. Brussels. www.nonviolentpeaceforce.org.

Nordquist, Kjell-Åke. 2008. Securing Independence and Peace in East Timor—Conflict Prevention through Non-Governmental Actors. In *Third Parties and Conflict Prevention*, ed. A. Mellbourn and P. Wallensteen, 186–201. Hedemora: Gidlunds.

Northcraft, G. B., and M. A. Neale. 1986. Opportunity Costs and the Framing of Resource Allocation Decisions. *Organisational Behaviour and Human Decisions* 37: 346–356.

Nowak A., and M. Lewenstein. 1994. Dynamical Systems: A Tool For Social Psychology? In *Dynamical Systems in Social Psychology*, ed. R. Vallacher and A. Nowak, 17–53. Burlington, MA: Academic Press.

Nowak, A., and R. R. Vallacher. 1998. *Dynamical Social Psychology*. New York: The Guilford Press.

Nowak, A., and R. R. Vallacher. 2000. Societal Transition: Toward a Dynamical Model of Social Change. In *The Practice of Social Influence in Multiple Cultures*, ed. W. Wosinska, R. B. Cialdini, D. W. Barrett, and J. Reykowski, 130–149. Mahwah, NJ: Lawrence Erlbaum Associates.

Nowak, A., R. R. Vallacher, L. Bui-Wrzosinska, and P. T. Coleman. 2007. Attracted to Conflict: A Dynamical Perspective on Malignant Social Relations. In *Understanding Social Change: Political Psychology in Poland*, ed. A. Golec and K. Skarzynska, 33–49. Hauppague, NY: Nova Science.

Nowak, A., R. R. Vallacher, M. Kus, and J. Urbaniak. 2005. The Dynamics of Societal Transition: Modeling Non-Linear Change in the Polish Economic System. *International Journal of Sociology* 35, no. 1: 65–88.

Noyek, A. M., H. Skinner, D. Davis, I. Clark, A. Sriharan, and C. G. Chalin. 2005. Building Bridges of Understanding through Continuing Education and Professional Development of Arabs and Israelis. *The Journal of Continuing Education in the Health Professions* 25, no. 2: 68–75.

Nye, J. S. Jr. 2004. *Soft Power: The Means to Success in World Politics*. New York: Public Affairs Press.

O'Connor, J. 1984. *Accumulation Crisis*. New York: Blackwell.

Oden, R. A., Jr. 1979. "The Contendings of Horus and Seth" (Chester Beatty Papyrus No. 1): A Structural Interpretation. *History of Religions* 18, no. 4: 352–369.

Odendaal, A. 2010. Local Peacebuilding in Ghana. http://www.gppac.net/page.php?id=1#par2544.

Odendaal, A., and R. Olivier. 2008. Local Peace Committees: Some Reflections and Lessons Learned. Report funded by USAID for the Nepal Transition to Peace (NTTP) Initiative, implemented by the Academy for Educational Development (AED) Kathmandu, Nepal, http://unpan1.un.org/intradoc/groups/public/documents/UN/UNPAN032148.pdf.

O'Fahey, R. S. 2004. Conflict in Darfur: Historical and Contemporary Perspectives. Paper presented at the Conference on Environmental Degradation and Conflict in Darfur and was included in conference proceedings *Environmental Degradation as a Cause of Conflict in Darfur*. Khartoum: University for Peace, 23–32.

Office of the President, Ministry of State for Provincial Administration and Internal Security. 2009. *National Policy on Peacebuilding and Conflict Management*. September. http://www.gppac.net/page.php?id=1#par2544.

Office of the UN Special Advisor on Africa. 2006. *Report on Expert Meeting on Natural Resources and Conflict in Africa*. Cairo, Egypt.

Ogbar, J.O.G. 2007. *Hip-Hop Revolution: The Culture and Politics of Rap*. Vol. 95. Lawrence: The University Press of Kansas.

Ogbu, K. 1978. *African Cultural Development*. Enugu: Four Dimensions Publishers.

Ojielo, O. 2010. Designing an Architecture for Peace: A Framework of Conflict Transformation in Ghana. *Legon Centre for International Affairs* 7, no. 1.

Olberding, J. C., and D. J. Olberding. 2010. Ripple Effects in Youth Peacebuilding and Exchange Programs: Measuring Impacts Beyond Direct Participants. *International Studies Perspectives* 11, no. 1: 75–91.

O'Leary, B. 2005. Debating Consociational Politics: Normative and Explanatory Arguments. In *From Power-Sharing to Democracy: Post-Conflict Institutions in Ethnically Divided Societies*, ed. S. Noel, 3–43. Toronto: McGill-Queens University Press.

O'Leary, B. 2008. The Logics of Power-Sharing, Consociation and Pluralist Federations. In *Settling Self-Determination Disputes: Complex Power-Sharing in Theory and Practice*, ed. M. Weller et al., 47–58. Leiden: Martinus Nijhoff.

O'Leary, B. 2009. *Testing Times for Power-Sharing*. New York: UNDPA/MSU.

O'Malley, P. 2007. *Shades of Difference: Mac Maharaj and the Struggle for South Africa*. New York: Penguin.

Omi, M., and H. Winant. 1994. *Racial Formation in the United States: From the 1960s to the 1990s*. London: Routledge.

O'Neill, W. G. 2005. *Mediation and Human Rights*. Geneva: The Centre for Humanitarian Dialogue.

Oo, Z., and W. Min. 2007. *Assessing Burma's Ceasefire Accords*. Washington, DC: Institute of Southeast Asian Studies.

Oppenheimer, L. 2006. The Development of Enemy Images: A Theoretical Contribution. *Peace and Conflict: Journal of Peace Psychology* 12, no. 3: 269.

Osgood, C. E. 1966. *Perspective in Foreign Policy*. Palo Alto, CA: Pacific Books.

Otterbein, K. F. 1970. *The Evolution of War: A Cross-Cultural Study*. New Haven, CT: Human Relations Area Files Press.

özür diliyorum. http://www.ozurdiliyoruz.com/.

Pain, D. 1997. *The Bending of Spears: Producing Consensus for Peace and Development in Northern Uganda*. London: International Alert and Kacoke Madit.

Pantham, T. 1987. Habermas' Practical Discourse and Gandhi's Satyagraha. In *Political Discourse: Exploration in Indian and Western Thought*, ed. P. Bhikhu and T. Pantham, 190. New Delhi: Sage Publications.

Papachristos, A. V. 2005. Interpreting Inkblots: Deciphering and Doing Something about Modern Street Gangs. *Criminology & Public Policy* 4, no. 3: 643–651.

Parel, A. 1997. *Hind Swaraj and Other Writings*. Cambridge: Cambridge University Press.

Paris, R. 2004. *At War's End: Building Peace After Civil Conflict*. Cambridge: Cambridge University Press.

Parker, K. 2010. The Quest to Sort Out Competing and Comparable Religions. *Washington Post*, May 9.

Parsons, C. 2008. France Urges U.N. Council to Act on Myanmar Cyclone. *Reuters*, May 7. http://www.reuters.com/article/idUSL07810481.

Pashayeva, G. 2010. Caucasus Edition: Reassessing the Nagorno-Karabakh Conflict in the Aftermath of the Russia-Georgia War. *Journal of Conflict Transformation* 2 no. 1: 2–3. http://www.president.az/articles/247/print?locale=az.

Patrick, S. 2006. Weak States and Global Threats: Fact or Fiction? *The Washington Quarterly* 29, no. 2: 27–53.

Peace on Facebook. http://peace.facebook.com/.

Pearce, W. B., and S. W. Littlejohn. 1997. *Moral Conflict: When Social Worlds Collide.* Thousand Oaks, CA: Sage.

Peck, C. 1993. Preventive Diplomacy. In *Cooperating for Peace: The Global Agenda for the 1990s and Beyond,* ed. G. Evans, 61–85. St. Leonards, Australia: Allen & Unwin.

Peck, C. 2001. The Role of Regional Organizations in Preventing and Resolving Conflict. In *Turbulent Peace: The Challenges of Managing International Conflict,* ed. C. Crocker, F. Hampson, and P. Aall, 561–584. Washington, DC: United Institute of Peace.

Perdue, P. C. 2005. *China Marches West: The Qing Conquest of Central Eurasia.* Cambridge, MA: Belknap Press of Harvard University Press.

Petersilia, J. 2006. *Understanding California Corrections.* Berkeley: California Policy Research Center.

Peterson, J. B. and J. Flanders. 2002. Complexity Management Theory: Motivation for Ideological Rigidity and Social Conflict. *Cortex* 38, no. 3: 429–458.

Pew Global Attitudes Project. 2004. A Global Generation Gap. http://pewglobal.org/2004/02/24/a-global-generation-gap/.

Philpott, D. 2004. The Catholic Wave. *Journal of Democracy* 15, no. 2: 32–46.

Philpott, D., M. D. Toft, and T. S. Shah. 2011. *God's Century: Resurgent Religion and Global Politics.* New York: W. W. Norton.

Piatt, B. 1997. *Black and Brown in America: The Case for Cooperation.* New York: New York University Press.

Pilisuk, M. 2010. *Peace Movements Worldwide.* 3 Volumes. Westport, CT: Praeger Publishers.

Ping-ti Ho. 2010. Uncovering the Mystery of the Causes of the Great Affair of Chinese History—Reconstructing the History of the Mohists in Qin (manuscript in Chinese), May.

Piombo, J. 2010. Peacemaking in Burundi: Conflict Resolution versus Conflict Management Strategies. *African Security* 3, no. 4: 239–272.

PITF State Failure Problem Set Datasets Posted on the Center for Systemic Peace website. www.systemicpeace.org/inscr.

du Plessis, J. 2001. Reflections on Stereotypes. *Wings, 9.* http://www.stratek.co.za/.%5Carchive%5Cjohanduplessis.html.

Polanyi, M. 1964. *Personal Knowledge: Towards a Post-Critical Philosophy.* New York: Harper and Row.

Pope, S. J. 2003. The Convergence of Forgiveness and Justice: Lessons from El Salvador. *Theological Studies* 64, no. 4: 812–836.

Popkin, M. 2000. *Peace without Justice: Obstacles to Building the Rule of Law in El Salvador.* University Park: Pennsylvania State University Press.

Potter, A. 2004. *Ceasefire Monitoring and Verification: Identifying Best Practice.* Background Paper, Mediators' Retreat. Oslo, Norway: Centre for Humanitarian Dialogue, June 10.

Potter, A. 2008. Gender Sensitivity: Nicety or Necessity in Peace-Process Management? Background Paper—The Oslo Forum Network of Mediators. Oslo, Norway: Royal Norwegian Ministry of Foreign Affairs and the Centre for Humanitarian Dialogue.

Prabhu, J. 2005. Trajectories of Hindu Ethics. In *The Blackwell Companion to Religious Ethics,* ed. William Schweiker, 355–367. Oxford: Blackwell Publishing.

Prashad, V. 2008. *The Darker Nations: A People's History of the Third World.* New York: New Press.

Praszkier, R., and A. Nowak. 2011. *Social Entrepreneurship: Theory and Practice.* New York: Cambridge University Press.

Praszkier, R., A. Nowak, and P. Coleman. 2010. Social Entrepreneurs and Constructive Change: The Wisdom of Circumventing Conflict. *Peace and Conflict: Journal of Peace Psychology* 16, no. 2: 153–174.

Praszkier, R., and A. Zablocka-Bursa. 2009. Social Capital Built by Social Entrepreneurs and the Specific Personality Traits that Facilitate the Process. *Psychologia Spoleczna* 4: 42–54.

Priests for Equality. 2009. *The Inclusive Bible: The First Egalitarian Translation.* Lanham, MD: Rowman & Littlefield.

Princen, T. 1992. *Intermediaries in International Conflict.* Princeton, NJ: Princeton University Press.

Prinsloo, E. D. 1998. Ubuntu Culture and Participatory Management. In *The African Philosophy Reader,* ed. P. Coetzee and A. Roux, 41–51. London: Routledge.

The Private Diplomacy Survey 2008: Mapping of 14 Private Diplomacy Actors in Europe and America. 2008. Helsinki: Crisis Management Initiative, November.

Program on International Policy Attitudes. 2009. *The GPI and Multi-National Attitude Research. University of Maryland.* http://www.visionofhumanity.org/info-center/vision-of-humanity-themes/economics-and-peace/the-global-peace-index-and-multi-national-attitude-research/?.

Pruitt, D. G. 1981. *Negotiation Behavior.* New York: Academic Press.

Pruitt, D. G. 1997. Ripeness Theory and the Oslo Talks. *International Negotiation* 2: 237–250.

Pruitt, D. G. 2005. *Whither Ripeness Theory?* Occasional Paper #25. Fairfax VA: Institute for Conflict Analysis & Resolution, George Mason University.

Pruitt, D. G. 2007a. Readiness Theory and the Northern Ireland Conflict. *American Behavioral Scientist* 50, no. 11 (July 1): 1520–1541.

Pruitt, D. G. 2007b. Social Conflict: Some Basic Principles. *Journal of Dispute Resolution* 151: 67–89.

Pruitt, D. G. 2011a. Communication Preliminary to Negotiation in Intractable Conflict. In *Psychological and Political Strategies for Peace Negotiation,* ed. Francesco Aquilar and Mauro Galluccio, 117–129. New York, NY: Springer.

Pruitt, D. G. 2011b. The South African Peace Process: An Urgency Theory Analysis. In *Peacemaking: From Practice to Theory,* vol. 2, ed. S. Allen Nan, Z. Cherian Mampilly, and A. Bartoli, 722–740. Santa Barbara, CA: Praeger.

Pruitt, D. G. and S. Hee Kim. 2004. *Social Conflict: Escalation, Stalemate and Settlement,* 3rd ed. Boston: McGraw Hill.

Public International Law & Policy Group. 2005. *Ceasefires: Peace Drafter's Handbook.* Washington, DC: The Public International Law & Policy Group.

Pugh, M., and W. Sidhu, eds. 2003. *The United Nations and Regional Security: Europe and Beyond.* Boulder, CO: Lynne Rienner.

Putnam, R. D. 1993. The Prosperous Community: Social Capital and Public Life. *The American Prospect* 13: 35–42.

Quinlan, A. 2010. Building Resilience in Ontario—More than Metaphor or Arcane Concept. *Resilience Science.* March 11. http://rs.resalliance.org/2010/03/11/building-resilience-in-ontario-%e2%80%93-more-than-metaphor-or-arcane-concept/.

Radzik, L. 2009. *Making Amends: Atonement in Morality, Law, and Politics.* Oxford: Oxford University Press.

Raiffa, H., J. Richardson, and D. Metcalfe. 2002. *Negotiation Analysis: The Science and Art of Collaborative Decision Making.* Boston: Harvard University Press.

Ramet, S. P. 1998. *Nihil Obstat: Religion, Politics, and Social Change in East-Central Europe and Russia*. Durham, NC: Duke University Press.

Ramsbotham, O. 2005. *Contemporary Conflict Resolution: The Prevention, Management and Transformation of Deadly Conflicts*, 2nd ed. Cambridge, UK: Polity.

Rawls, J., and S. Freeman. 1999. The Laws of Peoples. In *Collected Papers: John Rawls*, 529–564. Cambridge, MA: Harvard University Press.

Redekop, V. N. 2002. *From Violence to Blessing: How an Understanding of Deep-Rooted Conflict Can Open Paths to Reconciliation*. Ottawa: Novalis.

Redekop, V. N. 2007a. Reconciling Nuers with Dinkas: A Girardian Approach to Conflict Resolution. *Religion—An International Journal* 37: 64–84.

Redekop, V. N. 2007b. Teachings of Blessing as Elements of Reconciliation: Intra- and Inter Religious Hermeneutical Challenges and Opportunities in the Face of Violent Deep-Rooted Conflict. In *The Next Step in Studying Religion: A Graduate's Guide*, ed. M. Courville, 129–146. London: Continuum.

Redekop, V. N. 2008. A Post-Genocidal Justice of Blessing as an Alternative to a Justice of Violence: The Case of Rwanda. In *Peacebuilding in Traumatized Societies*, ed. B. Hart, 205–238. Lanham, MD: University Press of America.

Redekop, V. N. and S. Paré. 2010. *Beyond Control: A Mutual Respect Approach to Protest Crowd—Police Relations*. London: Bloomsbury Academic.

Reeves, M. 2008. *Somebody Scream!: Rap Music's Rise to Prominence in the Aftershock of Black Power*. New York: Farber and Farber.

Regan, A. 2010. *Light Intervention. Lessons from Bougainville*. Washington DC: US Institute of Peace Press.

Reporters Without Borders. 2009. Press Freedom Index 2009. *Reporters Without Borders for Press Freedom*. http://en.rsf.org/press-freedom-index-2009,1001.html.

Republic of the Philippines. 1997. *Agreement for General Cessation of Hostilities*. July 18. http://www.c-r.org/our-work/accord/philippines-mindanao/tripoli-agreement-peace.php.

Republic of the Philippines. 2010a. Guidelines for Mutual Understanding Between the Coordinating Committees on the Cessation of Hostilities of the Government of the Republic of the Philippines and the Moro Islamic Liberation Front for Ceasefire-Related Functions for the May 10, 2010 National Elections. April 23.

Republic of the Philippines. 2010b. Terms of Reference of the Civilian Protection Component (CPC) of the International Monitoring Team (IMT). May 5. http://www.scribd.com/doc/31303703/GRP-MILF-Terms-of-Reference-for-the-Civilian-Protection-Component.

Reychler, L., and T. Paffenholz, eds. 2001. *Peacebuilding: A Field Guide*. Boulder, CO: Lynne Rienner.

Reyntjens, F. 2000. *Burundi: Prospects for Peace*. London: Minority Rights Group International.

Reyntjens, F. 2009. *The Great African War: Congo and Regional Geopolitics, 1996–2006*. Cambridge: Cambridge University Press.

Riccardi, A. 1999. *Sant'Egidio: Rome and the World*. London: St. Paulus.

Riccardi, A. 2005. *La paix préventive: Raisons d'espérer dans un monde conflits*. Paris: Salvator.

Riccardi, A. 2009. *Living together*. Hyde Park, NY: New City Press.

Rice, S. E., and S. Patrick. 2008. *Index of State Weakness in the Developing World*. Washington, DC: Brookings Institution. http://www.brookings.edu/reports/2008/02_weak_states_index.aspx.

Richards, H. 1999. On the Concept of Peacemaking. *Paideusi—Journal for Interdisciplinary and Cross-Cultural Studies* 2: 25–44.

Richmond, O. P. 2004. The Globalization of Responses to Conflict and the Peacebuilding Consensus. *Cooperation and Conflict* 39, no. 2: 129–150.

Ricoeur, P. 2007 [1969]. *The Conflict of Interpretations: Essays in Hermeneutics.* Evanston, IL: Northwestern University Press.

Roberts, Nancy C. 2002. *The Transformative Power of Dialogue.* Boston: JAI Press.

Rogier, E. 2003. *Cluttered with Predators, Godfathers and Facilitators: The Labyrinth to Peace in the Democratic Republic of Congo.* Working Paper Series. The Hague: Netherlands Institute of International Relations, Clingendael.

Rogier, E. 2004. *Rethinking Conflict Resolution in Africa: Lessons from the Democratic Republic of the Congo, Sierra Leone and Sudan.* Working Paper Series. The Hague: Netherlands Institute of International Relations, Clingendael.

Romer, K., and A.M.N. Renzaho. 2007. Re-emerging Conflict in the Solomon Islands? The Underlying Causes and Triggers of the Riots of April 2006. *Journal of Peace Conflict & Development.* www.peacestudiesjournal.org.uk.

Rosenblum, N. L., and C. Taylor, eds. 1989. *Liberalism and the Moral Life.* Cambridge: Harvard University Press.

Rossabi, M., ed. 1983. *China among Equals: The Middle Kingdom and its Neighbors, 10th–14th Centuries.* Los Angeles: University of California Press.

Rotberg, R. I. 2003. *When States Fail: Causes and Consequences.* Princeton, NJ: Princeton University Press.

Rotblat, J. 1972. *Scientists in the Quest for Peace. A History of the Pugwash Conferences.* Cambridge, MA: The MIT Press.

Roth, N. 1994. *Jews, Visigoths, and Muslims in Medieval Spain.* Leiden, The Netherlands: E. J. Brill.

Rothchild, D., and P. G Roeder. 2005. Dilemmas of State-building in Divided Societies. In *Sustainable Peace: Power and Democracy after Civil Wars,* ed. D. Rothchild and P. G. Roeder, 1–26. Ithaca, NY: Cornell University Press.

Rubin, B. 1994. Religion and International Affairs. In *Religion, the Missing Dimension of Statecraft,* ed. D. Johnston and C. Sampson, 20–36. Oxford: Oxford University Press.

Rubin, B. 2002. *Blood on the Doorstep the Politics of Preventive Action.* New York: Century Foundation Press.

Rubin, J. Z., and J. Bercovitch. 2002. *Studies in International Mediation: Essays in Honor of Jeffrey Z. Rubin.* New York: Palgrave MacMillan.

Rubin, J. Z., D. G. Pruitt, and S. H. Kim. 1994. *Social Conflict: Escalation, Stalemate, and Settlement.* New York: McGraw-Hill.

Ruelle, D. 1989. *Elements of Differentiable Dynamics and Bifurcation Theory.* New York: Academic Press.

Ruvolo, M. 1997. Genetic Diversity in Hominoid Primates. *Annual Review of Anthropology* 26: 515–540.

Sagan, A. 2010. African Criminals/African Victims: The Institutionalised Production of Cultural Narratives in International Criminal Law. *Millennium-Journal of International Studies* 39, no. 1: 3–21.

Said, E. W. 1992. *The Question of Palestine.* New York: Vintage Books.

Salem, R. 1982. Community Dispute Resolution through outside Intervention. *Peace and Change* 8, no. 2: 91–104.

Salomon, G. 2002. The Nature of Peace Education: Not all Programs are Created Equal. In *Peace Education: The Concept, Principles, and Practices Around the World,* ed. G. Salomon and B. Nevo, 3–13. Mahwah, NJ: Lawrence Erlbaum Associates.

Samaddar, R. 2001. *A Biography of the Indian Nation, 1947–1997*. Thousand Oaks, CA: Sage Publications.

Samaddar, R. 2004. *The Politics of Dialogue—Living under the Geopolitical Histories of War and Peace in South Asia*. Aldershot, UK: Ashgate.

Sandole, D. 1999. *Capturing the Complexity of Conflict: Dealing with Violent Ethnic Conflicts in the Post-Cold War Era*. London: Pinter.

Sandquist, E. J., ed. 1996. *The Oxford W.E.B. Du Bois Reader*. New York: Oxford University Press.

Santa Cruz, A. 2005. *International Election Monitoring, Sovereignty, and the Western Hemisphere Idea: The Emergence of an International Norm*. New York: Routledge.

Santiago, D. 1993. *The Harvest of Justice: The Church of El Salvador Ten Years after Romero*. Mahwah, NJ: Paulist Press.

Satha Anand, C. 2001. The Nonviolent Crescent: Eight Theses on Muslim Nonviolent Action. In *Peace and Conflict Resolution in Islam: Precept and Practice*, ed. A. A. Said, N. C. Funk, and A. S. Kadayifci, 195–209. Lanham, MD: University Press of America.

Saunders, H. n.d. Sustained Dialogue: A Product of Experience. Kettering Foundation. http://www.kettering.org/foundation_programs/multinational_research/Sustained_Dialogue.

Saunders, H. 1999. *A Public Peace Process: Sustained Dialogue to Transform Racial and Ethnic Conflicts*. New York: Palgrave.

Sawyer, R. D. 1998. *The Tao of Spycraft: Intelligence Theory and Practice in Traditional China*. Boulder, CO: Lynne Rienner Publishers.

Sawyer, R. D. 1999. Chinese Warfare: The Paradox of the Unlearned Lesson. *American Diplomacy* 4, no. 4. http://www.unc.edu/depts/diplomat/AD_Issues/amdipl_13/china_sawyer.html.

Sawyer, R. D. 2006. Introduction. In *The Art of War*, by Sun Tzu. Lenox MA: Hard Press.

Scarry, E. 1987. *The Body in Pain: The Making and Unmaking of the World*. New York: Oxford University Press.

Schaap, A. 2005. *Political Reconciliation*. London: Routledge.

Scharmer, C. O. 2007. Addressing the Blind Spot of Our Time. In *Theory U: Leading from the Future as it Emerges*, 1–19. Cambridge, MA: Society for Organization Learning.

Schelling, T. 1978. *Micromotives and Macrobehavior*. New York: Norton.

Scheper, E. 2010. *Draft DPA Recommendations for Enhancing Gender Participation in Peacemaking and Peace-building*. Mimeo. New York: Mediation Support Unit (MSU), Department of Political Affairs (DPA).

Scherrer, C. P. 2002. *Genocide and Crisis in Central Africa: Conflict Roots, Mass Violence, and Regional War*. Westport, CT: Praeger.

Schirch, L. 2005. *Ritual and Symbol in Peacebuilding*. Sterling, VA: Kumarian Press.

Schmelzle, B. and M. Fisher, eds. 2009. *Peacebuilding at a Crossroads? Dilemmas and Paths for Another Generation*. Berlin: Berghof Research Center for Constructive Conflict Management.

Schmitt, M. N. 2007. 21st Century Conflict: Can the Law Survive? *Melbourne Journal of International Law* 8: 443–476.

Schulze, K. E. 2001. The East Timor Referendum Crisis and Its Impact on Indonesian Politics. *Studies in Conflict & Terrorism* 24, no. 1: 77–82.

Schuster, H. G. 1984. *Deterministic Chaos: An Introduction*. Weinheim, Germany: Physik Verlag.

Schwarz-Schilling, C. 2010. The Treaty of Shanyuan—Then and Now: Reflections 1,000 Years Later. http://www.eacrh.net/ojs/index.php/crossroads/article/view/2.

Sebenius, J. K. 2001. Six Habits of Merely Effective Negotiators. *Harvard Business Review* 79, no. 4: 87–97.

Sebenius, J. K. 2002. The Hidden Challenge of Cross-border Negotiations. *Harvard Business Review* 80, no. 3: 76–85.

Segal, J. 2004. The Uniquely Human in Human Nature. *Daedelus* 133, no. 4: 77–88.

Séjourné, L. 1983. La Traición de Quetzalcóatl. In *De Teotihuacán a Los Aztecas: Antología de Fuentes e Interpretaciones Históricas*, ed. Miguel León-Portilla, 236–242. Mexico City: Universidad Autónoma de México.

Selden, M. 2001. On Asian Wars, Reparations, Reconciliation. *Economic and Political Weekly* 36, no. 1: 25–26.

Sen, P. 2007. Ashoka's big Idea: Transforming the World through Social Entrepreneurship. *Futures* 39, no. 5: 534–553.

Serwer, D. 2010. *Kosovo: The Next Steps*. Peacebrief. http://www.usip.org/publications/kosovo-the-next-steps.

Sesay, M. 1995. Collective Security or Collective Disaster? Regional Peace-Keeping in West Africa. *Security Dialogue* 26, no. 2: 205–222.

Shah-Kazemi, R., and W. Berry. 2007. *My Mercy Encompasses All: The Koran's Teachings on Compassion, Peace and Love*. Berkeley, CA: Counterpoint Press.

Shakur, S. 2004. *Monster: The Autobiography of an L.A. Gang Member*. New York: Grove Press.

ShalomSalaam Social Movement (Global). *ShalomSalaam Social Movement (Global)*. https://www.facebook.com/group.php?gid=2225147640.

Sharp, G. 1989. The Intifadah and Nonviolent Struggle. *Journal of Palestine Studies* 19, no. 1: 3–13.

Sharp, G. 2005. *Waging Nonviolent Struggle: 20th Century Practice And 21st Century Potential*. Boston: Extending Horizons Books.

Sharp, G., and M. Finkelstein. 1973. *The Politics of Nonviolent Action*. Boston: Porter Sargent Publishers.

Shaw, T. M. 1995. New Regionalism in Africa as Responses to Environmental Crises: IGADD and Development in the Horn in the Mid-1990s. In *Disaster and Development in the Horn of Africa*, ed. J. Sorenson. New York: St. Martin's Press.

Sheppard, B. H. 1984. Third Party Conflict Intervention: A Procedural Framework. In *Research in Organizational Behavior*, vol. 6, ed. B. M. Staw and L. L. Cummings, 141–189. Greenwich, CT: JAI Press.

Sherif, M. 1966. *In Common Predicament: Social Psychology of Intergroup Conflict and Cooperation*. Boston: Houghton Mifflin.

Sherif, M., O. J. Harvey, B. J. White, W. E. Hood, and C. W. Sherif. 1961. *Intergroup Conflict and Cooperation: The Robber's Cave Experiment*. Norman: University of Oklahoma Press.

Sherif, M. 1961. *Intergroup Conflict and Cooperation: The Robber's Cave Experiment*. Norman: University of Oklahoma Press.

Sherif, M. 1966. A Theoretical Analysis of Individual-Group Relationship in a Social Situation. In *Concepts, Theory, and Explanation in the Behavioral Sciences*, ed. G. J. DiRenzo, 47–72. New York: Random House.

Shirky, C. 2008. *Here Comes Everybody: The Power of Organizing Without Organizations*. New York: Penguin Press.

Shriver, D. W. 1995. *An Ethic for Enemies: Forgiveness in Politics*. Cambridge, MA: Oxford University Press.

Simonson, I. and B. M. Staw. 1992. De-escalation Strategies: A Comparison of Techniques for Reducing Commitment to Losing Courses of Action. *Journal of Applied Psychology* 77, no. 4: 419–426.

Sisk, T. D. 1995. *Democratization in South Africa: The Elusive Social Contract.* Princeton, NJ: Princeton University Press.

Skinner, H., Z. Abdeen, H. Abdeen, P. Aber, M. Al-Masri, J. Attias, K. B. Avraham, et al. 2005. Promoting Arab and Israeli Cooperation: Peacebuilding through Health Initiatives. *Lancet* 365, no. 9466: 1274–1277.

Sleeter, C. E. 1996. *Multicultural Education as Social Activism.* Albany: State University of New York Press.

Slim, H. 2007. *A Guide to Mediation: Enabling Peace Processes in Violent Conflicts.* Geneva: The Centre for Humanitarian Dialogue (HDC).

Slim, H., and D. Mancini-Griffoli. 2008. *Interpreting Violence: Anti-Civilian Thinking and Practice and How to Argue Against It More Effectively.* Geneva: Centre for Humanitarian Dialogue.

Smith, A. 1991. *National Identity.* Reno: University of Nevada Press.

Smith, A. L., and D. R. Smock. 2008. *Managing a Mediation Process.* Washington DC: United States Institute of Peace.

Smith, D. L. 2007. *The Most Dangerous Animal: Human Nature and the Origins of War.* New York: St. Martin's Press.

Smith, J., C. Chatfield, and R. Pugnucco, eds. 1997. *Transnational Social Movements and Global Politics: Solidarity Beyond the State.* Syracuse, NY: Syracuse University Press.

Smith, J.D.D. 1997. *Stopping Wars: Defining the Obstacles to Cease-fire.* Boulder, CO: Westview Pr.

Smith, J., and H. Johnston, eds. 2002. *Globalization and Resistance: Transnational Dimensions of Social Movements.* Lanham, MD: Rowman & Littlefield.

Smith, M. J. 1992. Liberalism and International Reform. In *Traditions of International Ethics,* ed., T. Nardin and D. Mapel, 201–224. Cambridge: Cambridge University Press.

Smith, S. 2005. Engaging Armed Groups: Ceasefire Negotiations in Eastern Democratic Republic of Congo. *Conciliation Resource.* http://www.c-r.org/our-work/accord/engaging-groups/ceasefire-negotiations-drc.php.

Sobel, D. 1999. *Galileo's Daughter: A Historical Memoir of Science, Faith, and Love.* New York: Walker and Company.

Social Media for Social Change Conference. https://sites.google.com/a/ph-int.org/socialmedia2010/.

Soliya. n.d. Why We Do It. http://www.soliya.net/?q=why_we_do_it_overview.

Solomon, R. H. and N. Quinney. 2010. *American Negotiating Behavior.* Washington DC: USIP Press.

Somalia's President Quits Office. 2008. *BBC,* December 29, sec. Africa. http://news.bbc.co.uk/2/hi/7802622.stm.

Sovereignty. 2010. *Encyclopedia Britannica.* http://www.britannica.com/EBchecked/topic/557065/sovereignty.

Sparks, A. 1995. *Tomorrow is Another Country: The Inside Story of South Africa's Road to Change.* Chicago: University of Chicago Press.

SpearIt. 2006. God Behind Bars: Race, Religion & Revenge. *Seton Hall Law Review* 37: 497. http://heinonline.org/HOL/Page?handle=hein.journals/shlr37&id=503&div=&collection=journals.

Spergel, I. A. 1990. Strategies and Perceived Agency Effectiveness in Dealing with the Youth Gang Problem. In *Gangs in America,* ed. C. Ronald Huff, 288–309. Thousand Oaks, CA: Sage Publications.

Spergel, I. A. 1995. *The Youth Gang Problem: A Community Approach.* New York: Oxford University Press.

Spies, C. F. J. 2006. Revolutionary Change: The Art of Awakening Dormant Faculties in Others. In *Berghof Handbook Dialogue No. 5*. Berghof: Berghof Research Center for Constructive Conflict Management.

Srebrenica Genocide Blog. 2007. Published in 2007 on the 11th Anniversary of the Genocide Committed Against the Bosniaks of the "UN Safe Zone" of Srebrenica. http://srebrenica-genocide.blogspot.com/2008/05/united-nations-on-srebrenicas-pillar-of.html.

Stamnes, E. 2008. Operationalizing the Preventive Aspect of R2P. Norwegian Institute for International Affairs on the Responsibility to Protect. http://www.globalr2p.org/pdf/R2P-1-Stamnes.pdf.

Statement of the Bolivarian Republic of Venezuela: Ninth Open Debate on the Protection of Civilians in armed Conflict July 7. 2010. http://www.responsibilitytoprotect.org/Venezuala-%20Ninth%20Open%20Debate%20on%20the%20Protection%20of%20Civilains%20in%20Armed%20Conflict.pdf.

Statement of the President of the Security Council. 2010. Presented at the Security Council Meeting 6360, July 16, New York.

Staub, E. 2008. Promoting Reconciliation after Genocide and Mass Killing in Rwanda—and Other Post Conflict Settings: Understanding the Roots of Violence, Healing, Shared History, and General Principles. In *The Social Psychology of Intergroup Reconciliation*, ed. Nadler, A., T. F. Malloy, and J. D. Fisher, 867–894. New York: Oxford University Press.

Stedman J., and D. L. Weisel. 1998. *Addressing Community Gang Problems: A Practical Guide*. Washington, DC: Police Executive Research Forum (PERF). http://www.ncjrs.gov/App/Publications/abstract.aspx?ID=164273.

Stedman, S. J. 1991. *Peacemaking in Civil Wars: International Mediation in Zimbabwe, 1974–1980*. Boulder, CO: Lynne Rienner.

Stedman, S. J. 1997. Spoiler Problems in Peace Processes. *International Security* 22, no. 2: 5–53.

Stedman, S. J., D. S. Rothchild, and E. M. Cousens. 2002. *Ending Civil Wars: The Implementation of Peace Agreements*. Boulder, CO: Lynne Rienner.

Steiner, B. H. 2004. *Collective Preventive Diplomacy: A Study in International Conflict Management*. Albany: State University of New York Press.

Steyaert, C., and D. Hjorth. 2006. Introduction: What Is Social Entrepreneurship? In *Entrepreneurship as Social Change*, ed. C. Steyaert and D. Hjorth. Cheltenham, UK: Edward Elgar Publishing.

Strenger, C. 2010. Paranoid Vicious Circles. *Haaretz*, December 31.

Strogatz, S. 2003. *Sync: The Emerging Science of Spontaneous Order*. New York: Hyperion Books.

Structural Violence. *Wikipedia, the Free Encyclopedia*. http://en.wikipedia.org/wiki/Structural_violence.

Sudan: Reflecting on the IGAD Peace Process: An Interview with Nicholas (Fink) Haysom. 2006. *Conciliation Resource*. http://www.c-r.org/our-work/accord/sudan/igad-process.php.

Sullivan, Daniel. 2005. The Missing Pillars: A Look at the Failure of Peace in Burundi through the Lens of Arend Lijphart's Theory of Consociational Democracy. *The Journal of Modern African Studies* 43, no. 1: 75–96.

Supreme Court Refuses to Hear Petition by Jailed Bloggers, August 18. 2010. http://en.rsf.org/azerbaidjan-supreme-court-refuses-to-hear-18–08–2010,37894.html.

Sunzi. 1994. *The Art of War*. Trans. Ralph D Sawyer. Boulder, CO: Westview Press.

Sunzi. 2006 [sixth century B.C]. *The Art of War*. Lenox MA: Hard Press.

Svensson, I. 2006. Elusive Peacemakers: A Bargaining Perspective on Mediation in Internal Armed Conflicts. PhD diss., Uppsala University, Department of Peace and Conflict Research.

Svensson, I. 2007. Bargaining, Bias and Peace Brokers: How Rebels Commit to Peace. *Journal of Peace Research* 44, no. 2: 177–194.

Svensson, I. 2009. Who Brings Which Peace? Neutral versus Biased Mediation and Institutional Peace Arrangements in Civil Wars. *Journal of Conflict Resolution* 53, no. 3: 446–469.

Svensson, I., and P. Wallensteen. 2010. *The Go-Between. Ambassador Jan Eliason and Styles of Mediation*. Washington DC: USIP Press.

Swisspeace. 2009. *Peace Mediation Essentials: Dealing with the Past in Peace Mediation*. CSS & Swisspeace Negotiation and Mediation Resources. Zurich and Berne: Center for Security Studies; Berne: Swisspeace, and Swiss Federal Department of Foreign Affairs, September.

Sword, D. 2003. *Complex Conflict Analysis of Public Protest*. PhD diss. Toronto, CA: University of Toronto.

Tambo, A., ed. 1987. *Preparing for Power: Oliver Tambo Speaks*. London: Heinemann.

Taylor, C. 1996. Why Democracy Needs Patriotism. In *For love of Country: Debating the Limits of Patriotism*, ed. M. C. Nussbaum and J. Cohen. Boston: Beacon Press.

Teitel, R. G. 2003. Transitional Justice Genealogy. *Harvard Human Rights Journal* 16: 69.

Templeton, A. R. 1998. Human Races: A Genetic and Evolutionary Perspective. *American Anthropologist* 100, no. 3: 632–650.

Thom, R. 1975. *Structural Stability and Morphogenesis*. New York: Addison-Wesley.

Thornberry, T. P. 2003. *Gangs and Delinquency in Developmental Perspective*. Cambridge: Cambridge University Press.

Thucydides. 2009. *The History of the Peloponnesian War*. Trans. R. Crawley. Project Gutenberg eBook, November 4. http://www.gutenberg.org/files/7142/7142-h/7142-h.htm.

Tierney, B. 1997. *The Idea of Natural Rights: Studies on Natural Rights, Natural Law, and Church Law, 1150–1625*. Grand Rapids, MI: Wm. B. Eerdmans.

Tilly, C., and J. W. Zophy, eds. 1975. *The Formation of National States in Western Europe*. Princeton, NJ: Princeton University Press.

Tomuschat, C. 2008. *Human Rights: Between Idealism and Realism*. Oxford, UK: Oxford University Press.

Tonkinson, R. 1974. *The Jigalong Mob: Aboriginal Victors of the Desert Crusade*. Menlo Park, CA: Cummings.

Tonkinson, R. 1978. *Mardudjara Aborigines: Living the Dream in Australia's Desert*. New York: Holt, Rinehart and Winston.

The Transitional Federal Charter of the Somali Republic. Nairobi. 2004. February. http://www.ilo.org/wcmsp5/groups/public/—ed_protect/—protrav/—ilo_aids/documents/legaldocument/wcms_127637.pdf.

Transparency International. 2009. Corruption Perceptions Index. http://www.transparency.org/policy_research/surveys_indices/cpi/2009.

Treiber, A. K. 2007. *Considerations for Monitoring Gender-Based Violence as a Prohibited Act of Ceasefire Agreements in the Context of Darfur*. New York: United Nations Department of Political Affairs (DPA) and Mediation Support Unit (MSU).

Trostle, J. 1992. Research Capacity Building and International Health: Definitions, Evaluations and Strategies for Success. *Social Science and Medicine* 35, no. 11: 1321–1324.

Truong Buu Lam. 1968. Intervention Versus Tribute in Sino-Vietnamese Relations, 1788–1790. In *The Chinese World Order; Traditional China's Foreign Relations*, ed. J. K. Fairbank and Tung-tse Chu. Cambridge, MA: Harvard University Press.

Tutu, D. 1999. *No Future Without Forgiveness*. London: Rider.

UNICEF. 2006. *Uncounted Lives: Children, Women and Conflict in the Philippines*. Manila, Philippines. October.

United Nations. 1945a. *Charter of the United Nations*. October 24.

United Nations. 1945b. *Charter of the United Nations and Statute of the International Court of Justice*. New York: United Nations.

United Nations. 1991. *Agreements on a Comprehensive Political Settlement of the Cambodia Conflict*. Paris: United Nations.

United Nations. 2008. *Regional Confidence-Building Measures: Activities of the United Nations Standing Advisory Committee on Security Questions in Central Africa.* General Assembly Sixty-third session Item 92(g) of the Preliminary List. New York: United Nations, July 22.

United Nations. 2009a. *Draft—Confidence Building Measures (CBMs) in Peace Processes.* New York: United Nations Department of Political Affairs (DPA) Mediation Support Unit (MSU), January 22.

United Nations. 2009b. *Programme Evaluation of the Performance and the Achievement of Results by the United Nations Operation in Cote d'Ivoire.* General Assembly Sixty-third session Agenda item 128. New York: United Nations, February 9.

United Nations. 2009c. *Report of the Secretary-General on the Situation in the Republic of Bogaland.* Exercise CJSE 10. New York: United Nations.

United Nations. 2009d. *Ways to Further Promote Use of Mediation in Peaceful Settlement of Disputes.* Security Council 6108th Meeting. New York: United Nations Security Council, April 21.

United Nations. 2009e. *Why Dialogue Matters for Conflict Prevention and Peacebuilding.* New York: United Nations Development Programme.

United Nations. 2010. *Children and Armed Conflict: Report of the Secretary-General.* General Assembly Security Council Sixty-fourth Session Agenda Item 65(a)—Promotion and Protection of the Rights of Children. New York: United Nations.

United Nations Department of Peace-Keeping Operations-UNDPKO Office of the Military Adviser in collaboration with the DPA, Peacemaking Databank Team. 2006. *Military Operational Principles for Negotiating Ceasefire Agreements.* UN Peacemaker Operational Guidance Note. New York: United Nations, June 2.

United Nations-DPA. 2010. *Drafting Mediator's Guidance Notes.* Draft Guidelines. New York: United Nations.

United Nations Human Rights Council. 2008. 8th Special Session of the Human Rights Council: The Situation of the Human Rights in the East of the Democratic Republic of the Congo, Friday 28 November 2008. New York: UN Human Rights Council. http://www2.ohchr.org/english/bodies/hrcouncil/specialsession/8/index.htm.

United Nations Secretary-General. 1994. *Declaration on the Enhancement of Cooperation between the United Nations and Regional Arrangements or Agencies in the Maintenance of International Peace and Security.* A/RES/49/57. New York: UN General Assembly.

United Nations Secretary-General. 2001. *Prevention of Armed Conflict.* Report of the Secretary-General. A/55/985-S/2001/574. New York: United Nations.

United Nations Secretary-General. 2004. *Letter Dated 12 July 2004 from the Secretary-General Addressed to the President of the Security Council.* S/2004/567. New York: United Nations.

United Nations Secretary-General. 2006. *A Regional-Global Security Partnership: Challenges and Opportunities.* Report of the Secretary General to the UN Security Council. New York: United Nations, July 28. http://www.unhcr.org/refworld/docid/453780ed0.html.

United Nations Secretary-General. 2008. *Report of the Secretary-General on the Relationship between the United Nations and Regional Organizations, in particular the African Union, in the Maintenance of International Peace and Security.* S/2008/186. New York: United Nations, March 24.

United Nations Secretary-General. 2009a. *Implementing the Responsibility to Protect: Report of the Secretary General.* A/63/677. New York: United Nations, January 30.

United Nations Secretary-General. 2009b. *Report of the Secretary-General of the UN to the Security Council on Enhancing Mediation and Its Support Activities.* S/2009/189. April. New York: United Nations. http://daccess-ods.un.org/TMP/6862033.html.

United Nations Secretary-General. 2010. *Early Warning, Assessment and the Responsibility to Protect.* Report of the Secretary-General at the General Assembly's 64th session. A/64/864. New York: United Nations.

United Nations Security Council. 2004. *Security Council Reiterates Firm Support for Somali Reconciliation Process.* Security Council 4,915th Meeting. February 25. http://www.un.org/News/Press/docs/2004/sc8007.doc.htm.

United Nations Statistics Division—Demographic and Social Statistics. 2009. School Life Expectancy. *United Nations Statistics Division.* http://unstats.un.org/unsd/demographic/products/socind/education.htm.

United Nations-UNIFEM. 2009a. *Ceasefires—Addressing Conflict Related Sexual Violence.* New York: United Nations.

United Nations-UNIFEM. 2009b. *Conflict Related Sexual Violence and Peace Negotiations: Implementing Security Council Resolution 1820.* New York: United Nations.

United Nations-UNIFEM. 2009c. *Joint Strategy on Gender and Mediation.* New York: UN Development Fund for Women (UNIFEM) & the UN Department of Political Affairs (UNDPA).

UN Special Advisers of the Secretary-General on the Prevention of Genocide and the Responsibility to Protect on the Situation in Kyrgyzstan. 2010. United Nations Press Release. June 15. http://www.un.org/preventgenocide/adviser/pdf/Statement%20of%20Special%20Advisers%20Deng%20and%20Luck%20on%20the%20situation%20in%20Kyrgyzstan%2015%20June%202010.pdf.

Ury, W. 1999. *Violent Human Nature? Telling a New Story.* Presentation at Program on Negotiation, Harvard Law School October 1.

Ury, W. 2000. *The Third Side.* New York: Penguin Books.

Ury, W. 2007. *The Power of a Positive No: How to Say No and Still Get to Yes.* New York: Bantam Books.

U.S. Constitution, Art.1 sec.8 and Art.2.sec.2.

Ushahidi. http://www.ushahidi.com/.

Valdez, A. 2003. Toward a Typology of Contemporary Mexican American Youth Gangs. In *Gangs and Society: Alternative Perspectives,* ed. L. Kontos, D. Brotherton, and L. Barrios, 12–40. New York: Columbia University Press.

Vallacher, R. R., and A. Nowak. 2007. Dynamical Social Psychology: Finding Order in the Flow of Human Experience. In *Social psychology: Handbook of Basic Principles,* ed. A. W. Kruglanski and E. T. Higgins, 734–758. New York: Guilford Publications.

Vallacher, R. R., P. T. Coleman, A. Nowak, and L. Bui-Wrzosinska. 2010. Rethinking Intractable Conflict: The Perspective of Dynamical Systems. *American Psychologist* 65, no. 4: 262–278.

van Dijk, T. A., and R. Wodak. 2004. Politics, Ideology and Discourse. In *Encyclopedia of Language and Linguistics.* Atlanta, GA: Elsevier.

van Hofwegen, S. L. 2008. Unjust and Ineffective: A Critical Look at California's Step Act. *Southern California Interdisciplinary Law Journal* 18: 679. http://heinonline. org/HOL/Page?handle=hein.journals/scid18&id=685&div=&collection= journals.

van Tongeren, P. J. 2010. *Infrastructures for Peace.* Working Paper GPPAC. July. http:// www.gppac.net/page.php?id=1#par2544.

van Tongeren, P.J.M. 2001. Coordination and Codes of Conduct: The Challenge of Coordination and Networking. In *Peacebuilding: A Field Guide,* ed. L. Reychler and T. Paffenholz, 510–519. Boulder, CO: Lynne Reinner Publishers.

Varshney, A. 2002. *Ethnic Conflict and Civic Life: Hindus and Muslims in India.* New Haven, CT: Yale University Press.

Vasquez, J. A. 1993. *The War Puzzle.* Cambridge: Cambridge University Press.

Villa-Vicencio, C., and W. Verwoerd. 2000. *Looking Back, Reaching Forward: Reflections on the Truth and Reconciliation Commission of South Africa.* Cape Town, South Africa: University of Cape Town Press.

Vogel, G. 2004. The Evolution of the Golden Rule. *Science* 303, no. 5661: 1128–1131.

Volf, M. 1996. *Exclusion and Embrace: A Theological Exploration of Identity, Otherness, and Reconciliation.* Nashville: Abingdon Press.

Volf, M. 2006. *The End of Memory: Remembering Rightly in a Violent World.* Grand Rapids, MI: Eerdmans.

Volkan, V. 1998. *Bloodlines: From Ethnic Pride to Ethnic Terror.* Boulder, CO: Westview.

von Schorlemer, S. 2007. The Responsibility to Protect as an Element of Peace. *Policy Paper 28.* Bonn: Development and Peace Foundation.

Waaijman, K. 2002. *Spirituality: Forms, Foundations, Methods,* Trans. J. Vriend. Leuven: Peeters.

Wachira, G. 2008. Citizens in Action: Making Peace in the Post-Election Crisis in Kenya. http://bit.ly/KenyaCCP.

Wacquant, L. 2001. Deadly Symbiosis: When Ghetto and Prison Meet and Mesh. *Punishment and Society* 3, no. 1: 95–134.

Wade, G. 2009. Ming China, the "Tribute System" and the Rhetoric of Imperial China's Foreign Relations. In *The Nature of Political and Spiritual Relations Among Asian Leaders and Polities from the 14th to the 18th Centuries.* Paper prepared for the Roundtable on Institute of Asian Research, University of British Columbia, Vancouver, Canada, April.

Waldmeir, P. 1998. *Anatomy of a Miracle: The End of Apartheid and the Birth of the New South Africa.* New Brunswick, NJ: Rutgers University Press.

Wallensteen, P. 2009. The Strengths and Limits of Academic Diplomacy: The Case of Bougainville. In *Diplomacy in Theory and Practice, Essays in Honor of Christer Jönsson,* ed. K. Aggestam and B. Järnek, 258–281. Liber: Malmö.

Wallensteen, P. 2010. Experiments in Academic Diplomacy. In *Experiments with Peace. A Book Celebrating Peace at Johan Galtung's 80th Anniversary,* ed. J. Johansson, et al., 354–364. Oxford, England: Fahamu Books.

Wallensteen, P. 2011a. *Peace Research: Theory and Practice.* London: Routledge.

Wallensteen, P. 2011b. *Understanding Conflict Resolution. War, Peace and the Global System,* 3rd ed. London: Sage.

Wallensteen, P., and L. Harbom. 2010. Armed Conflicts, 1946–2009. *Journal of Peace Research* 47, no. 4: 501–509.

Wallerstein, I. M. 1974. *The Modern World-System*. Vol. 2. New York: Academic Press.

Wallerstein, I. M. 1997. *Modern World System: Capitalist Agriculture & the Origins of the European World Economy in the 16th Century*. Waltham, MA: Academic Press.

Walter, B. F. 2002. *Committing to Peace: The Successful Settlement of Civil Wars*. Princeton, NJ: Princeton University Press.

Walton, H., and S.D.B. Cook. 1971. *The Political Philosophy of Martin Luther King, Jr.* Westport, CT: Greenwood.

Walton, R. E., and R. B. McKersie. 1991. *A Behavioral Theory of Labor Negotiations: An Analysis of a Social Interaction System*. Ithaca, NY: Cornell University Press.

Waltz, K. 1979. *Theory of International Relations*. New York: Random House.

Walzer, M. 1977. *Just and Unjust Wars: A Moral Argument with Historical Illustrations*. New York: Basic Books.

Wang, G. 1983. The Rhetoric of a Lesser Empire: Early Sung Relations with its Neighbors. In *China Among Equals: The Middle Kingdom and its Neighbors, 10th–14th Centuries*, ed. M. Rossabi, 47–66. Los Angeles: University of California Press.

Wang, Yuan-Kang. 2010. *Harmony and War: Confucian Culture and Chinese Power Politics*. New York: Columbia University Press.

Wanis-St. John, A. 2005. Cultural Pathways in Negotiation and Conflict Management. In *The Handbook of Dispute Resolution*, ed. M. L. Moffitt and R. C. Bordone, 118–134. San Francisco: Jossey-Bass.

Wanis-St. John, A. 2011. *Back Channel Negotiation*. New York: Syracuse University Press.

Wanis-St. John, A., and D. Kew. 2008. Civil Society and Peace Negotiations: Confronting exclusion. *International Negotiation* 13, no. 1: 11–36.

Wasserstrom, S. 1995. *Between Muslim and Jew: The Problem of Symbiosis in Early Islam*. Princeton, NJ: Princeton University Press.

Weber, M. 1946. Politics as a Vocation. In *From Max Weber: Essays in Sociology*, ed. H. Gerth and C. W. Mills. New York: Oxford University Press.

Weber, M., and H. H. Gerth. 1968. *The Religion of China*. Glencoe, IL: Free Press.

Weber, M., H. H. Gerth, and C. W. Mills. 1958. *From Max Weber: Essays in Sociology*. London: Routledge.

Wehr, P., and J. P. Lederach. 1996. Mediating Conflict in Central America. In *Resolving International Conflict: The Theory and Practice of Mediation*, ed. J. Bercovitch, 55–74. Boulder, CO: Lynne Rienner Publishers.

Weigel, G. 2003. *The Final Revolution: The Resistance Church and the Collapse of Communism*. Cambridge, MA: Oxford University Press.

Weiner, E., ed. 1998. *The Handbook of Interethnic Coexistence*. New York: Continuum.

Weiss-Rosmarin, T. 1967. "Toward Jewish-Muslim Dialogue." *The Jewish Spectator*, September.

Welsh, D. 2009. *The Rise and Fall of Apartheid*. Charlottesville: University of Virginia Press.

Wennmann, A. 2010. *Development Assistance: Guidelines for Mediators*. Centre on Conflict, Development and Peace-building (CCDP) Issue Brief. Geneva: Graduate Institute of International and Development Studies, February.

Werdegar, M. M. 1999. Enjoining the Constitution: The Use of Public Nuisance Abatement Injunctions Against Urban Street Gangs. *Stanford Law Review* 51, no. 2: 409–445.

Werner, S., and A. Yuen. 2005. Making and Keeping Peace. *International Organization* 59, no. 2: 261–292.

Whitaker, B. E. 2010. Soft Balancing among Weak States? Evidence from Africa. *International Affairs* (London) 86, no. 5: 1109–1127.

Whitehead, N. L. 1990. The Snake Warriors—Sons of the Tiger's Teeth: A Descriptive Analysis of Carib Warfare, ca. 1500–1820. In *The Anthropology of War*, ed. J. Haas, 146–170. Cambridge: Cambridge University Press.

Whitfield, T. 2010. *External Actors in Mediation: Dilemmas and Options for Mediators*. Geneva: Centre for Humanitarian Dialogue, February.

Wilber, K. 2006. *Integral Spirituality: A Startling New Role for Religion in the Modern and Postmodern World*. Boston: Integral Books.

Williams, A. 2010. Strategic Planning in the Executive Office of the UN Secretary-General. *Global Governance* 16, no. 4 (December): 435–449.

Wilkinson, R. G., and K. E. Pickett. 2007. The Problems of Relative Deprivation: Why some Societies do Better than Others. *Social Science & Medicine* (1982) 65, no. 9 (November): 1965–1978. http://www.ncbi.nlm.nih.gov/pubmed/17618718.

Wilkinson, R. G., and K. E. Pickett. 2009. *The Spirit Level: Why Greater Equality Makes Societies Stronger*. London: Bloomsbury.

Wolfers, A. 1956. *The Anglo-American Tradition in Foreign Affairs: Readings from Thomas More to Woodrow Wilson*. Seattle, WA: Elliots Books.

Wolpert, S. 2001. *Gandhi's Passion: The Life and Legacy of Mahatma Gandhi*. New York: Oxford University Press.

Wolterstorff, N. 2008. *Justice: Rights and Wrongs*. Princeton, NJ: Princeton University Press.

Women War Peace. 2009. *Pre-Ceasefire Agreements, Ceasefires and Ceasefire Monitoring*. New York: United Nations.

Woocher, L. 2012 (forthcoming). The Responsibility to Prevent: Toward a Strategy. In *The Responsibility to Protect*, ed. W. A. Knight and F. E. London: Routledge.

Woocher, L., and P. Stares. 2010. *Enhancing International Cooperation for Preventing Genocide and Mass Atrocities: The Case for Transatlantic Cooperation*. Paper presented at the International Symposium on Preventing Genocide and Mass Atrocities, November 15, Paris, France.

Woodward, P. 2004. Somalia and Sudan: A Tale of Two Peace Processes. *The Round Table* 93, no. 375: 469–481.

Working with Armenia embassy project. n.d. Let's PeaceJam! http://ukinarmenia.fco.gov.uk/en/about-us/working-with-armenia/embassy-projects/project-stories/peace-jam.

World Economic Forum. 2009. *The Global Competitiveness Report 2009–2010*. Geneva: World Economic Forum.

World Health Organization. 2006. *World Health Report 2006: Working Together for Health*. World Health Organization.

World Public Opinion. 2008. *Freedom of the Media*. May 1. World Public Opinion.org.

World Public Opinion. 2009. *Most People Think Their Nation's Foreign Policy Is Morally No Better Than Average: Global Poll—World Public Opinion*. World Public Opinion.org. http://www.worldpublicopinion.org/pipa/articles/views_on_countriesregions_bt/584.php.

World Summit Outcome. 2005. http://www.un.org/summit2005/presskit/fact_sheet.pdf.

Wright, N. T. 2006. *Evil and the Justice of God*. Nottingham, UK: IVP Books.

Wright, Q. 1965. *Study of War*, 2nd ed. Chicago: University of Chicago Press.

Wright, R. 2009. *Iran's Green Movement*. Congressional Testimony, December. http://www.usip.org/publications/irans-green-movement.

Xocali: The Chronicle of Unseen Forgery and Falsifications. http://xocali.net/.

Yates, R.D.S. 2009. Law and the Military in Early China. In *Military Culture in Imperial China*, ed. N. di Cosmo, 23–44. Cambridge, MA: Harvard University Press.

Yawanarajah, N. 2009. *Draft Confidence Building Measure (CBMs) in Peace Processes*. Mediation Support Unit (MSU) and Department of Political Affairs (DPA). New York: United Nations.

Yoder, J. H. 1983. *What Would You Do?* Scottdale, PA: Herald Press.

Yogananda, P. 1995. *The Bhagavad Gita: God Talks with Arjuna: Royal Science of God Realization*. Los Angeles: Self Realization Fellowship.

Yoroms, G. 1993. ECOMOG and West African Regional Security: A Nigerian Perspective. *A Journal of Opinion* 21, no. 1: 84–91.

You and the Atomic Bomb by Orwell, G. http://forums.civfanatics.com/showthread.php?t=141639.

Young, C. 1994. *The African Colonial State in Comparative Perspective*. New Haven, CT: Yale University Press.

Zablocka-Bursa, A., and R, Praszkier. (forthcoming). Social Change Initiated by Social Entrepreneurs. In *Dynamical System Approach as Implemented in Social Sciences*, ed. A. Nowak, D. Bree, and K. Nowak-Winkowska. New York: Springer.

Zahar, M. J. 2008. Reframing the Spoiler Debate in Peace Processes. In *Contemporary Peacemaking; Conflict, Peace Processes and Post-War Reconstruction*, ed. J. Darby and R. Mac Ginty, chapter 12. Houndsmill, UK: Palgrave/Macmillan.

Zakaria, F. 1997. The Rise of Illiberal Democracy. *Foreign Affairs* 76, no. 6: 22–43.

Zartman, I. W. 1989. *Ripe for Resolution: Conflict and Intervention in Africa*. Cambridge, MA: Oxford University Press.

Zartman, I. W. 1995a. Negotiating the South African Conflict. In *Elusive peace: Negotiating an End to Civil Wars*, ed. W. Zartman, 147–174. Washington, DC: Brookings Institution.

Zartman, I. W., ed. 1995b. Elusive Peace: Negotiating an End to Civil Wars. Washington, DC: Brookings Institution Press.

Zartman, I. W. 2000a. Ripeness: The Hurting Stalemate and Beyond. In *Conflict Resolution after the Cold War*, ed. P. C. Stern and D. Druckman, 225–250. Washington, DC: National Academy Press.

Zartman, I. W. 2000b. *Traditional Cures for Modern Conflicts: African Conflict "Medicine."* Boulder, CO: Lynne Rienner.

Zartman, I. W. 2001. The Timing of Peace Initiatives: Hurting Stalemates and Ripe Moments. *Ethnopolitics* 1, no. 1: 8–18.

Zartman, I. W. 2006. Negotiating Internal, Ethnic and Identity Conflicts in a Globalized World. *International Negotiation* 11: 253–272.

Zelizer, C., and R. A. Rubenstein, eds. 2009. *Peacebuilding: Creating the Structure and Capacity for Peace*. Sterling, VA: Kumarian Press.

Index

Aall, Pamela, 693–94
Abdullah, Imam Muhammad, 517
Aboli, Sadaf, 12
Abraham Path Initiative, 529–30
Abraham's Path, 529–42; *vs.* Abraham Path Initiative, 529–30; broad coalition built around, 539–42; conclusion, 542; described, 529; history and evolution, 531–32; local decision making in, 536–38; as long-term endeavor, 539; meta challenges, 534–35; midlevel challenges, 535–36; negotiation theory and practice perspective, 536–38; peace contributions of, 530–31; power of, 540–41; range of people involved in, 541–42; sequencing negotiations to develop, 538–39; vertical and horizontal negotiations to develop, 532–34; vision of, 530
Abu Awwad, Ali, 235
Academic assertiveness, 466–67
Academic diplomacy, 457–76; academic assertiveness, 466–67; cases of, 466–73; diplomacy for a formula, 468–70; formulation requires elaboration, 470–73; introducing, 457–58; mediation in, 458–60; mediators in, 463–64; promise of, 473–76; quiet diplomacy, 467–68; seminars in,

460–62, 467–68; typology of, 464–66
Aceh, unfinished business in, 773
Aceh Monitoring Mission, 119
Acholi of Northern Uganda, 286–90
Acholi Religious Leaders' Peace Initiative, 129
Activists in social media, 478–80
Adams, Gerry, 672
Adamson, Daniel, 537
Adivasis, 6
Afghan Institute of Learning, 239–40
Afghanistan: Asad Danish operating in, 508; intractable conflicts in, 638; Jaghori District of, 492, 496, 499–500; peace agreements, 353; Taliban occupation, 492–93, 496, 499; U.S. policy in, 709–10, 714
Africa, 400–417. *See also* South African peace process; Sub-Saharan Africa; Ghana, 401–7; Great Lakes region, Ubuntu principles and, 295–307; Kenya, 401–5, 407–9; national architecture for peace, 406–7; peacemaking traditions in, 275–93; South Africa, 403–5
African Great Lakes region, Ubuntu principles and, 295–307; intergroup

conflicts impact on, 297–300; multicultural education and, 302–6
African National Congress (ANC), 722,
723, 724–26; exiles and negotiating,
732–33; *vs.* white urgency, 733–36
African traditions of peacemaking,
275–93; Acholi of Northern Uganda
and, 286–90; challenge of revitalizing,
291–92; contextualizing, 276; culture
and, 280–81; important lessons from,
292–93; limitations of, 290–91; *vs.*
official-vertical peacemaking, 291;
peacebuilding and, 277, 279; reconciliation and, 279–86; restorative
justice and, 282–83, 287–90; Ubuntu
societies and, 283–86; utility of,
290–92; vertical and horizontal
dimensions of, 276–77, 278–79, 292
African Union, 703; Constitutive Act of,
424; ECOWAS, 424; multiactor
approach in, 741; Panel of Eminent
Personalities, 426; R2P in, 424, 426
Agenda for Peace, An (Boutros-Ghali),
276, 429
Aggadic, 251
Ahimsa, 171–72
Ahmed, Sheikh Sharif Sheikh, 341
Ahtisaari, Martti, 116–19
Akhavan, Payam, 128, 131
Al-Aqsa Intifada, 38, 248
Al-As, Amr ibn, 251
Aliyev, Ilham, 480
Amidon, Elias, 531
Amir, Yehuda, 316
Amir, Yigal, 248
Amnesty International, 427
Analects, 212, 215
Analytic empathy, 316
Anand, Sukirat, 13
Ancient peacemakers, 563–81; bonobos,
573–74; chimpanzees, 568–70; *Epic of
Gilgamesh, The,* 577–78; gods,
heroes, histories, and images, 574–77;
humans as primates, 564–66; *Iliad,*
579–81; *Mahabharata, The,* 578–79; pri-
mate peace, 566–68; Rhesus monkeys,
570–72; stumptail monkeys, 572–73
Anderson, Mary, 380, 492–501
Anderson, Miriam, 344–75
Anhad (Act Now for Harmony and
Democracy), 8–9, 13

Annan, Kofi, 125, 392, 401, 422, 424, 426,
429, 713
Annual Report to the General Assembly,
1999 (Annan), 429–30
Anthropology examples of peacemaking, 550–59; ceremonies and symbolism, unifying, 554; compensation,
555–56; competition, ritualizing,
554–55; Expanding the Us, 551–52;
interconnections, nurturing, 552;
interdependence, 552–53; justice,
558–59; reconciliation rituals, 557–58;
restoration of peace, 555; structural
or institutional, 555; sustaining peace
and preventing war, 550–51; third
parties, 556; values, 553–54
Anticipatory capacity, 315
Apartheid laws, 722–23
Applied systems thinking (AST): in
dimensions of peacemaking, 622–36;
field, 623–24; interconnectedness, 623;
scale, 623; worldview, 624
Arafat, Yasser, 467–68, 708, 709, 746
Arai, Tatsushi, 310, 315
Arbenz, Jacobo, 752
Arbitration: as intervention type, 686; as
modality of decision making, 381–82
Arias, Oscar, 706–7
Aristotle, 613–14, 617–18; metaphysics, 614–15; philosopher-scientists,
614–16; praxis of peacemaking *vs.* its
poiesis, 548, 610; scientific investigation, 613
Ariyaratne, A. T., 192–210
Armed groups, interaction with,
498–500
Armengol, Fisas, 137
Armenia, 468–70; apology campaign
online, 485–86; Azerbaijani Film Festival, 487–88; Azerbaijani relations
with, 481–89; domestic violence and
physical abuse in army, 480; Eurovision song contest, 486–87; Khojali
massacre, 488
Arnault, Jean, 143
Arns, Evaristo, 267–68
Art in Action, 311, 312
Arts and movement-based approaches
to peacemaking, 308–25; applying, 318–19; cautions and caveats of,
317–18; conflict transformation and,

323–25; CRANE fieldwork in Sierra Leone of, 321–23; CRANE fieldwork in Vancouver, Canada of, 319–21; explained, 310–11; expressive arts as, 311–12; ourselves as physical beings and, 309–10; overview of, 308–9; reasons for success of, 312–14; shifting perception of "the other" and, 316; in Sub-Saharan Africa, 312; symbolic tools and cultural fluency in, 314–16
Asad, Hafez-al, 708
Ashoka: Innovators for the Public, 504
Assad Library speech, 84–85
Assis, Yom Tov, 251
Association of Southeast Asian Nations (ASEAN), 119, 141, 428
Atrocities, R2P and, 421–23
Attractors: collapse of complexity and, 642–43; conflict and peace in Mozambique, 640–41; constructive, 647–48; destructive, 648–49; dynamics, 641–42; initiatives, 646–47; landscapes, changing, 644–45; landscapes, navigating, 645–49; manifest and latent attractors of conflict, 643–44; recognizing systems, 645–46; systems of, 638–39; time scales, 646–47
Australopithecus, 566, 573
Autobiography of an L.A. Gang Member, The (Scott), 514
Awad, Mubarak, 235
Axelrod, Robert M., 570
Aylwin, Patricio, 267
Azerbaijan, 468–70; apology campaign online, 485–86; Armenian relations with, 481–89; Azerbaijani Film Festival, 487–88; Eurovision song contest, 486–87; Khojali massacre, 488; youth activists arrested in, 480

Baechler, Günther, 18–35
Baker, James, 681
Baldwin, Lewis V., 188
Bambaataa, Afrika, 514–15
Bandeba, Vincent, 295–307
Bangayimbaga, Apollinaire, 295–307
Ban Ki-Moon, 425, 426
Barak, Ehud, 708, 709, 746
Barnard, Niel, 725, 731, 736
Barnes, Catherine, 144
Bar-On, Dan, 247–49

Bar-Tal, D., 502
Barth, Karl, 259
Bartoli, Andrea, 107–21, 379–83, 545–49
Basic Human Needs theory (BHN), 187
Batarai, Babaram, 137
Beauregard, Mario, 588
Begin, Menachem, 151, 152
Beilin, Yossi, 746
Beliak, Haim, 254
Bellamy, Alex, 430
Belo, Bishop, 470
Benedict XV, Pope, 260
Bereaved Families Forum, 235
Between Muslim and Jew (Wasserstrom), 251
Bin Laden, Osama, 139
Bizos, George, 732
Black Spades, 514–15
Bleeker, Mô, 752, 757
Block, Thomas, 250, 251, 253, 254
Blogs/bloggers, 478, 480, 483–86, 490
Bloomfield, David, 693
Bohm, David, 148
Bolivia, UN's conflict management assistance in, 389
Bombande, Emmanuel, 389
Bonhoeffer, Dietrich, 260
Bonobos, 573–74
Borris, Eileen R., 66, 606, 607
Borrow, Rufus, 188
Bosnia-Herzegovina, 57, 421
Botha, P. W., 723, 725, 731
Bottom-up peacemaking, 277
Bougainville dispute, 466–67
Bougainville Revolutionary Army (BRA), 466–67
Boulding, Kenneth, 63
Boutros-Ghali, Boutros, 276, 429
Boyle, Greg, 518–19
Boyle, Robert, 616
Boys n the Hood (film), 517
Branch, Adam, 122–33
Brand-Jacobsen, Kai, 402
Brauer, Jurgen, 445
Brooks, E. Bruce, 215, 217
Brooks, Taeko, 215, 217
Brotherton, David, 519
Buber, Martin, 172
Bucher, Josef, 748
Buddha Dhamma, 192–93

Buddhism and peacemaking, 192–210; agenda for, 200–210; five-stage awakening process of, 203–4; insight meditation and, 207–9; loving kindness meditation and, 209–10; methods used in, 204–5; mindful breathing meditation and, 205–7; overview of, 192–93, 200–203; Principle of Paticcasamuppada and, 198–200; supremacy of the mind and, 193–98

Budrus, women peacebuilders in, 43–47

Building Peace: Sustainable Reconciliation in Divided Societies (Lederach), 400

Bui-Wrzosinska, Lan, 637–50

Bureau of Justice Assistance, 512

Burton, John, 107, 108–9, 187, 461, 462, 545, 549, 608, 668, 684–85, 695

Burundi: cultural competence in, enhancing, 303–4; empathetic ability strengthened in, 305–6; human diversity affirmed in, 304–5; human interconnectedness in, 305; unfinished business in, 773–77

Burundi, Ubuntu principles and, 295–307; intergroup conflicts and, 297–300; multicultural education and, 302–6; overview of, 295–96

Bush, George H. W., 676

Bush, George W., 710, 714

Cairo Agreement, 708

Calvin, John, 263

Cambodia, unfinished business in, 773–77

Camino de Santiago de Compostela, 531

Campbell, David, 247

Carnales, 519–20

Carnegie Commission on Preventing Deadly Conflict, 429

Carnegie Endowment for International Peace, 158

Carter, Jimmy, 112, 150, 151, 152, 707

Carter, Rosalynn, 112

Carter Center as NGO, 112–14; criteria for engagement by, 112–13; notable experiences of, 113–14; principles of, 112

Catholics, Polish: healing the history of, 254; psychological and historical issues of, 254–56

Caucasus Center for Peace-Making Initiatives (CCPR), 487

Caucasus Edition (IMAGINE Center), 482–84, 489

Cause and effect, Buddhism and chain of, 198

Causes, correlates differentiated from, 394–96

CDA Collaborative Learning Projects, 494, 500

Ceasefire agreements, mediating, 135–46; concepts and language of, 137–38; early recovery and development assistance in, 144–45; effective implementation and, 145–46; engaging belligerents and, 138–39; gender sensitivity and, 143–44; humanitarian assistance as point of entry to, 139–40; human rights and transitional justice in, 142–43; overview of, 135–36; ownership and, 138; protecting civilians and, 142; role of NGOs and civil society in, 144; structure of agreements for, 140–42; understanding operational environment and, 136–37

Cease-fire and peace implementation, 61

Ceasefire mediation, concepts of, 137–38

Ceasefire monitoring, 144

Center for Security Studies, 757

Centre for Humanitarian Dialogue (HD or "the Centre"), 114–16; policy program themes of, 115–16; principles and beliefs of, 114–15; violent conflict engagement by, 115

Ceremonies, unifying, 554

Challenges in peacemaking, 701–18; assessing interventions as, 710–11; interveners and interventions as, 702–10; managing obstacles to, 712–17; overview of, 701–2

Change process appropriate to relational paradigm, 154–57

Chatterjee, Bankim, 168

Chigas, Diana, 761–78

Chimpanzees, 568–70

China, Confucianism in, 211–24

Christian peacemaking, 257–71; concept of reconciliation in, 259–66; overview of, 257–59; practice of reconciliation in, 266–70

Christian reconciliation, 257–71; concept of, 259–66; practice of, 266–70

Christian tradition, Islamophobia in, 246–47

Civilian protection in R2P, 431–32

Civilization, Gandhi's definition of, 168

Civil Society Institute (Armenia), 485

Claes, Jonas, 380, 420–34

Classical era, Confucianism in, 213–17

Clinton, Bill, 258, 708, 709, 746

Clinton, Hillary, 480

Cobb, Sara, 328–42

Coetsee, Kobie, 725, 731, 736, 737

Coexistence in Islamic peacemaking, 231–33

Coleman, Peter, 637–50

Collaboration in Somalia, 337–39

Collaborative Learning Projects (CDA), 494

Collapse of complexity and attractors, 642–43

Collective action in social media, 478–79, 486

Colletta, Nat, 66, 135–46

Colombia: Ecuador–Colombia relations, 389–90; engaging the belligerents, 139; FARC, 53, 54, 57–58, 136, 493; indigenous communities, 493; peace agreements, 354–55; unifying identity of the peace villages in, 495–96

Combatants for Peace, 485

Common enemy, 576

Communication platforms online, 482

Community-based organizations (CBOs), 533

Community of Sant'Egidio as NGO, 109–11; early years of, 109; elements of success by, 110; information-gathering process of, 111; peace process involvement by, 109–10

Community strategies for conflict prevention, 492–501; conclusion, 500–501; evidence, origin of, 494; introduction, 492–94; strategic connectors, 494–500

Compensation, 555–56

Competition, ritualizing, 554–55

Competitive processes, 603

Complexity, collapse of, 642–43

Comprehensive Anti-Apartheid Act, 724

Comprehensive Peace Agreement, 748, 750–51

Conciliation, as intervention type, 686

Conciliation Resources, 484–85

Conflict: analysis and peacemaking interventions, 710–11; constructive, 602–5; destructive, 602–5; escalation and social media, 486–89; long-term, guidelines for working with, 645–49; narratives, 649; prevention (See Infrastructures for peace); resolution, 76–78, 157 (See also Noninstitutional organizations and conflict resolution); rules for managing, 608

Conflict Resolution, Arts and Intercultural Experience (CRANE), 319–23; Sierra Leone fieldwork of, 321–23; Vancouver, Canada fieldwork of, 319–21

Conflict Resolution: Track-Two Diplomacy (McDonald), 63

Conflict Transformation and Peace-Building Resource Centre in Stepanakert (Nagorno Karabakh), 485

Confucianism and peacemaking, 211–24; in classical era, 213–17; conceptions of peace and, 212–13; in eras of division, 222–24; in imperial era, 217–22; overview of, 211

Confucius, 212

Congress of South African Trade Unions (COSATU), 723

Constitutive Act of the African Union, 424

Constructive attractors, 647–48

Constructive conflict: development of, 604–5; processes in, 602–4

Consultation as intervention type, 686

Contingency model of third-party intervention, 689–92; evidence supporting, 694–97; variations and criticisms of, 692–94

Cooperative relations, 602

Correlates differentiated from causes, 394–96

Cosmopolitanism, 180

Costa Rica, GDP per capita, 447, 448

Cousins, Norman, 157

Crazy-patriot (blogger), 487

Creating Democracy, Celebrating Diversity campaign, 13

Creativity: Arai definition of, 310; in
    peacemaking, 630
Crimes against humanity, 420–28, 434
Criminality, 136, 145, 384, 455, 514, 523
Criminal trials and ICC, 123–25
Crips, 520
Crisis Management and Conflict Resolu-
    tion, 116
Crisis Management Initiative (CMI),
    116–19; Aceh peace process and, 118;
    categories of, 116–17; civil society
    actors roles in, 117; purpose of, 116;
    reasons for success of, 118–19
Criticality, 593–94, 598, 599
Crocker, Chester, 693–94
Crossette, Barbara, 427–28
Crude Law of Social Relations,
    Deutsch's, 604–5
Cultural competence, enhancing, 303–4
Cultural diversity in Islamic peacemak-
    ing, 231–33
Cultural fluency, key components of,
    315–16
Culture and peacemaking, 280–81
Curle, Adam, 107
Cyclone Nargis in Burma, R2P and,
    427–28
Cyprus: economic progress and, 770;
    UN's conflict management assistance
    in, 391
Czyzewski, Krzysztof, 507

Dalits, 6
Dancing at the Crossroads (DTC), 319,
    323–25
Danish, Asad, 508
Dannin, Robert, 518
Darby, John, 672
Dartmouth Conference, 158, 159
Decision making, modalities of, 381–82
Decommitment, 675–81; art and practice
    of, 675–77; strategies and tactics of,
    677–81
Deductive argumentation, 617–18
De Gruchy, John, 259–60
De Klerk, F. W., 725, 726, 731, 734, 735,
    737–38
De Mistura, Staffan, 26
Democratic Republic of the Congo
    (DRC), R2P in, 428–29

Deng, Francis, 425, 426, 427, 431, 432
Department for Political affairs (DPA),
    386–88, 390, 391, 397
Descartes, René, 616
De Soto, Alvaro, 143
Destructive attractors, 648–49
Destructive conflict: development of,
    604–5; processes in, 602–4
Deutsch, Karl, 680
Deutsch, Morton, 547, 601–9, 673; Crude
    Law of Social Relations, 604–5
Developmental initiatives, 647
De Waal, Frans B. M., 572, 573–74
De Waal, Thomas, 488
Dharnas, 9
Dholkia, Rahul, 14
Dialogue, 780–92; as continuum of war
    and peace, 781–86; defined, 780–81;
    position, 789; practitioner of, 789–92;
    risk and, 786–89; understanding, 791
Dialogue through Films (Conciliation
    Resources), 484–85
Diamond, Louise, 63–64, 65–66, 622–36
Dickman, Karen, 66
"Die, The" (Fiasco), 516
Digital Underground, 515–16
Diplomacy for a formula, 468–70
Discontinuities, identifying, 648
Dispute resolution, ceasefire agreements
    and, 141
District peace committees (DPC), 388,
    409
Diverse interveners, 703–4
Diverse interventions, 704–6
Diyya, 236
Dlakama, Alfonso, 641, 646
Doha Agreement, 229
Dosa (aversions), 193
Doxtader, Eric, 260
Drayton, William (Bill), 504
DuBois, W.E.B., 162
Du Toit, André, 264
Dynamical social psychology, 638
Dynamical systems perspective on
    peacemaking, 637–50. See also Intrac-
    table conflicts; conclusion, 649–50;
    conflict and peace in Mozambique,
    640–41; long-term conflicts, guide-
    lines for working with, 645–49
Dynamic librarian, 508

East Timor, 470–73

East Timor Study Group, 470–73

Eat the third party, 627

Economic Community of West African States (ECOWAS), 424

Economic domain, unfinished business in, 769–70

Economic security, 608

Economic value of peace, 444–45

Economy and environment as peace process topic, 743

Ecuador-Colombia, UN's conflict management assistance in, 389–90

Education and the media, 608

Egeland, Jan, 51–61

Einstein, Albert, 154, 310, 622, 628

Eisenhower, Dwight, 157

Elaboration required for formulation, 470–73

Elections, 395–96

Electronic mailing lists, 486

Eliasson, Jan, 459, 468–69

Eliatamby, Maneshka, 179–89

El-Kader, Abd, 239

ELN guerrillas, 53, 54

Embeddedness, 315

Emergent creativity, 592–94, 597–600

Empathic ability, strengthening, 305–6

Empowerment, 20

Energy dimension of peacemaking, 628–31

Engaging the parties, ceasefire mediation and, 138–38

Entry points, importance of, 393

Epic of Gilgamesh, The, 577–78

Episodic initiatives, 646–47

Eras of division, peacemaking in, 222–24

Escalation, stages of, 687–89

Esquipulos Agreement, 706–7

Ethnic cleansing, 420–28, 434, 626, 709

ETH Zurich, 757

Eurasia Partnership Foundation, 485

European Steel and Coal Commission, 530

Evans, Gareth, 424, 713

Evolutionary dimension of peacemaking, 631–35

Expanding the Us, 551–52

Experience, conceptualization of, 150–54

Exponential spread, 507

Expressive arts as peacemaking tool, 311–12

Expressive capacity, 315

External actors' roles and ceasefire mediation, 144

Extremists on both sides, curbing, 608–9

Facebook, 478, 480, 485–88

Fact-based analysis, 442–44

Fairbank, John K., 213, 218

FARC (Revolutionary Armed Forces of Colombia), 53, 54, 57, 136, 493

Fatwa, 228

Federal Department of Foreign Affairs (FDFA), 18

Fédération Internationales des Droits de l'Homme (FIDH), 427

Feedback loops: negative, introducing, 648–49; positive, decoupling, 648

Ferrer, Jorge, 588

Fiasco, Lupe, 516

Field in AST, 623–24

Firestone, Reuven, 246–47

Fisher, Roger, 152

Fisher, Ronald, 461, 683–98

Fitrah, 231

Five Percent Nation of Islam, 515

Folie à deux, 604

Ford, Gerald, 150, 151

Forgiveness: in Islamic peacemaking, 235–38; social-psychological perspective on, 606–7

Formulation requires elaboration, 470–73

Forsyth, P. T., 259

Foucault, Michel, 782–83

Four sublime values, Buddhism and, 196

Frente de Liberacao de Mozambique (FRELIMO), 640, 645–47, 706

Frequency of peace, 628–29

Fry, Douglas, 550–59

Gadres (support group), 752–53

Galileo Galilei, 612–14, 612–17

Galtung, Johan, 107, 186–87, 310

Gamaghelyan, Philip, 380, 477–90

Gandhi, Mahatma, 161–62, 628–29, 796; critique of modernity, 166–69; key ethical concepts of, 170–72; moral

universe of, 169–73; peacemaking
and, 165–76; Salt March *satyagraha*
and, 174–76

Gandhi, Mohandas Karamchand. *See*
Gandhi, Mahatma

"Gang Crackdown in Massachusetts
Prisons, The" (Kassel), 520

Gang intervention in United States,
511–24; anti-intervention promoted
through intervention, 521–22; conclusion and prospect for peace, 520–21;
criminal justice efforts, 512–14; cultural impacts, 514; ex-gang members used in, 519–20; hip-hop music,
514–16; programmatic approaches,
512; religion influencing gang culture, 516–19; theoretical and practical obstacles for success, 522–24; from
theory to practice, 511–12; validated
gang members in correctional facilities, 513–14

Gardell, Mattias, 516

G-Dog and the Homeboys (Boyle), 519

Gender and peacemaking, 344–75;
overview of, 344–45; reflecting international norms on women, 348–52,
372–75; sensitivity and mediation of
ceasefires, 143–44; women referenced
in peace agreements, 345, 366–71;
women's role in state, changes of,
345–48

Geneva Accords, 747

Geneva Initiative, 746, 747

Genocide, Rwandan, 420–28, 500, 590,
606

George, Alexander, 430–31

Georgia, UN's conflict management
assistance in, 391–92

Gerardi, Juan, 267

Getting to Yes (Fisher and Ury), 152,
531–32, 537–38

Geybullayeva, Arzu, 482

Ghai, Yash, 30

Ghana, 401–7; components of, 413–15;
conflicts in, 405–6; contribution to
peacebuilding, 407; National Architecture for Peace in, 406–7; Northern
Region Peace Advocacy Council, 389,
406; systemic approach to, 412; UN's
conflict management assistance in,
389

Ghose, Aurobindo, 168

Gillis, Margie, 313, 324

Giro, Mario, 92–105

Glasl, Friedich, 687–88

Glazer, Ilsa, 552

Glick, Thomas, 253

Globalization era, peacemaking in,
651–64; accomplishments of, 654–55;
cold war as example of, 655–56; ending of existing wars and, 656–57; protracted social conflict and, 656; rates
of consumption and, 653–54; separate peace and, 652; societal-systems
analysis and, 660–64; systemic peace
and, 658–59; warfare as meaning for,
651–54

Global Peace Index (GPI), 380, 438–55;
costs of violence identified with,
445–46; cumulative effects of peace
identified with, 446–48; data used
in research, 441; economic value of
peace identified with, 444–45; fact-
based analysis in, 442–44; indicator
movements, 453–55; overall findings,
452–53; peace measured by, 440–41;
sectoral analysis, 449–50; in strategic
business analysis, 450–51; in time-
series analysis, 451–52

Global Voices, 485

Gods, 574–77

Godse, Nathuram, 166

Goitein, Shelomo Dov, 250, 251–52, 253

Goldschmidt, Walter, 553, 554

Goldwyn, Sam, 676

Goncalves, Jaime, 640–41, 646

Google Docs, 483

Gopin, Marc, 76–90, 185. *See also* Syria,
Judaism and conflict resolution in;
Arafat encounter with, 82–83; childhood of, 78–79; conflict resolution
method developed by, 88; early
peacemaking experiences of, 80–81;
Kabawat, first encounter with, 83–84;
Lebanon War and, 79–80, 86; Mosque
in Aleppo and, 86–87; Syria and,
84–89

Gorbachev, Mikhail, 681

Gore, Al, 258

Government peacemaking roles, 55–56

Governments, non-monolithic, 394

Graffiti, 518–19

Graham, Billy, 247
Graham, Franklin, 247
Grassroots peacemaking, 277
Great Ages and Ideas of the Jewish People
  (Halkin), 253
Griffiths, Martin, 115
Gross domestic product (GDP), 444–49,
  451, 453, 454
Group awakening, principles of, 197–98
Group of Friends for the Guatemala
  Peace Process, 52
Guatemala peace process case study,
  751–53; conflict background, 751–52;
  mediation methodology, 752–53;
  overview of, 752
Guerrillas, 53, 54
Guinea-Conakry, UN's conflict manage-
  ment assistance in, 392
Gujarat: Parzania film contest and,
  14–15; pogram against Muslim popu-
  lation in, 7; rape of women in, 7
Gusmão, Xanana, 471, 472
Guyana, UN's conflict management
  assistance in, 389
Gyanendra, King, 19–21

Habermas, Jürgen, 782
Habibie, B. J., 471–72, 475
Hadith, 230
Hadjizadeh, Adnan, 480
Hagedorn, John M., 512, 514, 516
Hai Gaon, 253
Haiti, unfinished business in, 772–77
Hajj, 231, 237
Halachic, 251
Halkin, Abraham S., 253
Hampson, Fen, 693–94, 6903
Hanh, Thich Nhat, 627
Hans, Raj Kumar, 7
Hansson, Niklas, 144
Harare Declaration, 732, 737
Hardy, Thomas, 420
Harijan (newspaper), 161
Hart, James, 170
Harvard Negotiation Project, 531
Harvard Study Tour, 532
Harvey, R., 733
Hashmi, Shabnam, 6–17
Hassan, Abdiqasim Salad, 334
Hate-promoting websites, 487–88
Hawes, Dena, 310

Haysom, Nicolas "Fink," 750
Hedge, Harshvardhan, 7
*Here Comes Everybody: The Power of Orga-
  nizing without Organizations* (Shirky),
  477–78
Heroes, 574–77
Hidden dimensions of peacemaking,
  622–36; applied systems thinking,
  623–24; energy, 628–31; evolutionary,
  631–35; field, 623–24; inner, 624–27
Hind Swaraj (Gandhi), 166, 167–68
Hindu extremists, 15–16
Hip-hop music, 514–16
Histories, 574–77
Hodgson, Marshall G. S., 234
Hofstede, Geert H., 571, 572
Holl, Jane, 431
Holocaust, 421, 590, 745
Homeboy Industries (HBI), 516, 518–19
Homegirls Café, 518
Homicides, 451, 453
Homo sapiens, 564, 566, 568, 574
Horizontal peacemaking, 277, 278–79,
  292
Hostages, 577
Hottinger, Julian T., 750, 757
Howell, James C., 513, 514
Howell, Signe, 551
Hsiao Kung-chuan, 218
Hui, Victoria Tin-bor, 211–24
Human diversity, affirming, 304–5
Human interconnectedness, clarifying,
  305
Humanitarian assistance, ceasefire
  mediation and, 139–40
Humanization of the other, 608
Human maturation, 631–32
Human rights and mediation of cease-
  fires, 142–43
Human Rights Office of the Catholic
  Archdiocese of Guatemala, 267
Humans as primates, 564–66
Humper, Joseph, 268
Hussein, Saddam, 139
Hysteresis, 644–45

Iceberg model, 624–25
ICT for Peacebuilding initiative
  (ICT4Peace), 502
Identity development, 304
Ideological square, 488–89

Iklé, Fred, 671
Iliad (Homer), 579–81
Image of Enemy (Eurasia Partnership
    Foundation), 485
Images, 574–77
IMAGINE Center for Conflict Transfor-
    mation, 481–85
Imperial era, Confucianism in, 217–22
Implementation of Economic Activities
    as awakening stage, 203
Inclusive peacemaking, 161–64
India, economy of, 6
India, youth peacemaking in, 6–17;
    Anhad and, 8–9, 13; campaigns used
    in, 13–15; Creating Democracy, Cel-
    ebrating Diversity campaign and, 13;
    Gujarat relief camps and, 7; National
    Student's Festival for Peace, Justice
    and Communal Harmony, 13–14; rape
    and sodomy of women in, 7–8; Rock
    the Nation and, 14; Youth Aman
    Karwan and, 10–13
Indian Civil Disobedience Movement,
    174
Indian Constituent Assembly, 785
Indian Home Rule (Gandhi), 166
Indicator movements, 453–55
Indonesia, 470–73
Informal talks as peace process phase,
    742
Information-sharing platforms, 478
Infrastructures for peace, 384–417;
    advantages of, 413; components of,
    413–15; conclusion, 396–97; correlates
    differentiated from causes, 394–96;
    cost of prevention, 413; development
    and conflict, 411–12; elections, 395–96;
    electoral violence, 412; entry points,
    importance of, 393; governments and
    actors that are not monolithic, 394; ini-
    tiatives, 392–93; insiders, importance
    of accompaniment by, 393; interests
    and ownership in developing world,
    396; in Kenya, 407–9; mediation, lim-
    its of traditional, 384–85; national,
    defining, 385–87; national mandate,
    400, 404, 415; in Nepal, 411; in Nica-
    ragua, 409–10; in Philippines, 410–11;
    practices and pointers for further
    action, 392–94; at regional and global
    levels, 417; stakeholders included in,

413; systemic approach to, 412; *vs.*
    traditional approaches to conflict pre-
    vention, 387–89; UN assistance,
    examples of, 389–92; violent conflicts,
    expected increase in, 412–13
Initiatives: complementarity between
    national and international, 392–93;
    developmental, 647; episodic, 646–47;
    radical, 647
"In Larger Freedom" (Annan), 424
Inner dimension of peacemaking,
    624–27
Insiders, importance of accompaniment
    by, 393
Insight meditation (*vipassana*), 207–9
Insight theory, 618–19
Institute for Multi-Track Diplomacy, 64,
    107
Institute for Sustained Dialogue, The,
    107
Institutional peacemaking, 555
Institution building, 743
Instrumental reconciliation, 336
Interaction with armed groups, 498–500
Interactive conflict resolution, 157
Interconnectedness in AST, 623
Interconnections, 552, 597–99
Interdependence, 552–53, 577
Interests: in developing world, 396;
    stated *vs.* real in peace process, 59–60
Intergovernmental Authority on Devel-
    opment (IGAD), 750
Intergovernmental organizations, peace-
    making roles and, 55–56
Interhamwe, 493, 500
Intermarriage, 577
Internal conflicts, 453, 454–55, 459
International Alert in Brussels, 490
International Commission on Interven-
    tion and State Sovereignty (ICISS),
    422–24, 430, 432, 713
International Committee of the Red
    Cross (ICRC), 114
International Convention on the Elimi-
    nation of All Forms of Discrimination
    against Women (CEDAW), 347
International Criminal Court (ICC),
    279, 280, 289; accommodation to local
    power and, 127–30; accommodation
    to political power and, 126–27; crimi-
    nal trials and, 123–25; international

law enforcement and, 125–26; intervention by, and militarization by Uganda, 130–33; justice and peacemaking role of, 122–23; role of, in Uganda, 122–33

International law enforcement, dilemma of, 125–26

International Monetary Fund, 703

International nongovernmental organizations (INGOs), 703–4

International Rescue Committee, 428

International women's rights norms, defining, 348–49

Internet information wars, 488–89

Internet usage statistics, 482

Internet World Stats, 482, 489

Interpreting peacemaking, 545–49

Interveners, diverse, 703–4

Interventions in peacemaking, 702–10; Arias, Oscar in Central America, 706–7; assessing, 710–11; cases of, 706–10; cases of intervention, 706–10; changes for sustainable peace and, 711; Community of Sant'Egidio in Mozambique, 706; conflict analysis and, 710–11; diverse, 704–6; NATO bombing operations in Serbia and Kosovo, 709; overview of, 702–3; as peacemaking challenge, 702–10; types of, 686; U.S. and Soviet invasion of Afghanistan, 709–10, 714; U.S. government and Israeli-Arab conflict, 707–9; U.S-led invasion of Iraq, 710; Yugoslavia breakup as, 709

Intifada I, 45, 82–83, 235, 626

Intifada II, 709

Intimate contention, 576

Intractable conflicts: attractor dynamics, 641–42; attractors and collapse of complexity, 642–43; changing attractor landscapes, 644–45; conflict and peace in Mozambique, 640–41; in dynamical framework, 641–45; manifest and latent attractors of conflict, 643–44; navigating attractor landscapes, 645–49; systems of, 638–39

Iowa Peace Institute (IPI), 63

Islam and peacemaking, 228–41; appeal to gang members, 516–18; coexistence and cultural diversity in, 231–33; five pillars of, 231; forgiveness and reconciliation in, 235–38; non-violence and, 233–35; overview of, 228–30; peacemaking and, 228–41; positive influence on rehabilitation, 522; study of, 230–31; transformation and, 238–40

Islamic and Christian Spain in the Early Middle Ages (Glick), 253

Israel and Muslims, 247–49

Israeli-Arab conflict, U. S. intervention in, 707–8

Israel Oriental Studies II (Kister), 251

Israel-Palestine peace process case study, 745–48; actors involved in, 747; conflict background, 745–46; mediation methodology, 747–48; overview, 746

Ivekovic, Ivan, 783

Iyer, Raghavan, 170

Jafari, Sheherazade, 228–41

Jaghori District of Afghanistan, 492, 496, 499–500

Jakarta conference, 471

Jewish-Muslim reconciliation, 244–56; current state of, and Christian antagonism, 246–49; identities and, 251–52; parallel initiative to advance, 254–56; psychopolitical strategy for, 244–45, 249–54; Quran and, 251–54; religious ties between, 250

Jews, Polish: healing the history of, 254; psychological and historical issues of, 254–56

Jews, Visigoths and Muslims in Medieval Spain (Roth), 250, 253

Jews and Arabs: A Concise History of Their Social and Cultural Relations (Goitein), 250, 251–52

Jews of Islam, The (Lewis), 253–54

Jihad, 233–34

Jizya, 232

John Darby, 463, 672

Johnston, A. Iain, 213, 217

Judaism and conflict resolution, 76–90. *See also* Gopin, Marc; listening and confiding, 81–82; positive visioning and, 87; struggling with faith and, 87–88; in Syria, 84–89; values in, 76–78

Just Ice, 515

Justice: elements of, 558–59; and human rights as peace process topic, 743
Just Vision, 38, 47
Juul, Mona, 52

Kabawat, Hind, 83–84, 87–88
Kagame, Paul, 125
Kamil, Melek al, 258
Kang, David, 219, 220–21
Kant, Immanuel, 223, 259
Kashmir: dialogue and, 786–88; Multi-Track Diplomacy and, 67–72
Kassel, Phillip, 520
Keashly, Loraleigh, 686, 688, 689, 695, 697
Keller, Alexis, 746
Kelman, Herbert C., 244–45, 462, 685
Kenya, 401–9; bottom-up process to establish, 407–8, 415; challenges and dilemmas, 409; components of, 413–15; district peace committees, 388, 409; electoral violence, 412; local conflicts in, 407; National Peace Commission, 406–9; National Peace Forum, 408; NSC on Peacebuilding and Conflict Management, 408; Provincial Peace Fora, 409; R2P in, 426; systemic approach to, 412; UNDP Experience-Sharing Seminar on Building Infrastructures for Peace in Kenya, 401–2; UN's conflict management assistance in, 390; Wajir Peace and Development Committee, 407–8
Kettering Foundation, 107
Key actor identification, 136
Key people strategy, 763
Khamisa, Azim, 237–38
Khan, Abdul Ghaffar, 234–35, 239
Khan, Badshah, 234–35
Khojali massacre, 488
Khojali: The Chronicle of Unseen Forgery and Falsification, 488–89
Khrushchev, Nikita, 158
Kibaki, Mwai, 426
Kildoan Castle (ship), 166
Killelea, Steve, 380, 438–55
King, Martin Luther, Jr., 161, 179–89; global/international and cross-cultural conflict and, 183–86; PCAR legacy, 186–88; PCAR theory, 179–80; philosophical worldview of, 180–83

King, Mary Elizabeth, 37
Kishtainy, Khalid, 233
Kissinger, Henry, 150–51, 707
Kister, M. J., 251
Knill, Paolo, 311
Koirala, G. P., 24, 28
Kony, Joseph, 122, 139, 289
Kosovo, 421, 709, 764
Kouchner, Bernard, 428
Kriesberg, Louis, 63, 548, 692, 697, 701–18
KRS-ONE, 515
Kumar, Chetan, 380, 384–97, 384–99
Kumar, Rajni, 11
Kyrgyzstan: R2P in, 426–27; UN's conflict management assistance in, 390–91

Language of ceasefire mediation, 137–38
Latent attractors of conflict, 643–44, 647
Lauder, Ronald, 330, 708
Leaders, theories of changing and peacemaking, 670–73
LeBaron, Michelle, 308–25
Lederach, John Paul, 187, 238, 400–401, 404, 409, 463
Legal Recognition as awakening stage, 203
Lesotho, UN's conflict management assistance in, 391
Lessons learned from peace processes, 51–61; defining realistic goals, 57–58; external support, need for, 55; implementing deals and, 61; overview of, 51–52; parties willingness to end conflict, 53–54; post-cold war openings and, 52–53; rationality of actors involved, 54–55; setbacks expected as, 58–59; stated versus real interests, 59–60; states, IGOs, NGOs joining forces, 55–56; tension within parties and, 60; third party roles and, 56–57
Let's Peace Jam! (video conferences), 485
Levine, Stephen, 308, 311–12
Lewis, Bernard, 253–54
Liberal peace, explained, 259
Liberia, unfinished business in, 771, 773–77
Lincoln, Abraham, 239
Lobha (greed), 192
Local dialogues in Somalia, 338, 339

Local peace committees (LPCs): challenges of, 416–17; composition of, 415; conclusions and lessons learned from, 415–16; impact of, proven, 412, 415–16; lessons learned from, 404–5; in South Africa, 403–5; tasks of, 403–4

Local rituals in Somalia, 338, 339

Lochman, Jan Milic, 260

Locke, John, 259

Lonergan, Bernard, 592, 611, 618–19

Lord's Resistance Army (LRA), International Criminal Court and, 127–30

Loving kindness meditation (*Metta*), 196–97, 209–10

Luck, Edward, 425, 427, 431, 433

Lutheran World Federation, 52

Lu Xun, 224

Mack, Johnny, 179–89

MacLeod, Carrie, 308–25

Macy, Joanna, 632–33

Madhya Pradesh article, 16–17

Magnanimity, 576

Mahabharata, The, 578–79

Malcolm X (film), 517

Malley, Rob, 746

Mamdani, Mahmood, 125

Mampilly, Zachariah Cherian, 161–64

Mand, Jaswinder, 13

Mandela, Nelson, 265, 722–26, 730–38

Manifest attractors of conflict, 643–44

Maoists, 756, 786–88, 790

Marshall, Christopher, 260

Marshall, Monty, 651–64

Martin, Ian, 26, 31

Martti Ahtisaari Rapid Reaction Facility, 116

Masculine/feminine energies, 634

Mason, Simon J. A., 741–57

Mass atrocities, R2P and, 421–23

Mass Democratic Movement (MDM), 723

Mass Peace Meditations, 204–5

Mathematical reasoning, 614–17, 620

Mato Oput and restorative justice, 287–90

Maximalists, 430

Mays, Benjamin, 161

Mbeki, Thabo, 725–26, 733, 736, 738

McDonald, John, 62–75, 107

McGinnis, Martin, 672

MC Hammer, 516

McLoughlin, Mitchell, 672

Meaning, 380

Mediation, 381–82; in academic diplomacy, 458–60; of ceasefires, 135–46; as disinterested act, 103–5; Guatemala case study of, 751–53; Israel-Palestine case study of, 745–48; lessons learned from case studies on, 753–56; limits of, 384–85, 753–56; mediation methodology and, 743–44; methodology, dimensions of, 743–44; multiactor approach to, 741–42; multiphase approach to, 742–43; multitopic approach to, 743; NGOs and, 107–21; peacemaking through, 381–82, 741–57; potential of, 753–56; professionalism of, 104; Sudan case study of, 748–51

Mediation, peacemaking through, 741–57; Guatemala case study of, 751–53; Israel-Palestine case study of, 745–48; lessons learned from case studies on, 753–56; mediation methodology and, 743–44; multiactor approach to, 741–42; multiphase approach to, 742–43; multitopic approach to, 743; Sudan case study of, 748–51

Mediation and NGOs, 107–21; Carter Center and, 112–14; Centre for Humanitarian Dialogue and, 114–16; Community of Sant'Egidio and, 109–11; Crisis Management Initiative and, 116–19; overview of, 107–9

Mediation of ceasefires, 135–46; concepts and language of, 137–38; early recovery and development assistance in, 144–45; effective implementation and, 145–46; engaging belligerents and, 138–39; gender sensitivity and, 143–44; humanitarian assistance as point of entry to, 139–40; human rights and transitional justice in, 142–43; overview of, 135–36; ownership and, 138; protecting civilians and, 142; role of NGOs and civil society in, 144; structure of agreements for, 140–42; understanding operational environment and, 136–37

Mediation Support Project, 757

Mediators: in academic diplomacy, 463–64; ancient, 576

Mehmedovic, Hatidza, 39–41

Meir, Golda, 151

Melchin, Kenneth R., 618–20

Melkonian, Monte, 488

Menace II Society (film), 517–18

Mencius, 212, 216

Mencius collection of dialogues, 212, 216

Merritt, Richard, 680

Metaphysics: Aristotelian, 614–15; religious, 169–70

Method in peacemaking, 610–20; Galileo analogy, 612–17; scenarios in, 611–12

Metta, practice of, 196–97, 209–10

Mexican Mafia, 519–20

Michael, Murezi, 757

Micro-skills, 743

Middle East Peace Conference, 707–8

Middle East protests, 2011, 478

Middle East seminar, 467–68

Midrashic, 251

Military sophistication, 453, 455

Mill, John Stuart, 259

Millennium Development Goals (MDGs), 446

Miller, Tamar, 254

Millet system, 232–33

Milli, Emin, 480

Milosevic, Slobodan, 421, 709

Mimetic structures of violence, 586–87

Mindanao, unfinished business in, 773–77

Mindful breathing meditation (*anapana-sathi bhavana*), 205–7

Minds, theories about changing and peacemaking, 669–70

Minimalists, 430

Minsk Conference, 468

Mitchell, Christopher, 108, 668–82, 694

Modernity, Gandhi's critique of, 166–69

Modi, Narendra, 7, 11

Moghadam, Valentine, 783

Moha (ignorance), 193

Monitoring means of ceasefire agreement, 140–41

Monkeys: Rhesus, 570–72; stumptail, 572–73

Monnet, Jean, 530

Montville, Joseph, 62, 63, 244–56

Moral universe of Gandhi, 169–73

More people strategy, 763

Morrar, Ayed, 44–46

Morrar, Iltezam, 46

Moses, 251

Moses, Greg, 188

Mosque in Aleppo, 86–87

Mothers of Srebrenica, 39

Movement-based approaches to peacemaking. *See* Arts and movement-based approaches to peacemaking

Mozambique: Chidenguele District of, 493, 500; Community of Sant'Egidio peace efforts in, 94–96, 109, 111, 116; conflict and peace in, emergence of, 640–50; intervention in, illustrated case of, 706; NGOs role in conflicts, 120; peace agreements, 361, 369; Spirit of Mungoi, 493, 495, 498, 500; unfinished business in, 773–77

Mubarak, Hosni, 478

Mugabe, Robert, 733

Muhammad, Prophet, 230, 231, 233, 236–37, 239

Multiactor approach, 741–42

Multicultural education principles, 302–3; affirming human diversity, 304–5; clarifying human interconnectedness, 305; enhancing cultural competence, 303–4; identity development, 304; strengthening empathic ability, 305–6; Ubuntu reclaimed by using, 303–6

Multi-Party Negotiation Forum, 726

Multi-track diplomacy, 62–75; accomplishments of, 65–67; guiding principles of, 65; interns with, 66; Kashmir case study, 67–72; National Defense University and, 74–75; origins of, 62–64; publications by, 66–67; Punjab case study, 72–74; social media in, 477, 481; spreading the word about, 65–66

Mungoi, 493, 495, 498, 500

Murithi, Timothy, 275–93, 798

Muslim-Jewish-Christian antagonism, 246–49; Islamophobia and, 246–47; Israel and, 247–49

Mutual respect, 607–8

Mutual security, 607

Mutual trust and cooperation, 609

Nagorno-Karabakh conflict, 468–70, 474, 475, 481, 483, 484, 485, 488

Nan, Susan Allen, 330, 483, 610, 717

Nargis in Burma, R2P and, 427–28

Narrative approach to peacemaking, 328–42. *See also* Reconciliation

National Architecture for Peace in Ghana, 407

National Commission on the Disappearance of Persons (CONADEP), 269

National Council for East Timorese Resistance (CNRT), 471

National Defense University, 74–75

National dialogue in Somalia, 338, 339

National Dialogue Project, 768

National infrastructures for peace, defining, 385–87

National Peace Commission (NPC): establishing, 406–7; role in peace architecture, 408; Secretariat, 409

National Reconciliation Commission, 337, 339–40

National Security Ministry of Azerbaijan, 486–87

National sovereignty in R2P, 431–32

National Steering Committee (NSC) on Peacebuilding and Conflict Management, 408

National Student's Festival for Peace, Justice and Communal Harmony, 13–14

National truth commission in Somalia, 338

National unity reconciliation (NUR), 329

National War College (NWC), 74

Nation building, 714–15

Nation of Islam, 516, 517

Navigational capacity, 315–16

Nawan Zamana (newspaper), 13

Ndura, Elavie, 295–307

Negotiation, 381–82

Negotiation chains, 647–48

Negotiation phase as peace process phase, 742–43

Nepali Swiss Forum on Federalism (NSFF), 32

Nepal peace promotion in Switzerland, 18–35; confidence-building during King Gyanendra rule, 19–21; conflicting parties and dominant issues of, 18–19; Federalism and constituent assembly elections, 30–32; negotiations and peace agreement for, 24–30; shuttle diplomacy, ceasefire, and stronger democratic movement, 21–23; transition period for, 32–35

Nepal Transition to Peace Initiative, 24

Netanyahu, 708

Neutral Zone blog platform, 484

Neve Shalom, 80

New order, 577

Newton, Isaac, 616

Nicaragua, GDP per capita, 447, 448

Nigeria, UN's conflict management assistance in, 392

Nine-track model for diplomacy, 64

Nirvana, 195

Nixon, Richard, 150

Noble Eight-fold Path, 195, 199–200

No Future without Forgiveness (Tutu), 283

No More Prisons compilations, 516

Non-Aligned Movement (NAM), 424

Nongovernmental organizations (NGOs), 705; Carter Center, 112–14; Caucasus, 486, 487; Centre for Humanitarian Dialogue, 114–16; Community of Sant'Egidio, 109–11; Crisis Management Initiative, 116–19; effectiveness of, 119–21; expanding, 716; in Gadres, 752; GPI used by, 441; growth of, 459–60; Inter-NGO Consortium, 405; in Kenya, 408; mediation and, 107–21; in multiactor approach, 741–42; overview of, 107–9; peacemaking roles, 55–56; in R2P, 424, 430, 713; WANEP, 406

Noninstitutional organizations and conflict resolution, 92–105; Community of Sant'Egidio and, 94–96; listening and patience by, 98–103; mediation as disinterested act and, 103–5; model used by, 96–98; overview of, 92–94; reconciliation processes and, 105

Nonviolence in Islamic peacemaking, 233–35

Nonviolent action, women's roles in, 36–49; Budrus and, 43–47; link between nonviolent action and peacemaking, 37–39; opportunities, challenges, and recommendations for, 47–49; overview of, 36–37; Srebrenica and, 39–43

Nonviolent Peace Force (NPF), 144
Non-war identity, unifying, 494–96
Nordquist, Kjell-Åke, 469–72, 470–72
Normalcy, 496–97
North Atlantic Treaty Organization
    (NATO), 142, 421, 488, 596, 709
Northern Ireland, unfinished business
    in, 773–77
Northern Ireland Women's Initiative
    (NIWI), 352
Northern Region Peace Advocacy Coun-
    cil, 389, 406
Norwegian Channel, 52–53, 56
Nowak, Andrzej, 380, 502–9, 637–50
Noyek, Arnold, 502–3, 505
Nuba Mountains ceasefire agreement,
    749–50
Nunca Mais (Arns), 268

Obama, Barack, 127, 258, 480, 623, 679,
    709
Observing precepts, Buddhism and, 195
Obstacles to peacemaking, managing,
    712–17; inappropriate theorizing and,
    714–16; interveners interests and,
    712–13; structural issues and, 716–17
Odinga, Raila, 426
Office for Coordination of Humanitarian
    Assistance (OCHA), 140
Office of the Special Adviser on the Pre-
    vention of Genocide (OSAPG), 431
Olzack, Paul, 692–93
O'Malley, P., 733
Operational environment, understand-
    ing, 136–37
Organisation for Economic Co-Operation
    and Development, 714
Organization for Security and
    Co-operation in Europe (OSCE), 427,
    468, 633–34, 703, 705
Organization of American States, 703
Ortiz, Vanessa, 36–49
"The other," shifting perception of, 316
Other Walls: The Politics of the Arab-Israeli
    Peace Process, The (Saunders), 153
Otunbayeva, Roza, 427
Outcome Document (World Summit), 424
Owen, David, 58
Ownership: ceasefire mediation and,
    138; in developing world, 396
OZ (HBO series), 517

Palestine Liberation Organization
    (PLO), 467–68, 676, 708
Pantham, Thomas, 171
Papua New Guinea, 466–67
Parel, Anthony, 166
Partnership and collaboration in peace-
    making, 629–30
Parzania (film), 14–15
Passenger, The (Eurasia Partnership
    Foundation), 485
Paul, John II, Pope, 258, 260, 262,
    270
Paving the Way: Contributions of Interac-
    tive Conflict Resolution to Peacemaking
    (Fisher), 695
Paz, Yehudah, 506–7
Peace: agreements, 353–65; cumulative
    effects of, 446–48; dividend, sectoral
    analysis of, 449–50; economic value
    of, 444–45; in global context, 651;
    Global Peace Index used to measure,
    440–41; relative, 652; separate, 652;
    structural attributes of peaceful coun-
    tries, 443–44
Peacebuilder (newsletter), 66
Peacebuilding: in African, 277, 279; in
    Somalia, 334–35
Peace It Together, 318
Peacekeeping as intervention type,
    686
Peacemakers, ancient, 563–81
Peacemaking: African traditions of,
    275–93; anthropology examples of,
    550–59; arts and movement-based
    approaches to, 308–25; from bibli-
    cal literature, 596; Buddhism and,
    192–210; challenges in, 701–18; Chris-
    tian, 257–71; Confucianism and,
    211–24; defined, 546; Gandhi and,
    165–76; gender and, 344–75; in glo-
    balization era, 651–64; hidden dimen-
    sions of, 622–36; inclusive, 161–64;
    interpreting, 545–49; interveners and
    interventions in, 596, 702–11; Islam
    and, 228–41; Martin Luther King, Jr.
    and, 179–89; method in, 610–20; mul-
    ticultural education principles, 303–6;
    narrative approach to, 328–42;
    obstacles to, managing, 712–17; praxis
    of, vs. its poiesis, 548, 610, 617, 619,
    620; reconciliation and, 586, 594–95,

607–9; relational paradigm in, 148–60; social media and, 479, 480–86; social-psychological perspective on, 601–9; structural issues and, 716–17; theories of change in, 668–82; through mediation, 741–57; weak states and, 157–59

Peacemaking, conflict analysis, and conflict resolution theory and practice (PCAR), 179–80

Peace Meditational Walks, 204–5

Peace negotiations, linking ceasefires to, 137–38

Peace negotiations and peace agreement for Nepal, 24–30; crisis signs in peace process and, 27–28; drafting of peace agreement and, 29; interim constitution and, 30; Koirala and Prachanda confidence building and, 28–29; mediation between negotiation rounds and, 25; meeting between army general staff and CPNM and, 26–27; monitoring by UN and, 26, 27; 25-point ceasefire code of conduct, 24–25

Peace on Facebook page, 485

Peace process: goals, defining realistic, 57–58; phases, 742–43; topics, 743

Perdue, Peter, 221

Petersilia, Joan, 522

Philosopher-scientists, 614–16

Philpott, Daniel, 257–71

Physics, 613, 614, 624, 628, 631

Picard, Cheryl A., 618–20

Pillars of Shame, 40

Ping, Jean, 125

Pinochet, Augusto, 267

Poeisis, 311–12

Polish Jews and Catholics: healing the history of, 254; psychological and historical issues of, 254–56

Political domain, unfinished business in, 766–68

Political Instability Task Force (PITF), 659, 662

Politics of Dialogue, The (Samaddar), 780

Polska, Beit, 254

Positivity, 648

Postagreement phase as peace process phase, 743

Post-cold war foreign-policy activism, 52–53

Posterior Analytics (Aristotle), 613–14, 617–18

Posttraumatic stress syndrome (PTSD), 606, 626, 627

Power: constructive, 380; decision making in, 381; destructive, 380; in energy dimension of peacemaking, 629–30; integrative, 380; literature on, 380–81; mediation as intervention type, 686; power-sharing agreements in Somalia, 337, 338; structures, 380–81; victimization and, 382–83; weak, employing, 647

Prabhu, Joseph, 165–76

Practices and pointers for further action, 392–94

Praszkier, Ryszard, 380, 502–9

Praxis of peacemaking *vs.* its poiesis, 548, 610, 617, 619, 620

Prein, Hugo, 687, 688

Prenegotiation as peace process phase, 742

Prevention of Armed Conflict (Annan), 429

Preventive dialogue, 159

Price, Jamie, 548, 610–20

Primakov, Evgeny, 153

Primate peace, 566–68

Principia Mathematica (Newton), 616

Principle of Conditionality, 198

Principle of Paticcasamuppada, 198–200; explained, 198–99; Noble Eight-fold Path and, 199–200; outer world interdependency and, 200; overcoming ignorance and, 199

Prison Islam (Prislam), 522

Process design, 743–44

Processes, theories of changing and peacemaking, 673–75

Project Harmony International, 485

Pruitt, Dean, 670, 692–93, 722–39

Psychological Infrastructure Building as awakening stage, 203

Punjab Multi-Track Diplomacy, 72–74

Pure mediation as intervention type, 686

Purification of the mind, Buddhism and, 194

Quiet diplomacy, 467–68

Quran, 230–34, 240; forgiveness and, 235–36; Jewish references in, 251–54

Rabbo, Yasser Abed, 746
Rabin, Yitzhak, 248
Radical initiatives, 647
Ramos-Horta, José, 470
Rational bargaining, 784–85
Rawls, John, 259
Readiness, 727
Reagan, Ronald, 724
Realpolitik, 245
Reconciliation, 586, 594–95, 607–9;
    African traditions of peacemaking
    and, 279–86; concept of Christian,
    259–66; folk psychology and, 331; in
    Islamic peacemaking, 235–38; Jewish-
    Muslim, 244–56; as narrative process,
    331–33; practice of Christian, 266–70;
    rituals, 557–58; in Somalia, 333–42
Recovery of Historical Memory Project
    (REMHI), 267
Redekop, Vern Neufeld, 547, 585–600
Redemption (film), 521
Reflecting on Peace Practice Project
    (RPP), 761–78; addressing or neglect-
    ing unfinished business, 764–72;
    categories and issues of unfinished
    business in, 773–77; initial findings
    and issues, 762–63; linkages and dis-
    connects among tracks, 763–64; over-
    view of, 761–62
Regional peace committees (RPCs),
    403–4, 406
Relational paradigm in peacemaking,
    148–60; change process appropriate
    to, 154–57; conceptualization of
    experience and, 150–54; overview of,
    148–50; underlying causes of conflict
    and, 159–60; weak states and, 157–59
Relationship: Buddhism and, 195; con-
    cept of, 149–50; elements of, 149
Relative peace, 652
Religious metaphysics, 169–70
Reparations, 265
Reporters Without Borders, 480
Report of the Secretary-General's High-
    Level Panel on Threats, Challenges,
    and Change (2004), 424
Resistancia National Mocambicana
    (RENAMO), 640–41, 646–47, 706, 769
*Resolution of Conflict: Constructive and
    Destructive Processes, The* (Deutsch),
    602

Resolution on Srebrenica, 39
Responsibility to Protect (R2P), 420–34;
    civilian protection and national sover-
    eignty, 431–32; comprehensiveness of
    the responsibility to prevent, 429–30;
    conclusion, 434; effective catalyst
    for action, 432–33; four R2P crimes,
    420–28, 434; invocations, 425–29; from
    mass atrocities, 421–23; norm-based
    policy framework, 433; role in peace-
    making, 425–29, 432–33; three respon-
    sibilities in, 423–25; warning-response
    gap, 430–31
Restitution, 577
Restoration of peace, 555
Restorative justice, African traditions of,
    282–83; *Mato Oput* and, 287–90
"Return to Innocence Lost" (Roots), 516
Rhesus monkeys, 570–72
Riccardi, Andrea, 109
Ricigliano, R., 441
Ripeness theory, 726
Risk and dialogue, 786–89
Ritschl, Albrecht, 259
Ritualized combat, 576
Roberts, Rabia, 531
Rock the Nation (Anhad event), 14
Rodríguez, Carlos, 129
Roed-Larsen, Terje, 52
Roots, 516
Ross, Dennis, 708
Roth, Norman, 250, 253
Rothman, Jay, 316
Royal Society, 616
Ruch, Phillip, 40
Rules, procedures, and mechanisms of
    ceasefire agreement, 140
Rwanda: Arusha talks on, 103; churches'
    behavior during genocide, 269; cul-
    tural competence in, enhancing,
    303–4; empathetic ability strength-
    ened in, 305–6; genocide, 420–28, 500,
    590, 606; human diversity affirmed
    in, 304–5; human interconnectedness
    in, 305; Muslim identity in, 495, 500;
    peace agreement in, 362–63, 369–70;
    Ubuntu in, 295–307

Sadat, Anwar, 151, 152, 707
Sahnoun, Mohamed, 713
Said, Abdul Aziz, 228–41

St. Francis of Assisi, 258
St. Paul, 264
Salat, 231
Salt March *satyagraha*, 174–76; effects of, 176; facts about, 174–75; key features of, 175
Samaddar, Ranabir, 780–92
Samuel, Tamrat, 26
Sanliurfa tourism conference, 537–38
Sant'Egidio, Community of, 92–105; dialogue partners of, 98–103; Italian formula of conflict resolution by, 94–96, 97; mediation as disinterested act and, 103–5
Sarajevo, Bosnia, 37, 39, 493
Sargsyan, Serge, 488
Sarvodaya Movement, 192–210
Satha-Anand, Chaiwat, 234
Saturday Review of Literature, 157
Satya, 170
Satyagraha, 166, 170–71
Saunders, Hal, 461
Saunders, Harold, 107, 148–60
Savarkar, V. D., 166–67
Savimbi, Jonas, 139
Savun, Burcu, 145–46
Sawm, 231, 233
Sawyer, Ralph, 215
Scale in AST, 623
Scared Straight tactics, 519
Scarry, Elaine, 323
Schweitzer, Albert, 173
Scientific inquiry, 612–17
Scott, Monster Kody, 514, 517
Sectoral analysis, 449–50
Secular Voices (Anhad video), 13
Security as peace process topic, 743
Security Council, 712–13
Security domain, unfinished business in, 769
Security sector reform as peace process topic, 743
Segal, Zohra, 11
Self-constraints, 577
"Self-Destruction" (Stop the Violence), 515
Self-fulfilling prophecies, 603
Seminars in academic diplomacy, 460–62
Separate peace, 652
Separation of forces, 140

Setbacks expected during peace processes, 58–59
Shahada, 231
Shah-Kazemi, Reza, 236
Shalom-Salaam, 485
Shalom/Salam: A Story of a Mystical Fraternity (Block), 250, 251, 253
Shamir, Yaov, 256
Shaoxing Peace Accord, 222
Sharon, Ariel, 248, 709, 748
Sharp, Gene, 176
Sharpeville Massacre, 722
Shehadeh, Sheikh, 88–89
Sheppard, Blair, 687
Shirky, Clay, 477–78, 479
Shriver, Donald, 260
Shura, 492
Siegfried, Matthias, 757
Sierra Leone: CRANE fieldwork in, 321–23; UN's conflict management assistance in, 391
Sisk, Timothy, 733–34
Sitaula, K. B., 25
Skype, 482, 483
Sobel, Dava, 615
Social and cultural aspects as peace process topic, 743
Social change: social entrepreneurship used to facilitate, 504–5; social media and, 479–80
Social entrepreneurs: Asad Danish, 508; Krzysztof Czyzewski, 507; Yehudah Paz, 506–7
Social entrepreneurship, 502–9; Ashoka: Innovators for the Public, 504; conflict prevention in, 506–7; conflict transformation *vs.* conflict resolution in, 505–6; defined, 504; described, 503–4; mission pursued through building social capital, 506; new attractors built by, 505–6; social change facilitated by, 504–5
Social fabric domain, unfinished business in, 768–69
Social identity, 551–52
Social Infrastructure Building as awakening stage, 203
Social media, 477–90; activists in, 478–80; collective action in, 478–79, 486; conclusions, 489–90; conflict escalation and, 486–89; in multi-track

diplomacy, 477, 481; peacemaking and, 479, 480–86; social change and, 479–80; Web 2.0, 477–79

"Social Media for Social Change" (Project Harmony International), 485

Social networking websites, 478, 479, 482

Social-psychological perspective on peacemaking, 601–9; concluding thought, 609; constructive and destructive conflict, development of, 604–5; constructive and destructive conflict, processes in, 602–4; forgiveness, 606–7; reconciliation, 607–9

Societal-systems analysis, key elements of, 660–64

Society of Humanitarian Research (Azerbaijan), 485

Socioemotional reconciliation, 336

Soliya, 485

Solomon Islands: unfinished business in, 773–77; UN's conflict management assistance in, 390

Somalia, reconciliation in, 328–42; context for peacebuilding, 334–35; draft plan summary, 340–41; draft recommendations, 339–40; implications, 334; as narrative process, 331–33; national reconciliation process, 334–42; need for, prospective case study on, 333; paradox of peacemaking and, 328–30; story behind the draft plan, 341–42

South African peace process, 722–39; apartheid policies and, 723–24; CODESA negotiation sessions and, 726; infrastructures for peace in, 403–5; local peace committees in, 403–5; meetings with ANC leadership and, 724–25; regional peace committees in, 403–4; unfinished business in, 773–77; uprisings and, 722–23; urgency theory and, 726–39

South African Truth and Reconciliation Commission, 283, 286, 300, 329

SpearIt, 380, 511–24

Special Adviser for Peace Building in Nepal (SAPB), 18

Spergel, Irving A., 516, 524

Spirit of Mungoi, 493, 495, 498, 500

Spirituality, 588–91, 597–600

Srebrenica: atrocities in, 421, 422; women peacebuilders in, 39–43

Srebrenica-Potocari Memorial and Cemetery, 39

Sri Lanka, economic progress in, 770

State building, 714–15, 743

Stedman, Steven, 672

STEP Act, 512

Stoltenberg, Thorvald, 52, 58, 59

Stop the Violence, 515

Strategic business analysis, 450–51

Strategic connectors, 494–500; interaction with armed groups, 498–500; normalcy, 496–97; tradition, 497–98; unifying non-war identity, 494–96

Strenger, Carlo, 249

Structural peacemaking, 555, 716–17

Stumptail monkeys, 572–73

Sub-Saharan Africa: arts-based approaches to peace in, 312; ease of access to weapons of minor destruction in, 453; indicator movements in, 455; time-series analyses in, 451

Sudan peace process case study, 748–51; conflict background, 748; IGAD mediation team and, 750; issues addressed in, 750; mediation methodology, 750–51; Nuba Mountains ceasefire agreement and, 749–50; overview of, 748; peace structures in south and, 749

Sufism, 238

Sulha, 236

Sultanli, Jale, 481

Sumbeiywo, Lazaro, 750

Sunna, 230

Superordinate identities and goals, 648

Support, peacemaking and, 55

Supremacy of the mind, Buddhism and, 193–98; building right relationships, 195; chain of cause and effect, 198; four sublime values, 196; observing precepts, 195; practice of *Metta*, 196–97; principles of group awakening, 197–98; purification of the mind, 194; understanding "I," 194–95

Sustainable peace, changes needed for, 711

Sustained Dialogue process, 154–57

Svensson, Isak, 458–59

Swaraj, 176

Sweden, 468–70

Swiss Federal Department of Foreign
  Affairs (FDFA), 741, 744–45, 748–49,
  757
Swisspeace Bern, 757
Switzerland, Nepal peace promotion in,
  18–35; confidence-building during
  King Gyanendra rule and, 19–21; conflicting parties and dominant issues
  of, 18–19; Federalism and constituent
  assembly elections, 30–32; negotiations and peace agreement for, 24–30;
  shuttle diplomacy, ceasefire, stronger
  democratic movement and, 21–23;
  transition period for, 32–35
Symbolic tools, explained, 314–15
Symbolism, unifying, 554
Syria, Judaism and conflict resolution in,
  84–89; Assad Library speech, 84–85;
  Sheikh Shehadeh meetings and,
  88–89; United States political goals
  and, 85–86
Systems perspective on peacemaking:
  dynamical, 637–50; hidden dimensions of peacemaking, 622–36

Tahkim, 236
Tajikistan, unfinished business in,
  773–77
Taliban, 239, 492–93, 496, 499–500, 710
Tallgren, Immi, 123
Tambo, Oliver, 722, 725, 732–33
Tapas, 171
Tariq Khamisa Foundation, 238
Tawhid, 232, 233
Telescoping, 624
Tensions, peacemaking and, 60
Thakur, Ramesh, 424
Thatcher, Margaret, 733
Theistic-personalism, 180
Theories of change in peacemaking,
  668–82; decommitment and, 675–81;
  leaders and, 670–73; minds and,
  669–70; overview of, 668–69; pro-
  cesses and, 673–75
Thiong'o, Ngugi wa, 280
Third-party interventions, 56–57, 556,
  683–98; contingency model for,
  689–92; development and expres-
  sion of interactive conflict resolution,
  684–85; overview of, 683–84; stages
  of escalation and, 687–89; supporting

evidence for model of, 694–97; taxon-
  omy of, 685–87; variations and criti-
  cisms of model for, 692–94
Threat-to-care, 619–20
Throsby, David, 441, 450
Thurman, Howard, 161–62
Time-series analysis, 451–52
Timor Leste, UN's conflict management
  assistance in, 390
Tipping point, 646
Tobias, Channing, 161
Togo, UN's conflict management assis-
  tance in, 390
Tongeren, Paul van, 380, 400–417
Tonkinson, Robert, 553
Torricelli, Evangelista, 616
Track Two Diplomacy, 62–63
Tradition, 497–98
Transcend, 107
Transformation in Islamic peacemaking,
  238–40
Transitional Federal Charter, 334–35
Transitional justice and mediation of
  ceasefires, 142–43
Treaty of Hudaybiyya, 237
Truth and Reconciliation Commission
  (TRC), 260, 268
Truth-force, 166
Tulip Revolution, 427
Tutu, Desmond, 258, 260, 268, 270, 283,
  300
Tuzla, 39–42, 493, 496
25-point ceasefire code of conduct,
  24–25
Twitter, 478
Two New Sciences (Galileo), 613, 616

Ubuntu: African Great Lakes region
  principles, 295–307; Burundi principles, 295–307; five key stages of, 285;
  multicultural education uses, 303–6;
  peacemaking process, 283–86; principles of, 300–302; Rwandan principles,
  295–307
Uganda: International Criminal Court
  role in, 122–33; militarization by,
  130–33
Unbiased Media Coverage project, 485
Understanding "I" in Buddhism, 194–95
UN Development Programme (UNDP),
  386–95, 397; Experience-Sharing

Seminar on Building Infrastructures
for Peace in Kenya, 401–2; GPI data
used by, 441
Unfinished business: in Aceh, 773; in
Burundi, 773–77; in Cambodia,
773–77; categories and occurrences of,
765–66, 773–77; in economic domain,
769–70; in Haiti, 772–77; in Liberia,
771, 773–77; in Mindanao, 773–77;
in Mozambique, 773–77; nature of,
764–66; in Northern Ireland, 773–77;
in political domain, 766–68; in RPP,
773–77; in security domain, 769; significance of, 770–72; in social fabric
domain, 768–69; in Solomon Islands,
773–77; in South African, 773–77; in
Tajikistan, 773–77
UNHCHR, 429
Unidad Revolucionaria Nacional Guatemalteca, 752
Unifying non-war identity, 494–96
Unilateral decisions, 381–82
United Democratic Front (UDF), 723
United Nations, 654
United Nations (UN), 701, 703; Alliance
of Civilizations, 532, 534; Charter, 423,
425, 431, 661; conflict management
capabilities, 389–92; Department of
Political Affairs, 401, 432, 745; General
Assembly, 422, 423, 425, 426, 429, 431,
433, 713; Global Compact, 450–51;
MONUC, 429; ONUSAL, 142, 143;
R2P policies, 420–34; Security Council, 423, 426, 427, 431, 704; UNICEF,
140; World Summit, 2005, 420, 424,
425, 427, 434, 713; World Tourism
Organization, 532, 534
United States (U.S.): gang intervention
in, 511–24; ICC accommodations,
126–27; Israeli-Arab conflict and,
707–9; Judaism and conflict resolution
in Syria, political goals and, 85–86;
policy in Afghanistan, 709–10, 714
Unwitting commitments, 604
Upper Xingu River basin peace system,
551, 552–55
Uppsala Conflict Data Program (UCDP),
379, 458
Uppsala Conflict Peace Agreement
Dataset (UCDB), 345

Uppsala University: Department of
Peace and Conflict Research, 457,
467–68; Jakarta conference, 471
Uprising: Crips and Bloods Tell the Story
of America's Youth in the Crossfire, 519,
521
Urgency, sources of, 728–29
Urgency theory, 726–39; ANC negotiations and, 731–33; causes and consequences of, 728–29; distinctive ways
of, 727–28; stages to formal negotiation and, 736; white negotiations and,
729–31; white vs. ANC, 733–36
Ury, William, 152, 531, 537–38, 540, 565
Ushahidi, 480

Vallacher, Robin, 637–50
Values, 553–54
Van Antwerpen, Jonathan, 259
Vance, Cyrus, 151
Vancouver, Canada, CRANE fieldwork
in, 319–21
Van der Stoel, Max, 705
Van Dijk, T. A., 488
Van Tongeren, Paul, 400–417
Verification means of ceasefire agree-
ment, 140–41
Vertical peacemaking, 277, 278–79, 292
VHP (Vishwa Hindu Parishad), 11–12
Vibration, 628
Victimization, 382–83
Video-sharing websites, 478, 479
Village Self-Governance as awakening
stage, 204
Violence: costs of, 445–46; mimetic struc-
tures of, 586–87
Volf, Miroslav, 260

Waaijman, Kees, 588–89
Wallace, Marshall, 380, 492–501
Wallensteen, Peter, 380, 457–76, 470
Wang, Yuan-kang, 221
Wanis-St. John, Anthony, 547, 563–81
Waqf, 233
War crimes, R2P and, 420–28, 434
Warfare and peacemaking, 651–54
Warning-response gap, 430–31
Wasserstrom, Stephen, 251
Weak states, peacemaking and, 157–59
Web 1.0, 478

Web 2.0, 477–79
Weber, Max, 213
Weiss, Joshua, 380, 529–42
Weiss-Rosmarin, Trude, 251–52
Welsh, D., 730, 733–36
Wennmann, Achim, 144
"We're All in the Same Gang" (West Coast Allstars), 515–16, 521
West Bengal, dialogue and, 786–88
West Coast Allstars, 515–16
Where Do We Go from Here? Chaos or Community (King), 181–82
Where Elephants Weep (opera), 308
Wikipedia, 478
Wikis, 478
Wilber, Ken, 588–89
Williams, Abiodun, 380, 420–34
Williams, Stanley "Tookie," 520
Wilson, Woodrow, 259
Wolpert, Stanley, 175
Women: as Budrus peacebuilders, 43–47; conflict reference and, 346; envisaged state roles of, 345–48; long term reference and, 346–47; pogrom against, in Gujarat, 7; rape and sodomy of, in India, 7–8; referenced in peace agreements, 345, 366–71; reflecting international norms on, 348–52, 372–75; rights provisions in peace agreements of, 344–75; roles in nonviolent action, 36–49; as Srebrenica peacebuilders, 39–43; transition reference and, 346
Women of Srebrenica Association, 40–41
Woodrow, Peter, 761–78
World Bank, 703

World Food Program (WFP), 140
World of Gangs, A (Hagedorn), 512
World Trade Organization, 703
World Union of Progressive Judaism, 254
Worldview in AST, 624
Wren, Christopher, 616
Wright, Jaime, 267–68
Wujaha, 236
Wye River Memorandum, 708

Yacoobi, Sakena, 239–40
Yilmaz, 537–38
Youth 4 Peace, 11
Youth Aman Karwan, 10–13
Youth peacemaking in India, 6–17; Anhad and, 8–9, 13; campaigns used in, 13–15; Creating Democracy, Celebrating Diversity campaign and, 13; Gujarat relief camps and, 7; National Student's Festival for Peace, Justice Communal Harmony and, 13–14; rape and sodomy of women in, 7–8; Rock the Nation and, 14; Youth Aman Karwan and, 10–13
YouTube, 478, 480, 485
Yusuf, Abdullahi, 335
Yusuf, Hussein, 341

Zakat, 231, 232
Zartman, William, 669–70, 726–27, 728, 734, 735
Zelizer, Craig, 310
Zhongguo, peacemaking and, 223
Zulu Nation, 515

About the Editors

ANDREA BARTOLI is director and S-CAR's Drucie French Cumbie Chair. He has been at the School for Conflict Analysis and Resolution (S-CAR) at George Mason University since 2007. He works primarily on peacemaking and genocide prevention. An anthropologist from Rome, Dr. Bartoli completed his Italian *dottorato di ricerca* (PhD equivalent) at the University of Milan and his *laurea* (BA-MA equivalent) at the University of Rome.

ZACHARIAH CHERIAN MAMPILLY is an assistant professor of political science, international studies, and Africana studies at Vassar College. His research focuses on the nature of contemporary conflict processes with an emphasis on Africa and South Asia. His first book, *Rebel Rulers: Insurgent Governance and Civilian Life During War,* was based on field work behind insurgent lines in D.R. Congo, Sri Lanka, and Sudan. He received his PhD in political science from UCLA and his BA and MA from Tufts and Columbia, respectively.

SUSAN ALLEN NAN is assistant professor of conflict analysis and resolution at George Mason University. She is a scholar-practitioner of peacemaking, with current engagement in the South Caucasus region with Georgians and Ossetians. She has engaged practically in conflict contexts with the Alliance for Conflict Transformation, the Carter Center, and was a founding member of the Alliance for Peacebuilding. Dr. Nan holds a PhD and MS in conflict analysis and resolution from George Mason University.